The Trial Lawyer's Guide to the Attorney-Client Privilege and Work-Product Doctrine

REAGAN W. SIMPSON AND
ROBERT P. REDEMANN,
EDITORS

AMERICAN BAR ASSOCIATION
Tort Trial and Insurance
Practice Section

Cover design by ABA Design

Printed in the United States of America.

27 26 25 24 23 5 4 3 2 1

ISBN 978-1-63905-238-7

A catalog record for this book is on file with the Library of Congress.

CONTENTS

Preface xiii
About the Editors and Authors xv

CHAPTER 1
The Attorney-Client Privilege **1**
Reagan W. Simpson
I. The Elements of the Attorney-Client Privilege 1
A. Communications 3
B. Between an Attorney and a Client 5
1. Defining the Client 6
2. Defining the Attorney 8
C. In Confidence 10
D. For the Purpose of Securing or Providing Legal Advice 11
II. When the Attorney-Client Privilege Does Not Apply 13
III. Conclusion 14

CHAPTER 2
The Ethics Rule on Confidentiality and How It Differs from the Attorney-Client Privilege **15**
Arthur Garwin
I. Introduction 15
II. Model Rule 1.6—Confidentiality of Information 17
A. Public Information 19
B. Paragraph (a) Impliedly Authorized Disclosures 21
C. Authorized Disclosures 21
D. Paragraph (b) Exceptions 22
1. Physical Harm 22
2. Crime-Fraud Exception 23
3. Ethics Advice 25
4. Claim or Defense 27
5. Other Law or Court Order 28
6. Lawyer's Change of Employment 30
E. Paragraph (c) Inadvertent or Unauthorized Disclosures 30

CHAPTER 3
The Work-Product Privilege **33**
Robert P. Redemann
I. Basic Definition and Purpose 33
A. *Hickman v. Taylor* 33
B. Federal Rule of Civil Procedure 26(b)(3) 37
C. Selected State Rules 38
II. Elements of the Work-Product Privilege 39
A. The Need for Litigation 39
B. The Anticipation of Litigation 39
1. "Because of" Test 40
2. Primary-Purpose Test 41
3. Dual-Purpose Test 42
4. Sole-Purpose Test 43
C. Duration of the Privilege 43
D. Expectation of Confidentiality 45
III. Materials Beyond the Scope of Work Product 45
IV. Who Can Assert the Work-Product Privilege 46
V. Extent of Protection 47
A. Substantial Need 49
B. Undue Hardship 50
C. Substantial Equivalent 51
VI. Types of Documents Evaluated 52
A. Attorney Billing Records 52
B. Attorney Notes 53
C. Claim Files 53
D. Client Notes 54
E. Dual-Purpose Documents 54
F. Intangible Items 55
G. Internal Investigations 56
H. Pre-Litigation Investigations 57
I. Reports and Draft Reports 57
J. Reservation-of-Rights Letter 60
K. Reserves 61
L. Settlement Negotiations 62
M. Testing 64
N. Witness Identity 64
O. Witness Statements 65
VII. Conclusion 67

CHAPTER 4
The Common-Interest or Joint-Defense Privilege **69**
Reagan W. Simpson
I. Sorting Out the Two Privileges 69
II. The Common-Interest Privilege 71
III. The Joint-Defense Privilege 73
IV. The Joint-Defense Arrangement or Agreement 74
V. The Attorney-Client and Work-Product Privileges in Common-Interest or Joint-Defense Situations 76
VI. Waiver 79
VII. Conflicts of Interest That May Arise Because of a JDA 80
VIII. Discovery of Joint-Defense Agreements 82
IX. Conclusion 83

CHAPTER 5
Exceptions to Privileges **85**
Reagan W. Simpson and Robert P. Redemann
I. Crime-Fraud Exception 85
A. Overview of the Crime-Fraud Exception 85
B. Extending the Crime-Fraud Exception 87
C. Burden of Proof on the Crime-Fraud Exception 88
II. Attorney Misconduct Exception 91
III. Disputes between Attorney and Client 92
IV. Bad Faith 92
V. Impossibility 93
VI. Fiduciary Exception 95

CHAPTER 6
Waiver of Privileges **99**
Reagan W. Simpson
I. Waiver by Default 100
II. Waiver by Disclosure 105
III. Using Information with Witnesses, Including Experts 109
IV. Waiver When the Information Is at Issue 111
A. Relying on Advice of Counsel 112
B. Other Issues Involving Lawyers 113
V. Issues and Defenses That Implicate State of Mind or Knowledge 118
A. Good Faith 118
B. Bad Faith 119
C. Knowledge 120
D. Reliance 121
E. Contract Interpretation 122
VI. Who Can Waive 123
VII. Scope of Waiver 124

CHAPTER 7
Procedural Tools for Litigating Privileges **129**
Robert P. Redemann
I. Protective Orders 129
A. Before Discovery Begins 129
B. After Discovery Begins 130
II. Clawback Provisions 132
III. Interrogatories and Requests for Production 134
IV. Privilege Logs 135
V. Motions to Compel 138
VI. Choice of Law 139
VII. Quashing Depositions and Subpoenas 141
VIII. Motions in Limine 142
IX. Pretrial Orders 143
X. Objections 144
XI. Mandamus 144
XII. Practice Tips for Work-Product Disputes 146
A. Materials 146
1. Defending the Privilege 146
2. Attacking the Privilege 147
B. Because of Litigation 148
1. Defending the Privilege 148
2. Attacking the Privilege 149
C. By an Attorney, Agent, or Representative of a Party 150
1. Defending the Privilege 150
2. Attacking the Privilege 150
D. Substantial Need 150
1. Defending the Privilege 150
2. Attacking the Privilege 151
E. Undue Hardship 151
1. Defending the Privilege 151
2. Attacking the Privilege 151
F. Substantial Equivalent 152
1. Defending the Privilege 152
2. Attacking the Privilege 152
XIII. Conclusion 153

CHAPTER 8
The Attorney-Client Privilege in Organizations **155**
Douglas R. Richmond
I. Introduction 155
II. Organizational Clients and the Attorney-Client Privilege 157
A. The Control Group Test 157
B. The Subject Matter Test 158
C. The Modified Subject Matter Test, *Harper & Row* Test, or *Diversified Industries* Test 160
III. Employees and Officers versus the Corporation as the Client 161
IV. Former Employees and the Organization's Attorney-Client Privilege 164
V. In-House Lawyers and Privileged Communications 167
VI. Communications within a Corporate Family 173
A. The One-Client Approach 174
B. The Joint Client Approach 175
C. The Community-of-Interest Approach 179
VII. Corporate Succession 182
VIII. Dissolved Corporations 187
A. General Rules 188
B. An Illustrative and Explanatory Case 189
C. Summary 192
IX. Partnerships and the Attorney-Client Privilege 192
X. Limited Liability Companies 193
XI. Joint Ventures 195
XII. Conclusion 197

CHAPTER 9
Investigations **199**
David E. Bland and Scott G. Johnson
I. Introduction 199
II. Is the Investigating Attorney Acting as an Attorney? 201
A. Attorney Acting in Capacity of Attorney 202
B. Attorney Investigator Not Acting in Capacity of Attorney 206
C. Summary 210
III. Who Can Be Interviewed by the Attorney? 211
IV. What Must Be Disclosed 214

CHAPTER 10
Patent Matters **217**
George W. Jordan, III
I. Introduction and Overview 217
II. Communications Relating to Invention Process 218
A. The Privilege Standard Set Forth in the *Spalding* Decision 219
B. District Court Cases Applying *Spalding* 220
C. The Limits of the *Spalding* Decision 223
1. Forwarding Nonprivileged Records Not Privileged 223
2. Communications Lacking Confidential Information or Attorney Involvement Not Privileged 224
3. Primarily Business Documents Not Privileged 225
4. Facts about Prior Art Searches May Not Be Privileged 227
5. *Choice of Law Limitations* 228
D. Patent Prosecution Documents as Work Product 229
III. Communications with Patent Agents and Foreign Counsel as Privileged 231
A. Who Qualifies as an "Attorney" 231
B. Communications with U.S. Patent Agents 233
C. Communications with Foreign Patent Agents and Foreign Attorneys 236
1. Whose Law to Apply 238
2. Determining Privilege under Foreign Law 240
IV. Attorney-Client Privilege in Patent-Related Administrative Proceedings 247
A. Section 337 Investigations before the International Trade Commission 247
B. Proceedings before the Patent Trial and Appeal Board 250
C. PTAB Documents as Work Product 252
V. Design Around 254
VI. Waiver of Privilege or Immunity 255
A. Inadvertent versus Intentional Waiver 256
B. Advice-of-Counsel Defenses by Accused Infringer 261
1. The *EchoStar* Decision 263
2. The *Seagate* Decision 264
3. Post-*Seagate* Decisions 265
4. The *Halo* Decision 269
5. Post-*Halo* Decisions 270
6. Advice of Counsel after the AIA 272
C. Waiver Based on Crime-Fraud Exception 274
VII. Conclusion 279

CHAPTER 11
Litigating Attorney-Client Privileges under the United States Bankruptcy Code and the Federal Rules of Bankruptcy Procedure **281**
Toby L. Gerber and Jane A. Gerber
I. Privilege Disputes in Bankruptcy Are Different Than in Other Courts Because the Bankruptcy Code Operates to Transfer Control of the Privilege from a Debtor to Its Bankruptcy Fiduciary 282
II. The Attorney-Client Privilege of a Company in Bankruptcy Is Controlled by Whoever Manages the Company in Bankruptcy 283
III. The Attorney-Client Privilege of an Individual in Bankruptcy Generally Remains with the Individual unless the Bankruptcy Trustee Can Establish an Exception to the Privilege 285
IV. Balancing the Benefits of a Fiduciary's Control over the Attorney-Client Privilege against the Damage to the Corporate Debtor 287
V. Consideration of the Common Interest Doctrine in Bankruptcy 290

CHAPTER 12
Communications with Public Relations Consultants **293**
Mark D. Hinderks
I. The Nature of the Issue 293
II. The Attorney-Client Privilege and Third-Party Consultants 294
III. When Does a PR Consultant's Involvement Have a Sufficient Nexus to Legal Advice? 296
IV. The PR Firm as the "Functional Equivalent" of the Client 301
V. Application of the Work-Product Doctrine 304

CHAPTER 13
Insurance Settings **307**
Kirk Pasich
I. Introduction 308
II. Application of the Attorney-Client Privilege: The Majority View 310
III. Application of the Attorney-Client Privilege: The Minority View 317
IV. Witness Interviews by Insurers or Their Counsel 318
V. The Impact of an Insurer's Reservation of Rights or Declination on the Applicability of the Attorney-Client Privilege 321
VI. Application of the Work-Product Doctrine 327
VII. The Majority View: Information in an Insurer's Claim Files Is Collected in the Ordinary Course of Business 329

VIII. The Minority View: Information in an Insurer's Claim File Is Collected in Anticipation of Litigation 331
IX. The California View 333
X. Protection of the Work-Product Doctrine 333
XI. The Limited Protection View 334
XII. The Broad Protection View 334
XIII. The Intermediate View 335
XIV. Waiver of the Work-Product Doctrine under Federal Law 336
XV. Waiver of the Work Product Doctrine under California Law 338
XVI. Restatement of the Law Liability Insurance 340
XVII. Conclusion 341

CHAPTER 14
Class Actions **343**
Allan Kanner and Tibor L. Nagy, Jr.
I. Introduction 343
II. Communications with Nonclients Generally 344
A. Rules Against Solicitation, Contact with Represented Parties, and Misleading Statements 344
B. The Traditional Model: No-Comment Local Rules 346
C. *Gulf Oil Co. v. Bernard*: The No-Comment Model Is Cut Back 347
D. The Modern Model: Case Management 349
III. Communications with Putative Class Members 350
A. Precertification 350
1. *Jackson v. Motel 6 Multipurpose, Inc.* and *Abdallah v. Coca-Cola Co.* 352
2. *Hammond v. City of Junction City* 356
B. The Opt-Out Period 357
1. *Kleiner v. First National Bank of Atlanta* 358
2. *Georgine v. Amchem Products, Inc.* 360
C. Post-certification, Post-Opt-Out Period 362
IV. Opt-In Class Actions 362
V. Conclusion 367

CHAPTER 15
Choice of Law Issues **369**
Marcy Hogan Greer
I. Initial Questions Involving Choice of Law 369
II. State Courts 370
A. First Restatement 370
B. Second Restatement 371

C. Most Significant Relationship (MSR) 372
1. Section 139(1): Not Privileged in MSR State; Privileged in Forum 372
2. Section 139(2): Privileged in MSR State; Not Privileged in Forum 373
D. Third Restatement 375
E. Greater Interest/Government Interest Tests 375
III. Federal Courts 376
A. Federal Questions 377
B. Diversity 378
C. Communications Affecting Both Federal and State Claims 379
D. Transferred Cases 379
IV. Special Issues 379
A. Substantive Law versus Privilege Law 379
B. Other Countries' Laws 380
C. Discovery from Nonparties 382
V. Engaging the Choice of Law Analysis 382

PREFACE

This book is not a scholarly work on the attorney-client privilege or the work-product doctrine. Nor is it a 50-state survey. Even as to the jurisdictions on which this book is focused—federal courts and state courts in California, Illinois, New York, and Texas—there is no intent to be exhaustive.

Instead, the purpose of this book is to provide practical guidance to civil trial lawyers in litigating claims of confidentiality for attorney-client communications and attorney work product. It is a practice guide both for lawyers seeking to obtain such information and for those seeking to protect such information.

The book begins by discussing the basic elements of the attorney-client privilege and work-product doctrine. Following chapters deal with the common interest or joint defense privilege, waiver of privileges, exceptions to privileges, and procedural tools for litigating privileges. The next section of the book offers guidance concerning privilege issues in specific practice areas, namely, the representation of organizational clients, insurance disputes, bankruptcy matters, patent litigation, public relations related to litigation, and internal investigations in anticipation of litigation.

Three chapters do not squarely address privileges. Chapter 2 discusses the scope of confidential client information, which is broader than privileged communications. Ethical issues are at the heart of Chapter 2. Ethical issues are also a focus of Chapter 14 on class actions, which addresses communications by class counsel and defense counsel with claimants before and after class certification. Chapter 15, the last chapter, addresses choice of law issues on privileges.

The protection for attorney work product is technically not a privilege but a doctrine or a qualified immunity. But "like most courts, [this book] will for convenience [often] refer to . . . the 'work product privilege.'"[1] There is no consistency among judicial opinions, or sometimes even within the same opinion, on whether or not to hyphenate "work product" when it precedes "doctrine" or "privilege." This book favors hyphenation, but both forms will necessarily appear, without apology.

The Editors,
Reagan W. Simpson
Robert P. Redemann

1. N.Y. Times v. U.S. Dep't of Just., 939 F.3d 479, 489 n.4 (2019).

ABOUT THE EDITORS AND AUTHORS

Co-Editors and Authors

Reagan W. Simpson is a partner in the Houston, Texas, law firm of Yetter Coleman LLP, a litigation boutique. After graduating from the University of Texas with a bachelor's degree and from the University of Texas School of Law, he served as a law clerk to the late Thomas Gibbs Gee, Judge of the United States Court of Appeals for the Fifth Circuit. Reagan has spent the past 45 years trying cases to juries and appealing cases tried to juries. He is an Advocate in the American Board of Trial Advocates and a Member of the American Law Institute. He is certified in Civil Appellate and Civil Trial Law by the Texas Board of Legal Specialization. Reagan is a Fellow of both the American College of Trial Lawyers and the American Academy of Appellate Lawyers.

Robert P. Redemann is of-counsel with and a former shareholder in the Tulsa, Oklahoma, law firm of Perrine, Redemann, Berry, Taylor & Frette, PLLC. A graduate of the University of Wisconsin-Madison and the University of Tulsa, School of Law, he has been a trial lawyer since 1978 and has generally defended parties in civil lawsuits. He has experience in toxic torts, products liability, and employment law issues. He is a member of the Oklahoma Bar Association, the State Bar of Wisconsin, all Oklahoma federal court districts, the Tenth Circuit Court of Appeals and the United States Supreme Court. He serves the United States District Court for the Northern District of Oklahoma as an Adjunct Settlement Judge. He is active in the American Bar Association's Tort, Trial & Insurance Practice Section, the Oklahoma Bar Association, and the Tulsa County Bar Association.

Authors

David E. Bland is of counsel at Robins Kaplan LLP, practicing in the firm's Minneapolis office. He received his BA from the University of Minnesota in 1975 and his JD cum laude in 1979 from William Mitchell College of Law. His practice focuses on personal injury and products liability litigation, property and liability insurance coverage litigation, and directors' and officers' coverage litigation.

Arthur H. Garwin retired in 2016 from his position as Director, American Bar Association Center for Professional Responsibility. In 27 years at the ABA, he also served as Staff Counsel to the Task Force on the Future of Legal Education, Standing Committee on Professionalism, Commission on Multidisciplinary Practice, and Task Force on the Model Definition of the Practice of Law. He wrote numerous ABA Journal articles on professional responsibility; the ABA book *The Paralegal's Guide to Professional Responsibility*; and the chapter Confidentiality and Its Relationship to the Attorney-Client Privilege for prior editions of *The Attorney-Client Privilege in Civil Litigation*. He also was co-author and editor of the *Annotated Model Code of Judicial Conduct* (3rd edition); editor of *A Legislative History of the Model Rules of Professional Conduct, 1982–2013*; and contributor to the *Annotated Standards for Imposing Lawyer Sanctions* (2nd edition). He has BS and JD degrees from the University of Illinois and an MBA from Northwestern University. He practiced law for 15 years before moving to the ABA.

Jane A. Gerber is an Associate in the Dallas, Texas, office of McDermott Will & Emery LLP. She graduated from Wellesley College and from Washington University School of Law in St. Louis. During law school, Jane was Managing Editor of the Washington University *Global Studies Law Review*. Jane focuses her practice on restructuring and insolvency. She advises clients from the healthcare, consumer finance, automotive, restaurant and food retail, employment and real estate sectors in Chapter 11 proceedings, related adversary proceedings, distressed asset sales, and state court matters. Before joining McDermott, Jane clerked for Chief Judge Barbara J. Houser in the bankruptcy court for the Northern District of Texas and Judge Bill P. Parker in the bankruptcy court for the Eastern District of Texas, and interned for Chief Judge Brenda T. Rhoades in the bankruptcy court for the Eastern District of Texas.

Toby L. Gerber is a partner in the Dallas office of Norton Rose Fulbright. He concentrates his practice in bankruptcy, reorganization, and creditor rights. For more than 40 years, he has represented financial institutions, non-bank lenders, and a variety of other clients, including serving as lead counsel for syndicated and direct lenders and creditor groups structuring and restructuring major loan facilities, and in controversies throughout the United States and in numerous foreign jurisdictions. Toby is a fellow of the American College of Bankruptcy and is widely recognized for his work, including most recently by inclusion in Lawdragon 500 Leading US Bankruptcy and Restructuring Lawyers 2022, Lawyer of the Year—Bankruptcy and Creditors Rights, Insolvency and Reorganization Law (Dallas/Fort Worth), Best Lawyers 2022, The Best Lawyers in America, 2007–2022, and Chambers USA, Nationwide and Texas.

Marcy Hogan Greer is the Managing Partner of Alexander Dubose & Jefferson LLP, an appellate boutique. Her practice consistently includes class action and mass tort cases, including multidistrict litigation, in federal and state trial and appellate courts throughout the country. After completing a clerkship for the Honorable Carolyn Dineen King of the U.S. States Court of Appeals for the Fifth Circuit, she has been Board Certified in Civil Appellate Law by the Texas Board of Legal Specialization since 1997 and is a Member of the American Law Institute. In addition, Ms. Greer has been a member of the State Bar Pro Bono College for almost all of her career, requiring at least 75 hours of pro bono work each year. She designed, and was the original National Editor of, *A Practitioner's Guide to Class Actions* (ABA 2010), as well as the second edition (ABA 2017), and National Co-Editor of the third edition, which was published by the ABA in November 2021.

Mark D. Hinderks is a partner in the Kansas City office of Stinson LLP, leading its Legal Ethics and Professional Responsibility practice to provide opinions, expert witness services, training, and representation to law firms and law departments; and serving as one of its firm counsel. After graduating from the University of Kansas with undergraduate and law degrees, Mark practiced commercial litigation for over 30 years, becoming a Fellow of the American College of Trial Lawyers. He served as General Counsel of the firm, and in 2021 completed 11 years as the firm's Managing Partner. A frequent author and speaker on legal ethics, he co-founded "Ethics for Good," an ethics CLE stage show that has generated $850,000 for charities over the last 23 years, and currently authors "Dear Ethics Lawyer," a twice-monthly column circulating nationally with short form ethics questions and answers.

Scott G. Johnson is a partner at Robins Kaplan LLP, practicing in the firm's Minneapolis office. He received his BS magna cum laude from Winona State University in 1982 and his JD magna cum laude from William Mitchell College of Law in 1986. His practice focuses on property and liability insurance coverage litigation and subrogation.

George W. Jordan III is a senior counsel in the Houston office and intellectual property disputes group of Norton Rose Fulbright US LLP. Having spent the past 26 years managing patent litigation and licensing matters, he has litigated over 85 patent infringement cases. His privilege law experience includes leading large-scale document reviews, presenting training and best practices, and teaching a privilege seminar as an adjunct professor. He is a past Section Chair of the ABA Section of Intellectual Property Law and is registered to practice before the U.S. Patent and Trademark Office. George graduated from Duke University with a bachelor's degree in electrical engineering and from the University of Texas School of Law.

Allan Kanner is the founding member of Kanner & Whiteley, LLC, a national firm handling first-party insurance, natural resource damages, environmental, toxic torts, whistleblower, trials, and complex business litigation. Mr. Kanner is highly regarded nationally as a trial lawyer and legal strategist, especially in the fields of environmental law, consumer fraud, and complex litigation. He is an elected member of the American Law Institute, Law Dragon Hall of Fame member, a Leading Lawyer in America, and a Chambers & Partners' First Tier lawyer. In 2014, Law360 recognized Mr. Kanner as a "Titan of the Plaintiffs' Bar" (2014), www.law360.com/articles/585076/titan-of-the-plaintiffs-bar-allan-kanner; www.lawdragon.com/2017/10/01/lawyer-limelight-allan-kanner/. Many of his cases have become leading precedents or led to legislative and regulatory changes to better protect the public or the environment. He is frequently sought out as a teacher, lecturer, and author.

Tibor Nagy is a partner in Dontzin Nagy & Fleissig, LLP. He is a trial lawyer who represents plaintiffs and defendants in high-stakes litigation in state and federal courts throughout the United States. Mr. Nagy has been lead counsel in cases ranging from patent infringement to complex class actions. He regularly represents Fortune 500 companies, hedge funds, individual business owners, executives, inventors, patent owners, artists, and art galleries. He is a graduate of Yale Law School and Dartmouth College. Mr. Nagy was previously a partner in Susman Godfrey LLP. In 2017, he was named to *Benchmark Litigation*'s "Under 40 Hot List" and was also named an "Elite Boutique Trailblazer" by the *National Law Journal*. In 2021, Crain's *New York Business* named Mr. Nagy as one of its Notable Hispanic Leaders & Executives.

Kirk Pasich is a partner in the Los Angeles office of Pasich LLP. He conducts an active trial and appellate practice, representing insureds in complex insurance coverage matters. Kirk has been named by California Law Business to its "Legal Dream Team" as one of California's top 25 litigators, by Lawdragon as one of the nation's 500 leading lawyers, by Chambers USA: America's Leading Business Lawyers as one of the nation's Top 10 insurance coverage lawyers and "the market leader for policyholder representation in California," and by The International Who's Who of Insurance & Reinsurance Lawyers as one of the top 250 attorneys worldwide. Kirk also is the author of more than 500 articles on insurance and the author, co-author, and editor of several books, including *Casualty and Liability Insurance*; the American Bar Association's *Complex Insurance Coverage Litigation Handbook*; *Entertainment Law and Litigation*; and the *New Appleman Sports and Entertainment Insurance Law & Practice Guide*.

Doug Richmond is Managing Director of Aon's Professional Services Practice, the world's leading broker of insurance for law firms. Before joining Aon, he was a partner with Armstrong Teasdale LLP in Kansas City, Missouri, where he had a broad trial and appellate practice. He is the lead author of the book *Professional Responsibility in Litigation* (3rd edition 2021), published by the Tort Trial & Insurance Practice Section. Doug is a member of the American Law Institute and American Board of Trial Advocates and has served on the ABA's Standing Committee on Ethics & Professional Responsibility and the Standing Committee on Lawyers' Professional Liability. He earned his JD from the University of Kansas.

CHAPTER 1

The Attorney-Client Privilege

REAGAN W. SIMPSON

I. The Elements of the Attorney-Client Privilege

The attorney-client privilege is the "oldest of the privileges for confidential communications known to the common law," dating back to the days of Elizabethan England.[1] The privilege "has been a hallmark of Anglo-American jurisprudence for almost 400 years."[2] The purpose of the privilege is to encourage "full and frank communications between attorneys and their clients and thereby promote broader public interests in the observance of law and the administration of justice."[3] The attorney-client privilege is "quintessentially imperative" to our legal system.[4] "The attorney-client privilege continues indefinitely. Termination of the client-lawyer relationship, even for cause, does not terminate the privilege."[5]

Because the privilege hinders full discovery of the truth, however, it is narrowly construed.[6] As one court observed, the "attorney-client privilege is

---

1. Upjohn Co. v. United States, 449 U.S. 383, 389 (1981); *see also* United States v. Jicarilla Apache Nation, 564 U.S. 162, 165 (2011) ("The attorney-client privilege ranks among the oldest and most established evidentiary privileges known to our law."); United States v. Ivers, 967 F.3d 709, 716 (8th Cir. 2020); *In re* Grand Jury Subpoenas, 454 F.3d 511, 519 (6th Cir. 2006) (dating the privilege back to the Tudor dynasty).

2. Mitchell v. Superior Court, 691 P.2d 642, 645 (Cal. 1984).

3. *Upjohn Co. v. United States*, 449 U.S. 383, 389 (1981); *Swidler & Berlin v. United States*, 524 U.S. 399, 400 (1998).

4. Paxton v. City of Dallas, 509 S.W.3d 247, 261 (Tex. 2017).

5. Restatement (Third) of the Law Governing Lawyers § 77, cmt. b (2000).

6. *See, e.g.*, Eastman v. Thompson, 112 Fed. R. Serv. 3d 698 (C.D. Cal. 2022); Brown v. Barnes & Noble, Inc., 474 F. Supp. 3d 637, 648 (S.D.N.Y. 2019); National Rifle Ass'n of Am. v. Cuomo, 332 F.R.D. 420, 437 (N.D.N.Y. 2019); W. States Ins. Co. v. O'Hara, 828 N.E.2d 842, 847 (Ill. 2005) (noting that Illinois courts "strictly confine the privilege within its narrowest possible limits"; quotation omitted); Newman v. Highland Sch. Dist. No. 203, 381 P.3d 1188, 1191 (2016) ("It is a narrow privilege and protects

not without its costs. Since the privilege has the effect of withholding relevant information from the factfinder, it applies only where necessary to achieve its purpose."[7]

The criteria for the privilege have been consistently stated by courts and commentators as the following:

- Communications
- Between an attorney and a client
- In confidence
- For the purpose of seeking or providing legal advice[8]

In federal question cases, the attorney-client privilege is governed by federal common law.[9] In applying federal common law to issues of attorney-client privilege, federal courts usually rely on Proposed Federal Rule of Evidence 503, and particularly subdivision (b) of the proposed rule:

> A client has a privilege to refuse to disclose and to prevent any other person from disclosing confidential communications made for the purpose of facilitating the rendition of professional legal services to the client, (1) between himself or his representative and his lawyer or his lawyer's representative, or (2) between his lawyer and his lawyer's representative, or (3) by him or his lawyer to a lawyer representing another in a matter of common interest, or (4) between representatives of the client or between the client and a representative of the client, or (5) between lawyers representing the client.[10]

---

only communications and advice between attorney and client.") (internal quotes omitted); *In re* Grand Jury Subpoena, 204 F.3d 516, 519–20 (4th Cir. 2000); Hicks v. Bush, 452 F. Supp. 2d 88, 100 (D.D.C. 2006); Wood v. Superior Court of San Diego County, 46 Cal. App. 5th 562, 574 (2020); Feighan v. Feighan, 118 N.Y.S.3d 674, 676 (2020); United States v. Mejia, 655 F.3d 126, 132 (2d Cir. 2011).

7. Haines v. Liggett Group Inc., 975 F.2d 81, 84 (3d Cir. 1992) (citations and quotations omitted).

8. *See* United States v. Mejia, 655 F.3d 126, 132 (2d Cir. 2011); City of Wilmington v. United States, 141 Fed. Cl. 558, 562 (2019); *In re* Avandia Mktg. Sales Practices Prods. Liab. Litig., 415 F. Supp. 498, 505 (E.D. Pa. 2019) (quoting Rhone-Poulenc Rorer Inc. v. Home Indem. Co., 32 F.3d 851, 862 (3d Cir. 1994)); United States v. United Shoe Mach. Corp., 89 F. Supp. 357, 358–59 (D. Mass. 1950). *See, e.g.*, EEOC v. BDO USA, L.L.P., 876 F.3d 690, 695 (5th Cir. 2017); Cavallaro v. United States, 284 F.3d 236, 245 (1st Cir. 2002); United States v. Martin, 278 F.3d 988, 999 (9th Cir. 2002); United States v. Int'l Bhd. of Teamsters, 119 F.3d 210, 214 (2d Cir. 1997); *In re* Miller, 584 S.E.2d 772, 786 (N.C. 1994); People v. Simms, 736 N.E.2d 1092, 1117 (Ill. 2000); *In re* County of Erie, 473 F.3d 413, 419 (2d Cir. 2007); RESTATEMENT (THIRD) OF THE LAW GOVERNING LAWYERS § 68 (2000).

9. L&F Homes Dev., LLC v. City of Gulfport, 2012 WL 12919630, at *2 (S.D. Miss. Mar. 14, 2012); Blackmoon v. Charles Mix County, 2005 WL 8171368, at *1 (D.S.D. Sept. 14, 2005).

10. Blackmoon v. Charles Mix County, 2005 WL 8171368, at *1 (D.S.D. Sept. 14, 2005); *In re* Bieter Co., 16 F.3d 929, 935 (8th Cir. 1994).

As one court explained:

> Proposed Federal Rule of Evidence 503, which is also known as Supreme Court Standard 503, provides a useful starting place for our discussion. Although not enacted by Congress, "courts have relied upon it as an accurate definition of the federal common law of attorney-client privilege. . . . 'Consequently, despite the failure of Congress to enact a detailed article on privileges, Standard 503 should be referred to by the Courts.' 2 J. Weinstein, Evidence ¶ 503[02] at 503–17 (1975)." *United States v. Spector*, 793 F.2d 932, 938 (8th Cir. 1986) (citation omitted), cert. denied, 479 U.S. 1031, 107 S. Ct. 876, 93 L. Ed. 2d 830 (1987); *see United States v. (Under Seal)*, 748 F.2d 871, 874 n. 5 (4th Cir.1984) (Supreme Court Standard 503 "provides a comprehensive guide to the federal common law of attorney-client privilege"). . . .[11]

Although the basic elements of the privilege are nearly universal, how the elements are interpreted and applied varies with the jurisdiction. Chapter 15 of this book deals with choice of law issues. The basic elements of the attorney-client privilege will be discussed in this chapter. Chapters 8 through 14 of this book discuss specific ways in which the criteria are applied in certain practice areas.

A. Communications

Communications between the attorney and the client may be privileged, if the communications relate to the seeking or giving of legal advice in the attorney's professional capacity.[12] A "central inquiry is whether the communication is one that was made by a client to an attorney for the purpose of obtaining legal advice or services."[13] Thus, the privilege "protects the confidentiality of communications between attorney and client made for the purpose of obtaining legal advice."[14]

The facts underlying those communications are not protected.[15] To the extent that a communication by an attorney simply reveals the contents of

11. *In re* Bieter Co., 16 F.3d 929, 935 (8th Cir. 1994).

12. Wood v. Superior Court of San Diego County, 46 Cal. App. 5th 562, 576, 581–82 (2020) (observing that the privilege does not apply just because there is a conversation with an attorney).

13. *In re* Spalding Sports Worldwide, Inc., 203 F.3d 800, 805 (Fed. Cir. 2000); Ambac Assurance Corp. v. Countrywide Home Loans, Inc., 57 N.E.3d 30, 34 (N.Y. 2016).

14. Genentech, Inc. v. U.S. Int'l Trade Comm'n, 122 F.3d 1409, 1415 (Fed. Cir. 1997); Grand Design RV, LLC v. Thor Indus., Inc., 2022 WL 909647, at *5 (N.D. Ind. Mar. 28, 2022); Zen Design Group, Ltd. V. Scholastic, Inc. 327 F.R.D. 155, 159 (E.D. Mich. 2018).

15. Upjohn Co. v. United States, 449 U.S. 383, 395 (1981); Restatement (Third) of the Law Governing Lawyers § 69, cmt. d (2000). *See, e.g.*, *In re* County of Erie, 473 F.3d 413, 420 (2d Cir. 2007); United States v. Horvath, 731 F.2d 557, 562 (8th Cir. 1984); Skyline Wesleyan Church v. California Dep't

public information or information from a third party, it is not protected by the attorney-client privilege unless it also contains legal advice or responds to a request for advice.[16] The United States Supreme Court drew the distinction between privileged communications and facts:

> [The] protection of the privilege extends only to *communications* and not facts. A fact is one thing and a communication concerning that fact is an entirely different thing. The client cannot be compelled to answer the question, "What did you say or write to the attorney?" but may not refuse to disclose any relevant fact within his knowledge merely because he incorporated a statement of such fact into his communication to his attorney.[17]

In the criminal arena, of course, such facts as confession of guilt by the client will not come to light unless the client takes the stand. In civil cases, the client will be subject to discovery. During discovery, a client must disclose the facts it knows, including facts disclosed by the client to the attorney, but neither the client nor the attorney can be questioned about whether those facts were disclosed and what advice was given.[18]

Similarly, documents supplied to an attorney are not protected from disclosure in discovery, but whether they were provided to the attorney is likely a privileged matter.[19] One court noted that a "large set of lower courts have interpreted *Upjohn* to mean that even though the underlying content of the independently-discoverable attachments is not privileged, the act of sending the attachments is privileged."[20] Documents created by virtue of the attorney-client relationship may also be protected from disclosure by the work-product privilege, discussed in Chapter 3 of this book.

Examples of facts distinguished from communications are (1) the hiring of an attorney and a general description of the attorney's work;[21] (2) acts or services performed by an attorney during the representation;[22] (3) the subject

---

of Managed Health Care, 322 F.R.D. 571, 584–85, 2017 WL 4227026, at *10 (S.D. Cal. 2017); Dansko Holdings, Inc. v. Benefit Tr. Co., 2017 WL 5593321, at *7 (E.D. Pa. Nov. 21, 2017); Koumoulis v. Independent Fin. Mktg. Group, Inc., 295 F.R.D. 28, 45–46 (E.D.N.Y. 2013); Uber Techs., Inc. v. Google LLC, 27 Cal. App. 5th 953, 966 (2018); *In re* Alexander, 580 S.W.3d 858, 868 (Tex. App. 2019) (a person cannot cloak a material fact with the attorney-client privilege merely by communicating it to an attorney).

16. *See, e.g.*, Hickman v. Taylor, 329 U.S. 495, 508 (1947) (attorney-client privilege does not cover information attorney learns from witnesses).

17. Upjohn Co. v. United States, 449 U.S. 383, 395–96 (1981) (emphasis in original).

18. *See, e.g.*, Kan. Wastewater, Inc. v. Alliant Techsystems, Inc., 217 F.R.D. 525, 528–29 (D. Kan. 2003).

19. *See, e.g.*, Willis Elec. Co. v. Polygroup Trading, Ltd., 2021 WL 568454, at *6–7 (D. Minn. Feb. 16, 2021); Sneider v. Kimberly-Clark Corp., 91 F.R.D. 1, 4 (N.D. Ill. 1980); *In re* Ampicillin Antitrust Litig., 81 F.R.D. 377, 385 n.9 (D.D.C. 1978).

20. Willis Elec. Co. v. Polygroup Trading, Ltd., 2021 WL 568454, at *6–7 (D. Minn. Feb. 16, 2021) (citing cases at note 7).

21. *CoorsTek, Inc. v. Reiber*, 2010 WL 1332845, at *7 (D. Colo. Apr. 5, 2010).

22. *Id.* (citing Kovacs v. Hershey Co., 2006 WL 3054167, at *2 (D. Colo. Oct. 25, 2006)).

matter of meetings with an attorney, the persons present, the location of the meetings, or the persons arranging the meetings;[23] and (4) when legal services are rendered.[24] Contrast those facts with protected communications, such as a client's request that the attorney consider facts or documents, the client's discussion of the facts, and consideration given by the client to attorney's advice.[25] Finally, the absence of a communication is a fact and not a communication.[26]

B. Between an Attorney and a Client

Privileged communications are usually initiated by a client, but that is not always the case. For example, an attorney may realize that a client is facing a legal difficulty that the client does not appreciate, prompting the attorney to provide advice without a request from the client. The attorney-client privilege is "a two-way street, protecting both the client's communications to the attorney and the attorney's advice to the client."[27] The purpose of the privilege is to protect not only the giving of information to attorneys to enable them to give sound advice but also the giving of professional advice to those who can act upon it.[28] Some courts, however, protect communications from the attorney to the client only when the communication reflects client communications.[29]

---

23. *Id.* at *21 (quoting Burton v. R.J. Reynolds Tobacco Co., 170 F.R.D. 481, 484–85 (D. Kan. 1997)); *see also* Taylor Lohmeyer Law Firm P.L.L.C. v. United States, 957 F.3d 505, 510–11 (5th Cir. 2020) (client identities and fee arrangements are not protected as a general rule).

24. Sapia v. Bd. of Educ., 351 F. Supp. 3d 1125, 1132 (N.D. Ill. 2019).

25. *See* Chapter 5 for a discussion of the crime-fraud exception.

26. Dickinson v. Cosby, 37 Cal. App. 5th 1138, 1158 (2019) ("Thus, revealing that a particular communication did not occur would not necessarily result in a waiver of the privilege.").

27. People v. Radojcic, 998 N.E.2d 1212, 1221 (Ill. 2013); *see also* Saran v. Chelsea GCA Realty P'ship, L.P., 104 N.Y.S.3d 698, 700 (2019).

28. Upjohn Co. v. United States, 449 U.S. 383 (1981); SE Consulting, Inc. v. Frank Mercede & Sons, Inc., 838 A.2d 135, 167 (2004); *see, e.g.*, *In re* EchoStar Commc'ns Corp., 448 F.3d 1294, 1300–01 (Fed. Cir. 2006); Chaudhry v. Gallerizzo, 174 F.3d 394, 402 (4th Cir. 1999); *In re* Lindsey, 158 F.3d 1263, 1267 (D.C. Cir. 1998); United States v. Chen, 99 F.3d 1495, 1501 (9th Cir. 1996); United States v. Textron Inc., 507 F. Supp. 2d 138, 146 (D.R.I. 2007); Evans v. United Servs. Auto. Ass'n, 541 S.E.2d 782, 790 (N.C. Ct. App. 2001); *In re* Ford Motor Co., 988 S.W.2d 714, 718 (Tex. 1998); *In re* L.T.V. Sec. Litig., 89 F.R.D. 595 (N.D. Tex. 1981). *See also* RESTATEMENT (THIRD) OF THE LAW GOVERNING LAWYERS § 69, reporter's note, cmt. i (2000) ("Some decisions have protected a lawyer communication only if it contains or expressly refers to a client communication. That limitation is rejected here in favor of a broader rule more likely to assure full and frank communication (*see* § 68, Comment c). Moreover, the broader rule avoids difficult questions in determining whether a lawyer's communication itself discloses a client communication.").

29. *See* Brenton v. Dep't of State, 636 F.2d 600, 603 (D.C. Cir. 1981); United States v. Ramirez, 608 F.2d 1261, 1268 n.12 (9th Cir. 1979). Nationwide Mut. Ins. Co. v. Fleming, 924 A.2d 1259, 1264 (Pa. Super. Ct. 2007), *aff'd by an equally divided court*, 992 A.2d 65 (Pa. 2010) (holding that "the privilege protects confidential communications from an attorney to his or her client only to the extent that such communications contain and would thus reveal confidential communications from the client"); *see also* Harrisburg Auth. v. CIT Capital USA, Inc., 716 F. Supp. 2d 380 n.11 (M.D. Pa. 2010) (noting that the supreme court's decision in *Nationwide* did not decide whether the attorney-client privilege applies to communications from attorneys to clients); RESTATEMENT (THIRD) OF THE LAW GOVERNING LAWYERS § 69, reporter's note, cmt. i. (2000).

The Texas version of the attorney-client privilege goes further because it protects communications between the client's representatives as well as communications between the client and the client's representatives.[30] Those communications do not even involve the attorney, but the communications still must be for the purpose of gaining legal advice.[31]

1. Defining the Client

For purposes of the attorney-client privilege, the client includes someone who formally retains an attorney for legal advice.[32] The privilege extends further to a potential client,[33] and to agents or representatives of the client, particularly in the corporate context. As to potential clients, the Rules of Evidence in Texas and Alabama define "client" as someone who consults an attorney "*with a view* to obtaining professional legal services."[34] Once created, the privilege continues and does not end when the representation ends or even when the client dies.[35]

Because the privilege belongs to the client, the claim of privilege must be made by or on behalf of the client.[36] Although the privilege belongs to the client, the attorney may claim the privilege on behalf of the client and is presumed to have the authority to assert the attorney-client privilege in the absence of

---

30. *See* Tex. R. Evid. 503; *In re* Stephens Inc., 579 S.W.3d 438, 444–45 (Tex. App. 2019).

31. *Id.* at 445.

32. Wood v. Superior Court of San Diego County, 46 Cal. App. 5th 562, 574 (2020).

33. Restatement (Third) of the Law Governing Lawyers § 70, cmt. c (2000).

34. *See* Tex. R. Evid. 503(a)(1) (emphasis added); Ala. R. Evid. 502(a)(1) (emphasis added). *See* Barton v. U.S. Dist. Court, 410 F.3d 1104 (9th Cir. 2005).

35. It has been held that the privilege remains after the death of the client. Bunton v. Kruger, 8 N.E.2d 536, 545 (Ill. App. 2014) (noting that a personal representative of the estate may waive the privilege); Wesp v. Everson, 33 P.3d 191 (Colo. 2001); *In re* Busse's Estate, 75 N.E.2d 36 (Ill. App. 1947); Morrison v. State, 575 S.W.3d 1 (Tex. 2019); Eloise Bauer & Assocs. v. Elec. Realty Assocs., 621 S.W.2d 200, 204 (Tex. App. 1981). In Swidler & Berlin v. United States, 524 U.S. 399 (1998), the issue was whether a balancing test developed by the U.S. Court of Appeals for the D.C. Circuit was the appropriate method to determine whether an attorney's communications with a deceased client were discoverable. Under this test, issues of the significance of the statements bearing on crimes, as well as the scarcity of non-privileged evidence was to be considered (*see In re* Sealed Case, 124 F.3d 230 (D.C. Cir. 1997)), a test very similar to that of discovering attorney work product. The United States Supreme Court recognized that the privilege survives the death of the client. Swidler & Berlin, 524 U.S. at 410–11 (1998). The Court cited a draft of the Restatement that would *not* have extended the privilege after death, but the final Restatement does. *See* Restatement (Third) of the Law Governing Lawyers § 77, cmt. c (2000).

36. *See In re* Grand Jury Subpoena Duces Tecum, 391 F. Supp. 1029, 1034 (S.D.N.Y. 1975) (defendant need not be present for counsel to assert the privilege); Wood v. Superior Court of San Diego County, 46 Cal. App. 5th 562, 574 (2020); Sikes v. Segers, 587 S.W.2d 554, 559 (Ark. 1979); West v. Solito, 563 S.W.2d 240 (Tex. 1978).

evidence to the contrary.[37] Issues of successors that can claim the privilege can arise when mergers, corporate dissolutions, or bankruptcies occur.[38]

The privilege can extend to agents of the client.[39] The Eighth Circuit has held that even a nonemployee may qualify as a representative of the client for the purpose of the attorney-client privilege when the nonemployee is the functional equivalent of an employee, and a number of courts have followed that extension of the privilege.[40] Former employees may also be viewed as within the scope of the privilege.[41]

In the case of a corporation, it is generally held that the privilege may be asserted only by an authorized corporate representative on behalf of the corporation.[42] In the corporate setting, and in internal investigations conducted by corporations, issues surrounding the definition of the client become complex. The Supreme Court's decision in *Upjohn Co. v. United States*[43] remains the leading case on the scope of protection accorded internal corporate investigations under federal law. *Upjohn* rejected the control group test for the subject

37. *See, e.g.*, Ala. R. Evid. 502(c). *See also* Tex. R. Evid. 503(c) ("The person who was the lawyer or the lawyer's representative at the time of the communication is presumed to have authority to claim the privilege but only on behalf of the client."). This point was also made in *Cole v. Gabriel*, 822 S.W.2d 296, 296 (Tex. App. 1991, orig. proceeding) in a slightly different way when it was held that a lawyer had no standing to assert the attorney-client privilege in his individual capacity. *See also* Fisher v. United States, 425 U.S. 391, 402 (1976); Klitzman, Klitzman & Gallagher v. Krut, 744 F.2d 955, 962 (3d Cir. 1984); Haines v. Liggett Group Inc., 975 F.2d 81, 90 (3d Cir. 1992); *In re* Avandia Mktg. Sales Practices Prods. Liab. Litig., 415 F. Supp. 498, 505–06 (E.D. Pa. 2019).

38. *See, e.g.*, Knopf v. Sanford, 106 N.Y.S.3d 777, 814 (2019) (bankruptcy); Askari v. McDermott, Will & Emery, LLP, 114 N.Y.S.3d 412, 428–29 (2019) (merger and corporate dissolution).

39. United States v. Sanmina Corp., 968 F.3d 1107, 1116 (9th Cir. 2020).

40. *In re* Bieter Co., 16 F.3d 929, 937 (8th Cir. 1994); *accord* Berisha v. Lawson, 973 F.3d 1304, 1318 (11th Cir. 2020) (citing cases agreeing with the Eighth Circuit's extension to nonemployees functioning as employees); *accord* Narayanan v. Sutherland Global Holdings Inc., 285 F. Supp. 3d 604, 614–15 (W.D.N.Y. 2018).

41. *See* Collardey v. Alliance for Sustainable Energy, LLC, 406 F. Supp. 3d 977, 981 n.3 (D. Colo. 2019) (noting conflicting case law). The Restatement adopts the standard of "privileged persons" to refer to agents for clients and lawyers. *See* Restatement (Third) of the Law Governing Lawyers § 70.

42. *In re* Grand Jury Proceedings, 469 F.3d 24, 26 (1st Cir. 2006) (holding that the CEO of a corporation could not intervene in a proceeding to prevent counsel for the corporation from testifying to a conversation between the CEO and counsel in his personal capacity (absent evidence the counsel represented him in his personal capacity as well as the corporation)). In a context similar to that of the corporate world, it was held that White House lawyers could not claim that their conversations with the First Lady were privileged from disclosure in an investigation in which the President and First Lady were being investigated because the attorneys represented the White House and not the First Lady or the President. *In re* Grand Jury Subpoena Duces Tecum, 112 F.3d 910, 915–16 (8th Cir. 1997). *See also In re* Grand Jury Investigation, 599 F.2d 1224, 1236–37 (3d Cir. 1979) (applying control-group test).

43. 449 U.S. 383 (1981).

matter test.[44] Chapter 8 of this book deals with the attorney-client privilege in those situations.[45]

2. Defining the Attorney

The communication must involve an attorney or at least the process of obtaining advice from an attorney. For purposes of the privilege, the attorney must be acting in his or her professional capacity in giving legal advice during or related to the communication that it claimed to be privileged.[46] An attorney is, of course, someone who is authorized to practice law. There may be some professionals, such as patent agents, who are functionally engaged in the practice of law even though they are not attorneys.[47] If the client reasonably believes that a person is an attorney, the privilege still applies.[48] Some courts credit subjective belief, while others credit only objective belief in the status of the other person as an attorney.[49] Of course, the attorney must be acting for the client, so that a communication to an opposing counsel is not protected.[50]

As with the client, the privilege extends to an attorney's agents, such as paralegals, secretaries, non-attorney personnel, and outside parties whose assistance is necessary to provide services for attorneys, such as vendors who copy materials for production, IT professionals, and the like.[51] For example,

---

44. *Id.* at 390. As discussed in Chapter 8, the control group test is a minority view; the subject matter test is the clear majority rule. *See* RESTATEMENT (THIRD) OF THE LAW GOVERNING LAWYERS § 73, cmt. d (2000) (discussing control group test versus the subject matter test). Illinois follows the control group test. *See* Caldwell v. Advocate Condell Med. Ctr., 87 N.E.2d 1020, 1025 (Il. App. 2017); Claxton v. Thackston, 559 N.E.2d 82, 85 (Ill. App. 1990).

45. *See generally* RESTATEMENT (THIRD) OF THE LAW GOVERNING LAWYERS § 73 (2000) (discussing the privilege in connection with the organizational client).

46. Wood v. Superior Court of San Diego County, 46 Cal. App. 5th 562, 574, 581–82 (2020) (merely discussing a legal matter with an attorney is not enough); United States v. Sanmina Corp., 968 F.3d 1107, 1116 (9th Cir. 2020).

47. *See In re* Silver, 540 S.W.3d 530, 532 (Tex. 2018); *accord* Sperry v. State of Fla. *ex rel.* Fla. Bar, 373 U.S. 379 (1963); *In re* Queen's Univ. at Kingston, 820 F.3d 1287, 1294–1301 (Fed. Cir. 2016).

48. RESTATEMENT (THIRD) OF THE LAW GOVERNING LAWYERS § 72, cmt. e (2000).

49. *Id.*, reporter's note, cmt. b. *Compare* Alexander v. Superior Court, 685 P.2d 1309, 1314 (Ariz. 1984) (subjective) *with* United States v. Boffa, 513 F. Supp. 517, 523–25 (D. Del. 1981) (objective test).

50. RESTATEMENT (THIRD) OF THE LAW GOVERNING LAWYERS § 72, cmt. f (2000).

51. United States v. Sanmina Corp., 968 F.3d 1107, 1116 (9th Cir. 2020); *Rhone-Poulenc Rorer*, 32 F.3d at 862; *see also* Advanced Tech. Assoc., Inc. v. Herley Indus., Inc., 1996 WL 711018, at *5 (E.D. Pa. 1996); United States v. Kovel, 296 F.2d 918, 920–23 (2d Cir. 1961) (communications to accountant that enabled attorney to prepare defense in tax fraud case were protected by privilege); NXIVM Corp. v. O'Hara, 241 F.R.D. 109, 138 (N.D.N.Y. 2007); Broessel v. Triad Guar. Ins. Corp. 238 F.R.D. 215, 218–19 (W.D. Ky. 2006). *See also* Crow v. Crawford & Co., 269 S.W.2d 104 (Mo. Ct. App. 2008) (work by third-party administrator hired to investigate claims within attorney-client privilege). *But see* Reed Dairy Farm v. Consumers Power Co., 576 N.W.2d 709 (Mich. Ct. App. 1998) (holding that the attorney-client privilege did not attach to attorney's paralegal because, even though an employee of the attorney, he was not acting as an agent of the attorney, and the information sought was not the type that the attorney-client privilege was designed to protect); Lluberes v. Uncommon Prods., LLC, 663 F.3d 6, 24 (1st Cir. 2011) (declining to extend to a film script annotator the same status as accountants); United States v. Bergstein, 302 F. Supp. 3d 580 (S.D.N.Y. 2018).

communications made by the client to a private investigator employed by the client's attorney are protected by the attorney-client privilege to the same extent as if made to the attorney.[52] In some courts, the agent's assistance must, however, be "indispensable" to the provision of legal services for the privilege to apply.[53] Other courts take a broader view, as there are different approaches to the agency requirement:[54]

> The narrow approach applies the exception only to persons identified as "translators," meaning those who interpret information the client and attorney already possess. *See* [Michele DeStefano, *Claim Funders and Commercial Claim Holders: A Common Interest or a Problem?*, 63 DePaul L. Rev. 305, 331–41 (2014)]. In this category fall paralegals, law clerks, secretaries, and language translators, in addition to some non-attorney professionals such as accountants, depending on the tasks performed. *See, e.g.*, *Young v. Taylor*, 466 F.2d 1329, 1332 (10th Cir. 1972) (applying exception to secretaries and law clerks); *In re G–I Holdings Inc.*, 218 F.R.D. 428, 434 (D.N.J. 2003) (limiting exception to certain tasks performed by accountants).
>
> The second approach to the agency exception is to extend the waiver to a broader array of professionals with whom communication may be necessary for the provision of legal advice. For example, the Southern District of New York applied the agency exception to communications with a public relations firm in *In re Grand Jury Subpoenas Dated March 24, 2003*, 265 F. Supp. 2d 321, 326 (S.D.N.Y. 2003). In that case, the court noted that the firm provided much-needed "outside help" to assist the attorney, and that the firm's assistance "ha[d] a close nexus to the attorney's role in advocating the client's cause before a court or other decision-making body." *Id.* Similarly, the Third Circuit in *U.S. v. Alvarez* protected a client's communications with a psychiatrist because "the effective assistance of counsel with respect to the preparation of an insanity defense demands recognition that a defendant be as free to communicate with a psychiatric expert as with the attorney [the expert] is assisting." 519 F.2d 1036, 1046 (3rd Cir. 1975). . . .[55]

---

52. Sanchez v. Matta, 229 F.R.D. 649, 660 (D.N.M. 2004); Clark v. City of Munster, 115 F.R.D. 609, 613 (N.D. Ind. 1987); Am. Nat'l Watermattress Corp. v. Manville, 642 P.2d 1330, 1333–34 (Alaska 1982). It makes no difference whether the investigator is an employee of the attorney or is hired by the attorney to conduct the investigation.

53. United States v. Bergstein, 302 F. Supp. 3d 580 (S.D.N.Y. 2018) (quoting United States v. Kovel, 296 F.2d 918, 921 (2d Cir. 1961).

54. Diamond Resorts U.S. Collection Dev., LLC v. U.S. Consumer Attorneys, P.A., 2021 WL 505122, at *6 (S.D. Fla. 2021).

55. *Id.* (quoting *In re* Int'l Oil Trading Co., 548 B.R. 825, 834 (Bankr. S.D. Fla. 2016)).

The broader approach requires that the agent's participation be reasonably necessary rather than indispensable.[56]

C. In Confidence

The communication must be confidential to come within the attorney-client privilege. Unlike the work-product privilege, which remains even if the work product is shared with a non-adversary, the attorney-client privilege does not even attach if the communication is also made to a stranger to the attorney-client relationship.[57] A communication is not made in confidence unless there is a reasonable expectation of confidentiality.[58] Confidentiality may not exist even without the actual presence of a third party. In the governmental setting, a communication with an attorney may not be in confidence because of an open meetings or "sunshine" law.[59]

When a third party is involved in the communication, some courts will still recognize the confidentiality of the communication if the third party's presence was necessary to the rendition of legal services in order for the privilege to be maintained:

> [T]he third party must be nearly indispensable or serve some specialized purpose in facilitating the attorney-client communications. In other words, where the third party's presence is merely useful but not necessary, the privilege is lost.[60]

Other courts do not stress the indispensability of the third party as long as the third party is assisting the attorney in providing services.[61]

---

56. *See, e.g.*, Wyndham Vacation Ownership, Inc. v. Reed Hein & Assocs., 2019 WL 9091666, at *13–14 (M.D. Fla. Dec. 9, 2019); Louisiana Mun. Police Employers Retirement Sys. v. Sealed Air Corp., 253 F.R.D. 300, 311 (D.N.J. 2008).

57. *See, e.g.*, Protect Democracy Project, Inc. v. NSA, 10 F.4th 879, 891(D.C. Cir. 2021); Narayanan v. Sutherland Global Holdings Inc., 285 F. Supp. 3d 604 (W.D.N.Y. 2018) (unnecessary presence of accountant during communications negated privilege); Towne Place Condo. Ass'n v. Philadelphia Indem. Ins. Co., 284 F. Supp. 3d 889, 896 (N.D. Ill. 2018); Diamond Resorts U.S. Collection Dev., LLC v. U.S. Consumer Attorneys, P.A., 2021 WL 505122, at *5 (S.D. Fla. 2021).

58. People v. Henry, 103 N.Y.S.3d 656, 666 (2019); Restatement (Third) of the Law Governing Lawyers § 71, cmt. c (2000).

59. *See* Neu v. Miami Herald Pub. Co., 462 So. 2d 821, 823–24 (Fla. 1985); McKay v. Bd. of Cnty. Comm'rs, 746 P.2d 124, 126 (Nev. 1987). *But see* Dodson v. Floyd, 529 F. Supp. 1056, 1064–65 (N.D. Ga. 1981) (The plaintiff's argument that "open government" negates the existence of the attorney-client privilege as to matters discussed between county officials and county attorney is meritless). *See also* Multimedia Pub. of North Carolina, Inc. v. Henderson County, 525 S.E.2d 786 (N.C. App. 2000) (interpreting attorney-client exception to open meeting law).

60. Narayanan v. Sutherland Global Holdings Inc., 285 F. Supp. 3d 604, 611–12 (W.D.N.Y. 2018).

61. *See, e.g.*, Collardey v. Alliance for Sustainable Energy, LLC, 406 F. Supp. 3d 977, 980 (D. Colo. 2019) ("On the other hand, courts have extended the privilege to communications between a client

If the communication initially falls with the attorney-client privilege, the privilege will generally be waived by any later disclosure to third parties. A possible exception to waiver exists when the disclosure is to someone with a common interest. The common interest privilege is a complex subject that is covered by Chapter 4 of this book. Chapter 6 deals with the subject of waiver of privileges.

D. For the Purpose of Securing or Providing Legal Advice

A central inquiry in determining whether a communication is protected by the attorney-client privilege is whether the "communication" at issue (whether it is conveyed orally or in a document) "is one that was made by a client to an attorney for the purpose of obtaining legal advice or services."[62] That inquiry is necessary because the attorney-client privilege applies to communications to or from an attorney only to the extent that they reflect information obtained in confidence from the client for the purpose of obtaining legal advice, as opposed to business or tax advice.[63] Simply because an attorney may have been copied on a communication does not necessarily cloak that communication with privilege.

Legal advice must have been sought, requested, or provided for the communication to be privileged.[64] The privilege applies when the attorney's work

---

and a third party where the communication was made in confidence for the purpose of obtaining legal advice from the lawyer.") (quotation & citation omitted); United States v. Adlman, 68 F.3d 1495, 1499 (2d Cir. 1995) (recognizing that the attorney-client privilege can extend to communications with non-attorneys "when the purpose of the communication is to assist the attorney in rendering advice to the client").

62. *In re Spalding Sports Worldwide, Inc.*, 203 F.3d 800, 805 (Fed. Cir. 2000) (en banc); Allen v. Banner Life Ins. Co., 340 F.R.D. 232, 237 (D.N.J. 2022); Slaven v. Great Am. Ins. Co., 83 F. Supp. 3d 789, 793–94 (N.D. Ill. 2015) (discussing this requirement in depth); *see generally* Restatement (Third) of the Law Governing Lawyers § 72 (2000).

63. *See, e.g.*, Pinnacle Surety Servs., Inc. v. Manion Stigger, LLP, 370 F. Supp. 3d 745, 755 (W.D. Ky. 2019) *In re EchoStar Commc'ns Corp.*, 448 F.3d 1294, 1300 (Fed. Cir. 2006); Am. Standard, Inc. v. Pfizer, Inc., 828 F.2d 734, 745 (Fed. Cir. 1987); United States v. (Under Seal), 748 F.2d 871, 874 (4th Cir. 1984); *In re* Grand Jury Subpoena Duces Tecum Dated Sept. 15, 1983, 731 F.2d 1032, 1037 (2d Cir. 1984); Visa U.S.A., Inc. v. First Data Corp., 2004 WL 1878209, at *8 (N.D. Cal. Aug. 23, 2004) (concluding that where documents prepared with the assistance of attorneys would have been prepared in substantially identical form in making a business decision, no attorney-client or work-product protections applied); Galasso v. Cobleskill Stone Prods., Inc., 95 N.Y.S.3d 376 (2019) (valuation report prepared for tax reasons).

64. Sandra T.E. v. S. Berwyn Sch. Dist. 100, 600 F.3d 612, 620–22 (7th Cir. 2010); *In re* Grand Jury Subpoena, 599 F.2d 504, 511 (2d Cir. 1979) ("Participation of the general counsel does not automatically cloak the investigation with legal garb."); ABB Kent-Taylor, Inc. v. Stallings & Co., 172 F.R.D. 53, 57 (W.D.N.Y. 1996) ("The mere fact a communication is made directly to an attorney, or an attorney is copied in on a memorandum does not mean that the communication is necessarily privileged.") (citation omitted); *accord McCook Metals L.L.C. v. Alcoa Inc.*, 192 F.R.D. 242, 260 (N.D. Ill. 2000); U.S. Postal Serv. v. Phelps Dodge Ref. Corp., 852 F. Supp. 156, 160 (E.D.N.Y. 1994).

"pertains to a matter on which the attorney was consulted for his professional advice."[65] The legal advice need not be related to litigation.[66]

When there is a potential for business-related communications between client and attorney, an explicit request for legal advice is preferable and may be required.[67] Even when clients view the communication as being for the purpose of gaining legal advice, courts may deny protection if the subject matter can be classified as part of the client's "normal course of business."[68] In some cases, courts make rough assumptions as to whether the attorneys' work is protected, based less on the client's specific request for legal advice and more on whether the attorneys were outside or in-house counsel and, if the latter, the decision on privilege may depend on the positions held by in-house counsel within the client's business organization.[69]

---

65. FTC v. Boehringer Ingelheim Pharms., Inc., 892 F.3d 1264, 1266 (D.C. Cir. 2018) (at least a significant reason for the communication is to obtain legal advice); Lipton Realty, Inc. v. St. Louis Hous. Auth., 705 S.W.2d 565, 570 (Mo. App. 1986). *See also* Restatement (Third) of the Law Governing Lawyers § 72 (2000).

66. Heartland Alliance for Human Needs & Human Rights v. United States Immigration & Customs Enforcement, 406 F. Supp. 3d 90, 122 (D.D.C. 2019); Sapia v. Bd. of Educ., 351 F. Supp. 3d 1125, 1131 (N.D. Ill. 2019); Bloche v. Dep't of Defense, 414 F. Supp. 3d 6, 35 (D.D.C. 2019).

67. U.S. Postal Serv. v. Phelps Dodge Ref. Corp., 852 F. Supp. 156, 160 (E.D.N.Y. 1994) (noting that "house counsel have increased participation in the day-to-day operations of large corporations"; thus, "if the information-holder will communicate with the attorney even if the privilege does not exist, or if a nonlegal objective is sufficient to stimulate communication with the attorney, then there is no reason for the privilege to attach") (internal citation omitted). *See also* Shih v. Petal Card, Inc., 565 F. Supp. 3d 557, 566–67 (S.D.N.Y. 2021) ("Even where an attorney-client relationship exists, the client may not reflexively withhold every communication with its attorney as privileged.").

68. Some courts have held that certain types of tasks, such as preparing tax returns, are not within the privilege even if performed by lawyers. *See* Couch v. United States, 409 U.S. 322, 335, (1973); United States v. Arthur Young & Co., 465 U.S. 805, 817 (1984); United States v. Frederick, 182 F.3d 496, 500–01 (7th Cir. 1999); United States v. Davis, 636 F.2d 1028, 1043 (5th Cir. 1981); Evergreen Trading, LLC *ex rel.* Nussdorf, 80 Fed. Cl. 122, 130 (Fed. Cl. 2007).

69. *See, e.g.*, United States v. ChevronTexaco Corp., 241 F. Supp. 2d 1065, 1076 (N.D. Cal. 2002) (communications between a corporation and its outside legal counsel are presumed to be made in order to seek legal advice, but that presumption does not extend to communications with in-house counsel); *see also, e.g.*, Boca Investerings P'ship v. United States, 31 F. Supp. 2d 9, 12 (D.D.C. 1998) ("One important indicator of whether a lawyer is involved in giving legal advice . . . is his or her place in the corporation's organizational chart." There is a presumption that a lawyer in the legal department is giving legal advice, but an opposite presumption where a lawyer "works for the Financial Group or some other seemingly management or business side of the house."); Am. Oversight v. United States GSA, 311 F. Supp. 3d 327, 342 (D. D.C. 2018); Alison M. Hill, *A Problem of Privilege: In-House Counsel and the Attorney-Client Privilege in the United States and the European Community*, 27 Case W. Res. J. Int'l L. 145, 146 & n.6, 147, 164 n.92 (Winter 1995) (describing a 1982 European Court of Justice decision that lawyers employed by corporations would no longer be covered by the attorney-client privilege because their "independence" had thereby been compromised). *Cf.* Elizabeth G. Thornburgh, *Sanctifying Secrecy: The Mythology of the Corporate Attorney-Client Privilege*, 69 Notre Dame L. Rev. 157, 159 (1993) (arguing that "[O]nly elimination of the corporate attorney-client privilege can free the court system from the distortion and expense that was created by expanding the privilege to include corporate secrets.").

This element is frequently litigated, especially in corporate settings, which is the subject of Chapter 8 in this book. In general,

> in light of the two hats often worn by in-house attorneys, communications between a corporation's employees and its in-house counsel, though subject to the attorney-client privilege, must be scrutinized carefully to determine whether the predominant purpose of the communication was to convey business advice and information or, alternatively, to obtain or provide legal advice. If the former, the communication is not protected by the attorney-client privilege.[70]

II. When the Attorney-Client Privilege Does Not Apply

Some jurisdictions have adopted express statements of when the attorney-client privilege does not apply. A list of exceptions was in a proposed codification of the rules of privilege that was ultimately not accepted by Congress in enacting the Federal Rules of Evidence.[71] *Various state rules have adopted exceptions for certain types of communications:*

- Communications that aid in committing or planning to commit what the client knew or reasonably should have known to be a crime or fraud.
- Communications that are relevant to any of the following:
  - an issue between parties who claim through the same deceased client;
  - an issue of breach of duty by the attorney to the client or by the client to the attorney, arising from the attorney-client relationship;
  - an issue concerning the intention or competence of a client executing an attested document to which the attorney is an attesting witness, or concerning the execution or attestation of the document; or
  - a matter of common interest between two or more clients, or their successors in interest, if the communication was made by them to an attorney retained or consulted in common when offered in a civil action between the clients or their successors in interest.[72]

The crime-fraud exception is discussed at length in Chapter 5.

---

70. Brown v. Barnes & Noble, Inc., 474 F. Supp. 3d 637, 648 (S.D.N.Y. 2019).

71. *See Preliminary Draft of Proposed Rules of Evidence for the United States District Courts and Magistrates, 46 F.R.D. 161, 251 (1969); see also* Edward J. Imwinkelried, *Draft Article V of the Federal Rules of Evidence on Privileges, One of the Most Influential Pieces of Legislation Never Enacted: The Strength of the Ingroup Loyalty of the Federal Judiciary*, 28 Ala. L. Rev. 41 (2006).

72. Fla. Stat. § 90.502(4) (2014); Tex. R. Evid. 503(d); Ky. R. Evid. 503(d); La. Code Evid. art. 506(C).

III. Conclusion

This chapter has discussed the basic elements of the attorney-client privilege. The privilege applies to communications between attorneys and clients that are made in confidence for the purpose of obtaining or providing legal advice. There are, of course, matters of confidentiality between lawyers and client that are not related to legal advice. Chapter 2 of this book discusses the related subject of confidentiality outside the strict boundaries of the attorney-client privilege.

CHAPTER 2

The Ethics Rule on Confidentiality and How It Differs from the Attorney-Client Privilege

ARTHUR GARWIN

I. Introduction

Confidentiality and attorney-client privilege are related but distinct concepts that are frequently confused. This chapter describes the fundamentals of the ethics rule on confidentiality of information and points out the basic differences and interaction between it and the attorney-client privilege.

The attorney-client privilege applies "in judicial and other proceedings in which a lawyer may be called as a witness or otherwise required to produce evidence concerning a client."[1] This privilege "protects against compelled disclosure of a relatively narrow category of communications between lawyer and client."[2] Compelled disclosure might occur in a deposition, for example, or in response to a subpoena. If a lawyer is asked a question in a deposition or at a trial that arguably calls for an answer containing privileged information, the lawyer is obligated to refuse to answer (unless the client agrees to waive the privilege), and force a ruling by the court. If the court agrees that the testimony would be privileged, the court will sustain the objection and effectively order the lawyer not to answer.

Confidentiality is a principle of legal ethics that governs whether a lawyer may reveal information related to a client representation. Confidentiality rules are not limited to judicial or other proceedings, but rather apply in all

1. ABA Model Rules of Prof'l Conduct Rule 1.6 cmt. 3 (2020).

2. Thomas D. Morgan, Lawyer Law, Comparing the ABA Model Rules of Professional Conduct with the ALI Restatement (Third) of the Law Governing Lawyers 243 (2005).

representational contexts.[3] In addition, confidentiality applies to all information related to a representation,[4] whatever its source, and not merely to client communications.[5] The exceptions are drawn narrowly and the scope of confidentiality is applied expansively.[6] Because confidentiality is an ethics rule, the ramification of a breach by the lawyer of the lawyer's duty of confidentiality is a possible disciplinary action and sanction against the lawyer.

Everything that is privileged is also protected by the confidentiality principle, but the converse is not true.[7] The confidentiality rule covers far more than communications between a client and a lawyer. And the duty to maintain confidentiality does not expand the scope of the privilege.[8]

"Attorney-client privilege has numerous exceptions, which courts apply liberally. Much of what would be confidential ultimately proves to be subject

---

3. *See* X Corp. v. Doe, 805 F. Supp. 1298 (E.D. Va. 1992) (Whereas "the attorney client-privilege is . . . applied in the litigation context by judges, not lawyers, for the purpose of deciding whether to compel the disclosure of putatively privileged material . . . the . . . standard for disclosure of confidential information is one that is applied in the first instance by lawyers, not judges, as they struggle with the decision whether voluntarily to disclose certain confidential information they believe reflects an ongoing or future fraud. Judges apply the . . . standard in the second instance only to review post hoc whether a voluntary disclosure was ethically appropriate or, as here, to decide whether to enjoin a potential voluntary disclosure. . . ."). *See also* Fred C. Zacharias, *Harmonizing Privilege and Confidentiality*, 41 S. Tex. L. Rev. 69 (1999) (discussing why confidentiality rules developed so broadly); Fred C. Zacharias, *Rethinking Confidentiality*, 74 Iowa L. Rev. 351 (1989) (discussing why the client protective basis for this broad development may be misplaced).

4. "In contrast to both the attorney-client privilege . . . and Rule 1.9(c)(1) . . . Rule 1.6 contains no exception permitting disclosure of information previously disclosed or publicly available." Ellen J. Bennett & Helen W. Gunnarsson, Annotated Model Rules of Prof'l Conduct, at 111 (9th ed. 2019). *See also* Fred C. Zacharias, *The Fallacy That Attorney-Client Privilege Has Been Eroded: Ramifications and Lessons for the Bar*, Prof'l Law., 1999 Symposium Issue 39.

5. *See* ABA Model Rules of Prof'l Conduct Rule 1.6 (reprinted in section II); Rule 1.18(b) (regarding confidentiality and prospective clients). *See also* Restatement (Third) of the Law Governing Lawyers § 59 (2000). The attorney-client privilege and the rule of confidentiality also apply to prospective clients. *See id.* § 70 (2000) (regarding the attorney-client privilege and prospective clients). For purposes of this discussion, references will be made only to current or former clients.

6. Fred C. Zacharias, *Harmonizing Privilege and Confidentiality*, 41 S. Tex. L. Rev. 69 (1999). *See also* Restatement (Third) of the Law Governing Lawyers § 59 cmt. b (2000) ("The expansive definition of client information not protected by the attorney-client privilege that nonetheless a lawyer is obliged to keep confidential comes primarily from the law of agency and rules of professional regulation."); Ronald D. Rotunda & John S. Dzienkowski, Legal Ethics: The Lawyer's Deskbook on Professional Responsibility § 1.6-1 (2018–2019 ed., ABA) ("The attorney is the agent of her client, who is the principal. Under a general rule of agency law, the agent must neither use nor disclose 'information confidentially given to him by the principal or acquired by him during the course of or on account of his agency. . . .'" (quoting Restatement (Third) of the Law of Agency § 8.05)).

7. "The confidentiality rule . . . applies not only to matters communicated in confidence by the client but also to all information relating to the representation, whatever its source." ABA Model Rules of Prof'l Conduct Rule 1.6 cmt. 3 (2020). *See also* Laws. Manual on Prof'l Conduct (ABA/BNA) 55:301 *et seq.* (2022) (comparing the protection afforded under the ethics rules with that afforded by the attorney-client privilege in regard to client identity; client's whereabouts; financial, billing, and fee data; and publicly available or previously disclosed information).

8. Adams v. Franklin, 924 A.2d 993 (D.C. 2007).

to discovery or production in court."[9] But even if a court orders a lawyer to disclose confidential information, the lawyer may not reveal that same information outside the scope of the proceeding.

Moreover, the privilege protects only the communications themselves, not underlying facts, the disclosure of which may be compelled from those who communicated them to the attorney.[10] Thus, the other side can ask your client: "Is X true?" and demand an answer (in a formal proceeding), unless something like the Fifth Amendment applies. But it cannot ask the client: "Did you tell your lawyer whether X is true?" Furthermore, as explained in the example in the following excerpt, even a lawyer could be compelled to testify about the facts if he or she gained knowledge of them without a communication from the client:

> For example, a lawyer's observations about a client's physical condition are not privileged, even though the lawyer presumably would not have been in a position to make the observations absent a relationship of confidentiality and trust. At the same time, and conversely, a genuine communication from a client to a lawyer retains its privileged character, even if it is made demonstratively, through body language or gestures, rather than with words. Thus, as explained in illustrations accompanying Restatement of the Law Governing Lawyers § 69, Comment *e*, if a client—in response to his attorney's question—silently rolls up his sleeve to reveal a tattoo, the lawyer could not be compelled to testify about the tattoo. But the opposite would be true if the same client visited his lawyer's office wearing a short-sleeve shirt, and the lawyer noticed the tattoo.[11]

II. Model Rule 1.6—Confidentiality of Information

The Model Rules of Professional Conduct were adopted by the American Bar Association in 1983, replacing the Model Code of Professional Responsibility. Since then every state has adopted the Model Rules format and Model Rule 1.6, or some modified version of it.[12] A few jurisdictions, however, retain the Model

---

9. Fred C. Zacharias, *Harmonizing Privilege and Confidentiality*, 41 S. Tex. L. Rev. 69 (1999) ("[A]ttorney-client privilege rules are products of lawsuits. Courts and legislators make the rules. Whoever adopts the rules initially, it is judges who interpret them and flesh them out. Because privilege applies only when one client attempts to prevent the other side's access to potentially probative evidence in litigation, courts implementing privilege are cognizant of secrecy's negative attributes. Thus, judges tend to interpret attorney-client privilege narrowly.").

10. *See* Upjohn Co. v. United States, 449 U.S. 383, 395 (1981).

11. Geoffrey C. Hazard, Jr., W. William Hodes & Peter R. Jarvis, The Law of Lawyering § 10.07.9, at 10-48 (4th ed. 2018) (endnote omitted).

12. *See* ABA, CPR Policy Implementation Comm., Variations of the ABA Model Rules of Professional Conduct, Rule 1.6 (Jan. 2, 2020), http://www.americanbar.org/groups/professional_responsibility/policy/rule_charts.html.

Code language of "confidences," defined as "information protected by the attorney-client privilege," and "secrets," defined as "other information gained in the professional relationship that the client has requested be held inviolate or the disclosure of which would be embarrassing or would be likely to be detrimental to the client," which is less inclusive than the current Model Rules.

Model Rule 1.6, as originally adopted, contained only two exceptions: current (b)(5) and a less permissive version of (b)(1). In 2002, the ABA added current (b)(4) and (b)(6). Then, in 2003, the ABA added (b)(2) and (b)(3) (see further discussion about the context of these additions at section II.D.2, Crime-Fraud Exception). More than half the states have adopted some version of paragraphs (b)(2) and (b)(3), although there remains considerable variation in the language from jurisdiction to jurisdiction.

ABA Model Rule 1.6: Confidentiality of Information

(a) A lawyer shall not reveal information relating to the representation of a client unless the client gives informed consent, the disclosure is impliedly authorized in order to carry out the representation or the disclosure is permitted by paragraph (b).

(b) A lawyer may reveal information relating to the representation of a client to the extent the lawyer reasonably believes necessary:

(1) to prevent reasonably certain death or substantial bodily harm;

(2) to prevent the client from committing a crime or fraud that is reasonably certain to result in substantial injury to the financial interests or property of another and in furtherance of which the client has used or is using the lawyer's services;

(3) to prevent, mitigate or rectify substantial injury to the financial interests or property of another that is reasonably certain to result or has resulted from the client's commission of a crime or fraud in furtherance of which the client has used the lawyer's services;

(4) to secure legal advice about the lawyer's compliance with these Rules;

(5) to establish a claim or defense on behalf of the lawyer in a controversy between the lawyer and the client, to establish a defense to a criminal charge or civil claim against the lawyer based upon conduct in which the client was involved, or to respond to allegations in any proceeding concerning the lawyer's representation of the client;

(6) to comply with other law or a court order; or

> (7) to detect and resolve conflicts of interest arising from the lawyer's change of employment or from changes in the composition or ownership of a firm, but only if the revealed information would not compromise the attorney-client privilege or otherwise prejudice the client.
>
> (c) A lawyer shall make reasonable efforts to prevent the inadvertent or unauthorized disclosure of, or unauthorized access to, information relating to the representation of a client.

As stated in the Model Rules, the duty of confidentiality is subject to several exceptions. In the case of each exception, the disclosure is permitted only to the extent the lawyer reasonably believes necessary.

A. Public Information

The Restatement of the Law Governing Lawyers states, "The law generally provides that a client communication cannot become public and still remain protected by the attorney-client privilege. . . . The scant case authority is divided on the question whether the definition of confidential client information includes publicly available information. . . ."[13] Rule 1.6 is silent on the subject of previously disclosed information, but *Lawyer Law: Comparing the ABA Model Rules of Professional Conduct with the ALI Restatement (Third) of the Law Governing Lawyers* states, "Unlike the rules relating to attorney-client privilege and work-product protection, failure to protect confidential client information adequately does not make the information less confidential. The lawyer's obligation to protect the information continues even after its initial disclosure."[14]

This question of confidentiality of public information is particularly relevant in the context of the conflicts rules, where, for example, information protected by Model Rule 1.6 figures in the equation of whether a duty to a former client under Model Rule 1.9(b) prohibits representation.[15] In discussing disqualification of lawyers due to conflicts with duties owed to former clients,

---

13. Restatement (Third) of the Law Governing Lawyers § 59 cmt. d (2000).

14. Thomas D. Morgan, Lawyer Law: Comparing the ABA Model Rules of Professional Conduct with the ALI Restatement (Third) of the Law Governing Lawyers 293 (2005). *See also* Ellen J. Bennett & Helen W. Gunnarsson, Annotated Model Rules of Prof'l Conduct, at 111–12 (9th ed. 2019).

15. ABA Model Rules of Prof'l Conduct Rule 1.9 (2020):

> (b) A lawyer shall not knowingly represent a person in the same or a substantially related matter in which a firm with which the lawyer formerly was associated had previously represented a client
>
> (1) whose interests are materially adverse to that person; and
>
> (2) about whom the lawyer had acquired information protected by Rules 1.6 and 1.9(c) that is material to the matter

the comment to Model Rule 1.9 states: "Information that has been disclosed to the public or to other parties adverse to the former client ordinarily will not be disqualifying."[16] As expressed by the Restatement:

> The absence of a similarly limiting provision in ABA Model Rule 1.8(b), which applies to ongoing representations, is not inconsistent. Any such lawyer use would be impermissible on the broad ground under ABA Model Rule 1.7 that a lawyer may not use even publicly known information to the detriment of a current client, whether to further a personal interest of the lawyer or to further the interest of another client. Revealing client information adversely in a way that is gratuitous or negligent would violate the duty to take all reasonably available steps to advance the client's lawful objectives.[17]

However, this conclusion derives from the duty of loyalty, not confidentiality.[18] Model Rule 1.6 does not put generally known information outside the boundaries of confidentiality. Though the duty that would be violated would be that of loyalty to the client, rather than confidentiality, the result is the same and the duties are inextricably bound in this context.

Hazard, Hodes, and Jarvis, in *The Law of Lawyering*, criticize what they perceive to be the too-broad nature of the confidentiality rule in regard to public information:

> [R]ead literally and in isolation, the rule is so stringent as to approach the unworkable and the unrealistic. . . .
>
> . . . [T]he overinclusion of "too much" material within the universe of protected confidential information can have awkward consequences. If a lawyer is charged with disclosing information that is technically protected by Rule 1.6, but would not be protected under a sensible reading of the rule, there will be inevitable pressure to force the situation into one of the other recognized exceptions to reach the proper result. Over the long run, this could harm the basically well-balanced regime of limited and narrow exceptions.[19]

---

16. ABA Model Rules of Prof'l Conduct Rule 1.9 cmt. 3 (2020). *See also* ABA Formal Op. 479 (2017). "Information is generally known within the meaning of Model Rule 1.9(c)(1) if it is widely recognized by members of the public in the relevant geographic area or it is widely recognized in the former client's industry, profession, or trade. For information to be generally known it must previously have been revealed by some source other than the lawyer or the lawyer's agents. Information that is publicly available is not necessarily generally known."

17. Restatement (Third) of the Law Governing Lawyers § 59 cmt. d (2000) (citations omitted).

18. "Loyalty and independent judgment are essential elements in the lawyer's relationship to a client." ABA Model Rules of Prof'l Conduct Rule 1.7 cmt. 1 (2020).

19. Geoffrey C. Hazard, Jr., W. William Hodes & Peter R. Jarvis, The Law of Lawyering § 10.16, at 10-100 (4th ed. 2018) (endnotes omitted).

Nevertheless, the ABA Standing Committee on Ethics and Professional Responsibility has concluded that "[l]awyers who blog or engage in other public commentary may not reveal information relating to a representation that is protected by Rule 1.6(a), including information contained in a public record, unless disclosure is authorized under the Model Rules."[20]

B. Paragraph (a) Impliedly Authorized Disclosures

Model Rule 1.6(a) specifically permits disclosure of client information when "impliedly authorized in order to carry out the representation." Comment 5 to the rule and ABA Formal Opinion 08-453 make it clear that disclosures between lawyers within a firm are impliedly authorized, except, of course, that disclosure may not be made to a lawyer in the firm who has been screened from participation in the matter because of a conflict.

The comment also states that "[e]xcept to the extent that the client's instructions or special circumstances limit that authority . . . a lawyer may be 'impliedly authorized' to admit a fact that cannot properly be disputed or to make a disclosure that facilitates a satisfactory conclusion to a matter."[21] Thus, for example, the District of Columbia Bar Legal Ethics Committee has stated that an attorney may disclose confidential information of a deceased client if "the attorney has reasonable grounds for believing that release of the information is impliedly authorized in furthering the interests of the former client in settling her estate."[22] The ABA Standing Committee on Ethics and Professional Responsibility has said that a lawyer hired by an insurance company to defend an insured "may disclose the insured's confidential information . . . to the insurer if the lawyer reasonably believes that doing so will advance the interests of the insured" and will not "affect a material interest of the insured adversely."[23] On the other hand, the Committee also has stated that "[a] lawyer should not, absent informed client consent, reveal to a judge the limits of the lawyer's settlement authority or the lawyer's advice to the client regarding settlement."[24]

C. Authorized Disclosures

As paragraph (a) of Rule 1.6 indicates, if disclosure is not impliedly authorized or otherwise permitted by the rule's exceptions (see section D, which follows),

---

20. ABA Formal Ethics Op. 480 (2017).
21. ABA Model Rules of Prof'l Conduct Rule 1.6 cmt. 5 (2020).
22. D.C. Ethics Op. 324 (2004). *See also* Haw. Ethics Op. 38 (1999); Kan. Ethics Op. 01-01 (2001).
23. ABA Formal Ethics Op. 01-421 (2001). *See generally* Restatement (Third) of the Law Governing Lawyers § 61 (2000) (permitting disclosure that advances client's interests). *See also* ABA Informal Ethics Op. 86-1518 (1986) (interpreting exception for disclosures impliedly authorized as permitting lawyer to disclose to opposing counsel, without client consultation, inadvertent omission of contract provision).
24. ABA Formal Ethics Op. 93-370 (1993).

then client consent is required. That consent must be informed, which means that "the lawyer has communicated adequate information and explanation about the material risks of and reasonably available alternatives to the proposed course of conduct."[25]

What is adequate information and explanation in the context of Rule 1.6? At a minimum, it should include mention of the risk of information being disclosed to others, of the possible loss of the attorney-client privilege, and of information that is disclosed being used to the client's disadvantage.[26]

D. Paragraph (b) Exceptions

1. Physical Harm

Paragraph (b)(1) was amended in February 2002, pursuant to the Report with Recommendation of the Commission on Evaluation of the Rules of Professional Conduct (Ethics 2000 Commission). Prior to the amendment, the rule permitted disclosure "to prevent the client from committing a criminal act that the lawyer believes is likely to result in imminent death or substantial bodily harm." The exception was broadened in three ways. First, the word "imminent" was replaced with "reasonably certain." Thus, the exception now authorizes disclosure to prevent serious physical harm that may occur at a later date.[27] For example, "a lawyer who knows that a client has accidentally discharged toxic waste into a town's water supply may reveal this information to the authorities if there is a present and substantial risk that a person who drinks the water will contract a life-threatening or debilitating disease and the lawyer's disclosure is necessary to eliminate the threat or reduce the number of victims."[28]

Second, there is no longer a requirement that the client be the one who will cause this level of harm. It could be the client's uncle or business partner whom the client would prefer to protect. Third, the criminal-act requirement was removed.

The hypothetical often used to illustrate perceived problems related to this exception prior to the 2003 rule change was derived from the case of *Spaulding v. Zimmerman.*[29]

> In that celebrated case, lawyers were defending the driver in a civil suit arising out of a serious automobile accident. The defendant's doctor examined the plaintiff and discovered a life-threatening aortic

---

25. ABA Model Rules of Prof'l Conduct Rule 1.0(e) (2020).

26. Ellen J. Bennett & Helen W. Gunnarsson, Annotated Model Rules of Prof'l Conduct, at 117–18 (9th ed. 2019). *See also* ABA Formal Ethics Op. 473 (2016).

27. Ellen J. Bennett & Helen W. Gunnarsson, Annotated Model Rules of Prof'l Conduct, at 119 (9th ed. 2019).

28. ABA Model Rules of Prof'l Conduct Rule 1.6 cmt. 6 (2020).

29. Spaulding v. Zimmerman, 116 N.W.2d 704 (Minn. 1962).

> aneurysm that was probably—but not certainly—caused by the accident. The plaintiff's own doctor had not discovered the aneurysm, and plaintiff's lawyers had (mistakenly) not requested the defense team's medical reports. A settlement agreement was worked out and approved by the court, while the plaintiff and his lawyers were still in the dark about plaintiff's true medical condition.
>
> * * *
>
> No confidentiality issue was presented in the actual case, because the lawyers unilaterally decided not to disclose, but it is certainly possible that even if the clients had been told about the aneurysm, they would have embargoed the information. In that event, the ultimate question would have to be faced: would the lawyers have discretion to disclose against the wishes of their clients in this extraordinary circumstance, or would they be prohibited by the rules of ethics from doing what is morally right?[30]

Under the current rule, the lawyers would have the discretion to disclose.

2. Crime-Fraud Exception

Paragraphs (b)(2) and (b)(3) of Model Rule 1.6 were adopted by the ABA House of Delegates and added to the rule in August 2003 pursuant to the Report with Recommendation of the ABA Task Force on Corporate Responsibility.[31] These changes, which were driven by the "issues relating to corporate responsibility arising out of the unexpected and traumatic bankruptcy of Enron and other Enron-like situations,"[32] were consistent with the existing rules in many states.

Paragraph (b)(2) addresses preventing a client's action that is going to cause harm, whereas paragraph (b)(3) addresses preventing, mitigating, or rectifying harm resulting from an action by the client that has already occurred. In both instances, the exception applies only when the lawyer's services have been or are being used in furtherance of the crime or fraud. So, if a client merely tells his lawyer that he is about to commit a crime or fraud (presumably one that would not result in reasonably certain death or substantial bodily harm and

30. Geoffrey C. Hazard, Jr., W. William Hodes & Peter R. Jarvis, The Law of Lawyering § 10.29, at 10-141 to 10-144 (4th ed. 2018) (endnote omitted). For a thorough examination of this case, including interviews with some of the historical characters, see Roger Cramton & Lori Knowles, *Professional Secrecy and Its Exceptions*: Spaulding v. Zimmerman *Revisited*, 83 Minn. L. Rev. 63 (1998).

31. *See* ABA, Library of Adopted Policies, https://www.americanbar.org/content/dam/aba/directories/policy/annual-2003/2003_am_119a.pdf (last visited July 17, 2022). The ABA House of Delegates had previously rejected the same recommendation made by the Ethics 2000 Commission two years earlier.

32. *Id.* (quoting Robert Hirshon, President of the American Bar Association, Charge to ABA Task Force on Corporate Responsibility, Mar. 28, 2002).

thus be covered under paragraph (b)(1)), paragraph (b)(2) does not provide a vehicle for the lawyer to reveal that confidential information. Likewise, if the client "confesses" to the lawyer about a completed crime or fraud, the lawyer cannot reveal information in order to prevent, rectify, or mitigate the financial harm if the lawyer's services have not been used in furtherance thereof.

While these exceptions are discretionary in form, it is possible that lawyers will convert "may reveal" into "must reveal" to avoid getting sued or prosecuted later themselves. In addition, Model Rule 4.1(b) provides that "in the course of representing a client a lawyer shall not knowingly fail to disclose a material fact when disclosure is necessary to avoid assisting a criminal or fraudulent act by a client, unless disclosure is prohibited by Rule 1.6." Thus, if it is permissive to reveal under Rule 1.6, it becomes mandatory under Rule 4.1 if the information to be revealed is material and the disclosure is necessary to avoid assisting the client's criminal or fraudulent act. This assumes, of course, that the lawyer's participation was "innocent," because otherwise the lawyer would have been an accessory to the crime or fraud and would have violated Rule 1.2(d) (which states that "a lawyer shall not counsel a client to engage, or assist a client, in conduct that the lawyer knows is criminal or fraudulent") at the time the lawyer provided the services, and violated Rule 1.16(a) by not withdrawing.

The crime-fraud exception to the confidentiality rule is similar to, but not the same as, the crime-fraud exception to the attorney-client privilege. The confidentiality exception

> applies only when the likelihood of financial loss is great and the lawyer reasonably believes that use or revelation is necessary to prevent the crime or fraud or to prevent, rectify, or mitigate the loss it causes. . . . In contrast, the crime-fraud exception to the attorney-client privilege . . . applies without regard to the consequences of the intended act so long as the act itself is a crime or fraud. That exception to the attorney-client privilege applies only when a client consults a lawyer with intention to obtain assistance to commit a crime or fraud or so uses the lawyer's services, whereas the [confidentiality exception] applies regardless of the client's intention at the time of consultation. . . . Finally, [the confidentiality exception] is limited to client acts in which a lawyer's services are employed; the crime-fraud exception [to the attorney-client privilege] applies whether or not the lawyer's services are so employed. Due to the several differences . . . a finding that a lawyer permissibly used or disclosed confidential client information . . . and a determination whether [the exception to the attorney-client privilege] applies must be made independently.[33]

33. Restatement (Third) of the Law Governing Lawyers § 67, at 507 (2000).

Two examples from the Restatement of the Law Governing Lawyers illustrate how these exceptions operate.

In the first instance, a lawyer prepares an opinion letter on behalf of a client. The lawyer later receives information that gives him reason to believe that the transaction for which he wrote the letter was criminal or fraudulent, a fact that the lawyer did not know at the time he wrote the letter. Because the lawyer's services were used, the lawyer has discretion to disclose the information in order to prevent, mitigate, or rectify any substantial injury to the financial interests or property of another that is reasonably certain to result or has resulted from the transaction.[34]

In the second instance, a client seeks assistance from a lawyer in defending against charges by a regulatory agency of participation in a scheme to defraud. The loss to the victim has already occurred. Though the lawyer comes to believe that the client's acts were fraudulent and caused the harm, she does not have discretion to disclose the client's confidential information because her services were not used in furtherance of the fraud.[35]

3. Ethics Advice

Paragraph (b)(4) of Model Rule 1.6 was added in February 2002 pursuant to the Report with Recommendation of the Ethics 2000 Commission. "Although disclosure to secure ethics advice will '[i]n most situations' be impliedly authorized, Rule 1.6(b)(4) permits disclosure even without implicit authorization[36] 'because of the importance of a lawyer's compliance with the Rules of Professional Conduct.'"[37] "Moreover, clients are adequately protected by the requirement that such disclosures be made only when protected by the attorney-client evidentiary privilege."[38] This is so because the person consulted will also be a lawyer, who will establish a new attorney-client privilege with the inquiring lawyer. The second lawyer also will be subject to a new confidentiality obligation vis-à-vis the inquiring lawyer under Rule 1.6.

The following illustration from *The Law of Lawyering* provides a good example of how this exception operates.

> Lawyer L is representing a client in a difficult matter involving novel and complex legal issues. Opposing counsel has also threatened—informally so far—to move to disqualify L, claiming that L violated the rules of professional conduct. L retains another lawyer to provide

34. *Id.* at 508.

35. *Id.* at 508–09.

36. See discussion at section II.B regarding impliedly authorized disclosure.

37. Ellen J. Bennett & Helen W. Gunnarsson, Annotated Model Rules of Prof'l Conduct, at 123 (9th ed. 2019) (quoting ABA Model Rules of Prof'l Conduct Rule 1.6 cmt. 9).

38. ABA, Ctr. for Prof'l Responsibility, Model Rule 1.6: Reporter's Explanation of Changes, http://www.americanbar.org/groups/professional_responsibility/policy/ethics_2000_commission/e2k_rule16rem.html (last visited July 17, 2022).

> himself with legal advice about handling the legal issues in the underlying case. Shortly thereafter, L informally consults [a professional responsibility] expert . . . about the ethical issues that have arisen.
>
> * * *
>
> The disclosures L must make to the consulting lawyer are in furtherance of the main representation, and are accordingly "impliedly authorized" under Rule 1.6(a), even when the consultation is not revealed to the client. . . .
>
> The analysis does not change merely because the consultation with the legal ethics expert is an informal one. The law professor probably needs to be given some client information in order to be able to respond properly, and the law professor—being a lawyer as well—must also abide by normal confidentiality and conflict of interest rules. The consultation and attendant disclosures are again "impliedly authorized" in the sense of Rule 1.6(a), because disqualification of L would adversely affect the client. However, out of an abundance of caution, L should reveal only such details as are necessary to a full understanding of the issues involved. L should not reveal the identity of his client unless it is germane.[39]

The ABA Standing Committee on Ethics and Professional Responsibility has suggested that the exception provided by paragraph (b)(4) provides a basis for the revelation of confidential information to an intermediary lawyer for the purpose of determining what conflicts may exist when lawyers change firms.[40] The Opinion, however, does not require the use of an intermediary lawyer when checking for conflicts between the incoming lawyer and the new firm. The Committee allows that the situation does not really fit into any of the rule's exceptions, but that "[b]ecause conflicts information is needed to detect and resolve conflicts of interest when lawyers move between firms, as a general matter and subject to [certain] limitations . . . , disclosure of conflicts information otherwise protected by Rule 1.6 should be considered permissible as necessary to comply with the Rules."[41] In 2012, the ABA, in recognition of the Committee's statements, adopted a new exception to Model Rule 1.6 (discussed in subsection II.D.6, Lawyer's Change of Employment).

39. Geoffrey C. Hazard, Jr., W. William Hodes & Peter R. Jarvis, The Law of Lawyering § 10.22, at 10-118, 10-119 (4th ed. 2018).

40. ABA Formal Ethics Op. 09-455 (2009).

41. *Id.* at 3.

4. Claim or Defense

Paragraph (b)(5) contains the only exception to Rule 1.6 that neither has been added nor amended since the original adoption of the rule in 1983 (although it has been renumbered).[42] Perhaps the most common use of this exception is to allow a lawyer to reveal confidential information to collect a fee.[43] However,

> [t]his right to use confidences . . . does not create a right to blackmail the client. The lawyer may not state to the client: "Pay the fee or I will reveal to your employer your income tax problems." The lawyer may only exercise the right to reveal client information to the extent that it is reasonably *necessary to establish or collect the fee. There must not be any extortion or unnecessary disclosure.*[44]

Similarly, if the lawyer seeks to withdraw from the representation of a client for nonpayment of fees in a civil litigation, the lawyer may "disclose only such confidential information as is reasonably necessary for the court to make an informed decision on the motion."[45]

The exception also applies to other kinds of claims. For example, the ABA Standing Committee on Ethics and Professional Responsibility has concluded that "a retaliatory discharge or similar claim by a former in-house lawyer against her employer is a 'claim' under Rule 1.6 (b)."[46]

The self-defense portion of the exception permits disclosure to defend claims brought against the lawyer by clients or third parties,

> for example, a person claiming to have been defrauded by the lawyer and client acting together. The lawyer's right to respond arises when an assertion of such complicity has been made. Paragraph (b)(5) does not require the lawyer to await the commencement of an action or proceeding that charges such complicity, so that the defense may be

---

42. *See* ABA, A Legislative History: The Development of the ABA Model Rules of Professional Conduct, 1982–2013, at 105–52 (2013).

43. "This aspect of the rule expresses the principle that the beneficiary of a fiduciary relationship may not exploit it to the detriment of the fiduciary." Model Rules of Prof'l Conduct Rule 1.6 cmt. 11 (2020).

44. Ronald D. Rotunda & John S. Dzienkowski, Legal Ethics: The Lawyer's Deskbook on Professional Responsibility § 1.6-12(c) (2018–2019 ed., ABA) (footnote omitted) (emphasis in original).

45. ABA Formal Ethics Op. 476 (2016).

46. ABA Formal Ethics Op. 01-424 (2001). "Whether, and to what extent, former in-house counsel may sue their former employers for employment-related matters varies among jurisdictions, and has changed over time. "The Model Code version of the exception, DR 4-101(C)(4), applied only to fee disputes and self-defense. This meant that wrongful discharge suits were not permitted unless they could be maintained without violating client confidences." Ellen J. Bennett & Helen W. Gunnarsson, Annotated Model Rules of Prof'l Conduct, at 125 (9th ed. 2019).

> established by responding directly to a third party who has made such an assertion.[47]

While formal proceedings are not required to assert the exception, such as when the lawyer is being investigated by a government agency, it has been held, though not universally, that public criticism, and, in particular, the online variety, is not enough to allow disclosure.[48]

5. Other Law or Court Order

Paragraph (b)(6) was added in February 2002 pursuant to the Report with Recommendation of the Ethics 2000 Commission. It distinguished the prior position as follows:

> Prior to the amendment, the Rule did not address whether lawyers are permitted or required to disclose information when such disclosure is required by other law or a court order. Former Comment [20], however, stated that a lawyer must comply with the final orders of a court or other tribunal requiring the lawyer to give information about the client, and former Comment [21] referred to other law that may supersede Rule 1.6. The Commission recommended that the text of Rule 1.6 be amended explicitly to permit, but not require, disclosure to comply with law or court orders. No change in substance was intended. See also Comments [12] and [13].[49]

However, similar to the crime-fraud exceptions described earlier, this exception, while discretionary in form, in practice converts "may reveal" into "must reveal" because of the "other law" or "court order" that applies. For example, in the case of a court order, the conversion may take place as follows. Someone demands that a lawyer provide information about a client. The lawyer's first response, instinctually, is: "Sorry, it's privileged." Only after a court rules that there is no privilege does the lawyer retreat to: "Okay, but it's still confidential." However, then the court says: "Fine. It may be confidential, so you can't reveal the information to your wife or your golfing buddies—but I'm ordering you to answer anyway, because we're in court, and in court only the evidence rules apply. And by the way, even though it's confidential, there's an exception that allows you to disclose in situations just like this one." Then

---

47. ABA Model Rules of Prof'l Conduct Rule 1.6 cmt. 10 (2020). *See also* Geoffrey C. Hazard, Jr., W. William Hodes & Peter R. Jarvis, The Law of Lawyering § 10.37, Disclosure of Client Confidences as a Matter of Preemptive Self-Defense (4th ed. 2018).

48. *See, e.g.*, *In re* Skinner, 758 S.E.2d 788 (Ga. 2014). *Cf. In re* Discipline of Draskovich, 439 P.3d 1177 (Nev. 2021). *See also* ABA Formal Ethics Op. 496 (2021).

49. ABA, Ctr. for Prof'l Responsibility, Model Rule 1.6: Reporter's Explanation of Changes, http://www.americanbar.org/groups/professional_responsibility/policy/ethics_2000_commission/e2k_rule16rem.html (last visited July 17, 2022).

the lawyer says (to himself): "I think that 'may disclose' just turned into 'must disclose,' because the judge is going to hold me in contempt if I don't comply. And I won't get into trouble with the lawyer disciplinary authorities if I do testify, because of the permission given me under the court order exception to the confidentiality rule."

a. Other Law

The Annotated Model Rules of Professional Conduct provides the following examples of this exception:

> [T]he Internal Revenue Code, . . . 26 U.S.C. § 6050, . . . compels lawyers to disclose, through IRS Form 8300, the identities of clients and the amounts and payment dates of all cash fees in excess of $10,000.
>
> * * *
>
> The issue also arises in connection with statutes requiring that child abuse be reported. See, e.g., N.Y. City Ethics Op. 1997-2 (1997) (lawyer employed by social service agency may disclose information relating to abuse of minor client to social service agency if required by law).[50]

And even though the other law may require disclosure, the lawyer "must discuss the matter with the client to the extent required by Rule 1.4."[51]

b. Court Order

As noted at the beginning of this chapter, the attorney-client privilege applies in judicial proceedings. Nevertheless, in that context, "[a]lthough a determination of whether a lawyer must reveal client information . . . will turn on rules of evidence rather than rules of ethics, the lawyer's ethical duty of confidentiality governs important aspects of the lawyer's response to a demand for information."[52]

In that regard, the lawyer, "[a]bsent informed consent of the client to do otherwise, . . . should assert on behalf of the client all nonfrivolous claims that the order is not authorized by law or that the information sought is protected against disclosure by the attorney-client privilege or other applicable law."[53]

---

50. Ellen J. Bennett & Helen W. Gunnarsson, Annotated Model Rules of Prof'l Conduct, at 129 (9th ed. 2019).

51. ABA Model Rules of Prof'l Conduct Rule 1.6 cmt. 12 (2020).

52. Ellen J. Bennett & Helen W. Gunnarsson, Annotated Model Rules of Prof'l Conduct, at 110 (9th ed. 2019).

53. ABA Model Rules of Prof'l Conduct Rule 1.6 cmt. 15 (2020). *See also* N.Y. State Ethics Op. 1239 (Mar. 22, 2022) ("An attorney in receipt of a court order directing production of his hard drive containing the confidential information of clients who have not waived privilege or consented to

However, the scope of the protection offered by the attorney-client privilege is not increased by application of the duty of confidentiality, which will thus not provide a reason for noncompliance with a court order.[54] Nevertheless, "a lawyer may reveal information related to the representation of a client [only] to the extent the lawyer reasonably believes necessary."[55]

Legal Ethics: The Lawyer's Deskbook on Professional Responsibility provides an example of how the limitation upon this exception might work in practice. In the course of representing a client regarding a business proposal, a lawyer uncovers information from third parties that relates to the representation. Pursuant to a criminal investigation, a court later orders the lawyer to reveal this information to a grand jury on the grounds that it is not protected by the evidentiary privilege, having not been the result of a communication between the client and the lawyer. The lawyer obeys the court order. Later, reporters ask him whether he complied. He answers: "Yes." Then they ask him what he said to the grand jury. If the lawyer tells them, the lawyer will commit a disciplinary violation by revealing information relating to the representation that remains protected by the confidentiality rule.[56]

6. Lawyer's Change of Employment

Paragraph (b)(7) was added to Model Rule 1.6 in August 2012 pursuant to the Report with Recommendation of the Commission on Ethics 20/20. This addition built upon ABA Ethics Opinion 09-455 (Disclosure of Conflicts Information When Lawyers Move between Law Firms). The commission decided to amend the rule to provide "a firmer doctrinal basis" for the revelation of information in the change of employment situation "and more readily available guidance on the limitations on such disclosures."[57] Notably, this is the one place where the attorney-client privilege is mentioned in a Model Rule itself, as opposed to one of its comments, suggesting the overriding importance of not compromising the privilege in this context.

E. Paragraph (c) Inadvertent or Unauthorized Disclosures

Paragraph (c) of Model Rule 1.6 also was added in August 2012 pursuant to the Report with Recommendation of the Commission on Ethics 20/20. It was thought necessary "in light of the increase in electronic storage and dissemination of information."[58] It was a matter of putting in the rule for purposes of

---

disclosure, has the obligation to advise non-waiving clients of the existence of the court order . . . [and take] reasonable steps necessary to avoid or limit production of confidential information. . . .").

54. Adams v. Franklin, 924 A.2d 993 (D.C. 2007).

55. ABA Model Rules of Prof'l Conduct Rule 1.6(b) (2020).

56. Ronald D. Rotunda & John S. Dzienkowski, Legal Ethics: The Lawyer's Deskbook on Professional Responsibility § 1.6-1 (2018–2019 ed., ABA).

57. ABA, A Legislative History: The Development of the ABA Model Rules of Professional Conduct, 1982–2013, at 146 (2013).

58. *Id.*

clarity that which was already recognized in the comments to the rule regarding the need to make reasonable efforts to protect information relating to the representation.

If an opposing lawyer inadvertently transmits confidential information, Model Rule 4.4(b) comes into play, requiring notification to the sender of the occurrence. However, the comment to the rule specifically acknowledges that any "additional steps, such as returning the document or deleting electronically stored information, is a matter of law beyond the scope of these Rules, as is the question of whether the privileged status of a document or electronically stored information has been waived."[59]

59. *See* Chapter 6 on Waiver for a discussion of this topic.

CHAPTER 3

The Work-Product Privilege

ROBERT P. REDEMANN

This chapter focuses on the origin, purpose, and elements of the work-product doctrine, which is referred to in this book by its most common name, the work-product privilege, although it is more accurately a qualified discovery and evidentiary immunity.[1] This chapter further examines the various courts' interpretations of those elements, selected states' rules regarding the work-product privilege, and cases regarding specific types of documents evaluated by the courts.

I. Basic Definition and Purpose

A. *Hickman v. Taylor*

The work-product privilege is designed to achieve two major goals, the primary one of which is "safeguarding the fruits of an attorney's trial preparations."[2] Its other major goal is to prevent "freeloading" off an opponent's work efforts.[3] Other goals have been described as freedom to evaluate a case thoroughly and record thoughts, strategies, and mental impressions.[4] Yet another goal is to provide a "breathing space for attorneys to prepare witnesses for depositions."[5]

1. Jane Doe 1 v. Baylor Univ., 335 F.R.D. 476, 487 (W.D. Tex. 2020) ("The doctrine does not place work product outside the scope of discovery, but instead 'creates a form of qualified immunity from discovery' for materials prepared in anticipation of litigation) (quoting Chiasson v. Zapata Gulf Marine Corp., 988 F.2d 513, 514 n.2 (5th Cir. 1993)). *See also* Neonode Smartphone, LLC v. Apple, Inc., 2022 WL 1285429, at * 3 (N.D. Cal. Apr. 29, 2022); Murphy v. Gorman, 271 F.R.D. 296. 311 (D.N.M. 2010) (quoting Moore's Federal Practice that the "work product doctrine is not actually a privilege, but rather a qualified immunity from discovery").

2. Judicial Watch, Inc. v. Consumer Fin. Protection Bureau, 985 F. Supp. 2d 1, 8 (D.C. 2013) (quotation omitted from United States v. AT&T Co., 642 F.2d 1285, 1299 (D.C. Cir. 1980)).

3. Diaz v. Devlin, 327 F.R.D. 26, 29 (D. Mass. 2018).

4. United States v. Nobles, 422 U.S. 225, 237 (1975).

5. Sporck v. Peil, 759 F.2d 312, 317 (3d Cir.1985); *see also In re* Xarelto (Rivaroxaban) Prods. Liab. Litig., 314 F.R.D. 397 (E.D. La. 2016).

Overall, the work-product privilege has been described as a positive for the adversary system, because it encourages each party to prepare its best case in confidence:

> In contrast [to the attorney-client privilege], the work-product doctrine promotes the adversary system directly by protecting the confidentiality of papers prepared by or on behalf of attorneys in anticipation of litigation. *Appleton Papers, Inc. v. E.P.A.*, 702 F.3d 1018, 1022 (7th Cir. 2012); *Westinghouse Elec. Corp. v. Republic of Philippines*, 951 F.2d 1414, 1428 (3rd Cir. 1991); *E.E.O.C. v. FAPS, Inc.*, 2012 WL 1656738, 28 (D.N.J. 2012).[6]

Recognized by the United States Supreme Court in *Hickman v. Taylor*,[7] the Court first noted that it was faced with a balancing task between various safeguards to protect the privacy of a person's work and the public policy supporting reasonable and necessary inquiries. "Properly to balance these competing interests is a delicate and difficult task."[8] This difficult balancing task is involved in all court decisions where the work-product privilege is asserted and challenged.

Hickman v. Taylor involved the death of a crewman during the sinking of a tug and the litigation that followed. Shortly after the sinking, the tug owners employed an attorney "to defend them against potential suits by the representatives of the deceased crewmen" and to sue for damages to the tug.[9] After a public hearing regarding the incident, at which four of the survivors gave testimony, the attorney took private statements from them with "an eye toward the anticipated litigation."[10]

A Jones Act case was filed for the death of one of the crewmen against the tug owners and a railroad. The plaintiff's attorney made a demand for the statements taken by the interviewing attorney, both in an interrogatory and during the deposition of the interviewing attorney. The interviewing attorney refused to produce the statements, and the district court held him in contempt and ordered him jailed. An appeal of the lower court's order to the Third Circuit Court of Appeals[11] resulted in a reversal, with that court stating: "Information

---

6. Miller UK Ltd. v. Caterpillar, Inc., 17 F. Supp. 3d 711, 736 (N.D. Ill. 2014). This is true not only in civil litigation but also in criminal cases. *See* United States v. Nobles, 422 U.S. 225, 238 (1975) ("Although the work-product doctrine most frequently is asserted as a bar to discovery in civil litigation, its role in assuring the proper functioning of the criminal justice system is even more vital. The interests of society and the accused in obtaining a fair and accurate resolution of the question of guilt or innocence demand that adequate safeguards assure the thorough preparation and presentation of each side of the case.").

7. 329 U.S. 495 (1947).

8. *Id.* at 497.

9. *Id.* at 498.

10. *Id.*

11. 153 F.2d 212.

here sought was part of the 'work product of the lawyer' and hence privileged from discovery under the Federal Rules of Civil Procedure."[12]

The Supreme Court, after noting that the factual information sought was available to the requester through the public hearing and his own investigation, stated:

> Here is simply an attempt, without purported necessity or justification, to secure written statements, private memoranda and personal recollections prepared or formed by an adverse party's counsel in the course of his legal duties. . . . As such, it falls outside the arena of discovery and contravenes the public policy underlying the orderly prosecution and defense of legal claims. Not even the most liberal of discovery theories can justify unwarranted inquiries into the files and the mental impressions of an attorney.[13]

The Court explained what it meant by an orderly prosecution and defense of claims:

> [I]t is essential that a lawyer work with a certain degree of privacy, free from unnecessary intrusion by opposing parties and their counsel. Proper preparation of a client's case demands that he assemble information, sift what he considers to be the relevant from the irrelevant facts, prepare his legal theories and plan his strategy without undue and needless interference.[14]

The work product of the lawyer included in that preparation consists of, "interviews, statements, memoranda, correspondence, briefs, mental impressions, personal beliefs, and countless other tangible and intangible ways. . . ."[15] Commenting on how disclosure of these materials would affect the legal profession, the Court wrote:

> Were such materials open to opposing counsel on mere demand, much of what is now put down in writing would remain unwritten. An attorney's thoughts, heretofore inviolate, would not be his own. Inefficiency, unfairness and sharp practices would inevitably develop in the giving of legal advice and in the preparation of cases for trial. The effect on the legal profession would be demoralizing. And the interests of the clients and the cause of justice would be poorly served.[16]

---

12. 329 U.S. at 499–500.
13. *Id.* at 510.
14. *Id.* at 510–11.
15. *Id.* at 511.
16. *Id.*

The Court's language has been interpreted to incorporate an "anti-freeloading" concept, that one's adversary should not be able to profit from an attorney's diligence and preparation. In the concurring opinion by Justice Jackson, he wrote:

> The real purpose and the probable effect of the practice ordered by the district court would be to put trials on a level even lower than a "battle of wits." I can conceive of no practice more demoralizing to the Bar than to require a lawyer to write out and deliver to his adversary an account of what witnesses have told him.[17]

The Court then turned to the other policy of free and fair disclosure of all relevant facts in the preparation of a case and performed its balancing function. It noted there are limitations on this privilege:

> We do not mean to say that all written materials obtained or prepared by an adversary's counsel with an eye toward litigation are necessarily free from discovery in all cases. Where relevant and non-privileged facts remain hidden in an attorney's file and where production of those facts is essential to the preparation of one's case, discovery may properly be had.[18]

However, the burden rests on the one seeking to invade the privacy of the attorney to establish adequate reasons to justify the intrusion.[19]

The Court established a variety of concepts that consistently appear in the cases involving the assertion and challenge to the claim of attorney work product:

1. The privilege arises within the context of actual or anticipated litigation.
2. The information sought must be attorney work product;
3. An attempt to secure the information without necessity or justification falls outside of proper discovery.
4. No discovery theory justifies the unwarranted inquiry into the files and mental impressions of an attorney.
5. In order to do her job, a lawyer must have a degree of privacy free from intrusion by an opposing party.
6. Work product can include both tangible and intangible items.
7. Without the needed privacy, inefficiency, unfairness, and sharp practices are likely to develop.

---

17. 329 U.S. at 516.
18. *Id.*
19. *Id.*

8. Not all written materials prepared by an attorney for litigation are necessarily free from discovery.
9. Relevant, and privileged, facts necessary to develop a case may be subject to discovery;
10. The burden of proving justification for production of work product rests on the party seeking to invade the privileged information.
11. Justice is best served when each party does its own preparation, as opposed to freeloading off the other party.
12. It is the court that decides whether or not the privilege has been appropriately invoked.

"Although 'the attorney-client privilege and the work product doctrine spring from the same common law origin' the work product doctrine under contemporary law 'is distinct from and broader than the attorney-client privilege.'"[20] The idea that this privilege is broader than the attorney-client privilege stems from the fact that it can include third parties working for the attorney on behalf of the client and, in most cases, continues to exist after the attorney-client relationship no longer exists. "[T]he work product privilege 'functions not merely and (perhaps) not mainly to assist the client in obtaining complete legal advice but in addition to establish a protected area in which the lawyer can prepare his case free from adversarial scrutiny.'"[21]

B. Federal Rule of Civil Procedure 26(b)(3)

The discovery rules, as interpreted by the Court in *Hickman* and subsequent cases, have resulted in multiple revisions to Federal Rule of Civil Procedure 26, but the balancing requirement has remained. Current Rule 26(b)(3)[22] has incorporated the privilege and the limitation that not all material is exempt from discovery under all situations, as explained in *Hickman*. The rule's language states:

> Ordinarily, a party may not discover documents and tangible things that are prepared in anticipation of litigation or for trial by or for another party or its representative (including the other party's attorney, consultant, surety, indemnitor, insurer, or agent). But, subject to Rule 26(b)(4), those materials may be discovered if:

---

20. *In re* Murphy, 560 F.2d 326, 337 (8th Cir. 1977) (quotations omitted from *In re Grand Jury Proceedings*, 473 F.2d 840, 844 (8th Cir. 1973) and United States v. Nobles, 422 U.S. 225, 238 n.11 (1975)).

21. Lamar Advertising of South Dakota Inc. v. Kay, 267 F.R.D. 568, 575 (D. S.D. 2010) (quoting *In re* Special September 1978 Grand Jury (II), 640 F.2d 49, 62 (7th Cir. 1980)).

22. Rule 26 was last revised in 2015, with the latest revision to 26(b)(3) occurring in 2007. *See* Advisory Committee Notes 2007.

(1) they are otherwise discoverable under Rule 26(b)(1); and
(2) the party shows that it has substantial need for the materials to prepare its case and cannot, without undue hardship, obtain their substantial equivalent by other means.[23]

The rule has also been expanded to address the question of expert trial preparation[24] and the procedure to be used when claiming the privilege or protecting trial preparation materials.[25]

C. Selected State Rules

Several states, following the lead of the federal rules, have developed their own versions of Rule 26, but with slightly differing language. For instance, the Texas rule defines an attorney's work product as "core work product" that is not discoverable,[26] while other work product can be obtained upon a showing of substantial need and undue hardship in acquiring the information through alternative means.[27] Under the California statute, "[a] writing that reflects an attorney's impressions, conclusions, opinions, or legal research or theories is not discoverable under any circumstances," and other attorney work product is not discoverable unless the court finds that denial will unfairly prejudice a party's case or will result in an injustice.[28]

Illinois has a Supreme Court rule that states: "Material prepared by or for a party in preparation for trial is subject to discovery only if it does not contain or disclose the theories, mental impressions, or litigation plans of the party's attorney."[29] New York has a statute that reads: "The work product of an attorney shall not be obtainable,"[30] and materials otherwise discoverable and prepared in anticipation of litigation or for trial by or for a party's representative, including an attorney, may be obtained, but only on a showing of substantial need and undue hardship in acquiring the same or similar information.[31]

Most other states have similar rules in place, all with the balancing of full disclosure with the need for some privacy and the refusal to allow freeloading.

---

23. Fed. R. Civ. P. 26(b)(3)(A).
24. Fed. R. Civ. P. 26(b)(4).
25. Fed. R. Civ. P. 26(b)(5). This rule requires that a party claiming the privilege must "(i) expressly make the claim; and (ii) describe the nature of the [materials] . . . in a manner that . . . will enable other parties to assess the claim."
26. Tex. R. Civ. P. 192.5(b)(1).
27. Tex. R. Civ. P. 192.5(b)(2).
28. West's Ann. Cal. Civ. P. Code § 2018.030.
29. ILCS S. Ct. Rule 201, (b)(2).
30. McKinney's CPLR § 3101, (b).
31. McKinney's CPLR § 3101, (d)(2).

II. Elements of the Work-Product Privilege

A. The Need for Litigation

As mentioned in *Hickman v. Taylor*, the privilege extends to material developed in anticipation of litigation or during litigation.[32] This is mirrored in Federal Rule of Civil Procedure 26(b)(3), which states: "Ordinarily, a party may not discover documents and tangible things that are prepared in anticipation of litigation or for trial. . . ." In the recent Ninth Circuit case of *United States v. Sanmina Corp.*,[33] the Circuit Court of Appeals stated: "The work-product doctrine is a 'qualified' privilege that protects 'from discovery documents and tangible things prepared by a party or his representative in anticipation of litigation,'" and "the primary purpose of the work-product rule is to 'prevent exploitation of a party's efforts in preparing for litigation.'"[34] The *Hickman* court majority opinion never mentioned exploitation directly, but it may be inferred from the need for privacy and the worry that "sharp practices" might develop without protection from intrusion by opposing counsel. It may also be inferred from the statement in the concurring opinion by Justice Jackson: "Discovery was hardly intended to enable a learned profession to perform its functions either without wits or on wits borrowed from the adversary."[35]

B. The Anticipation of Litigation

Clearly, if suit is filed and a document is prepared by an attorney for that suit, the litigation requirement to assert the work-product privilege has been satisfied. If suit has not yet been filed, then another evaluation must take place to determine if the material sought to be protected was created in anticipation of litigation.

It has been said that it is "admittedly difficult to reduce to a neat general formula the relationship between preparation of a document and possible litigation necessary to trigger the protection of the work product doctrine."[36] The courts have developed several different tests since *Hickman* in an attempt to help parties understand when a document has been created in anticipation of litigation. These tests include:

---

32. 329 U.S. 495 at 498.

33. 968 F.3d 1107 (9th Cir. 2020).

34. *Id.* at 1119. *See also* Adams v. Mem'l Herman, 973 F.3d 343, 349 (5th Cir. 2020) ([The privilege] protects materials prepared in anticipation of litigation, whether those materials were prepared by the attorney or by agents of the attorney. *In re* Grand Jury Proceedings, 601 F.2d 162, 171 (5th Cir. 1979)).

35. Hickman v. Taylor, 329 U.S. 495, 516 (1947).

36. United States v. Davis, 636 F.2d 1028, 1040 (5th Cir. 1981).

- The "because of" test,[37]
- The "primary-purpose" test,[38]
- The "dual-purpose" test,[39] and
- The "sole-purpose" test.[40]

Just as the burden is on the party wishing to claim the privilege, "the burden of showing that the materials were prepared in anticipation of litigation is on the party asserting privilege."[41] The burden to provide sufficient evidence to the court to support the claim of privilege is present in all of the tests, not just the primary-purpose test, although the nature of the evidence can vary, as described next.

The individual circumstances of each case will control the outcome, and courts within districts have not always been consistent in applying the following tests for what constitutes the necessary anticipation of litigation.

1. "Because of" Test

The Ninth Circuit Court of Appeals has stated that "a document . . . should be deemed prepared 'in anticipation of litigation' and thus [be] eligible for work product protection . . . if in light of the nature of the document and the factual

---

37. Am. Civil Liberties Union of N. California v. United States Dep't of Justice, 880 F.3d 473, 485 (9th Cir. 2018) (When a document was not prepared exclusively for litigation, it "should be deemed prepared 'in anticipation of litigation' and thus eligible for work product protection . . . if 'in light of the nature of the document and the factual situation in the particular case, the document can be fairly said to have been prepared or obtained because of the prospect of litigation.'" (quoting Charles A. Wright, Arthur R. Miller & Richard L. Marcus, 8 Federal Practice & Procedure § 2024 (2d ed. 1994)) (Internal case citation omitted.).

38. United States v. Davis, 636 F.2d 1028, 1040 (5th Cir. 1981) (We conclude that litigation need not necessarily be imminent, as some courts have suggested . . . as long as the primary motivating purpose behind the creation of the document was to aid in possible future litigation.) (citations omitted). *But see* United States v. Willis, 565 F. Supp. 1186, 1203 (S.D. Iowa 1983) (the *Davis* holding appears to be at odds with the Wigmore test adopted by the Eighth Circuit. . . . This analysis appears to suggest that the *Davis* court viewed tax preparation by attorneys in a vacuum—as the only service provided to a particular client—rather than as an integral part of the total legal services lawyers provide their clients.).

39. *See In re* Grand Jury Subpoena (Mark Torf/Torf Environmental), 357 F.3d 900, 910 (9th Cir. 2004). (The documents are entitled to work product protection, because taking into account the facts surrounding their creation, their litigation purpose so permeates any non-litigation purpose that the two purposes cannot be discretely separated from the factual nexus as a whole.)

40. Judicial Watch, Inc. v. U.S. Dep't of Homeland Security, 926 F. Supp. 2d 121, 138 (D.D.C. 2013) (the motivational element demands that the document be prepared or obtained *because of* the prospect of litigation. In this respect, the proponent bears the burden of "showing that the documents were prepared for the purpose of assisting an attorney in preparing for litigation, and not some other reason." (Internal citation omitted.) (citing Alexander v. F.B.I., 192 F.R.D. 42, 46 (D.D.C. 2000)).

41. Alexander v. F.B.I., 192 F.R.D. 42, 46 (D.D.C. 2000) (citing Compagnie Francaise d'Assurance v. Phillips Petroleum Co., 105 F.R.D. 16, 40 (S.D.N.Y. 1984)).

situation in the particular case, the document can be fairly said to have been prepared or obtained because of the prospect of litigation."[42]

The Second Circuit, in approving the " because of" language used by the Wright and Miller treatise,[43] and while noting such language was also used by the Third, Fourth, Seventh, Eighth, and D.C. Circuits, has construed the phrase "in anticipation of litigation" to mean that "in light of the nature of the document and the factual situation in the particular case, the document can fairly be said to have been prepared or obtained *because of* the prospect of litigation."[44]

This test has been called "more lenient," because material developed for litigation can also be used for an ordinary business purpose without losing its protected status.[45] Because it looks at both the nature of the document and the circumstances surrounding its origin, it is important to provide such facts to the court so that the court has a full appreciation of the document's creation.

2. Primary-Purpose Test

Earlier decisions in the Seventh and D.C. Circuits used a slightly different standard, under which "[t]he mere contingency of litigation alone is not enough to warrant protection under the work product doctrine. Rather, the primary motive behind the creation of the document or investigation must be to aid in the adversarial trial process itself."[46] The Fifth Circuit seems to have adopted this approach, as well.[47]

The purpose of the material in question must be examined. The court in *Pinnacle Surety Services, Inc. v. Manion Stigger, LLP*[48] stated that "'an ordinary business purpose' does not suffice," and that "the burden is on the party

---

42. Am. Civil Liberties Union of N. California v. United States Dep't of Justice, 880 F.3d 473, 485 (9th Cir. 2018) (quotation omitted from Charles A. Wright, Arthur R. Miller & Richard L. Marcus, 8 Federal Practice & Procedure § 2024 (2d ed. 1994)).

43. Charles A. Wright, Arthur R. Miller & Richard L. Marcus, 8 Federal Practice & Procedure § 2024, at 343 (1994).

44. United States v. Adlman,134 F.3d 1194, 1202 (2d Cir. 1998). The Adlman court notes that the Fifth Circuit, at the time, seemed to choose a different test. That was, "The 'primarily to assist in litigation' formulation is exemplified by a line of cases from the United States Court of Appeals for the Fifth Circuit. *United States v. Davis,* 636 F.2d 1028 (5th Cir.), *cert. denied,* 454 U.S. 862, 102 S. Ct. 320, 70 L. Ed. 2d 162 (1981)." 134 F.3d at 1198.

45. U.S. v. DeLoitte, LLP, 610 F.3d 129, 138 (D.C. Cir. 2010) (a document can contain protected work-product material even though it serves multiple purposes, so long as the protected material was prepared because of the prospect of litigation).

46. Ferguson v. Lurie, 139 F.R.D. 362, 367 (N.D. Ill. 1991) (citing EEOC v. Commonwealth Edison, 119 F.R.D. 394, 395 (N.D. Ill. 1988); Janicker v. George Washington Univ., 94 F.R.D. 648, 650 (D.D.C. 1982)). *But see* U.S. v. Adlman, 134 F.3d 1194, 1200 (2d Cir. 1998), wherein the need for a specific adversary process is discussed and discarded.

47. *See* United States v. Davis, 636 F.2d 1028 (5th Cir. 1981); United States v. El Paso Co., 682 F.2d 530 (5th Cir. 1982).

48. 370 F. Supp. 3d 745 (W.D. Ky. 2019).

claiming protection to show that anticipated litigation was the driving force behind the preparation of each requested document."[49] In essence, the courts are weighing the purposes for which the material was created to see which is the more likely motivation.

3. Dual-Purpose Test

In the recent case *South Fifth Towers, LLC v. Aspen Insurance UK Ltd.*,[50] the Sixth Circuit explained that anticipation of litigation is judged from the perspective of the creator of the document, but in an objective way. In discussing whether a document was created for more than one purpose, the court said: "Our test 'asks (1) whether a document was created because of a party's subjective anticipation of litigation, as contrasted with an ordinary business purpose, and (2) whether that subjective anticipation of litigation was objectively reasonable.'"[51]

South Fifth Towers owned an apartment building that suffered water damage during a storm. Its insurer, Aspen Insurance, declined to cover the cost of demolition and repair. During the litigation that followed, South Fifth requested both attorney and investigator documents from Aspen, for which Aspen claimed either the attorney-client privilege or work-product privilege. The dispute was presented to a magistrate judge, who reviewed the documents in camera and determined that all of the materials but one were protected by the privileges. The district court affirmed the magistrate's decision when appealed, and the Sixth Circuit affirmed the district court's ruling.

South Fifth argued that the attorney and investigators' documents were created for a business purpose, specifically handling the claim, and that both the magistrate judge and district court over-relied on a letter from South Fifth's attorney to Aspen's attorney before the creation of the documents to reach their decisions. The Sixth Circuit explained:

> The letter warned that failure to attend to South Fifth's insurance claim would "lead to the conclusion that Aspen is in breach of its policy." . . . As the district court observed, given that "breach of contract" is a common cause of action in insurance disputes, it was reasonable for the Magistrate Judge to find that a letter warning the opposing party that it would be "in breach of its policy . . . created both a subjective and objectively reasonable anticipation of litigation."[52]

This statement incorporates both the subjective test (the factual situation as perceived by the party) and the objective test (the document can be fairly said to be created for litigation).

---

49. 370 F. Supp.3d at 755.
50. 763 Fed. Appx. 401 (6th Cir. 2019).
51. *Id.* at 405 (quoting United States v. Roxworthy, 457 F.3d 590, 594 (6th Cir. 2006)).
52. *Id.* at 406 (quotations omitted).

Thus, while looking at the perspective of Aspen's attorney when receiving the letter, the subjective view, the court still required that perspective to pass an objective test, as well, for the privilege to attach. This double test is required to prevent blanket statements about the fear of litigation from totally blocking all attempts to appropriately challenge the invocation of the privilege simply because of a party's viewpoint of the circumstances. It is part of the balancing test the court goes through.

4. Sole-Purpose Test

The sole-purpose test is the most restrictive of the tests. "[T]o qualify [for the work-product privilege] the documents had to be prepared in order to assist an attorney in preparing for a trial or for use at that trial. If the documents were prepared for some other reason, the work-product privilege did not apply merely because a lawyer prepared them at some point during the pendency of litigation."[53] "[T]he documents must at least have been prepared with a specific claim supported by concrete facts which would likely lead to litigation in mind."[54] "To demonstrate that this privilege is applicable, it must be shown that the material was prepared exclusively in anticipation of litigation."[55] To satisfy this test, an affidavit regarding the facts and the likely litigation is suggested.

C. Duration of the Privilege

While considered broader[56] than attorney-client privilege but narrowly construed.[57] The work-product privilege is of continuing duration.[58]

> Were the work product protection not continuing, a situation would result in which a client's communications to an attorney, which must be full, frank and open, are protected, Tex. R. Civ. Evid. 503, but the same attorney's work product done in furtherance of such attorney-client relationship is not. This anomaly clearly cannot be allowed.[59]

---

53. Athridge v. Aetna Cas. & Sur. Co., 184 F.R.D. 200, 205 (D.D.C. 1998).

54. Coastal States Gas Corp. v. Dep't of Energy, 617 F.2d 854, 865 (D.C. Cir. 1980).

55. Fields v. First Liberty Ins. Corp., 954 N.Y.S.2d 427, 431 (S. Ct. N.Y. 2012).

56. "[T]he work-product doctrine is distinct from and broader than the attorney-client privilege." United States v. Nobles, 422 U.S. 225, 238 n.11 (1975); *In re* Grand Jury Proceedings, 601 F.2d 162, 171 (5th Cir. 1979).

57. "[C]ourts have always construed the privilege narrowly, *Swidler & Berlin*, 524 U.S. at 411, 118 S. Ct. 2081, and will not apply it 'unless to do so will serve a public good transcending the normally predominant principle of utilizing all rational means for ascertaining truth.' *Shaffer*, 662 F.3d at 446." Pearlshire Capital Group, LLC v. Zaid, 490 F. Supp. 3d 1299, 1307 (N.D. Ill. 2020).

58. *See* Humphreys v. Caldwell, 888 S.W.2d 469, 471 (Tex. 1994).

59. Owens-Corning Fiberglass Corp. v. Caldwell, 818 S.W.2d 749, 751 (Tex. 1991).

The Eighth Circuit also supported the position of permanent privilege for attorney work product[60] when it noted:

> The work product privilege would be attenuated if it were limited to documents that were prepared in the case for which discovery is sought. What is needed, if we are to remain faithful to the articulated policies of Hickman, is a perpetual protection for work product, one that extends beyond the termination of the litigation for which the documents were prepared. Any less protection would generate the very evils that the Court in Hickman attempted to avoid.[61]

The Illinois Supreme Court has also taken this position[62] and held that it also extends to nonrelated litigation when they cited the Eighth Circuit case *In re Murphy*.[63] "If work product is protected in related, but not unrelated future cases, an attorney would be hesitant to assemble extensive work product materials because of the concern that the materials will not be protected in later, unrelated litigation. The unrelatedness of the subsequent litigation provides an insufficient basis for disregarding the privilege."[64]

While the privilege may extend to nonrelated litigation, several cases have held that it does not extend to nonparties. In a Michigan case, where a widow brought an action against the police officers for the death of her husband, she subpoenaed the records of the local prosecutor who had done an investigation to determine whether or not to bring charges against the officers. The prosecutor resisted, claiming work-product privilege.

The court ordered production, because while Michigan's work-product rule is similar to the federal rule, "the court rule prohibits the discovery of materials compiled by a *party* or a party's representative in anticipation of litigation absent a showing of substantial need for the materials and inability to obtain the materials through other means. The court rule does not apply the same restrictions to the work product of an attorney for a nonparty."[65] A similar outcome occurred in a Ninth Circuit case, where materials prepared by attorneys for the California Public Utilities Commission were deemed not protected from discovery under the work-product doctrine in a case between

60. *In re* Murphy, 560 F.2d 326 (8th Cir. 1977).

61. *Id.* at 334 (footnote omitted).

62. Fischel & Kahn, Ltd. v. Van Straaten Gallery, Inc., 727 N.E.2d 240, 247 (Ill. 2000) ("We agree with the rationale expressed in *Murphy* and conclude that the work product privilege extends to all subsequent litigation. *See, e.g.*, Midland Investment Co. v. Van Alstyne, Noel & Co., 59 F.R.D. 134 (S.D.N.Y. 1973); Philadelphia Electric Co. v. Anaconda American Brass Co., 275 F. Supp. 146 (E.D. Pa. 1967).")

63. 560 F.2d 326 (8th Cir. 1974).

64. 727 N.E.2d at 246–47.

65. Matter of Subpoena Duces Tecum to the Wayne County Prosecutor, 477 N.W.2d 412, 414–15, 191 Mich. Ct. App. 90 (1991).

two private corporations.[66] The court there declined to extend the privilege, stating: "Although some courts have extended the work product privilege outside the literal bounds of the rule, we conclude that the rule, on its face, limits its protection to one who is a party (or a party's representative) to the litigation in which discovery is sought."[67]

D. Expectation of Confidentiality

In order for the privilege to attach to materials, there must be an expectation of privacy, similar to that for the attorney-client privilege. In *United States v. Sanmina*,[68] a work-product waiver case, the need for an expectation of confidentiality was discussed. The Court stated:

> The second inquiry is "whether the disclosing party had a reasonable basis for believing that the recipient would keep the disclosed material confidential." This "reasonable expectation of confidentiality" could "derive from common litigation interests between the disclosing party and the recipient," or it "may be rooted in a confidentiality agreement or similar arrangement between the disclosing party and he recipient."[69]

III. Materials Beyond the Scope of Work Product

"The doctrine does not place work product outside the scope of discovery, but instead 'creates a form of qualified immunity from discovery' for materials prepared in anticipation of litigation."[70] As noted in *Hickman v. Taylor*, the facts surrounding a case are not afforded protection. "Mutual knowledge of all the relevant facts gathered by both parties is essential to proper litigation. To that end, either party may compel the other to disgorge whatever facts he has in his possession."[71] This is true even if the facts are contained in a document that is itself not discoverable.[72] Also, "[a] party should not be allowed to conceal critical, non-privileged, discoverable information, which is uniquely within the knowledge of the party and which is not obtainable from any other source, simply by imparting the information to its attorney and then attempting to hide behind the work product doctrine after the party fails to remember the information."[73]

---

66. *In re* Subpoena Served on California Public Util. Comm'n, 892 F.2d 778 (9th Cir. 1989).
67. *Id.* at 781.
68. 968 F.3d 1107 (9th Cir. 2020).
69. 968 F.3d at 1121 (citations omitted).
70. Doe 1 v. Baylor Univ., 335 F.R.D. 476, 487 (2020) (Chiasson v. Zapata Gulf Marine Corp., 988 F.2d 513, 514 n.2 (5th Cir. 1993)).
71. 329 U.S. 495, 507.
72. Fed. R. Civ. P. 26(b)(3), Advisory Committee Notes (1970).
73. Xerox Corp. v. Int'l Bus. Machs., 64 F.R.D. 367, 381–82 (1974).

Witness statements and affidavits prepared by an attorney have been generally held to be outside the scope of protection from the work-product privilege.[74] One court has noted: "An affidavit, after all, purports to be a statement of facts within the personal knowledge of the *witness*, and not an expression of the opinion of counsel."[75] On the other hand, *Hickman* involved an attorney's notes while taking witness statements. The nature of the materials (notes rather than a mere recordation of the witness's words) was partially determinative of the work-product claim outcome.

Similarly, the identity of witnesses is not protected and is a required disclosure under federal rules.[76] This can also be true of non-testifying experts, as noted in *Curtis v. Superior Court of Los Angeles*.[77] "The identity of Curtis's non-testifying expert is not entitled to absolute work product protection because it is not 'a writing' that would reveal Curtis's 'impressions, conclusions, opinions, or legal research or theories.'"[78]

When an attorney-produced witness statement appears to be the mere recordation of a witness's testimony, or if the attorney takes or obtains a statement from every witness to an incident, that statement will typically not be protected under the privilege, because, like in *Curtis*, the statements are factual recitations and do not reveal the mental impressions of the attorney. If the attorney includes specific questions about possible theories or defenses or only selectively interviews certain witnesses, there is a much greater chance that the statements will be protected.

IV. Who Can Assert the Work-Product Privilege

The answer to this question depends upon your jurisdiction. In the recent California case *Curtis v. The Superior Court of Los Angeles*,[79] the Court of Appeals stated: "The work product privilege is held by the attorney, not the client . . .

---

74. Murphy v. Walmart, 259 F.R.D. 421, 431 (S.D. 2009) (In light of the majority view expressed above, the court is reluctant to extend the protections of the work product doctrine to third-party witness affidavits that are, by their very nature, "statement[s] of facts within the personal knowledge of the witness[es].") (Citations omitted). ("That attorney prepared affidavits comprised of factual statements are not protected by the work-product doctrine appears to be the majority view." Diaz v. Devlin, 327 F.R.D. 26, 30 (D. Mass. 2018)) (citing Murphy).

75. Infosystems, Inc. v. Ceridan Corp., 197 F.R.D. 303, 306 (E.D. Mich. 2000).

76. Fed. R. Civ. P. 26(a)(1)(A)(i) ("a party must . . . provide to the other parties: (i) the name . . . of each individual likely to have discoverable information . . . that the disclosing party may use to support its claims or defenses."

77. 276 Cal. Rptr. 3d 676 (Cal. Ct. App. 2021).

78. *Id.* at 680. The identity was provided protection as "qualified work product protection" and, therefore, subject to disclosure upon a finding of unfair prejudice. The court found such prejudice. *Id.* at 692–93.

79. 276 Cal. Rptr. 3d 676 (2021). *But see* Fellows v. Superior Court (1980), 166 Cal. Rptr. 274, 278 (work-product privilege belongs to attorney, but may be waived by client in possession of the work product) (disapproved on other grounds in Coito v. Superior Court, 278 P.3d 860 (2012)).

plaintiff could not invoke work product privilege to suppress answers given by plaintiff's former attorney in deposition because attorney is holder of the privilege."[80] The work-product privilege is most often asserted by the attorney, but the Fifth Circuit found it broader than that: "In contrast to the attorney-client privilege, the work product privilege belongs to both the client and the attorney, either one of whom may assert it. Thus, a waiver by the client of the work product privilege will not deprive the attorney of his own work product privilege, and vice versa."[81]

The better approach seems to recognize that the work-product privilege is a shared privilege. This is so because Rule 26(b)(3)(A) applies to materials prepared in anticipation of litigation or for trial, "by or for another party or its representative (including the other party's attorney, consultant, surety, indemnitor, insurer or agent)." A party may hire a consultant, expert, or accountant in anticipation of litigation before hiring an attorney, and the work product generated by someone pre-attorney can still be protected if it conforms to the requirements of Rule 26. However, it is not the type of information that reflects the "mental impressions" of the attorney, and the attorney cannot so claim in a discovery dispute, although a client can.

A variety of materials produced by non-attorneys have been held to be protected by the work-product privilege. Such materials include staff memoranda,[82] as well as materials generated by independent auditors,[83] litigation consultants, in-house technical assistants, technical consulting firms, and insurers,[84] to name a few. The key determination is whether or not the material is so intertwined with legal analysis as to warrant protection.[85] That determination must be done by the court.

V. Extent of Protection

The work-product privilege is at odds with a major goal of the adversary system—to uncover all relevant facts to promote a fair outcome, which is accomplished by full disclosure. This goal is the rationale behind the scope of discovery articulated in Rule 26(b)(1), which allows discovery of "any non-privileged matter that is relevant to any party's claim or defense," and reflects that:

---

80. 276 Cal. Rptr. 3d at 688.

81. *In re* Grand Jury Proceedings, 43 F.3d 966, 972 (5th Cir. 1994).

82. Martin v. Office of Special Counsel, Merit Sys. Protection Bd., 819 F.2d 1181, 1183 (D.C. Cir. 1982) (the Freedom of Information Act context).

83. U.S. v. Deloitte, 610 F.3d 129 (D.C. Cir 2010) (requiring remand to District Court for more thorough evidentiary basis to classify audit as protected).

84. *In re* Cendant Corp, Secs. Litig., 343 F.3d 658, 665 (3d Cir. 2003).

85. US v. ISS Marine Servs., 905 F. Supp. 2d 121, 134 (D.C. Cir. 2012) (Auditor's report not be protected.).

> [I]t cannot be stressed enough that there is no presumption in favor of finding a document to be immune from discovery under either the attorney-client privilege or the work product doctrine. Both evidentiary privileges operate in derogation of the search for the truth and run counter to the public's right to every person's evidence.[86]

Because of this, the privilege is to be narrowly construed.[87] How that privilege is applied depends on the nature of the work product and whether it is opinion work product or non-opinion fact work product.[88]

In keeping with the language in *Hickman*,[89] the current Rule 26(b)(1)(A) makes a distinction between factually developed work product and opinion work product, also sometimes called "core work product."[90]

> [T]he work-product doctrine affords special or heightened protection to materials that reveal an attorney's mental impressions or opinions. *Admiral Ins. Co.*, 881 F.2d at 1494; Fed. R. Civ. P. 26(b)(3)(B). Such materials are generally referred to as "opinion" or "core" work product and are distinguished from "fact" work product. Fact work-product may be ordered produced upon a showing of substantial need for the information and that the information cannot be otherwise obtained without undue hardship. *Admiral Ins. Co.*, 881 F.2d at 1494; Fed. R. Civ. P. 26(b)(3)(A)(ii). Opinion or core work product, however, is discoverable only "when mental impressions are at issue in a case and the need for the material is compelling."[91]

As mentioned earlier, opinion work product may be never discoverable, as announced in Texas Rule of Civil Procedure 192.5(b)(1),[92] or it can be discoverable under rare circumstances, when "mental impressions are at issue and the need for the material is compelling."[93] Thus, in some jurisdictions, the privilege is more absolute than in others.

---

86. Pearlshire Capital Group, LLC v. Zaid, 490 F. Supp. 3d 1299, 1307 (N.D. Ill. 2020) (citations omitted). *See also* Holladay v. Royal Caribbean Cruises, Ltd., 334 F.R.D. 628, 631 (S.D. Fla. 2020).

87. *Id.*

88. *In re* Grand Jury Subpoena, 870 F.3d 312, 316 (4th Cir. 2017); *In re* Int'l Sys. & Controls Corp. Sec. Litig., 693 F.2d 1235, 1240 (5th Cir. 1982).

89. 329 U.S. 495 (1947).

90. Tex. R. Civ. P. 192.5(b)(1) states: "Core work product—the work product of an attorney or an attorney's representative that contains the attorney's or the attorney's representative's mental impressions, opinions, conclusions, or legal theories—is not discoverable." *See also* Crosby v. City of New York, 269 F.R.D. 267, 277–78 (S.D.N.Y. 2010).

91. McKenzie Law Firm, PA v. Ruby Receptionists, Inc., 333 F.R.D. 638, 641 (D. Ore. 2019).

92. *See also In re* Allstate Fire & Cas. Co., 617 S.W.3d 635, 647 (Tex. App. 2021) ("Core work product is sacrosanct and its protection impermeable.").

93. 333 F.R.D. at 641.

Factual work product, on the other hand, can be compelled "if: (i) [it is] otherwise discoverable under Rule 26(b)(1); and (ii) the party shows that it has a substantial need for the materials to prepare its case and cannot, without undue hardship, obtain their substantial equivalent by other means."[94] All state rules also allow for the conditional discovery of facts, even if they are the work product of a party or attorney.

A. Substantial Need

Substantial need has been said to be "the least uniformly applied by the courts."[95] While Rule 26(b)(3) does not define what constitutes substantial need, the Advisory Committee Notes offer some direction by noting cases involving decisions on substantial need.[96] These circumstances have included: not finding "special circumstances" where plaintiff possessed substantially similar materials, and impeachment value was deemed speculative;[97] allowing discovery of an opponent's witness statements where the witnesses refused to speak with the movant;[98] finding no "special circumstances" sufficient to support disclosure of witness statements, where plaintiff had deposed those same witnesses, and plaintiff's purported need for materials for purposes of impeachment was speculative;[99] and granting discovery of accident report materials where information contained therein was not otherwise available.[100] The Committee also cited *Southern Ry. v. Lanham*,[101] as describing circumstances where substantial need was sufficient to make witness statements subject to discovery.

Most often, "substantial need" or a close variant must be proven to gain access to factual work product. This is the part of the policy that discourages living off the wits of an opponent, which the courts have found abhorrent. "Substantial need is demonstrated where the factual material contained in the otherwise protected documents is 'essential to the preparation of one's case.'"[102] "Thus, a substantial need exists where the material 'is crucial to the determination of whether the defendant could be held liable for the acts alleged, or carries great probative value on contested issues.'"[103]

---

94. Fed. R. Civ. P. 26(b)(3)(a). *See also* Tex. R. Civ. P. 192.5(b)(1).
95. Special Project, *The Work Product Doctrine*, 68 Cornell L. Rev. 760, 802 (1983).
96. Fed. R. Civ. P. 26(b)(3) Advisory Committee Notes (1970).
97. Guilford Nat'l Bank v. S. Ry., 297 F.2d 921, 923–27 (4th Cir. 1962).
98. Mitchell v. Bass, 252 F.2d 513, 518–19 (8th Cir. 1958).
99. Hauger v. Chicago, R.I. & Pac. R.R., 216 F.2d 501, 505–06 (7th Cir. 1954).
100. Burke v. United States, 32 F.R.D. 213, 215 (E.D.N.Y. 1963).
101. 403 F.2d 119 (5th Cir. 1968).
102. Securities Exchange Commission, 337 F.R.D. 70, 78 (S.D.N.Y 2020) citing Hickman v. Taylor, 329 U.S. 495, 511 (1947).
103. S.E.C. v. Collector's Coffee, Inc., 337 F.R.D. 70, 78 (S.D.N.Y. 2020) (citation and internal quotation marks omitted).

Another court identified specific, if broad, requirements to find substantial need, stating: "A non-exhaustive list of factors are assessed in determining substantial need including: (1) the importance of the materials to the party seeking them for case preparation, (2) the difficulty the party will have obtaining them by other means, and (3) the likelihood that the party, even if he obtains the information by independent means, will not have the substantial equivalent of the documents he seeks."[104] An explanation of at least one idea of importance appeared in a New York court's opinion: "The importance of the documents requested cannot be understated because 'it is beyond dispute that [Plaintiffs] need the information requested,' and that they 'contain[ ] the evidence upon which [Plaintiffs] base[ ] their complaint.' *Resolution Tr. Corp. v. Heiserman*, 151 F.R.D. 367, 375 (D. Colo. 1993)."[105] When the information in the documents is so crucial that a cause of action or defense cannot be presented without it, and the information is not obtainable otherwise, the privilege protection is no longer appropriate. The burden of showing substantial need is on the party seeking the material.[106]

The cases demonstrate the need for clear and thorough evidence by the party seeking disclosure, which is not always readily available without seeing the documents. "Whether a particular document is shielded from disclosure necessarily is a fact-specific determination that most often requires an *in camera* inspection."[107] "[A] moving party's burden is generally met if it demonstrates that the materials are relevant to the case, the materials have a unique value apart from those already in the movant's possession, and 'special circumstances' excuse the movant's failure to obtain the requested materials itself."[108] Those facts need to be provided to the factfinder.

If the materials sought are attorney "opinion work product—that is, 'the mental impressions, conclusions, opinions, or legal theories of a party's attorney or other representative concerning the litigation'—that requires a higher standard of 'a highly persuasive showing' or extraordinary justification to secure its release."[109]

B. Undue Hardship

In *Burrow v. Forjas Taurus SA*,[110] a gun manufacturer and importer products liability case, the plaintiffs sought an internal investigation done by defendants after the plaintiffs' firearms expert inspected a revolver of the type involved in

---

104. *See* Burrow v. Forjas Taurus S.A., 334 F. Supp. 3d 1222, 1229 (S.D. Fla. 2018). *See also* F.T.C. v. Boehringer Ingelheim Pharm., Inc., 778 F.3d 142, 155 (D.C. Cir. 2015).

105. *Id.* at 1230.

106. 337 F.R.D. at 78.

107. Fields v. First Liberty Ins. Corp., 954 N.Y.S.2d 427, 431 (N.Y. Sup. Ct. 2012).

108. 778 F.3d at 155. *See also* Cooper v. Rezutko, 2022 WL 406387, at *7 (N.D. Ind. Feb. 10, 2022) (where work-product protection was disallowed based upon the requesting party's substantial need).

109. U.S. v. Petit, 438 F. Supp. 3d 212, 215 (S.D.N.Y. 2020).

110. 334 F. Supp. 3d 1222 (S.D. Fla. 2018).

two drop-fire incidents. While the defendants argued that the documents were created for litigation, plaintiffs argued that they were created for the business purposes of (1) improving the product, (2) protecting future gun owners, and (3) avoiding negative publicity.[111] "Application of this exception [to work product privilege] requires a fact-based inquiry into the needs of the party seeking discovery as well as into the hardship that might be avoided by allowing discovery."[112]

The court found that the plaintiffs were seeking the engineering reports and technical papers to determine defendants' knowledge about potential product defects and propensity to fail. In describing undue hardship, the court stated:

> Since Defendants have already performed their extensive research using their unique testing protocols, there is no persuasive reason to withhold those items any longer. Plaintiffs lack the facilities, equipment, technology, staffing, and expertise to replicate Defendants' testing and analysis. Plaintiffs have little to no knowledge, when compared to Defendants, of what type of tests Defendants performed, how they were performed, or the results.[113]

Evidence about what a party does not have or cannot do may often be required to show undue hardship.

C. Substantial Equivalent

In the case *Diaz v. Devlin*,[114] the defendant moved to compel the affidavit of a nonparty witness to a no-knock event at an apartment complex. The plaintiff's attorney drafted an affidavit, which the witness signed. At the witness's deposition, he was asked about the contents of the affidavit, as it had been identified in discovery responses but not produced. The witness said he could not remember. The magistrate judge made the initial determination to order production of the affidavit. On appeal, the district court found, after an in camera review, that the information contained in the affidavit was factual, and also that the failure of the witness to remember created a substantial need and substantially the same information could not be obtained without undue hardship on the defendants.[115]

Similarly, in *Burrow v. Forjas Taurus*,[116] the court stated: "While Defendants suggest that Plaintiffs can obtain the same information via other means—such

111. *Id.* at 1228.
112. *Id.* at 1229.
113. *Id.* at 1233.
114. 327 F.R.D. 26 (D. Mass. 2018).
115. *Id.* at 31–32.
116. Burrow v. Forjas Taurus, SA, 334 F. Supp. 3d 1222 (S.D. Fla. 2018).

as depositions or affidavits—nothing can provide a substantial equivalent of the raw data and technical information contained within the documents themselves."[117] Documents that have unique information vital to a claim are more likely subject to production.

VI. Types of Documents Evaluated

The types of specific documents that can be protected are almost limitless, but their treatment falls into groups. The two main groups are those produced by an attorney and those produced by the client or its representative.[118]

Each class of documents is further divided into two main sections—those that contain factual information and those that contain case-specific attorney mental impressions, strategies, and evaluations. The class of documents produced by the client or non-attorney representatives is more likely to be evaluated in the context of whether the document has a business purpose or is a litigation document, though attorney-produced documents often undergo this analysis, as well, especially if created by an in-house attorney. The same type of documents may have different protection status depending on their origin.

As might be expected, documents that contain mental impressions, strategies, and evaluations and were created for specific litigation are more likely to be protected. Dual-purpose materials, business-purpose materials, and materials directed or generated by a non-attorney are more likely to not be protected. Following, in alphabetical order, are some common examples of the types of documents evaluated by the courts.

A. Attorney Billing Records

Attorney billing records have been held to be work product in Texas. *In re National Lloyds Insurance Co.*[119] dealt with the issue of whether or not attorney billing records could be protected by work-product privilege. In that case, the plaintiff homeowners sought attorney billing records as part of their claim against the insurer for alleged underpayment of claims and for attorney fees.

In denying the homeowners access to the attorney billing records, the Texas Supreme Court stated: "[W]e hold that a request to produce all billing records invades a party's work product privilege because, cumulatively, billing records constitute a mechanical compilation of information that, at least

117. 334 F. Supp. 3d at 1232.

118. U.S. v. Nobles, 422 U.S. 225, 238–39 (1975) ("[T]he doctrine is an intensely practical one, grounded in the realities of litigation in our adversary system. One of those realities is that attorneys often must rely on the assistance of investigators and other agents in the compilation of materials in preparation for trial. It is therefore necessary that the doctrine protect material prepared by agents for the attorney as well as those prepared by the attorney himself.").

119. 532 S.W.3d 794 (Tex. 2017).

incidentally, reveals an attorney's strategy and thought processes."[120] The court continued: "[A]s a whole, billing records represent the mechanical compilation of information that reveals counsel's legal strategy and thought processes, at least incidentally,"[121] and, as such, it is core work product.

B. Attorney Notes

In *Alexander v. F.B.I.*,[122] the notes taken by an attorney at meetings with corporate client's employees were protected by work-product doctrine. In that case, plaintiffs alleged their privacy interests were violated when the FBI handed over investigation files of appointees and government employees during the Reagan and Bush administrations to the Clinton Whitehouse. Intervenors, third-party contractors, sought the work-product privilege for various documents listed on intervenor's outside counsel's privilege log. The court held:

> The notes made by an attorney from communications with a client or with the representatives of a client are protected under the work product doctrine. Here the notes taken by counsel reflect their understanding of issues raised by representatives of the client. This type of mental impression, gleaned from client and witness interviews, have been held to be protected under the work product doctrine.[123]

C. Claim Files

Claim files can be protected under the work-product privilege in some instances. For example, in *In re Mid-Continent Insurance Co.*,[124] the insured in an underinsured and bad-faith case subpoenaed the insurer's entire claim file when the insurer's custodian of records was noticed for deposition. The insurer moved to quash the notice on the ground of work-product privilege. The lower court denied the motion and found the claim file to not be work product, and the insurer appealed. Because part of the file was created prior to the claim of bad faith, one of the issues was whether the work-product rule could apply to the underlying claim file.

On this issue, the court wrote: "The work product privilege is not necessarily specific to the claim for which it is sought, but is specific for the claim for which it was created. Once it is created as work product in relation to a claim, it remains work product and protected by a privilege from disclosure from

120. *Id.* at 803.
121. *Id.* at 804.
122. 198 F.R.D. 306, 49 Fed. R. Serv. 3d 18 (D.D.C. 2000).
123. *Id.* at 313.
124. 549 S.W.3d 730 (Tex. App. 2017).

any claim."[125] The court further found that if the materials were not core work product, the insured failed to show "both that a substantial need for the materials exists and that materials equivalent to those sought cannot be obtained without substantial hardship."[126] Failure to meet this "heavy burden" resulted in the protection being granted.

D. Client Notes

In *WebXchange, Inc. v. Dell, Inc.*,[127] the defendants sought plaintiff's communications with and documents from a non-testifying expert. The court found plaintiff had sustained its burden to show the documents were protected, as they had been done at the request of counsel for potential litigation.[128] Thus, it seems that even a client's notes regarding strategy or mental impressions can be protected under the right circumstances. Just as an opponent should not be allowed to "freeload" off of an attorney's efforts, a similar argument can be made for work done by a client in the litigation effort.

E. Dual-Purpose Documents

In *Bradley v. Melroe*,[129] the plaintiff sought the investigation materials of a product manufacturer of accidents on the same machine prior to his injury. The court viewed this as a self-critical analysis work-product issue and applied the concept that the work-product privilege of Rule 26(b)(3) applies to "material prepared by or for *any* litigation or trial so long as it was prepared by or for a party to the subsequent litigation."[130] Production of the factual information in the reports was required, but all mental impressions, opinions, evaluations, recommendations, and theories were redacted.[131]

Materials developed by attorneys while doing investigations have been held to be protected by work-product privilege. "Work-product protection applies to attorney-led investigations when the documents at issue 'can fairly be said to have been prepared or obtained because of the prospect of litigation.'"[132]

A Seventh Circuit case involved an attorney-led investigation into allegations of sexual misconduct at an elementary school. The school district hired a law firm to do the investigations. The firm conducted oral interviews in which

125. *Id.* at 733.
126. *Id.* at 735.
127. 264 F.R.D. 123 (D. Del. 2010).
128. *Id.* at 128.
129. 141 F.R.D. 1 (D.D.C. 1992).
130. *Id.* at 2 (where the court cites to F.T.C. v. Grolier, Inc., 462 U.S. 19, 25 (1988)) (citing Charles A. Wright & Arthur R. Miller, Federal Practice & Procedure § 202, at 201 (1970)).
131. *Id.* at 3.
132. Sandra T.E. v. South Berwyn Sch. Dist., 600 F.3d 612, 622 (7th Cir. 2010) (citing Logan v. Commercial Union Insurance Co., 96 F.3d 971, 976–77 (7th Cir. 1996)).

the attorneys made notes of the interviews and presented an oral summary to the school board. The court noted: "There is a distinction between precautionary documents 'developed in the ordinary course of business' for the 'remote prospect of litigation' and documents prepared because 'some articulable claim, *likely* to lead to litigation, [has] arisen.' Only documents prepared in the latter circumstances receive work-product protection."[133]

While some documents have been recognized to have a dual nature, the cases are not uniform in granting such documents protection from disclosure. In analyzing whether or not the work-product privilege should apply to dual-purpose documents, the Ninth Circuit stated that it would make the analysis under the "because of" test.[134] The court wrote:

> The "because of" standard does not consider whether litigation was a primary or secondary motive behind the creation of a document. Rather, it considers the totality of the circumstances and affords protection when it can fairly be said that the "document was created because of anticipated litigation, and would not have been created in substantially similar form but for the prospect of that litigation[.] *Adlman*, 134 F.3d at 1195.[135]

The court further explained this application: "In the 'because of' Wright & Miller formulation, 'the nature of the document *and* the factual situation of the particular case' are key to a determination of whether work product protection applies. Wright & Miller § 2024 (emphasis added). When there is a true independent purpose for creating a document, work product protection is less likely, but when two purposes are profoundly interconnected, the analysis is more complicated."[136] As with other aspects of the work-product privilege, the court needs evidence of the facts surrounding the creation of the material to be able to decide whether or not the work-product privilege should apply.

F. Intangible Items

Though Federal Rule of Civil Procedure 26(b)(3) does not specifically list intangible material, *Hickman v. Taylor* does mention it,[137] and the cases have universally held that intangible items are also protected.[138]

---

133. *Id.*

134. The "because of test" is the most widely used test when determining whether or not a document was created in anticipation of litigation.

135. *In re* Grand Jury Subpoena (Mark Torf/Torf Environmental Management, 357 F.3d 900, 908 (9th Cir. 2004). *See* United States. v. Adlman, 134 F.3d 1194 (2d Cir. 1998).

136. *Id.*

137. 329 U.S. 495, 511 (1947).

138. Adams v. Mem'l Hermann, 973 F.3d 343, 349–50 (5th Cir. 2020). This case's Footnote 4 further supports this, "*Nobles*, 422 U.S. at 237; *see also* 8 Charles A. Wright, Arthur R. Miller & Richard Marcus, Federal Practice & Procedure § 2024, at 494–95 (3d ed. 2010) ("Rule 26(b)(3)

G. Internal Investigations

"As a general rule, '[i]nvestigatory reports and materials are not protected by the attorney-client privilege or the work-product doctrine merely because they are provided to, or prepared by, counsel.'"[139] To have the attorney-client privilege apply, the materials must be communications seeking legal advice, and to have the work-product privilege apply, they must be created in anticipation of litigation. But, "[i]nterview notes and memoranda produced in the course of . . . internal investigations have long been considered classic attorney work product."[140]

In the case *In re Symbol Technologies, Inc. Securities Litigation*,[141] an internal investigation was held to be protected by the work-product privilege under the circumstances. The company previously had a history of accounting improprieties, prior investigation by the Securities Exchange Commission investigation, and class action litigation by shareholders over its accounting practices, and then instituted a new internal investigation regarding questions over a quarterly report. "Based upon the particular circumstances in this case, and in light of the fact that '[n]othing' in Rule 26(b)(3) states or suggests that documents prepared 'in anticipation of litigation' with the purpose of assisting in the making of a business decision do not fall within its scope, the Court finds that the documents at issue are protected by the work product privilege."[142] The court noted that in view of its recent past difficulties, the company had every reason to expect litigation to occur. "Symbol had every conceivable reason to believe that once the issues were publicly disclosed, it could be facing the real prospect of additional shareholder suits as well as further investigations by both the SEC and the U.S. Attorney's Office."[143]

In a wrongful-termination case,[144] the court stated: "Records from internal investigations arising after the filing of administrative complaints are widely

---

itself provides protection only for documents and tangible things. . . . Nonetheless, *Hickman v. Taylor* continues to furnish protection for work product within its definition that is not embodied in tangible form. . . ."); United States v. Deloitte, LLP, 610 F.3d 129, 136 (D.C. Cir. 2010) ("Thus *Hickman* provides work-product protection for intangible work product independent of Rule 26(b)(3)."); *In re* Seagate Tech., LLC, 497 F.3d 1360, 1376 (Fed. Cir. 2007), *abrogated on other grounds by* Halo Elecs., Inc. v. Pulse Elecs., Inc., — U.S. ——, 136 S. Ct. 1923 (2016); *In re* Cendant Corp. Sec. Litig., 343 F.3d 658, 662 (3d Cir. 2003); United States v. One Tract of Real Prop., 95 F.3d 422, 427 (6th Cir. 1996)."

139. Cicel (Beijing) Science & Tech. Co., v. Misonix, Inc., 331 F.R.D. 218, 230 (E.D.N.Y. 2019) (citing OneBeacon Ins. Co. v. Forman Int'l, Ltd., 2006 WL 3771010, at *5 (S.D.N.Y. Dec. 15, 2006)).

140. 331 F.R.D. 218, 232 (E.D.N.Y. 2019) citing *In re* General Motors LLC Ignition Switch Litig., 80 F. Supp. 3d 521 (S.D.N.Y. 2015) at 532.

141. 2016 WL 8377036 (E.D.N.Y. Sept. 30, 2016).

142. *Id.* at *9 (citation omitted).

143. *Id.*

144. Claiborne v. Southeastern Pennsylvania Transp. Auth., 2021 WL 2646894, at *2 (E.D. Pa. June 28, 2021), citing Martin v. Bailys Park Palace Hotel & Casino, 393 F.2d 1252, 1261 (3d Cir. 1993) (internal report after OSHA made inquiry regarding possibly unsafe working conditions was work product and potentially protected), and Lafate v. Vanguard Group, Inc., 2014 WL 5023406, at *6 (E.D. Pa. Oct.

considered to have been prepared in anticipation of litigation and thus are subject to special protections as work product."

H. Pre-Litigation Investigations

In re Turkey Antitrust Litigation[145] involved two subpoenas to a third party investigator for the results of its investigation done on behalf of plaintiffs' attorney shortly before the named plaintiff engaged the attorney in a class-action suit. The defendants seeking the materials argued that Rule 26(b)(3) required, at the least, that there be an actual "party" in the case before the work-product protection could attach under the terms of the rule and that the materials were merely business development.[146] In granting the motions to quash, the court wrote that an overly literal interpretation of Rule 26(b)(3) could lead to discovery problems and that the rule was not a limiting codification of *Hickman v. Taylor.*[147] In fact, the court went on to note that another way to look at the issue was that the codification of the *Hickman* ruling by Rule 26(b)(3) was incomplete, and in the appropriate case, extended beyond the wording of the rule.[148]

I. Reports and Draft Reports

Reports often have more than one purpose. This dual-purpose issue is pervasive in the cases examining whether or not a report should be covered by the work-product privilege. Unless specifically created, directed, or requested by counsel, the likelihood that a report will be afforded work-product protection decreases. Reports often fail the balancing test between being created for litigation and being created to help a business improve. It is this business function that creates uncertainty in the application of the privilege. However, reports created by attorneys have enjoyed more acceptance as work product, and even reports created by non-attorneys can receive at least partial protection. Nonetheless, while reports can be afforded the privilege, the imminent approach of litigation does not automatically qualify a company's internal report as work product.[149]

7, 2014) (materials prepared and obtained during investigation into EEOC complaint were created because of the prospect of litigation).

145. 2022 WL 797180 (N.D. Ill. Mar. 16, 2022).

146. *Id.* at *2.

147. 329 U.S. 495 (1947).

148. 2022 WL 797180, at *9 (N.D. Ill. Mar. 16, 2022). The court found additional support for its decision in Rule 26(b)(1) and Rule 45(d). For a decision using a more literal interpretation of the terms of Rule 26(b), see Castro v. Sanofi Pasteur, Inc., 2013 WL 1707094 (N.D. Ill. Apr. 19, 2013), which was distinguished by *In re Turkey Antitrust Litigation.*

149. EEOC v. Commonwealth Edison, 119 F.R.D. 394, 395 (N.D. Ill. 1988) (citing Janicker v. George Washington Univ., 94 F.R.D. 648, 650 (D.D.C. 1982); Soeder v. Gen. Dynamics Corp., 90 F.R.D. 253, 255 (D. Nev. 1980)).

In the case *Hernandez v. Office of the Commissioner of Baseball*,[150] umpire Hernandez sued the commissioner for failure to assign him to a World Series game and as crew chief. Hernandez produced an expert report by Dr. Gregory W. Baxter, who was later deposed. During the deposition, Baxter was asked if he had reviewed any documents for the deposition, and he referenced a memorandum he had created after his report was submitted regarding his methodology to review umpire performance evaluations.[151] He did this to better prepare for the deposition. While there is work-product protection for drafts of reports,[152] and for communications between an attorney and an expert,[153] the court here found that because Baxter had stated the memo was to himself, the claim that it was created around the time Baxter was going to have to discuss the case with Hernandez's attorney did not make it a "communication" under Rule 26 (b)(4)(C).[154] "[A]s a general matter, an expert's notes are not protected by 26(b)(4)(B) or (C), as they are neither drafts of an expert report nor communications between the party's attorney and the expert witness."[155]

Two engineering reports, including a draft report, were the subject of discovery contests in two *Holladay v. Royal Caribbean Cruises, Ltd.* cases, when an injured passenger sought copies of them at different times. The court utilized an exception to the work-product rule in the first instance and found that the draft report was not done in anticipation of litigation in the second instance to require the production of both.

In the first case,[156] the court ordered Royal Caribbean to produce an engineering report in its possession because the subject of the report, a ride upon which plaintiff was injured, had been dismantled prior to plaintiff's expert having a chance to examine it. The court found that while determining whether or not work-product privilege applied, its decision on the question of privilege did not matter:

> because Plaintiff has demonstrated a substantial need for the Report and an inability to obtain a substantial equivalent even with undue hardship.
>
> Plaintiff satisfies the three factors used to assess substantial need: the importance of the materials to the party seeking them for case preparation, (2) the difficulty the party will have obtaining them by other means, and (3) the likelihood that the party, even if he obtains

150. 335 F.R.D. 45 (S.D.N.Y. 2020).
151. *Id.* at 46–47.
152. Fed. R. Civ. P. 26(b)(4)(B).
153. Fed. R. Civ. P. 26(b)(4)(C).
154. 335 F.R.D. at 48–49.
155. Dongguk Univ. v. Yale Univ., 2011 WL 1935865, at *1 (D. Conn. May 19, 2011).
156. Holladay v. Royal Caribbean Cruises, Ltd., 333 F.R.D. 588 (S.D. Fla. 2019).

> the information by independent means, will not have the substantial equivalent of the documents he seeks.[157]

In the second case,[158] a draft engineering report created by Celtic, an engineering firm hired by Royal Caribbean, was the subject. Royal Caribbean argued that the post-accident report was work product, because it hired Celtic as a consulting expert and it was prepared in anticipation of litigation. It further indicated it hired Celtic and the first engineering firm to determine how the accident involving the plaintiff happened.[159]

Plaintiff countered that (1) Royal Caribbean had used Celtic regularly as its engineering firm, (2) it arranged for Celtic to review the ride before the plaintiff's incident, (3) Royal Caribbean produced the first pre-incident report, (4) Celtic's post-incident assessment was just part of its on-going business relationship with Royal Caribbean, and (5) the report was prepared in the ordinary course of business to improve the attraction's performance, to protect passengers from potential harm, and to protect the long-term interests of the company.[160]

The court analyzed where the Eleventh Circuit stood on the issue of what test to use to determine if a document was created in anticipation of litigation and concluded that it was unsettled.[161] After reviewing the various tests used, the court chose to not adopt any test with a specific name and, instead, "to confine the ruling to the unique facts of this specific fact pattern."[162] The court then explained how it viewed the draft Celtic report:

> In contrast, the Celtic Draft Report mentions nothing about an incident, a fall, injuries, or Holladay. Although its "Overview" mentions that the Sky Pad was "closed during the entire duration of the visit" (by Celtic engineers), it does not expressly say or even implicitly suggest *why* the attraction was closed. It does not say that the project concerned Holladay's fall, nor does it mention that the equipment caused an injury.
>
> Instead, it simply mentions that the scope of work "includes in field condition survey of the Sky Pad on the Mariner of the Seas *and* Independence of the Seas" (emphasis added). There is no mention of any incident, litigation or threatened litigation over the Sky Pad attraction on the other ship (i.e., the *Independence of the Seas*). Nor does it mention threatened litigation or a Royal Caribbean concern over

157. *Id.* at 593–94 (citation omitted).
158. Holladay v. Royal Caribbean Cruises, Ltd., 334 F.R.D. 628 (S.D. Fla. 2020).
159. *Id.* at 630.
160. *Id.*
161. *Id.* at 631–32.
162. *Id.* at 633.

imminent litigation involving Holladay's fall on the *Mariner of the Seas*. Royal Caribbean has not explained why, if the primary purpose of Celtic's retention was to prepare for anticipated litigation, Celtic would have been asked to evaluate an attraction on a *second* ship where **no** incident was reported.[163]

This passage shows the extreme importance of both developing and presenting competent evidence to a court to show why the balancing of various requirements necessary to invoke the work-product protection should be decided one way or the other. The court noted what the Celtic Report did not do, implying that had it done so, the result might have been different. Specifically, the report did not mention the incident, a fall, injuries, or the plaintiff, Holladay. It did not say why the attraction was closed, that it concerned Holladay's fall, or that it caused an injury. Last, it made no reference to the Holladay litigation and did not explain why it included an examination of the same attraction on another ship.

In *Brooklyn Union Gas Co. v. American Home Assurance Co.*,[164] it was noted that the work-product privilege only attaches to work done by an attorney working as such. The court stated that "attorney work product applies only to documents prepared by counsel acting as such, and to materials uniquely the product of a lawyer's learning and professional skills, such as those reflecting an attorney's legal research, analysis, conclusions, legal theory or strategy."[165] The court further stated that "[d]ocuments prepared in the ordinary course of an insurance company's investigation to determine whether to accept or reject coverage and to evaluate the extent of a claimant's loss are not privileged and are, therefore, discoverable. In addition, such documents do not become privileged 'merely because an investigation was conducted by an attorney.'"[166] Because the nature of attorney involvement is not always clear, the court in *Venture v. Preferred Mutual Ins.*[167] allowed the plaintiff in a bad-faith insurance case to inquire of an attorney whether he was acting as an investigator, an attorney, or in some hybrid role.[168]

J. Reservation-of-Rights Letter

A reservation-of-rights letter was found to be work product in the case *In re Madrid*.[169] In that case, an insured driver, Madrid, was a defendant in an auto

163. *Id.*

164. 803 N.Y.S.2d 532 (N.Y. App. Div. 2005).

165. *Id.* at 534.

166. *Id.* (citing "Spectrum Sys. Int'l Corp. v. Chem. Bank, 78 N.Y.2d 371, 379, 575 N.Y.S.2d 809, 581 N.E.2d 1055 [1991]; *accord* Bertalo's Rest. v. Exchange Ins. Co., 240 A.D.2d 452, 455, 658 N.Y.S.2d 656 [1997], *appeal dism.* 91 N.Y.2d 848, 667 N.Y.S.2d 683, 690 N.E.2d 492 [1997])."

167. 61 N.Y.S.3d 210 (N.Y. App. Div. 2017).

168. *Id.* at 210.

169. 242 S.W.3d 563 (Tex. App. 2007).

negligence action. The plaintiff in that suit requested a copy of the reservation-of-rights letter Madrid's insurer had sent to him. The lower court ordered production, and Madrid sought mandamus to block the court's order.

In the hearing on the motion to compel production of the letter, an affidavit was provided to the court from the insurance adjuster who had written the reservation-of-rights letter. In that affidavit, he stated the letter was written after the negligence suit had been filed; it was a communication between an insurer, its insured, and the insured's attorney; and it was for the purposes of the trial.[170] The court found that because the letter related to the current litigation, specifically the defense of the negligence case, the letter was work product. It did not find it to be "core work product," the mental impressions, opinions, conclusions, or legal theories of an attorney or an attorney's representative, so not absolutely protected. However, the plaintiff failed to show he had "a substantial need of the materials in the preparation of his case and that he [was] unable without undue hardship to obtain the substantial equivalent of the material by other means."[171]

K. Reserves

One example of a reserve being held to be work product was in the case *In re BP Products North America, Inc.*[172] This case involved an explosion in Texas City, Texas. Shortly after the explosion, BP reported to the Securities Exchange Commission that it had set a reserve of $700 million to resolve personal injury and other losses. The plaintiffs in the action sought the materials BP used to arrive at this figure. BP claimed work product and attorney-client privileges. Plaintiffs argued that the methodology to determine the $700 million was merely business advice and not eligible for either privilege. Plaintiffs further argued that BP had waived the privileges by submitting the reserve amount to the SEC. The lower court ordered production, and BP appealed.

The in-house BP attorney who had determined the amount testified in an affidavit that he had been working in his role as an in-house BP attorney and as an attorney who would be involved in the lawsuits, already filed, regarding the incident. He also testified that he had used his experience in the cases and work-product materials to make his determination and that the documents prepared and mental impressions developed were in anticipation of litigation and trial of the cases stemming from the incident.[173] Plaintiffs argued that the attorney's affidavit merely stated conclusions and did not have the detail necessary to support the protection of the privilege.

In dispensing with the plaintiffs' arguments, and after noting BP had the burden to make a prima facie case that the privilege applied, the court found

---

170. *Id.* at 565–66.
171. *Id.* at 569.
172. 263 S.W.3d 106 (Tex. App. 2006).
173. *Id.* at 109–10.

adequate support in the attorney's affidavit to invoke the privilege. The court noted that the affiant was an attorney, was working on the cases, had formed mental impressions and documents based upon his experience with the cases, and those documents were made in anticipation of further litigation and trial.[174]

In addressing the waiver claim, the court held that because BP had only disclosed the amount of the reserve and none of the underlying documents or methodology, it had not waived the work-product privilege.[175]

New York has also found reserves to be privileged, because "the court's ruling precluding discovery of the reserves placed on the plaintiff's insurance claims was based on the notion that such specific figures represent work product, since they are normally created because of the anticipation of litigation. Indeed, that is the generally accepted rule. *See, e.g., Simon v. G.D. Searle & Co.*, 816 F.2d 397, 401–02 (8th Cir.1987); *In re Pfizer Inc. Secs. Litig.*, 1994 WL 263610, *1–2 (S.D.N.Y. June 6, 1994)."[176] In *Luxottica of America, Inc. v. Allianz Global Risks US Ins. Co.*, the court wrote: "Reserves are generally considered privileged as work product because it reflects an assessment of the value of the claim taking into account the likelihood of an adverse judgment."[177]

In Illinois, which has a narrower scope to work-product privilege than the federal courts,[178] a court held that because the evidence did not show that reserve information "necessarily reflect[ed] the theories, mental impressions, or litigation plans *of defense counsel or coverage counsel*," it was not protected under the work-product privilege.[179] In California, reserves may be disclosed after the court makes an in camera review to determine if either an absolute or qualified privilege exists; thus, it is on a case-by-case basis.[180]

L. Settlement Negotiations

The work-product privilege was not extended to materials regarding settlement negotiations in *Central Nat'l Ins. Co. of Omaha v. Medical Protective Co. of Fort Wayne, Indiana.*[181] The case involved an excess insurance carrier seeking damages for an underlying carrier's failure to settle a medical-malpractice claim. As part of the discovery, the excess carrier sought information and documents regarding the settlement negotiations, which the underlying carrier refused on the grounds of attorney-client and work-product privileges. The

174. *Id.* at 113–14.

175. *Id.* at 116–17.

176. Lava Trading Inc. v. Hartford Ins. Co., 2005 WL 6689, at *2 (S.D.N.Y. Jan. 11, 2005); *accord* Fox Paine & Co., LLC v. Houston Cas. Co., 37 N.Y.S.3d 207 (Sup. Ct. N.Y. 2016), 2016 WL 1602747 (Apr. 21, 2016), which found reserves not to be protected because they were not the work of an attorney.

177. 2022 WL 1204870, at *3 (S.D. Ohio Apr. 22, 2022).

178. Depositors Ins. Co. v. Canal Ins. Co., 2013 WL 5509108 (Ill. App. Ct. Oct. 1, 2013).

179. *Id.* at *3.

180. Lipton v. Superior Court, 56 Cal. Rptr. 2d 341, 48 Cal. App. 4th 1599, 1620 (Cal. Ct. App. 1996), *distinguished by* Costco Wholesale Corp. v. Superior Court, 219 P.3d 736 (Cal. 2009).

181. 107 F.R.D. 393 (E.D. Mo. 1985).

court analogized the situation to that of an insured and an insurer and held that in a claim for failure to settle, the attorney-client privilege did not apply. As to the work-product claim, the court found that while the mental impressions of the attorney were sought, the work-product privilege is a qualified one and may be defeated by a showing of good cause. In this case, the essence of the claim by the excess carrier involved the communications it sought, and that provided the good cause needed to overcome the claim of privilege.[182]

A settlement brochure that was voluntarily given to defense counsel was considered work product, but the disclosure to the adverse party waived the work-product protection.[183]

Notwithstanding, where there was an agreement to confine the use of a work-product document solely for settlement negotiations, it has been held that the privilege was not waived.[184] This comports with an early Maryland District Court case, which stated:

> During settlement negotiations, the confidentiality necessary to be present to assert an attorney-client or work product privilege is not lost by disclosure of pertinent information to opposing counsel or control group members. Any question of waiver of the attorney-client privilege or work product immunity during settlement negotiations must be considered in light of the importance of facilitating such settlement.[185]

A letter sent by Mobil's wholly owned German subsidiary tax counsel to Mobil officers and members of Mobil's tax department, which discussed the state of settlement negotiations with a German taxing authority, was found to be protected by both the attorney-client and work-product privilege.[186]

Not all courts have found work-product protection in the settlement context. Contrary to *Akamai*, another California court found material disclosed during settlement negotiations to be discoverable. In a case that involved whether or not a settlement by other parties was in good faith, the court noted that "the weight of authority overwhelmingly holds that '[d]isclosure to an adversary waives the work product protection as to items actually disclosed, even where disclosure occurs in settlement.'"[187] The court also found that while the documents were privileged, the requesting party had shown compelling need, and the holder of the documents had waived its privilege by divulging

---

182. *Id.* at 395.

183. Khandji v. Keystone Resorts Mgmt., Inc., 140 F.R.D. 697 (D. Colo. 1992).

184. Akamai Techs., Inc. v. Digital Island, Inc., 2002 WL 1285126 (N.D. May 30, 2002) *distinguished by* City of Colton v. American Promotional Events, Inc., 2011 WL 13223879 (C.D. Cal. Oct. 24, 2011).

185. Burlington Indus. v. Exxon Corp., 65 F.R.D. 26, 45, 19 Fed. R. Serv. 2d 533 (E.D. Md. 1974).

186. U.S. v. Mobil Corp., 149 F.R.D. 533, 539 (N.D. Tex. 1993).

187. City of Colton v. American Promotional Events, Inc., 2011 WL 13223879, at *6 (C.D. Cal. Oct. 24, 2011) (citing *In re* Qwest Commc'ns Int'l, Inc., 450 F.3d 1179, 1186 (10th Cir. 2006)).

them to an adversary.[188] The court further found that even though the settling parties had entered into a confidentiality agreement, it was not binding on the other parties or the court.[189]

M. Testing

In a patent infringement case,[190] the plaintiff sought a "privilege log identifying certain testing and/or analysis conducted 'for this litigation' by defendant or on defendant's behalf, as well as related correspondence, that ha[d] been withheld on grounds of privilege."[191] The defendant's testifying expert, Richard Hillstead, instructed defendant's employee Kshitija Garde "to perform a physical test of the accused Defendant products and a finite element analysis of the same products on his behalf in preparing his opinions for his rebuttal expert report."[192] During Garde's deposition, plaintiff's counsel inquired if there was additional testing or analysis that had not been disclosed to expert Hillstead. Defendant's counsel objected and instructed Garde not to respond based upon attorney-client and work-product privilege.

The court noted that courts in its circuit had routinely denied requests for post-litigation logs and then wrote: "[C]ounsel's communications with the client and work product developed once the litigation commences are presumptively privileged and need not be included on any privilege log. [A] rule requiring creation of an ongoing log of all post-complaint privileged communications would have a chilling effect on the attorney-client relationship."[193]

In *Bennet v. State Farm Fire & Casualty Co.*,[194] the court issued an order "precluding the deposition of a nonparty witness concerning the results of soil boring tests performed at the property and preventing the disclosure of an investigation report prepared by the plaintiffs' engineering expert based upon those test results. The plaintiffs established that the data sought was generated solely in anticipation of litigation or for trial."[195]

N. Witness Identity

In a case involving an attempt to have a 30(b)(6) witness testify to an internal investigation, the court wrote that the defendant "[was] correct that the identity of the individuals its outside counsel [had] selected to interview [was]

---

188. *Id.*
189. *Id.* at *7.
190. Colibri Heart Valve, LLC. v. Medtronic CoreValve, LLC, 2021 WL 6882375 (C.D. Cal. Dec. 6, 2021).
191. *Id.* at *2.
192. *Id.*
193. *Id.* at *3.
194. 122 N.Y.S.3d 321 (N.Y. App. Div. 2020).
195. *Id.* at 324.

itself protected work product."[196] But, the court qualified that, stating "some courts have found that the identities of interviewed witnesses are fact work product that may be discoverable if there is a sufficient need for the information. *See, eg, In re Harmonic, Inc Sec Litig*, 245 FRD 424, 427 (ND Cal 2007) (citing cases and finding that identities of confidential witnesses were either not protected work product or fact work product discoverable due to need)."[197]

O. Witness Statements

Coito v. Superior Court[198] is instructive in several ways regarding witness statements. The issue of work-product privilege arose when a wrongful-death plaintiff sought witness statements taken by investigators employed by defense counsel and the identity of witnesses from whom defense counsel had statements. The court held:

> the recorded witness statements are entitled as a matter of law to at least qualified work product protection. The witness statements may be entitled to absolute protection if defendant can show that disclosure would reveal its "attorney's impressions, conclusions, opinions, or legal research or theories." If not, then the items may be subject to discovery if plaintiff can show that "denial of discovery will unfairly prejudice [her] in preparing [her] claim . . . or will result in an injustice."[199]

As to the identity of the witnesses who had given statements to defense counsel, the court stated that information was "not automatically entitled as a matter of law to absolute or qualified work product protection. In order to invoke the privilege, defendant must persuade the trial court that disclosure would reveal the attorney's tactics, impressions, or evaluation of the case (absolute privilege) or would result in opposing counsel taking undue advantage of the attorney's industry or efforts (qualified privilege)."[200]

The court first examined whether absolute privilege might apply and determined that a witness statement taken by an attorney may be entitled to absolute privilege because it may show, by the questions asked or not asked, an attorney's focus in a case and reveal a strategy. Additionally, the statements may be inextricably bound with the attorney's mental impressions, opinions,

---

196. *In re* Cathode Ray Tube (CRT) Antitrust Litig., MDL 1917, 2015 WL 13631248, at *5 (N.D. Cal. Oct. 5, 2015) (citing *In re* MTI Tech Corp Sec Litig. II, 2002 WL 32344347 (C.D. Cal. June 13, 2002) and Mitchell Eng'g v. City and County of San Francisco, 2010 WL 1853493 (N.D. Cal. May 6, 2010)).

197. *In re* Cathode Ray Tube (CRT) Antitrust Litig., MDL 1917, 2015 WL 13631248, at *5 (N.D. Cal. Oct. 5, 2015).

198. 278 P.3d 860, 54 Cal. 4th 480, 142 Cal. Rptr. 3d 607.

199. *Id.* at 863.

200. *Id.*

evaluations, legal research, and theory of the case. Redaction alone of the attorney's questions may not protect information gleaned from the witnesses' answers, and the line of questioning may expose what theories an attorney thinks helpful to the case and which ones are to be discarded. In fact, which witnesses an attorney has chosen to interview may reveal case strategies.[201]

Then the court analyzed the documents under a qualified privilege and explained why it ruled that an attorney-garnered witness statement was entitled to the qualified privilege as a matter of law. Such a ruling supported the two policies the court saw in the California statute.[202] First, one of policies supporting the work-product privilege was to deter opposing counsel from benefitting from the diligence and work an attorney went through to get a witness statement. "Absent a showing that a witness is no longer available or accessible, or some other showing of unfair prejudice or injustice, the Legislature's declared policy is to prevent an attorney from free riding on the industry and efforts of opposing counsel."[203]

The second policy is to encourage attorneys to investigate both the favorable and unfavorable aspects of their case as a way of determining the truth of the case. This policy would suffer if attorneys did not have the privacy to explore their cases freely, because if the witness interviews were always discoverable, they would avoid a thorough interview for fear of exposing a weakness in their case.[204] The court remanded the case with the direction to the lower court to review the witness interviews to determine whether or not absolute privilege applied to all or some parts of the statements, and if it did not, then to determine whether or not the seeking party could make an adequate showing of unfair prejudice or injustice such that discovery should be allowed.[205]

Memoranda of witnesses' oral statements to an investigator and notes by the attorneys of their pretrial preparation were held to be work product.[206] Documents protected by the work-product privilege do not need to be created personally by attorneys. They may be created by or for a party, or the party's representative, as long as they are created in anticipation of litigation.[207]

The 1970 Advisory Committee Notes[208] cite to *Southern Ry. v. Lanham*[209] as a case discussing when witness statements may be discoverable. The Note gives

---

201. *Id.* at 869.

202. West's Ann. Cal. C.C.P. § 2018.030 (2005), which reads "(a) A writing that reflects an attorney's impressions, conclusions, opinions, or legal research or theories is not discoverable under any circumstances. (b) The work product of an attorney, other than a writing described in subdivision (a), is not discoverable unless the court determines that denial of discovery will unfairly prejudice the party seeking discovery in preparing that party's claim or defense or will result in an injustice."

203. *Id.* at 870.

204. *Id.*

205. *Id.* at 872–73.

206. Soter v. Cowles Pub. Co., 130 P.3d 840, 845 (Wash. App. 2006).

207. *Id.*

208. Fed. R. Civ. P. 26(b)(3) Advisory Committee's Notes (1970).

209. 403 F.2d 119 (5th Cir. 1968).

examples, such as when a witness has given a contemporaneous statement to the event and is only available to the party seeking discovery substantially later, or when a witness is reluctant or hostile, or when the witness has had a lapse of memory or is deviating from his/her previous statement.

VII. Conclusion

The one thing that all the cases have in common is that it takes evidence for the court to properly apply the balancing test that *Hickman v. Taylor* and the Federal Rules of Civil Procedure require. The court cannot make the necessary determinations without the evidence provided by privilege logs; attorney, client, and witness affidavits; depositions; and live testimony. When making a claim in the work-product-privilege arena, there must be supporting evidence to gain or challenge the protection.

CHAPTER 4

The Common-Interest or Joint-Defense Privilege

REAGAN W. SIMPSON

I. Sorting Out the Two Privileges

The history and elements of the common-interest and joint-defense privileges are set out in a lengthy Third Circuit opinion styled *In re Teleglobe Communications Corp.*[1] As that opinion recounts, the origins of the privileges began with the recognition in all U.S. jurisdictions of a privilege to share attorney-client communications as between co-clients of the same lawyer in regard to a legal proceeding. When two or more parties employ a lawyer as their common counsel, communications to that attorney are confidential and privileged as against all common adversaries,[2] but not if there is later adversity between the jointly represented parties.[3]

That sharing privilege was expanded when courts in most jurisdictions came to recognize a joint-defense privilege among multiple defendants that hired separate attorneys to defend against the same lawsuit, the recognition coming first in criminal cases and then in civil cases.[4] The privilege was expanded further by the recognition in section 76 of the Restatement (Third) of the Law Governing Lawyers of the common-interest privilege, which can relate to a common defense of litigation but can also apply outside of litigation even into transactional matters. The existence of a broader sharing-privilege

1. 493 F.3d 345, 362–66 (3d Cir. 2007).
2. *Id.*; John Morrell & Co. v. Local Union 304A, 913 F.2d 544, 555–56 (8th Cir. 1990).
3. *See, e.g.*, Feighan v. Feighan, 180 A.D.3d 873, 874 (N.Y. App. 2020); *In re* Alexander, 580 S.W.3d 858, 865 (Tex. App. 2019).
4. *In re* Teleglobe Commc'ns Corp., 345, 363–64 (3d Cir. 2007); Jared S. Sunshine, *Seeking Common Sense for the Common Law of Common Interest in the D.C. Circuit*, 65 Cath. U. L. Rev. 833, 838–49 (2016) (distinguishing among the co-client privilege, the joint-defense privilege, and the common-interest privilege).

beyond litigation has been well received by many federal courts but has a spotty record in state courts.[5] Thus, it is important for the practitioner to know the scope of the privilege adopted in the relevant jurisdiction.

As will be discussed more in depth later, these two privileges are not independent privileges but operate to prevent waiver from sharing protected information as long as the sharing occurs within an allied group.[6] Their greatest utility is expanding the attorney-client privilege beyond the strict confines of the attorney-client relationship.[7] The privileges are also invoked to protect disclosures of work product,[8] but work product must arise from litigation, and preserving protection for shared work product does not require either the common-interest or joint-defense privilege because work product is waived only when its disclosure is to an adversary or substantially increases the chance of disclosure to an adversary.[9]

Less confusion would exist in the case law if courts adopted common-interest as the name of the privilege rather than referring to the joint-defense privilege. One court has expressly stated that the term "common-interest" privilege is preferred to "joint-defense" privilege.[10] Another court lamented that federal courts confuse the joint-client privilege with the common-interest privilege.[11] Yet, many courts continue to refer to the joint-defense privilege, which "protects communications between two or more parties and their respective counsel if they are engaged in a joint-defense effort."[12] Thus, the two terms are often used interchangeably,[13] and joint defense is often the term used because litigation is usually present in common-interest situations. For that reason, a somewhat overlapping discussion of each sharing privilege appears next.

---

5. *See generally* N. Neary, *The Last Man Standing: Kansas's Failure to Recognize the Common Interest Doctrine*, 65 U. Kan. L. Rev. 795 (2016) (containing an extensive discussion of the joint-defense and common-interest privileges and their status in many other jurisdictions and urging Kansas to adopt some form of the privilege); *see also* Robert R. McCormick Found. v. Arthur J. Gallagher Risk Mgmt. Servs., 110 N.E.3d 1081, 1085–86 (Ill. App. 2018) (noting that every federal circuit and almost all states have recognized some form of the privilege).

6. *See In re* Pac. Pictures Corp., 679 F.3d 1121, 1129 (9th Cir. 2012); Fellowship of Christian Athletes v. San Jose Unified Sch. Dist. Bd. of Educ., 2022 WL 1189886, at *2 (N.D. Cal. Apr. 21, 2022).

7. United States v. Patel, 509 F. Supp. 3d 1334, 1340 (2020).

8. *See, e.g.*, Blackmon v. Bracken Constr. Co., 338 F.R.D. 91, 96 (2021).

9. *See, e.g.*, Samuels v. Mitchell, 155 F.R.D. 195, 200 (N.D. Cal. 1994) ("[T]he work product privilege is not automatically waived by any disclosure to third persons. Rather, the courts generally find a waiver only if the disclosure 'substantially increases the opportunity for potential adversaries to obtain the information.'" (citation and quotation omitted)).

10. Kansas City Power & Light v. United States, 139 Fed. Ct. Cl. 546, 563 (2018); *accord* United States v. Schwimmer, 892 F.2d 237, 243–44 (2d Cir. 1989) referring to the joint-defense privilege as "more properly identified as the 'common interest rule'").

11. Prudential Defense Solutions, Inc. v. Graham, 2021 WL 405988, at *3 (E.D. Mich. 2021).

12. *In re* Sealed Case, 29 F.3d 715, 719 n.5 (D.C. Cir. 1994).

13. *See, e.g.*, Allendale Mut. Ins. Co. v. Bull Data Sys., Inc., 152 F.R.D. 132, 140 (N.D. Ill. 1993); Boyd v. Comdata Network, Inc., 88 S.W.3d 203, 213 n.13 (Tenn. 2002).

II. The Common-Interest Privilege

A number of courts have recognized a "common-interest" privilege.[14] The common-interest privilege protects privileged attorney-client communications when disclosed to a third party if the third party "shares a common interest with the disclosing party which is adverse to that of the party seeking discovery."[15] In *Lawson v. Spirit AeroSystems, Inc.*, the court provided a good overview of the common-interest privilege:

> The common-interest doctrine is an exception to waiver that may protect information and documents shared outside of the attorney-client relationship. *See In re Teleglobe Commc'ns Corp.*, 493 F.3d 345, 362–66 (3d Cir. 2007) (discussing the history and the contours of the joint-client and common interest doctrines); *see also In re Qwest Commc'ns Int'l Inc.*, 450 F.3d 1179, 1195 (10th Cir. 2006). . . . To be protected, communications must be made in the course of a "joint effort with respect to a common legal interest" and for the purpose of furthering that effort. *United States v. BDO Seidman, LLP*, 492 F.3d 806, 815–16 (7th Cir. 2007). Courts have generally required that the nature of the parties' common interest "be identical, not similar, and be legal, not solely commercial." Teleglobe Commc'ns, 493 F.3d at 365 (quoting *Duplan Corp. v. Deering Milliken, Inc.*, 397 F. Supp. 1146, 1172 (D.S.C. 1974)). . . .[16]

More succinctly, the common-interest privilege arises when (1) parties undertake a joint effort (2) with respect to an identical legal interest, as opposed to a business interest, and (3) the withheld communications are made to further said ongoing legal enterprise.[17] Not all jurisdictions require the common interest to be identical.[18]

The common interest must be legal in nature, as noted previously. As an example, in *Fresenius Med. Care Holdings v. Roxane Labs. Inc.*,[19] the court noted that a "common *legal* interest" may exist in the advancement of patents,

---

14. *See, e.g.*, B.E. Meyers & Co. v. United States, 41 Fed. Cl. 729, 732 (Fed. Cl. 1998) (finding that the common-interest doctrine is "well recognized in all circuits that have considered it"); Wilson P. Abraham Constr. Corp. v. Armco Steel Corp., 559 F.2d 250, 253 (5th Cir. 1977); Ploen v. AIG Specialty Ins. Co., 2022 WL 220832, at *4 (D. Minn. June 21, 2022). For a general survey of the common-interest privilege, see N. Neary, *The Last Man Standing: Kansas's Failure to Recognize the Common Interest Doctrine*, 65 U. Kansas L. Rev. 795 (2016). The Illinois Appellate Court, First Division surveyed the doctrine and its genesis in Selby v. O'Dea, 90 N.E.2d 1144 (2017).

15. Allendale Mut. Ins. Co. v. Bull Data Sys., Inc., 152 F.R.D. 132, 140 (N.D. Ill. 1993); Christian Athletes v. San Jose Unified Sch. Dist. Bd. of Educ., 2022 WL 1189886, at *2 (N.D. Cal. Apr. 21, 2022).

16. 410 F. Supp. 3d 1195, 1209 (2019).

17. United States v. BDO Seidman, LLP, 492 F.3d 806, 815–16 (7th Cir. 2007).

18. GUS Consulting GMBH v. Chadbourne & Parke LLP, 20 Misc. 3d 539, 542, 858 N.Y.S.2d 591 (Sup. Ct. N.Y. 2008) (not requiring "a total identity of interest among" the parties) (citing Eugenia VI Venture Holdings, Ltd. v. Chabra, 2006 WL 1096825, at *1 (S.D.N.Y. 2006)).

19. 2007 WL 895059 (S.D. Ohio Mar. 21, 2007).

whereas a common commercial interest is not enough for the common-interest privilege to apply.[20] As another court remarked:

> Although the distinction between a common legal, as opposed to commercial, interest is somewhat murky, a common legal interest has been defined as one in which the parties have been, or may potentially become, co-parties to a litigation . . . or have formed a coordinated legal strategy.'" *Fresh Del Monte Produce, Inc. v. Del Monte Foods, Inc.*, No. 13 Civ. 8997 JPO GWG, 2015 WL 3450045, at *3 (S.D.N.Y. May 28, 2015) (quoting *In re Subpoena Duces Tecum Served on N.Y. Marine & Gen. Ins. Co.*, No. M 8-85 MHD, 1997 WL 599399, at *4 (S.D.N.Y. Sept. 26, 1997) (citations and internal quotation marks omitted).[21]

Generally, to establish the common-interest privilege, courts require the parties to demonstrate that the communications (1) were intended to be kept confidential, (2) were made in the pursuit of a joint legal effort, and (3) were intended to advance a common interest.[22] When those elements are met, the exchange of information between various co-defendants and their attorneys "is not made for the purpose of allowing unlimited publication and use, but rather, the exchange is made for the limited purpose of assisting in their common cause."[23]

Under the broad view of the common-interest privilege, the privilege is not limited to litigation settings.[24] Section 76 of the Restatement (Third) of the Law Governing Lawyers explicitly states that the common-interest privilege does not require existing litigation or the status of those sharing information as co-parties:

> The common interest privilege . . . protects from discovery communications among clients and attorneys "allied in a common legal cause." *In re Regents of Univ. of Cal.*, 101 F.3d 1386, 1389 (Fed. Cir. 1996) (citation omitted). The privilege "applies in civil and criminal litigation, and even in purely transactional contexts." *In re Teleglobe Commc'ns Corp.*, 493 F.3d 345, 364 (3d Cir. 2007), as amended (Oct. 12, 2007) (citations omitted).[25]

---

20. *Id.* at 3 (emphasis added); *see also* Golden Door Properties, LLC v. Superior Court, 53 Cal. App. 5th 733, 782 (2020) (requiring common legal interest); Sandoz v. Lannett Co., 2021 WL 5139975, at *2 (E.D. Pa. Nov. 4, 2021); United States v. Patel, 509 F. Supp. 3d 1334, 1344–48 (2020) (not finding a common legal interest).

21. Covey v. Colonial Pipeline Co., 336 F.R.D. 514, 521 (N.D. Ala. 2020).

22. *See* United States v. Bay State Ambulance & Hosp. Rental Serv., Inc., 874 F.2d 20, 28 (1st Cir. 1989); United States v. Evans, 113 F.3d 1457, 1467–68 (7th Cir. Ill. 1997); Roller Bearing Co. of Am. v. Raytheon Co., 2022 WL 3088538, at *4. (D. Mass. Aug. 3, 2022).

23. John Morrell & Co. v. Local Union 304A, 913 F.2d 544, 555–56 (8th Cir. 1990) (quoting Wilson P. Abraham Constr. Corp. v. Armco Steel Corp., 559 F.2d 250 (5th Cir. 1977)).

24. *In re* Sealed Case, 29 F.3d 715, 719 (D.C. Cir. 1994).

25. 10x Genomics, Inc. v. Celsee, Inc., 505 F. Supp. 3d 334, 337 (D. Del. 2020).

Nevertheless, the common-interest privilege most often occurs in the context of litigation, and a number of courts do limit the common legal interest to an interest in regard to a lawsuit and reject the broader common-interest privilege, or define it to be nothing more than a different name for the joint-defense privilege.[26] One utility of the broader common-interest privilege in litigation is that it can extend protection to cooperating plaintiffs as well as to cooperating defendants.[27] The Texas version of the common-interest privilege requires a pending action but is not limited to defendants and thus could include allied plaintiffs and other allied parties.[28]

III. The Joint-Defense Privilege

As noted earlier, the joint-defense privilege is an expansion of the co-client privilege when parties are represented by the same lawyer.[29] Many court decisions, together with rules and statutes, recognize that attorneys aligned in a joint-defense posture "may exchange privileged communications and attorney work product in order to prepare a common defense without waiving the privilege."[30] Similarly, the joint-defense privilege protects information communicated by a client to counsel for co-defendants.[31] When the joint-defense privilege applies, it protects communications to an attorney to establish a common defense strategy, even though the attorney represents a different client that may have adverse interests.[32] One court has held that the "question in

---

26. *See, e.g.*, Infinite Energy Inc. v. Econnergy Energy Co., 2008 WL 2856719, at *2 (N.D. Fla. July 23, 2008) ("The interest must, therefore, relate to litigation for this privilege to apply . . . .") (citing Bank Brussels Lambert v. Credit Lyonnais (Suisse), 160 F.R.D. 437 (S.D.N.Y.1995). *See generally* N. Neary, *The Last Man Standing: Kansas's Failure to Recognize the Common Interest Doctrine*, 65 U. Kansas L. Rev., 795 (2016) (surveying many jurisdictions, the author notes that that Texas and New York recognize only the joint-defense privilege, Delaware by statute recognizes the broad common-interest privilege, and Kansas state courts, as distinguished from Kansas federal courts, seems not to recognize any form of common-interest protection.

27. Sedlacek v. Morgan Whitney Trading Group, 795 F. Supp. 329, 331 (C.D. Cal. 1992).

28. Tex. R. Evid. 503(b)(1)(C).

29. The common-interest doctrine is an expansion of the joint-defense privilege. Neary, *supra* note 5, at 802; *see* Jared S. Sunshine, *Seeking Common Sense for the Common Law of Common Interest in the D.C. Circuit*, 65 Cath. U.L. Rev. 833, 838–49 (2016) (distinguishing among the co-client privilege, the joint-defense privilege, and the common-interest privilege).

30. Schachar v. Am. Acad. of Ophthalmology, Inc., 106 F.R.D. 187, 191 (N.D. Ill. 1985); John Morrell & Co. v. Loc. Union 304A of United Food & Com. Workers, AFL-CIO, 913 F.2d 544 (8th Cir. 1990); Fellowship of Christian Athletes v. San Jose Unified Sch. Dist. Bd. of Educ., 2022 WL 1189886, at *2 (N.D. Cal. Apr. 21, 2022).

31. Eisenberg v. Gagnon, 766 F.2d 770, 787–88 (3d Cir. 1985).

32. *Id.* at 787–88. *See also* Hunydee v. United States, 355 F.2d 183, 184–85 (9th Cir. 1965); Haines v. Liggett Grp., Inc., 975 F.2d 81, 94 (3d Cir. 1992) (tobacco company defendants exchanged information among various attorneys representing them in order to adequately prepare a joint defense); *see also* United States v. Schwimmer, 892 F.2d 237, 244–45 (2d Cir. 1989) (protecting communications made to an accountant aiding attorneys conducting a joint defense); Fresenius Med. Care Holdings v. Roxane Labs. Inc., 2007 WL 895059, at *2 (S.D. Ohio Mar. 21, 2007) ("the purpose of the [common-interest] doctrine is to permit persons with similar legal interests, but represented by different counsel, to enjoy

determining whether a document is part of the joint defense effort is not the party to whom the document was directed, but whether the document reflects material [that] is part of the joint-defense effort."[33]

Thus, when the defendants choose to have their independent counsel work together in a shared defense arrangement, information passed between them is privileged to the extent that it is part of an ongoing and joint effort to set up a common defense strategy.[34] In a joint-defense arrangement, the attorney-client privilege protects communications by a client to his own lawyer, even though the attorney may later share that information with co-defendants.[35]

In order to invoke the joint-defense privilege, it is necessary to prove a joint-defense agreement.[36] The agreement may be shown by conduct.[37] A written agreement is preferable, however, so that the agreement is more easily proved and its scope is defined.

As with the common-interest privilege, the joint-defense privilege does not apply when the shared interest is commercial or personal rather than legal in nature.[38] For example, there was no protectable common "legal" interest when family members financially assisted other family members in a dissolution action seeking property in a marital estate.[39]

IV. The Joint-Defense Arrangement or Agreement

The joint-defense privilege is often accompanied by a formal joint-defense arrangement, usually called a joint-defense agreement, or JDA. The joint-defense arrangement or agreement may provide for sharing of costs and promote the development of litigation strategy. Further, a joint-defense agreement may minimize the potential for friction and discord among defendants (which often plays a major role in assisting the plaintiff in establishing his case) and may serve to discourage piecemeal settlements (which help to finance the plaintiff's action against the remaining defendants).

---

the same ability to communicate confidentially about their common interests with multiple attorneys that each client enjoys separately").

33. Ohio-Sealy Mattress Mfg. Co. v. Kaplan, 90 F.R.D. 21, 29 (N.D. Ill. 1980) (citing *In re* Grand Jury Subpoena Duces Tecum, 406 F. Supp. 381, 393–94 (S.D.N.Y. 1975)); *see also In re* Sealed Case, 120 F.R.D. 66, 71 (N.D. Ill. 1988) (discussing *Ohio-Sealy Mattress*).

34. *See, e.g.*, Brossel v. Triad. Guar. Ins. Corp., 238 F.R.D. 215, 219–20 (W.D. Ky. 2006); City of Kalamazoo v. Mich. Disposal Serv. Corp., 125 F. Supp. 2d 219, 234 (D. Mich. 2000) (quoting from joint-defense agreement and rejecting argument that only the group itself was the law firm's client).

35. Waller v. Fin. Corp. of Am., 828 F.2d 579, 583 n.7 (9th Cir. 1987); United States v. McPartlin, 595 F.2d 1321, 1336 (7th Cir. 1979) (citing cases); Sedalcek v. Morgan Whitney Trading Grp., 795 F. Supp. 329 (C.D. Cal. 1992); Selby v. O'Dea, 90 N.E.3d 1144, 1155–56 (Il. App. 2017) (citing United States v. McPartlin).

36. *See* N. Am. Rescue Prods., Inc. v. Bound Tree Med., LLC, Inc., 2010 WL 1873291, at *4 (S.D. Ohio May 10, 2010) ("some evidence" is required); Brossel v. Triad. Guar. Ins. Corp., 238 F.R.D. 215, 219–20 (W.D. Ky. 2006).

37. *See* United States v. Gonzalez, 669 F.3d 974, 981 (9th Cir. 2012).

38. Nidec Corp. v. Victor Co., 249 F.R.D. 575, 579 (N.D. Cal. 2007).

39. Keller v. Keller, 63 Conn. L. Rptr. 474, 2016 WL 7742915, at *5 (Conn. Super. Ct. 2016).

Joint-defense arrangements may range from engaging a single defense counsel for all purposes to a much more organized defense committee that assigns the lead role on particular projects. While the extent to which a joint or coordinated defense is feasible will depend on the facts in each case, it is important to recognize that such arrangements can offer significant benefits and advantages to all parties.

Even if a joint-defense arrangement or agreement is informal rather than written, it is still valid,[40] as long as confidentiality can be inferred from circumstances, such as when a disclosure is made among parties having a strong incentive "in sharing the fruit of trial preparation efforts."[41] Although a written agreement is not required,[42] a well-written agreement provides better evidence of the scope of defense protection.[43] As one court observed, "A written agreement is the most effective method of establishing the existence of a common interest agreement, although an oral agreement whose existence, terms and scope are proved by the party asserting it, may provide a basis for the requisite showing."[44]

One reason to have a written agreement is to impose an express duty of confidentiality.[45] When the transfer of information to parties with common interests is conducted under a confidentiality agreement, the case against waiver is strengthened.[46] Having a signed nondisclosure agreement was described by the court as "a guarantee of confidentiality."[47] Specific suggestions to consider for a written agreement are as follows:[48]

1. The agreement should cover all participants, including attorneys, clients, and support staff. Clients should sign or there should at least be a representation that all clients agree.

---

40. *See* Safeco Ins. Co. of Am. v. M.E.S., Inc., 2013 WL 12362006, at *10 (E.D.N.Y. Feb. 12, 2013); Trading Techs. Int'l v. eSpeed, 2007 WL 1302765, at *2 (N.D. Ill. May 1, 2007).

41. United States v. Gulf Oil Corp., 760 F.2d 292, 296 (Temp. Emer. Ct. App. 1985); *see also* Eugenia VI Venture Holdings v. Chabra, 2006 WL 1096825, at *2 (S.D.N.Y. Apr. 25, 2006) (inferring common interest from circumstances).

42. Old Tampa Bay Enters., Inc. v. Gen. Elec. CO., 745 So. 2d 517, 518 (Fla. App. 1999); *In re* Riverkeeper, Inc. v. Port Auth. of New York & New Jersey, 111 N.Y.S.3d 523, 528 (2019) ("The party asserting the common interest rule bears the burden of showing that there was an agreement, though not necessarily in writing . . . ."; quoting Denney v. Jenkens & Gilchrist, 362 F. Supp. 2d 407, 415 (S.D.N.Y. 2004).

43. *See, e.g., In re* Grand Jury Subpoena (Newparent), 274 F.3d 563, 569 (2001) (noting lack of specificity that arose from oral joint-defense agreement).

44. Intex Recreation Corp. v. Team Worldwide Corp., 471 F. Supp. 2d 11, 16 (D.D.C. 2007).

45. *See* United States v. Stepney, 246 F. Supp. 2d 1069, 1076 (N.D. Cal. 2003).

46. AT&T, 642 F.2d at 1299–1300.

47. United States v. Gulf Oil Corp., 760 F.2d 292, 296 (Temp. Emer. Ct. App. 1985); Bank Brussels Lambert v. Chase Manhattan Bank, N.A., 1998 WL 567862, at *2 (S.D.N.Y. 1998) (noting that parties to JDA did not waive work product with disclosure to third party, as documents were produced pursuant to confidentiality agreement).

48. Such suggestions are found in Stephen A. Messer & Scott J. Seagle, *Combining Forces: A Primer on the Joint Defense Agreement in Civil Litigation*, Trial Advocacy Q. (Summer 2011) (available in Westlaw).

2. State the common interest in defending current or potential litigation. And what will be done to promote the common interest, such as exchange of work product. The agreement should provide that the parties will reasonably cooperate with each other in the defense of the parties' common interests, including the sharing of information protected by the attorney-client privilege to assert joint defenses to the claims in the litigation.
3. Include a confidentiality clause that binds all members not to disclose information in any form outside the group and to use the information only for the common purpose. The clause should state that no one member may waive privileges for shared information without consent from all members. Consider requiring notice if a request for the information comes from a party, governmental agency, or court.
4. Each party should acknowledge that it is represented by its own counsel, and that the other attorneys owe an unqualified duty of loyalty to their clients that are the other parties to the agreement, so that attorneys may, in representing their clients, take positions adverse to the other parties. This should include a waiver of conflict of interest to allow an attorney to take such positions.
5. Decide how to handle the potential for later adversity between or among the members. The law allows members to use information if later disputes arise, but parties can agree otherwise.
6. Consider addressing what members can do individually in the litigation, such as engaging in settlement discussions and whether advance notice of negotiations or settlements is required.
7. Address withdrawing from the agreement, whether withdrawal requires advance notice, return of or destruction of documents, and continuation of confidentiality.
8. Address what happens if attorneys involved in the joint defense change firms and specifically what happens if an attorney joins a firm that represents parties adverse to the common group.
9. Address cost-sharing—whether it is expected, and, if so, what costs will be shared and how.

How to fashion a joint-defense agreement is not an easy task, especially in light of issues of waiver and conflicts of interest that are discussed later in this chapter. The agreement should be written with care, tailored to the particular case, and should take into account what may happen as the litigation evolves.

V. The Attorney-Client and Work-Product Privileges in Common-Interest or Joint-Defense Situations

As noted at the beginning of this chapter, the common-interest and joint-defense privileges are not stand-alone privileges. They stand on top of underlying privileges. The most important aspect of the privileges is to prevent waiver of the attorney-client privilege when communications are made outside the strict attorney-client relationship. As one court aptly noted, the "common interest privilege, although often referred to as a privilege, is not an independent privilege, but an exception to the general rule that a voluntary disclosure of privileged material to a third party waives the attorney-client privilege."[49]

As also discussed earlier, the common-interest or joint-defense privilege is much less important for protecting shared work product. The work-product privilege is not waived when it is shared with non-adversaries unless the disclosure substantially increases the chance of its disclosure to an adversary.[50] Thus, a common legal interest or a joint-defense arrangement is not necessary to prevent waiver of the work-product privilege.[51]

Nevertheless, a proven common legal interest or a joint-defense arrangement does assist in proving that the disclosure did not in any way expose the work product to an adversary. Of course, work product must be conducted in anticipation or in furtherance of litigation, so the common interest is necessarily limited to litigation when the common-interest privilege is being invoked to protect work product, and because litigation is a necessary element, courts will more often refer to the joint-defense privilege rather than the common-interest privilege when addressing a claim of waiver of work product.

Returning to the attorney-client privilege, the main utility of the common-interest or joint-defense privilege is to expand the attorney-client privilege beyond the strict attorney-client relationship. If the attorney-client communication at issue is not connected to litigation, and the common-interest privilege is available in the jurisdiction, then the common-interest privilege should be invoked, if it is available in the jurisdiction. If the attorney-client communication is connected to litigation, then either the common-interest or the joint-defense privilege can be invoked, depending again on the jurisdiction.

The joint-defense arrangement protects disclosures when made in the course of formulating a common legal strategy[52] or otherwise furthering the parties' joint interest in the litigation.[53] The joint defense, then, requires the existence of threatened or current litigation.[54] Some courts have defined

---

49. United States v. Patel, 509 F. Supp. 3d 1334, 1340 (2020).

50. *See, e.g.*, Samuels v. Mitchell, 155 F.R.D. 195, 200 (N.D. Cal. 1994) ("[T]he work product privilege is not automatically waived by any disclosure to third persons. Rather, the courts generally find a waiver only if the disclosure 'substantially increases the opportunity for potential adversaries to obtain the information.'" (citation and quotation omitted)).

51. Blattman v. Scaramellino, 891 F.3d 1, 5 (1st Cir. 2018) (disclosure of work-product to a third-party does not necessarily waive the protection; only disclosing material in a way inconsistent with keeping it from an adversary waives work product protection; quotation omitted); United States v. AT&T Co., 642 F.2d 1285 (D.C. Cir. 1980).

52. *See* United States v. Bergonzi, 216 F.R.D. 487, 495 (N.D. Cal. 2003).; Libbey Glass, Inc. v. Oneida Ltd., 197 F.R.D. 342, 348 (N.D. Ohio 1999).

53. Nidec Corp. v. Victor Co., 249 F.R.D. 575, 578 (N.D. Cal. 2007); Lectrolarm Custom Sys., Inc. v. Pelco Sales, Inc., 212 F.R.D. 567, 572 (E.D. Cal. 2002).

54. *In re* Grand Jury Subpoena, 274 F.3d 563, 575 (1st Cir. 2001); Fojtaksi v. NCL (Bahamas) Ltd., 262 F.R.D. 650, 654 (S.D. Fla. 2009).

potential litigation narrowly.[55] If the disclosure is for any other non-litigation purpose, there is no privilege, because the disclosure was not for the purpose of the common interest in defending the lawsuit.[56]

Courts do not always agree on whether a common or joint legal interest exists between the parties sharing privileged information. The disagreement results in part from judicial confusion between the joint-defense privilege, which requires litigation, and the broader common-interest privilege, which does not require litigation that is being jointly defended.

For example, in *D'Ippolito v. Cities Service Co.*,[57] the plaintiff in a private suit raised the work-product privilege to prevent disclosure of an exhibit, but the plaintiff conceded that he had voluntarily disclosed the exhibit to attorneys in the antitrust division of the Department of Justice. The court found waiver because the government was not a party to the lawsuit. This holding illustrates a narrow interpretation of "common interest," which limits it to co-parties.

On similar facts, another judge in the same court refused to find waiver in *G.A.F. Corp. v. Eastman Kodak Co.*[58] In settling the issue for the Second Circuit, the appellate court declined to adopt a "per se" rule regarding whether all voluntary disclosures to the government operate to waive the protections of the work-product rule and held that the privilege was waived on the facts because the disclosure occurred when the government agency was adverse to the disclosing party.[59]

In still another case, the D.C. Circuit in *United States v. AT&T Co.* adopted the *G.A.F.* standard of waiver, reasoning that the purpose of the work-product privilege is to protect information from opponents—not necessarily all other parties. In this light, the court held that "[a] disclosure made in the pursuit of such trial preparation, and not inconsistent with maintaining secrecy against opponents, should be allowed without waiver of the privilege."[60]

Holdings would perhaps be more consistent if courts would use the term common-interest privilege rather than joint-defense privilege. As for practitioners, they should be careful about which privilege they assert, and if an opponent asserts only a joint-defense privilege, then the assertion of privilege may be subject to attack if the common interest is not actually defending the lawsuit.

---

55. *E.g.*, *In re* Santa Fe Int'l Corp., 272 F.3d 705, 710–14 (5th Cir. 2001).
56. Nidec Corp. v. Victor Co., 249 F.R.D. 575, 578 (N.D. Cal. 2007).
57. 39 F.R.D. 610 (S.D.N.Y. 1965).
58. 85 F.R.D. 46 (S.D.N.Y. 1979).
59. *In re* Steinhardt Partners, L.P., 9 F.3d 230, 236 (2d Cir. 1993).
60. United States v. AT&T Co., 642 F.2d 1285, 1299 (D.C. Cir. 1980).

VI. Waiver

Waiver of privilege is discussed in Chapter 6. Obviously, neither the joint-defense privilege nor the common-interest privilege erases the normal waiver rules. Disclosure outside of the joint-defense or common-interest setting can effect a waiver, whether the disclosure is intentional, mistaken, or inadvertent. Further, the normal rules apply on whether the work-product privilege applies in later litigation.

What is different is the question of whether waiver by one member of the joint-defense or common-interest group results in a waiver by all members. Generally, "the joint defense privilege cannot be waived without the consent of all parties to the defense."[61] Similarly, it has been held that a subsidiary could not later waive a joint-defense privilege without the consent of its former parent.[62]

The exception to this rule is when the members of the joint-defense group later litigate against each other about the same subject matter.[63] There must be actual adversity for this exception to apply, not just an "ill feeling" or a "divergence of interests."[64] Otherwise, "joint defense would become impractical since no defendant would be protected against a co-defendant trading a waiver in order to obtain a separate settlement."[65]

Once co-defendants take action against each other, neither "can reasonably be allowed to deny to the other the use of information which he already has by virtue of the former's known disclosure."[66] Under the joint-defense privilege,

61. Ohio-Sealy Mattress Mfg. Co. v. Kaplan, 90 F.R.D. 21, 29 (N.D. Ill. 1980) (citing *In re* Grand Jury Subpoena Duces Tecum, 406 F. Supp. 381, 393–94 (S.D.N.Y. 1975)); Mackenzie-Childs LLC v. Mackenzie-Childs, 262 F.R.D. 241 (W.D.N.Y. 2009); Interfaith Housing Del., Inc. v. Town of Georgetown, 841 F. Supp 1393, 1400–01 (D. Del. 1993) (citing many cases for the inability of one member of the joint-defense group to waive privileges as to all other members and stating: "This holding is in accord with the vast majority of other decisions which address the issue."). *See also* IBJ Whitehall Bank & Trust v. Corey & Assocs., 1999 WL 617842, at *5–6 (M.D. Ill, Aug. 12, 1999) (discussing issue of whether communications between non-lawyers are included; finding that it does, so there was no waiver; rejecting contrary decisions in Schachar v. Am. Academy of Opthalmology, Inc., 106 F.R .D. 187, 191–92 (N.D.Ill.1985) (holding that an attorney must be party to the communications in order for the privilege to attach); John Labatt Ltd. v. Molson Breweries, 898 F. Supp. 471, 476–77 (E.D. Mich. 1995) (holding that communications only privileged if the party receiving privileged information is a "conduit" to other attorneys)).

62. Medcom Holding Co. v. Baxter Travenol Labs., Inc., 689 F. Supp. 841, 845–46 (N.D. Ill. 1988).

63. United States v. Moscony, 697 F. Supp. 888, 894 (E.D. Pa. 1988); Friday Investments, LLC v. Bally Total Fitness of the Mid-Atlantic, Inc., 788 S.E.2d 170, 177 (N.C. App. 2016) (no privilege applies to "disputes inter sese.").

64. *In re* Sealed Case, 120 F.R.D. 66, 71 (N.D. Ill. 1988).

65. *Id.* (citing *In re* Grand Jury Subpoena Duces Tecum dated Nov. 16, 1974, 406 F. Supp. 381, 394 (S.D.N.Y. 1975).

66. *In re* Grand Jury Subpoena Duces Tecum, 406 F. Supp. 381, 394 (S.D.N.Y. 1975); *see also* IBJ Whitehall Bank and Trust Co. v. Corey & Assocs., Inc., 1999 WL 617842, at *3 (M.D. Ill. Aug. 12, 1999); *In re* Ginn-LA St. Lucie Ltd., LLLP, 439 B.R. 801, 805–06 (Bankr. S.D. Fla. 2010).

communications between co-defendants are privileged only as to third parties. When co-defendants reposition themselves to take action against each other, there is a restructuring of the parties' rights to make their interests adverse and any information exchanged between them in a previous litigation is no longer privileged. Use of shared defense information against a group member can prove to be damaging in a multiparty case. An example would be when a joint defense has been undertaken, and one or several co-defendants later assert indemnity claims against one another.

As the Restatement (Third) of the Law Governing Lawyers points out, however, the parties may agree otherwise as to the ability to use shared information in a later dispute between or among them.[67] The parties should consider whether to include a confidentiality provision that waives the right to use shared information in a later dispute in order to prevent a member from trading a waiver for a settlement or some other advantage.[68]

VII. Conflicts of Interest That May Arise Because of a JDA

Common-interest or joint-defense arrangements can cause conflicts of interest problems for lawyers and clients. The issue arises more often in the setting of litigation, so the discussion in the case law on this issue is usually phrased in terms of the joint-defense privilege.

In some joint-defense settings, counsel can operate by agreement as "common" counsel for the entire group, in which case, the common counsel cannot later act adverse to any member of the group on a related matter.[69] Otherwise, a joint-defense arrangement does not automatically establish a direct attorney-client privilege between all parties to the arrangement and their respective attorneys.[70] Nevertheless, a joint-defense arrangement "may create an implied attorney-client relationship with co-defendants."[71] California, however, does not recognize this extension of the attorney-client relationship,[72] although it does recognize that the joint-defense privilege applies to attorney-client communications.[73]

When an implied attorney-client relationship is recognized, conflicts of interest can arise in later proceedings. If adversity develops, one of the members

67. Restatement (Third) of the Law Governing Lawyers § 76(2) (1998).

68. *See In re* Sealed Case, 120 F.R.D. 66, 71 (N.D. Ill. 1988).

69. City of Kalamazoo v. Mich. Disposal Serv. Corp., 151 F. Supp. 2d 913, 914 (D. Mich. 2001).

70. *See, e.g.*, Essex Chem. Corp. v. Hartford Accident & Indem. Co., 993 F. Supp. 241, 254–55 (D.N.J. 1998).

71. Wood v. Superior Court of San Diego County, 46 Cal. App. 5th 562, 586 (2020) (discussing the federal standard); City of Kalamazoo v. Mich. Disposal Serv. Corp., 125 F. Supp. 2d 219, 234 (D. Mich. 2000), *aff'd*, 151 F. Supp. 2d 913 (D. Mich. 2001).

72. Wood v. Superior Court of San Diego County, 46 Cal. App. 5th 562, 586 (2020) ("California requires a genuine attorney-client relationship for the privilege to apply.").

73. Golden Door Properties, LLC v. Superior Court, 53 Cal. App. 5th 733, 782 (2020).

of the arrangement may seek to disqualify counsel for another member on the ground that continued representation violates the implied attorney-client privilege between members of the arrangement and their respective attorneys.[74] The disqualification may extend to the lawyer's entire firm.[75]

For example, the Fifth Circuit in *Wilson P. Abraham Construction Corp. v. Armco Steel Corp.*[76] held that when information is exchanged between co-defendants and attorneys in a joint-defense setting, "this exchange is not made for the purpose of allowing unlimited publication and use, but rather, the exchange is made for the limited purpose of assisting in their common cause. In such a situation, an attorney who is the recipient of such information breaches his fiduciary duty if he later, in his representation of another client, is able to use this information to the detriment of one of the co-defendants."[77] The opposite side of the coin, of course, is the effect on the client who hired the lawyer subject to the conflict of interest.

Even if there is not a direct or implied attorney-client relationship created by a joint defense or common-interest arrangement, an attorney may still be disqualified if the attorney cannot disprove receipt of any confidential information via participation in the group effort.[78] Such a showing would generally be hard to make because the entire purpose of a joint-defense agreement is to share confidential information.[79]

Regardless of how the ethical rules are applied, however, it is advisable to cover this situation in a written agreement. But the best way to deal with the issue is not always clear. If a joint-defense agreement includes a waiver of conflicts, to free lawyers to represent their clients, the waiver may later cause a much bigger problem than adversity between or among group members. One court upheld a waiver of conflict when an attorney left the group and joined the other side of the litigation.[80] The provision interpreted by the court provided: "The parties expressly acknowledge and agree that nothing in this Agreement, nor compliance with the terms of this Agreement by either party, shall be used as a basis to seek to disqualify the respective counsel of such party in any future litigation."[81] Thus, in the case of a joint-defense agreement, the members should carefully consider how to deal with conflicts of interest.

---

74. *Id.* at 242–43; United States v. Henke, 222 F.3d 633, 637–38 (9th Cir. 2000); *In re* Gabapentin Patent Litig., 407 F. Supp. 2d 607, 615 (D.N.J. 2005).

75. *See In re* Gabapentin Patent Litig., 407 F. Supp. 2d 607, 615 (D.N.J. 2005); Nat'l Med. Enters., Inc. v. Godbey, 924 S.W.2d 123, 133 (Tex. 1996); Meza v. H. Muehlstein & Co., 176 Cal. App. 4th 969, 978–83 (Cal App. 2000); *see generally Obligations of a Lawyer Who Formerly Represented a Client in Connection with a Joint Defense Consortium*, ABA Comm. on Ethics & Prof's Resp., Formal Op. 395 (1995).

76. 559 F.2d 250 (5th Cir. 1977).

77. *Id.* at 253.

78. Essex Chem. Corp. v. Hartford Accident & Indem. Co., 993 F. Supp. 241, 252 (D.N.J. 1998).

79. *See* City of Kalamazoo v. Mich. Disposal Serv. Corp., 125 F. Supp. 2d 219, 235 (D. Mich. 2000), *aff'd*, 151 F. Supp. 2d 913 (D. Mich. 2001).

80. *In re* Shared Memory Graphics LLC, 659 F.3d 1336, 1339 (Fed. Cir. 2011).

81. *Id.* at 1340.

VIII. Discovery of Joint-Defense Agreements

Courts have considered motions to compel production of JDAs. A number of courts have held that standard or "garden variety" JDAs, with "boilerplate" terms are not relevant to any issue in the case and thus are not discoverable regardless of any privilege issue.[82] In *Essex Chem Corp. v. Hartford Accident & Indemnity*,[83] the court refused to require a party even to answer interrogatories about the existence of a joint-defense agreement. A JDA may, however, contain provisions that are not work product at all, in which case a portion of the agreement may be discoverable.[84]

Other courts have focused on whether the JDA may contain provisions such as tolling agreements that would be relevant to show bias for impeachment purposes.[85] Another court allowed discovery of a tolling agreement, which results from some level of adversity between the members of the group, but the court did limit its order to the tolling agreement.[86] One court has invoked the substantial need requirement that applies to work product.[87]

In *Blackmon v. Bracken Construction Co.*,[88] the court agreed that other courts had denied discovery JDAs, but the court noted that in those cases, the relevant parts of the JDA had already been disclosed, namely, the parties to the agreement, the date the agreement was reached, and its general scope. The court then held that the plaintiffs were entitled to the same information because that information was relevant to the privileged status of documents, some of which may have predated the JDA. That information was not viewed as protected by the attorney-client privilege, and the court held that there was substantial need for the information that justified discovery of the information despite the existence of qualified work-product protection.

---

82. Wausau Underwriters Ins. Co. v. Reliable Transp. Specialists, 2018 WL 4235077, at *1 (E.D. Mich. Sept. 6, 2018); Biovail Labs. Int'l, SRL v. Watson Pharms. Inc., 2010 WL 3447187, at *1–2 (S.D. Fla. Aug. 30, 2010) (examining agreement in camera to determine if it contained anything other than "boilerplate terms"); Ford Motor Co. v. Edgewood Properties, Inc., 257 F.R.D. 418, 428 (D.N.J. 2009); Broessel v. Triad Guar. Ins. Co., 238 F.R.D. 215, 218 (W.D. Ky. 2006); Innovative Legal Mktg., LLC v. Mkt. Masters-Legal, 2011 WL 13118266, at *1 (E.D. Va. Sept. 23, 2011); AI Credit Corp. v. Providence Wash. Ins. Co., 1997 WL 231127, at *4 (S.D.N.Y. May 7, 1997) (noting that joint defense agreements are generally privileged) United States v. Bicoastal Corp., 1992 WL 693384, at *5 (W.D.N.Y. Sept. 28, 1992).

83. 975 F. Supp. 650 (D.N.J. 1997), *rev'd on other grounds*, 993 F. Supp. 241 (D.N.J. 1998).

84. Biovail Labs. Int'l, SRL v. Watson Pharms. Inc., 2010 WL 3447187, at *1–2 (S.D. Fla. Aug. 30, 2010) (ordering production of tolling provisions).

85. AMEC Civil, LLC v. DMJM Harris, Inc., 2008 WL 817059 D.N.J. July 11, 2008) (noting that settlement or tolling provisions may be relevant on that ground).

86. Tribune Co. v. Purcigliolotti, 1997 WL 54810, at *3 (S.D.N.Y. Sept. 3, 1997).

87. Generac Power Sys., Inc. v. Kohler Co., 2012 WL 5463913, at *2 (E.D. Wis. Nov. 8, 2012) (finding no evidence of substantial need especially since agreement was signed after litigation began).

88. 338 F.R.D. 91, 94–95 (M.D. La. 2021).

IX. Conclusion

The common-interest and joint-defense privileges assist in protecting the underlying privileges for attorney-client communications and attorney work product. The common-interest privilege is especially needed to preserve the confidentiality of attorney-client communications that would otherwise lose their protection when disclosed outside the confines of the attorney-client relationship. Work product does not lose its protection as long as disclosure does not expose it to an adversary, and a joint-defense agreement serves only to reinforce an argument against waiver. Of course, the elements of the underlying attorney-client and work-product privileges must still be met because the common-interest and joint-defense privileges are not independent privileges.

The joint-defense arrangement or agreement is a specific vehicle that assists multiple defendants in defending against a common plaintiff or a common set of plaintiffs. Memorializing a defense arrangement in writing helps to guard against waiver, can address in advance issues that may later arise during the litigation, and can specify how the parties will share information and perhaps the costs of litigation. The agreement must be tailored to the case and must deal with issues of waiver of privilege and future potential conflicts of interest.

CHAPTER 5

Exceptions to Privileges

REAGAN W. SIMPSON AND ROBERT P. REDEMANN

As discussed in Chapter 3 on the work-product privilege, non-core attorney work product can be discovered if there is substantial need for information not otherwise available. A prime example is Federal Rule of Civil Procedure 26(b)(4)(ii), which allows discovery if a party shows "substantial need for the materials to prepare its case and cannot, without undue hardship, obtain their substantial equivalent by other means." Such a provision in a rule of civil procedure could be viewed as exception to privilege but is more properly an element of a qualified privilege. This chapter discusses true exceptions, although some exceptions may overlap with the substantial need concept addressed in Chapter 3 or with principles of waiver addressed in Chapter 6.

I. Crime-Fraud Exception

A. Overview of the Crime-Fraud Exception

The attorney-client privilege is the oldest and most universally accepted privilege recognized by the common law,[1] and the crime-fraud exception, in turn, is the oldest exception.[2] The crime-fraud exception prevents clients from using legal advice and attorney work product to perpetrate or plan unlawful activity and then use the privilege as a shield from disclosure.[3] For example, the exception applied when there was evidence of "an ongoing or imminent crime or fraud" in a "pervasive and systematic scheme to destroy or alter

1. Upjohn Co. v. United States, 449 U.S. 383, 389 (1981).

2. *See generally* Auburn K. Daily & S. Britta Thornquist, *Has the Exception Outgrown the Privilege?: Exploring the Application of the Crime-Fraud Exception to the Attorney-Client Privilege*, 16 Geo. J. Legal Ethics 583, 584 (2003) (discussing its 18th-century English common law roots); 8 J.H. Wigmore, Wigmore on Evidence § 2298 (John T. McNaughton rev. 1961).

3. The exception applies to work product as well as attorney-client communications. *See, e.g., In re Grand Jury Subpoena, 419 F.3d 329, 335 (5th Cir. 2005); In re* Int'l Sys. & Controls Corp. Sec. Litig., 693 F.2d 1235, 1242 (5th Cir. 1982).

subpoenaed evidence," coupled with "routinely perjured testimony" by the party's archivist, "all with the knowledge and participation of [the party's] legal department."[4]

The exception applies to communications to further future or ongoing criminal or fraudulent conduct, including other wrongful conduct such as intentional torts.[5] For example, courts have held that communications in furtherance of document spoliation are not privileged under the crime-fraud exception.[6] Exceptions to the exception include communications regarding *past* crime or fraud.[7] Another exception is when the communication is not for the purpose of furthering conduct but to seek legal advice to determine the legality of conduct before taking action.[8] The attorney's innocence or guilt is irrelevant to applying the crime-fraud exception.[9] The focus is on the client's conduct and intentions.[10] Beyond the scope of this book is any discussion of when lawyers are allowed or must disclose planned criminal conduct.[11]

To invoke the crime-fraud exception, the party asserting the exception must first demonstrate "a factual basis" for a "good faith belief by a reasonable person" that a crime or fraud has been committed.[12] If that threshold is met, the court will conduct an in camera review to determine whether the party asserting the exception has made a "prima facie showing" that (1) "the client was committing or intending to commit a fraud or crime" and (2) "the attorney-client communications were in furtherance of that alleged crime or fraud."[13]

---

4. United States v. Zolin, 491 U.S. 554, 563 (1989); *In re* Sealed Case, 754 F.2d 395, 399, 400 (D.C. Cir. 1985). *See also In re* Diasonics Sec. Litig., 110 F.R.D. 570, 575 (D. Colo. 1986) (exception applied where fiduciaries accused of creating false financial statements sought legal assistance in rescinding a sale "for their own personal benefit," in conflict with the interests of the company's shareholders).

5. *In re* Grand Jury Subpoena, 419 F.3d 329, 335 (5th Cir. 2005); *In re* Grand Jury Subpoena, 223 F.3d 213, 217 (3d Cir. 2000); *In re* Sealed Case, 754 F.2d 395, 399 (D.C. Cir. 1985); Ross v. Superior Court of Riverside County, 77 Cal. App. 5th 667 (2022); *see also* Rambus, Inc. v. Infineon Techs. AG, 220 F.R.D. 264, 281 (E.D. Va. 2004) (internal citations omitted) ("The term crime/fraud exception, however, is a bit of a misnomer."); Int'l Tel. & Tel. Corp. v. United Tel. Co. of Fla., 60 F.R.D. 177, 180 (M.D. Fla. 1973) ("substantial abuses of the attorney-client relationship"); New York Tile Wholesale Corp. v. Herrick Feinstein, LLP, 205 A.D.3d 723 (2022).

6. *E.g.*, Rambus, Inc. v. Infineon Techs. AG, 220 F.R.D. 264, 286 (E.D. Va. 2004).

7. United States v. Zolin, 491 U.S. 554, 562 (1989); *In re* Grand Jury Subpoena, 745 F.3d 681, 687 (3d Cir. 2014); *In re* Sealed Case, 754 F.2d 395, 399 (D.C. Cir. 1985); *In re* John Doe Corp., 675 F.2d 482, 491 (2d Cir. 1982).

8. *In re* BankAmerica Corp. Sec. Litig., 270 F.3d 639, 643 (8th Cir. 2001); United States v. Jacobs, 117 F.3d 82, 88 (2d Cir. 1997), *abrogated on other grounds by* Loughrin v. United States, 134 S. Ct. 2384 (2014).

9. United States v. Doe, 429 F.3d 450, 454 (3d Cir. 2005).

10. *In re* Grand Jury Subpoena, 745 F.3d 681, 691 (3d Cir. 2014); *In re* Grand Jury Proceedings, 417 F.3d 18, 23 (1st Cir. 2005); *In re* BankAmerica Corp. Sec. Litig., 270 F.3d 639, 642 (8th Cir. 2001); United States v. Chen, 99 F.3d 1495, 1504 (9th Cir. 1996); *In re* Grand Jury Proceedings v. (Under Seal), 102 F.3d 748, 750–51 (4th Cir. 1996); *In re* Grand Jury Proceedings, 680 F.2d 1026, 1028 (5th Cir. 1982).

11. *See ABA* Model Rules of Prof'l Conduct Rule 1.13 & 1.6.

12. United States v. Scarfo, 2022 WL 2763761, at *17 (3d Cir. July 15, 2022) (citing Haines v. Liggett Grp. Inc., 975 F.2d 81, 96 (3d Cir. 1992)).

13. *Id.* (quotation omitted and altered).

B. Extending the Crime-Fraud Exception

A significant difference, however, can be found among jurisdictions as to the conduct that falls within the exception. Some jurisdictions require that the conduct invoked for the exception must satisfy statutorily or judicially recognized elements of a particular crime or fraud.[14] Most courts apply a broader view.[15] Thus, in these jurisdictions, legal advice sought with fraudulent intent does not receive the benefit of the attorney-client privilege, regardless of whether the client happens to succeed in inducing reliance.

Questions arise whether the exception extends to conduct at the margin between fraudulent conduct and tortious conduct, whether intentional, in bad faith, or just merely tortious. Some courts have leaped from applying the exception to cases of crime or fraud to allegations of tortious conduct that meets a high standard of culpability, such as an intentional tort[16] or bad faith.[17] In *Koch v. Specialized Care Servs., Inc.*,[18] the court quoted and discussed section 82 of the Restatement (Third) of the Law Governing Lawyers:

> Clearly, the Restatement view recognizes the benefit of expanding the crime-fraud exception in certain circumstances while acknowledging that some authorities would construe it narrowly. Indeed, the Reporter's Note indicates that "[t]he authorities disagree whether the exception should include more than crimes and frauds." However, for purposes of a general rule, the Restatement confines section 82 to crimes and frauds because of the inherent difficulty in "formulat[ing]

---

14. *See, e.g., In re* Napster, Inc. Copyright Litig., 479 F.3d 1078, 1093–96 (9th Cir. 2007), *abrogated on other grounds by* Mohawk Indus., Inc. v. Carpenter, 558 U.S. 100 (2009); Union Carbide Corp. v. Dow Chem. Co., 619 F. Supp. 1036, 1051 (D. Del. 1985); Research Corp. v. Gourmet's Delight Mushroom Co., 560 F. Supp. 811, 820 (E.D. Pa. 1983).

15. *See, e.g., In re* Grand Jury, 705 F.3d 133, 155–57 (3d Cir. 2012) (granting the exception where there was a "reasonable basis to suspect" that a corporation committed tax evasion); United States v. Martin, 278 F.3d 988, 1001 (9th Cir. 2002) ("reasonable cause to believe that the attorney's services were utilized in furtherance of . . . defrauding a legitimate business"); *In re* Sealed Case, 754 F.2d 395, 399 (D.C. Cir. 1985) (extending the exception to "crime, fraud or other misconduct"); Cooksey v. Hilton Int'l Co., 863 F. Supp. 150, 151 (S.D.N.Y. 1994) (applying the exception to "intentional torts moored in fraud"); Volcanic Gardens Mgmt. Co. v. Paxson, 847 S.W.2d 343, 347 (Tex. Ct. App. 1993) (refusing to limit the application of the exception only in cases of common law or criminal fraud).

16. Diamond v. Stratton, 95 F.R.D. 503, 505 (S.D.N.Y. 1982); *see* Coleman v. Am. Broad. Cos., 106 F.R.D. 201, 207 (D.D.C. 1985) (listing other decisions applying the exception to tort allegations).

17. *Freedom Trust v. Chubb Group of Ins. Cos.*, 38 F. Supp. 2d 1170, 1173 n.3 (C.D. Cal. 1999). *See also* Koch v. Specialized Care Servs., Inc., 437 F. Supp. 2d 362, 373, 375 (D. Md. 2005) (Evidence codes and cases are divided on extending the crime-fraud exception to wrongs that, although criminal or fraudulent, "have hallmarks of clear illegality, and the threat of serious harm." Argues that exception should be expanded because "legislatures classify illegal acts as crimes or frauds for purposes and policies different from those defining the privilege." Court from this leaped to conclusion that "limiting the exception to crimes and frauds produces an exception narrower than principle and policy would otherwise indicate"; endorses view that "any distinction between crimes and frauds and other wrongdoings" is an "overly crude boundary.").

18. 437 F. Supp. 2d 362 (D. Md. 2005).

> a broader exception that is not objectionably vague." Thus, the Restatement does not outrightly reject expanding outside the traditional notions of crime or fraud; however, it recognizes that such an expansion should be on a factual, case-by-case basis and is not easily codified into language suitable for purposes of the Restatement.[19]

After quoting the comment to section 82 as stating the "prevailing view" that the exception is limited to crimes and frauds, the court doubts that is an accurate assessment and refers to the Reporter's Note as proof of its doubt:

> The Reporter's Note to "comment d" lists substantial authority in favor of an expanded crime-fraud exception and then notes several model and state evidence codes that limit the exception to only crimes and frauds. The Court believes that, on balance, the authority in favor of a limited exception is not substantial enough to support the conclusion that it is the prevailing view, at least as of 2005. Restatement (Third) Law Governing Law. § 82 cmt. d.[20]

Expansions of the crime-fraud exception are important given the increasing allegations of commercial fraud and bad faith.[21]

C. Burden of Proof on the Crime-Fraud Exception

The burden of proof for the crime-fraud exception is important. The issue is how much evidence is needed to invoke the exception.

The consensus seems to be that the parties seeking discovery need only meet a burden of making out a prima facie case of the underlying crime or fraud.[22] One court held that the "prima facie case" required to defeat the privilege consisted of "requiring that the evidence in favor of [the] proposition be sufficient to support a finding in its favor, if all of the evidence to the contrary

---

19. 437 F. Supp. 2d at 375.

20. *Id.* at 375 & n.17.

21. *See* State *ex rel.* Allstate Ins. Co. v. Madden, 601 S.E.2d 25, 45 (W. Va. 2004) (Albright, J., dissenting) (Intent requirement for crime-fraud exception "bears emphasis in light of the fact that there appears to be a concerted attempt underway to use the crime-fraud exception to gain access to the insurance claims file . . . or what is referred to by lawyers in bad-faith litigation as the 'ticket to the gold mine.'").

22. *See, e.g.*, United States v. Scarfo, 2022 WL 2763761, at *17 (3d Cir. July 15, 2022); *In re* Grand Jury Subpoena, 745 F.3d 681, 691 (3d Cir. 2014); Walker v. Charter Commc'ns, LLC, 2022 WL 1439125, at *2 (9th Cir. May 6, 2022); *In re* Napster, Inc. Copyright Litig., 479 F.3d 1078, 1093–96 (9th Cir. 2007), *abrogated by* Mohawk Indus., Inc. v. Carpenter, 558 U.S. 100 (2009); *In re* Grand Jury Subpoena, 220 F.3d 406, 410 (5th Cir. 2000). In *In re Methyl Tertiary Butyl Ether (MTBE) Products Liability Litigation*, the court articulated the New York rule, which requires that "the moving party . . . establish probable cause that the disputed communications 'were intended in some way to facilitate or to conceal the [fraudulent] activity.'" 180 F. Supp. 3d 273, 282 (S.D.N.Y. 2016).

be disregarded."[23] In other words, the privilege could be done away with by meeting the motion to dismiss standard, without necessarily proving any facts, and without considering any evidence to the contrary.

Another court required only that there be a showing of "some foundation in fact" to constitute a prima facie case to abrogate the privilege.[24] By contrast, other courts refuse to allow the exception based on strained inferences,[25] and several courts have adopted a rule that requires parties to show by a preponderance of the evidence that the exception applies.[26] Another issue is whether any heightened pleading or proof standards that apply to the underlying crime or fraud apply equally to invoking the exception to the privilege.[27]

Federal lower courts follow *United States v. Zolin*.[28] *Zolin* held that, in deciding to allow the exception, courts could consider "any relevant evidence, lawfully obtained, that has not been adjudicated to be privileged."[29] This, of course, includes the contested communications themselves, which must be reviewed by the court in camera.[30] Further, *Zolin* specified that the party contesting privilege "must present evidence sufficient to support a reasonable belief that *in camera* review may yield evidence that establishes the exception's

---

23. United Servs. Auto. Ass'n v. Werley, 526 P.2d 28, 32 n.15 (Alaska 1974); *cf.* Laser Indus., Ltd. v. Reliant Techs., Inc., 167 F.R.D. 417, 425 (N.D. Cal. 1996) (courts would reason unreliably if they were permitted to consider only the evidence of the party trying to penetrate the privilege, without regard to the opposing party's evidence).

24. United States v. Hallinan, 290 F. Supp. 3d 355, 365 (E.D. Pa. 2017); *In re* Economou, 362 B.R. 893, 898 (Bankr. N.D. Ill. 2007) (prima facie case showed that client had transferred property while mortgage was in default, and that attorney assisted client in scheme by preparing documents to implement transfers.); United States v. Skeddle, 989 F. Supp. 890, 901–02 (N.D. Ohio 1997) (requiring reasonable basis); Caldwell v. Dist. Court, 644 P.2d 26, 32 (Colo. 1982). *See also* Koch v. Specialized Care Servs., Inc., 437 F. Supp. 2d 362, 373 (D. Md. 2005) (exception can apply even if proponent does not plead a specific crime or cause of action in fraud); *but see* United Bank v. Buckingham, 301 F. Supp. 3d 547, 553–54 (D. Md. 2018) (*Koch* rule should be restricted to cases of actual fraud, in which fraudulent acts were performed with wrongful intent).

25. *In re* Sealed Case, 107 F.3d 46, 50 (D.C. Cir. 1997) (court refused to infer that legal advice was sought in order to further illegal conduct from fact that client discussed campaign finance laws with counsel, and then "within weeks" violated those laws).

26. *See, e.g.*, *Laser Indus., Ltd. v. Reliant Techs., Inc.*, 167 F.R.D. 417, 432 (N.D. Cal. 1996); *In re* Napster, Inc. Copyright Litig., 479 F.3d 1078, 1094 (9th Cir. 2007), *abrogated by* Mohawk Indus., Inc. v. Carpenter, 558 U.S. 100 (2009); Swortwood v. Tenedora de Empresas, S.A. de C.V., 2014 WL 895456, at *12 (S.D. Cal. Mar. 6, 2014), *clarified on denial of reconsideration by* Swortwood v. Empresas, S.A. de C.V., 2014 WL 12026069 (S.D. Cal. Apr. 18, 2014).

27. *See* State *ex rel.* Allstate Ins. Co. v. Madden, 601 S.E.2d 25, 48 (W. Va. 2004) (Maynard, C.J., dissenting) (Since a cause of action for fraud requires proof by clear and convincing evidence, insofar as the misdeed upon which a party bases his or her assertion of the crime-fraud exception also consists of fraudulent conduct, then the proper quantum of proof likewise would be clear and convincing evidence.).

28. 491 U.S. 554 (1989).

29. *Id.* at 575; *see also* Roe v. White, 2014 WL 842790, at *2 (N.D. Cal. Feb. 28, 2014).

30. *See, e.g.*, *In re* BankAmerica Corp. Sec. Litig., 270 F.3d 639, 644 (8th Cir. 2001) ("We have found no case in which this court affirmed an order to produce documents under the crime-fraud exception where the district court did not first review the documents in camera.").

applicability."[31] Once this showing is made, however, the contested communications themselves "may provide the evidentiary basis for the ultimate showing that the crime-fraud exception applies."[32] That is, the court held that independent evidence of the crime or fraud was not required to apply the exception.

Zolin, however, did not resolve the question of ultimate burden of proof, and different standards have emerged:

- Requiring presentation of "evidence which, if believed by the fact-finder, would be sufficient to support a finding that the elements of the crime-fraud exception were met."[33]
- Evidence "must be such as to subject the opposing party to the risk of non-persuasion if the evidence as to the disputed fact is left unrebutted."[34]
- Parties must "demonstrate that there is a factual basis for a showing of probable cause to believe that crime or fraud has been committed and that the communications in question were in furtherance of the fraud or crime," after which a decision regarding the exception is left to the discretion of the trial court.[35]
- Party must offer "evidence that if believed by the trier of fact would establish the elements of an ongoing or imminent crime or fraud," and then a decision is left to the trial court's discretion.[36]
- Parties "must present the district court with sufficient evidence to make its prima facie case . . . [and] must persuade the court to find that the communications with the lawyer were in furtherance of an intended or present illegality and that there is some relationship between the communications and the illegality."[37]

The question arises about what happens after prima facie proof is presented. In *Gutter v. E.I. du Pont de Nemours*,[38] a securities class action, the court held that the prima facie evidence of the exception required that the burden of

31. 491 U.S. at 574–75; *see also In re* Grand Jury Subpoena, 745 F.3d 681, 688–89 (3d Cir. 2014).

32. 491 U.S. at 574 n.12.

33. *In re* Grand Jury Investigation, 445 F.3d 266, 274 (3d Cir. 2006).

34. *In re* Grand Jury Proceedings #5 Empaneled January 28, 2004, 401 F.3d 247, 251 (4th Cir. 2005) (quoting Duplan Corp. v. Deering Milliken, Inc., 540 F.2d 1215, 1220 (4th Cir. 1976).

35. United States v. Chervin, 2011 WL 4424297, at *3 (S.D.N.Y. Sept. 21, 2011); United States v. Jacobs, 117 F.3d 82, 87 (2d Cir. 1997).

36. *In re Grand Jury Subpoenas, 144 F.3d 653, 600 (10th Cir. 1998); In re* Sealed Case, 107 F.3d 46, 50 (D.C. Cir. 1997); United States v. Philip Morris USA, Inc., 2004 WL 5355972, at *36 (D.D.C. Feb. 23, 2004).

37. United States v. Martin, 278 F.3d 988, 1001 (9th Cir. 2001).

38. 124 F. Supp. 2d 1291 (S.D. Fla. 2000); *see also* JTR Enters., LLC v. An Unknown Quantity of Colombian Emeralds, Amethysts & Quartz Crystals, 297 F.R.D. 522, 527 (S.D. Fla. 2013).

persuasion shift to the party asserting the privilege to give a reasonable explanation of its conduct.[39]

II. Attorney Misconduct Exception[40]

In a corollary to the crime-fraud exception, attorney misconduct can give rise to a loss of work-product protection. In *Moody v. I.R.S.*,[41] Moody sought all documents regarding him under a Freedom of Information Act request. The IRS resisted production of all documents based on exemption 5 of the act, which gives agency-deliberative documents the same protection as that provided by Rule 26(b) of the Federal Rules of Civil Procedure, including work-product protection. The document in question detailed a meeting between a government attorney and the federal judge overseeing the receivership of W.L. Moody & Sons, Banker, regarding enforcement of a summons on the bank's receiver. The document was in the form of a memorandum dated two days before the petition to enforce the summons was filed.

The court found such a meeting inappropriate and possibly an ethical violation. The court noted, "a lawyer's unprofessional behavior may vitiate the work product privilege."[42] The court agreed that it would be destructive to allow the privilege, designed to uphold the integrity of the adversarial system, to be used to cover up an activity destructive of the system's integrity and sent the matter back to the lower court to determine if the government attorney's actions were actually unprofessional.

The holding in *Moody* has been called into doubt,[43] but it has also been cited favorably in later cases.[44] In one of those cases, *Wilson v. Lamb*,[45] an attorney surreptitiously recorded the statements of two employees of a defendant prior to filing suit and then refused to produce them. In affidavits, the employees indicated they would not have given the statements if they had known they were being recorded. The court directed production of the statements on two grounds: the unprofessional behavior of the attorney and the right of a witness to a copy of his statement under Federal Rule of Civil Procedure 26(b)(3).[46]

---

39. *Id.* at 1307.

40. G. Michael Halfenger, *The Attorney Misconduct Exception to the Work Product Doctrine*, 58 U Chi. L. Rev. 1079 (1991).

41. 654 F.2d 795 (D.C. Cir. 1981).

42. *Id.* at 800.

43. Bartko v. U.S. Dep't of Justice, 2014 WL 12787631, at *8 (D.D.C. Oct. 4, 2014).

44. Wilson v. Lamb, 125 F.R.D. 142, 143 (E.D. Ky 1989); H.L. Hayden Co. of New York, Inc. v. Siemens Medical Sys., Inc., 108 F.R.D. 686, 690 (S.D.N.Y. 1985) (behavior of the attorney destroyed the privilege.) Haigh v. Matsushita Elec. Corp. of America, 676 F. Supp. 1332, 1357–59 (E.D. Va. 1987).

45. 125 F.R.D. 142, (E.D. Ky 1989).

46. *Id.* at 143.

III. Disputes between Attorney and Client

In cases where the client and attorney become adversaries, the reasoning for the privilege breaks down. The majority view is that, while both can be said to hold the privilege, the material produced by the attorney belongs to the client, because without the client's seeking legal counsel, the materials would not have been created.[47] To put it succinctly, "the work product doctrine does not apply to the situation in which a client seeks access to documents or other tangible things created or amassed by his attorney during the course of the representation."[48] The minority view is that the material belongs to the attorney, unless the client is suing the attorney.[49]

California has codified the majority. "In an action between an attorney and a client or a former client of the attorney, no work product privilege under this chapter exists if the work product is relevant to an issue of breach by the attorney of a duty to the client arising out of the attorney-client relationship."[50] When a client has made a complaint against an attorney and there is an investigation, California has statutorily removed any claim of work product.[51]

IV. Bad Faith

As mentioned in Chapter 6 on waiver, the issue of bad faith in a case can cause the work-product privilege protection to be challenged. In *Nationwide Mutual Insurance Co. v. Smith*,[52] an insurance bad-faith case, the court noted, "To establish that the insurer acted in bad faith, the plaintiff must show whether [the insurer] sought and followed [the] advice and recommendation of its agents, adjusters and attorneys. Therefore, all such information is relevant and good cause [is] established for its production."[53] Subsequent cases have restricted the position adopted in *Nationwide* to hold that attorney work product is not relevant and the privilege stands unless an insurer uses the defense of reliance on advice of counsel.[54]

---

47. Resolution Trust Corp. v. H----, P.C., 128 F.R.D. 647 (N.D.Tex.1989); In the Matter of Kaleidoscope, Inc., 15 B.R. 232 (Bankr. N.D. Ga. 1981); O&C Creditors Group, LLC v. Stephens & Stephens XII, LLC, 42 Cal. App. 5th 546, 562 (2019).

48. Swift, Currie, McGehee & Hiers v. Henry, 581 S.E. 2nd 37, 40 (Ga. 2003).

49. *Id.* at 39. Even in this situation there may be "good cause" to keep the privilege in place. For instance, if disclosure would violate an attorney's duty to a third party, if the material is evaluative of the client, or if the material is simply preliminary impressions designed to help the attorney determine a strategy. *Id.*

50. Cal. Civ. Pro. Code § 2018.080 (2005).

51. Cal. Civ. Pro. Code § 2018.070 (2005) (allowing the State Bar to discover the work product of an attorney against whom disciplinary charges are pending when it is relevant to issues of breach of duty by the lawyer and requisite client approval has been granted; filing a complaint is considered the requisite client approval).

52. 174 F.R.D. 250, 253 (D. Conn. 1993).

53. *Id.* at 253 (internal quotes omitted).

54. Martin. v. Am. Bankers Life Assur. Co. of Florida, 184 F.R.D. 263 (D.V.I. 1999). For more cases restricting the broad concept stated in *Nationwide*, see Rhone–Poulenc Rorer, Inc. v. Home Indem. Co.,

In *Nei v. Travelers Home and Marine Insurance Co.*,[55] an underinsured unfair claims practices and bad faith suit, the plaintiff sought historical materials, including attorney work-product information and his complete claim file. The court noted that in order for the attorney work product to be unprotected, the insurer would have to raise the defense of reliance on advice of counsel.[56]

The defense was raised in *High Country Paving, Inc. v. United Fire & Casualty Co.*,[57] and production was required. Thus, the bad-faith exception may not be a separate exception. It may well be a variant of the "at issue" exception or the substantial need exception.[58]

V. Impossibility

As mentioned earlier, a party may be able to obtain work-product materials if the materials are relevant, necessary for the party to proceed, and there is no way to obtain the materials without great cost or in substantially similar form. Though labeled a separate exception, in Illinois even opinion work product can be discoverable, if there is a showing of impossibility.[59] The "impossibility" being a lack of ability to find the material from other sources. While labeled an "exception," this is really just a form of the requirement of need found in Federal Rule Civil Procedure 26(b)(3)(A)(ii).[60]

---

32 F.3d 851, 863 (3d Cir.1994); Northwood Nursing and Convalescent Home, Inc. v. The Cont'l Ins. Co., 161 F.R.D. 293, 298 (E.D. Pa. 1995); Dixie Mill Supply Co. Inc. v. Cont'l Cas. Co., 168 F.R.D. 554, 556–57 (E.D. La. 1996); Ferrara & DiMercurio, Inc. v. St. Paul Mercury Ins. Co., 173 F.R.D. 7, 11–12 (D. Mass. 1997).

55. 326 F.R.D. 652 (D. Mont. 2018).

56. Barnard Pipeline, Inc. v. Travelers Property Cas. Co of Am., 2014 WL 1576543, at *5 (D. Mont. Apr. 17, 2014) ("unless the insurer relies on the advice of counsel defense "the insurer, not the attorneys, [makes] the ultimate decision to deny coverage," and therefore "attorney mental impressions and opinions are not directly at issue" in insurance bad faith claims. The insured cannot establish a compelling need for opinion work product of an insurer's attorneys and the work product doctrine thus protects such materials from disclosure) (citations omitted).

57. 414 F. Supp. 3d 1299, 1304–05 (D. Mont. 2019) (United Fire's reliance on an advice of counsel defense has placed "the attorney's mental impressions and opinions . . . directly at issue in the case." Therefore, United Fire is required to disclose work product related to the underlying claim.") (citation omitted). Further, they found a compelling need for the materials to be disclosed.

58. Burrow v. Forjas Taurus S.A., 334 F. Supp. 3d 1222, 1230 (S.D. Fla. 2018) (referring to substantial need.); Barnard Pipeline, Inc. v. Travelers Property Cas. Co of Am., 2014 WL 1576543, at *5 (D. Mont. Apr. 17, 2014) (same).

59. Doe v. Township High School 211 (34 N.E.3d 652, 674 (Ill. App. 2015) (citing Waste Mgmt., Inc. v. Int'l Surplus Lines Ins. Co., 579 N.E. 2d 322, 330 (Ill. 1991) ("Opinion or 'core' work product which consists of materials generated in preparation for litigation which reveal the mental impressions, opinions, or trial strategy of an attorney, is subject to discovery upon a showing of impossibility of securing similar information from other sources."). *See* Huebner v. Family Video Movie Club, Inc., 2019 WL 2409005 at *6 (Ill. App. June 5, 2019) (impossibility not shown and work product protection remained).

60. This provision reads, "the party [requesting the materials must] show[] that it has substantial need for the materials to prepare its case and cannot, without undue hardship, obtain their substantial equivalent by other means."

The uniqueness of evidentiary materials may also play a role and have some influence on a court's decision. The court in *Burrow v. Forjas Taurus S.A.*,[61] citing a line of cases,[62] stated as much:

> While all of the cases above involve many different causes of action, the reasons why these items were compelled—notwithstanding the work product doctrine—remain the same. That reasoning is premised on the determination of whether certain types of items—including investigative reports, technical data, photos, and videos—are so unique and essential to the facts of a case that they must be produced. Courts have often compelled the production of *photographs* and videos because other discovery devices cannot act as an adequate substitute for the unique content found therein. *See, e.g., Zoller v. Conoco, Inc.*, 137 F.R.D. 9, 10 (W.D. La. 1991).[63]

Thus, uniqueness, because it makes it impossible for a party to obtain the substantial equivalent, may be persuasive to overcome privilege.

---

61. 334 F. Supp. 3d 1222 (S.D. Fla. 2018).

62. *Id.* at 1230–31 ("As further support that Plaintiffs have demonstrated a substantial need, our review of the relevant case law suggests that engineering reports, pictures, and videos should be produced in cases like these because parties seeking discovery have few ways to acquire this information or a substantial equivalent thereof."). *See, e.g.*, Gillespie v. Charter Commc'ns, 133 F. Supp. 3d 1195 (E.D. Mo. 2015) (ordering the production of incident reports in a discrimination case because plaintiff had no other means to obtain the documents requested); F.T.C. v. Boehringer Ingelheim Pharm., Inc., 778 F.3d 142, 157–58 (D.C. Cir. 2015) (finding that the FTC had shown a substantial need and undue hardship for materials relating to financial analyses and forecasts in an unfair trade practices case); United States v. ISS Marine Servs., Inc., 905 F. Supp. 2d 121, 142 (D.D.C. 2012) (ordering the production of an audit report in a case where the federal government sought to enforce a subpoena on the basis that a report was the only evidence available to determine when a contractor became aware of any potential overpayments made on the government contract, which went to the heart of the government's case); Huggins v. Fed. Express Corp., 250 F.R.D. 404, 407 (E.D. Mo. 2008) (ordering the production of photographs because of the plaintiff's inability to obtain equivalent information in a negligence case); *see also* Harris v. Provident Life & Accident Ins. Co., 198 F.R.D. 26 (N.D.N.Y. 2000) (ordering the production of medical reports because they were critical to the defense in showing that the insured did not have a latex allergy and that there was no breach of a disability insurance policy); Peterson v. Wallace Computer Servs., Inc., 984 F. Supp. 821, 826 (D. Vt. 1997) (finding in a sexual harassment suit by a former employee that a plaintiff had a substantial need to review notes and memoranda prepared by the employer's employees during their investigation into the plaintiff's sexual harassment allegations); Nationwide Mut. Fire Ins. Co. v. Smith, 174 F.R.D. 250, 253 (D. Conn. 1997) (ordering the production of information about meetings and conversations with experts in a bad faith action where insureds were entitled to discovery about how the insurer processes fire claims and why it denies those claims); Varuzza by Zarrillo v. Bulk Materials, Inc., 169 F.R.D. 254, 257 (N.D.N.Y. 1996) (ordering the production of a statement that the plaintiff gave to an insurance investigator following an accident in a personal injury case because although the statement fell within the scope of the work product doctrine, defendants needed the statement to assist in filling the gaps in plaintiff's testimony and for impeachment purposes)."

63. Burrow v. Torjas Taurus, S.A., 334 F.3d 1222 (S.D. Fla. 2018) at 1231 (emphasis in original).

VI. Fiduciary Exception

As discussed at length in *Tyler Group Partners, LLC v. Madera,*[64] some courts recognize an exception to the attorney-client privilege for communications to a fiduciary when the information is sought by the beneficiary.[65] Whether it applies to attorney work product is not settled.[66]

There are two grounds for this exception: (1) the fiduciary has a duty to disclose all relevant information to those who are owed a duty by the fiduciary, and (2) the fiduciary is acting on behalf of those who are owed the fiduciary duty.[67] The fiduciary exception has its origins in English trust law, which viewed the fiduciary relationship between a trustee and a trust beneficiary as providing an exception to the privilege with respect to communications between the trustee and the trust's attorney.[68]

The theory behind the exception is that the trustee is acting for the beneficiary when seeking legal advice.[69] Thus, the lawyer "may not withhold work product from his own client. Moreover, that principle has been applied to bar such immunity claims by counsel for a fiduciary in the face of the beneficiaries' demand for access."[70] In 1970, the Fifth Circuit extended the fiduciary exception to the corporate environment in *Garner v. Wolfinbarger71* for the first time, allowing shareholders to use the exception to pierce the corporate attorney-client privilege.

The fiduciary exception has been adopted by a minority of states. Often, adopting jurisdictions make a distinction between when the fiduciary is acting on behalf of the beneficiaries or doing routine administration and when the

64. 564 F. Supp. 3d 964, 991–92 (D.N.M. 2021).

65. *See* Gamache v. Hogue, 112 Fed. R. Serv. 3d 744 (M.D. Ga. 2022) (nothing that, while the Eleventh Circuit has not adopted the exceptions, district courts in that circuit have done so); Washington-Baltimore Newspaper Guild, Local 35 v. Washington Star Co., 543 F. Supp. 906, 909 (D.D.C. 1982); Riggs Nat'l Bank v. Zimmer, 355 A.2d 709, 714 (Del. Ch. 1976); *In re* Long Island Lighting Co.), 129 F.3d 268, 272 (2d Cir. 1997); Hoopes v. Carota (1988) 142 A.D.2d 906, 531 N.Y.S.2d 407, 409, *aff'd,* 74 N.Y.2d 716, 544 N.Y.S.2d 808, 543 N.E.2d 73 (1989); United States v. Evans 796 F.2d 264, 265–66 (9th Cir.1986); *see also* Navajo Nation v. U.S. Dep't of Interior, 26 F.4th 794 (9th Cir. 2022) (discussing consideration of the privilege in United States v. Jicarilla, 564 U.S. 162 (2011).

66. Murphy v. Gorman, 271 F.R.D. 296, 320–22 (D.N.M. 2010) (discussing the case law extensively and rejecting the exceptions application to attorney work product).

67. United States v. Mett, 178 F.3d 1058, 1065 (9th Cir. 1999).

68. Nama Holding, LLC v. Greenberg Traurig LLP, 133 A.D.2d 46, 52–53 (N.Y. 2015); *see also* Craig C. Martin & Matthew H. Metcalf, *The Fiduciary Exception to the Attorney–Client Privilege,* 34 Tort & Ins. L.J. 827, 832–33 (1999); Riggs Nat'l Bank of Washington, D.C. v. Zimmer, 355 A.2d 709, 712 (Del. Ch. 1976).

69. Riggs Nat'l Bank v. Zimmer, 355 A.2d 709, 714 (Del. Ch. 1976). *Riggs* remains good law. *See* J.P. Morgan Trust Co. v. Fisher, 2019 WL 6605863, at *1 (Del. Ch. Dec. 5, 2019). *See also In re* Estate of McAleer, 248 A.3d 416, 428–36 (Pa. 2021) (holding to *Riggs* but noting split opinions in many states).

70. Lawrence v. Cohn, 2002 WL 109530, at *6 (S.D.N.Y. Jan. 25, 2002); *see also* Corbell v. Norton, 213 F.R.D. 1 (D.D.C. 2003).

71. 430 F.2d 1093 (5th Cir. 1970).

fiduciary is consulting an attorney to protect himself from possible claims by the beneficiaries. In the latter case, the rationale that the attorney is working, ultimately, for the beneficiaries is not present.

Further, when the attorney-client communication relates to the litigation brought against the fiduciary by those to whom the fiduciary duty is owed, courts tend to recognize the privilege.[72] The Ninth Circuit explained the difference in applying the privilege in that situation:

> On the one hand, where an ERISA trustee seeks an attorney's advice on a matter of plan administration and where the advice clearly does not implicate the trustee in any personal capacity, the trustee cannot invoke the attorney-client privilege against the plan beneficiaries. On the other hand, where a plan fiduciary retains counsel in order to defend herself against the plan beneficiaries (or the government acting in their stead), the attorney-client privilege remains intact.[73]

This conclusion aligns with an earlier Fifth Circuit decision that did not allow the exception to be used to gain privileged information developed for the trustee in defending against an action brought by plan beneficiaries against the trustee.[74] Thus, when the attorney-client communication relates to the subject matter that creates the fiduciary duty, such as the administration of a plan by a trustee, the privilege is more likely to be applied than when the communication relates to the trustee's personal defense in a suit brought by those to whom the duty is owed, such as beneficiaries of the plan that a trustee is administering.

Other courts have rejected the exception outright.[75] For example, the Texas Supreme Court explained its rejection:

> The attorney-client privilege serves the same important purpose in the trustee-attorney relationship as it does in other attorney-client relationships. A trustee must be able to consult freely with his or her attorney to obtain the best possible legal guidance. Without the privilege, trustees might be inclined to forsake legal advice, thus adversely affecting the trust, as disappointed beneficiaries could later pore over the attorney-client communications in second-guessing the trustee's actions.[76]

---

72. *See* Paskoski v. Johnson, 626 So. 2d 338, 339 (Fla. App. 1993); Wilbur v. ARCO Chem. Co., 974 F.2d 631, 645 (5th Cir. 1992).

73. United States v. Mett, 178 F.3d 1058, 1064 (9th Cir. 1999).

74. Wildbur v. ARC Chem. Co., 974 F.2d 631, 645 (5th Cir. 1992).

75. Wells Fargo Bank v. Superior Court, 990 P.2d 591, 594, 596 (Cal. 2000); Huie v. DeShazo, 922 S.W.2d 920, 924–25 (Tex. 1996).

76. Huie v. DeShazo, 922 S.W.2d 920, 924 (Tex. 1996).

Murphy v. Gorman[77] predicted that New Mexico would not accept the privilege. The opinion contains an extensive discussion of the exception and refers to many other states as adopting or rejecting the exception. The court further concluded that the exception does not apply under federal law to work product, and cites cases on both sides of that issue.[78]

The California Supreme Court rejected the exception in *Wells Fargo v. Superior Court*[79] on the ground that the court lacked power to change a statutory privilege, noting that courts adopting the exception were not so constrained.[80] Other state courts have taken the same position or have determined that a statute or rule prohibits recognition of the exception.[81]

As discussed, the fiduciary exception applies to attorney-client communications. The exception has generally not been extended to apply to work product. In *Jicarilla Apache Nation v. United States*,[82] the federal claims court specifically noted, "the court agrees with the wide majority of courts that have held that the fiduciary exception does not apply to work product immunity."[83] The court opined that the strong admonition from the United States Supreme Court given in *Upjohn v. United States* that attorney opinion work product is entitled to "special protection"[84] was sufficient to overcome the arguments supporting the fiduciary exception. Specifically, the court noted,

> In refusing to apply the fiduciary exception to work product, other cases have observed that the exception, as applied to the attorney-client privilege, is based upon a mutuality of interest between the fiduciary and the beneficiaries. They have logically opined that "once there is sufficient anticipation of litigation to trigger the work product immunity, . . . this mutuality is destroyed, making it unreasonable "to indulge in the fiction that counsel, hired by [the fiduciary], is also constructively hired by the same party counsel is expected to defendant against."[85]

77. 271 F.R.D. 296, 320 (D.N.M. 2010).
78. *See id.* at 320–22.
79. 990 P.2d 591 (Cal. 2000).
80. *Id.* at 594, 596.
81. *In re* Estate of McAleer, 248 A.3d 416, 432–33 (Pa. 2021).
82. 88 Fed. Cl. 1 (Fed. Cl. 2009)
83. *Id.* at 12–13 (footnote omitted).
84. Upjohn v. United States, 449 U.S. 383 at 400–01 (1981).
85. Jicarilla Apache Nation v. United States, 88 Fed. Cl. 1, 12 (Fed. Cl. 2009) (citations omitted).

CHAPTER 6

Waiver of Privileges

REAGAN W. SIMPSON

Tips for Asserting Protection	**Tips for Opposing Protection**
• Make timely objections • Follow all procedures for asserting privileges • Guard against inadvertent sending of privileged information and promptly take steps to correct • Negotiate a strong clawback provision • Be careful of defenses that will make privileges at issue in the case (e.g., advice of counsel and state of mind defenses, issues that implicate knowledge, contract interpretation)	• Assert waiver for any procedural default (e.g., failing to object timely, insufficient privilege log) • Argue lack of care as to inadvertent or mistaken disclosure • Seek privilege information when a privilege might be at issue (e.g., advice of counsel and state of mind defenses, issues that implicate knowledge, contract interpretation)

Privileges, of course, can be waived. That is true for both the attorney-client privilege and the work-product privilege. But waiver principles do not apply equally to those two privileges because of their different purposes.

The work-product privilege "upholds the fairness of the adversarial process by allowing litigators to creatively develop legal theories and strategies—without their adversaries invoking the discovery process to pry into the litigators' minds and free-ride off them."[1] By contrast, the attorney-client privilege is not limited to the adversarial process; "it is not so much concerned with the fairness of litigation as it is with providing a sanctuary for candid communication about any legal matter, not just pending litigation."[2] Thus, a waiver of the attorney-client privilege does not necessarily compromise work-product immunity, and the scope of waiver for each privilege differs because of their different purposes.

1. *In re* Grand Jury, 13 F.4th 710, 715 (9th Cir. 2021).
2. *Id.* at 716.

The burden of proof on waiver may also differ. One court stated this difference: "Unlike the attorney-client privilege, the burden of proving waiver of work product immunity falls on the party asserting waiver."[3] That comment no doubt arises because a party must in the first instance prove that an attorney-client communication did not include persons outside the attorney-client relationship. In some situations, however, the burden of proving non-waiver may seem to fall on the party asserting work-product protection, or, at least, the burden shifts to that party after a showing of waiver.[4] Two aspects of the burden of proof are clear. When a party is seeking work product based on substantial need, that party has the burden of showing the need.[5] Likewise, the burden of proving privilege is always on the party asserting it.[6] Whoever has the burden must present sufficiently detailed evidence to prevail in asserting protection.[7]

I. Waiver by Default

Lawyers can waive the attorney-client and work-product privileges by various procedural defaults, essentially by failing to assert a privilege or failing to comply with the rules for asserting the privilege. Examples of such procedural defaults are:

- Failing to object to questions at depositions.
- Failing to object to discovery requests.
- Failing to follow procedures for claiming protection, such as listing a document on a sufficiently detailed privilege log.
- Failing to present sufficient evidence to support the privilege.
- Producing privileged documents in response to discovery.
- Failing to object to questions at trial.[8]

3. S.E.C. v. Brady, 238 F.R.D. 429, 444 (N.D. Tex. 2006); *accord* Ecuadorian Plaintiffs v. Chevron Corp., 619 F.3d 373, 379 & n.10 (5th Cir. 2010); Jolivet v. Compass Group USA, Inc., 2021 WL 5176930, at *7 (N.D. Tex. Sept. 14, 2021); McKenzie Law Firm, P.A. v. Ruby Receptionists, Inc., 333 F.R.D. 638, 641–42 (D. Ore. 2019) (noting also that the party asserting work-product protection has the burden of showing that the elements of the privilege have been met).

4. Target Corp. v. ACE Am. Ins. Co., 2021 WL 6062553, at *4 (D. Minn. Dec. 22, 2021).

5. Klosin v. E.I. Du Point De Nemours & Co., 2021 WL 4271920l, at *9 (W.D.N.Y. Sept. 20, 2021) (burden on party seeking work-product information based on substantial need).

6. *See, e.g.*, *In re* E.I. DuPont de Nemours & Co., 136 S.W.3d 218, 223, 225 (Tex. 2004); *In re* Grand Jury Subpoena Duces Tecum, 112 F.3d 910, 925 (8th Cir. 1997).

7. Wright v. Allstate Fire & Cas. Ins. Co., 2022 WL 1213444 (W.D. Wash. Apr. 25, 2022). ("In the end, the failure to provide sufficient detail for a court to evaluate claims of attorney-client privilege or work-product waives any claimed protection." (citing Baxter Healthcare Corp. v. Fresenius Med. Care Holding, Inc., 2008 WL 5214330, at *1 (N.D. Cal. Dec. 12, 2008)).

8. *See, e.g.*, Burlington N. & Santa Fe Ry. Co. v. U.S. Dist. Ct. for Dist. of Mont., 408 F.3d 1142, 1147–49 (9th Cir. 2005) (rejecting a per se waiver rule deeming privilege waived under Federal Rule 34 where a privilege log required by Federal Rule 26 is not produced within Federal Rule 34's 30-day time limit but affirming the district court's holding that a party had waived privilege where privilege logs were

Failure to follow such required procedural steps may waive any complaint of the trial court's action regarding the privilege.[9]

The party resisting discovery of material claimed to be privileged must specifically claim the privilege relied on and establish the justification for its imposition.[10] In written discovery, the discovery response must identify the privilege and identify each document to which the privilege applies. General objections will most likely not suffice. Simply listing documents under the heading "Attorney-Client/Attorney Work Product" is generally insufficient to protect documents from discovery. A global claim that a list of documents is protected by one or more privileges is also too general to prevent their discovery. Further, merely attaching something to a privileged document does not, by itself, make the attachment privileged.[11]

Producing privileged documents by mistake in discovery has always been a fear of lawyers, especially in cases with large numbers of documents and time pressures on productions. It is, as one court noted, "a specter that haunts every document intensive case."[12] The term "mistake" is used here rather than "inadvertent" because a production of a document to the opposing counsel in discovery was intended in the sense that the documents were intentionally made available to the opponent, albeit by mistake in the case of the privileged document. Inadvertent production or disclosure occurs when there was no

---

provided five months late); Texas Tech Univ. Health Sciences Ctr. v. Niehay, 641 S.W.3d 761, 790–91 (Tex. App. 2022) (failure to object to deposition question); *In re* Halliburton Energy Servs., Inc., 2022 WL 2513478 (Tex. App. July 7, 2022, orig. proceeding) (privilege logs were sufficient to void waiver); *West v. Solito*, 563 S.W.2d 240 (Tex. 1978); Young v. Taylor, 466 F.2d 1329 (10th Cir. 1972) (failure to object during examination of defendant attorney waived privilege as to testimony of attorney's secretary regarding privileged conversation she heard between two defendants); Drimmer v. Appleton, 628 F. Supp. 1249 (S.D.N.Y. 1986) (failure to object to testimony at hearing on motion in Nevada to enforce settlement agreement waived privilege in subsequent New York trial on settlement agreement); Munguia-Brown v. Equity Residential, 337 F.R.D. 509, 516–17 (N.D. Cal. 2021) (boilerplate objections, insufficient privilege log, and tardy assertion of privilege); Carlson v. Colorado Center for Reproductive Med., LLC, 112 Fed. R. Serv. 3d 1175 (D. Colo. 2022) (privilege log insufficient); Custer v. Cerro Flow Prods., Inc., 136 N.E.3d 1108, 1117 (Ill. App. 2019) (discussing procedures for claiming privilege); *In re* Stephens Inc., 579 S.W.3d 438, 445 (2019) (same; listing documents on privilege log and producing evidence in support of privilege); Parneros v. Barnes & Noble, Inc., 332 F.R.D. 482, 491 (S.D.N.Y. 2019) (New York law requires party to prove no waiver of privilege); Diamond Resorts U.S. Collection Dev., LLC v. U.S. Consumer Attorneys, 519 F. Supp. 3d 1184, 1194, 1197–98 (S.D. Fla. 2021) (objecting, listing document on privilege log, typically with an affidavit, and requesting *in camera* review); Slocum v. Int'l Paper Co., 2021 WL 5861499, at *4 (E.D. La. June 28, 2021) (privilege log found insufficient because it contained conclusory statements rather than factual descriptions supporting claim of privilege).

9. *See* People v. Agado, 964 P.2d 565 (Colo. App. 1998); Cacamo v. Liberty Mut. Fire Ins. Co., 798 So. 2d 1210 (La. App. 2001); Loftin v. Martin, 776 S.W.2d 145 (Tex. 1989); Weisel Enters., Inc. v. Curry, 718 S.W.2d 56 (Tex. 1986) (per curiam).

10. Maura Strassberg, *Privilege Can Be Abused: Exploring the Ethical Obligations to Avoid Frivolous Claims of Attorney-Client Privilege*, 37 Seton Hall L. Rev. 413 (2007) (noting that the privilege should not be frivolously claimed).

11. *In re* Human Tissue Prods. Liab. Litig., 255 F.R.D. 151 (D.N.J. 2008), *aff'd*, 2009 WL 1097671 (D.N.J. 2009).

12. F.D.I.C. v. Marine Midland Realty Credit Corp., 138 F.R.D. 479, 479–80 (E.D. Va. 1991).

intent to deliver the information to the opposing lawyer, as when the opposing lawyer is accidentally copied on a sensitive email. Courts, however, use the terms interchangeably.

Courts have taken three positions on mistaken or inadvertent disclosure as discussed in *Bank Brussels Lambert v. Credit Lyonnais (Suisse) S.A.*,[13] namely: (1) disclosure automatically voids the privilege; (2) disclosure does not void the privilege unless it was the result of an intentional and voluntary waiver of the privilege; and (3) disclosure results in a waiver if reasonable precautions against disclosure were not taken.[14] The court in *Bank Brussels Lambert* adopted the third approach, which it said "best reconciles the principles underlying the attorney-client privilege with the realities of document production in complex litigation."[15] The third approach, sometimes called the totality of circumstances test, is the majority position, as one court noted:

> Like most courts elsewhere, courts within the Ninth Circuit have embraced the totality of the circumstances approach. In the Ninth Circuit, the inadvertent production of privileged documents is neither a necessary nor a sufficient condition for finding that the privilege was waived. Instead, in determining whether a privilege has been waived by the inadvertent production of privileged documents, courts within the Ninth Circuit consider "the circumstances surrounding the disclosure," including whether the privilege holder has made efforts "'reasonably designed' to protect and preserve the privilege."[16]

The specter of mistaken production in discovery has led to "clawback" rules and agreements. Federal Rule of Civil Procedure 26(b)(5) allows a party that has mistakenly produced a document or information to notify the opposition and the basis for the privilege. After notification, the other side must then return the document or information and not use or disclose it until the claim of privilege is resolved and must take reasonable steps to retrieve the document or information it has disclosed. Obviously, the document or information may

---

13. 160 F.R.D. 437 (S.D.N.Y. 1995). This case was discussed at length in Curto v. Med. World Commc'ns, 783 F. Supp. 373, 379–80 (E.D.N.Y. 2011).

14. *Id.* at 442–44; *see also* Amgen, Inc. v. Hoechst Marion Roussel, Inc., 190 F.R.D. 287, 291 (D. Mass. 2000) (discussing the three positions on waiver); Berg v. Molex, Inc., 875 F. Supp. 261 (D. Del. 1995) (same); FDIC v. Singh, 140 F.R.D. 252, 253 (D. Me. 1992) (same); Redland Soccer Club, Inc. v. Dep't of Army, 55 F.3d 827, 856 (3d Cir. 1995) (waiver not found when attaching privileged documents was not a "voluntary" waiver); Mendenhall v. Barber-Greene Co., 531 F. Supp. 951, 954–55 (N.D. Ill. 1982) (mere inadvertent production is not a waiver of privilege); Wichita Land & Cattle Co. v. Am. Fed. Bank, 148 F.R.D. 446, 457 (D.D.C. 1992) (even inadvertent disclosure waives privilege; collecting cases).

15. 160 F.R.D. at 443.

16. U.S. *ex rel.* Bagley v. TRW, Inc., 204 F.R.D. 170, 177 (C.D. Cal. 2001) (citations and quotations omitted; containing an excellent discussion of the approaches to mistaken or inadvertent production with citations to numerous cases); *accord* Tyler Group Partners, LLC v. Madera, 2021 WL 4479606, at *50 (D.N.M. Sept. 30, 2021).

be disclosed to the court in order to resolve whether the document or information is privileged or if the privilege has been waived despite the clawback.

Similarly, under Federal Rule of Evidence 502, an inadvertent disclosure does not waive the privilege if three standards are satisfied:

- The disclosure is inadvertent;
- The holder of the privilege . . . took reasonable steps to prevent disclosure; and
- The holder [of the privilege] promptly took reasonable steps to rectify the [mistaken disclosure], including (if applicable) following Federal Rule of Civil Procedure 26(b)(5)(B).[17]

Additionally, the rule contemplates that litigants may enter agreements about mistaken production of privileged information.[18] When federal courts issue such orders consistent with or without the parties' agreement, Rule 502(d) provides that the order is enforceable in subsequent federal and state court proceedings.[19] Further, subdivision (c) of Rule 502 addresses the effect in federal court of privilege disclosures that occur in state court.[20] Overall, Rule 502 "aims to reduce the time and effort lawyers spend screening documents before producing them by limiting the risk that disclosure of documents or information protected by the attorney-client privilege or work-product doctrine will result in broad waiver of that protection."[21]

As an example of how courts apply such rules, in *Ergo Licensing, LLC v. Carefusion 303, Inc.*,[22] the district court found no waiver by including 31 pages of privileged material in the production of a 540-page document using a three-factor test. That test inquired whether the disclosure was inadvertent, whether "the holder of the privilege took reasonable steps to prevent the disclosure," and whether "the holder promptly took steps to rectify the error."[23]

Despite such procedural protections, courts can still find waiver, depending on such factors as the care taken in the production process, the time it took to request the return of the information, and the nature of the information. That results in uncertainty, and parties can avoid such uncertainty by agreeing to a more ironclad procedure. Some court rules may be more ironclad.

For example, Texas Rule of Civil Procedure 193.3(d) flatly says that a "Privilege Is Not Waived by Production." At the same time, however, the rule

17. *See* Fed. R. Evid. 502(b). *See also* Paula Schaefer, *The Future of Inadvertent Disclosure: The Lingering Need to Revise Professional Conduct Rules*, 69 Md. L. Rev. 195, 217–18 (2010).

18. *See* Fed. R. Evid. 502(e); Fed. R. Civ. P. 26(f).

19. *See* Fed. R. Evid. 502(d).

20. *See* Fed. R. Evid. 502(c).

21. *Id.*

22. 263 F.R.D. 40 (D. Me. 2009).

23. *Id.* at 46. *See also* Kansas City Power & Light Co. v. United States, 139 Fed. Cl. 546, 561 (2018) (waiver may occur when party does not seek return of privileged document that the party produced).

requires the producing party to give notice of the mistake within ten days (or any shorter time set by the court) after actual discovery of the problem. Then if the producing party asserts the privilege, the opposing party must return the document pending a final ruling by the court on the assertion of the privilege. Thus, as with Federal Rule 26(b)(5), the requirement of returning the document or information appropriately depends on notification by the producing party rather than imposing a burden in the first instance on the recipient. Other clawback rules exist in many states.[24]

Ethical issues are not clear in this situation. ABA Model Rule of Professional Responsibility 4.4(b) states: "A lawyer who receives a document or electronically stored information relating to the representation of the lawyer's client and knows or reasonably should know that the document or electronically stored information was inadvertently sent shall promptly notify the sender." The phrase "inadvertently sent" seems to refer to accidental transmissions, not including a privileged document in information that was intended to be sent. The comment to the rule seems to enlarge the rule to cover not just accidental transmission but a specific type of intended transmission, that is, when "electronically stored information is accidentally included with information that was intentionally transmitted," the latter of which is still a form of inadvertence as distinguished from production of a document with a productional label affixed indicating an intention to produce. The comment further warns that court rules may impose sanctions or subject the lawyer-recipient to disqualification in certain situations:

> [2] Paragraph (b) recognizes that lawyers sometimes receive a document or electronically stored information that was mistakenly sent or produced by opposing parties or their lawyers. A document or electronically stored information is inadvertently sent when it is accidentally transmitted, such as when an email or letter is misaddressed or a document or electronically stored information is accidentally included with information that was intentionally transmitted. If a lawyer knows or reasonably should know that such a document or electronically stored information was sent inadvertently, then this Rule requires the lawyer to promptly notify the sender in order to permit that person to take protective measures. Whether the lawyer is required to take additional steps, such as returning the document or electronically stored information, is a matter of law beyond the scope of these Rules, as is the question of whether the privileged status of a document or electronically stored information has been waived. Similarly, this Rule does not address the legal duties of a lawyer who receives a document or electronically stored information

24. *See, e.g.*, Custer v. Cerro Flow Prods., Inc., 136 N.E.3d 1108, 1117 (Ill. App. 2019) (discussing Illinois Supreme Court Rule 201(p)).

that the lawyer knows or reasonably should know may have been inappropriately obtained by the sending person. For purposes of this Rule, "document or electronically stored information" includes, in addition to paper documents, email and other forms of electronically stored information, including embedded data (commonly referred to as "metadata"), that is subject to obligation under this Rule only if the receiving lawyer knows or reasonably should know that the metadata was inadvertently sent to the receiving lawyer.

[3] Some lawyers may choose to return a document or delete electronically stored information unread, for example, when the lawyer learns before receiving it that it was inadvertently sent. Where a lawyer is not required by applicable law to do so, the decision to voluntarily return such a document or delete electronically stored information is a matter of professional judgment ordinarily reserved to the lawyer. *See* Rules 1.2 and 1.4.

Nevertheless, the ethical duties are not well defined. One court observed, "If the holder of the attorney-client privilege has not waived the privilege, lawyers representing an adverse party who have received such information knowing it is privileged have an ethical duty not to use it. It does not matter whether the information has been provided deliberately or inadvertently."[25] Although that court accorded the same treatment to both deliberate or inadvertent production, the court's observation began with an important "If." Waiver of privilege may be more likely when the production is deliberate, albeit mistaken, rather than merely inadvertent.

In litigation, the party opposing the withholding of the information should try to take advantage of any procedural default. The party seeking to retain the privilege must try to excuse the default and must be ready to address and present evidence showing circumstances that tend to excuse the default, the prejudice caused by not respecting the privilege, and the lack of prejudice to the party seeking the evidence.

II. Waiver by Disclosure

A party can waive a privilege by voluntary disclosure outside of discovery.[26] In the context of the attorney-client privilege, the privilege does not even

25. Wu v. O'Gara Coach Co., LLC v. Ra, 30 Cal. App. 5th 1115, 1128 (2019).

26. *See, e.g.*, *In re* King's Daughters Health Sys. Inc., 31 F.4th 520 (6th Cir. 2022) (partial disclosure to government waived privilege); Gamache v. Hogue, 112 Fed. R. Serv. 3d 744 (M.D. Ga. 2022) (disclosure to counterparties); Ross v. Superior Court of Riverside County, 77 Cal. App. 5th 667 (2022); Getz v. Superior Court, 287 Cal. Rptr. 3d 722, 737 (2021); United States v. Sanmina Corp., 968 F.3d 1107, 1116 (2020).

attach if a third party is included in the attorney-client communication.[27] A privilege-ending disclosure occurs also when an attorney-client communication is disclosed to the third party after the original communication, as when an attorney-client letter is sent to a third party.[28]

Whether someone is a third party is another issue. An employee or agent of the client's lawyer is not a third party for this purpose. Nor is a third party an employee of the client, except if the jurisdiction limits the privilege to the control group. This issue is discussed in depth in the chapter on the common interest or joint defense privilege.

By contrast, disclosure of the work-product privilege does not automatically waive the privilege. While the attorney-client privilege is generally waived upon disclosure to third parties,[29] the work-product doctrine is considered waived when protected materials are disclosed to an adversary,[30] or when a disclosure is made to a third party that "substantially increases the likelihood that work product will fall into the hands of the adversary."[31] In some cases, an issue may arise about whether the recipient of the information was or was not an adversary.[32]

Disclosures outside the discovery process can be inadvertent, just as they can be during discovery. Today's technology increases the chance of inadvertent disclosure outside of the discovery process. Following are some of the more frequently encountered "high-risk" areas for inadvertent disclosure of information:

- Including an adverse counsel or party on an email
- Using means of communication accessible by third parties[33]
- Responding to a government investigation[34]

---

27. *See, e.g.*, Towne Place Condo. Ass'n v. Philadelphia Indem. Ins. Co., 284 F. Supp. 3d 889, 896 (N.D. Ill. 2018). Prudential Defense Solutions, Inc. v. Graham, 2021 WL 405988, at *4 (E.D. Mich. Feb. 5, 2021); Walsh v. CSG Partners, LLC, 544 F. Supp. 3d 389, 391 (S.D.N.Y. 2021).

28. *In re* Columbia/HCA Healthcare Corp. Billing Practices Litig., 293 F.3d 289, 304–05 (6th Cir. 2002).

29. *See, e.g.*, Protect Democracy Project, Inc. v. NSA, 10 F.4th 879, 891 (D.C. Cir. 2021); Narayanan v. Sutherland Global Holdings Inc., 285 F. Supp. 3d 604 (W.D.N.Y. 2018) (unnecessary presence of accountant during communications negated privilege); Towne Place Condo. Ass'n v. Philadelphia Indem. Ins. Co., 284 F. Supp. 3d 889, 896 (N.D. Ill. 2018); Diamond Resorts U.S. Collection Dev., LLC v. U.S. Consumer Attorneys, P.A., 2021 WL 505122, at *5 (S.D. Fla. 2021).

30. *See* Ayers Oil Co. v. Am. Bus. Brokers, Inc., 2009 WL 4725297, at *3 (E.D. Mo. Dec. 2, 2009); Peralta v. Cendant Corp., 190 F.R.D. 38, 42 (D. Conn. 1999).

31. Nidec Corp. v. Victor Co. of Japan, 2007 WL 2156256, at *2 (N.D. Cal. July 26, 2007) (no waiver when disclosure did not increase probability of reaching adversary); *accord* Bank Brussels Lambert v. Credit Lyonnais (Suisse), S.A., 160 F.R.D. 437, 448 (S.D.N.Y. 1995).

32. *See* Pilkington N. Am., Inc. v. Mitsui Sumitomo Ins. Co, 341 F.R.D. 10 (S.D.N.Y. 2022).

33. Eastman v. Thompson, 112 Fed. R. Serv. 3d 698 (C.D. Cal. 2022) (considering whether expectation of privacy existed in using employer-monitored email system; finding no access to emails by third parties).

34. *See* United States v. Reyes, 239 F.R.D. 591 (N.D. Cal. 2006); *Axelson, Inc. v. McIlhaney*, 755 S.W.2d 170 (Tex. App. 1988, orig. proceeding).

- Supplying information to a government agency
- Submitting insurance renewals
- Replying to an inquiry from an auditor or accountant
- Submitting public financial disclosure documents
- Disclosing information to third parties not working under the attorney or at the attorney's direction, or for nonlegal purposes
- Posting information on a website[35]
- Posting information on social media[36]
- Using a computer system belonging to an employer or someone outside the scope of the privilege[37]
- Otherwise disclosing information in a way that is likely to reach outside the scope of the privilege[38]

As discussed in the preceding section, waiver is not automatic in most courts, and the same factors that are applied in the discovery context apply here as well. Logically, mere inadvertence outside of discovery should be more forgivable than mistaken production in document production, because, in the latter situation, lawyers are on notice of the care needed to prevent production of privileged information.

The factors to be considered in deciding whether an inadvertent disclosure waives a privilege are the ones set forth in Federal Rule of Evidence 502:

(1) the disclosure is inadvertent;
(2) the holder of the privilege or protection took reasonable steps to prevent disclosure; and
(3) the holder promptly took reasonable steps to rectify the error, including, (if applicable) following Federal Rule of Civil Procedure 26(b)(5)(B).[39]

Cases apply this reasonableness standard in varying ways.[40]

---

35. *See* Kintera, Inc. v. Convio, Inc., 219 F.R.D. 503 (S.D. Cal. 2003).

36. Allen v. PPE Casino Resorts Maryland, LLC, 543 F. Supp. 3d 91, 93 (D. Md. 2021) ("Generally, social media content, even where designated as 'non-public,' is neither privileged nor protected by any right of privacy . . . .").

37. *Holmes v. Petrovich Dev. Co.*, 119 Cal. Rptr. 3d 878 (2011). *But see* Stengart v. Loving Care Agency Inc., 990 A.2d 650 (N.J. 2010) (communications between attorney and client sent on employer's computer were privileged because employer's privacy policy was ambiguous).

38. *United States v. Ruehle*, 583 F.3d 600 (9th Cir. 2009) (statements made by a corporation's chief financial officer (CFO) to in-house counsel were not privileged because the CFO understood that in-house counsel would disclose the information to third-party auditors).

39. *See* Fed. R. Evid. 502(b). *See also* Paula Schaefer, *The Future of Inadvertent Disclosure: The Lingering Need to Revise Professional Conduct Rules*, 69 Md. L. Rev. 195, 217–18 (2010); Novaryis Pharms. Corp. v. Superior Court, 2021 WL 191877, at *1 (Cal. App. May 13, 2021) (inadvertent production after reasonable screening measures does not waiver privilege).

40. *See* Mt. Hanley Ins. Co. v. Felman Prod. Inc., 2010 WL 1990555 (S.D. W. Va. May 18, 2010); Edelen v. Campbell Soup Co., 265 F.R.D. 676 (N.D. Ga. 2010); Spicker v. Quest Cherokee, 2009 WL 2168892 (D. Kan. 2009); Rhodes Indus., Inc. v. Bldg. Materials Corp. of Am., 254 F.R.D. 216 (E.D. Pa. 2008); Sitterson v. Evergreen Sch. Dist., 196 P.3d 735 (Wash. Ct. App. 2008).

Ethical duties are again implicated, and in this context, as distinguished from intended productions of documents, the recipient usually knows that the disclosure was not intended. That is no doubt why ABA Rule 4.4 puts the duty to notify on the recipient. In extreme cases, disqualification results from the use of privileged material inadvertently sent. For example, the Texas Supreme Court listed these factors as relevant regarding whether to disqualify counsel that used obviously privileged information sent inadvertently:

- Whether the attorney knew or should have known that the material was privileged
- The promptness with which the attorney notifies the opposing side that he or she has received its privileged information
- The extent to which the attorney reviews and digests the privileged information
- The significance of the privileged information; that is, the extent to which its disclosure may prejudice the movant's claim or defense, and the extent to which return of the documents will mitigate that prejudice
- The extent to which movant may be at fault for the unauthorized disclosure
- The extent to which the nonmovant will suffer prejudice from the disqualification of his or her attorney[41]

In light of the case law, the attorney responsible for a large document production should create a plan (preferably reduced to writing) for the production of documents that will minimize the chances of a mistaken production of a privileged document. Also, an attorney who discovers that he or she has mistakenly produced a privileged document should immediately master the governing procedures and, if necessary, file any appropriate motion with the court. The attorney should then become familiar with the burdens of proof expected by courts dealing with mistaken disclosure issues. Further, the attorney should assemble, by admissible affidavit or declaration, the evidence needed to sustain that burden, file the proof in a timely manner, and have the motion set for hearing.

Another attorney-client privilege issue that has seen litigation is whether emails regarding action against the employer and sent between client and attorney on the client's employer's computer are protected by the attorney-client privilege. *Holmes v. Petrovich Development Co.*[42] held that emails sent by an employee to her attorney regarding possible legal action against her employer were not subject to attorney-client privilege because the employee used her work computer even though she knew that the company's policy prohibited the use of company email for personal reasons.[43]

41. *In re* Meador, 968 S.W.2d 346, 351–52 (Tex. 1998).
42. *Holmes v. Petrovich Dev. Co., 119 Cal. Rptr. 3d 878 (2011).*
43. *Id.* at 895–99.

III. Using Information with Witnesses, Including Experts

Privileges may be waived by using the information at trial or in a deposition, as for example in refreshing the witness's recollection. Federal Rule of Evidence 612 provides that an adverse party is entitled to review any writing used by a witness to refresh recollection. Likewise, courts typically consider the work-product doctrine to be inadequate protection from disclosure when work-product documents have been used to prepare a witness for depositions.[44] Some courts have even found that the use of work-product materials for deposition purposes is an automatic waiver of the protection, meaning that a party requesting disclosure does not have to show a substantial need or undue hardship.[45]

The consequence of providing information to experts is a separate subject, though related to waiver of privileges. Generally, in many state courts, privileged material provided to a testifying expert must be produced upon request by opposing counsel.[46] For example, the court in *Vaughan Furniture Co. v. Featureline Manufacturing, Inc.* outlined a broad scope of a waiver of the work-product immunity, stating that the waiver applied "to those documents which the expert reviewed at any time and which would be relevant to the formulation of [the attorney's] expert opinion."[47] The sole limitation on disclosure was items unrelated to the subject matter of the expert's opinion.

The rules in federal courts are different. As amended in 2010, Federal Rule of Civil Procedure 26(a)(2)(B)(ii) requires disclosure of the "facts or data

---

44. *See* FED. R. EVID. 612. *See generally San Diego Unified Port Dist. v. Monsanto Co., 2018 WL 3656298, at *3 (S.D. Cal.* Aug. 2, 2018) (also discussing the foundational elements of waiver under Federal Rules of Civil Procedure 612); Nutramax Lab., Inc. v. Twin Lab., Inc., 183 F.R.D. 458 (D. Md. 1998); Shipes v. BIC Corp., 154 F.R.D. 301 (M.D. Ga. 1994); Margaret Hall Found., Inc. v. Strong, 121 F.R.D. 141 (D. Mass. 1988); Redvanly v. NYNEX Corp., 152 F.R.D. 460 (S.D.N.Y. 1993); Begner v. State Ethics Comm'n, 552 S.E.2d 431 (Ga. Ct. App. 2001).

45. *See* Berkey Photo, Inc. v. Eastman Kodak Co., 74 F.R.D. 613, 617 (S.D.N.Y. 1977) (Although the court did not order disclosure in *Berkey*, it stated, "To put the point succinctly, there will be hereafter powerful reasons to hold that materials considered work product should be withheld from prospective witnesses if they are to be withheld from opposing parties."). *See also In re* Rivastigmine Patent Litig., 486 F. Supp. 2d 241, 243 (S.D.N.Y. 2007) (citing *Berkey* and stating that the key consideration is whether the document had a sufficient impact on the testimony); Nutramax Labs., Inc. v. Twin Labs. Inc., 183 F.R.D. 458, 467–69 (D. Md. 1998) (discussing *Berkey* and the "apparent conflict" between Federal Rule of Evidence 612 and the work-product doctrine); Arkwright Mut. Ins. Co. v. Nat'l Union Fire Ins. Co., 1994 WL 51004, at *17 (S.D.N.Y. Sept. 16, 1994) (not all compilations of documents reveal attorney work product).

46. *See DeLuca v. State Fish Co., 217 Cal. App. 4th 671, 689 (2013) ("As a general rule, neither the attorney-client privilege nor the work product protection will prevent disclosure of statements to, or reports from, a testifying expert."); accord In re* Christus Spohn Hosp. Kleberg, 222 S.W.3d 434 (Tex. 2007); People v. Wagener, 752 N.E.2d 430, 437 (Il. 2001) ("Any attorney-client privilege which might have protected the conversations between defendant and attorney Gooch was waived by the disclosure of the statement to defendant's testifying expert witnesses.").

47. 156 F.R.D. 123, 128 (M.D.N.C. 1994). *See also* E.I. DuPont de Nemours & Co. v. Kolon Indus., Inc., 269 F.RD. 600, 608 (E.D. Va. 2010) (citing but distinguishing *Vaughn Furniture* and similar cases).

considered by the witness" in forming opinions,[48] which limits what can be discovered but does not require that the expert relied upon the information.[49] The precise scope of "facts or data" is subject to debate, as the comments to the rule seem to expand the phrase to mean "factual ingredients."[50]

Protection of work product is expressly covered by Rule 26(b)(4)(B) & (C), which provides additional protections from waiver for drafts of expert reports and communications between the expert and hiring counsel required for providing a report:

> (B) Trial-Preparation Protection for Draft Reports or Disclosures. Rules 26(b)(3)(A) and (B) protect drafts of any report or disclosure required under Rule 26(a)(2), regardless of the form in which the draft is recorded.
>
> (C) Trial-Preparation Protection for Communications Between a Party's Attorney and Expert Witnesses. Rules 26(b)(3)(A) and (B) protect communications between the party's attorney and any witness required to provide a report under Rule 26(a)(2)(B), regardless of the form of the communications, except to the extent that the communications:
>
> > (i) relate to compensation for the expert's study or testimony;
> >
> > (ii) identify facts or data that the party's attorney provided and that the expert considered in forming the opinions to be expressed; or
> >
> > (iii) identify assumptions that the party's attorney provided and that the expert relied on in forming the opinions to be expressed.

The preceding provisions follow the general rule that core attorney work product containing mental impressions of counsel is protected from discovery.[51]

The Federal Rule 26's provisions on experts are often more protective than state court rules,[52] which has led some lawyers to enter into agreements to

48. Fed. R. Civ. P. 26(a)(2(B)(ii) (emphasis added).

49. United States *ex rel.* Wall v. Vista Hospice Care, 319 F.R.D. 498, 506 (N.D. Tex. 2016) (quoting and discussing Advisory Committee Comments).

50. Fed. R. Civ. P. 26(a)(2)(B), Advisory Committee Notes, 2010 Amendments. *See, e.g.*, Republic of Ecuador v. For Issuance of a Subpoena Under 28 U.S.C. Sec. 1782(a), 735 F.3d 1179, 1187 (10th Cir. 2013) (noting that "factual ingredients" is far more than just "facts or data").

51. McClurg v. Mallinckrodt, LLC, 2018 WL 3047014, at *4 (E.D. Mo. June 20, 2018); Republic of Ecuador v. Mackay, 742 F.3d 860, 869 (9th Cir. 2014).

52. Blayne R. Thompson & Maria Wycoff Boyce, *Expert Communications and Draft Reports: Key Discovery Distinctions between State and Federal Courts in Texas*, The Advocate (Texas) (Spring 2018) (warning of substantial differences between federal and Texas state practice, the latter of which allows broad discovery of materials provided to experts).

apply the federal rules in state court. Therefore, it is important for the lawyer to know and follow the governing rules.

Federal Rule 26(b)(4)(D) prohibits all discovery of experts "retained or specially employed" only for trial preparation and who will not testify at trial. Except for such experts who conduct physical or mental examinations under Rule 35, these consulting experts are off limits unless the party seeking discovery shows "exceptional circumstances under which it is impracticable for the party to obtain facts or opinions on the same subject by other means."[53] Questions have arisen whether this limitation or any limitation applies to non-testifying informally consulted experts and non-testifying employee/in-house experts.[54]

IV. Waiver When the Information Is at Issue

Privileges do not shield facts, and privileged information can itself become relevant to the factual disposition of a case. In some situations, a party is affirmatively trying to use favorable privileged information as the proverbial sword while still relying on the privilege to shield unfavorable facts.[55] Courts do not allow such gamesmanship. In other situations, the waiver results naturally from a seemingly neutral defense, so that the waiver is not intended and may even be surprising. Sometimes, whether privileged information is "at issue" overlaps with the "need" exception discussed later in this chapter. A key question is whether the court will require that a party is actually relying on ordinarily protected information to support the issue in question or if the information is merely relevant to the issue.[56]

---

53. Fed. R. Civ. P. 26(b)(4)(D).

54. One commentator has called the distinction "murky" between retained and informally consulted experts but generally concludes discovery is not allowed of the latter category, which is not addressed by the Federal Rule 26. *See* Virginia B. Maurer, *Compelling the Expert Witness: Fairness and Utility Under the Federal Rules of Civil Procedure*, 19 Georgia. L. Rev. 71, 90 n.73 (1984) (citing cases on informal experts). *See also In re* Abilify (Aripiprazole) Prods. Liab. Litig., 2017 WL 2225614, at *2–3 (N.D. Fla. May 15, 2017) (seeming to recognize that informal experts are off limits but not extending that rule to a pre-retention communications with a later-retained expert).

For an extended discussion of in-house experts, see Edward J. Winkelried & Andrew Amoroso, *The Application of the Attorney-Client Privilege to Interactions Among Clients, Attorneys, and Experts in the Age of Consultants: The Need for a More Precise, Fundamental Analysis*, 48 Houston L. Rev. 265 (2011).

55. Allstate Ins. Co. v. Levesque, 263 F.R.D. 663, 667 (M.D. Fla. 2010); *see* GAB Bus. Servs., Inc. v. Syndicate, 809 F.2d 755 (11th Cir. 1987); HSH Nordbank AG N.Y. Branch v. Swerdlow, 259 F.R.D. 64, 74 (S.D.N.Y. 2009) (holding that in an order to prevent the attorney-client privilege from at once being used as a shield and a sword, the "at issue" doctrine precludes a party from disclosing only self-serving communications while barring discovery of other communications that an adversary could use to challenge the truth of the claim).

56. *See Bacchi v. Massachusetts Mut. Life Ins. Co., 110 F. Supp. 3d 270, 275–76 (D. Mass. 2015) (comparing In re* County of Erie, 546 F.3d 222, 227–28 (2d Cir. 2008), *with* Heartn v. Rhay 68 F.R.D. 574, 577 (E.D. Wash. 1975)).

A. Relying on Advice of Counsel

When a party attempts to rely on the advice or opinions of counsel, most courts find that its opponent is entitled to discover the analyses underlying that opinion.[57] Thus, courts will freely find that the advising attorney's work product—even opinion work product—is discoverable.[58]

For example, in *Handgards, Inc. v. Johnson & Johnson*,[59] a patent infringement case, Johnson & Johnson called as witnesses three of its lawyers to testify about the legal advice they gave Johnson & Johnson. The court held that Johnson & Johnson's "deliberate injection of the advice of counsel into a case waived the attorney-client privilege as to communications and documents relating to the advice and the entire litigation files in the prior cases."[60] Other cases are to the same effect.[61]

An express disclaimer of reliance on the advice of counsel may not insulate protected information. If there is any indication that the party did rely on counsel, or if the court concludes that reliance on counsel was necessarily involved, then the door is likely to be opened.[62]

Avoiding the loss of the privilege requires that the courts restrict the situations in which an opposing party can force abrogation of the privilege by way of its allegations against the privilege holder. For example, the advice of counsel is not necessarily "interjected into" a case by a responding party's denial of allegations, where the responding party may have had legal advice regarding those allegations.[63]

A party can, in essence, volunteer reliance on attorney advice when that is the only logical support for its position. For example, in *Dawson v. New York Life Insurance Co.*,[64] potentially protected information was central to supporting (and refuting) the qualified privilege claim. Although the defendant

---

57. *See In re* Arizona, 2022 WL 1117113 (9th Cir. Apr. 14, 2022) ("The district court was well within its discretion to decide both that the State defendants raised an advice of counsel defense and that fairness mandated that Toomey have access to the documents underlying that defense."); 2138747 Ontario Inc. v. Lehman Bros. Holdings, Inc., 205 A.D.3d 403 (2022); Garfinkle v. Arcata Nat'l Corp., 64 F.R.D. 688, 689 (S.D.N.Y. 1974) (holding that defendant's reliance on attorney's opinion letter entitled plaintiff to examine the surrounding circumstances: "[Plaintiff] cannot be limited to the letter itself—the finished product. He is entitled to know how the letter came into being.").

58. Chiron Corp. v. Genentech, Inc., 179 F. Supp. 2d 1182, 1190 (E.D. Cal. 2001).

59. 413 F. Supp. 926 (N.D. Cal. 1976).

60. *Id.* at 929.

61. *See, e.g.*, Coleco Indus., Inc. v. Universal City Studios, Inc., 110 F.R.D. 688, 691–92 (S.D.N.Y. 1986) ("a consistent line of cases has developed an exception to the work-product privilege where the party raises an issue which depends upon an evaluation of the legal theories, opinions and conclusions of counsel"; citing *Handgards, Inc. Johnson & Johnson*, 413 F. Supp. 926, 929 (N.D. Cal. 1976)); *Panter v. Marshall Field & Co.*, 80 F.R.D. 718, 722 (N.D. Ill. 1978).

62. SEC v. Welliver, 2012 WL 8015672, at *8–11 (D. Minn. Oct. 26, 2012); *In re Consol. Litig. Concerning Int'l Harvester's Disposition of Wisconsin Steel*, 666 F. Supp. 1148 (N.D. Ill. 1987).

63. Twin City Fire Ins. Co. v. Burke, 63 P.3d 282, 286–87 (Ariz. 2003) (en banc). Note, however, that the conduct of the defendant in this case was not directly at issue.

64. 901 F. Supp. 1362 (N.D. Ill. 1989).

did not explicitly volunteer that it would rely on attorney-client information, that reliance was implied when all of the relevant deponents (the defendant's employees) stated that they either (1) directly relied on attorney information to prepare allegedly defamatory statements or (2) knew of the attorney information before making such statements.[65]

Dawson was not followed in *United States ex rel. Derrick v. Roche Diagnostics Corp.*[66] for allowing waiver merely because protected information was relevant rather than actually being relied upon as required in opinions by the Third and Seventh Circuits. The *Derrick* court stressed that fairness was a consideration in deciding waiver issues.[67]

Thus, while courts clearly consider whether reliance on an attorney is volunteered, a party should be careful to not implicitly "volunteer" such reliance. In contrast, a party may be able to avoid a requirement to produce its privileged information by explicitly volunteering not to rely on the advice of counsel in support of a good-faith defense. Of course, the disclaimer may strip the client of a needed defense. Further, the tactic may not work when an expressly pleaded defense implicates advice of counsel.

B. Other Issues Involving Lawyers

In some situations, lawyers may be inextricably involved in conduct at issue. One example is *AM International, Inc. v. Eastman Kodak Co.*[68] Because Kodak alleged that AM International, Inc. (AMI) knowingly filed suit based on invalid patents, the court found that discovery from AMI was appropriate. Since this allegation put the opinions of AMI's attorneys directly at issue, and Kodak's need was "compelling," the court ordered the relevant work product produced. In a nutshell, "[a]n attorney's work product is discoverable where such information is directly at issue and the need for production is compelling."[69]

---

65. *Id.* at 1367; *see also* United States v. Bilzerian, 926 F.2d 1285, 1293–94 (2d Cir. 1994) (holding that privilege was waived because defendant's good faith testimony "would have put [their] knowledge of the law and the basis for his understanding of what the law required at issue"); Robinson v. De Niro, 2022 WL 704922, at *6 (S.D.N.Y. Mar. 9, 2022) (favorably citing *Bilzerian*); Claffey v. River Oaks Hyundai, 486 F. Supp. 2d 776, 778 (N.D. Ill. 2007) (noting that the attorney-client privilege may be waived when a company relies on consultations with counsel as part of its defense); *In re* Omnicom Group, Inc. Sec. Litig., 233 F.R.D. 400, 413–14 (S.D.N.Y. 2006) (recognizing potential for waiver but not finding record sufficient to hold that the privilege was waived); Roehrs v. Minn. Life Ins. Co., 228 F.R.D. 642, 646–47 (D. Ariz. 2005) (requiring production of notes from the insurance adjusters to the insurer's lawyers and the lawyers' replies because the adjusters had testified that they relied on the insurer's lawyers' statements in denying the plaintiff's claims).

66. 2019 WL 1789883, at *2 (N.D. Ill. Apr. 24, 2019) (referring to Garcia v. Zenith Elecs. Corp., 58 F.3d 1171, 1175 n.1 (7th Cir. 1995), and Rhone-Poulenc v. Rorer Inc. v. Home Indem. Co., 32 F.3d 851, 863 (3d Cir. 1994)).

67. 2019 WL 1789883, at *4.

68. 217 U.S.P.Q. (BNA) 1001 (N.D. Ill. 1982).

69. *Id.* at 1002. For another example of waiver by opponent's pleadings, see *Bird v. Penn Cent. Co.*, 61 F.R.D. 43, 46–48 (E.D. Pa. 1973).

Another example is *United States v. Exxon Corp.*[70] The government accused Exxon of overcharging its customers. As a defense, Exxon contended that it did not cause other owners of oil interests to raise their prices. Holding that Exxon's defense effected a waiver, the court reasoned that "[w]hether Exxon had an overall scheme to pressure other interest owners to adopt certain pricing policies can only be effectively determined by exploring attorney-client discussions wherein such a scheme *may* have been concocted."[71] Another court declined to extend this holding when a company was asserting only "routine defense" to agency action, holding that a waiver does not occur merely because privileged information may be relevant to a defense.[72]

Yet another example is *Rutgard v. Haynes*,[73] a legal malpractice case. The plaintiff claimed the malpractice resulted in damages for settlement payments negotiated by another attorney in a malicious prosecution case. The court found that the reasonableness of the attorney's actions in negotiating the settlement was at issue in the malpractice action, and thus, privileged information in the malicious prosecution suit was discoverable.[74] *Rutgard* has been described as an "outlier" for characterizing two separate representations as one matter.[75]

Further, lawyers may also know facts, and in-house counsel may have played roles other than as counsel in their employer's business activities. Attorneys who hold multiple roles in a company and then serve as the company's representative under Federal Rule of Civil Procedure 30(b)(6) may also face these issues. In *Adler v. Wallace Computer Services, Inc.*,[76] Wallace's general counsel—and vice president—served as the company's Rule 30(b)(6) representative. The court held that in this second role, the attorney waived Wallace's attorney-client privilege by answering deposition questions based on privileged information.[77] Because of those disclosures, the court granted the plaintiff's motion to compel answers to questions that the attorney had declined to answer on the basis of attorney-client privilege.

---

70. 94 F.R.D. 246 (D.D.C. 1981).

71. *Id. at 249. For* commentary critical of the decision, see Note, *Developments in the Law—Privileged Communications*, 98 HARV. L. REV. 1450, 1642 (1985). For another example of a court finding privilege waived due to a "causation" defense, see *Tackett v. State Farm Fire & Casualty Insurance Co.*, 653 A.2d 254 (Del. 1995) (holding that an insurer waived the attorney-client privilege by making factual representations that implicitly relied upon legal advice as justification for nonpayment of claims).

72. United States v. Ohio Edison Co., 2002 WL 1585597, at *4–5 (S.D. Ohio July 11, 2002).

73. 185 F.R.D. 596, 599 (S.D. Cal. 1999).

74. *Id.* at 599–600.

75. Woodbury Knoll, LLC v. Shipman & Goodwin, LLP, 305 Conn. 750, 782–86 (2012); Dana v. Piper, 173 Wash. App. 761, 773 (Wash. Ct. App. 2013).

76. 202 F.R.D. 666 (N.D. Ga. 2001).

77. *Id.* at 674–75.

Likewise in *State ex rel. United Hospital Center, Inc. v. Bedell*,[78] the court found waiver when the hospital designated its general counsel to testify as a corporate representative:

> We hold therefore that when a corporation, partnership, association or governmental agency designates an attorney to testify on its behalf at a deposition pursuant to West Virginia Rule of Civil Procedure 30(b)(6), such corporation, partnership, association or governmental agency waives the attorney-client privilege and work product doctrine with regard to matters, set forth in the notice of deposition, about which the attorney was designated to testify.[79]

On the one hand, when a party wants to call one of its own counsel, the decision raises issues of waiver. On the other hand, when an opponent seeks to depose counsel for the other party, the other party should consider opposing the deposition or seeking protection in advance of the deposition.

In-house counsel can safely answer purely factual questions that do not ask for the substance of communications between attorney and client.[80] If an in-house counsel testifies to any portion of an attorney-client communication, the privilege is waived and counsel cannot then refuse to fill in the remaining facts by claiming attorney-client privilege.[81] Accordingly, a party should be wary of relying on counsel as witnesses, unless the party has carefully isolated the in-house lawyer from privileged information that the party does not wish the other side to discover.

When counsel does serve as a witness for a party, courts may wait to see the nature of the testimony before deciding whether the party has waived privileges. The court so held in *In re Application for an Order for Judicial Assistance in a Foreign Proceeding in the Labor Court of Brazil*.[82] Other courts do not wait until a party's lawyer has actually been placed on the witness stand before allowing discovery of privileged material. Once a party indicates that counsel may testify, the opposing party is entitled to pretrial discovery of the issues related to the attorney's proposed testimony.[83] In *Secure Energy v. Coal Synthetics*[84] the topic of the upcoming testimony had been disclosed, so the court could rule on the issue of waiver of privilege.[85]

---

78. 484 S.E.2d 199.
79. *Id.* at 216.
80. Stamps.Com Inc. v. Endicia, Inc., 2008 WL 11338241, at *3 (C.D. Cal. Oct. 6, 2008); Sony Elecs., Inc. v. Soundview Techs., Inc., 217 F.R.D. 104, 110 (D. Conn. 2002).
81. *Adler*, 202 F.R.D. at 675.
82. 244 F.R.D. 434 (N.D. Ill. 2007).
83. Coleco Indus., Inc. v. Universal City Studios, Inc., 110 F.R.D. 688, 691–92 (S.D.N.Y. 1986) (citing *Handgards, Inc. Johnson & Johnson*, 413 F. Supp. 926, 929 (N.D. Cal. 1976)).
84. 2010 WL 199953 (E.D. Mo. Jan. 13, 2010).
85. *Id.* at *1–2.

In *Shelton v. American Motors Corp.*,[86] the Eighth Circuit formulated a three-part test for determining when opposing counsel may be deposed. A party must show that (1) no other means exist to obtain the information, (2) the information is relevant and nonprivileged, and (3) the information is crucial to the case.[87]

The Eighth Circuit later limited the *Shelton* framework to depositions of attorneys involved in the current matter. Thus, in *Pamida v. E.S. Originals, Inc.*,[88] the circuit court found the *Shelton* factors unnecessary when attorneys were to be deposed concerning their knowledge of a concluded action that was relevant to an ongoing action. In these scenarios, the party seeking the deposition need only show either waiver of privilege or substantial need and undue hardship under Federal Rule of Civil Procedure 26(b)(3).[89] However, if the court finds the underlying matter to be a current matter relevant to the case, the *Shelton* factors may still apply.[90]

Shelton has been cited many times. A number of courts have rejected it.[91] An extended discussion of Shelton in *Phillips v. Indianapolis Life Insurance Co.*[92] provides a summary of why Shelton has not always found acceptance:

> The Seventh Circuit has never addressed *Shelton*'s propriety. The only decision from this District to have done so, *Cook Inc. v. C.R. Bard, Inc.*, 2003 WL 23009047 (S.D.Ind.2003) (Barker, J.), rejected it. According to that case, counsel in this District seldom try to depose opposing counsel; therefore, this District does not need the Shelton rule. *Id.* at *1. Instead, it cautioned counsel to "think carefully before noticing such a deposition" because sanctions would be readily employed "if, in retrospect, it is apparent that the deponent had so little relevant, non-privileged information that the deposition was no more than a waste of everyone's time." *Id.* at *2.
>
> The Court likewise rejects *Shelton*. The Federal Rules have the force of statute. . . . Shelton's heightened burden-of-proof rule finds no support in the plain text of the Federal Rules of Civil Procedure.

86. 805 F.2d 1323, 1327 (8th Cir. 1986) (deposition appropriate only in limited circumstances; trial counsel is not "absolutely immune" from being deposed). *See also* Simmons Foods, Inc. v. Willis, 191 F.R.D. 625, 630 (D. Kan. 2000) (noting that *Shelton* test is majority rule).

87. *Shelton v. Am. Motors Corp.*, 805 F.2d 1323, 1327 (8th Cir. 1986); *see also* Nguyen v. Excel Corp., 197 F.3d 200, 208–09 (5th Cir. 1999) (counsel deposed when executives were unable to respond to queries without stating reliance on counsel or consulting with counsel).

88. 281 F.3d 726 (8th Cir. 2002).

89. *Id.* at 730–31.

90. Seipler v. Cundiff, 2011 WL 4954224, at *5 (N.D. Ill. Oct. 18, 2011).

91. *See, e.g.*, *In re* Subpoena Issued to Dennis Friedman, 350 F.3d 65, 67 (2d Cir. 2003) (We conclude that the deposition-discovery regime of the Federal Rules of Civil Procedure requires a more flexible approach to attorney depositions than the rigid *Shelton* rule.).

92. 2009 WL 1564384 (S.D. Ind. June 3, 2009).

> *See* Fed. R. Civ. Pro. 30(a)(1) (permitting a party to "depose any person" by issuing a notice of deposition and, if necessary, a subpoena (emphasis added)). And, in any event, this magistrate agrees with Cook that the Shelton rule is unnecessary given the rarity of attorney depositions in this District and given the Court's ability to sanction counsel for proceeding with a frivolous deposition, see Fed. R. Civ. Pro. 26(g)(1)(B)(i), (iii).[93]

In *ATS Products, Inc. v. Champion Fiberglass, Inc.*,[94] the court discussed *Shelton* extensively and decided to apply the less stringent approach used by in *Pamida v. E.S. Originals, Inc.*[95] *when the Eighth Circuit reexamined Shelton and limited its application to pending cases.*

In *Sterne Kessler Goldstein & Fox, PLLC v. Eastman Kodak Co.*,[96] the attorney was not currently counsel to a party but had been involved in a somewhat related matter. The court ruled under Rule 26 that the deposition of counsel was not appropriate. Other courts refused to apply *Shelton* altogether, instead requiring attorneys to attend depositions and have privilege objections raised contemporaneously.[97] Other courts conduct a full evaluation of the circumstances as opposed to the application of a rote test.[98] Still other courts have implemented a flexible application of the *Shelton* factors, taking additional factors into consideration.[99]

Just as a party can waive the attorney-client privilege by putting its lawyer on the stand, one can also waive the privilege by calling as a witness some third party. An example would be an investigator hired by the attorney, whose communications are otherwise protected by the attorney-client privilege.[100]

---

93. *Id.* at *1–2.

94. 2015 WL 356161, at *3–6 (N.D. Cal. June 8, 2015).

95. 281 F.3d 726 (8th Cir. 2002).

96. 276 F.R.D. 376, 382 (D.D.C. 2011).

97. Taylor Mach. Works, Inc. v. Pioneer Distrib. Inc., 2006 WL 1686140, at *2 (C.D. Ill. June 19, 2006).

98. *See id.* at *3–4.

99. *See id.* at *3 (synthesizing additional factors considered by multiple courts). These factors include the need to take the deposition, the lawyer's role in the underlying action and in the primary action, the risk of encountering privilege and interfering in the attorney-client relationship, avoiding unnecessary expense, and the means and extent of discovery already conducted to obtain the information to be gleaned from the attorney.

100. Clark v. City of Munster, 115 F.R.D. 609, 615 (N.D. Ind. 1987) (cited with approval in Thacker Eng'g, Inc. v. Chicago Hous. Auth., 1988 WL 84714, at *8 (N.D. Ill. Aug. 11, 1988); *see also* Brown v. Trigg, 791 F.2d 598, 601–02 (7th Cir. 1986) (defendant in adult trial for felony murder waived attorney-client privilege and work-product protection by having administrator of the polygraph test testify at juvenile court waiver hearing).

V. Issues and Defenses That Implicate State of Mind or Knowledge

A. Good Faith

Hearn v. Rhay was a civil rights action brought against prison officials by an inmate who alleged that his confinement in a mental health unit constituted "cruel and unusual punishment" and violated his right to due process.[101] Defendants asserted the affirmative defense of "qualified immunity,"—that is, they contended that they acted in good faith, pursuant to their understanding of the law, and were therefore immune from the suit for damages.[102] The plaintiff sought discovery of all the legal advice the defendants received on the legality of his confinement in the mental health unit. Finding the plaintiff's argument persuasive, the court held that the defendants waived any attorney-client privilege by asserting their qualified immunity as a defense.[103]

Nevertheless, many courts refuse to follow *Hearn*, either rejecting its formulation or finding it too liberally applied.[104] The Second Circuit notes that there are very few instances in which the *Hearn* factors do not apply, thereby eroding the attorney-client privilege.[105] In *Bacchi v. Massachusetts Mutual Life Insurance Co.*,[106] *the court concluded that the more accepted test requires that the privileged information be actually relied upon rather than merely relevant to the claim or defense, citing the Second Circuit's decision in In re County of Erie.*[107]

"Good faith" is a common defense to numerous torts outside the civil rights context but may be susceptible to *Hearn*'s holding. For example, in *McLaughlin v. Lunde Truck Sales, Inc.*,[108] the defendants argued that they acted in good-faith reliance on representations made by the plaintiff's agents and offered an affidavit by their former attorney to support that position. The court held that the defendants waived their attorney-client privilege by asserting

---

101. 68 F.R.D. 574, 577 (E.D. Wash. 1975).

102. *Id.*

103. *Id.* at 581. The court noted that advice of counsel was relevant to the subjective component of the qualified privilege.

104. *See, e.g.*, *In re* Itron, Inc., 883 F.3d 553, 563–65 (5th Cir. 2018); *In re* County of Erie, 546 F.3d 222, 227–28 (2d Cir. 2008); Rhone-Poulenc Rorer Inc. v. Home Indem. Co., 32 F.3d 851, 864 (3d Cir. 1994); Windsor Secs., LLC v. Arent Fox LLP, 273 F. Supp. 3d 512, 521–22 (S.D.N.Y. 2017); United States v. Ohio Edison Co., 2002 WL 1585597, at *4–5 (S.D. Ohio July 11, 2002); Ryall v. Appleton Elec. Co., 153 F.R.D. 66, 663 n.1 (D. Colo. 1994); Remington Arms Co. v. Liberty Mut. Ins. Co., 142 F.R.D. 408, 413–14 (D. Del. 1992); Standard Chartered Bank PLC v. Ayala Int'l Holdings (U.S.) Inc., 111 F.R.D. 76, 81 (S.D.N.Y. 1986); McCarthy v. Slade Assocs., 972 N.E.2d 1037, 1049 (Mass. 2012); Public Serv. Co. of N.M. v. Lyons, 10 P.3d 166, 172–73 (N.M. Ct. App. 2000).

105. *In re* County of Erie, 546 F.3d 222, 227 (2d Cir. 2008); *see also* Windsor Secs., LLC v. Arent Fox LLP, 273 F. Supp. 3d 512, 521–22 (S.D.N.Y. 2017).

106. *110 F. Supp. 3d 270, 275–76 (D. Mass. 2015).*

107. 546 F.3d 222, 227–28 (2d Cir. 2008).

108. 714 F. Supp. 916 (N.D. Ill. 1989); *accord* United States v. Kmart Corp., 2017 WL 3034342, at *2–3 (S.D. Ill. July 17, 2017) (citing *McLaughlin* but not finding waiver as Kmart was not "wielding any swords").

good faith and by "injecting their former counsel's affidavit in support of their good faith defense."[109]

In some circumstances, a careful attorney may be able to craft a good-faith defense and not waive attorney-client privilege.[110] In *Cardtoons, L.C. v. Major League Baseball Players Association*,[111] the plaintiff planned to print parody baseball cards, which sparked a cease-and-desist letter from the defendant. The plaintiff responded with a suit alleging a multitude of claims, including several that required proof of the defendant's intent, and the defendant denied the alleged intent rather than affirmatively asserting a good-faith defense. The court held that the mere fact that privileged communications would make it easier for the plaintiff to prove its case was not enough to waive the defendant's attorney-client privilege.[112] Nevertheless, the court warned that the issue of waiver could be teed up again if the defendant relied on attorney work product at trial to support a good-faith argument.[113]

B. Bad Faith

The opposite of good faith is bad faith. When a party is accused of bad-faith conduct, there is a potential for privileged information to be discoverable and admissible. Such a determination requires inquiries into "any investigations conducted by the [defendant], the information available to the company at the time its decision was made, and the manner in which the company arrived at its decision, including reliance on advice of counsel."[114] That is, the operative facts in a bad-faith case include all steps the client took to reach the decision in question.[115]

In turn, the courts have held that "bad faith actions . . . can only be proved by showing exactly how the company processed the claim, how thoroughly it was considered and why the company took the action it did."[116] From that, it followed that documents held by the accused party were freely discoverable.[117] Some courts have dismissed out of hand claims of privilege in bad-faith cases, even where part of the materials in question were attorney-client letters: "the time-worn claims of . . . attorney-client privilege cannot be

---

109. 714 F. Supp. at 919.

110. *See* Kaiser Found. Health Plan, Inc. v. Abbott Labs., Inc., 552 F.3d 1033, 1043 (9th Cir. 2009) (no waiver found where the client "did not actually rely on an advice-of-counsel defense"); *see also* United States v. Newell, 315 F.3d 510, 525 (5th Cir. 2002) (attorney-client privilege not waived when party showed that good-faith defense "was not based on advice of counsel, but rather on a simple lack of knowledge of the wrongdoing and absence of intent to participate in it").

111. 199 F.R.D. 677 (N.D. Okla. 2001).

112. *Id.* at 681–83.

113. *Id.* at 683.

114. *In re* Bergeson, 112 F.R.D. 692, 697 (D. Mont. 1986); *see also* Omni Health Solutions, LLC v. Zurich Am. Ins. Co., 2018 WL 4701791, at *4 (M.D. Ga. Oct. 1, 2018).

115. *City of Elmira v. Larry Walter, Inc.*, 453 N.Y.S.2d 259, 260 (N.Y. App. Div. 1982).

116. Brown v. Superior Court, 670 P.2d 725, 734 (Ariz. 1983) (en banc) (construing work-product privilege).

117. *Id.*

invoked to the [defendant's] benefit where the only issue in the case is whether the company breached its duty of good faith in processing the insured's claim."[118] On the other hand, courts have acknowledged that "it would be a rare confidential communication that would not satisfy the relevancy test."[119] Also, attorney-client communications have "pragmatic importance," but if the privilege could be abrogated on that ground, "the privilege would have little meaning."[120]

C. Knowledge

A party may also make state of mind an issue by trying to toll a statute of limitations. Adopting *Hearn*'s reasoning, the district court in *Connell v. Bernstein-Macaulay, Inc.*[121] found that the privilege was waived when the plaintiffs claimed that the defendants were estopped from asserting the statutory bar, since the defendants had convinced the plaintiffs to withhold their suit while the defendants tried to remedy the situation. The court found that the plaintiffs waived protection on the issue of whether they had withheld suit solely or principally because of the defendants' persuasion:

> [W]here a litigant seeks to avoid a statutory protection which has been established for the benefit of his adversary [by a claim of estoppel]; and where it appears that there is a good faith basis for believing that invasion of the attorney-client privilege would shed light on the validity of such claim of estoppel; the party making such assertion must be deemed to have waived the privilege.[122]

The *Connell* court seemed reluctant to permit an assertion of attorney-client privilege to defeat the public policy reflected in the limitations statute.[123]

---

118. Silva v. Fire Ins. Exch., 112 F.R.D. 699, 700 (D. Mont. 1986); *but see* Spargo v. State Farm Fire & Cas. Co., 2017 WL 2695292, at *4 (D. Nev. June 22, 2017) (stating that *Silva* court cited no authority for quoted statement).

119. Dontzin v. Myer, 694 A.2d 264, 268 (N.J. Super. App. Div. 1997).

120. Twin City Fire Ins. Co. v. Burke, 63 P.3d 282, 287 (Ariz. 2003) (en banc).

121. 407 F. Supp. 420 (S.D.N.Y. 1976). *Connell,* though, can be viewed as an express rather than implied reliance case, making *Hearn*'s holding not on point. *See In re* County of Erie, 546 F.3d 222, 227–28 (2d Cir. 2008).

122. 407 F. Supp. at 423 (footnote omitted).

123. Other cases involving tolling provisions include *Conkling v. Turner*, 883 F.2d 431 (5th Cir. 1989) (by claiming that the statute was tolled until his attorney informed him of defendant's alleged fraud, plaintiff waived the privilege); *Byers v. Burleson*, 100 F.R.D. 436 (D.D.C. 1983) (by claiming that the statute was tolled while he was allegedly unaware of grounds for legal malpractice action, plaintiff waived the privilege); and *Russell v. Curtin Matheson Scientific, Inc.*, 493 F. Supp. 456 (S.D. Tex. 1980) (by claiming that 180-day notice requirement was tolled because the Department of Labor affirmatively misled them as to that requirement, plaintiffs waived the privilege for communications that occurred more than 180 days prior to actual filing of notice).

Compare *Connell's* broad holding with *Darius v. City of Boston.*[124] The *Darius* defendant sought privileged materials concerning a meeting with counsel to establish that plaintiffs knew of their causes of action prior to the expiration of the statute. The Massachusetts Supreme Court refused the defendant's motion for production, finding that what counsel may have told the plaintiffs about their causes of action did not change what plaintiffs knew or should have known prior to the expiration of the statute, and what plaintiffs told their counsel about what they knew "strike[s] at the very core of the privilege."[125]

In *Sprint Communications Co. v. Charter Communications, L.P.,*[126] the court held that asserting lack of knowledge in response to a limitations defense was not the type of affirmative injecting of an issue that waived the attorney-client privilege. In so holding, the court recognized *Hearn v. Rhay*[127] as valid authority but did not find any of the element of the *Hearn* test to have been met.

Akin to knowledge is mental capacity. In *Meyer v. Gwinnett County Police Department,*[128] the court found the attorney-client privilege to have been waived when the party asserting the privilege had injected his mental capacity as an issue.

D. Reliance

Courts have found waiver of privilege as a result of estoppel claims in other contexts as well. For example, when the defendant in a patent infringement action claimed that the plaintiff was estopped from enforcing its patent because of the defendant's detrimental reliance on the plaintiff's previous inaction, the court in *Southwire Co. v. Essex Group Inc.* found waiver as to any documents that tended to show the defendant had instead relied on legal advice about the patent invalidity.[129]

Despite some objective evidence showing reliance on inaction, the *Southwire* court found that, in fairness, the plaintiff should be permitted discovery of privileged documents to show the defendant's subjective intent.[130] The court found the claim of waiver particularly compelling in view of the defendant's reliance on the opinions of its lawyers as a defense to a different claim, that of willful infringement.[131] This alternative theory gave some credence to the plaintiff's claim that the defendant relied on something other than the plaintiff's inaction. Results on this issue in other courts have been mixed.[132]

124. 741 N.E.2d 52 (2001).
125. *Id.* at 57.
126. 2022 WL 594823 (D. Kan. Feb. 28, 2022).
127. 68 F.R.D. 574, 577 (E.D. Wash. 1975).
128. 2022 WL 2439590 (11th Cir. July 5, 2022).
129. 570 F. Supp. 643, 649–50 (N.D. Ill. 1983).
130. *Id.* at 649.
131. *Id.* at 645–46, 649–50.
132. Chamberlain Group v. Interlogix, Inc., 2002 WL 467153, at *1–3 (N.D. Ill. Mar. 27, 2002) (collecting and discussing cases).

The issue of implied waiver has arisen in cases of alleged fraud as well. In *Sedco International, S.A. v. Cory*,[133] the Eighth Circuit held that an investor asserting fraudulent inducement, "at most, waived his right to assert the privilege to prevent disclosure of communications which might have proven he did not rely on [his opponent's] statements or that such reliance was unreasonable." However, the court refused to compel disclosure of privileged communications, finding that none of those communications could possibly show that the investor relied on anything other than the alleged misstatements.[134]

Some later opinions have followed *Sedco*'s in determining whether an implied waiver has occurred, including from allegations of fraud.[135] Other courts have adopted *Sedco*'s factual finding that privileged matters were not relevant to the issue of reliance.[136]

E. Contract Interpretation

State-of-mind issues also arise in connection with contract disputes. In many cases, one party will try to introduce extrinsic evidence of an agreement's underlying understanding or intent. Because attorneys often play a role in contract negotiation, their advice is arguably intertwined with the client's contractual intent. Thus, several courts have found the party employing such a strategy waived its attorney-client privilege.[137]

For example, *Sax v. Sax*[138] involved a dispute regarding a memorandum agreement between Lawrence Sax and John Sax. Lawrence Sax sued to enforce the agreement; John Sax alleged, among other things, that the agreement was invalid because it was vague and the parties did not have a mutual understanding of its terms.[139]

The district court observed that "John Sax ha[d] raised an issue of his lack of understanding of the Memorandum Agreement in circumstances in which

---

133. 683 F.2d 1201, 1206 (8th Cir. 1982).

134. *Id.* at 1206–07.

135. *See, e.g.*, Sedillos v. Bd. of Educ. of Sch. Dist. No. 1, 313 F. Supp. 2d 1091, 1093–94 (D. Colo. 2004); Synalloy Corp. v. Gray, 142 F.R.D. 266, 270 (D. Del. 1992) (also discussing Hearn v. Rhay, 68 F.R.D. 574 (E.D. Wash. 1975)); FDIC v. Wise, 139 F.R.D. 168, 171–72 (D. Colo. 1991) (also discussing Hearn v. Rhay, 68 F.R.D. 574 (E.D. Wash. 1975)).

136. *See, e.g.*, Pippenger v. Gruppe, 883 F. Supp. 1201, 1204–06 (S.D. Ind. 1994) (also discussing Hearn v. Rhay, 68 F.R.D. 574 (E.D. Wash. 1975)).

137. *See, e.g.*, Liberty Int'l Underwriters Canada v. Scottsdale Ins. Co., 2014 WL 6991329, at *4–5 (D.N.J. Dec. 10, 2014); Blitz v. 970 Realty Assocs., 233 N.J. Super. 29, 34–36 (App. Div. 1989); Pitney-Bowes, Inc. v. Mestre, 86 F.R.D. 444 (S.D. Fla. 1980), *aff'd on other grounds*, 701 F.2d 1365 (11th Cir. 1983); *see also* Medtronic, Inc. v. Intermedics, Inc., 162 F.R.D. 133 (D. Minn. 1995) (holding that defendant's potential use of extrinsic evidence would effect a waiver of attorney-client privilege, and giving defendant ten days to notify plaintiff whether it would use such evidence at trial). Indeed, where the contract in question is a settlement agreement, the scope of this waiver may extend to attorney work product. *But see* Dontzin v. Myer, 694 A.2d 264, 269–70 (N.J. Super. App. Div. 1997) (reversing order that privilege must be waived in a contract interpretation case).

138. 136 F.R.D. 542 (D. Mass. 1991).

139. *Id.* at 543.

perhaps the only person who would have explained the agreement to him was his attorney."[140] As a result, the court held that he had implicitly waived his attorney-client privilege.[141]

In retaliation, John Sax then filed a motion challenging Lawrence Sax's privilege claims. This time, the district judge ruled differently, finding that Lawrence Sax had simply sought a declaration that the agreement, as written, was valid—without relying on extrinsic evidence, his attorney's advice, or his own state of mind—the court upheld his privilege claims.[142]

VI. Who Can Waive

The attorney-client privilege belongs to the client. The client's attorney, of course, can waive a privilege on behalf of the client.[143] The work-product privilege belongs to the attorney, although it can be waived by the client as well as by the attorney.[144]

It has been held that an employee whose communications have been claimed as privileged under the attorney-client privilege on behalf of the corporation may waive that privilege.[145] Most courts, however, follow the principles of the *Restatement (Third) of the Law Governing Lawyers*,[146] which provides that only an authorized agent of the corporation may waive the privilege of the corporation.[147]

When corporate employees are being deposed, the corporate attorney should be prepared to object and instruct the employee (or former employee) not to answer a question that calls for the disclosure of privileged attorney-client communications. If necessary, the attorney should terminate the deposition, seek a protective order from the court,[148] or contact the court for instructions on how to protect the privileged information. Failure to take these measures and allowing the testimony despite objection will, in most cases, be construed by the court as waiver of the privilege.[149]

---

140. *Id.* at 544.

141. *Id. Sax is discussed in a later case as employing the Hearn test rather than the more accepted test of requiring reliance rather just relevance with respect to privileged information, see Bacchi v. Mass. Mut. Life Ins. Co., 110 F. Supp. 3d 270, 275–76 (D. Mass. 2015).*

142. *Id.*

143. *See, e.g.*, Shaffer v. Pennsbury Sch. Dist., 525 F. Supp. 3d 573, 577 (E.D. Pa. 2021).

144. Curtis v. Superior Court, 62 Cal. App. 5th 453, 469 (2021).

145. Jonathan Corp. v. Prime Comp., Inc., 114 F.R.D. 693, 700 (E.D. Va. 1987).

146. Restatement (Third) of the Law Governing Lawyers § 78 (2000).

147. *See* Commodity Futures Trading Comm'n v. Weintraub, 471 U.S. 343, 349 (1985) (recognizing that "[T]he power to waive the corporate attorney-client privilege rests with the corporation's management and is normally exercised by its officers and directors."); Texas Tech Univ. Health Sciences Ctr. v. Niehay, 641 S.W.3d 761, 790 (Tex. App. 2022).

148. *E.g.*, Fed. R. Civ. P. 26(c).

149. Perrignon v. Bergen Brunswig Corp., 77 F.R.D. 455, 459 (N.D. Cal. 1978).

VII. Scope of Waiver

In general, a waiver of privilege may extend to all communications on the same subject matter. Federal Rule 502(a) provides the general rule for federal courts:

> (a) **Disclosure Made in a Federal Proceeding or to a Federal Office or Agency; Scope of a Waiver.** When the disclosure is made in a federal proceeding or to a federal office or agency and waives the attorney-client privilege or work-product protection, the waiver extends to an undisclosed communication or information in a federal or state proceeding only if:
>
> (1) the waiver is intentional;
>
> (2) the disclosed and undisclosed communications or information concern the same subject matter; and
>
> (3) they ought in fairness to be considered together.

Application of this rule, however, can be elusive and unpredictable. In applying Federal Rule of Evidence 502(a), one court noted:

> [A]s to determining subject matter, "[t]here is no bright line test for determining what constitutes the subject matter of a waiver, rather courts weigh the circumstances of the disclosure, the nature of the legal advice sought and the prejudice to the parties of permitting or prohibiting further disclosures." *Fort James* [*Corp. v. Solo Cup Co.*], 412 F.3d [1340,] 1349 [(Fed. Cir. 2005)]. Third, the fairness inquiry requires a consideration of whether "further disclosure of related, protected information" is necessary "to prevent a selective and misleading presentation of evidence to the disadvantage of the adversary." Fed. R. Evid. 502(a) advisory committee's note (2007); *see also In re EchoStar Commc'ns Corp.*, 448 F.3d 1294, 1303 (Fed. Cir. 2006) (noting that the "overarching goal" of subject matter waiver is "to prevent a party from using the advice he received as both a sword, by waiving privilege to favorable advice, and a shield, by asserting privilege to unfavorable advice").[150]

The advisory committee note to Rule 502(a) mentioned in the preceding passage discusses the meaning of Rule 502(a):

150. Kansas City Power & Light Co. v. United States, 139 Fed. Cl. 546, 561–62 (2018).

Subdivision (a). The rule provides that a voluntary disclosure in a federal proceeding or to a federal office or agency, if a waiver, generally results in a waiver only of the communication or information disclosed; a subject matter waiver (of either privilege or work product) is reserved for those unusual situations in which fairness requires a further disclosure of related, protected information, in order to prevent a selective and misleading presentation of evidence to the disadvantage of the adversary. *See, e.g., In re United Mine Workers of America Employee Benefit Plans Litig.*, 159 F.R.D. 307, 312 (D.D.C. 1994) (waiver of work product limited to materials actually disclosed, because the party did not deliberately disclose documents in an attempt to gain a tactical advantage). Thus, subject matter waiver is limited to situations in which a party intentionally puts protected information into the litigation in a selective, misleading and unfair manner. It follows that an inadvertent disclosure of protected information can never result in a subject matter waiver. *See* Rule 502(b). The rule rejects the result in *In re Sealed Case*, 877 F.2d 976 (D.C. Cir. 1989), which held that inadvertent disclosure of documents during discovery automatically constituted a subject matter waiver.

The language concerning subject matter waiver—"ought in fairness"—is taken from Rule 106, because the animating principle is the same. Under both Rules, a party that makes a selective, misleading presentation that is unfair to the adversary opens itself to a more complete and accurate presentation.

To assure protection and predictability, the rule provides that if a disclosure is made at the federal level, the federal rule on subject matter waiver governs subsequent state court determinations on the scope of the waiver by that disclosure.[151]

When there is no bright-line rule and fairness is the test for the scope of waiver, there is little chance of any meaningful way to predict what the scope of waiver may be, allowing both sides to argue their position based on the facts. Some general observations can be made, however.

- Disclosure of attorney-client communications usually results in waiver of communications on the same subject matter.[152]

---

151. *See also* SEC v. Collector's Coffee Inc., 338 F.R.D. 309, 316–17 (S.D.N.Y. 2021) (applying the advisory committee's note).

152. *See, e.g., In re* Keeper of the Records, 348 F.3d 16, 24–25 (1st Cir. 2003); Pittman v. Frazer, 129 F.3d 983, 987 (8th Cir. 1997) (referring to "broad concepts of subject matter waiver" as to disclosure of attorney-client communications) (citation omitted); Genentech, Inc. v. United States Int'l Trade Comm'n, 122 F.3d 1409, 1416–17 (Fed. Cir. 1997) (quoting commentator that when attorney-client communication is disclosed, the privilege is gone); United States v. Jones, 696 F.2d 1069, 1072 (4th Cir.

- Nevertheless, principles of fairness may militate against subject matter waiver for disclosure of attorney-client communications.[153]
- Subject matter waiver tends not to be applied to disclosure of work-product information.[154] As noted in *Munguia-Brown v. Equity Residential*,[155] courts tend to narrow the scope of waiver of disclosed work product. While Federal Rule of Evidence 502(a) applies the fairness test to both the attorney-client and work-product privileges, fairness concepts may apply differently to attorney-client communications, factual work product, and opinion work product.[156]
- Nevertheless, disclosure of work product for apparent tactical reasons can lead to subject matter waiver.[157]
- Because of an enhanced interest in protecting against disclosure of trial strategy, the waiver of work product will end once the lawsuit is filed.[158]
- Courts are especially reluctant to extend subject matter waiver to opinion work product,[159] but some courts may extend waiver in certain cases to core work product.[160]

1982); Cox v. Administrator U.S. Steel & Carnegie, 17 F.3d 1386, 1422 (11th Cir.), *opinion modified on rehearing*, 30 F.3d 1347 (11th Cir. 1994); Brasfield & Gorrie, LLC v. Hirschfeld Steel Group LP, 2021 WL 5449203, at *4 (N.D. Ala. Nov. 22, 2021); *In re* Sealed Case, 676 F.2d 793, 809 (D.C. Cir. 1982); Nat'l Steel Prods. Co. v. Superior Court, 164 Cal. App. 3d 476, 485 (1985); *In re* Bryan, 61 P.3d 641 656 (Kan. 2003).

153. *See In re* von Bulow, 828 F.2d 94, 103 (2d Cir. 1987) (citing cases; dealing with extrajudicial disclosure); *see also In re* Keeper of the Records, 348 F.3d 16, 24–25 (1st Cir. 2003) (also dealing with extrajudicial disclosure); Center Partners, Ltd. v. Growth Head GP, 981 N.E.2d 345, 364 (Ill. 2012) (excellent discussion of novel issue of extrajudicial disclosure, held not to effect subject matter waiver, and subject matter waiver in general).

154. Pittman v. Frazer, 129 F.3d 983, 987 (8th Cir. 1997); Brasfield & Gorrie, LLC v. Hirschfeld Steel Group LP, 2021 WL 5449203, at *3 (N.D. Ala. Nov. 22, 2021) ("Due to the sensitive nature of work-product materials and the policy behind maintaining their secrecy, generally speaking, when the work product protection has been waived, it is limited to the information actually disclosed, not subject matter waiver.") (citations and quotation omitted); *In re* Bexar County Criminal Dist. Attorney's Office, 224 S.W.3d 182, 190–91 (Tex. 2007) (waiver of work product limited to produced documents themselves); *In re* Arterial Vascular Eng'g, Inc., 2001 WL 1609684, at *1 (Tex. App. Dec. 18, 2001) (noting that subject matter waiver does not apply to work product under California law, as it does with waiver of the attorney-client privilege).

155. 337 F.R.D. 509, 516–17 (N.D. Cal. 2021).

156. *Id.*; *see also* New York Times Co. v. United States Dep't of Justice, 939 F.3d 479, 496 (2d Cir. 2019) ("We have subsequently clarified, however, that implied waiver of the work product privilege based on the 'fairness' or 'at-issue' doctrine is not nearly so broad. To find implied waiver, we look for specific instances of unfairness that undermine the adversarial process, and this is inherently a case-by-case determination.") (citations omitted).

157. *See* United States v. John Rodgers, 2022 WL 1074013, at *8–9 (E.D. Tex. Apr. 8, 2022) (noting that disclosure of work product generally results in waiver of only document disclosed absent deliberate disclosure for tactical advantage) (citing Doe 1 v. Baylor Univ., 320 F.R.D. 430, 442 (W.D. Tex. 2017).

158. Aspex Eyewear, Inc. v. E'Lite Optik, Inc., 276 F. Supp. 2d 1084, 1095 (D. Nev. 2003).

159. *See* Brasfield & Gorrie, LLC v. Hirschfeld Steel Group LP, 2021 WL 5449203, at *4 (N.D. Ala. Nov. 22, 2021); *In re* Martin Marrieta Corp., 856 F.2d 619, 625–26 (4th Cir. 1988); *In re* EchoStar Commc'ns Corp., 448 F.3d 1294, 1302 (Fed. Cir. 2006) (work-product waiver extends only to factual work product on the same subject matter).

160. *See, e.g.*, Munguia-Brown v. Equity Residential, 337 F.R.D. 509, 516–17 (N.D. Cal. 2021).

The scope of waiver is often broad when a party is relying on advice of counsel as a defense. Generally, the waiver extends to the subject matter of the advice.[161] The waiver is "at least to the extent of all information respecting communication between client and attorney up until the time the attorney's opinion is rendered."[162] When advice of counsel is given after litigation has begun, the waiver cannot be limited to pretrial communications.[163] Furthermore, if a party relying on advice of counsel changes its position from what was originally stated in the advice-of-counsel opinion, fairness dictates that the court extend the waiver post-suit.[164]

Relying on advice of counsel may waive both the attorney-client and the work-product privileges,[165] as may calling an attorney to testify.[166] A limit may exist if the work product was not shared with the client, so that it has less probative value on the issue of the client's reliance on counsel.[167] A more typical limit is that the work product of trial counsel remains protected, as distinguished from the work product of the opinion counsel.[168] However, even trial counsel's opinion work product is still subject to disclosure if the opposing party can make the appropriate showing under Federal Rule of Civil Procedure 26(b)(3) that the party seeking discovery has substantial need of the materials in the preparation of the party's case and that the party is unable without undue hardship to obtain the substantial equivalent of the materials by other means.[169]

In addition, an opposing party might gain access to the advice and opinions of *other* attorneys consulted by that client and to communications and analyses given *after* the opinion on which the client relies.[170] Once again, the rationale is fairness—courts find that the jury, in assessing whether a party

---

161. *See, e.g.*, Nomura Asset Capital Corp. v. Cadwalader, Wickersham & Taft, LLP, 62 A.D.3d 581, 582, 880 N.Y.S.2d 617 (2009).

162. Micron Separations Inc. v. Pall Corp., 159 F.R.D. 361, 362 (D. Mass. 1995); *accord* Michlin v. Canon, Inc., 208 F.R.D. 172, 173 (E.D. Mich. 2002).

163. K.W. Muth Co. v. Bing-Lear Mfg. Group, LLC, 219 F.R.D. 554, 574 (E.D. Mich. 2003).

164. *BASF Aktiengesellschaft* v. Reilly Indus., Inc., 283 F. Supp. 2d 1000, 1006 (S.D. Ind. 2003).

165. *In re* Seagate Tech., 497 F.3d 1360, 1370 (Fed. Cir. 2007); Munguia-Brown v. Equity Residential, 337 F.R.D. 509, 516–17 (N.D. Cal. 2021).

166. Hernandez v. Tanninen, 604 F.3d 1095, 1100 (9th Cir. 2010) (waiver of both privileges limited to subject matter of attorney's testimony).

167. *BASF Aktiengesellschaft* v. Reilly Indus., Inc., 283 F. Supp. 2d 1000, 1005 (S.D. Ind. 2003) (citations omitted); Aspex Eyewear, Inc. v. E'Lite Optik, Inc., 276 F. Supp. 2d 1084, 1091–92 (D. Nev. 2003); City of Glendale v. Nat'l Union Fire Ins. Co., 2013 WL 1797308, at *7 (D. Ariz. Apr. 29, 2013).

168. *In re* Seagate Tech., 497 F.3d 1360, 1375 (Fed. Cir. 2007).

169. *Id.* at 1376 (Fed. Cir. 2007) (waiver can extend to trial counsel if a party or attorney engages in "chicanery"); *BASF Aktiengesellschaft* v. Reilly Indus., Inc., 283 F. Supp. 2d 1000, 1006 (S.D. Ind. 2003) (citing cases that extend waiver to trial counsel waiver extended to trial counsel but only to the extent documents were communicated to defendants and contained conclusions or advice that contradict or cast doubt on the earlier opinions).

170. *See* Micron Separations, Inc. v. Pall Corp., 159 F.R.D. 361, 363–65 (D. Mass. 1995); *see also* Pro-Com Heating, Inc. v. GHP Group, Inc., 2016 WL 3659137, at *5 (W.D. Ky. May 11, 2016) (no waiver as to irrelevant information).

was "reasonable" in relying on one attorney's advice, is entitled to know if the client received overwhelming advice to the contrary from other attorneys,[171] or if the client subsequently learned that this original advice was wrong.[172]

Returning to an earlier observation, without a bright-line rule and with fairness being the main determinant, there is considerable room for argument on both sides of the scope of waiver. To lend certainty to the issue, the parties may agree to the scope of waiver, although the agreement binds only the parties to the agreement.[173]

---

171. *See* SEC v. Forma, 117 F.R.D. 516, 523 n.5 (S.D.N.Y. 1987).
172. *See* Micron Separations, Inc. v. Pall Corp., 159 F.R.D. 361, 363 (D. Mass. 1995).
173. *In re* King's Daughters Health Sys, Inc., 2022 WL 1122869, at * 5 (6th Cir. Apr. 15, 2022).

CHAPTER 7

Procedural Tools for Litigating Privileges

ROBERT P. REDEMANN

This chapter discusses procedural tools that are used when litigating the application of privileges. Those seeking to protect a claimed privilege must use the tools properly. Those seeking the information that is claimed as privilege should take advantage of any deficiencies in the use of these tools. Privileges are usually litigated during discovery but they can also be litigated during a trial. The following sections generally follow the timeline of when a procedure is likely to occur in the life of a case. Following them, the chapter offers some practice tips for those litigating privileges.

I. Protective Orders

While a protective order may be sought anytime during the life of a case, there are three times when a protective order is most likely to be entered. These times are before discovery starts, when an issue arises after discovery commences, or during trial. The following sections discuss these times.

A. Before Discovery Begins

The best time to "litigate" discovery disputes is before discovery actually commences. All federal jurisdictions and many states require an early conference in cases to give counsel a chance to discuss the issues in a case, including anticipated discovery issues.[1] During this conference, if you suspect you may have discovery issues, it is wise to raise the issues and discuss how to resolve them. This is also a chance to propose either a joint discovery order or an agreed upon protective order to present to the court. These orders can detail a variety

1. Fed. R. Civ. P. (26)(f).

of things, such as how a discovery dispute should be handled prior to going to the court for resolution; specific meet and confer requirements; limits or expansions on local discovery rules, such as numerical limits on discovery requests and depositions; inadvertent disclosure and clawback procedures, especially if the rules don't address those; the way to designate both confidential documents and attorney's eyes only documents and a procedure for challenging such designations; and the procedure for returning or destroying documents once the case ends.

Most courts will look favorably on agreed orders, though protective orders may have a more difficult time than discovery orders because they often hide information from the public which is contrary to the concept of full public disclosure.

Even if the order is agreed upon by the parties, the court still has an obligation to independently ascertain whether or not good cause is shown and whether the totality of the circumstances supports the breadth of the protection in the order. Federal Rule of Civil Procedure 26(c) requires this, though some courts will find the parties' agreement on the issues to satisfy the good cause requirement. To ensure the entry of an agreed to order and to support the finding of good cause, evidence should be prepared and presented to the court, when requesting a pre-discovery protective order. While the necessary evidence varies, affidavits from experts, parties, and witnesses are helpful. Often, the court also seeks attorney observations and estimations.

B. After Discovery Begins

Federal Rule of Civil Procedure 26(c) addresses protective orders. The order may be sought in the court where the action is pending or where the responder is located.[2] The motion for it must include a certification that the moving party has conferred or attempted to confer with the other parties involved in an attempt to resolve the issue without court intervention.[3] The court may issue a protective order, after a finding of good cause, to protect the respondent from (1) annoyance, (2) embarrassment, (3) oppression, or (4) undue burden or expense.[4] The order can be very broad or narrowly tailored to fit the situation.[5]

---

2. Fed. R. Civ. P. 26(c)(1); Rule 30(d)(3) motion to terminate or limit; Rule 45(d)(3)(A) provides for a motion to quash in the place of the production.

3. Fed. R. Civ. P. 26(c)(1).

4. *Id.*

5. The rule allows the court the flexibility by (1) forbidding the disclosure or discovery; (2) specifying the terms of disclosure or discovery including time, place, and allocation of expenses; (3) selecting a different discovery method; (4) forbidding inquiry into specific matters or limiting discovery or disclosure to certain matters; (5) identifying who may be present while discovery is conducted; (6) requiring the sealing of a deposition until order of the court; (7) requiring a trade secret or other confidential research, development, or commercial information not be revealed or revealed

If the motion is denied in whole or part, the court may order any party or person, on just terms, to provide or permit discovery.[6]

The recent case of *Singer v. Lagas*,[7] arose from a collision between a pickup truck and a tractor trailer. The plaintiff, a passenger in the pickup, filed a 30(B)(6)[8] deposition notice along with a Request for Production of Documents that listed 140 topics for deposition and requests for production of documents. Defendant trucking company moved for a protective order and stay in the deposition. The parties narrowed the scope of dispute, but the motions went forward to determine the remaining issues. Prior to analyzing the motions, the court summarized the concepts underlying protective orders. The court wrote:

> The decision to enter a protective order is within the court's broad discretion. Pursuant to Federal Rule of Civil Procedure 26(c), a "court may, for good cause, issue an order to protect a party or person from annoyance, embarrassment, oppression, or undue burden or expense[.]" Despite this broad discretion, "a protective order is only warranted when the movant demonstrates that protection is necessary under a specific category set out in Rule 26(c)." In addition, the party seeking a protective order bears the burden of establishing good cause. The moving party must make "a particular and specific demonstration of fact, as distinguished from stereotyped and conclusory statements." Even upon a showing of good cause, however, the Court also considers other factors that were or could have been presented by the party seeking discovery to determine whether the totality of the circumstances justifies the entry of a protective order. The court has broad discretion "to decide when a protective order is appropriate and what degree of protection is required." The Supreme Court has recognized "[t]he trial court is in the best position to weigh the fairly competing needs and interests of the parties affected by discovery. The unique character of the discovery process requires that the trial court have substantial latitude to fashion protective orders."[9]

---

only in a certain way; and (8) requiring parties to simultaneously file documents or information in sealed envelopes to be opened as the court directs.

6. Fed. R. Civ. P. (c)(2).

7. 2022 WL 1063715 (D. Kan. Apr. 8, 2022).

8. Fed. R. Civ. P. 30.

9. 2022 WL 1063715, at *1 (D. Kan. Apr. 8, 2022) (citations omitted). *See also* Waters v. AIG Claims, Inc., 338 F.R.D. 156 (M.D. Ala. 2020) ("[T]he party seeking the protective order must show good cause by demonstrating a particular need for protection" because "[b]road allegations of harm, unsubstantiated by specific examples or articulated reasoning, do not satisfy the Rule 26(c) test."); Trinos v. Quality Staffing Servs. Corp., 250 F.R.D. 696, 698 (S.D. Fla. 2008) (citing Cipollone v. Liggett Group, Inc., 785 F.2d 1108, 1121 (3d Cir. 1986)). The district court also has a duty to balance the interests of the parties. Farnsworth v. Procter & Gamble Co., 758 F.2d 1545, 1547 (11th Cir. 1985).

This passage describes the following, which should be kept in mind:

1. The court is the fact finder and is given broad latitude. Hence, you must present evidence to the court to support your motion. Attorney characterizations of specific facts may carry the day, but evidence in the form of affidavits or testimony that demonstrate a particular and specific fact is stronger, for example, the cost of responding to a specific discovery request and the basis of its calculation. Conclusory statements about the difficulty of responding to a request are not facts that will persuade the court.
2. Rule 26(c) lists specific items from which a party may be protected.
3. Protective orders can only be granted upon a showing of good cause and it is the moving party's burden to show that. Since the court has broad discretion, "good cause" can also be broad but the more categories from Rule 26(c) that you can fairly include in a motion, the better the chance of showing good cause.
4. While good cause is the basic consideration, it is not necessarily all that the court may consider. It can look at other factors that were or could have been presented by a party to determine whether in light of the totality of the circumstances a protective order is appropriate and the extent of any protection granted. This allows the court leeway to make its decision on factors other than just those presented by the parties, for example, the need for transparency in the courts or a strong public interest in the proceedings or the need for privacy or protection of proprietary interests.
5. Appeal from a decision on a motion for protective order will rarely succeed because the court is granted so much discretion.

II. Clawback Provisions

In federal courts before the 2006 amendments to Rule 26, the parties were on their own to develop procedures regarding inadvertently produced work-product material. This was usually done by agreed protective orders that included provisions for the segregation and return of the inadvertently produced work-product materials. This option is still available today but the federal rules, at least, have included guidance on this issue.[10]

Federal Rule of Civil Procedure 26(b)(5)(B) states that if information is produced that the producing party claims is privileged, the party may notify the

10. Fed. R. Civ. P. 26(b)(5). The Advisory Committee Notes indicated that it had been advised that the cost and delay in discovery had increased due to the work necessary to prevent waiver of work-product privilege. This coupled with volume of electronically kept data and the need to review all of it spurred the Committee to add a procedure for after produced claims of privilege.

receiving party of the claim and the basis for it.[11] The receiving party upon notice has duties and options. The receiving party is required to (1) promptly sequester, return, or destroy the material and any copies it has made; (2) must not use or disclose the material until the claim is resolved; (3) must take reasonable steps to retrieve the information if disclosed to others; and may (4) promptly present the material, under seal, to the court for a determination of the claim. The producing party must preserve the information until the claim is resolved.

The American Bar Association has also commented on inadvertent disclosures. ABA Model Rule of Professional Conduct 4.4(b) states that, "A lawyer who receives a document or electronically stored information relating to the representation of the lawyer's client and knows or reasonably should know that the document or electronically stored information was inadvertently sent shall promptly notify the sender." Different jurisdictions have differing approaches to inadvertent disclosure and rulings on whether it constitutes a waiver.[12]

State Compensation Ins. Fund v. WPS, Inc.[13] addressed the California requirements for an attorney receiving privileged materials inadvertently. The court wrote:

> When a lawyer who receives materials that obviously appear to be subject to an attorney-client privilege or otherwise clearly appear to be confidential and privileged and where it is reasonably apparent that the materials were provided or made available through inadvertence, the lawyer receiving such materials should refrain from examining the materials any more than is essential to ascertain if the materials are privileged, and shall immediately notify the sender that he or she possesses material that appears to be privileged. The parties may then proceed to resolve the situation by agreement or may resort to the court for guidance with the benefit of protective orders and other judicial intervention as may be justified. We do, however, hold that whenever a lawyer ascertains that he or she may have privileged attorney-client material that was inadvertently provided by another, that lawyer must notify the party entitled to the privilege of that fact.[14]

In essence this is a case made "clawback" provision.

Provisions in a protective order that stated an inadvertent disclosure did not waive the work product or the attorney client privilege and, further stating

---

11. *Id.* at 26(b)(5)(B).
12. See Chapter 6 regarding waiver.
13. 82 Cal. Rptr. 2d 799 (Cal. Ct. App. 1999).
14. *Id.* at 808.

that, after notice by the receiving party, the material disclosed would not be considered inadvertent if the producing party did not request the material back within ten days of notice have been used.[15] In *Radiance Aluminum*, the receiving party communicated evidence of fraud in discovery to the producing party who realized the reference was to privileged materials. In a letter within ten days of discovery of the inadvertent disclosure, the producing party demanded the materials destroyed under the case's protective order clawback provision. The receiving party refused and used the documents in a deposition a short time later. Producing party eventually issued two amended clawback letters and receiving party refused claiming the documents were not privileged and the clawback demand was tardy.

In determining that the clawback request was timely, the court pointed to the volume of documents produced and the three clawback letters, one within ten days, the second within five weeks, and the third within seven weeks of the first notice. The court determined that the producing party had complied with the requirements of both Federal Rule of Civil Procedure 26(b)(5)(B) and Federal Rule of Evidence 502(b)(3) in its efforts to clawback the documents.[16] The court noted that the receiving party's attorney's belief that the documents were not privileged was not a sufficient reason to justify failure to comply with the clawback request letter.[17] In granting the producing party's motion to compel, the court said, "The claw-back provision of Rule 26(b) cannot be read to allow the recipient to continue to use the disputed materials pending a finding of privilege by the Court."[18]

III. Interrogatories and Requests for Production

As previously mentioned, the burden to show that a claim of privilege is appropriate rests on the party who is claiming the privilege. The first step in proving that privilege applies typically takes place in the form of an objection to a discovery request and a statement that the response or material sought is requesting either attorney-client communications or work-product material and enough information regarding the specific document that the other parties or the court can make a determination whether or not the privilege has grounds to be applied. This is usually done in a form known as a privilege log. Failure to object and state the specific grounds for the objection can constitute waiver of the privilege.

---

15. Radiance Aluminum Fence, Inc. v. Marquis Metal Material, Inc., 335 F.R.D. 371, 374 (E.D. Mich. 2020).
16. *Id.* at 376.
17. *Id.* at 376–77.
18. *Id.*

IV. Privilege Logs

Federal Rule of Civil Procedure 26(b)(5) describes what a party must do when documents are withheld. The rule only recognizes two categories of documents as appropriate for withholding; privileged or trial preparation.

If documents are withheld, a party must do two things. First, the claim of privilege or trial preparation protection must be expressly made.[19] Second, they must describe the nature of the document, communication, or tangible thing, without revealing privileged or protected material, such that the description will enable the other parties to assess the claim.[20]

The claim and description are usually done in a privilege log, which itemizes the documents for ease of reference. The claim must be specific, that is, what privilege or protection is being asserted.[21] Failure to be specific can lead to waiver of the claim.[22] Additionally, all objections must be made at once. In a case where a party first asserted the attorney-client privilege and when that was deemed not to apply, asserted the work-product privilege, the court said, "the work product objection did not come into existence in any form until after the Court's finding that attorney-client privilege had been waived. That was tactical manipulation. Accordingly, the Court finds that Defendants have waived any work product protection over [the] documents."[23]

Failure to produce a log can result in waiver.[24] Failure to include a document can also result in a waiver.[25] Though it has also been held that, "'[i]t has been observed that 'only "flagrant" violations of these rules should result in a waiver of privilege.'"[26] "Whether waiver is warranted depends on such factors

19. Fed. R. Civ. P. 26(b)(5)(A)(i).

20. *Id.* at 26(b)(5)(A)(ii).

21. ("Broad allegations of harm, unsubstantiated by specific examples or articulated reasons, do not satisfy the Rule 26(c) test.") (citation omitted). Nei v. Travelers Home & Marine Ins. Co., 326 F.R.D. 652, 664 (D. Mont. 2018).

22. See Chapter 6 on Waiver.

23. Munguia-Brown v. Equity Residential, 337 F.R.D. 509, 515 (N.D. Cal. 2021).

24. Brown v. Barnes & Noble, Inc., 474 F. Supp. 3d 637, 646–47 (S.D.N.Y. 2019). However, here the court did not rule there was waiver because the parties had engaged in protracted negotiations over electronic discovery protocol and the remedy was to give additional discovery time.

25. Waiver of privilege may also occur where a party fails to list withheld documents on its privilege log. Pursuant to Federal Rule of Civil Procedure 26(b)(5)(A), a party who withholds documents on the account of privilege must "describe the nature of the documents, communications, or tangible things not produced or disclosed—and do so in a manner that, without revealing information itself privileged or protected, will enable other parties to assess the claim." Fed. R. Civ. P. 26(b)(5)(A). Cicel (Beijing) Science & Technology Co., Ltd. v. Misonix, Inc., 331 F.R.D. 218, 227 (E.D.N.Y. 2019). As in many cases, here the court allowed a supplemental privilege log to be filed. *Id.* at 236. *See also* Urban 8 Fox Lake Corp. v. Nationwide Affordable Housing Fund 4, LLC., 334 F.R.D. 149, 160 (N.D. Ill. 2020), Tex. R. Civ. P. 193.3(b) also describes what must be included in a claim of privilege.

26. Dey, L.P. v. Sepracor, Inc., 2010 WL 5094406, at *2 (S.D.N.Y. Dec. 8, 2010) (quoting Pern-America, Inc. v. Sunham Home Fashions, LLC, 2007 WL 3226156, at *2 (S.D.N.Y. Oct. 31, 2007)).

as the length of the delay, the willfulness of the transgression, and the harm to other parties."[27] Failure to include adequate description can also be waiver.[28]

In *Trumand v. City of Orem*,[29] the court listed the specific defects in the original privilege log and specifically told the attorney what to include, such as witnesses' identities, if the document pertained to a specific witness or the author of a document with handwritten notes. Such aid from the court is not common and the danger of waiver for failure to provide adequate information is real.

"The Ninth Circuit has rejected a *per se* waiver rule when documents are not identified in a privilege log. *See Burlington N. & Santa Fe Ry. Co. v. U.S. Dist. Court for Dist. of Mont.*, 408 F.3d 1142, 1149 (9th Cir. 2005). Factors to be considered in deciding whether waiver has occurred include the timeliness of objections and whether the parties and the Court have enough information to evaluate any work product claim"[30] (citation omitted).

A Florida court explained the procedure for the assertion of the privilege and how the privilege log is the initial proof:

> The first step in this process is to provide a privilege log. *See* S.D. Fla. L.R. 26.1(e)(2)(C). Sometimes, the privilege log will be sufficiently detailed to meet the proponent's burden. Typically, however, the log should be supported by "affidavit or other evidence identifying each document or communication claimed to be protected by the privilege and setting forth sufficient facts to allow a judicial determination as to whether the particular communication or document is, in fact, privileged." *Reed Hein*, 2019 WL 9091666, at *7 (citing *Purdee*, 2008 WL 11350099, at *1 and *Bridgewater*, 286 F.R.D. at 639 ("The party claiming the privilege must provide the court with underlying facts demonstrating the existence of the privilege, which may be accomplished by affidavit.")). Additionally, the party may request that the Court conduct an *in camera* review of the allegedly privileged documents; *in camera* review, however, "is not to be used as a substitute for a party's obligation to justify its withholding of documents." *CSX Transp. Inc. v. Admiral Ins. Co.*, No. 93-132-CIV-J-10, 1995 WL 855421, at *5 (M.D. Fla. July 20, 1995) (citing *Diamond State Ins. Co. v. Rebel Oil Co., Inc.*, 157 F.R.D. 691, 700 (D. Nev. 1994))."[31]

As the wording of Rule 26(b)(5) is somewhat broad as to what is an appropriate description of the material sought to be protected, there have been cases examining this. One example is *Federal Trade Commission v. Boehringer*

27. Universal Standard, Inc., v. Target Corp., 331 F.R.D. 80, 85 (S.D.N.Y. 2019) (citations omitted).
28. *Id.*
29. 362 F. Supp. 3d 1121, 1138–39 (2019).
30. Continental Circuits, LLC. v. Intel Corp., 435 F. Supp. 3d 1014, 1022 (D. Ariz. 2020).
31. Diamond Resorts U.S. Collection Dev., LLC v. US, 519 F. Supp. 3d 1184 (S.D. Fla. 2021).

Ingelheim Pharmaceuticals, Inc.,[32] where the FTC challenged Boehringer's claim of privilege. The court examined the privilege log, which Boehringer had offered to supplement—an offer not taken by the FTC. The court noted that Boehringer had supplemented the document descriptions with affidavits, "with specific explanations of its claims of privilege for each of the documents in the sample."[33] Boehringer's efforts were found adequate.

If responding to a subpoena with a claim of privilege, a privilege log is required. A privilege log under the subpoena rule[34] is the same as one under the general discovery rule.[35]

If the claim of privilege includes a work-product objection, the Sixth Circuit described what was necessary to show that the documents in question were made in anticipation of litigation. "[A] party may satisfy its burden of showing anticipation of litigation in any of the traditional ways in which proof is produced in pretrial proceedings such as affidavits made on personal knowledge, depositions, or answers to interrogatories, and that the showing can be opposed or controverted in the same manner."[36]

Commenting on the strength an affidavit adds to the proof of privilege, an Illinois court stated:

> Where an "undisputed affidavit . . . is specific and detailed to indicate that the documents were prepared in anticipation of litigation or trial," then the party claiming work product protection has met its burden. *Toledo Edison*, 847 F.2d 335, at 341. However, application of the privilege will be rejected where the "only basis" for the claim is an affidavit containing "conclusory statement [s]." *Guardsmark*, 206 F.R.D. at 210; *accord Bowne*, 150 F.R.D. at 474; *Senate of P.R. ex rel. Judiciary Comm. v. U.S. Dep't of Justice*, 823 F.2d 574, 586 (D.C. Cir. 1987) (rejecting party's "bare assertion" that documents were withheld in anticipation of litigation where facts of case raised "enough questions as to its accuracy to render it insufficient as a matter of law").[37]

Thus "bare assertions" and "conclusory statements" are not sufficient. Specific facts are needed.

Care must be taken in deciding what to include in a privilege log. Clearly, documents containing facts only do not qualify for the privilege and should

---

32. 892 F.3d 1264 (D.D.C. 2018).

33. *Id.* at 1270.

34. Fed. R. Civ. P. 45.

35. Texas Brine LLC & Occidental Chem. Corp., 879 F.3d 1224, n.3 (10th Cir. 2018).

36. United States v. Roxworthy, 457 F.3d 590, 597 (6th Cir. 2006) (citing *Toledo Edison v. G A Techs, Inc.*, 847 F.2d 335, 339, and *Bowne of New York City, Inc. v. AmBase Corp.*, 150 F.R.D. 465, 473 (S.D.N.Y. 1993) (internal quotes omitted) ("In requiring a party to prove the factual basis for its claims of privilege, the courts generally look to a showing based on affidavits or equivalent statements that address each document at issue.").

37. *Id.* at 597.

not be listed. Documents that are not created in anticipation of litigation or as part of an attorney-client communication should also not be included. Overly zealous inclusions can result in penalties. Of course, invalid claims of privilege are sanctionable, as they serve to withhold from the other side discoverable materials. But generally, "sanctions may only be imposed where a party displays wilfulness, [sic] bad faith, or fault." *Am. Nat. Bank & Tr. Co. of Chicago v. Equitable Life Assur. Soc. of U.S.*, 406 F.3d 867, 877–78 (7th Cir. 2005); *Langley v. Union Elec. Co.*, 107 F.3d 510, 514 (7th Cir. 1997)[38] (citation omitted).

V. Motions to Compel

Motions for an order compelling disclosure or a discovery response are authorized by Federal Rule of Civil Procedure 37(a) and its subsections.[39] Other selected state jurisdictions have a similar procedure.[40]

If there is a suspicion that the other party has not provided a complete privilege log or none at all, the usual procedure, after conferring with them, is to file a motion to compel. The motion can be to compel production, allow an inspection, compel a response, or to compel a more complete privilege log. Most courts require the parties to attempt to resolve or limit discovery disputes before a motion to compel is ripe for filing. This step is typically not optional and requires a conference of the parties' counsel.[41]

Motions to compel have been used to secure a variety of things. As one example, in Illinois, documents from an insured's insurance company regarding a claim against the insured,[42] a metallurgical report containing mathematical calculations, formulae, photographs, industry standards,[43] materials and communications with a party's attorney (owing to waiver) and presenting the party's attorney for deposition[44] have all been required to be produced or occur. Other states have required similar productions. The motion can also be used to compel a physical examination. Motions to compel have also been

38. Urban 8 Fox Lake Corp. v. Nationwide Affordable Housing Fund 4, LLC., 334 F.R.D. 149, 164 (N.D. Ill. 2020).

39. Fed. R. Civ. P. 37(a)(3)(B)(i) when a deponent fails to answer under Rules 30 or 31, (ii) when a corporation fails to make a designation under Rule 30(b)(6) or 31(a)(4), (iii) when a party fails to answer an interrogatory under Rule 33, or (iv) when a party fails to produce documents or fails to respond to a request or to permit an inspection under Rule 34.

40. New York's can be found at N.Y. C.P.L.R. 3124, Illinois' at Ill. S. Ct. Rule 219, Texas' at Tex. R. Civ. P. 215.1, and California's at Cal. St. Civ. Rule 3.1345.

41. For example, Federal Rule of Civil Procedure 37(a)(1) requires, "The motion must include a certification that the movant has in good faith conferred or attempted to confer with person or party failing to make disclosure or discovery in an effort to obtain I without court action."

42. Western States Ins. Co. v. O'Hara, 828 N.E.2d 842 (App. Ct. Ill. 2005).

43. Consolidation Coal Co. v. Bucyrus-Erie Co., 432 N.E.2d 250 (Ill. 1985).

44. Stewart Title Guar. Co. v. CVOF71, LLC, 2012 WL 6962893 (App. Ct. Ill. Jan. 30, 2012).

used to force a party to return or destroy inadvertently produced privileged materials.[45]

Even if the motion is not successful, as long as it is reasonable, the movant may be entitled to a reasonable attorney fee.[46]

VI. Choice of Law

Another procedural tool is a motion to apply, or a notice of the application of, a law different from that of the forum on the issue of privilege. Originally, privileges were viewed as procedural, so the default was to the forum's law, but the modern rule is to consider policy issues.[47] The older procedural view is still followed and can be found in decisions by courts in California and New York.[48]

A detailed treatment of this subject is found in Chapter 15 of this book. A few comments are appropriate here by way of introduction to the issue.

Federal Rule of Evidence 501 addresses choice of law in a confusing way, leading to four different interpretations:

> [I]n civil actions and proceedings, with respect to an element of a claim or defense as to which State law supplies the rule of decision, the privilege of a witness, person, government, State, or political subdivision thereof shall be determined in accordance with State law.

The four interpretations were discussed in *Magten Asset Management Corp. v. Northwestern Corp.*:[49]

---

45. Radiance Aluminum Fence, Inc. v. Marquis Metal Material, Inc., 335 F.R.D. 371, 374 (E.D. Mich. 2020).

46. Building a Better Redondo v. City of Redondo Beach, 2021 WL 632685, at *9–10 (Cal. App. Feb. 18, 2021) (unpublished and not citable in California).

47. McCormick on Evidence § 73.2 (8th ed.). For extended discussions of the subject, see Earl C. Dudley, Jr., *Federalism and Federal Rule of Evidence 501: Privilege and Vertical Choice of Law*, 82 Geo. L.J. 1981 (1994); Donald W. Price, *A Choice of Law Analysis of Evidentiary Privileges*, 50 La. L. Rev. 157 (1989); Olin Guy Wellborn III, *The Federal Rules of Evidence and the Application of State Law in the Federal Courts*, 55 Tex. L. Rev. 371 (1977).

48. Truckee Carson Irrigation Dist. v. Sierra Pac. Power Co., 2010 WL 4461659, at *2 (Cal. App. Nov. 9, 2010) (Although the court found a choice of law analysis unnecessary, it nevertheless stated, "in the issue of the attorney-client privilege, a choice of law approach is procedural not substantive" and "[t]he law is well settled that in procedural matters, the law of the forum state applies."); Ambac Assurance Corp. v. Nomura Credit & Capital, Inc., 175 A.D.3d 1165 (N.Y. App. 2019) (noting that New York courts routinely decide privilege issues based on the law of the place where the evidence will be introduced at trial, or the place where the discovery proceeding is located) (citations omitted). *But see* First Interstate Credit Alliance, Inc. v. Arthur Andersen & Co., 542 N.Y.S.2d 901, 902–03 (N.Y. Sup. Ct.) (without engaging in choice-of-law analysis per se, the court applied Maryland's accountant privilege).

49. 2007 WL 9811154 (D. Del. June 8, 2007).

> [T]he leading treatise on federal practice and procedure has stated that there are four possible interpretations of Rule 501's requirement that state law be applied to privilege disputes. These four options are: (a) that the privilege law of the state providing the rule of decision on the merits should apply (the position that the Committee Notes seem to suggest); (b) that the state privilege law of the forum should apply because issues of privilege and evidence are procedural issues; (c) that the courts should apply the forum state's conflict of laws doctrine as to the privilege issue, as opposed to the substantive law issue—in other words, a separate choice of law analysis should be performed with respect to privilege as opposed to the substantive law governing the merits of the litigation in the unlikely event that the factors affecting choice of law would be different for privilege than merits; and (d) the ambiguity in Rule 501 should simply lead the federal courts to rely on federal common law as to privilege issues. *See* C. Wright & K. Graham, *Federal Practice and Procedure*, § 5435 (2007 ed.).[50]

The complexities in the choice of law issues surrounding privileges often allow both sides to mount arguments for their position. The main point is that an attorney should always determine what choice of law analysis is adopted by the court where the issue arises. Chapter 15 provides detailed guidance on this issue.

Although this book refers to the work-product doctrine as a privilege for the sake of convenience, it is a qualified immunity, as stated in Chapter 3 of this book.[51] That has led courts to decide that questions of the applicability of protection for attorney work product are procedural in nature and thus depend on the forum's law.[52] Nevertheless, courts refer to choice of law issues when discussing the protection for work product, so there is room to argue choice of law on protection for work product in some jurisdictions and on some issues.[53]

50. *Id.* at *3.

51. *See* Jane Doe 1 v. Baylor Univ., 335 F.R.D. 476, 487 (W.D. Tex. 2020); Murphy v. Gorman, 271 F.R.D. 296, 311 (D.N.M. 2010).

52. *See* Philips N. Am. LLC v. Fitbit LLC, 2022 WL 252392, at *14 (D. Mass. Jan. 27, 2022); *accord* Gucci Am., Inc. v. Guess?, Inc., 271 F.R.D. 58, 73 & n.7 (S.D.N.Y. 2010) (although the court noted that choice-of-law analysis would yield the same answer).

53. *See* Raymer v. Zurich Am. Ins. Co., 2010 WL 11651883, at *3 (E.D. Ky. Apr. 5, 2010) (directing the parties to address choice-of-law issues regarding both privilege and work-product protection); Cozort v. State Farm Mut. Auto. Ins. Co., 233 F.R.D. 674, 676 (M.D. Fla. 2005) (applying state law when information was developed in state litigation) (discussed along with conflicting cases in Sanh Ngoc Do v. Allstate Property & Cas. Ins. Co., 2008 WL 11336323, at *2 (M.D. Fla. Dec. 11, 2008); Allianz Ins. Co. v. Guidant Corp., 869 N.E.2d 1042, 1048 (Ill. App. 2007) ("The principal issue on appeal is whether, under Illinois choice-of-law rules, the law of Illinois or the law of a foreign jurisdiction applies in determining whether the materials . . . are protected by the attorney-client privilege or the work-product doctrine.").

VII. Quashing Depositions and Subpoenas

While there are other grounds on which to seek to quash a subpoena, one of the grounds is that it, "requires disclosure of privileged or other protected matter, if no exception or waiver applies."[54] To show that matter is entitled to a claim of privilege, the objecting party must (1) expressly make the claim and (2) describe the nature of the withheld material, without revealing the privileged portion, with enough detail to allow the other parties (and the court) to assess the claim.[55] This can be done with a privilege log, affidavit, or testimony, but it must be specific.

Texas Brine LLC and Occidental Chemical Corp.,[56] involved a subpoena issued by Occidental to a nonparty consultant, Frontier International Group, LLC, which had done work for Texas Brine on an emergency basis and for litigation support in a negligence case due to the appearance of a sinkhole that was alleged to have damaged property. Texas Brine filed a motion to quash. Texas Brine did not produce a privilege log and asserted only a blanket claim of privilege including both attorney-client and work-product privileges.[57] The court issued an order requiring Texas Brine to submit a privilege log for any communications it believed were privileged and granted the motion and denied the motion in part.[58] Frontier produced over 20,000 documents but withheld some and produced a privilege log for those.

The Tenth Circuit noted that the lower court, though it did not have to, granted Texas Brine a second chance to produce a privilege log, but instead it appealed, effectively arguing it did not have to produce either privileged documents or a privilege log. The court stated, "Why Texas Brine believes it can assert a blanket claim of privilege over its communications with Frontier without complying with Fed. R. Civ. P. 45(e)(2)(A) or Fed. R. Civ. P. 26(b)(5)(A) is beyond us."[59] As a result, the court denied Texas Brine's appeal as being untimely because it had an insufficient record, specifically, a privilege log, to determine the appropriateness of the lower court's order.[60]

The Advisory Committee's Note to Rule 45 also mentions the need for privilege logs, the waiver effect of failing to provide one, and the possibility of being in contempt[61] "The operative language is mandatory and, although the

54. Fed. R. Civ. P. 45(d)(3)(A)(iii).
55. *Id.* at 45(e)(2)(A).
56. Texas Brine, LLC & Occidental Chem. Corp., 879 F.3d 1224 (10th Cir. 2018).
57. *Id.* at 1226–27.
58. *Id.* at 1228.
59. *Id.* at 1229–30.
60. *Id.* at 1230.
61. ("A person claiming a privilege or protection who fails to provide adequate information about the privilege or protection claim to the party seeking the information is subject to an order to show cause why the person should not be held in contempt under subdivision [(g)].") Advisory Committee Notes, subdiv. d (1991).

rule does not spell out the sufficiency requirement in detail, courts consistently have held that the rule requires a party resisting disclosure to produce a document index or privilege log."[62] A party that fails to submit a privilege log is deemed to waive the underlying privilege claim.[63] While neither Rule 26(b)(3) nor Rule 45 require an affidavit to support the claims of privilege in a log, providing the court with such supportive material could help persuade the court of the viability of the privilege claim.

A recent class action ERISA[64] case involving a subpoena to an attorney examined under what conditions an attorney may be forced to give a deposition when privileges were claimed. In *Gamache v. Hogue*,[65] plaintiffs filed an action against the administrators of their retirement plan. Plaintiffs issued a subpoena to their employer's attorney, Moore. Moore contended that none of his work involved the retirement plan or its administrators or its administration.

The plaintiffs had written to the administrators requesting ownership information and Moore responded on behalf of the administrators. The court noted that nonparties may be compelled to testify under Federal Rule of Civil Procedure 45, if they have relevant nonprivilege matter and the Federal Rules are to be construed liberally to allow robust discovery.[66] While the deposition of another party's attorney can invite delay, disruption, harassment, and possible disqualification of the attorney, there is nothing in the Federal Rules that prevents the taking of another party's attorney's deposition as long as the deposition seeks only relevant nonprivileged information.[67] The court found that the attorney-client privilege existed between Moore and the administrators but as he was giving legal advice to plan administrators in the execution of their plan duties, the common law fiduciary exception applied.[68] After balancing all interests, including the claim of undue burden raised by Moore, the court denied the motion to quash.

VIII. Motions in Limine

If privileged material or communications are revealed during discovery, a party may consider a motion in limine to prevent or limit the use of the material during trial. As with all motions, the burden rests on the party seeking the relief and if the motion is to exclude or limit evidence, the party has the burden to show that evidence is "irrelevant or should be excluded."[69] Once again,

62. *In re* Grand Jury Subpoena, 274 F.3d 563, 575 (1st Cir. 2001); *see also* Dorf & Stanton Commc'ns, Inc. v. Molson Breweries, 100 F.3d 919, 923 (Fed. Cir. 1996).

63. *In re* Grand Jury Subpoena, 274 F.3d at 576.

64. Employee Retirement Income Security Act, 29 U.S.C. §§ 1001 *et seq.* (1994).

65. ___ F. Supp. 3d____, 112 Fed. R. Ser. 3d 744, 2022 WL 989483 (M.D. Ga. Mar. 30, 2022).

66. *Id.* at *2 (citing Akridge v. Alfa Mut. Ins. Co., 1 F.4th 1271, 1276–77 (11th Cir. 2021)).

67. *Id.* at *3.

68. *Id.* at *6. See Chapter 5 on exceptions.

69. Samuel v. Century Hill, Inc., 2021 WL 1564723, at *2 (Sup. Ct. V.I. Apr. 14, 2021).

generalized statements regarding the material or communication's privileged status should be avoided. Specific items of evidence and the harm anticipated from their disclosure should be included in the motion, if necessary, under seal, to help the court see the totality of the circumstances. "In limine motions are designed to facilitate the management of a case, generally by deciding difficult evidentiary issues in advance of trial."[70] Specifically, they, "allow the trial court to rule in advance of trial on the admissibility and relevance of certain forecasted evidence."[71]

Motions in limine can be effective. In *Feinwachs v. Minnesota Hospital Association*,[72] District Court Judge Wright evaluated a magistrate judge's order finding that communications between a party and his counsel were not protected under work-product privilege because the attorney-client privilege, which also had been asserted, was found to be waived because District Court Judge Tunheim found disclosure to an adverse party. As such, the magistrate judge found that the law of the case was determinative. Judge Wright wrote that because Judge Tunheim had not specifically ruled on the work-product privilege claim presented and deferred a ruling, that the law of the case doctrine was not controlling.[73] As the communication in the contested material was clearly done in anticipation of litigation and because the disclosure was not intended, as Eighth Circuit case law required, the privilege was not waived and the materials were protected.[74]

Because, "a trial court's ruling on a motion *in limine* is preliminary and may change depending on what actually happens in trial"[75] a party must be ready to re-argue its position at trial.[76]

IX. Pretrial Orders

Federal Rule of Civil Procedure 26(f)(3)(D) directs the parties to discuss in their discovery conference whether or not any agreement made pursuant to Federal Rule of Evidence 502, regarding the disclosure of privileged material during trial or other hearing, should be included in a court's order, such as the pretrial

70. Tung v. Chicago Title Co., 278 Cal. Rptr. 3d 182, 199–200, 63 Cal. App. 5th 734 (Ct. of App. Cal. 2021).

71. Samuel v. Century Hill, Inc., 2021 WL 1564723, at *2 (Sup. Ct. V.I. Apr. 14, 2021).

72. 2019 WL 4298085 (D. Minn. Sept. 11, 2019).

73. *Id.* at *3.

74. *Id.* at *7. Judge Wright also wrote, "Under Eighth Circuit law, a party must *intend* for an adversary to see work product in order to waive the work product protection through disclosure. Grundacker v. Unisys Corp., 151 F.3d 842, 848 (8th Cir. 1998) ("Although disclosure to an adversary ordinarily waives work product protection, there must be an intention that the opposing party see the work product.")."

75. Samuel v. Century Hill, Inc., 2021 WL 1564723, at *2 (Sup. Ct. V.I. Apr. 14, 2021).

76. Oral motions in limine have been allowed. Wilkinson v. British Airways, 740 N.Y.S.2d 294, 296, 292 A.D. 2d 263 (Sup. Ct. N.Y. 2002) ("there is no requirement that an *in limine* motion be made in writing and be in accordance with CPLR 2214.").

order. This is an opportunity for the parties to discuss and plan protections for both the intentional and inadvertent disclosure of privileged material at trial or during testimonial discovery. Federal Rule of Evidence 502 specifically limits the effect of an agreement regarding privileged material only to the parties to the agreement unless it is incorporated into a court's order.[77] If a broader scope of confidentiality is needed, a court's order is a possibility.

X. Objections

Objections to discovery requests for privileged material are allowed in discovery and at trial. In fact, it is the objection that starts the evaluation process for claims of privilege. An objection to an interrogatory must, "be stated with specificity. Any ground not stated in a timely objection is waived unless the court, for good cause, excuses the failure."[78]

An objection to a request for production of a document must, "state with specificity the grounds for objecting to the request, including the reasons."[79] It must also state whether or not any materials are being withheld on the basis of that objection.[80]

Similarly, at trial, in order to preserve an error for appeal, a party must, "timely object . . . and state the specific ground."[81] Thus in all three instances, the claim of privilege must be raised as the grounds for objection, along with any other objections, or it can be deemed waived.

XI. Mandamus

Mandamus may be sought to challenge a court's ruling on some discovery orders.[82] However, it is an extraordinary writ and the success rate is not high.

Regarding the use of mandamus, the U.S. Supreme Court has said, "this Court has required that a party seeking issuance have no other adequate means to attain the relief he desires, and that he satisfy the 'burden of showing that [his] right to issuance of the writ is clear and indisputable.'"[83]

77. Fed. R. Evid. 502(e).

78. Fed. R. Civ. P. 33(b)(4).

79. *Id.* 34(b)(2)(B).

80. *Id.* 34(b)(2)(C).

81. Fed. R. Evid. 103(a)(1).

82. "It is generally inappropriate to review discovery orders by mandamus. However, mandamus may be appropriate where a discovery order 'raises a novel and important question of power to compel discovery, or . . . reflects substantial uncertainty and confusion in the district courts.' 16 Charles Alan Wright, Arthur R. Miller & Edward H. Cooper, *Federal Practice and Procedure: Jurisdiction and Related Matters* § 3935.3 (2d ed. 1996) (citing Schlagenhauf v. Holder, 379 U.S. 104, 111, 85 S. Ct. 234, 13 L. Ed. 2d 152 (1964)." *In re* MSTG, Inc., 675 F.3d 1337, 1341 (Fed. Cir. 2012).

83. Allied Chem. Corp. v. Daiflon, 449 U.S. 33, 35–36 (1980) (citations omitted).

> In a mandamus action in which petitioner seeks to have discovery orders involving a claim of privilege reviewed, we have held that review is appropriate when: (1) disclosure of the allegedly privileged or confidential information renders impossible any meaningful appellate review of the claim of privilege or confidentiality; and (2) the disclosure involves questions of substantial importance to the administration of justice.[84]

While showing that a lack of meaningful review may exist because of the immediacy of a discovery response and the time to appellate review is distant, a party must also show how their appeal relates to questions of substantial importance to the administration of justice[85] to qualify for mandamus relief.

In a discovery dispute between Alcon Laboratories and Johns Hopkins over alleged patent infringement, Alcon sought a writ of mandamus to overturn a magistrate judge's ruling. The appellate court noted:

> Mandamus may be used in "extraordinary circumstances" to correct an unlawful disclosure of privileged communications. *Mohawk Indus., Inc. v. Carpenter*, 558 U.S. 100, 111 (2009). That standard is an exacting one, requiring petitioner to establish that there are no adequate alternative legal channels through which it may obtain the same relief and that the disclosure order "'amount[s] to a judicial usurpation of power or a clear abuse of discretion,' or otherwise works a manifest injustice." *Id.* at 110 (citing *Cheney v. U.S. Dist. Court for the Dist. of Columbia*, 542 U.S. 367, 390 (2004)); *see also Kerr v. U.S. Dist. Court for the N. Dist. of Cal.*, 426 U.S. 394, 403 (1976).[86]

Alcon asserted an advice of counsel defense and produced two opinion letters and designated their in-house counsel as their only witness on the issue of mental state. In response, Johns Hopkins filed a motion to compel to which Alcon objected and produced only a privilege log. The magistrate judge found for Johns Hopkins but only ordered Alcon to produce the specific documents identified by Johns Hopkins and those documents on the privilege log which concerned advice of counsel.[87] The appellate court found no abuse of discretion in the lower court's ruling and denied mandamus.

84. *In re* Qwest Commc'ns Int'l, Inc., 450 F.3d 1179, 1182–83 (10th Cir. 2006) (mandamus denied).

85. Issues of first impression, such as determining whether or not there is settlement negotiation privilege *In re* MSTG, Inc., 675 F.3d 1337 (Fed. Cir. 2012); and maintenance of the attorney client privilege up to its proper limits has substantial importance to the administration of justice. *In re* Spalding Sports Worldwide, Inc., 203 F.3d 800, 804 (Fed. Cir. 2000).

86. *In re* Alcon Labs., Inc., 2018 WL 7485446, at *1 (Fed. Cir. Feb. 14, 2018) (mandamus denied).

87. *Id.*

XII. Practice Tips for Work-Product Disputes

All discovery disputes involving the assertion of or challenge to the work-product privilege are decided by a fact finder. This means there is a need for evidence. If challenged, the initial burden to show the privilege is appropriate falls on the party asserting the privilege.[88]

To show that the privilege applies, a party must show that (1) materials, typically documents or tangible items, (2) have been created in anticipation of or in response to litigation, (3) by a party or party's representative, such as an attorney, consultant, insurer. Additionally, under Federal Rule of Civil Procedure 26(b)(3)(i) and (ii), materials may be discoverable if they fulfill the requirements of Rule 26(b)(1), and a party shows it (1) has a substantial need for the materials to prepare its case, and (2) it cannot, without undue hardship, obtain the substantial equivalent by other means. The following contains a few thoughts on these elements.

A. Materials

1. Defending the Privilege

To identify documents or other tangible items to be eligible for the privilege they must be listed somewhere, typically in a privilege log. Items left out of a privilege log, or for which the work-product privilege has not been listed as reason for non-production, may have the privilege waived. A presenting attorney must be careful to include both the item and the claim in the privilege log.

Additionally, there must be enough of a description of the item that both opposing parties and discovery dispute fact finders have adequate information to be able to determine if this item is the kind that may be subject to a claim of privilege. Generalized identifications, such as "claim file" or "investigation," are likely not enough. Such a lack of detailed description of the item is likely to require supplementation or possibly a waiver of the claim. Remember: the privilege log is your first piece of evidence in any discovery dispute about the privilege; as such, you need to make the entry detailed enough that a fact finder can easily determine the nature of the item. Unlike the limited stating of an objection in court, here, evidence is being offered and a detailed objection should be helpful.

Consider showing the draft privilege log to another attorney not involved in the matter to review the log entries to see if they can determine the nature of the item.

---

88. "The party asserting the privilege 'me[ets] its burden of providing a factual basis for asserting the privileges when it produce[s] a detailed privilege log stating the basis of the claimed privilege for each document in question, together with an accompanying explanatory affidavit of its . . . counsel.'" Murphy v. Kmart Corp., 259 F.R.D. 421, 428 (S.D. 2009) (citations omitted).

2. Attacking the Privilege

First, remember that what you may be entitled to involves the facts surrounding the case. Attorney evaluations, strategies, and trial preparation are only rarely disclosed, and then because there is a factual element to them. Pursuing nonfactual attorney-created material is not justified except under highly unique circumstances.

If the need to challenge the work-product privilege arises, the usual method is by filing a motion to compel. Most jurisdictions have procedural steps a party must go through before the contest is ripe for filing. After the initial evaluation of the responder's discovery responses is made and if found wanting, every jurisdiction requires an attempt by the parties to resolve any issues before bringing them to the court's attention. The extent of the effort can vary by jurisdiction, but, at a minimum, it requires notice to the responder that their discovery response is inadequate and how it is inadequate. Most jurisdictions require a conference between the parties and many require an in-person conference. Most jurisdictions allow the responder to explain their response or to alter it before a motion to compel may be filed. Failure to conduct the required conference can result in a denial of the motion on procedural grounds.

If a motion to compel is filed and the responding party can make a *prima facie* showing that the materials are privileged, then the burden to show that they are not or that the privilege has been waived falls to the party seeking their disclosure.

If a party becomes aware that the responder has left out materials from the privilege log, the responder may have waived the privilege and, in challenging the privilege, this should be raised. If there is evidence of missing files, like an underwriting file in an insurance breach case, and there is an inadequate explanation as to why they are missing, such evidence should be included in the motion to compel and a waiver argument should be included. Generalized or overly broad designation by category of the nature of the documents requested is little help to a fact finder and the lack of detailed description of the claimed privilege documents suggests inadequate or faulty review by the producing party. If the fact finder is shown several examples of vague material description, the privilege may be waived or the responder may have to supplement their privilege log.

Similarly, boilerplate or oft-repeated identically worded objections, without adequate detail as to the characteristics of each document that establish why the privilege might apply, can be used as evidence to show lack of adequate review and overly broad claims of privilege. Overly broad claims of privilege can often make all the claims suspect in the fact finder's eyes.

Though not commonly raised, materials that are not tangible, such as oral questions and responses to an attorney's or investigator's questions, can be claimed to be outside the work-product privilege under a strict construction of the discovery rules. If there is a reason to believe such material exists, the argument can be made that they fall outside the privilege.

Since the fact finder needs evidence, a detailed explanation of why it is suspected that materials may be missing is necessary. This may include evidence from an investigator, the party, an expert, or even an attorney in the form of an affidavit about what seems to be missing. If there are materials that infer other materials exist but are not on the privilege log, they can be identified in an affidavit and included as exhibits. The initial response by a party to a discovery request is their first best chance to object to the production of material based on work-product privilege, and failure to do so can be a waiver of that privilege.

B. Because of Litigation

1. Defending the Privilege

There are three main time periods in determining whether material has been developed because of litigation. In reverse chronological order, they are after suit has been filed, post-incident but pre-suit, and pre-incident.

The easiest to apply is when the lawsuit is filed. Materials developed after suit has been filed are generally considered to be because of litigation.

Because your privilege log is your first piece of evidence, if the material was created after the initiation of the suit, listing both the date the item was created and stating as part of the objection that it was created after the suit was filed will help the fact finder identify the item as privileged. Some states allow some time to pass after filing to achieve service on a defendant. Documents created in this time period, that is, before service, may require additional explanation on the privilege log to show the defendant had knowledge of the filing even though service had not yet been achieved or because the item falls into the second main time period. The additional evidence may be an affidavit from the defendant regarding their knowledge of the filing of the suit prior to service.

The next major time period is after the incident giving rise to the lawsuit but before filing. Once again, the statements in your privilege log will be used as evidence by any fact finder. As such, the date of the creation of the item and its author and, if applicable, its recipient needs to be clearly shown. Also, additional explanation about the defendant's state of knowledge regarding the anticipation of a suit being filed, or information about when an attorney was hired, or an explanation that the item was created at the direction of the attorney, or that it contains evaluative or strategy information are all helpful to the fact finder. Generalized statements that are repetitive are not as convincing as individualized statements regarding a specific document's creation. If challenged, an affidavit from the attorney or client including the creation details can also be helpful.

The last major time period is prior to any specific incident actually occurring. This period often includes things such as an investigation into a party's policies and adherence to them; often in employment, discrimination, or sexual misconduct cases. There are also expert reviews of products, safety procedures, and policies. These are the most difficult to shield because they often appear to be done as part of an organization's effort to be law and regulation complaint or to improve its products or performance. Once again, adequate description in the objection of the time of document creation, its purpose and attorney involvement, especially outside attorney involvement, is an aid to the fact finder. There may also be a strong attorney-client privilege basis for nondisclosure and that needs to be stated in the objection as well.

Some documents are created for more than one purpose: a business purpose and a litigation purpose.[89] The more evidence presented to show that the major reason was one of litigation, the better the chance a fact finder will determine the material to be protected.

2. Attacking the Privilege

Showing that the privilege does not apply after the lawsuit has been filed is difficult. Typically, this might occur if the material is shared with a nonparty who is not involved with the suit or if the material is put at issue by a party, such as a claim or defense in a summary judgment proceeding. Additional ways may include a party sharing the material with a regulating entity, using it for another purpose, such as public relations, or presenting it during the deposition of their own or an opposing party's expert.

Showing that one of these situations exists, again by affidavit or transcript, gives the fact finder the evidence they need to determine that the privilege has been waived.

In the next major time period, after the incident but before suit is filed, it is often less difficult to show that materials were prepared for a purpose other than litigation. A common example is facts surrounding an accident contained in witness statements collected by an insurance adjuster. It is the requirement and business of an insurer to investigate claims, and, even if directed to do so by an attorney, the information collected is usually not privileged. The identity of witnesses is another example. Showing that the materials were created in the course of business can be done through affidavits by your experts or witness testimony transcripts.

If you become aware of materials created before the incident triggering the lawsuit, a strong claim that they are not protected by work-product privilege can be made. A typical example is an outside investigation carried out by a law firm or outside engineering company to determine an organization's adherence to it policies. Here testimony of a party is a powerful piece of evidence for a fact finder to consider. Having a party explain the purpose behind an

---

89. *See* Goosby v. Branch Banking & Trust Co., 309 F. Supp. 3d 1223, 1229–35 (S.D. Fla. 2018) (discussing the dual-purpose doctrine versus the primary-purpose doctrine, both of which are discussed, along with other tests in Chapter 3).

investigation that occurs prior to any litigation may show that the material was not developed "because of" litigation. If such testimony is not yet available, showing the time periods involved places a heavy burden on the proponent claiming the privilege to show how litigation is involved.

C. By an Attorney, Agent, or Representative of a Party

1. Defending the Privilege

The more distant the creator of the materials sought to be protected is from a party or its attorney, the greater the chance the materials will not be protected. The party seeking the protection of the privilege must provide enough information to the fact finder such that they can clearly see the connection to or direction from the party or its attorney to create the material in question. Here documentary evidence such as emails, letters, and reports can help establish the chain of authority from client to individual that supports the closeness of relationship or control necessary to establish the privilege. If the privilege log is not detailed enough, affidavits or testimony from the client, the attorney, and the creator of the document regarding the direction and control they exercised over the creator of the material is necessary.

2. Attacking the Privilege

Conversely, when attacking the privilege, evidence that the creator of the materials acted on their own authority, or in keeping with a party's policies, or without contact from a party or a party's attorney is the most useful. A non-witness accountant, insurance adjuster, nonparty entity, or nonparty witness are a few examples. Showing the distance of the relationship or the fact that there is no relationship between the document creator and the party or its attorney supports the view that privilege is not appropriately extended to their materials.

D. Substantial Need

1. Defending the Privilege

If faced with a claim of substantial need, a party must show the court why the need is either not "substantial" or not really a need at all. A focus on the elements of the case and an explanation as to why the materials do not support those elements, even if produced, is helpful to the court. If similar but non-protected material has been previously produced, a discussion of how those materials satisfy any need the seeker of material has is good to include.

An emphasis in argument on how one of the major goals of the work-product privilege is to prevent freeloading and a demonstration of how the seeker may obtain the materials in some other way will both have some persuasive value. An emphasis, if appropriately made, as to how the material is inextricably intertwined with attorney evaluation, strategy, and thoughts may also help the court understand the full circumstances surrounding the claim of need. Showing the court that the case can continue without these materials can destroy the need claim.

2. Attacking the Privilege

When seeking materials that are claimed to be privileged but that may be discoverable, typically fact-related information, the party seeking the materials may be entitled to their disclosure even though the materials would normally qualify for protection. Under the Federal Rules of Civil Procedure and most states' rules, materials that are not attorney thoughts, strategy, evaluations, etc., may be disclosed upon a showing by the seeker that there is a substantial need for the materials to prepare its case. If the protection of the privilege is found by the court, evidence of the substantial need for the materials for case preparation needs to be shown.

This can be done by a detailed showing to the court of how the specific material in question supports a contention or element of the theory of recovery or addresses an element of a defense raised by the holder of the materials. It must also show why it is necessary for this specific case. Fishing expeditions or attempts to garner materials for another or different case are outside the scope of this requirement. Testimony, affidavits, and witness statements may also be used to show why the evidence is crucial to the case, and an explanation of why the case cannot continue without it are persuasive to the courts. If the case can continue without these materials, the court is not likely to require their production, so a clear case of the "substantial need" must be made.

E. Undue Hardship

1. Defending the Privilege

Because "undue hardship" is hard to show, arguments showing how the time, resources, other procedural or discovery mechanisms available to the seeker of the materials are plentiful and unused should be brought to the court's attention. Any contradictory facts regarding resources, expert's bias, or misjudgments regarding time and expenses would also be helpful. Showing easy availability of witnesses and any failure by the seeker to fully document and support their undue hardship claim should be highlighted. Again, the U.S. Supreme Court's comments in *Hickman* about an attorney's right to prepare their case in privacy and the anti-freeloading comments in the case law should be included.

2. Attacking the Privilege

Showing "undue hardship" is not an easy task. However, the court may be persuaded if the seeker of the materials can show that all the holders of the materials are controlled by the defendant and that extensive, and a case-inappropriate amount of discovery, such as third-party subpoenas, would have to be undertaken to gain the materials. Additionally, an affidavit or testimony from an expert explaining the necessary work and expense that would have to be done to gain the information could be helpful. Likewise, an accountant may be able to show the court the types and kinds of unreasonable expense that would have to be expended to gain the information.

In certain cases, testimony or an affidavit from the plaintiff as to their financial condition may be an appropriate piece of evidence. Rule 26(b)(1) also includes considerations of the parties' access to relevant information and the parties' resources, which could be mentioned. And any argument should include, somewhere, a mention of Federal Rule of Civil Procedure 1, which calls for the speedy and inexpensive resolution of all cases and why that should be applied to this case specifically.

F. Substantial Equivalent

1. Defending the Privilege

As with substantial need, showing the court that other similar evidence is available to the requesting party can defeat the substantial equivalent element. This can be done through expert affidavit or testimony regarding how substitute material could be used to acquire equivalent knowledge. Additionally, arguments showing the discovery alternatives available to the requester or why the information sought is generic can also be utilized. Because it's hard to show a negative, an emphasis on the burden undertaken by the requester to show that other discovery material or testimony is not the substantial equivalent can be used.

2. Attacking the Privilege

This is also a hard requirement for the seeker of the materials to overcome, but it can be done. Success has most usually occurred when the evidence has been temporally short, or isolated from the seeker. Examples include (1) photographs taken immediately after an accident, even at the direction of an attorney, showing the conditions at the time, which may have since changed; (2) access to machinery or processes being limited because of control by the other party; (3) a party's testing of products immediately after an incident and subsequent modification, making a similar testing not comparable; or (4) a party's control of a product or process known only to them, as in the case of specialized machines or secret processes. Showing an inability to recreate or a specialized uniqueness in the material sought helps the court understand why there is no substantial equivalent.

Once again, an affidavit or testimony showing a sequence of events or circumstances that make the evidence sought unique and not reproducible can fulfill this requirement. Expert testimony or affidavits regarding specialized products or processes and the inability to reproduce tests or generate data could also help the court understand why no substantial equivalent exists or can be obtained reasonably.

XIII. Conclusion

Because there are many ways to both attack and defend privileges and the court decisions are necessarily fact dependent, at least a few of the arguments and procedural tools mentioned can be used to urge your position.

CHAPTER 8

The Attorney-Client Privilege in Organizations

DOUGLAS R. RICHMOND

I. Introduction

Organizational clients, like individuals, are entitled to assert the attorney-client privilege concerning communications within its scope. For example, corporations,[1] partnerships,[2] limited liability companies,[3] governmental

1. Jacobson Warehouse Co. v. Schnuck Mkts., Inc., 13 F.4th 659, 676 (8th Cir. 2021) (applying Missouri law); Affiniti Colo., LLC v. Kissinger & Fellman, P.C., 461 P.3d 606, 614 (Colo. App. 2019); Nemours Found. v. Martinez Arroyo, 292 So. 3d 6, 8 (Fla. Dist. Ct. App. 2019); St. Simons Waterfront, LLC v. Hunter, Maclean, Exley & Dunn, P.C., 746 S.E.2d 98, 103 (Ga. 2013); Harris Mgmt., Inc. v. Coulombe, 151 A.3d 7, 15 (Me. 2016); Att'y Gen. v. Facebook, Inc., 164 N.E.3d 873, 887 n.12 (Mass. 2021); Frank v. Morgans Hotel Group Mgmt. LLC, 116 N.Y.S.3d 889, 891 (Sup. Ct. 2020) (quoting Rossi v. Blue Cross & Blue Shield of Greater N.Y., 540 N.E.2d 703, 704–05 (N.Y. 1989)); Hermanson v. Multi-Care Health Sys., Inc., 475 P.3d 484, 488 (Wash. 2020); State *ex rel.* HCR Manorcare, LLC v. Stucky, 776 S.E.2d 271, 282 (W. Va. 2015).

2. *See, e.g., In re* Bieter Co., 16 F.3d 929, 935–40 (8th Cir. 1994) (applying the attorney-client privilege to communications with a partnership's independent consultant).

3. *See, e.g.,* Carpenters Pension Tr. v. Lindquist Fam. LLC, 2014 WL 1569195, at *3–4 (N.D. Cal. Apr. 18, 2014) (applying corporate attorney-client privilege law to an LLC); *In re* Haynes, 577 B.R. 711, 736–37 (Bankr. E.D. Tenn. 2017) (applying the subject matter test for the privilege to an LLC); *In re* Newman, 500 B.R. 328, 330 (Bankr. D. Conn. 2013) (stating that an LLC may claim the attorney-client privilege); Fla. Marlins Baseball Club, LLC v. Certain Underwriters at Lloyd's London Subscribing to Policy No. 893/HC/97/9096, 900 So. 2d 720, 721 (Fla. Dist. Ct. App. 2005) (upholding the privilege with respect to an LLC's in-house lawyer).

bodies,[4] and private associations[5] can all invoke the privilege. Assuming a communication otherwise qualifies as privileged, it does not matter whether the lawyer involved is in-house or outside counsel.[6]

As artificial constructs, organizations cannot speak; their ability to communicate depends on employees who are empowered to act on their behalf. It is therefore important for lawyers to understand who among the entity's employees speaks for it, so that communications between the entity's lawyers and those employees may be protected against discovery by third parties under the entity's attorney-client privilege. And, as organizations experience the inevitable turnover in their workforces, it is essential to understand when, if ever, the attorney-client privilege attaches to communications between the organization's lawyers and its former employees.

Of course, those are not the only attorney-client privilege issues that arise when a lawyer represents an organization. Whether the privilege attaches to in-house lawyers' communications is a concern where those lawyers also dispense business advice. The application of the attorney-client privilege to communications between members of a corporate family may pivot on the privilege test a court applies. Where a corporation merges or sells its assets to another entity, post-transaction control of the predecessor corporation's privilege can become a hotly contested issue. When a corporation dissolves, the ability to thereafter invoke or waive its attorney-client privilege can be a flashpoint. Finally, the application of the attorney-client privilege to partnerships, limited liability companies, and joint ventures is a vital issue as businesses increasingly choose these organizational forms over incorporation, yet there is relatively little law on-point.

---

4. *See, e.g.*, Sandra T.E. v. S. Berywn Sch. Dist. 100, 600 F.3d 612, 621 (7th Cir. 2010) (explaining the importance of recognizing the attorney-client privilege where government agencies are concerned); Banks v. Off. of the Senate Sergeant-at-Arms, 222 F.R.D. 1, 3 (D.D.C. 2004) (proclaiming "no doubt" that government agencies may invoke the privilege); Wood v. Super Court of San Diego County, 259 Cal. Rptr. 3d 798, 808 (Ct. App. 2020) ("It is well-settled that a public entity enjoys an attorney-client relationship with its lawyers and the attorney-client privilege protects communications made in the course of that relationship."); Affiniti Colo., LLC v. Kissinger & Fellman, P.C., 461 P.3d 606, 614 (Colo. App. 2019) (noting that the privilege applies to public entities); Suffolk Constr. Co. v. Div. of Cap. Asset Mgmt., 870 N.E.2d 33, 38 (Mass. 2007) (stating that communications between governmental entities and their counsel are protected under normal attorney-client privilege rules); Nelson v. City of Billings, 412 P.3d 1058, 1068 (Mont. 2018) (stating that the attorney-client privilege "protect[s] governmental agencies and employees like any other party to civil litigation"); Paxton v. City of Dallas, 509 S.W.3d 247, 260 (Tex. 2017) (explaining the importance of the privilege in the governmental context).

5. *See, e.g.*, Fouts v. Breezy Point Condo. Ass'n, 851 N.W.2d 845, 849 (Wis. Ct. App. 2014) (stating that a private association may invoke the attorney-client privilege in a case involving a condominium association).

6. F.T.C. v. Boeringher Ingelheim Pharms., Inc., 892 F.3d 1264, 1267 (D.C. Cir. 2018); Cormack v. United States, 117 Fed. Cl. 392, 397 (Fed. Cl. 2014).

II. Organizational Clients and the Attorney-Client Privilege

The essential question in many privilege cases involving corporations is whether lawyers' communications with corporate employees are protected by the corporation's attorney-client privilege. It is therefore an appropriate place to start a discussion of the attorney-client privilege in the organizational setting.

In deciding whether communications between lawyers for an organization and employees of the organization are protected against disclosure by the organization's attorney-client privilege, courts have generally applied two tests: the "control group" test and the "subject matter" test. Some courts have adopted a third test that closely tracks the subject matter test, and which is often described as the "modified subject matter test." The subject matter tests now represent the clear majority rule, although a few jurisdictions still follow the control group approach.

A. The Control Group Test

The control group test as initially conceived is perhaps best exemplified by the decision in *City of Philadelphia v. Westinghouse Electric Corp.*[7] The *Westinghouse* court reasoned that if the employee communicating with a corporation's lawyer is positioned "to control or even to take a substantial part in a decision about any action which the corporation may take" based on the lawyer's advice, "or if he is an authorized member of a body or group which has that authority, then, in effect, he is (or personifies) the corporation when he makes his disclosure to the lawyer" and the privilege applies.[8] In short, for a communication to be privileged under the control group test, it must be made by an employee who "has the authority to control, or substantially participate in, a decision regarding action to be taken on the advice of a lawyer, or is an authorized member of a group that has such power."[9] Only these employees qualify as the client for privilege purposes. At base, then, the control group test as originally conceived requires that the employee a lawyer communicates with be a member of senior management with ultimate decision-making authority for the communication to be privileged.[10] Distribution of a privileged communication outside the control group destroys the privilege with respect to that communication.[11]

---

7. 210 F. Supp. 483 (E.D. Pa. 1962).
8. *Id.* at 485.
9. Natta v. Hogan, 392 F.2d 686, 692 (10th Cir. 1968) (footnote omitted).
10. Consol. Coal Co. v. Bucyrus-Erie Co., 432 N.E.2d 250, 257–58 (Ill. 1982); *see, e.g.*, Garrison v. Gen. Motors Corp., 213 F. Supp. 515, 518 (S.D. Cal. 1963) (determining that GMC's "officers, directors, [and] department heads" constituted the corporation's control group).
11. Call One Inc. v. Berkley Ins. Co., 2022 WL 879208, at *3 (N.D. Ill. Feb. 28, 2022).

Unfortunately, the control group test limits lawyers' ability to communicate freely with clients' mid- and low-level employees, thereby limiting the lawyers' access to potentially crucial information.[12] These restrictions, in turn, impair lawyers' ability to properly advise their clients.

Some courts, correctly recognizing that organizational decision-making tends to be more collaborative and dispersed than it once might have been, have relaxed the control group test. In *Caldwell v. Advocate Condell Medical Center*,[13] for example, the court explained that under the Illinois version of the control group test, employees whose advisory role to senior management in an area is such that a final decision would not normally be made without considering their opinions, and whose opinions in fact form the basis of any final decision by senior managers with decision-making authority, are properly within the control group.[14] Accordingly, at least under Illinois law, the control group may extend beyond the actual organizational decision-makers.[15] Deciding which employees occupy an advisory role sufficient to qualify as control group members for privilege purposes is a fact-intensive analysis.

B. The Subject Matter Test

In comparison to the control group test, the subject matter test affords significantly broader privilege protection. Under the subject matter test, a lawyer's communication with any employee may be privileged if (1) the lawyer is representing the corporation in his or her capacity as a lawyer; (2) the communication is intended to secure legal advice for the corporation; (3) the employee is communicating with the lawyer at a superior's request or direction; and (4) the employee's duties or responsibilities include the subject of the communication. Applying this test, the employee's position or status is irrelevant to the privilege analysis. The attorney-client privilege extends not only to the company's top executives, officers, and directors but also to mid-level and lower-level employees. This approach makes sense; after all, lawyers representing an organization may need to gather information from employees at all levels of the organization to effectively carry out the representation. The Supreme Court embraced the subject matter approach in *Upjohn Co. v. United States*.[16] In *Upjohn*, the court rejected the control group test in favor of a subject matter approach essentially because, as just suggested, the control group test

12. Upjohn Co. v. United States, 449 U.S. 383, 391–92 (1981).

13. 87 N.E.3d 1020 (Ill. App. Ct. 2017).

14. *Id.* at 1036 (citing Consol. Coal Co. v. Bucyrus-Erie Co., 432 N.E.2d 250, 258 (Ill. 1982)).

15. *See* Mlynarski v. Rush Presbyterian-St. Luke's Med. Ctr., 572 N.E.2d 1025, 1028 (Ill. App. Ct. 1991) ("Under the control-group test, there are two tiers of corporate employees whose communications with the corporation's attorney are protected. The first tier consists of the decision-makers, or top management. The second tier consists of those employees who directly advise top management, and upon whose opinions and advice the decision-makers rely.").

16. 449 U.S. 383, 394 (1981).

"overlooks the fact that the privilege exists to protect not only the giving of professional advice to those who can act on it but also the giving of information to the lawyer to enable him to give sound and informed advice."[17]

By rejecting the control group test in favor of a subject matter test, the *Upjohn* court arguably steered attorney-client privilege analysis back toward the privilege's original purpose. To explain, the privilege initially developed to protect clients' confidential communications to their lawyers, rather than the other way around.[18] The hierarchical control group test, in contrast, emphasizes employees' ability or power to act on the lawyer's advice, thereby emphasizing the lawyer's advice to the client, rather than the client's communications to the lawyer.[19] Indeed, the Supreme Court specifically noted this flaw in embracing the subject matter test.[20]

Although the Supreme Court rejected the control group test in favor of some form of subject matter test, the Court declined to formulate a specific test.[21] Regardless, it is clear following *Upjohn* that a lawyer's confidential communications with any employee are privileged when they concern matters within the scope of the employee's responsibilities and the employee knows that the communications are intended to enable or facilitate the lawyer's representation of the corporation.[22] In this way, the subject matter test is a functional test that focuses on employees' roles and responsibilities and the information they possess, rather than a hierarchical test that concentrates on employees' ranks or status for privilege purposes.

---

17. *Id.* at 390.

18. *See* United States v. United Shoe Mach. Corp., 89 F. Supp. 357, 358–59 (D. Mass. 1950) (listing attorney-client privilege elements).

19. Thomas E. Spahn, The Attorney-Client Privilege and the Work Product Doctrine: A Practitioner's Guide 111 (2013).

20. *See* Upjohn Co. v. United States, 449 U.S. 383, 390 (1981) (observing that the control group test "overlooks the fact that the privilege exists to protect not only the giving of professional advice to those who can act on it but also the giving of information to the lawyer to enable him to give sound and informed advice").

21. *Id.* at 396.

22. *See, e.g.*, Grand Canyon Skywalk Dev. LLC v. Cieslak, 2015 WL 4773585, at *8 (D. Nev. Aug. 13, 2015) ("*Upjohn* holds that the privilege applies to communications with corporate employees, regardless of their position, when the communications concern matters within the scope of the employee's corporate duties and the employee is aware that the information is being furnished to enable the attorney to provide legal advice to the corporation."); MGA Entm't, Inc. v. Nat'l Prods. Ltd., 2012 WL 3150532, at *2 (C.D. Cal. Aug. 2, 2012) ("According to the Supreme Court, the privilege applies to communications by any corporate employee regardless of position when the communications concern matters within the scope of the employee's corporate duties and the employee is aware that the information is being furnished to enable the attorney to provide legal advice to the corporation."); United States v. Ghavami, 882 F. Supp. 2d 532, 538–39 (S.D.N.Y. 2012) ("Within a corporation . . . the attorney-client privilege protects communications by corporate employees to counsel for the corporation who is acting as a lawyer, as long as the communications are made at the direction of corporate superiors in order to secure legal advice and the employees are aware that they are being questioned in connection with the provision of such advice.").

C. The Modified Subject Matter Test, *Harper & Row* Test, or *Diversified Industries* Test

The third test is often called the "modified subject matter test" even though the test predates the Supreme Court's decision in *Upjohn*. It is also described as "modified *Harper & Row* test," or the "*Diversified Industries* test," after the federal cases from which it derives: *Harper & Row Publishers, Inc. v. Decker*[23] and *Diversified Industries, Inc. v. Meredith*.[24] The *Harper & Row* and *Diversified Industries* courts were persuaded that the control group test was undesirable, first, because it inhibits the free flow of material information from employees to the corporation's lawyers and thereby defeats the purpose of the attorney-client privilege by impairing the lawyers' ability to muster the facts necessary to properly advise their client.[25] Second, it potentially dissuades employees from speaking with corporate counsel "in a good faith effort to promote compliance with the complex laws governing corporate activity."[26] These courts favored "a more reasoned approach" to corporate attorney-client privilege questions that focused on "why an attorney was consulted, rather than with whom the attorney communicated."[27] The *Diversified Industries* court thus formulated the following corporate privilege test:

> [T]he attorney-client privilege is applicable to an employee's communication if (1) the communication was made for the purpose of securing legal advice; (2) the employee making the communication did so at the direction of his corporate superior; (3) the superior made the request so that the corporation could secure legal advice; (4) the subject matter of the communication is within the scope of the employee's corporate duties; and (5) the communication is not disseminated beyond those persons who, because of the corporate structure, need to know its contents.[28]

The modified *Harper & Row* test or *Diversified Industries* test is essentially the subject matter test with the "need to know" element added,[29] hence the

23. 423 F.2d 487 (7th Cir. 1970).

24. 572 F.2d 596 (8th Cir. 1977).

25. *Id.* at 609.

26. *Id.*

27. *Id.* (referring to the *Harper & Row* test).

28. *Id.*; *see also* Herrera v. Jarden Corp., 334 So. 3d 637, 644 (Fla. Dist. Ct. App. 2022) (reciting this test for the attorney-client privilege under Florida law).

29. *See* S. Bell Tel. & Tel. Co. v. Deason, 632 So. 2d 1377, 1383 n.10 (Fla. 1994) (explaining that the *Diversified Industries* court "modified the subject matter test in an effort to focus on why the attorney was consulted and to prevent the routine channeling of information through the attorney to prevent subsequent disclosure").

modified subject matter test label.[30] In applying this test, the "need to know" refers to certain employees' need for the lawyer's advice to perform their duties or to act upon the lawyer's advice for the organization's benefit—not to the lawyer's need for the information known by the employees.[31] As a practical matter, the higher or more senior an employee's role in the organization, the more likely that a court will find that the employee had a need to know—that is, a need for the lawyer's guidance.

III. Employees and Officers versus the Corporation as the Client

Regardless of whether a jurisdiction favors the subject matter test or the control group test, a question may arise as to whether a corporate officer or employee who confides in corporate counsel is doing so in a representative role, or rather as an individual. Absent a lawyer's express agreement to represent an officer or employee individually (in addition to representing the corporation), courts presume that the officer or employee consulted with the lawyer in the officer's or employee's corporate capacity rather than her individual capacity.[32] Consequently, the officer or employee cannot assert a personal attorney-client privilege to prevent disclosure of those communications.

Employees or officers may, however, be able to demonstrate that their communications with corporate counsel are protected by an individual privilege despite courts' default position. In deciding whether officers or employees can assert an individual attorney-client privilege over communications with corporate counsel, most courts have adopted the *Bevill* test,[33] named after the

30. One court has credited the *Harper & Row* court with formulating the subject matter test and stated that the modified subject matter test originated with the *Diversified Industries* court. *See* Keefe v. Bernard, 774 N.W.2d 663, 671–72 (Iowa 2009) (discussing the various attorney-client privilege tests).

31. *See* Diversified Indus., Inc. v. Meredith, 572 F.2d 596, 610–11 (8th Cir. 1977) (noting that the corporation carefully avoided disseminating the information at issue beyond those employees immediately concerned with the matter); United States v. Am. Tel. & Tel. Co., 86 F.R.D. 603, 620 (D.D.C. 1979) ("The privilege applies to the communication only if the employee is the source of the information going to the attorney or is a regular conduit for such information, or, in response, if the information is revealed in the attorney's advice and the employee to whom the information is disclosed has a 'need to know' the information to carry out his own duties.").

32. *See In re* Grand Jury Subpoena, 274 F.3d 563, 571 (1st Cir. 2001) ("The default assumption is that the attorney only represents the corporate entity, not the individuals within the corporate sphere, and it is the individuals' burden to dispel that presumption. . . . This makes perfect sense because an employee has a duty to assist his employer's counsel in the investigation and defense of matters pertaining to the employer's business.") (citation omitted); Pearlshire Capital Group, LLC v. Zaid, 490 F. Supp. 3d 1299, 1309 (N.D. Ill. 2020) (quoting *In re* Grand Jury Subpoena, 274 F.3d at 571); *In re* Grand Jury Investigation, 2019 WL 2179116, at *15–16 (D.D.C. Mar. 4, 2019) (quoting *In re Grand Jury Subpoena* and later reiterating "the default rule that the General Counsel represents the entity and not individuals within the entity").

33. *See, e.g.*, United States v. Graf, 610 F.3d 1148, 1161 (9th Cir. 2010); *In re* Grand Jury Subpoena, 274 F.3d 563, 571–72 (1st Cir. 2001); *In re* Grand Jury Subpoenas, 144 F.3d 653, 659 (10th Cir. 1998); United

Third Circuit case effectively adopting it, *In re Bevill, Bressler & Schulman Asset Management Corp.*[34] Under *Bevill*, corporate officers or employees must pass a five-part test to invoke a personal attorney-client privilege: (1) they must show that they approached the lawyer for the purpose of seeking legal advice; (2) they must prove that when they approached the lawyer, they clarified that they were seeking legal advice in their individual capacities rather than in their representative capacities; (3) they must establish that the lawyer opted to communicate with them in their individual capacities despite knowing that a conflict of interest could arise; (4) they must demonstrate that their conversations with the lawyer were confidential; and (5) they must show that the substance of their communications with the corporation's lawyer did not concern matters within the corporation or its general affairs.[35] The *Bevill* principles apply equally where an organization other than a corporation is concerned.[36]

Officers or employees fail the *Bevill* test if they cannot prove any of the five elements,[37] but the fifth element has proven to be especially difficult for those looking to establish a personal attorney-client privilege.[38] In many instances, officers or employees discuss company affairs with a lawyer for the corporation with the embedded purpose of evaluating their personal liability or

---

States v. Int'l Bhd. of Teamsters, 119 F.3d 210, 214–15 (2d Cir. 1997); Sovereign Holdings, Inc. v. Deck, 2018 WL 4441468, at *9–12 (D.S.D. Sept. 17, 2018); Paolini v. Albertson's, Inc., 2002 WL 35650974, at *1 (D. Idaho May 8, 2002) (noting that the Idaho Supreme Court had yet to rule on when an attorney-client relationship will arise between corporate counsel and a corporate employee and thus looking to the law of other jurisdictions); *Ex parte* Smith, 942 So. 2d 356, 359–61 (Ala. 2006); Zielinski v. Clorox Co., 504 S.E.2d 683, 686 (Ga. 1998); Maleski *ex rel.* Chronister v. Corp. Life Ins. Co., 641 A.2d 1, 4–5 (Pa. Commw. Ct. 1994). *But see* United States v. Balsiger, 2013 WL 3490873, at *8–9 (E.D. Wis. July 10, 2013) (adopting a slightly different test).

34. 805 F.2d 120 (3d Cir. 1986).

35. *Id.* at 123 (quoting *In re* Grand Jury Investig. No. 83-30557, 575 F. Supp. 777, 780 (N.D. Ga. 1983)).

36. *See* Rutherford v. Palo Verde Health Care Dist., 2014 WL 12632901, at *5 (C.D. Cal. Apr. 17, 2014) (referring to a public health care district).

37. *See, e.g.*, United States v. Merida, 828 F.3d 1203, 1210–11 (10th Cir. 2016) (failing at least four of the five *Bevill* elements); Sovereign Holdings, Inc. v. Deck, 2018 WL 4441468, at *11–12 (D.S.D. Sept. 17, 2018) (failing the second, third, and fifth *Bevill* prongs); United States v. Head, 2013 WL 5739095, at *3 (E.D. Cal. Oct. 22, 2013) (holding that the defendant failed the second prong of the *Bevill* test because he could not prove that he informed the lawyer that he was seeking legal advice in his personal capacity).

38. *See, e.g.*, Grassmueck v. Ogden Murphy Wallace, P.L.L.C., 213 F.R.D. 567, 572 (W.D. Wash. 2003) (holding that the law firm could not show that documents alleged to be personally privileged were segregable from issues related to the former executive's corporate capacities and thus the fifth *Bevill* element was not satisfied); United States v. Head, 2013 WL 5739095, at *3 (E.D. Cal. Oct. 22, 2013) (failing the fifth *Bevill* element because the letters at issue demonstrated that "the substance of their communications were within the general affairs of the company"); *In re* Equaphor Inc., 2012 WL 1682583, at *4 (Bankr. E.D. Va. May 14, 2012) ("[The law firm's] defense of the officers in this case was directly related to the affairs of the corporation; indeed, the only reasons the [i]ndividual [d]efendants were sued (or at least the *sine qua non* of their having been named as defendants) was that they occupied positions as officers and directors of the company. There has been no showing that any of the advice sought from [the law firm] was personal in nature, and not related to the [i]ndividual [d]efendants' positions as officers and directors of the company.").

consequences arising out of those affairs. In such cases, courts often hold that the officers or employees cannot stake privilege claims because the communications did not involve their purely personal interests.[39] In other words, only communications involving officers' or employees' purely personal interests can be the subject of individual attorney-client privilege claims. Other courts, however, do not read *Bevill's* fifth element so grudgingly. As the Tenth Circuit has alternatively explained:

> The fifth prong of *In Matter of Bevill*, properly interpreted, only precludes an officer from asserting an individual attorney client privilege when the communication concerns the corporation's rights and responsibilities. However, if the communication between a corporate officer and corporate counsel specifically focuses upon the individual officer's personal rights and liabilities, then the fifth prong of *In Matter of Bevill* can be satisfied even though the general subject matter of the conversation pertains to matters within the general affairs of the company. For example, a corporate officer's discussion with his corporation's counsel may still be protected by a personal, individual attorney-client privilege when the conversation specifically concerns the officer's personal liability for jail time based on conduct interrelated with corporate affairs. Such a conversation would satisfy the fifth prong of [the] *In Matter of Bevill* test because the officer's potential prison sentence is outside the scope of the corporation's concerns and affairs.[40]

If corporate constituents can establish the five *Bevill* factors, such that they enjoy an individual attorney-client privilege with corporate counsel, their communications with the lawyer regarding their personal interests will remain privileged, even if the corporation waives its attorney-client privilege. If a jurisdiction has not adopted the *Bevill* test, an officer or employee attempting to assert an individual attorney-client privilege must at the very least be prepared to demonstrate that she made clear to corporate counsel that she was seeking legal advice on personal matters.[41]

---

39. *See, e.g.*, *In re* Grand Jury Subpoenas, 144 F.3d 653, 659 (10th Cir. 1998) ("[W]e conclude that a limited attorney-client privilege exists between Intervenor and [two lawyers]. Our holding is an extremely limited one and does not extend to communications . . . in which both corporate and individual liability were discussed. It includes only that very small portion of communications in which Intervenor sought legal advice as to his personal liability without regard to any corporate considerations."); Transcont'l Refrigerated Lines, Inc. v. New Prime, Inc., 2014 WL 2471936, at *7 (M.D. Pa. June 3, 2014) (stating that the plaintiff's former president and sole shareholder could only assert an attorney-client privilege "to the extent that his communications with [the plaintiff's law firm] involved purely personal interests").

40. *In re* Grand Jury Proc., 156 F.3d 1038, 1041 (10th Cir. 1998); *see also In re* Grand Jury Subpoena, 274 F.3d 563, 572 (1st Cir. 2001) (adopting this interpretation).

41. *See* United States v. Adams, 2018 WL 5311410, at *9 (D. Minn. Oct. 27, 2018) (quoting United States v. Int'l Bhd. of Teamsters, 119 F.3d 210, 215 (2d Cir. 1997)).

Although courts' default assumption that a corporation's lawyer represents the corporation and not individual employees or officers is sensible where large, publicly traded companies are concerned, the situation is arguably different where a lawyer represents a closely held corporation. Nonetheless, where individuals choose the benefits of corporate form for their businesses—such as protection against personal liability—it is appropriate to treat them as corporate officers for privilege purposes. Accordingly, courts generally apply the default assumption to closely held corporations.[42] Shareholders of closely held corporations cannot base personal attorney-client privilege claims solely on their ownership status or decision-making powers.[43] Instead, they must satisfy all five *Bevill* factors to establish a personal attorney-client privilege. In addition, a court may consider who paid the lawyer's fees, who the lawyer understood to be her client, and whether the lawyer communicated with only the corporate officer or also with other employees in deciding whether a shareholder in a close corporation has an individual attorney-client privilege with corporate counsel.[44]

IV. Former Employees and the Organization's Attorney-Client Privilege

Once most courts adopted the subject matter test in one form or another, it was inevitable that they would extend the attorney-client privilege to an organization's former employees in some situations.[45] Indeed, it is now the case that lawyers' communications with former employees about events or matters that occurred while the former employees worked for the organization generally are privileged if they otherwise satisfy the subject matter test or modified subject matter test.[46] The privilege generally does not, however, cloak

42. Sovereign Holdings, Inc. v. Deck, 2018 WL 4441468, at *12 (D.S.D. Sept. 17, 2018).

43. MacKenzie-Childs LLC v. MacKenzie-Childs, 262 F.R.D. 241, 255 (W.D.N.Y. 2009).

44. Sovereign Holdings, Inc. v. Deck, 2018 WL 4441468, at *12 (D.S.D. Sept. 17, 2018).

45. For a comprehensive discussion of the attorney-client privilege in the former employee context, see Douglas R. Richmond, *The Attorney-Client Privilege and Former Employees*, 70 Cath. U. L. Rev. 39 (2020).

46. *See, e.g.*, *In re* Allen, 106 F.3d 582, 606 (4th Cir. 1997) (stating that the *Upjohn* analysis applies to former employees); United States v. Chen, 99 F.3d 1495, 1502 (9th Cir. 1996) (quoting *In re* Coordinated Pretrial Proc., 658 F.2d 1355, 1361 n.7 (9th Cir. 1981)); Corcoran v. HCA-HealthONE LLC, 2022 WL 1605296, at *2–4 (D. Colo. May 20, 2022) (balancing the corporate entity's privilege with the adversary's right to know if the witnesses' testimony was influenced in any way); Hof as the Tr. of the Estate of FoodServiceWarehouse.Com v. LaPorte, 2020 WL 5594126, at *5 (E.D. La. Sept. 18, 2020) ("To the extent [a former board member's and a former employee's] communications with the Trustee's counsel concern their actions during their employment with [the debtor], those communications are privileged even if they were also discussing recent testimony. Parsing such a communication to extract some 'unprivileged' portion is not possible."); Jacobs v. Alam, 2020 WL 3064435, at *6 (E.D. Mich. June 9, 2020) (applying the attorney-client privilege to a former employee); Hairston v. Royal Bldg. Prods., Inc., 2019 WL 1550790, at *1–2 (W.D. Va. Feb. 15, 2019) (following *In re Allen*, 106 F.3d at 606); Subramanian v. Lupin Inc., 2019 WL 1771556, at *2–3 (S.D.N.Y. Apr. 23, 2019) (recognizing the attorney-client privilege in the former client context, but noting that absent a privilege log or the submission of

communications between an organization's lawyer and a former employee regarding matters or issues that occurred or arose after the former employee left the organization.[47]

---

particular communications, it could not rule); MF Global Holdings Ltd. v. Pricewaterhouse Coopers LLP, 232 F. Supp. 3d 558, 569 (S.D.N.Y. 2017) (quoting Indergit v. Rite Aid Corp., 2016 WL 6441566, at *3 (S.D.N.Y. Oct. 31, 2016)); Hanover Ins. Co. v. Plaquemines Parish Gov't, 304 F.R.D. 494, 498–500 (E.D. La. 2015) (predicting how the Louisiana Supreme Court would rule); Goswami v. DePaul Univ., 2014 WL 1307585, at *1–2 (N.D. Ill. Mar. 31, 2014) (explaining that Illinois' control group test did not apply; federal law controlled the privilege question); Winthrop Res., Inc. v. Commscope, Inc. of N.C., 2014 WL 5810457, at *2–3 (W.D.N.C. Nov. 7, 2014) (adopting the reasoning of Peralta v. Cendant Corp., 190 F.R.D. 38 (D. Conn. 1999)); Gary Friedrich Enters., LLC v. Marvel Enters., Inc., 2011 WL 2020586, at *5 (S.D.N.Y. May 20, 2011) (applying the attorney-client privilege where the former employee was deposed regarding his work while employed by the defendant); New York v. Salazar, 2011 WL 13205947, at *5 (N.D.N.Y. June 23, 2011) ("Cason's discussions with counsel for the DOI that occurred during the course of his employment with DOI and those of whose 'nature and purpose' was for the DOI's counsel to learn facts related to this lawsuit that the defendant Cason was aware of as a result of his employment, regardless of when they occurred, are privileged."); Weber v. FUJIFILM Med. Sys. U.S.A., 2011 WL 3163597, at *7 (D. Conn. July 27, 2011) (declining to revisit an earlier decision recognizing the privilege); Gioe v. AT&T, Inc., 2010 WL 3780701, at *1 (E.D.N.Y. Sept. 20, 2010) ("[I]nformation obtained by the former employee during the period of employment, including information conveyed by counsel during that period, remains privileged."); *In re* Flonase Antitrust Litig., 723 F. Supp. 2d 761, 765 (E.D. Pa. 2010) ("Because [the witness's] testimony concerned matters within the scope of her former responsibilities with [the] defendant corporation and because her conversations with defense counsel may be relevant to [the] defendant's legal strategy, her communications with defense counsel fall within the attorney-client privilege."); Fisher v. Halliburton, 2009 WL 483890, at *2 (S.D. Tex. Feb. 25, 2009) ("[A]ll communications between Richard and the defendants' counsel are protected as privileged provided they relate to events concerning Richard's duties while employed by defendants."); Misner v. Potter, 2008 WL 11380016, at *2 (D. Utah June 19, 2008) ("[U]nder . . . *Upjohn* and its progeny, the attorney-client privilege applies to confidential communications concerning matters within the scope of the employee's corporate duties whether or not they are currently employed."); Export-Import Bank of the United States v. Asia Pulp & Paper Co., Ltd., 232 F.R.D. 103, 112 (S.D.N.Y. 2005) ("Virtually all courts hold that communications between company counsel and former company employees are privileged if they concern information obtained during the course of employment."); United States *ex rel.* Hunt v. Merck-Medco Managed Care, LLC, 340 F. Supp. 2d 554, 558 (E.D. Pa. 2004) (following the majority approach); Cool v. BorgWarner Diversified Transmission Prods., Inc., 2003 WL 23009017, at *2 (S.D. Ind. Oct. 29, 2003) (citing *In re Allen*, 106 F.3d at 606); Miramar Constr. Co. v. Home Depot, Inc., 167 F. Supp. 2d 182, 184–85 (D.P.R. 2001) (applying Puerto Rico law and reasoning that applying the privilege to communications with former employees was consistent with the underlying purposes of the attorney-client privilege, but declining to extend the privilege to a former independent contractor); *In re* Maxus Energy Corp., 2021 WL 856040, at *3 (Bankr. D. Del. Mar. 8, 2021) ("[T]wo types of information remain privileged after a pre-deposition preparation session of a former employee of a corporation: (a) privileged information that the former employee received during his or her employment; and (b) communications designed to allow the employer's counsel to ascertain facts relevant to the lawsuit that the former employee witnessed while employed.") (footnote omitted); E.I. DuPont de Nemours & Co. v. Medtronic Vascular, Inc., 2012 Del. Super. LEXIS 129, at *18–20 (Del. Super. Ct. Mar. 13, 2012) (enforcing Medtronic's privilege because the communications with the former employee directly related to knowledge she obtained or conduct that occurred while she was in Medtronic's employ); Radovic v. City of N.Y., 642 N.Y.S.2d 1015, 1017 (Sup. Ct. 1996) (reasoning that the witness's status as a former employee was of "no consequence" from a privilege perspective); Morris v. Scenera Res., LLC, 2011 WL 3808544, at *6 (N.C. Super. Ct. Aug. 26, 2011) (relying on *In re Allen*, 106 F.3d at 606).

47. Those communications may, however, be protected by the lawyer's work product immunity. *See, e.g.*, Kraus Indus., Inc. v. Moore, 2012 WL 1408815, at *6 (W.D. Pa. Feb. 11, 2008) ("[T]o the extent that Defendants seek disclosure of communications between [the former employee] and counsel for

Peralta v. Cendant Corp.[48] is the seminal case on former employees and the attorney-client privilege.[49] In that case, Ramon Peralta sued Cendant for employment discrimination. His lawyer deposed Peralta's former supervisor, Randi Klaber, who no longer worked for Cendant. Peralta's lawyer asked Klaber if she had discussed the deposition with anyone. Klaber said that she had spoken with Cendant's lawyer, Maureen Bresnan.[50] When Peralta's lawyer asked Klaber about that conversation, Bresnan instructed Klaber not to answer the question. After a break, Peralta's lawyer asked Klaber what, if anything, she had discussed with Bresnan over the break. Bresnan again instructed Klaber not to answer. The parties then engaged the court, which concluded that under federal law, "any privileged information" Klaber obtained while employed by Cendant, "including any information conveyed by counsel during that period, remain[ed] privileged upon the termination of her employment."[51] The court reasoned that distinguishing between lawyers' privileged and nonprivileged communications with former employees should be relatively easy "if the essential point is kept in mind: did the communication relate to the former employee's conduct and knowledge, or communication with [the organization's] counsel, during his or her employment? If so, such communication[s] [are] protected from disclosure by [the organization's] attorney-client privilege under *Upjohn*."[52]

While *Peralta* reflects the majority rule,[53] other courts have taken a narrower view of the privilege where former employees are concerned.[54] A few

---

the Plaintiff occurring after [the former employee's] employment at Kraus in which counsel communicated conclusions, opinions, or legal theories regarding the instant litigation, the same is protected by the work product doctrine and not subject to discovery."); *see also* Gary Friedrich Enters., LLC v. Marvel Enters., LLC, 2011 WL 2020586, at *6 (S.D.N.Y. May 20, 2011) (discussing work product immunity in the former employee context).

48. 190 F.R.D. 38 (D. Conn. 1999).

49. Although *Peralta* is the seminal case on privileged communications with former employees, like all federal district court decisions, it is neither authoritative nor precedential. *See* Intervarsity Christian Fellowship/USA v. Univ. of Iowa, 5 F.4th 855, 865–66 (8th Cir. 2021) ("'A decision of a federal district court judge is not binding precedent in either a different judicial district, the same judicial district, or even upon the same judge in a different case.'" (quoting Camreta v. Greene, 563 U.S. 692, 730 n.7 (2011))); Vertex Surgical, Inc. v. Paradigm Biodevices, Inc., 648 F. Supp. 2d 226, 231 (D. Mass. 2009) ("As Judges Posner and Easterbrook have repeatedly and accurately observed, with characteristic bluntness, district court decisions are neither authoritative nor precedential.").

50. Peralta v. Cendant Corp., 190 F.R.D. 38, 39 (D. Conn. 1999). Bresnan only represented Cendant; she did not also represent Klaber. *Id.*

51. *Id.* at 41.

52. *Id.*

53. *See* Export-Import Bank of the U.S. v. Asia Pulp & Paper Co., Ltd., 232 F.R.D. 103, 112 (S.D.N.Y. 2005) ("Virtually all courts hold that communications between company counsel and former company employees are privileged if they concern information obtained during the course of employment.").

54. *See, e.g.*, Infosys., Inc. v. Ceridian Corp., 197 F.R.D. 303, 305–06 (E.D. Mich. 2000) (suggesting that the attorney-client privilege applies only where the former employee spoke with a lawyer at management's direction while employed by the organization, the former employee has a present connection

courts have refused to recognize the privilege in the former employee context.[55] Plus, the privilege generally does not protect a lawyer's communications with former employees in a jurisdiction that employs the control group test.[56] Given these variations between jurisdictions, lawyers should be cautious about what they say to clients' former employees. Even in courts that follow the majority rule, the privilege does not protect communications between an organization's lawyer and a former employee whom the lawyer does not represent that "bear on or otherwise potentially affect" the person's testimony, either "consciously or subconsciously."[57] For example, a lawyer's efforts to refresh a former employee's recollection before the former employee's deposition generally are discoverable. In short, lawyers are wise to assume that communications with former employees who they do not represent will not be privileged and plan their interactions accordingly.

V. In-House Lawyers and Privileged Communications

Many corporations and other organizations employ their own law departments.[58] Insofar as those lawyers are providing legal advice to the corporation, their communications with other corporate employees generally are protected by the corporation's attorney-client privilege.[59] In-house lawyers may, however, have nonlegal roles in addition to their legal responsibilities. For example, a general counsel may also supervise the corporation's compliance office, government relations or public relations operations, human resources group, or risk management department. In addition, in-house lawyers frequently dispense business advice as well as legal advice. Plus, in some instances whether a communication or a task is a business function or a legal one may depend on the context.[60] All this may cause some confusion within the organization

---

or agency relationship with the organization, or the communication concerns a confidential matter that was uniquely within the former employee's knowledge when she worked for the organization).

55. *See, e.g.*, United States v. Philip Morris USA, Inc., 2005 WL 8156890, at *3 (D.D.C. Jan. 21, 2005); Clark Equip. Co. v. Lift Parts Mfg. Co., 1985 WL 2917, at *5 (N.D. Ill. Oct. 1, 1985); Newman v. Highland Sch. Dist. No. 203, 181 P.3d 1188, 1192–94 (Wash. 2016).

56. *See, e.g.*, Barrett Indus. Trucks, Inc. v. Old Republic Ins. Co., 129 F.R.D. 515, 517–18 (N.D. Ill. 1990) (applying Illinois law).

57. Peralta v. Cendant Corp., 190 F.R.D. 38, 42 (D. Conn. 1999).

58. Courts treat in-house lawyers in corporations and in other types of organizations equally when it comes to the attorney-client privilege. *See, e.g.*, Klaassen v. Anderson, 2016 WL 3881334, at *3 (D. Kan. July 18, 2016) (involving a university medical center).

59. F.T.C. v. Boeringher Ingelheim Pharms., Inc., 892 F.3d 1264, 1267 (D.C. Cir. 2018); Cormack v. United States, 117 Fed. Cl. 392, 397 (Fed. Cl. 2014); Frank v. Morgans Hotel Group Mgmt. LLC, 116 N.Y.S.3d 889, 891 (Sup. Ct. 2020). Communications with an in-house lawyer may be privileged even if the lawyer is not currently an active member of any state bar. Gucci Am., Inc. v. Guess?, Inc., 2011 WL 9375, at *4 (S.D.N.Y. Jan. 3, 2011). The test in that situation is "whether the client had a reasonable belief that it was communicating with an attorney." *Id.* at *5 (footnote omitted). This is a case- and fact-specific inquiry.

60. *In re* Appraisal of Dole Food Co., 114 A.3d 541, 561 (Del. Ch. 2014).

because the privilege does not attach to all communications with a lawyer.[61] To be privileged, a communication must be made to provide or obtain legal advice.[62] The attorney-client privilege does not cover purely business or operational communications with an in-house lawyer.[63] Similarly, a lawyer's mere participation in a communication does not render the communication privileged.[64]

In dispensing legal and business advice, in-house lawyers may not neatly segregate their communications; an email message, letter, memorandum, or other document may contain a mix of business and legal advice. In other instances, the business and legal issues on which an in-house lawyer is consulted are interwoven. In both situations, the question then becomes whether the communication is privileged in its entirety, as corporations often contend. Courts considering this issue usually apply the "primary purpose" or "predominant purpose" test.[65] Under this test, "the attorney-client privilege applies to the entirety of a document only if the predominant purpose of the communication is to render or solicit legal advice."[66] Phrased slightly differently, where the predominant or primary purpose of a communication is the solicitation or delivery of legal advice, then the entire document or other communication is privileged. Passages or portions of the communication that do not embody legal advice are not severable.[67] The primary or predominant purpose of a communication may be informed by whether the lawyer holds dual positions—one plainly legal and the other plainly business—as well as by the client's needs or objectives that animate the advice.[68]

As originally crafted and typically applied, the primary purpose test holds that the privilege does not protect a document in its entirety "if legal advice

---

61. L.A. County Bd. of Supervisors v. Superior Court, 386 P.3d 773, 779 (Cal. 2016); Gross v. Parson, 624 S.W.3d 877, 890 (Mo. 2021).

62. State *ex rel.* Adel v. Adleman, 503 P.3d 120, 126 (Ariz. 2022); St. Simons Waterfront, LLC v. Hunter, Maclean, Exley, & Dunn, P.C., 746 S.E.2d 98, 106 (Ga. 2013).

63. Margulis v. Hertz Corp., 2017 WL 772336, at *5 (D.N.J. Feb. 28, 2017).

64. BankDirect Cap. Fin., LLC v. Cap. Premium Fin., Inc., 326 F.R.D. 176, 181 (N.D. Ill. 2018).

65. *In re* Grand Jury, 23 F.4th 1088, 1092 (9th Cir. 2021) (describing the "primary-purpose test"); F.T.C. v. Boeringher Ingelheim Pharms., Inc., 892 F.3d 1264, 1267 (D.C. Cir. 2018) (applying the "primary purpose" test); Alomari v. Ohio Dep't of Pub. Safety, 626 F. App'x 558, 570 (6th Cir. 2015) (referring to the predominant purpose test); *In re* County of Erie, 473 F.3d 413, 420 (2d Cir. 2007) (considering the communication's "predominant purpose"); Harrington v. Freedom of Info. Comm'n, 144 A.3d 405, 417 (Conn. 2016) (referring to the communication's primary purpose); *In re* Appraisal of Dole Food Co., 114 A.3d 541, 561 (Del. Ch. 2014) (describing the predominant purpose test); *In re* Polaris, 967 N.W.2d 367, 407 (Minn. 2021) (adopting the predominant purpose test); Saran v. Chelsea GCA Realty P'ship, L.P., 104 N.Y.S.3d 698, 700 (App. Div. 2019) (stating that the critical inquiry is whether a communication is "primarily or predominantly of a legal character"); *see also* Exxon Mobil Corp. v. Hill, 751 F.3d 379, 382 (5th Cir. 2014) (applying a "manifest purpose" standard).

66. *In re* Polaris, 967 N.W.2d 367, 407 (Minn. 2021).

67. *In re* County of Erie, 473 F.3d 413, 420 (2d Cir. 2007).

68. *Id.* at 421.

is merely *one purpose* and not the primary purpose of the communication."[69] The District of Columbia Circuit, however, applies a slightly altered version of the primary purpose test, and holds that courts should determine whether providing or securing legal advice "'was *one of* the significant purposes of the attorney-client communication.'"[70] This adjusted approach is intended to help "reduce uncertainty regarding the attorney-client privilege."[71] The D.C. Circuit's modification of the primary purpose test has yet to attract other federal appellate courts,[72] although some district courts have embraced it with respect to privilege claims arising out of internal investigations.[73]

Because, as noted earlier, communications with corporate counsel often weave together legal and business issues, a court applying the primary purpose or predominant purpose test should resolve any doubts in favor of recognizing the attorney-client privilege.[74] Furthermore, a court's refusal to protect an entire document under the primary purpose or predominant purpose test does not mean that the corporation's attorney-client privilege is thereby lost. Rather, absent some applicable exception, the privilege will still protect those portions of the document that reflect legal advice.[75] The corporation's lawyers will be entitled to redact privileged portions of any documents before producing them to an adversary.[76]

As the primary purpose doctrine highlights, in-house lawyers' potential dual roles (legal versus business) can complicate courts' attorney-client privilege analysis.[77] As a result, and even though courts commonly recognize that communications by corporate employees with in-house counsel are entitled to the protection of the attorney-client privilege, they sometimes articulate specific rebuttable presumptions when analyzing in-house lawyers' privilege

---

69. *In re* Polaris, 967 N.W.2d 367, 408 (Minn. 2021) (emphasis added).

70. F.T.C. v. Boeringher Ingelheim Pharms., Inc., 892 F.3d 1264, 1267 (D.C. Cir. 2018) (quoting *In re* Kellogg, Brown & Root, Inc., 756 F.3d 754, 760 (D.C. Cir. 2014)).

71. *Id.* at 1268.

72. *See In re* Grand Jury, 23 F.4th 1088, 1092 (9th Cir. 2021) ("None of our other sister circuits have openly embraced *Kellogg* yet.") (footnote omitted).

73. *See, e.g.*, *In re* Smith & Nephew Birmingham Hip Resurfacing Hip Implant Prods. Liab. Litig., 2019 WL 2330863, at *2 (D. Md. May 31, 2019); Edwards v. Scripps Media, Inc., 2019 WL 2448654, at *1–2 (E.D. Mich. June 10, 2019); *In re* Gen. Motors LLC Ignition Switch Litig., 80 F. Supp. 3d 521, 530 (S.D.N.Y. 2015).

74. Carhartt, Inc. v. Innovative Textiles, Inc., 333 F.R.D. 113, 117 (E.D. Mich. 2019) (quoting Ganley v. Mazda N. Am. Ops., 2007 WL 9706988, at *5 (N.D. Ohio Nov. 15, 2007)).

75. *In re* Polaris, 967 N.W.2d 367, 408 (Minn. 2021) (citing *In re* Vioxx Prods. Liab. Litig., 501 F. Supp. 2d 789, 798 (E.D. La. 2007)).

76. *In re* County of Erie, 473 F.3d 413, 421 n.8 (2d Cir. 2007); Harrington v. Freedom of Info. Comm'n, 144 A.3d 405, 416 (Conn. 2016).

77. *See* Shenwick v. Twitter, Inc., 2018 WL 5750119, at *1 (N.D. Cal. Oct. 30, 2018) ("In the in-house context, where the corporation is the client, the privilege protects communications seeking legal advice from in-house counsel, but the matter is complicated by the fact that in-house counsel may play different roles within the company, some of which are not related to the provision of legal advice.").

claims. First, some courts presume that outside lawyers' communications with corporate employees are privileged while leaning the other way where in-house lawyers are concerned.[78] As an Oklahoma federal court explained:

> Many courts have relied on two rebuttable presumptions (though often not stated expressly) regarding the role of the lawyer in determining the nature of the advice: (1) if outside counsel is involved, the confidential communication is presumed to be a request for and the provision of "legal advice"; and (2) if in-house counsel is involved, the presumption is that the attorney's input is more likely business than legal in nature.[79]

Second, other courts have formulated presumptions based on in-house lawyers' legal roles within their companies' law departments and business roles outside their law departments.[80] As one court described this method:

> Because an in-house lawyer often has other functions in addition to providing legal advice, the lawyer's role on a particular occasion will not be self-evident as it usually is in the case of outside counsel. A court must examine the circumstances to determine whether the lawyer was acting as a lawyer rather than as business advisor or management decision-maker. One important indicator of whether a lawyer is involved in giving legal advice or in some other activity is his or her place on the corporation's organizational chart. There is a

78. *See, e.g.*, Dolby Labs. Licensing Corp. v. Adobe Inc., 402 F. Supp. 3d 855, 866 (N.D. Cal. 2019) ("[U]nlike communications with outside counsel, which are presumed to be made for the purpose of seeking legal advice, there is no presumption that communications with in-house counsel are protected by attorney-client privilege."); Cintron v. Title Fin. Corp., 2018 WL 6605901, at *2 (D. Mont. Dec. 17, 2018) ("Generally, it is presumed that communications between an attorney and her client are privileged, but that presumption 'does not extend to communications with in-house counsel' because those communications 'might well pertain to business rather than legal matters,' and '[t]he privilege does not protect an attorney's business advice.'" (quoting United States v. ChevronTexaco Corp., 241 F. Supp. 2d 1065, 1076 (N.D. Cal. 2002))); Stevens v. Corelogic Inc., 2016 WL 397936, at *4 (S.D. Cal. Feb. 1, 2016) ("'Because in-house counsel may operate in a purely or primarily business capacity in connection with many corporate endeavors,' it is not presumed that all communications involving in-house counsel pertain to legal matters and are protected by the attorney-client privilege." (quoting *Chevron*, 241 F. Supp. 2d at 1076)); Dewitt v. Walgreen Co., 2012 WL 3837764, at *3 (D. Idaho Sept. 4, 2012) ("[C]ommunications between in-house counsel and corporate representatives, unlike those between a client and outside counsel, are not presumed to be made for the purpose of obtaining legal advice."); *Chevron*, 241 F. Supp. 2d at 1076 ("Because in-house counsel may operate in a purely or primarily business capacity in connection with many corporate endeavors, the presumption that attaches to communications with outside counsel does not extend to communications with in-house counsel.").

79. Lindley v. Life Inv. Ins. Co. of Am., 267 F.R.D. 382, 389 (N.D. Okla. 2010).

80. *See, e.g.*, Breneisen v. Motorola, Inc., 2003 WL 21530440, at *3 (N.D. Ill. July 3, 2003) ("Generally, there is a presumption that a lawyer in the legal department of the corporation is giving legal advice, and an opposite presumption for a lawyer who works on the business or management side. However, the lawyer's position in the corporation is not necessarily dispositive.").

> presumption that a lawyer in the legal department or working for the general counsel is most often giving legal advice, while the opposite presumption applies to a lawyer . . . who works for the Financial Group or some other seemingly management or business side of the house. . . . A lawyer's place on the organizational chart is not always dispositive, and the relevant presumption therefore may be rebutted by the party asserting the privilege.[81]

Relatedly, some courts apply a heightened standard when deciding whether the attorney-client privilege applies to corporate employees' communications with an in-house lawyer.[82] For instance, when evaluating whether the privilege protected the communications of an in-house lawyer who was also the company's vice president, who was told by the company's president and other personnel "about virtually all company business activities," and who had certain nonlegal responsibilities, a federal court stated that the company could "shelter [the in-house lawyer's] advice only upon *a clear showing* that [he] gave it in a professional legal capacity."[83] Similarly, a New York court observed that because in-house lawyers may serve as corporate officers "with mixed business responsibility, and their involvement in the company may blur the line between legal and nonlegal communications, there is a heightened need to apply the privilege cautiously in the case of in-house counsel."[84] Absent such elevated scrutiny, the court speculated, a company might use "the mere participation of an attorney" in a communication "to seal off disclosure."[85]

In fact, courts need not presume anything regarding allegedly privileged communications with in-house lawyers.[86] Nor do courts need to apply a more stringent standard of review when evaluating attorney-client privilege claims that involve corporate employees' communications with in-house counsel. Courts typically construe the privilege narrowly because it limits full

81. Boca Investerings P'ship v. United States, 31 F. Supp. 2d 9, 12 (D.D.C. 1998) (citations omitted).

82. *See, e.g.*, First Fin. Bank, N.A. v. Citibank, N.A., 2012 WL 626272, at *4 (S.D. Ind. Feb. 4, 2012) (requiring a "stronger showing" for attorney-client privilege protection where the in-house lawyer whose communications are at issue has a business role and another lawyer serves as the company's general counsel); Oracle Am., Inc. v. Google, Inc., 2011 WL 3794892, at *4 (N.D. Cal. Aug. 26, 2011) (establishing that an internal communication involving in-house counsel is privileged requires a clear showing that the communication was made to obtain or provide legal advice).

83. *In re* Sealed Case, 737 F.2d 94, 99 (D.C. Cir. 1984) (emphasis added).

84. Saran v. Chelsea CGA Realty P'ship, L.P., 104 N.Y.S.3d 698, 700 (App. Div. 2019).

85. *Id.* (citing Rossi v. Blue Cross & Blue Shield of Greater N.Y., 540 N.E.2d 703, 705 (N.Y. 1989)).

86. *See, e.g.*, Davis v. PMA Cos., 2012 WL 3922967, at *3 (W.D. Okla. Sept. 7, 2012) ("[T]he Court does not presume that an in-house attorney's involvement was primarily for business purposes, but instead looks at each communication to determine whether it was made for the purpose of seeking or providing legal advice."); Lindley v. Life Inv. Ins. Co. of Am., 267 F.R.D. 382, 391 (N.D. Okla. 2010) (declining to apply "the presumptions regarding the status of the attorney (whether in-house or outside counsel)" and instead considering the lawyer's status as "one of many factors in determining whether the communication at issue was made for the purpose of seeking or providing legal advice").

disclosure of the truth.[87] The client must assert the privilege with respect to each challenged communication and the court must scrutinize each communication independently.[88] Whether the privilege applies to a communication is a fact-intensive inquiry.[89] These established principles, which apply to outside lawyers as well as in-house counsel, fully protect against the potential gamesmanship that concerns some courts where in-house lawyers are involved in disputed communications.

In-house lawyers who want to ensure that their internal communications are protected by the attorney-client privilege rather than potentially being exposed to discovery as business or other nonlegal advice should consider several precautionary measures. First, they should maintain an active law license in at least one jurisdiction.[90] Even if this measure is not required, it supports the proposition that the in-house lawyer is first and foremost a lawyer. Second, they should make clear that any employees with whom they communicate in any format or situation understand the purpose of the communication. If a written communication (including email messages) is intended to convey legal advice, the lawyer should indicate that its sole purpose is legal and label the communication as privileged. If a communication has dual purposes the lawyer should attempt to distinguish them. Third, in-house lawyers with business responsibilities should maintain separate files—including email folders—for business matters and legal matters where feasible. Fourth, in-house lawyers should not casually label documents as privileged, and they should discourage colleagues with whom they communicate from doing the same. An attorney-client privilege label or legend should be reserved for documents or communications that embody legal advice. Indiscriminate identification of documents as privileged arguably lessens the chance that any individual document will be afforded the privilege protection it allegedly deserves. Fifth, when discussing legal matters, in-house lawyers should exclude from the discussion anyone whose presence might waive the privilege. Sixth, if an in-house lawyer attends a company's board of directors or management meetings for the purpose of providing legal advice, the minutes of those meetings

---

87. United States v. Ivers, 967 F.3d 709, 716 (8th Cir. 2020); State v. Kosuda-Bigazzi, 250 A.3d 617, 640 (Conn. 2020); Hill, Kertscher & Wharton, LLP v. Moody, 839 S.E.2d 535, 539 (Ga. 2020); Underwood Props., LLC v. City of Hackensack, 269 A.3d 509, 516 (N.J. Super. Ct. App. Div. 2022). *But see* Fresenius Med. Care Holdings, Inc. v. Hood, 269 So. 3d 36, 63 (Miss. 2018) ("The Court interprets the scope of the attorney client privilege under Mississippi law broadly.").

88. Oldham v. Pedrie, 411 P.3d 933, 941–42 (Colo. App. 2015) (quoting Wesp v. Everson, 33 P.3d 191, 197 (Colo. 2001)); Brown v. Katz, 868 N.E.2d 1159, 1167 (Ind. Ct. App. 2007).

89. Towne Place Condo. Ass'n v. Phila. Indem. Ins. Co., 284 F. Supp. 3d 889, 895 (N.D. Ill. 2018); Kern v. Superior Court, 141 Cal. Rptr. 3d 504, 529 (Ct. App. 2012).

90. *See* ABA Model Rules of Prof'l Conduct Rule 5.5(d) (2021) (allowing in-house lawyers who are licensed in one United States jurisdiction to practice in another jurisdiction without engaging in the unauthorized practice of law).

should reflect that the lawyer attended in her role as corporate counsel and discussions were for the purpose of obtaining legal advice.

Additionally, companies may wish to consider educating employees on communicating with in-house counsel. For example, employees should be counseled on (1) the appropriate labeling of communications as privileged; (2) separating requests for legal advice or assistance from other business communications; (3) making requests for legal advice as specific as possible; and (4) confining any communications with counsel to only those people who need to know that legal advice or assistance has been requested.

VI. Communications within a Corporate Family

Corporations are not necessarily unitary entities; in fact, many have parents or subsidiaries. Related corporations are often described as being members of a corporate family. Communications between corporate family members are in many instances protected by the attorney-client privilege.[91] This is an exception to the general rule that disclosure of a privileged communication to a third party waives the privilege, which some courts call the disclosure rule.[92] In a discussion focusing on waiver but applicable to the privilege in the corporate context more broadly, the court in *Teleglobe Communications Corp. v. BCE, Inc. (In re Teleglobe Communications Corp.)*[93] outlined the theories courts apply to protect confidential communications among corporate family members: (1) the corporate family members constitute one client; (2) the corporate family members are joint clients; and (3) the corporate family members share a community of interest.[94] In many cases, however, courts do not specify the theoretical basis for their recognition of the privilege in the corporate family context.[95]

---

91. *See* Crabb v. KFC Nat'l Mgmt. Co., 1992 WL 1321, at *3 (6th Cir. Jan. 6, 1992) ("It is well settled that attorney-client privilege is not waived merely because the communications involved extend across corporate structures to encompass parent corporations, subsidiary corporations, and affiliated corporations.").

92. *See* MA Equip. Leasing I, LLC v. Tilton, 980 N.E.2d 1072, 1081 (Ohio Ct. App. 2012) ("While a client's disclosure of confidential information normally precipitates a waiver of the attorney-client privilege, courts often apply exceptions to the disclosure rule when communications are shared with a corporate parent, subsidiary, or affiliate.").

93. 493 F.3d 345 (3d Cir. 2007).

94. *Id.* at 370.

95. *See, e.g.*, Amorim Holding Financeira S.G.P.S., S.A. v. C.P. Baker & Co., Ltd., 2011 WL 5879433, at *3 (D. Mass. Nov. 22, 2011) ("Because Plaintiff and Amorim Holding II are related through common ownership and control, communications between Plaintiff's in-house counsel and the Amorim II employees are treated in the same way as communications between Plaintiff's in-house counsel and Plaintiff's employees."); Guy v. United Healthcare Corp., 154 F.R.D. 172, 177–78 (S.D. Ohio 1993) ("The disclosure of otherwise privileged materials to a parent by a wholly owned subsidiary will not result in a waiver of the attorney-client privilege.").

A. The One-Client Approach

The first corporate family privilege theory—the one-client approach—traces back to *United States v. United Shoe Machinery Corp.*,[96] long regarded as an important attorney-client privilege case. In *United Shoe*, the parties disputed the privilege's application to several categories of documents. In evaluating United Shoe's privilege claims, the court reasoned that "the client [was] United Shoe Machinery Corporation and all its subsidiaries and affiliates considered collectively."[97] This was a relatively easy call for the court based on the facts: the corporations "all used the same outside and inside counsel. The legal affairs of [the] corporations were closely related. Except for convenience in billing and formal accounting there was no attempt [by their lawyers] to regard one particular corporation as 'the client.'"[98]

United Shoe was followed nearly 30 years later by *United States v. American Telephone & Telegraph Co. (AT&T)*,[99] where the court adopted a list of guidelines for applying the attorney-client privilege to communications among related corporations. According to the *AT&T* court:

> The cases clearly hold that a corporate "client" includes not only the corporation by whom the attorney is employed or retained, but also parent, subsidiary, and affiliate corporations. . . . The cases in which the issue has arisen as to the identity of the client also involved facts in which the two related corporations had a substantial identity of legal interest in the matter in controversy. . . . But if there is no such community of interest in seeking advice, . . . the question of closeness of affiliation may arise.
>
> In the facts of this case, both parties contend that the wholly-owned and majority-owned affiliates of AT&T have close and long-standing relationships with each other, although they differ as to the legal significance of that intimacy. For purposes of the attorney-client privilege rule, however, the positions of both parties imply that these affiliates be considered part of AT&T as a single client.
>
> As for the companies in which AT&T owns a minority interest, apparently AT& T's interest in no case exceeds 30 percent. . . . These companies appear to have an autonomous corporate life of their own and, therefore, should be treated as independent of AT&T. . . .
>
> Despite the fact that the minority-owned companies affiliated with AT&T . . . will most likely have had a "substantial identity of legal interest" with the AT&T system in the matters that will be brought into question . . . the defendants still insist that AT&T as

---

96. 89 F. Supp. 357 (D. Mass. 1950).
97. *Id.* at 359.
98. *Id.*
99. 86 F.R.D. 603 (D.D.C. 1979).

> "client" should include collectively all member corporations of the Bell system. Defendants contend that to distinguish between member corporations on the basis of percentage of ownership exalts form over substance. We do not agree.
>
> The cases referring to parent, subsidiary, and affiliate corporations in regard to the attorney-client privilege simply reach the conclusion that there was a single client without examining this question. . . . If analysis begins with the proposition that corporations under unified control are "one" even though comprised of components held in varying degrees of ownership, then a minority-owned company can be assimilated to one in which substantial, although not majority, ownership is held. On the other hand, if analysis begins with the proposition that formerly distinct corporations are separate persons except as specific legal purpose warrants treating them as one, then a different conclusion is reached.
>
> A minority-owned company by hypothesis has independent stockholders, and those stockholders, by our analysis, will have some added protection in the fact that an attorney serving their corporation is bound to regard that company as being distinct from an individual corporate stockholder that, for practical purposes, may control the company but not own a majority of the stock. Hence, we conclude that the legal form should be given effect in such a context. . . .[100]

The *AT&T* opinion is not a model of clarity. Among other things, the court did not discuss whether the corporations shared common inside or outside counsel. Nonetheless, *AT&T* enjoys some currency with courts, which continue to recognize the one-client approach.[101] The one-client approach also finds support in the Restatement (Third) of the Law Governing Lawyers.[102]

B. The Joint Client Approach

Next, there is the joint client approach, under which members of a corporate family are treated as joint clients for attorney-client privilege purposes.[103]

---

100. *Id.* at 616–17.

101. *See, e.g.*, Pasadena Ref. Sys. Inc. v. United States, 2011 WL 1938133, at *2 (N.D. Tex. Apr. 26, 2011) ("[C]orporations related through common ownership or control are treated as one entity for attorney-client privilege purposes."); Va. Elec. & Power Co. v. Westmoreland-LG & E Partners, 526 S.E.2d 750, 755 (Va. 2000) (taking the one client approach without expressly adopting it).

102. *See* Restatement (Third) of the Law Governing Lawyers § 73 cmt. d (2000) (stating that when a parent corporation owns a controlling interest in a subsidiary, the parent's agents who are responsible for the subsidiary's legal matters are considered the subsidiary's agents, and the subsidiary's agents who are responsible for the parent's affairs are also considered agents of the parent for privilege purposes).

103. *See, e.g.*, Robinson Mech. Contractors Inc. v. PTC Grp. Holding Corp., 2017 WL 2021070, at *2–3 (E.D. Mo. May 12, 2017) (involving a parent and a subsidiary corporation that the court considered

Teleglobe Communications Corp. v. BCE, Inc. (In re Teleglobe Communications Corp.)[104] is the leading joint client case.

Teleglobe began with a complaint in a Chapter 11 bankruptcy case. The debtors were the wholly owned United States subsidiaries of a Canadian telecommunications company formerly known as Teleglobe, Inc. (Teleglobe). Teleglobe was, in turn, a wholly owned subsidiary of Bell Canada Enterprises, Inc. (BCE). When the debtors sued BCE in an adversary action, a dispute arose over communications between BCE lawyers and Teleglobe lawyers, officers, and directors that BCE withheld on attorney-client privilege grounds. Ultimately, BCE was ordered to produce numerous documents in discovery that it contended were privileged, and it took an interlocutory appeal to the Third Circuit. BCE's appeal raised "core questions about the proper operation of a corporate family's centralized in-house legal department."[105] Answering those questions required the court to delve into "a variety of concepts related to the co-client (or joint-client) privilege."[106] In doing so, the court applied Delaware law. Where there was no Delaware law on-point, the court predicted that Delaware would follow federal common law and the law of other states.

With respect to the co-client or joint-client privilege, the *Teleglobe* court observed that it is often expedient for two or more people to consult a single lawyer.[107] The rules of professional conduct allow a lawyer to serve multiple clients on the same matter so long as all clients consent, and there is no significant risk of the lawyer being unable to fulfill her duties to them all. Just as in single-client representations, the lawyer and co-clients begin their relationship when the co-clients express their wish for joint representation, and the lawyer consents.[108]

In comparison, the community-of-interest approach allows lawyers representing different clients with similar legal interests to safely share information.[109] As the court explained, two aspects of the community-of-interest approach stand out. First, to be protected, the communication must be shared with the lawyer for the other member of the community of interest.[110] Sharing the communication directly with a community member may void the privilege. Second, all community members must have a common legal interest in the shared communication.[111]

joint clients because they shared in-house counsel and had a common interest); Davis v. PMA Cos., 2012 WL 3922967, at *3 (W.D. Okla. Sept. 7, 2012) (adopting the joint client approach).

104. 493 F.3d 345 (3d Cir. 2007).

105. *Id.* at 359.

106. *Id.*

107. *Id.* at 362.

108. *Id.*

109. *Id.* at 364.

110. *Id.*

111. *Id.*

The *Teleglobe* court carefully pointed out that because the community-of-interest extension of the privilege only applies when clients are separately represented, it generally does not apply in cases that "revolve around corporate family members' use of common attorneys (namely, centralized in-house counsel)."[112] Second, while in both the joint client and community-of-interest contexts courts refer to the clients' common interests, the concepts are not the same. Specifically, "because co-clients agree to share all information related to the matter of common interest with each other and to employ the same attorney, their legal interests must be identical (or nearly so) in order that an attorney can represent them all with the candor, vigor, and loyalty that our ethics require."[113] Under the community-of-interest approach, on the other hand, because the clients have separate lawyers, courts can afford to relax the degree to which clients' interests must align without worrying that their lawyers' loyalty and zealous representation will suffer.[114]

Returning to the joint-client privilege, the court noted that it only protects communications from compelled disclosure to third parties.[115] When former co-clients sue each other, the default rule is that all communications made during the joint representation are discoverable. Here, BCE argued that the default rule should be flipped when the joint clients are a parent company and its wholly owned subsidiary; that is, courts should presume that communications generated during the joint representation are not discoverable in later litigation between the entities. BCE contended that no parent would want its subsidiary to be able to invade the privilege in subsequent litigation, so courts should not presume that intent. Furthermore, because parents and wholly owned subsidiaries share the same interests, the parent's intent (to shield information) should control.[116] The court ultimately rejected BCE's argument and predicted that Delaware courts would apply the adverse litigation exception even where the joint clients are wholly owned by the same entity. That determination left the court to pull together the various privilege and waiver principles in the modern parent-subsidiary corporation environment.

Because parent corporations often centralize the delivery of legal services to their corporate families in a single in-house legal department, the *Teleglobe* court deemed it important to consider how the disclosure rule affected information sharing among corporate affiliates.[117] "Recognizing that any other result would wreak havoc on corporate counsel offices," the *Teleglobe* court observed that "courts almost universally hold that intra-group information sharing does not implicate the disclosure rule."[118] Rephrased, the general rule

---

112. *Id.* at 365 (footnote omitted).
113. *Id.* at 366 (citing F.D.I.C. v. Ogden Corp., 202 F.3d 454, 461 (1st Cir. 2000)).
114. *Id.*
115. *Id.*
116. *Id.*
117. *Id.* at 369.
118. *Id.*

holds that information sharing among members of a corporate family does not waive the attorney-client privilege like disclosure to an unrelated third party would. The *Teleglobe* court considered this result to be unassailable.[119] The question was how to reach it.

The court first considered the one-client approach. In doing so, it observed that within a wholly owned corporate family, it superficially makes sense to hold that the family is one client for privilege purposes and that the privilege is held solely by the parent because all fiduciary duties flow to the parent.[120] At the same time, treating corporate family members as one client disregards corporate form.[121] It is a fundamental principle of corporate law that courts must respect entity separateness unless doing so would be seriously inequitable.[122] In tort litigation, for example, a court likely would not treat the debtors, Teleglobe, and BCE as one entity. The *Teleglobe* court therefore stated that absent some compelling reason to disregard corporate form, courts should treat the members of a corporate family as the separate entities they are and not as one client.[123]

The community-of-interest approach fared no better in the court's eyes. The court reasoned that the community-of-interest privilege necessarily fails as a matter of law where intra-company communications are concerned, because it only comes into play when parties are represented by separate counsel, which often is not the case with parent and subsidiary corporations.[124] Moreover, the community-of-interest privilege only applies when the different lawyers disclose information to one another, not when the parties communicate directly. Lastly, "it assumes too much" to think that corporate family members necessarily have a substantially similar legal interest (as the community-of-interest privilege requires) in all their communications.[125]

The court's dislike of the one-client and community-of-interest approaches prompted the court to reject the disclosure rule in the corporate family setting on the basis that the members of a corporate family are joint clients.[126] The court reasoned that the joint client approach reflected both the separateness of each corporation and the reality that they are all represented by the same in-house counsel (regardless of whether the lawyer offices with the parent or a subsidiary).[127]

---

119. *Id.*

120. *Id.* at 370.

121. *Id.* at 371.

122. *Id.* (first citing Pauley Petrol., Inc. v. Cont'l Oil Co., 239 A.2d 629, 633 (Del. Ch. 1968); then citing *In re* Owens Corning, 419 F.3d 195, 211 (3d Cir. 2005)).

123. *Id.* at 372.

124. *Id.*

125. *Id.*

126. *Id.*

127. *Id.*

In the end, the court held that the district court could only compel BCE to produce disputed documents because of the adverse-litigation exception to the co-client privilege if it found that BCE and the debtors were jointly represented on a matter of common interest that the documents addressed.[128] Thus, the primary issue on remand would be whether BCE and the debtors were jointly represented. As a rule—both as embodied in *Teleglobe* and elsewhere—the existence of a joint or co-client relationship is a fact-specific inquiry.[129] Courts cannot assume as a matter of law that corporate family members share a common legal interest sufficient to be considered joint clients.[130]

C. The Community-of-Interest Approach

Finally, for now, there is the community-of-interest approach to protecting the privilege in the corporate family realm. Although the *Teleglobe* court rejected the community-of-interest approach, other courts have adopted it, as *Duplan Corp. v. Deering Milliken, Inc.*[131] illustrates.

Duplan was a patent-antitrust case. The court applied the community-of-interest test in deciding whether communications between a parent and subsidiary corporation were privileged when the corporations did not employ a common lawyer. In a confusing and poorly written opinion, the court held that there was a sufficient community of interest between a French corporation, which was a patent owner, and some of its subsidiaries for the attorney-client privilege to apply to communications between them.[132] As the court explained:

> A community of interest exists among . . . separate corporations where they have an identical legal interest with respect to the subject matter of a communication between an attorney and a client concerning legal advice. The third parties receiving copies of the communication and claiming a community of interest may be distinct legal entities from the client receiving the legal advice and may be a non-party to any anticipated or pending litigation. The key consideration is that the nature of the interest be identical, not similar, and be legal, not solely commercial. The fact that there may be an overlap of a commercial and a legal interest . . . does not negate the effect of the legal interest in establishing a community of interest.[133]

---

128. *Id.* at 386–87.
129. Newmark Group, Inc. v. Avison Young (Canada) Inc., 2020 WL 5514156, at *15 (D. Nev. Sept. 14, 2020); Margulis v. Hertz Corp., 2017 WL 772336, at *7 (D.N.J. Feb. 28, 2017).
130. MA Equip. Leasing I, LLC v. Tilton, 980 N.E.2d 1072, 1085 (Ohio Ct. App. 2012).
131. 397 F. Supp. 1146 (D.S.C. 1974).
132. *Id.* at 1184–85.
133. *Id.* at 1172.

Continuing, the *Duplan* court reasoned that while an interest of a third-party corporation from a commercial standpoint normally would not establish a community of interest sufficient to recognize the privilege, the fact that here the communications were among corporations under common ownership or control justified treating "such inter-related corporate communications in the same manner as intra-corporate communications."[134] In summary, if a corporation with a legal interest in an attorney-client communication shares the communication with a related corporation, the attorney-client privilege is not waived as a result.[135] If, on the other hand, the communications were shared with an unrelated corporation, the privilege would be lost.[136]

Unfortunately, the community-of-interest approach can yield inconsistent results, as *Somers v. QVC, Inc.*[137] reflects. *Somers* concerned QVC's alleged monopolization of the direct response television programming market and control over the sale of nutritional supplements in that market. The plaintiffs alleged that QVC and the Home Shopping Network (HSN) began violating antitrust law when QVC's corporate parent, Qurate, acquired HSN.

The plaintiffs filed a motion to compel discovery when QVC withheld communications based on the attorney-client privilege. The plaintiffs sought (1) communications between an in-house HSN lawyer, Gassett, and QVC employees; and (2) communications from a QVC lawyer, LaMonaca, and HSN employees. The plaintiffs argued that the privilege did not apply because HSN and QVC were separate entities, and the lawyers were communicating with employees from a sister company rather than their respective clients.[138]

QVC replied that its interests and HSN's interests were generally aligned as wholly owned subsidiaries of the same corporate parent and were specifically aligned regarding the delivery of consistent legal advice. QVC noted that after Qurate acquired HSN, the QVC and HSN legal teams were consolidated into one legal department. QVC asserted that this structure satisfied any requirement of aligned interests. QVC and HSN also reached an "Affiliate Company Shared Services Agreement," which defined their shared "business operations" and "administrative services" to include in-house legal services.[139] The agreement specifically provided "that 'legal communications among and between them, including those made as a consequence of the Services Agreement, [were] made pursuant to a joint client/attorney client privilege.'"[140]

QVC argued that because QVC and HSN were both wholly owned subsidiaries of Qurate, they had the same interests because "all of the duties owed to the subsidiaries flow back up to the parent," and "the only interest of a wholly

---

134. *Id.* at 1184.
135. *Id.* at 1185.
136. *Id.*
137. 2021 WL 3487315 (E.D. Pa. Aug. 9, 2021).
138. *Id.* at *1.
139. *Id.*
140. *Id.* (quoting the agreement).

owned subsidiary is in serving its parent."[141] According to QVC, because it and HSN shared Qurate's interests—ranging from consistent contract interpretation to avoiding liability arising out of on-air product claims—Gassett's and LaMonaca's communications in furtherance of those goals were privileged.[142] The court disagreed in part:

> Nowhere in QVC's brief does it identify or explain how QVC has any interest whatsoever in "consistent interpretation" of contracts to which it is not a party, or how HSN has a legal interest in a sister entity complying with its contracts with third parties. Qurate—the parent company—undoubtedly has an interest in all its subsidiaries complying with their own contracts. However, there is no clear interest for sister companies to comply with each other's contracts; nor is it clear that Qurate has an interest in one subsidiary complying with another subsidiary's contract. The Court concludes that QVC has no cognizable legal interest in a contract between HSN and its vendor, just as Qurate has no legal interest in QVC complying with HSN's contracts. While Qurate, HSN, and QVC may all share an interest in not alienating a profitable partner, this is a business or commercial interest, not a legal interest. When a communication pertains to business or commercial advice, that communication will not be privileged. . . . A private agreement between these entities that their communications are privileged does not alter this conclusion.[143]

In contrast, the court agreed that emails that pertained to compliance with regulations and assessing legal risks associated with approving on-air claims regarding the plaintiffs' nutritional supplements were privileged. Qurate had an interest in all its subsidiaries complying with the law, as it is possible it could be responsible for liabilities or fines incurred by a subsidiary.[144] Similarly, where QVC and HSN communicated regarding their conflict with the plaintiffs, the companies shared a legal interest in defending themselves in potential litigation. To the extent that HSN and QVC communicated regarding a shared interest in defending themselves in litigation with the plaintiffs, those exchanges were privileged.[145]

As suggested earlier, *Somers* is a somewhat muddled decision. The court initially focused on the joint client approach, but its analysis seemed to drift toward the community-of-interest approach. QVC appeared to argue for the community-of-interest approach, as suggested by the court's description

141. *Id.* at *4.
142. *Id.*
143. *Id.*
144. *Id.*
145. *Id.* at *5.

of Gassett's and LaMonaca's different roles and employers. The court also appeared to embrace the community-of-interest approach by recognizing the privilege where litigation was concerned. After all, courts often confine any common interest extension of the privilege to litigation matters.[146] In any event, it is reasonable to believe that many courts would decide *Somers* differently under either the joint client or community-of-interest approaches and more generously enforce QVC's attorney-client privilege based on the corporate family's combined legal department's representation of both wholly owned subsidiaries.

VII. Corporate Succession

Corporations commonly merge, sell their assets, or are acquired by other companies. In such instances, a question that sometimes arises is whether the successor corporation may assert the predecessor corporation's attorney-client privilege. As a rule, when control of a corporation passes to new management, authority to assert or waive the corporation's attorney-client privilege also passes to new management.[147] This is certainly true in the case of mergers,[148] but it may also be true in the case of asset sales.[149] Where an asset sale is concerned, "[i]f the practical consequences of the transaction result in the transfer of control of the business and the continuation of the business under new

146. *See, e.g.*, Brinkmann v. Petro Welt Trading Ges.M.B.H., 324 So. 3d 574, 579 (Fla. Dist. Ct. App. 2021) (quoting AG Beaumont 1, LLC v. Wells Fargo Bank, N.A., 160 So. 3d 510, 512 (Fla. Dist. Ct. App. 2015)); Ambac Assurance Corp. v. Countrywide Home Loans, Inc., 57 N.E.3d 30, 38–39 (N.Y. 2016) (explaining why common interest arrangements should be confined to pending litigation or matters where litigation is reasonably anticipated).

147. Hillman Group, Inc. v. KeyMe, LLC, 439 F. Supp. 3d 845, 853–54 (E.D. Tex. 2020); Great Hill Equity Partners IV, LP v. SIG Growth Equity Fund I, LLLP, 80 A.3d 155, 162 (Del. Ch. 2013); Bridlington Co., L.L.C. v. S. Disposal Servs., L.L.C., 216 So. 3d 219, 223 (La. Ct. App. 2017); Girl Scouts-W. Okla. v. Barringer-Thomson, 252 P.3d 844, 847–48 (Okla. 2011); State v. Doyle, 235 A.3d 482, 503–04 (R.I. 2020); *In re* Cap Rock Elec. Coop., Inc., 35 S.W.3d 222, 228 (Tex. App. 2000).

148. Venture Law Group v. Superior Court, 12 Cal. Rptr. 3d 656, 660–61 (Ct. App. 2004).

149. *See, e.g.*, United States v. Adams, 2018 WL 1255003, at *3–4 (D. Minn. Mar. 12, 2018) (involving asset purchase agreements under which the buyer acquired essentially every asset necessary to continue the seller's business); MacKenzie-Childs LLC v. MacKenzie-Childs, 262 F.R.D. 241, 252–53 (W.D.N.Y. 2009) (holding that the privilege passed with the transfer of "substantially all of the assets" of the company; the purchaser continued the seller's business); Am. Int'l Specialty Lines Ins. Co. v. NWI-I, Inc., 240 F.R.D. 401, 408 (N.D. Ill. 2007) ("[B]ecause the practical consequences of the Asset Purchase Agreement resulted in the transfer of control of Old FTL's business and the continuation of that business under new management, the authority to assert or waive the attorney-client privilege transferred to New FTL."); Postorivo v. AG Paintball Holdings, Inc., 2008 WL 343856, at *2 (Del. Ch. Feb. 7, 2008) (involving the sale of "substantially all of the assets" of the corporation). *Cf.* Goodrich v. Goodrich, 960 A.2d 1275, 1283 (N.H. 2008) ("A pure asset sale transfers only ownership over property, not control of the establishing corporation itself, and, accordingly, does not transfer the attorney-client privilege. . . . If, however, an entity acquires control of the establishing corporation's business operations, rights and liabilities, it is generally accepted that it also acquires authority over the attorney-client privilege.") (citations omitted).

management, the authority to assert or waive the attorney-client privilege will follow as well."[150] In deciding whether the practical consequences of a transaction result in the transfer of control of the business, courts may consider such factors as the extent of the assets acquired, including whether stock was sold; whether the successor entity continues to sell the same product or deliver the same service as the predecessor entity; whether the successor retains the predecessor's customers and employees; and whether the successor uses the same patents and trademarks that the predecessor company used.[151]

Tekni-Plex, Inc. v. Meyner & Landis[152] is the leading case on the transfer of corporate attorney-client relationships. Tekni-Plex, Inc. (old Tekni-Plex) manufactured and packaged industrial products. For years, old Tekni–Plex had 18 shareholders and was managed by a five-member board of directors. Tom Y.C. Tang was both a director and a shareholder of the company. In 1986, Tang became the sole shareholder of old Tekni-Plex. From that time until the company's sale in 1994, Tang was also old Tekni-Plex's president, chief executive officer, and sole director. Meyner & Landis (M&L), a New Jersey law firm, began representing old Tekni-Plex in 1971. M&L handled various matters for old Tekni-Plex, including environmental permitting and compliance issues.

In March 1994, Tang and old Tekni-Plex entered into a merger agreement with TP Acquisition Co. (Acquisition), whereby Tang sold old Tekni-Plex to Acquisition for $43 million. M&L represented both old Tekni-Plex and Tang in the transaction.[153]

Acquisition was a shell corporation created by the buyers solely to acquire old Tekni-Plex. Under the parties' merger agreement, old Tekni-Plex merged into Acquisition, with Acquisition the surviving corporation, and old Tekni-Plex ceased its separate existence.[154] Old Tekni-Plex conveyed to Acquisition all its assets, liabilities, and rights. In return, Acquisition paid Tang the purchase price "in complete liquidation of Tekni-Plex," and Tang's shares in old Tekni-Plex—which were the only shares outstanding—were canceled.[155]

After the merger, Acquisition changed its name to Tekni-Plex, Inc. (new Tekni-Plex).[156] In June 1994, new Tekni-Plex initiated an arbitration proceeding against Tang, alleging that he breached representations and warranties in the merger agreement concerning old Tekni-Plex's compliance with environmental laws. Tang's alleged misrepresentations involved the status of environmental permitting and compliance by old Tekni-Plex with respect to a laminator machine at its Somerville, New Jersey, plant. New Tekni-Plex

150. Soverain Software LLC v. Gap, Inc., 340 F. Supp. 2d 760, 763 (E.D. Tex. 2004).
151. John Crane Prod. Solutions, Inc. v. R2R and D, LLC, 2012 WL 3453696, at *3 (E.D. Tex. Aug. 14, 2012).
152. 674 N.E.2d 663 (N.Y. 1996).
153. *Id.* at 665.
154. *Id.*
155. *Id.*
156. *Id.*

asserted that old Tekni-Plex had misled government regulators regarding the nature of discharges from the laminator when it was initially permitted several years before the merger and that Tang had similarly misrepresented the nature of such discharges to new Tekni-Plex in the merger agreement.[157] M&L had advised old Tekni-Plex on environmental compliance and assisted it in obtaining the permit for the laminator.[158]

Tang hired M&L to represent him in the arbitration. New Tekni-Plex moved to disqualify M&L, but the arbitrator determined that he lacked authority to rule on the motion. New Tekni-Plex thus moved for an order to show cause in a New York trial court to enjoin M&L from representing Tang in any action against new Tekni-Plex and for an order disqualifying M&L from representing Tang in the then pending arbitration. The trial court enjoined M&L from representing Tang in the arbitration, further enjoined M&L from disclosing to Tang any information obtained from old Tekni-Plex, and ordered M&L to deliver to new Tekni-Plex all the firm's files concerning its representation of old Tekni-Plex.[159] After the Appellate Division affirmed the trial court's orders, the case made its way to New York's highest court, the Court of Appeals.

The Court of Appeals agreed with the lower courts that M&L should be disqualified from representing Tang in the arbitration.[160] As for confidential communications between old Tekni-Plex and M&L during M&L's representation of old Tekni-Plex on environmental matters, authority to assert the attorney-client privilege passed to new Tekni-Plex.[161]

The *Tekni-Plex* court began its analysis by observing that lawyers' duty of confidentiality continues after a representation concludes and that "a lawyer may not reveal information confided by a former client, or use such information to the disadvantage of the former client or the advantage of a third party."[162] Continuing, the court noted that DR 5-108(A)(1) of New York's Code of Professional Responsibility provided that, absent a former client's consent, a lawyer could not "represent another person in the same or a substantially related matter in which that persons interests are materially adverse" to the former client's interests.[163] A party seeking to disqualify an opponent's lawyer under DR 5-108(A)(1) had to show (1) the existence of a prior attorney-client relationship with the lawyer, (2) that the matters in both representations were substantially related, and (3) that the current and former client's interests were materially adverse.[164] The moving party's satisfaction of the three-part test

157. *Id.*
158. *Id.* at 669.
159. *Id.* at 666.
160. *Id.*
161. *Id.*
162. *Id.*
163. *Id.* at 667.
164. *Id.*

created an irrebuttable presumption of disqualification.[165] With that foundation laid, the *Tekni-Plex* court capsulized the relationship between M&L and old Tekni-Plex regarding lawyers' duty of confidentiality and the attorney-client privilege:

> M&L represented old Tekni-Plex for over 20 years on a variety of legal matters. As counsel to the corporation, the law firm's duties of confidentiality and loyalty ran to old Tekni-Plex on these matters. . . . Concomitantly, the attorney-client privilege attached to any confidential communications that took place between M&L and [old] Tekni-Plex corporate actors in the course of this representation. . . . The power to assert or waive the privilege, moreover, belonged to the management of old Tekni-Plex, to be exercised by its officers and directors . . . .[166]

Tang and M&L argued that Acquisition's purchase of old Tekni-Plex should not be held to transfer M&L's attorney-client relationship with old Tekni-Plex to new Tekni-Plex because (1) the transaction was a mere asset sale; and (2) by virtue of the deal, M&L's sole former client, old Tekni-Plex, ceased to exist.[167] The court was not persuaded, explaining that "[w]hen ownership of a corporation changes hands, whether the attorney-client relationship transfers as well to the new owners turns on the practical consequences rather than the formalities of the particular transaction."[168] As the Supreme Court had previously established in *Commodity Futures Trading Commission v. Weintraub*,[169] where the successor entity "makes efforts to run the pre-existing business entity and manage its affairs, successor management stands in the shoes of prior management and controls the attorney-client privilege with respect to matters concerning the company's operations."[170] The *Tekni-Plex* court reasoned that in such cases, the predecessor company's attorney-client relationship logically continues with the new entity.[171] In contrast, a mere transfer of assets with no effort to continue the preexisting business generally does not transfer the attorney-client relationship.[172]

The *Tekni-Plex* court then dismissed new Tekni-Plex's characterization of old Tekni-Plex's merger with Acquisition and linked the businesses of old Tekni-Plex and new Tekni-Plex:

165. *Id.*
166. *Id.* at 668 (citations omitted).
167. *Id.*
168. *Id.*
169. 471 U.S. 343 (1985).
170. *Tekni-Plex*, 674 N.E.2d at 668.
171. *Id.*
172. *Id.*

> Here, [Tang and M&L] emphasize that old Tekni-Plex merged into Acquisition and ceased to exist as a separate legal entity. That Acquisition, rather than old Tekni-Plex, was designated the surviving corporation, however, is not dispositive. Acquisition was a mere shell corporation, created solely for the purpose of acquiring old Tekni-Plex. Following the merger, the business of old Tekni-Plex remained unchanged, with the same products, clients, suppliers and non-managerial personnel. Indeed, under the Merger Agreement, new Tekni-Plex possessed all of the rights, privileges, liabilities and obligations of old Tekni-Plex, in addition to its assets. Certainly, new Tekni-Plex is entitled to access . . . any relevant pre-merger legal advice rendered to old Tekni-Plex that it might need to defend against these liabilities or pursue any of these rights.
>
> As a practical matter, then, old Tekni-Plex did not die. To the contrary, the business operations of old Tekni-Plex continued under the new managers. Consequently, control of the attorney-client privilege with respect to any confidential communications between M&L and corporate actors of old Tekni-Plex concerning these operations passed to the management of new Tekni-Plex. . . . An attorney-client relationship between M&L and new Tekni-Plex necessarily exists.[173]

Once the court established a former attorney-client relationship between M&L and new Tekni-Plex, the dominos fell quickly. Because M&L had advised old Tekni-Plex on the same environmental compliance issues that undergirded new Tekni-Plex's misrepresentation claims against Tang, and because the firm's proposed representation of Tang was plainly adverse to new Tekni-Plex, the court concluded that M&L should be disqualified from representing Tang in the arbitration.[174]

Finally, the court had to determine whether the trial court properly enjoined M&L from revealing to Tang any confidential communications obtained from old Tekni-Plex and whether new Tekni-Plex owned the confidences created during M&L's prior representation of old Tekni-Plex. This required the court to separately analyze M&L's general business communications with old Tekni-Plex and those communications related to the merger negotiations.

With respect to M&L's general business communications with old Tekni-Plex, the court reiterated that new Tekni-Plex's management continued old Tekni-Plex's business operations. Thus, control of the attorney-client privilege concerning confidential communications arising out of those operations—including pre-merger communications between old Tekni-Plex and M&L regarding the company's environmental compliance—passed to new Tekni-Plex's management. New Tekni-Plex thus had the power to assert the

173. *Id.* at 669 (citation omitted).

174. *Id.* at 669–70.

attorney-client privilege to prevent M&L from sharing such confidential communications with Tang.[175] This result was consistent with new Tekni-Plex's right to invoke the pre-merger attorney-client relationship of old Tekni-Plex on the basis that new Tekni-Plex might be required to prosecute or defend third-party suits involving the assets it acquired, and the liabilities it assumed, from old Tekni-Plex through the merger.[176]

As for communications between old Tekni-Plex and M&L concerning the merger transaction, new Tekni-Plex did not assume old Tekni-Plex's control of the attorney-client privilege.[177] New Tekni-Plex's claims against Tang did not derive from the rights it inherited from old Tekni-Plex, but rather from the rights retained by Acquisition in connection with the transaction. Furthermore, under the merger agreement, old Tekni-Plex's rights with respect to disputes arising from the merger remained independent from—and, in fact, adverse to—Acquisition's rights. Accordingly, in the current dispute, new Tekni-Plex could not "both pursue the rights of the buyer (Acquisition) and simultaneously assume the attorney-client rights that the buyer's adversary (old Tekni-Plex) retained regarding the transaction."[178]

Tekni-Plex has been described as "a wake-up call for transactional lawyers."[179] Although the court's holding was analytically unremarkable—at least in the merger realm (where the surviving corporation assumes its vanishing partner's attributes)—it raised confidentiality and disqualification issues that many transactional lawyers had never studiously considered.[180] For a company that is selling all its assets to another company that will carry on its business or which will be merged out of existence, and which wishes to retain control of its attorney-client privilege concerning pre-transaction communications, a possible solution is to contractually exclude from the transferred assets any attorney-client communications that it wishes to retain as its own.[181]

VIII. Dissolved Corporations

Beyond the results of mergers or asset sales, corporations may cease activities for various reasons. Perhaps the business a corporation was formed to operate fails. A corporation may be administratively dissolved for noncompliance with state law. Whatever the circumstances, questions may arise around the defunct corporation's attorney-client privilege. For example, a representative

175. *Id.* at 670.
176. *Id.*
177. *Id.* at 671.
178. *Id.*
179. Henry S. Bryans, *Business Successors and the Transpositional Attorney-Client Relationship*, 64 Bus. Law. 1039, 1046 (2009).
180. *Id.*
181. *See* Great Hill Equity Partners IV, LP v. SIG Growth Equity Fund I, LLLP, 80 A.3d 155, 161–62 (Del. Ch. 2013) (suggesting this option).

of a defunct corporation—such as a former officer or director, or the corporation's former lawyer—may receive a subpoena seeking documents that would be privileged if the corporation still existed. These representatives may have an interest in withholding the information sought by the third party. For instance, they might be concerned about personal liability based on the corporation's demise or some preceding act or event. Because lawyers' duty of confidentiality continues after a representation concludes,[182] as does the attorney-client privilege,[183] a lawyer for a defunct corporation normally must resist a third party's efforts to obtain ostensibly privileged materials.[184] Those efforts, in turn, require courts to address the application of the defunct corporation's attorney-client privilege, if any. "If any" is the critical qualifier here. Although an individual client's attorney-client privilege clearly survives the client's death,[185] the survival of a corporation's attorney-client privilege following its "death" is not so clear-cut.

A. General Rules

Whether the attorney-client privilege survives a corporate dissolution is a question of law.[186] Courts take two approaches to the question.[187] First, communications between a corporation and its lawyer retain their privileged status after the corporation dissolves or ceases normal business operations so long as the corporation retains some form of continued existence evidenced by having someone with the authority to speak for the "client."[188] That person may be a bankruptcy trustee, a receiver or statutory liquidator, a person managing the corporation during the windup process, or some other person

182. *In re* Bryan, 61 P.3d 641, 658 (Kan. 2003); ABA Model Rules of Prof'l Conduct Rule 1.6 cmt. 20 (2021).

183. O'Boyle v. Borough of Longport, 94 A.3d 299, 309 (N.J. 2014); CLL Acad., Inc. v. Acad. House Council, 231 A.3d 884, 888 (Pa. Super. Ct. 2020).

184. *See* State v. Gonzalez, 234 P.3d 1, 11 (Kan. 2010) ("There is some overlap between the ethical duty of confidentiality and the attorney-client privilege. By definition, all communications protected by the attorney-client privilege will be confidential and covered by the ethical duty. . . . That overlap is the reason why the ethical duty of confidentiality requires an attorney to invoke the attorney-client privilege when it is applicable.") (citation omitted); McNelis v. Crain, 78 N.E.3d 1237, 1241 (Ohio Ct. App. 2016) (explaining that because a lawyer's duty to preserve a client's confidences survives the termination of the attorney-client relationship and the attorney-client privilege does not cease upon the client's death, the lawyer had a responsibility to maintain the decedent's confidences).

185. Swidler & Berlin v. United States, 524 U.S. 399, 405 (1998); *In re* Estate of Rabin, 474 P.3d 1211, 1218 (Colo. 2020); CLL Acad., Inc. v. Acad. House Council, 231 A.3d 884, 888 (Pa. Super. Ct. 2020); Morrison v. State, 575 S.W.3d 1, 26 (Tex. App. 2019).

186. Affiniti Colorado, LLC v. Kissinger & Fellman, P.C., 461 P.3d 606, 611 (Colo. App. 2019); Red Vision Sys., Inc. v. Nat'l Real Estate Info. Servs., L.P., 108 A.3d 54, 60 (Pa. Super. Ct. 2015).

187. *See* Official Comm. of Admin. Claimants *ex rel.* LTV Steel Co. v. Moran, 802 F. Supp. 2d 947, 948–49 (N.D. Ill. 2011) (discussing the competing scenarios).

188. Favila v. Katten Muchin Rosenmann LLP, 115 Cal. Rptr. 3d 274, 298–99 (Ct. App. 2010); Affiniti Colorado, LLC v. Kissinger & Fellman, P.C., 461 P.3d 606, 614–17 (Colo. App. 2019); Red Vision Sys., Inc. v. Nat'l Real Estate Info. Servs., L.P., 108 A.3d 54, 68 (Pa. Super. Ct. 2015).

or group who succeeds to the defunct corporation's management.[189] Second, and alternatively, if a corporation is dissolved or has ceased to operate and has neither a legal successor nor remaining managers authorized to handle its post-dissolution windup, then the inoperative corporation enjoys no attorney-client privilege,[190] absent a contrary state statute.[191] In the case of a truly defunct corporation, there is no longer any "client" to assert or waive the privilege.[192] Furthermore, and perhaps more important, all the policy reasons that support recognition of the attorney-client privilege vanish.[193] In fact, where a corporation truly is "dead," courts generally presume that its attorney-client privilege no longer exists.[194]

B. An Illustrative and Explanatory Case

Affiniti Colorado, LLC v. Kissinger & Fellman, P.C.[195] highlights the various concerns or issues in play when a dissolved corporation's claimed attorney-client privilege is disputed. In 2015, Affiniti sued a corporation named EAGLE-Net for breach of contract and won a judgment. The litigation exhausted EAGLE-Net's assets, and, in May 2017, EAGLE-Net's board of directors resolved to dissolve EAGLE-Net and divest it of its assets. In June 2017, the dissolution process ended, and EAGLE-Net ceased to exist.

During the contract litigation, Affiniti learned that EAGLE-Net had not obtained the approval required to grant Affiniti a security interest in its assets, contrary to statements allegedly made in an opinion letter written by EAGLE-Net's general counsel, Kenneth S. Fellman, of Kissinger & Fellman, P.C. (collectively Fellman). Because of the resulting difficulties in collecting its judgment against EAGLE-Net, Affiniti sued Fellman for negligent misrepresentation.

---

189. Red Vision Sys., Inc. v. Nat'l Real Estate Info. Servs., L.P., 108 A.3d 54, 68 (Pa. Super. Ct. 2015).

190. Jiaxing Super Lighting Elec. Appliance Co., Ltd. v. Lunera Lighting, Inc., 2021 WL 2711229, at *2–3 (N.D. Cal. July 1, 2021); United States v. Walters, 2020 WL 1934803, at *2 (S.D. Miss. Apr. 21, 2020) (applying federal law to an administratively dissolved corporation); Express Homebuyers USA, LLC v. WBH Mktg., Inc., 2018 WL 4922467, at *2 (S.D. Fla. Feb. 9, 2018) (applying federal privilege law); Sec. & Exch. Comm'n v. Carrillo Huettel LLP, 2015 WL 1610282, at *2–3 (S.D.N.Y. Apr. 8, 2015) (applying federal law); Affiniti Colorado, LLC v. Kissinger & Fellman, P.C., 461 P.3d 606, 614–17 (Colo. App. 2019); John Doe Corp 1 v. Huizenga Mgrs. Fund, LLC, 188 N.E.3d 1259, 1278–81 (Ill. App. Ct. 2021); Red Vision Sys., Inc. v. Nat'l Real Estate Info. Servs., L.P., 108 A.3d 54, 68 (Pa. Super. Ct. 2015).

191. *See, e.g.*, PCS Nitrogen, Inc. v. Ross Dev. Corp., 2011 WL 3665335, at *4 (D.S.C. Aug. 19, 2011) (relying on a South Carolina statute permitting a dissolved corporation to be sued); Wallace v. Huntington Nat'l Bank, 2010 WL 3603494, at *7 (S.D. Ohio Sept. 10, 2010) (applying an Ohio statute); Reilly v. Greenwald & Hoffman, LLP, 127 Cal. Rprtr. 3d 317, 324 (Ct. App. 2011) (discussing a California statute).

192. *In re* Fundamental Long Term Care, Inc., 2012 WL 4815321, at *9 (Bankr. M.D. Fla. Oct. 9, 2012); Red Vision Sys., Inc. v. Nat'l Real Estate Info. Servs., L.P., 108 A.3d 54, 68 (Pa. Super. Ct. 2015).

193. United States v. Cole, 569 F. Supp. 3d 696, 701 (N.D. Ohio 2021); *In re* Fundamental Long Term Care, Inc., 2012 WL 4815321, at *9 (Bankr. M.D. Fla. Oct. 9, 2012); John Doe Corp 1 v. Huizenga Mgrs. Fund, LLC, 188 N.E.3d 1259, 1278–79 (Ill. App. Ct. 2021).

194. Abdo v. Fitzsimmons, 2019 WL 10910805, at *1 (N.D. Cal. Oct. 2, 2019).

195. 461 P.3d 606 (Colo. App. 2019).

After Affiniti sought communications between Fellman and EAGLE-Net in discovery, Fellman moved for a protective order based on the attorney-client privilege. The trial court denied Fellman's motion and Fellman took an interlocutory appeal to the Colorado Court of Appeals.

On appeal, Fellman contended that because the attorney-client privilege applies equally to corporations and individuals, and because the privilege survives the death of an individual, the privilege must necessarily survive the dissolution of a corporation.[196] As part of this contention, Fellman further asserted that Kenneth Fellman was authorized to invoke the privilege because of his status as EAGLE-Net's former general counsel.[197]

The *Affiniti Colorado* court observed that in *Swidler & Berlin v. United States*,[198] the Supreme Court had found that a posthumous privilege, subject to a few exceptions, was well settled at common law. In doing so, the Court reasoned that posthumous recognition of the attorney-client privilege was justified because the privilege encourages frank and open communication between clients and their lawyers and that "'[c]lients may be concerned about reputation, civil liability, or possible harm to friends or family.'"[199] The Colorado Supreme Court had adopted the *Swidler & Berlin* reasoning several years earlier in *Wesp v. Everson*.[200] Thus, to summarize, both *Swidler & Berlin* and *Wesp* recognized that a posthumous privilege was justified to (1) ensure full and frank communication between clients and lawyers; (2) protect a client's reputation; (3) avoid civil liability; and (4) avoid embarrassment and potential harm to the late client's friends and family.[201]

The same reasoning, however, does not equally apply to defunct corporations.[202] First, although full and frank communications between corporations and their lawyers unquestionably are important, a corporation's privilege is held by its managers, who often change over time. Thus, no individual manager can be assured that future managers will not waive the privilege and reveal confidential information.[203] Second, dissolved corporations do not have friends or family who could be embarrassed or harmed by the disclosure of confidential attorney-client communications, nor do they have a reputation to protect following dissolution.[204] Third, because there are usually no assets left to preserve and no directors, the protections of the attorney-client privilege are

---

196. *Id.* at 613.
197. *Id.*
198. 524 U.S. 399 (1998).
199. Affiniti Colorado, LLC v. Kissinger & Fellman, P.C., 461 P.3d 606, 614 (Colo. App. 2019) (quoting Swidler & Berlin, 524 U.S. at 407).
200. Wesp v. Everson, 33 P.3d 191, 200 (Colo. 2001).
201. Affiniti Colorado, LLC v. Kissinger & Fellman, P.C., 461 P.3d 606, 614–15 (Colo. App. 2019).
202. *Id.* at 615.
203. *Id.*
204. *Id.*

less meaningful to a typical dissolved corporation.[205] Fourth, the truth-seeking goals of the justice system outweigh a defunct corporation's need for privilege protection.[206]

The *Affiniti Colorado* court acknowledged that other courts had concluded that, while the attorney-client privilege normally does not survive a corporation's dissolution, there may be instances where the privilege remains in force because an individual with the authority to act on the corporation's behalf is around to invoke or waive it.[207] But not so here. Fellman admitted in the trial court that EAGLE-Net had been dissolved, that it no longer represented EAGLE-Net, and that EAGLE-Net's dissolution rendered it unable to consent to the firm's assertion or waiver of the privilege.[208] EAGLE-Net was not still winding up its affairs, nor was it in bankruptcy or enmeshed in similar proceedings. Thus, the trial court's finding that EAGLE-Net was a dissolved corporation with no managers to act on its behalf was supported by the record.[209]

Clinging to hope, Fellman argued that, as EAGLE-Net's former general counsel, it was authorized to invoke the privilege on EAGLE-Net's behalf.[210] In doing so, the firm relied on case law holding that a successor-in-interest, bankruptcy trustee, person managing a corporation's windup, or statutory liquidator had the authority to invoke or waive the attorney-client privilege during post-dissolution proceedings. Fellman also argued without support that the court should recognize a "former general counsel exception" that would permit a dissolved corporation's former general counsel to invoke the corporation's privilege.[211] The court rejected the firm's argument because it was inconsistent with precedent precluding former corporate directors and managers from invoking a defunct corporation's attorney-client privilege,[212] and it contradicted the Supreme Court's position that former corporate managers cannot assert the privilege to protect their own interests.[213]

In conclusion, the *Affiniti Colorado* court affirmed the trial court's order permitting the discovery of Fellman's communications with EAGLE-Net. In doing so, the court aligned itself with the majority of courts that have considered the operation of the attorney-client privilege where a dissolved corporation is concerned.

---

205. *Id.* (quoting City of Rialto v. United States Dep't of Def., 492 F. Supp. 2d 1193, 1200 (C.D. Cal. 2007)).

206. *Id.* at 616.

207. *Id.*

208. *Id.* at 617.

209. *Id.*

210. *Id.*

211. *Id.*

212. *Id.* (first citing Commodity Futures Trading Comm'n v. Weintraub, 471 U.S. 343, 354–56 (1985); then citing Genova v. Longs Peak Emergency Physicians, P.C., 72 P.3d 454, 463 (Colo. App. 2003)).

213. *Id.* (citing Commodity Futures Trading Comm'n v. Weintraub, 471 U.S. 343, 353–54 (1985)).

C. Summary

Again, confidential communications between a corporation and its lawyer that reflect the solicitation or delivery of legal advice generally retain their privileged status after the corporation dissolves or ceases normal business operations if the corporation lingers on in some form as evidenced by the presence of someone authorized to speak on its behalf.[214] If a corporation is dissolved or has ceased operations and has neither a legal successor nor remaining management with authority to conduct its post-dissolution windup, however, then it enjoys no attorney-client privilege, absent a contrary state statute. In deciding whether a defunct corporation still exists for attorney-client privilege purposes, courts consider practical realities rather than legal technicalities.[215]

IX. Partnerships and the Attorney-Client Privilege

Naturally, not all organizations are incorporated; many businesses and firms are structured as partnerships. With respect to partnerships, organizational structure may drive application of the attorney-client privilege where partners are concerned. In general partnerships, all partners may assert the privilege concerning communications with lawyers about partnership affairs.[216] Limited partnerships spawn differing views. There is authority for the proposition that limited partners, like general partners, are co-holders of the partnership's attorney-client privilege.[217] There is also a competing view that limited partners are generally analogous to corporate shareholders, and therefore cannot invoke (or waive) the limited partnership's attorney-client privilege.[218] Under the second approach, among the partners of a limited partnership, only general partners may invoke the partnership's attorney-client privilege.[219] The second approach makes more sense. As a rule, it is the general partners in a limited partnership who are liable for partnership debts and transact the partnership's

214. *But see* United States v. Head, 2013 WL 5739095, at *3 (E.D. Cal. Oct. 22, 2013) ("Head has been convicted of both conspiracy to commit mail fraud and mail fraud in another case related to his work at Head Financial and is indicted in the instant case on similar charges. Given these circumstances, Head may not invoke the privilege on behalf of Head Financial."); PCS Nitrogen, Inc. v. Ross Dev. Corp., 2011 WL 3665335, at *4 (D.S.C. Aug.19, 2011) (determining that a former director of a dissolved corporation could not invoke the privilege when circumstances suggested that it would be used to protect his own interests and those of other former directors and not the interests of the dissolved corporation).

215. Jiaxing Super Lighting Elec. Appliance Co., Ltd. v. Lunera Lighting, Inc., 2021 WL 2711229, at *2 (N.D. Cal. July 1, 2021); *In re* KiOR, Inc., 631 B.R. 313, 325 (Bankr. D. Del. 2020); John Doe Corp 1 v. Huizenga Mgrs. Fund, LLC, 188 N.E.3d 1259, 1279 (Ill. App. Ct. 2021).

216. Restatement (Third) of the Law Governing Lawyers § 73 cmt. d (2000).

217. *See, e.g.*, Roberts v. Keim, 123 F.R.D. 614, 625 (N.D. Cal. 1988) (concluding that limited partners and general partners were co-holders of the attorney-client privilege).

218. *In re* Subpoena Duces Tecum Served on Rosenman & Colin, 1996 WL 527331, at *7 (S.D.N.Y. Sept. 16, 1996); Restatement (Third) of the Law Governing Lawyers § 73 cmt. d (2000).

219. Restatement (Third) of the Law Governing Lawyers § 73 cmt. d (2000).

business. Limited partners, in contrast, invest in the partnership, but generally are not active in the partnership's business operations and face no potential liability for partnership debts beyond the loss of their investments. With such limited responsibilities and liability exposure, limited partners are analogous to corporate shareholders,[220] who, absent some additional role, cannot claim or waive the corporation's attorney-client privilege.[221]

Regardless of whether a partnership is general or limited, its employees may function as its agents for attorney-client privilege purposes.[222] Whether a partnership employee's exchanges with partnership counsel are privileged is generally evaluated under the tests that courts apply to corporations.[223]

X. Limited Liability Companies

In addition to corporations and partnerships, businesses and firms are frequently structured as limited liability companies (LLCs). An LLC has attributes of both partnerships and corporations. Like a partnership, an LLC is a pass-through entity for tax purposes, and interests in the LLC are generally nontransferrable. Aside from tax implications and the inalienability of equity interests, however, LLCs are generally thought to more closely resemble corporations.[224] Like a corporation, formation of an LLC requires its organizers to file a document (articles of organization) with a central state agency (usually the Secretary of State) and LLC members enjoy limited liability. Furthermore, like corporations, limited liability companies are entities distinct from their members. They can sue and be sued in their own names, and members' liability protections can be forfeited in the same circumstances that would justify piercing the corporate veil.[225] The alter ego doctrine typically applies to LLCs

---

220. MapleWood Partners, L.P. v. Indian Harbor Ins. Co., 295 F.R.D. 550, 587 n.155 (S.D. Fla. 2013).

221. *See generally* United States v. Campbell, 73 F.3d 44, 47 (5th Cir. 1996) (rejecting the argument that a limited partnership is more like an individual than a corporation, reasoning that like a corporation, a limited partnership is an inanimate entity that can act only through its agents, and therefore concluding the bankruptcy trustee of the debtor-partnership had the authority to waive the attorney-client privilege on the partnership's behalf).

222. Restatement (Third) of the Law Governing Lawyers § 73 cmt. d (2000).

223. *See, e.g.*, *In re* Bieter Co., 16 F.3d 929, 935 (8th Cir. 1994) (stating that although the *Diversified Industries* test is expressly applicable to corporations and their employees, it "is no less instructive as applied to a partnership, or some other client entity . . . and its employees"); United States v. Daugerdas, 757 F. Supp. 2d 364, 370 (S.D.N.Y. 2010) ("As an initial matter . . . Field's privilege claim is properly evaluated under the *Teamsters* standard [governing communications between corporate employees and corporate counsel], notwithstanding that BDO is a partnership rather than a corporation.").

224. Although they may resemble corporations in many respects, LLCs are *not* corporations. Block v. Black Ent. Television, LLC, 2018 WL 3797568, at *6 (D. Or. June 26, 2018) ("LLCs are not corporations, and are formed, or organized, rather than incorporated.").

225. *In re* Senior Cottages of Am., LLC, 482 F.3d 997, 1001 (8th Cir. 2007) (discussing Minnesota law); *see also* Abrahim & Sons Enters. v. Equilon Enters., LLC, 292 F.3d 958, 962 (9th Cir. 2002) (emphasizing that LLCs and their actions are separate and distinct from their members and their members' actions).

just as it does to corporations.[226] Many LLCs are managed like corporations. State LLC statutes may be adapted from state corporation law statutes.[227] On balance then, and despite LLCs' similarities to partnerships in some respects, it is understandable that courts typically treat LLCs like corporations for attorney-client privilege purposes.[228] *Montgomery v. eTreppid Technologies, LLC*[229] leads this line of authority.

Montgomery was an intellectual property dispute between eTreppid and a former member and manager, David Montgomery. eTreppid objected to some of Montgomery's discovery requests based on attorney-client privilege. The essential question for the court was the identity of the client for attorney-client privilege purposes. As a preliminary matter, the parties disagreed over whether an LLC should be treated as a corporation or a partnership for purposes of federal privilege law.[230] This was an issue of first impression for the court.

Montgomery argued that an LLC is more closely analogous to a partnership because, like partners in a partnership, LLC members owe each other fiduciary duties. Unfortunately, he cited no supporting authority, nor did he cite any case law applying partnership law to LLCs. Rather, he simply compared eTreppid's organizational structure to a partnership.[231]

eTreppid contended that under federal common law, partnerships and limited partnerships are treated as corporations for attorney-client privilege purposes. The court agreed.[232] Furthermore, the court's careful review of eTreppid's operating agreement indicated that eTreppid functioned more like a corporation than a partnership.[233] eTreppid's organization was based on a corporate structure, with the management committee being compared to a corporate board of directors and a chief executive officer, and the manager being compared to a president and chief operating officer. Like a corporate board of directors, the management committee acted by vote and formulated policies and procedures. The management committee thereafter supervised eTreppid's management in implementing those policies and procedures, just

---

226. Gardner *ex rel.* L.G. v. Eighth Jud. Dist. Ct., 405 P.3d 651, 735–36 (Nev. 2017).

227. *See, e.g.*, *In re* Senior Cottages of Am., LLC, 482 F.3d 997, 1001 (8th Cir. 2007) (citing MINN. STAT. ANN. § 322B.01 note (West 2001)).

228. *See, e.g.*, Carpenters Pension Tr. v. Lindquist Fam. LLC, 2014 WL 1569195, at *3–4 (N.D. Cal. Apr. 18, 2014) (applying corporate attorney-client privilege law to an LLC); *In re* Haynes, 577 B.R. 711, 736–37 (Bankr. E.D. Tenn. 2017) (reasoning that an LLC's privilege must be analyzed under *Upjohn*); Fla. Marlins Baseball Club, LLC v. Certain Underwriters at Lloyd's London Subscribing to Pol'y No. 893/HC/97/9096, 900 So. 2d 720, 721 (Fla. Dist. Ct. App. 2005) (treating an LLC identically to a corporation in upholding the privilege with respect to communications with an in-house lawyer).

229. 548 F. Supp. 2d 1175 (D. Nev. 2008).

230. *Id.* at 1178.

231. *Id.* at 1181.

232. *Id.* (first citing Hopper v. Frank, 16 F.3d 92, 94–97 (5th Cir. 1994); then citing United States v. Campbell, 73 F.3d 44, 47 (5th Cir. 1996); and then citing *In re* Bieter Co., 16 F.3d 929, 935 & n.7 (8th Cir. 1994)).

233. *Id.* at 1182.

as a board of directors oversees corporate officers. eTreppid's members, like corporate shareholders, had no personal liability. eTreppid appointed a resident agent just as a corporation does, had to file articles of organization with the Nevada Secretary of State like corporate procedure with respect to articles of incorporation, and had an operating agreement akin to corporate bylaws. The only comparison to a partnership was eTreppid's tax treatment.[234]

The *Montgomery* court additionally observed that federal and state courts had regularly applied corporate law to LLCs in other situations, including veil-piercing, application of the alter ego doctrine, determining standing, business judgment rule battles, and derivative actions.[235] The court therefore concluded that eTreppid should be treated like a corporation for attorney-client privilege purposes under federal common law.[236]

Montgomery is well-reasoned. There is no reason to think that other courts will generally reach different conclusions on this privilege issue. That said, it is perhaps possible that a particular LLC's operating agreement or organizational or operational structure might point a given court toward a different result.

XI. Joint Ventures

Finally, both organizations and individuals sometimes form joint ventures to capitalize on business opportunities. A joint venture is often described as an association or agreement between two or more people or entities to engage in a single undertaking for profit. With slight variation between jurisdictions, the elements of a joint venture are (1) an express or implied agreement; (2) a common purpose or community of interest in the venture; (3) an agreement to share profits and losses; and (4) a mutual right of control or management. Joint ventures are commonly described as being "in the nature of a partnership,"[237] as "a type of partnership,"[238] or as a "limited-purpose partnership."[239] Because joint ventures are similar to partnerships, they are generally governed by the same legal principles.[240] That said, when it comes to the attorney-client privilege, the structure of the joint venture can significantly affect the analysis.

If the joint venturers create an entity such as an LLC to achieve their goal, then they will be subject to the attorney-client privilege principles applicable to LLCs. In the more common scenario where the participants form the joint venture contractually rather than forming a distinct legal entity,

---

234. *Id.* at 1182–83.

235. *Id.* at 1183.

236. *Id.*

237. Weyers v. Cmty. Mem. Hosp., Inc., 971 N.W.2d 155, 165 (Neb. Ct. App. 2022).

238. TooBaRoo, LLC v. W. Robidoux, Inc., 614 S.W.3d 29, 39 (Mo. Ct. App. 2020).

239. C.N. v. S.R., 230 A.3d 1003, 1008 (N.J. Super. Ct. Ch. Div. 2020).

240. Shoreline Found., Inc. v. Brisk, 278 So. 3d 68, 73 (Fla. Dist. Ct. App. 2019); Bosch v. NorthShore Univ. Health Sys., 155 N.E.3d 486, 505 (Ill. App. Ct. 2019); Peoples Tr. & Sav. Bank v. Sec. Sav. Bank, 815 N.W.2d 744, 756 (Iowa 2012).

application of the privilege will be a case-specific inquiry. In the contractual context, the critical question is who the lawyer or lawyers represent; after all, to enjoy the protections of the attorney-client privilege, a person must be a client of the lawyer in the matter.[241]

If the joint venturers engage a single lawyer for the joint venture, there are three possible approaches, none of which has been developed in the case law. First, given their similarities, the same attorney-client privilege rules that apply to general partnerships should govern the joint venture. Second, each venturer is a co-client of the lawyer and the attorney-client privilege rules that apply to joint representations generally apply to the joint venture, both during its formation and thereafter.[242] Or, third, each venturer is a co-client of the lawyer during the preparation of the joint venture agreement and the joint venture either becomes the lawyer's sole client or another co-client upon its formation with the resulting privilege implications. The third approach assumes that (1) the jurisdiction recognizes the joint venture as a legal entity,[243] and (2) the venturers desire the lawyer's continued representation. Again, the outcome in any case will pivot on the facts.

There are, of course, other alternatives. Most obviously, each venturer may be represented by its own lawyer during the preparation of the joint venture agreement and thereafter, with there never being a single lawyer for the joint venture. In that instance, if the lawyers for the respective parties hope to protect their communications with each other as privileged, they will generally need to reach some sort of common interest agreement. Such an arrangement may or may not be effective depending on the jurisdiction and the facts. For

241. *See* Bare v. Cruz, 2012 WL 1138591, at *3 (E.D. Pa. Apr. 2, 2012) ("First and foremost, the attorney-client privilege applies only if an attorney-client relationship exists.") (footnote omitted); Roehrs v. Minn. Life Ins. Co., 228 F.R.D. 642, 646 (D. Ariz. 2005) ("Of course, there must be an attorney-client relationship before the privilege exists."); Grassmueck v. Ogden Murphy Wallace, P.L.L.C., 213 F.R.D. 567, 571 (W.D. Wash. 2003) ("[T]here can be no assertion of attorney-client privilege if there is no attorney-client relationship."); *In re* Paul Abbott Co., 767 N.W.2d 14, 18 (Minn. 2009) ("An attorney-client relationship must exist before communications can be considered privileged.").

242. *Cf.* Al-Yusr Townsend & Bottum Co. v. United Mid E. Co., 1995 WL 592548, at *4 (E.D. Pa. Oct. 4, 1995) (indicating that Pennsylvania cases in analogous contexts supported the conclusion that an attorney-client relationship exists between a lawyer representing a joint venture and the individual members of the joint venture); Franklin v. Callum, 804 A.2d 444, 448 (N.H. 2002) (stating that the project there resembled a joint venture and explaining that a lawyer who represents members' joint interests in an unincorporated association represents each individual member of the association as to matters of association business).

243. *Compare* Coleman v. Querbes Co. No. 1, 218 So. 3d 665, 673 (La. Ct. App. 2017) ("A joint venture is *a juridical person* created by an agreement between two or more persons to combine their efforts or resources in determined proportions and to collaborate at mutual risk for their common profit or commercial benefit.") (emphasis added), *and* Bank One Texas, N.A. v. Stewart, 967 S.W.2d 419, 443 (Tex. App. 1998) ("[A] joint venture, like a partnership, is an entity legally distinct from the partners."), *with* Jerry Dickerson Presents, Inc. v. Concert S. Chastain Promotions, 579 S.E.2d 761, 770 (Ga. Ct. App. 2003) ("Generally, a 'joint venture' is not a legal entity separate from those parties that compose it.") (footnote omitted), *and* Costa v. Borges, 179 P.3d 316, 320 (Idaho 2008) (explaining that a joint venture is not an entity separate and distinct from its members).

example, many jurisdictions require either reasonably anticipated or pending litigation for a common interest agreement to be enforceable, while some others do not.[244]

XII. Conclusion

The application and operation of the attorney-client privilege can pose a range of complex and challenging issues for lawyers who represent organizations. Many cases turn on their facts. In other situations, jurisdictional variations in privilege law may force lawyers to recalibrate their advice or analysis. Fortunately, in many instances, there is a developed body of case law that lawyers may rely on to guide their thinking. Where there is not, lawyers must be prepared to argue by analogy, always keeping in mind the essential principles of the attorney-client privilege.

---

244. *Compare* Brinkmann v. Petro Welt Trading Ges. M.B.H., 324 So. 3d 574, 579 (Fla. Dist Ct. App. 2021) (requiring litigation for the common interest exception to privilege waiver to apply), *and* Ambac Assur. Corp. v. Countrywide Home Loans, Inc., 57 N.E.3d 30, 38–39 (N.Y. 2016) (explaining why common interest arrangements should be confined to pending litigation or matters where litigation is reasonably anticipated), *with In re* Teleglobe Commc'ns Corp., 493 F.3d 345, 364 (3d Cir. 2007) ("[T]he community-of-interest privilege allows attorneys representing different clients with similar legal interests to share information without having to disclose it to others. It applies . . . *even in purely transactional contexts.*") (emphasis added), *and* United States v. BDO Seidman, LLP, 492 F.3d 806, 816 (7th Cir. 2007) (stating that "communications need not be made in anticipation of litigation to fall within the common interest doctrine") (footnote omitted), *and* Hanover Ins. Co. v. Rapo & Jensen Ins. Servs., Inc., 870 N.E.2d 1105, 1110 (Mass. 2007) (adopting the position that the common interest doctrine is not limited to situations involving litigation or impending litigation).

CHAPTER 9

Investigations

DAVID E. BLAND AND SCOTT G. JOHNSON

I. Introduction

Both in-house and outside counsel are often asked by their clients to participate in or conduct investigations in myriad different matters. Examples include the following:

- A potential medical malpractice claim against a hospital[1]
- Allegations of sexual molestation by an elementary school teacher[2]
- The drowning of a 13-year-old[3]
- A large corporation facing a wage and hour issue[4]
- The alleged backdating of stock options[5]
- A potential arson on behalf of a property insurance carrier[6]
- Alleged child sexual abuse by a college football coach[7]
- A hotel's potential liability for sexual harassment[8]
- A multinational corporation accused of making questionable payments to a foreign governmental official to secure government business[9]
- Allegations that laboratory managers impeded a separate internal ethics investigation[10]

1. Frankfort Reg'l Med. Ctr. v. Shepherd, 2016 WL 3376030 (Ky. June 16, 2016); Samaritan Found. v. Goodfarb, 862 P.2d 870 (Ariz. 1993); Hyams v. Evanston Hosp., 587 N.E.2d 1127 (Ill. App. Ct. 1992).
2. Sandra T.E. v. S. Berwyn Sch. Dist. 100, 600 F.3d 612 (7th Cir. 2010).
3. Coito v. Superior Court, 278 P.3d 860 (Cal. 2012).
4. Costco Wholesale Corp. v. Superior Court, 219 P.3d 736 (Cal. 2009).
5. United States v. Ruehle, 583 F.3d 600 (9th Cir. 2009).
6. Dunn v. State Farm Fire & Cas. Co., 927 F.2d 869 (5th Cir. 1991); Burr v. United Farm Bureau Mut. Ins. Co., 560 N.E.2d 1250 (Ind. Ct. App. 1990); State *ex rel.* U.S. Fid. & Guar. Co. v. Canady, 460 S.E.2d 677 (W. Va. 1995).
7. Bagwell v. Pa. Office of Attorney Gen., 116 A.3d 145 (Pa. Commw. Ct. 2015).
8. O'Gorman v. Kitchen, 2021 WL 1292907 (S.D.N.Y. Apr. 7, 2021).
9. Upjohn Co. v. United States, 449 U.S. 383 (1981).
10. Gingrich v. Sandia Corp., 165 P.3d 1135 (N.M. Ct. App. 2007).

Attorneys then communicate the results of their investigations to their clients.[11] When the client's adversary seeks discovery of the communications between the client and the attorney investigator in subsequent litigation, a dispute often arises as to what documents or information must be produced.

Most attorney-client-privilege disputes arise in the context of a corporation or other business entity on one or both sides of the dispute. The Supreme Court's decision in *Upjohn Co. v. United States*[12] is the most frequently cited case on the application of the attorney-client privilege where the client is a business entity.

Upjohn addressed the federal common law attorney-client privilege.[13] *Upjohn* is not binding on state courts[14] or on federal courts in diversity cases.[15] Some state courts have followed the *Upjohn* approach,[16] others have modified the *Upjohn* test,[17] and others have rejected it.[18]

Two legal issues most frequently arise when a court is called upon to determine whether documents generated during an investigation conducted by an attorney are discoverable. The first issue is whether the attorney is acting in the capacity of an attorney while conducting the investigation and reporting its results. The second issue is who the attorney can interview within the scope of the attorney-client privilege. A third issue, the application of the work-product doctrine, is raised in some cases.[19]

---

11. *See In re* Allen, 106 F.3d 582, 602 (4th Cir. 1997) (noting that "[c]ourts have consistently recognized that investigation may be an important part of an attorney's legal services to a client").

12. 449 U.S. 383 (1981).

13. Stillmunkes v. Givaudan Flavors Corp., 2009 WL 936605, at *4 (N.D. Iowa Apr. 7, 2009); Dietz v. FDIC, 1992 WL 26712, at *1 (N.D. Ill. Feb. 7, 1992).

14. Fed. R. Evid. 501 ("But in a civil case, state law governs privilege regarding a claim or defense for which state law supplies the rule of decision."); *see, e.g.*, Hartsock v. Goodyear Dunlop Tires N. Am. Ltd, 672 F. App'x 223, 226 (4th Cir. 2016); Doe v. Archdiocese of Milwaukee, 772 F.3d 437, 440 (7th Cir. 2014); Babasa v. LensCrafters, Inc., 498 F.3d 972, 974 (9th Cir. 2007).

15. Under the Federal Rules of Evidence, *Upjohn* will govern in any case in federal court where there is federal question jurisdiction, but state law will control in those federal cases where there is diversity jurisdiction. *See* Fed. R. Evid. 501; *see, e.g.*, Nakajima v. Gen. Motors Corp., 857 F. Supp. 100, 104 (D.D.C. 1994); Barrett Indus. Trucks, Inc. v. Old Republic Ins. Co., 129 F.R.D. 515, 516–17 (N.D. Ill. 1990); Command Transp., Inc. v. Y.S. Line (USA) Corp., 116 F.R.D. 94, 95, 97 n.10 (D. Mass. 1987).

16. *See, e.g.*, Lexington Pub. Library v. Clark, 90 S.W.3d 53, 59 (Ky. 2002); Wardleigh v. Dist. Court, 891 P.2d 1180 (Nev. 1995).

17. Keefe v. Bernard, 774 N.W.2d 663 (Iowa 2009) (privilege applies only to those whose conduct creates potential liability to the corporation); Newman v. Highland Sch. Dist. No. 203, 381 P.3d 1188 (Wash. 2016) (privilege does not protect communications with former employees who are only fact witnesses).

18. Harris Mgmt., Inc. v. Coulombe, 151 A.3d 7 (Me. 2016).

19. United States v. Nobles, 422 U.S. 225, 238 n.11 (1975) ("[T]he work-product doctrine is distinct from and broader than the attorney-client privilege.") (relying on Hickman v. Taylor, 329 U.S. 495, 508 (1947)).

II. Is the Investigating Attorney Acting as an Attorney?

Case law universally holds that the attorney-client privilege attaches only to communications made by or to an attorney acting in his or her "capacity as such."[20] The role an attorney plays is a key factor that courts consider in deciding these issues.

Thus, the threshold issue in virtually every case is whether an attorney hired to conduct an investigation is acting in his or her capacity as an attorney. Generally, an attorney acts in the capacity of an attorney when he or she is being consulted by a client for the purpose of obtaining legal services or advice.[21] The privilege will not apply to attorney-client communications in cases where the client hires the attorney for business or personal advice or to perform the work of a nonlawyer.[22] Many courts dealing with attorney investigations, however, have had great difficulty in drawing the line between attorneys who are rendering legal advice and those who are merely performing the ordinary business of claims investigation for their clients.[23]

The disagreement among legal scholars highlights how important the resolution of this question is. Indeed, Charles Wright and Kenneth Graham express the view that "no privilege applies where the lawyer's primary function is as a detective. Where the lawyer is retained for the purposes of litigation, the privilege should apply only where the investigation is one that cannot

---

20. *See* 8 John H. Wigmore, Evidence in Trials at Common Law §§ 2300–2304, at 580–89 (James McNaughton rev. ed. 1961 & Supp. 2014). *See also* Edward J. Imwinkelried, The New Wigmore: A Treatise on Evidence: Evidentiary Privileges § 6.2.4 (4th ed. 2022).

21. *See* Cicel (Beijing) Sci. & Tech. Co. v. Misonix, Inc., 331 F.R.D. 218, 230 (E.D.N.Y. 2019); Hairston v. Royal Bldg. Prod., Inc., 2019 WL 1550790, at *1 (W.D. Va. Feb. 15, 2019); Henson v. Wyeth Lab., Inc., 118 F.R.D. 584, 587 (W.D. Va. 1987); Heathcoat v. Santa Fe Int'l Corp., 532 F. Supp. 961, 964 (E.D. Ark. 1982); Westinghouse Elec. Corp. v. Kerr-McGee Corp., 580 F.2d 1311, 1319–20 (7th Cir. 1978); *see also* United States *ex rel.* Fago v. M & T Mortg. Corp., 238 F.R.D. 3, 10–11 (D.D.C. 2006) (holding that communications with counsel concerning legal advice were protected by attorney-client privilege but communications made by and to the same lawyer with respect to business matters were not protected by privilege).

22. *See, e.g.*, United States v. Sawyer, 853 F. Supp. 2d 1014 (E.D. Cal. 2012) (communications between defendant and his girlfriend/lawyer not protected when discussing personal matters in jail); *Westinghouse*, 580 F.2d at 1320; NXIVM Corp. v. O'Hara, 241 F.R.D. 109, 130 (N.D.N.Y. 2007) (holding that communication with lawyer who was "coordinating media, public relations, lobbying, and other non-legal services" were not privileged); *see also* SmithKline Beecham Corp. v. Apotex Corp., 194 F.R.D. 624 (N.D. Ill. 2000) (holding that attorney-authored meeting agendas were not protected by the attorney-client privilege in patent infringement suit because it was unlikely that legal advice was involved); *Henson*, 118 F.R.D. at 587. *See generally* 8 John H. Wigmore, Evidence in Trials at Common Law §§ 2296–2299 (James McNaughton rev. ed. 1961 & Supp. 2014).

23. *See, e.g.*, St. Paul Reinsurance Co. v. Commercial Fin. Corp., 197 F.R.D. 620, 641–42 (N.D. Iowa 2000); Goodyear Tire & Rubber Co. v. Chiles Power Supply, Inc., 190 F.R.D. 532, 535 (S.D. Ind. 1999) (noting that there is no bright-line rule for courts deciding whether an attorney is acting in his or her capacity as such).

be carried out by non-lawyer investigators."[24] But even the authors openly acknowledge their disagreement on the issue.[25] This position was roundly criticized by the Ninth Circuit in *United States v. Rowe*[26] and, as set forth in more detail in the following, appears to be the minority view. On the other hand, the American Law Institute favors the broad approach that protects all communications from lawyer to client.[27] The institute favors the broad approach because it "avoids difficult questions in determining whether a lawyer's communication itself discloses a client communication."[28]

A. Attorney Acting in Capacity of Attorney

As the *Upjohn* Court stated, "The first step in the resolution of any legal problem is ascertaining the factual background and sifting through the facts with an eye to the legally relevant."[29] Relying on this reasoning, the Fourth Circuit explained that clients "often do retain lawyers to perform investigative work because they want the benefit of a lawyer's expertise and judgment," and "if a client retains an attorney to use her legal expertise to conduct an investigation, that lawyer is indeed performing legal work."[30]

A good illustration of this can been seen in *Sandra T.E. v. South Berwyn School District 100*,[31] where the Seventh Circuit analyzed the issue of whether an attorney investigator is acting in the capacity of an attorney in the context of claims of sexual molestation made against an elementary school teacher and his school district employer.[32] The school board hired Sidley Austin LLP to conduct an investigation and provide legal advice to the district.[33] The board

---

24. 24 C. Wright & K. Graham, Federal Practice and Procedure § 5478, at 229 (1986 & Supp. 2022).

25. *See id.* at n.178.

26. 96 F.3d 1294, 1296 n.1 (9th Cir. 1996). *See also* State *ex rel.* Toledo Blade Co. v. Toledo-Lucas County Port Auth., 905 N.E.2d 1221 (Ohio 2009) (specifically rejecting Wright and Graham's approach).

27. Restatement (Third) of the Law Governing Lawyers § 69 (2000 & Supp. 2022).

28. *Id.* at cmt. i, illus. 7.

29. Upjohn Co. v. United States, 449 U.S. 383, 390–61 (1981); *see also* Trammel v. United States, 445 U.S. 40, 51 (1980) ("The lawyer-client privilege rests on the need for the advocate and counselor to know all that relates to the client's reasons for seeking representation if the professional mission is to be carried out.").

30. *In re* Allen, 106 F.3d 582, 604 (4th Cir. 1997). *Accord* Random Ventures, Inc. v. Advanced Armament Corp., 2013 U.S. Dist. LEXIS 20513 (S.D.N.Y. Feb. 5, 2013); Yerger v. Liberty Mut. Grp., Inc., 2013 U.S. Dist. LEXIS 136291 (E.D.N.C. Sept. 24, 2013). As one lawyer put it, "I don't think I've ever given a legal opinion without performing an investigation or collecting information because you can't give a legal opinion in a vacuum." Harlandale Indep. Sch. Dist. v. Cornyn, 25 S.W.3d 328, 333 (Tex. App. 2000).

31. 600 F.3d 612 (7th Cir. 2010).

32. The teacher ultimately confessed to the crimes he was charged with and received a sentence of 20 years. *Id.* at 615.

33. *Id.* at 616. "The School Board wanted Sidley to review the criminal charges filed against [teacher], investigate the actions of school administrators in response to the allegations of sexual abuse, examine whether any district employees had failed to comply with district policies or federal or state law, and analyze the effectiveness of the District's existing compliance procedures."

sent a letter to all parents advising them of Sidley's retention. Sidley interviewed both current and former employees of the district and some third-party witnesses. Sidley did not record the interviews, but the Sidley attorneys took notes during the interviews and later drafted memoranda summarizing them. Sidley provided the school board with a written executive summary as well as an oral report of the legal advice it was retained to provide.[34]

The victims and their families sued the school district in January 2005. Plaintiffs first sought production of the Sidley materials from a Sidley partner by way of a deposition subpoena with an accompanying request for documents. Sidley turned over more than 1,000 pages of documents but withheld the witness interview summaries and other internal legal memoranda. Plaintiffs moved to compel production of the materials, and the trial court so ordered, finding that Sidley was hired as an "investigator, not as an attorney."[35]

The Seventh Circuit, however, reversed, concluding that Sidley was acting as an attorney while investigating the details of the allegations of sexual molestation.[36] The court reasoned that "Sidley's investigation of the factual circumstances surrounding the abuse was an integral part of the package of legal services for which it was hired and a necessary prerequisite to the provision of legal advice about how the District should respond."[37] The court noted that Sidley told each employee it interviewed that it was acting as the school board's attorney, not the employees'; Sidley marked all communications to the board as "privileged"; and Sidley presented its findings and recommendations to the board in a closed session not open to the public. The court found these facts were indicative of an attorney-client relationship.[38]

The court reached a similar result in *Costco Wholesale Corp. v. Superior Court*.[39] There, Costco hired an outside law firm to provide legal advice about whether certain managers were exempt from the wage and overtime laws. Counsel interviewed two warehouse managers about their job duties and ultimately provided Costco with a 22-page opinion.[40] Several years later, several Costco employees filed a class action against Costco alleging they were miscategorized as exempt employees. Predictably, the employees sought production of counsel's earlier report. Costco objected on both attorney-client and work-product grounds.[41]

The court-appointed discovery referee reviewed the report and first found that much of the report "constitutes attorney client communications and/or the type of attorney observations, impressions and opinions plainly protected

34. *Id.*
35. *Id.* at 616–17.
36. *Id.* at 618–21.
37. 600 F.3d at 620.
38. *Id.*
39. 219 P.3d 736 (2009).
40. *Id.* at 740.
41. *Id.*

as work product." Nevertheless, the referee ordered that a heavily redacted version of the report containing "factual information about various employees' job responsibilities" be provided to plaintiffs.[42] The trial court adopted the referee's findings, and the intermediate appellate court denied Costco's petition for relief. The California Supreme Court granted review.[43]

The supreme court held that (1) the entire report was protected from discovery, (2) the trial court could not review the report itself to determine the privilege question,[44] and (3) the party claiming the privilege need not prove it will be harmed in order to obtain the appellate court's review.[45] The court reasoned that Costco hired counsel to provide a legal opinion. The court concluded that "[t]he attorney-client privilege attaches to a confidential communication between the attorney and the client and bars discovery of the communication irrespective of whether it includes unprivileged material."[46] The court rejected plaintiffs' argument that the dominant purpose of the attorney's efforts was not to provide legal advice but to provide business advice: "Here, [counsel] was presented with a question requiring legal analysis and was asked to investigate the facts she needed to render a legal opinion."[47]

The New York Court of Appeals provided an excellent analysis of the legal counsel "acting as such" requirement in *Spectrum Systems International Corp. v. Chemical Bank.*[48] There, Chemical Bank retained a law firm to "perform an investigation and render legal advice to Chemical regarding possible fraud by its employees and outside vendors, and to counsel Chemical with respect to litigation options."[49] The law firm interviewed Chemical's employees, a former Chemical officer, and representatives of Spectrum itself and reported the results of its investigation. After Spectrum sued Chemical and learned about the report, Spectrum requested it in discovery. Chemical moved for a protective order. The trial court, without ever viewing the documents, ordered the documents produced.[50] The intermediate appellate court affirmed, and Chemical appealed to the New York Court of Appeals.

The court of appeals reversed, concluding that the report was legal advice: "The critical inquiry is whether, viewing the lawyer's communication in its full content and context, it was made in order to render legal advice or services

42. *Id.*

43. *Id.*

44. Cal. Evid. Code § 915(a)–(b). *Contra* Genovese v. Provident Life & Accident Ins. Co., 74 So. 3d 1064, 1068 (Fla. 2011) (Pariente, J., concurring).

45. *Costco Wholesale Corp. v. Superior Court,* 219 P.3d at 740.

46. *Id.* at 741.

47. *Id.* at 743. This court did not reach the work-product issue because of its ruling on the attorney-client privilege. *See also* Los Angeles County Bd. of Supervisors v. Superior Court, 386 P.3d 773, 780 (Cal. 2016) (the privilege only protects information communicated "for the purpose of legal consultation.").

48. 581 N.E.2d 1055 (N.Y. 1991).

49. *Id.* at 1058.

50. *Id.* at 1058–59.

to the client."[51] Applying this rule, the court concluded "that the facts were selected and presented in the [law firm's] report as the foundation for the law firm's advice, and that the communication was primarily and predominantly of a legal character."[52] The court further held that the prospect of litigation was irrelevant to the issue of privilege even though it may be relevant to a work-product claim.[53]

Other cases reach conclusions similar to *Sandra T.E., Costco, and Spectrum Systems*. In *Fay Avenue Properties, LLC v. Travelers Property Casualty Co.*,[54] the court concluded that a law firm hired by Travelers to investigate an insurance claim and take examinations under oath was hired primarily to provide legal coverage advice to Travelers.[55] Similarly, in *Rattner v. Chubb National Insurance Co.*,[56] the court found that documents prepared by an attorney hired by an insurance company to investigate a potential arson fire loss were privileged because the attorney's investigation "related to the rendition of legal services."[57] In *Hawker v. BancInsurance, Inc.*,[58] the court held that outside counsel hired after the defendant received a claim notice was acting in a legal capacity, and communications with the defendant were protected. Similarly, in *Hanson v. First National Bank*,[59] the court agreed that the defendant's chairman did not have to testify to what outside counsel told him following an investigation of a fired director. In *Salvation Army v. Superior Court*,[60] the court refused to order production of interview tapes recorded by an outside attorney's investigator, concluding they were prepared to assist outside counsel to provide legal advice following a near drowning.[61] In *In re General Motors LLC Ignition Switch Litigation*,[62] the court held that notes and memoranda relating to witness interviews conducted by outside counsel during their investigation of an ignition switch defect were protected by the attorney-client privilege and

51. *Id.* at 1061 (citations omitted).

52. *Id.* at 1061.

53. *Id.* at 1061–62. However, the common-interest doctrine that allows parties with a common interest to share privileged information without waiving the privilege applies only to information shared when there is anticipated litigation, not simply a business transaction that both parties are interested in completing. Ambac Assurance Corp. v. Countrywide Home Loans, Inc., 57 N.E.3d 30 (N.Y. 2016).

54. 2014 WL 2738682 (S.D. Cal. June 17, 2014).

55. *Id.* at *16–17. *Accord* Reynolds v. State, 963 So. 2d 908 (Fla. Dist. Ct. App. 2007).

56. 2017 WL 1836444 (E.D. Va. May 8, 2017).

57. *Id.* at *5 (quoting *In re* Allen, 106 F.3d 582, 603 (4th Cir. 1997)).

58. 2013 WL 6843088 (E.D. Cal. Dec. 27, 2013). *Accord* Hawes v. Langston, 853 So. 2d 1237, 1244 (Miss. 2003) ("[T]the privilege relates to and covers *all information* regarding the client received by the attorney in his professional capacity and in the course of his representation of the client.") (emphasis in original).

59. 2011 WL 13228436 (S.D. W. Va. Dec. 19, 2011).

60. 273 P.2d 656 (Ariz. Ct. App. 2012).

61. *Id.* at 662. *See also* State v. von Bulow, 475 A.2d 995, 1005 (R.I. 1984) (finding that an attorney hired to investigate the circumstances surrounding Martha von Bulow's comatose condition was acting as an attorney during his investigation).

62. 80 F. Supp. 3d 521 (S.D.N.Y. 2015).

work-product doctrine even where legal advice was not the sole purpose of the investigation.[63] Lastly, in *Optimize Technology Solutions, LLC v. Staples, Inc.*,[64] the court held that a client's communications with a nonlicensed lawyer were protected because the client believed it was consulting a lawyer. One court has recently decided that even if an investigation is undertaken because a company policy requires it, it is protected.[65]

Finally, in *City of Petaluma v. Superior Court*,[66] a California intermediate appellate court considered whether the attorney-client privilege extended to an employer's pre-litigation investigation of an employee's harassment and discrimination claims conducted by an outside attorney who was specifically directed not to provide legal advice. In finding the investigation privileged, the court concluded that the rendering of legal advice was not required for the privilege to apply.[67] As support, the court relied on the California statute that defined "client" for purposes of the attorney-client privilege and work-product doctrine to mean a person who retains a lawyer for securing "legal service or advice."[68] The court said that the statute supported the conclusion that an attorney-client relationship can exist where an attorney provides a legal service without also providing legal advice.[69] The appellate court reasoned that the outside attorney was retained to provide a legal service because "she was hired to act as an attorney in bringing her legal skills to bear to assist the City in developing a response" to the employee's claim.[70]

B. Attorney Investigator Not Acting in Capacity of Attorney

Courts have not permitted clients to cloak a routine business investigation with attorney-client privilege protection simply by retaining an attorney to conduct that investigation.[71] Many of these cases have arisen in the context of an insurance company client where the courts have found that the attorney's investigation was part of the insurer's ordinary business of claims investigation.[72]

---

63. *Id. at 526–30.*
64. 2014 WL 2728596 (E.D. Tex. June 16, 2014).
65. *In re* Kellogg Brown & Root, Inc., 756 F.3d 754, 760 (D.C. Cir. 2014). *Accord* Miniex v. Houston Hous. Auth., 2019 WL 2524918, at *4 (S.D. Tex. Mar. 1, 2019).
66. 204 Cal. Rptr. 3d 196 (Cal. Ct. App. 2016).
67. *Id.* at 205.
68. *Id.* (quoting in part Cal. Evid. Code § 951).
69. *Id.* ("The rendering of legal advice is not required for the privilege to apply.").
70. *Id.*
71. *See, e.g.*, Griffith v. Davis, 161 F.R.D. 687, 697 (C.D. Cal. 1995) ("defendant . . . cannot prevent disclosure of an administrative investigation by having its litigation counsel (or an agent of its litigation counsel) conduct that investigation").
72. St. Paul Reinsurance Co. v. Commercial Fin. Corp., 197 F.R.D. 620, 642 (N.D. Iowa 2000) (holding that communications to attorney acting as a claims investigator were not protected by attorney-client privilege); Bertalo's Rest. Inc. v. Exch. Ins. Co., 658 N.Y.S.2d 656, 659 (N.Y. App. Div. 1997). California has recognized the importance of files created in the investigation of a claim filed by an

Mission National Insurance Co. v. Lilly[73] is an often-cited example in the insurance context. There, Mission insured a nightclub in northern Minnesota that was destroyed by fire. Because Mission retained the Cozen & O'Connor law firm "as a matter of course to conduct its claims adjustment investigations in a geographic area including Minnesota for all claims exceeding $25,000,"[74] the Cozen firm investigated the loss and corresponded with Mission. After Mission sued for declaratory relief, the insured sought production of Mission's claim file, including correspondence from Cozen's office.[75] The court concluded that the Cozen firm was not acting as counsel but was performing a business function of Mission, thereby rendering the results of Cozen's investigation discoverable: "It is not the precepts of law that give rise to the difficulty in this case; instead, the difficulty exists because of plaintiffs [sic] decision, immediately upon receiving notice of the fire, to employ attorneys to fulfill its ordinary business function of claims investigation."[76]

The South Dakota Supreme Court reached a similar result in *Dakota, Minnesota & Eastern Railroad Corp. v. Acuity.*[77] There, Acuity hired a law firm to provide a coverage opinion on the extent of coverage under the policy's uninsured motorist coverage available to an employee of Dakota, Minnesota & Eastern (DME) allegedly injured when a "phantom vehicle" cut him off. DME deposed Acuity's claims representative, who knew little about the investigation even though he was the sole Acuity claims person because he delegated the investigative work to counsel. The supreme court reversed a summary judgment in favor of Acuity, holding that "where an insurer unequivocally delegates its initial claims function and relies exclusively upon outside counsel to conduct

insured by promulgating regulations that require insurance companies to investigate every filed claim and maintain claims files containing all documents, notes, and work papers relevant to each claim. *See* Cal. Code Regs. tit. 10, §§ 2695.1–.11 (2022). The Washington Supreme Court recently held that, in insurance bad-faith cases, there is a rebuttable presumption that "there is no attorney-client privilege relevant between the insured and the insurer in the claims adjusting process, and that the attorney-client and work product privileges are generally not relevant." Cedell v. Farmers Ins. Co., 295 P.3d 239, 246 (Wash. 2013). The insurer can rebut this presumption by showing that the attorney was not involved in investigating or evaluating the claim but provided the insurer with advice as to its own potential liability. *But see* W. Bend Mut. Ins. Co. v. Higgins, 9 So. 3d 655, 658 (Fla. Ct. App. 2009) ("We see nothing in Ruiz to suggest that a first-party insurer against whom a bad faith claim has been made is subject to the exposure of all its communications with its own counsel.").

73. 112 F.R.D. 160 (D. Minn. 1986). *Lilly* remains a frequently cited decision. *See, e.g.*, Strand v. Usana Health Scis., Inc., 2021 WL 3055608 (D. Utah July 20, 2021); Carlson v. BNSF Ry. Co., 2021 WL 3030644 (D. Minn. July 19, 2021); Solano-Sanchez v. State Farm Mut. Auto Ins. Co., 2021 WL 229400 (E.D. Pa. Jan. 22, 2021); Buckley LLP v. Series 1 of Oxford Ins. Co. NC LLC, 2020 WL 6696138 (N.C. Super. Nov. 9, 2020).

74. *Id.* at 162.

75. *Id.* at 162–63.

76. *Id.* at 163. The court also relied on the fact that Mission retained other counsel to handle the lawsuit that Lilly filed. *Id.*

77. 771 N.W.2d 623 (S.D. 2009).

the investigation and determination of coverage, the attorney-client privilege does not protect such communications."[78]

In *U.S. Bank N.A. v. PHL Variable Insurance Co.*,[79] the court considered whether a report prepared by outside counsel hired by a life insurance company was privileged. The underlying dispute concerned whether a $3 million life insurance policy initially issued by PHL to a trust and later sold to U.S. Bank constituted an improper stranger-originated life insurance (STOLI) purchase. U.S. Bank challenged PHL's assertion that the attorneys were retained for the purpose of seeking legal advice, pointing to contemporaneous documents suggesting that the advice was "business-oriented."[80] The court found that this evidence rebutted the presumption that communications between an attorney and client are for the purposes of legal advice.[81] With the exception of a few portions that summarized legal advice, the court ordered production of the attorneys' report.[82]

This rule is not applied exclusively to insurance company investigations. *United States v. ISS Marine Services, Inc.*[83] exemplifies a situation where such an investigation was not privileged. Two ISS employees reported that some of ISS's business practices in Dubai might violate the law. ISS's management contacted its regular outside counsel, who talked with the reporting employees. Counsel prepared a proposal to investigate the allegations and report to management. The investigation was undertaken by an ISS employee.[84]

Thereafter, the Navy began an investigation to determine whether ISS had overcharged the Navy for work ISS had performed. The government issued a subpoena seeking all audit reports ISS had. When ISS refused to produce the audit report claiming attorney-client privilege, the government petitioned for an order compelling ISS to produce it. The court granted the government's petition and ordered ISS to produce the report.[85]

The court concluded that the report was not privileged. First, the court rejected ISS's claim that it could exclude counsel from actually performing the investigation but retain counsel to "consult" on the investigation in order to protect the report. The court reasoned that "[w]hen a company fails to involve lawyers directly in an internal investigation, the company faces a higher burden to demonstrate that the attorney-client privilege applies to the results of

---

78. *Id.* at 638.

79. 2016 WL 1258466 (D. Minn. Mar. 30, 2016).

80. *Id.* at *6. For example, one email stated that PHL retained "an outside firm 'Bracewell and Giuliani' to review our current procedures and provide recommendation to us on how to improve the detection and prevention of life insurance sales intended to be investor owned." *Id.*

81. *Id.* at *7.

82. *Id.* at *12–14.

83. 905 F. Supp. 2d 121 (D.D.C. 2012).

84. *Id.* at 124–25.

85. *Id.* at 126.

that investigation."[86] Second, the court rejected the concept that counsel could coach the investigation at arm's length. Rather, the court concluded that "when an attorney is absent from the information-gathering process, 'the original communicator has no intention that the information be provided to a lawyer for the purposes of legal representation.'"[87]

Two recent opinions in New York have distinguished the *Spectrum Systems* case discussed previously. First, in *Brooklyn Union Gas Co. v American Home Insurance Co.*,[88] the court decided that documents prepared by attorneys hired by an insurance company to investigate the circumstances of a loss were acting as claims investigators, not legal counsel.[89] Second, in *Vector Capital Corp. v. Ness Technologies, Inc.*,[90] Vector sued Ness for breach of contract for failing to provide relevant information to allow Vector to decide whether to take over Ness. The court held that report of Vector's due diligence investigation of Ness, prepared by counsel, was discoverable as a document prepared in the ordinary course of Vector's business.[91]

More recently, in *Gawel v. Radius Health, Inc.*,[92] Radius hired a law firm to conduct an investigation after it received an anonymous complaint about alleged misconduct by plaintiff, who was then its employee. The law firm interviewed several employees of Radius and then provided its findings to Radius.[93] Radius terminated plaintiff who then filed suit. During discovery, plaintiff requested all of the law firm's communications with Radius. Radius agreed that the investigative report prepared by the law firm was not privileged and produced it. Radius, however, contended that law firm's recommendations concerning remedial measures was privileged. The court disagreed, concluding that all of the law firm's work for Radius was done as an investigator, not as legal counsel.[94] The court did permit Radius to redact limited portions of the recommendations because the court found that a few communications were providing legal advice.[95]

In *Aerojet Rocketdyne, Inc. v. Global Aerospace, Inc.*,[96] Global retained a law firm to investigate and evaluate Aerojet's claim for coverage under a liability

86. *Id.* at 130.

87. *Id.* (quoting Nesse v. Shaw Pittman, 206 F.R.D. 325, 330 (D.D.C. 2002)).

88. 803 N.Y.S.2d 532 (N.Y. App. Div. 2005).

89. *Id.* at 534. *But see In re* Residential Capital, LLC, 575 B.R. 29, 40–42 (S.D.N.Y. 2017) (when attorney is a claims handler and also provides legal advice, the privilege remains intact as to the legal advice).

90. 2014 WL 171160 (S.D.N.Y. Jan. 9, 2014).

91. *Id.* at *5–6.

92. 2021 WL 3810545 (S.D. Cal. Aug. 26, 2021).

93. *Id.* at *1.

94. *Id.* at *3.

95. *Id.* at *4.

96. 2019 WL 4929930 (E.D. Cal. Oct. 7, 2019).

insurance policy Global issued. The law firm was retained the day after Global received Aerojet's claim, and the evidence suggested that the law firm was investigating the claim in conjunction with Global's claims group. After the claim was denied and litigation ensued, Global objected to producing any of the documents the law firm authored, claiming those documents were protected by the attorney-client privilege. The court first determined that New Jersey law applied, and then determined that the law firm was conducting a claims investigation and was not providing legal advice.[97] The court first noted that Global did not have an engagement letter describing the law firm's role, which the court deemed significant.[98] The court rejected Global's argument that it was always anticipating litigation when a claim was submitted because that would lead to a situation where Global's obligation to investigate a claim would always be protected behind the attorney-client privilege or the work-product doctrine.[99] The district court affirmed the magistrate judge's order.[100]

C. Summary

The *Sandra T.E.*, *Costco*, and *Spectrum Systems* cases illustrate that the communications between attorney and client relating to the attorney's investigation will be protected by the attorney-client privilege only as long as the attorney is acting in his or her capacity as an attorney. The *Lilly*, *Acuity*, *ISS Marine*, *U.S. Bank*, *Gawel*, *and Aerojet* cases, however, demonstrate that not all attorneys conducting investigations on behalf of clients are acting in the capacity of an attorney. Where, as in *Lilly*, *Acuity*, *ISS Marine*, *U.S. Bank*, *Gawel*, *and Aerojet*, the attorney is performing an investigation that can be generally considered part of the client's ordinary business practices, a client cannot shield the results of that investigation simply by having an attorney conduct the investigation. To obtain attorney-client privilege protection of attorney-client investigative communications, the party seeking to invoke the privilege must carry the burden of establishing that the attorney's investigation was conducted to render legal advice to the client.

---

97. *Id.* at *6.

98. *Id.* Several courts have looked to the engagement letter to determine whether the letter clearly defines the scope of the attorney's work for the client. *See, e.g.*, B.L. v. Schuhmann, 2020 WL 6293582 (W.D. Ky. Oct. 27, 2020); U.S. *ex rel.* Wollman v. Mass. Gen. Hosp., Inc., 475 F. Supp. 3d 45 (D. Mass. 2020); Estate of Paterno v. NCAA, 168 A.3d 187 (Pa. Super. Ct. 2017).

99. *Id.* In reaching its decision, the court relied heavily on Payton v. New Jersey Turnpike Authority, 691 A.2d 321 (N.J. 1997), where the New Jersey Supreme Court rejected the Turnpike Authority's argument that its entire investigation into a sexual harassment complaint was privileged because it was undertaken by lawyers. The court held that "when an attorney conducts an investigation not for the purpose of preparing for litigation or providing legal advice, but rather for some other purpose, the privilege is inapplicable." *Id.* at 551.

100. Aerojet Rocketdyne, Inc. v. Glob. Aerospace, Inc., 2021 WL 134551 (E.D. Cal. Jan. 14, 2021).

As the foregoing cases demonstrate, the fact that a lawyer investigates, in his or her capacity as a lawyer, for a corporate client does not necessarily mean that the communications to or from that lawyer will always be protected. In those jurisdictions that follow *Upjohn*, an attorney can be more confident that the communications with the client's employees will be protected. In a control group jurisdiction, the communications will not be protected by the attorney-client privilege unless the communicator or recipient of the communication from the attorney is within the narrowly defined control group or is the person whose conduct gave rise to the potential liability.

In sum, there is nothing attorneys can do to absolutely ensure that the results of their investigation will be protected by the work-product doctrine. There are, however, steps an attorney can take to help establish that investigation materials were prepared in anticipation of litigation. For example, the attorney can, upon receiving a request to evaluate and investigate on behalf of a client, send a confirming letter to the client that notes that the attorney is investigating and evaluating the matter in anticipation of litigation, specifying the precise claims the attorney "anticipates." The attorney can make sure he or she is not performing a task that the client would perform as a regular part of its business if it had not hired the attorney, especially if the client is an insurance company. The lawyer can also make sure that any related claims are considered to protect the work product of all of those involved. The lawyer should determine the law applicable to statements from nonclients before deciding whether to take them and how to record them. Finally, while the work-product doctrine may shield *documents* from discovery, most courts hold that an opposing party can, by interrogatories or by deposition, discover factual information learned during an investigation.[101]

III. Who Can Be Interviewed by the Attorney?

The second issue concerns what individuals the investigating attorney can interview and keep the results of the investigation within the scope of the attorney-client privilege. This issue arises in two contexts: first, interviews of former or nonemployees and, second, interviews of witnesses to an event who have no independent liability for it. *Upjohn* left open the question of whether communications with a corporation's former employees are protected by the attorney-client privilege.[102] Because this issue had not been addressed in the

101. *See, e.g.*, Raso v. CMC Equip. Rental, Inc., 154 F.R.D. 126, 128 (E.D. Pa. 1994); Eoppolo v. Nat'l R.R. Passenger Corp., 108 F.R.D. 292, 294 (E.D. Pa. 1985).

102. The *Upjohn* Court noted that seven of the 86 employees interviewed by counsel had terminated their employment by the time they were interviewed. *Upjohn*, 449 U.S. at 394 n.3.

courts below, the *Upjohn* Court declined to opine on it.[103] But many courts look to the reason the Court rejected the control group test when determining what communications are within the attorney-client privilege.[104]

Peralta v. Cendant Corp.[105] is an early decision that determined whether the attorney-client privilege applied to communications with former employees. The issue arose during the former employee's deposition. The court indicated that this case involved federal law, and rejected opinions decided under state law that held the privilege did not apply as contrary to *Upjohn.*[106] The court relied on Chief Justice Burger's concurring opinion in *Upjohn* to conclude that any privileged information the former employee knew of remain privileged after her termination. And the former employee could not be questioned about discussions she had with her employer's attorneys after she left the company that relate to the reasons for plaintiff's termination.[107]

Hanover Insurance Co. v. Plaquemines Parish[108] is a case addressing this issue under state law. There, Hanover provided a performance bond for a construction project funded by the parish. Disputes arose and litigation ensued between the bonding company, the parish, and the contractor and subcontractors.[109] The issue was this: "are conversations between counsel for a corporation and the corporation's former employees entitled to the attorney-client privilege."[110] The court determined that there was no existing

---

103. In a concurring opinion, Chief Justice Burger suggested that the *Upjohn* rule should apply to communications with former employees otherwise falling within the framework of *Upjohn. See id.* at 402–03.

104. The Court rejected the control group test because it did not protect communications between and investigating attorney and the employees of the corporation whose actions may create corporate liability. 449 U.S. at 684–85. *See, e.g., In re* Coordinated Pretrial Proceedings, 658 F.2d 1355, 1365 n.7 (9th Cir. 1981) ("Former employees, as well as current employees, may possess the relevant information needed by corporate counsel to advise the client with respect to actual or potential difficulties. Again, the attorney-client privilege is served by the certainty that conversations between the attorney and client will remain privileged after the employee leaves.") (decided before *Upjohn*).

105. 190 F.R.D. 38 (D. Conn. 1999).

106. *Id.* at 40. The court rejected the reasoning of Barrett Indus. Trucks v. Old Republic Ins. Co., 129 F.R.D. 515 (N.D. Ill. 1990), Connolly Data Systems v. Victor Technologies, 114 F.R.D. 89 (S.D. Cal. 1987), and Clark Equipment Co. v. Lift Parts Mfg. Co., 1985 WL 2917 (N.D. Ill., Oct. 1, 1985).

107. *Id.* at 41. As another court stated, Peralta protected communications about "the former employee's conduct and knowledge, or communication with defendant's counsel, during his or her employment." Cyphert v. Scotts Miracle-Gro Co. (*In re* Morning Song Bird Food Litig.), 2017 WL 7512980, at *3 (S.D. Fla. Nov. 29, 2018). *See also* Jacobs v. Alam, 2020 WL 3064435, at *5–6 (E.D. Mich. June 9, 2020) (holding that "privileged communications between an employee and corporate counsel should not automatically lose their protected status upon the employee leaving the company"). *But see* Infosystems, Inc. v. Ceridian Corp., 197 F.R.D. 303, 305–06 (E.D. Mich. 2000) (noting that *Peralta* failed to include a key element from *Upjohn*—that the communication from the former employee be at the direction of management).

108. 304 F.R.D. 494, 496 (E.D. La. 2015).

109. *Id.* at 495.

110. *Id.* at 496.

state court precedent, so it had to predict what the Louisiana Supreme Court would decide as required by the *Erie* doctrine.[111] The court concluded that Louisiana would recognize the existence of a privilege between a corporation's counsel and a former employee when the former employee's conduct may give rise to corporate liability.[112]

Other federal and state courts have reached the same conclusion.[113] Furthermore, the Fourth Circuit noted in *In re Allen*[114] that courts that have declined to apply the attorney-client privilege to communications between the client's attorney and former employees have done so because they were following state law or because the former employee was not an employee when the relevant conduct occurred.[115]

But the court in *Newman v. Highland School District No. 203*[116] took a different approach to the question of whether communications with former employees are protected by the attorney-client privilege. There, Newman suffered permanent brain injury at a school football game and sued the school district for damages.[117] Highland's counsel interviewed several former coaches and also appeared as their counsel at their depositions. Newman sought production of communications between defense counsel and the former employees. The district moved for a protective order claiming that the communications

111. *Id.* at 497. The court noted that the Louisiana Supreme Court had issued a single paragraph order with no facts or context that stated, in part, "a protective order is entered in their favor preventing any discovery regarding privileged communications between relators' corporate counsel and any former employees relating to the subject matter of this lawsuit." Turner v. Lowery, 703 So. 2d 1 (La. 1997). Turner cited *Upjohn* and *In re Allen*, 106 F.3d 582 (4th Cir. 1997).

112. *Id.* at 499–500.

113. *See, e.g.*, Miramar Constr. Co. v. Home Depot, Inc., 167 F. Supp. 2d 182 (D.P.R. 2001); Guillen v. City of Chi., 956 F. Supp. 1416, 1425 (N.D. Ill. 1997); Command Transp., Inc. v. Y.S. Line (USA) Corp., 116 F.R.D. 94, 96–97 (D. Mass. 1987); Porter v. Arco Metals Co., 642 F. Supp. 1116, 1118 (D. Mont. 1986); Denver Post Corp. v. Univ. of Colo., 739 P.2d 874, 880 (Colo. Ct. App. 1987). *But see* Newman v. Highland Sch. Dist. No. 203, 381 P.3d 1188, 1191 (Wash. 2016) (no protection for communications with nonmanagerial former employees) (holding that no privilege can attach to communications with former employees absent special circumstances). For cases reaching similar conclusions but in different contexts, *see Peralta v. Cendant Corp.*, 190 F.R.D. 38 (D. Conn. 1999) (holding that the attorney-client privilege attaches to communications with former employees only if the communications relate to knowledge obtained during employment or the communications were held with the employee prior to termination and were privileged at that time); *Camden v. State*, 910 F. Supp. 1115 (D. Md. 1996); and *Fruehauf Trailer Corp. v. Hagelthorn*, 528 N.W.2d 778 (Mich. Ct. App. 1995). *See also* Winthrop Res. Corp. v. CommScope, Inc. of N.C., 2014 WL 5810457 (W.D.N.C. Nov. 7, 2014) (following *Peralta*).

114. 106 F.3d 582 (4th Cir. 1997).

115. *Id.* at 606 (citing Nakajima v. Gen. Motors Corp., 857 F. Supp. 100, 104 (D.D.C. 1994) (District of Columbia law); Barrett Indus. Trucks v. Old Republic Ins. Co., 129 F.R.D. 515, 517–18 (N.D. Ill. 1990) (Illinois law); Connolly Data Sys. v. Victor Techs., 114 F.R.D. 89, 93–94 (S.D. Cal. 1987) (California law)).

116. 381 P.3d 1188 (Wash. 2016).

117. *Id.* at 1190.

were protected by the attorney-client privilege. The trial court disagreed and denied Highland's motion for the protective order.[118]

The court affirmed the trial court's decision in a 5–4 decision. The court rejected *Upjohn*'s flexible approach and held that the attorney-client privilege does not protect communications with former employees after their employment is terminated.[119] The court reasoned that the termination of the employment relationship terminates any agency relationship between the former employee and the employer. Because there is no agency relationship, "a former employee is no different from other third-party fact witnesses to a lawsuit, who may be freely interviewed by either party."[120] Notably, the court indicated that the former employees were "fact witnesses in this litigation."[121]

The significance of *Newman* is uncertain. The Washington Supreme Court distinguished *Newman* in *Hermanson v. MultiCare Health System, Inc.*,[122] holding that *Newman* did not apply to an independent contractor physician who still had a principal-agent relationship with the defendant hospital.[123] More recently, *Newman* was rejected by the federal court in Colorado that chose to apply *Peralta* instead.[124] At least one commentator has suggested that *Newman* will not be widely accepted.[125]

IV. What Must Be Disclosed

If the Court's admonition in *Upjohn* that the protection of the attorney-client privilege applies only to communications and not facts is correct, then the obvious answer is that the communication should never be produced, but the party must always provide requested information in response to interrogatories or in depositions. The *Upjohn* Court clearly stated that the witnesses interviewed by counsel could be deposed and had to answer questions;[126] what the government could not obtain were the questionnaires those witnesses filled out.

---

118. *Id.*

119. *Id.* at 1191. The court relied on the RESTATEMENT (THIRD) OF THE LAW GOVERNING LAWYERS § 73 (2000).

120. *Id.* at 1193.

121. *Id.* at 1191.

122. 475 P.3d 484 (Wash. 2020).

123. *Id.* at 489. The court also relied on the RESTATEMENT (THIRD) OF THE LAW GOVERNING LAWYERS § 73 (2000).

124. Corcoran v. HCA-Healthone LLC, 2022 WL 1605296, at *6–8 (D. Colo. May 20, 2022), relying in part on B. Lesback & J. Lesback, *Privileged Communication with Current and Former Corporate Employees*, 51 COLO. LAW. 42 (May 2022). Newman was also discussed and rejected in a trial court decision. Mayotte v. Brattleboro Mem. Hosp., 2022 WL 1242631, at *1 (Vt. Super. Ct. Feb. 10, 2022).

125. Douglas R. Richmond, *The Attorney-Client Privilege and Former Employees*, 70 CATH. U. L. REV. 39, 57 (2021) ("The importance of the decision in *Newman* is debatable.").

126. Upjohn Co. v. United States, 449 U.S. 383, 395–96 (1981).

Those resisting discovery usually make two arguments: first, the information is protected by the attorney-client privilege, and, second, the information falls within the work-product protection afforded by Federal Rule of Civil Procedure 26(b)(3) and its state law counterparts. As explained earlier in more detail, the attorney-client privilege is narrow in scope, while the work-product doctrine is broader.[127] An adversary can obtain ordinary work product if that party can show substantial need and the inability to obtain the substantial equivalent by other means.[128] But the attorney-client privilege is absolute.[129] Thus, the discovery issue may be resolved differently if the court takes one approach or the other.[130]

Even if attorney-client-privileged communications contain discoverable factual information, it does not necessarily mean that communications containing those facts "are fair game in discovery."[131] Some courts hold that

---

127. *See, e.g.*, Wynn Resorts, Ltd. v. Eighth Judicial Dist. Court of Nev., 399 P.3d 334, 347 (Nev. 2017). A detailed discussion of the intricacies of the work product doctrine is contained in Chapter 3 of this treatise.

128. Fed. R. Civ. P. 26(b)(3)(A)(ii).

129. The protection afforded by the attorney-client privilege is absolute unless waived. Westinghouse Elec. Corp. v. Republic of Philippines, 951 F.2d 1414, 1429 (3d Cir. 1991). There is no "substantial need" exception to the attorney-client privilege. Phila. Indem. Ins. Co. v. Olympia Early Learning Ctr., 2013 WL 3338503 (W.D. Wash. July 2, 2013). *Accord* Abington Emerson Cap., LLC v. Landash Corp., 2019 WL 6167085, at *5 (S.D. Ohio Nov. 20, 2019). *See also* Siddall v. Allstate Ins. Co., 15 Fed. App'x 522, 523 (9th Cir. 2001) ("[A] substantial need does not, as a matter of law, provide a legal basis for piercing the attorney-client privilege."). Nor is a witness's unavailability a reason to require production of an attorney-client-privileged statement to counsel. Admiral Ins. Co. v. U.S. Dist. Ct., 881 F.2d 1486, 1494 (9th Cir. 1989) ("An unavailability exception is, therefore, inconsistent with the nature and purpose of the privilege."). *See also* Genovese v. Provident Life & Accident Ins. Co., 74 So. 3d 1064, 1068–69 (Fla. 2011). Generally, even a shareholder cannot obtain privileged materials from the corporation. Espinoza v. Hewlett-Packard Corp., 32 A.3d 365 (Del. 2011).

130. If a court finds that the attorney-client privilege applies, there is no reason to also consider whether the document is protected by the work-product doctrine. *See, e.g.*, Buxbaum v. St. Vincent's Health Servs. Inc., 2013 WL 74733 (D. Conn. Jan. 7, 2013). *See also* E.E.O.C. v. George Washington Univ., 2022 WL 3980991, at *15 ("The finding that all the withheld documents listed on the January 2022 Privilege Log are privileged obviates the need to address work product protection."). *Contra*, E.E.O.C. v. Lutheran Soc. Servs., 186 F.3d 959, 969 (D.C. Cir. 1999) ("We find the entire report protected by the work product privilege. We therefore have no need to consider whether the attorney-client privilege also protects the report."). *Accord*, Leberman v. Alabama Bd. of Pardons, 2020 WL 12991595, at *3 n.5 (M.A. Ala. Oct 10, 2020).

131. Documents in a party's counsel's files are within the scope of documents that must be produced in response to a discovery request directed to that party. Rule 34 of the Federal Rules of Civil Procedure, for example, requires parties to produce requested documents that are within their possession, custody, or control. *See* Fed. R. Civ. P. 34. "Control" is broadly construed to mean not only physical possession but also the legal or practical right to obtain them from another source on demand. *See, e.g.*, Golden Trade v. Lee Apparel Co., 143 F.R.D. 514, 525 (S.D.N.Y. 1992); M.L.C., Inc. v. N. Am. Philips Corp., 109 F.R.D. 134, 136 (S.D.N.Y. 1986). *See also* Hanson v. Gartland S.S. Co., 34 F.R.D. 493, 496 (N.D. Ohio 1964).

the written communications do not have to be produced at all,[132] but rather, the client must disclose the discoverable factual information in either depositions or interrogatory responses.[133] Other courts require the written communication to be produced with the exception of those portions relating to legal advice, which are to be redacted.[134]

132. *See, e.g.*, E.E.O.C. v. George Washington Univ., 2022 WL 3980991, at *14 (D.D.C. Sept. 1, 2022) (privileged information correctly withheld).

133. *See, e.g.*, Arkwright Mut. Ins. Co. v. Nat'l Union Fire Ins. Co., 1994 WL 510043 (S.D.N.Y. Sept. 16, 1994). In *Arkwright*, National Union sought production of documents in the possession of Arkwright's counsel in prior litigation and in possession of counsel hired by Arkwright to conduct a subrogation investigation. National Union argued that some of the claimed attorney-client-privileged documents lost their privilege because they contain discoverable factual information. The court rejected National Union's argument, noting "[t]hat principle simply means that Arkwright must, in either depositions or interrogatory responses, disclose relevant facts if National Union inquires, not that any privileged communications containing facts are fair game in discovery." *Id.* at *8. *See also* Bovis Lend Lease, LMB, Inc. v. Seasons Contracting Corp., 2002 WL 31729693, at *18 (S.D.N.Y. Dec. 5, 2002). *But see* Green v. Kroger Co., 2022 WL 1078024, at *3 (S.D. Tex. Apr. 11, 2022) where the judge ruled that an employee tasked by in-house counsel to develop the position statement required by the EEOC in a harassment claim did not have to answer questions in his deposition about what documents he reviewed or what witnesses he interviewed in order to prepare the statement.

134. *See, e.g.*, Wagner Aeronautical, Inc. v. Dotzenroth, 2022 WL 4004188, at *5 (S.D. Cal. Sept. 1, 2022) (privileged information to be redacted from email chain then produced); Homeland Ins. Co. v. Clinical Pathology Labs, Inc., 2022 WL 3567740, at *2 (W.D. Tex. Aug. 18, 2022) (same); Carte Blanche (Singapore) PTE, Ltd. v. Diners Club Int'l, Inc., 130 F.R.D. 28, 31 (S.D.N.Y. 1990) (information the court called "factual" obtained from third parties must be disclosed).

CHAPTER 10

Patent Matters

GEORGE W. JORDAN, III

I. Introduction and Overview

Because clients depend on attorneys to be heavily involved with patents, attorney-client privilege disputes arise in patent litigation more often other civil litigation. For clients interested in seeking patent protection, attorneys are involved in patentability decisions, drafting patent applications, filing patent applications, and prosecuting patent applications before the U.S. Patent and Trademark Office to seek patent issuance. For clients interested in avoiding infringement of another's patents, attorneys can be involved in the process of designing around patents or involved in providing opinions of counsel that might be relied upon for an advice of counsel defense. Therefore, in patent litigation, either side or both sides might have attorney-client communications, attorney declarations, and attorney witnesses involved.

Such attorney-client privilege disputes tend to implicate two competing policies. On the one hand, the purpose of the privilege is "to encourage clients to make full disclosure to their attorneys."[1] Consequently, protection of the privilege promotes broader societal interests in the administration of justice and encourages clients to observe the law.[2] On the other hand, the discovery provisions in the Federal Rules of Civil Procedure "are to be applied as broadly and liberally as possible" and, consistent with the breadth of discovery, "the privilege limitation must be restricted to its narrowest bounds."[3] One court summarized these competing interests when it aptly observed that "lawyers love to know the secret communications between opposing parties and

1. Fisher v. United States, 425 U.S. 391, 403 (1976).
2. Hunt v. Blackburn, 128 U.S. 464, 470 (1888).
3. Hickman v. Taylor, 329 U.S. 495, 506 (1947).

their counsel" but "[m]otions to penetrate clearly applicable privileges can be tools for harassment—and can chill the communications that the privileges are designed to encourage."[4]

Likewise, heavy attorney involvement tends to explain why work-product immunity disputes are commonplace in patent litigation. For clients that anticipate patent litigation, attorneys are often involved in preparing for litigation, including with respect to validity investigations, infringement investigations, and opinions of counsel.

II. Communications Relating to Invention Process

Accused patent infringers invariably wish to discover documents and communications relating to the creation and patenting of the invention that is the subject of litigation. Such communications may be relevant to a myriad of substantive patent law issues, including claim interpretation, validity, and inequitable conduct. Not surprisingly, there are a number of specific types of communications that are commonly the subject of discovery requests in patent cases. Whether a privilege attaches to such communications depends upon (1) the timing of the communication, (2) the context and subject matter of the communication, and (3) the identities of the parties to the communication. The party seeking to avoid discovery of the privileged documents bears the burden of establishing privilege.[5]

For example, usually the inventors or assignees will possess documents and communications relating to some technical problem that they (or their employer) wish to solve. As part of their efforts to solve that problem, the inventors may create laboratory notebooks, research memoranda, and similar types of records documenting their work, including tests they have conducted and their findings and conclusions. Such "purely" technical documents and "purely" technical communications may not qualify as privileged because they ordinarily do not request legal advice or services or responses to such requests.[6]

As time goes on in the "invention" process, however, the line between what constitutes a purely "technical" document or communication not deserving of a privilege and what constitutes a communication of technical information for the purpose of legal advice begins to blur. For example, a question

---

4. Laser Indus. Ltd. v. Reliant Techs., Inc., 167 F.R.D. 417, 424 (N.D. Cal. 1996) (denying motion to pierce patent holder's attorney-client privilege).

5. *See In re Diagnostics Sys. Corp.*, 328 F. App'x 621, 623 (Fed. Cir. 2008) ("[T]he case turns on whether [the party] met its burden to establish privilege for each of the documents remaining in dispute.").

6. *See, e.g.*, Meds. Co. v. Mylan Inc., 936 F. Supp. 2d 894, 901 (N.D. Ill. 2013) ("[T]echnical information does not make the document privileged"); Shire Develop. Inc. v. Cadila Healthcare Ltd., 2012 WL 5247315, at *4, (D. Del. June 15, 2012) ("[T]here can be no real dispute that purely factual information is not privileged. Indeed, as Plaintiffs admit, tests, testing results, and formulation strategies are not privileged in and of themselves.").

may be raised during the development process regarding whether the results of the technical work, as reflected in the "purely" technical documents or communications, demonstrate or result in a patentable invention. The scientists, chemists, and engineers working on the technical project usually are unable to make such an assessment. They require the advice of an attorney or patent agent. The question often arises in patent cases whether, and to what extent, the substance of various communications and associated documents relating to or documenting the inventive process is privileged. The federal circuit's en banc decision in *In re Spalding Sports Worldwide, Inc.*[7] is the appropriate starting point for addressing such issues.[8]

A. The Privilege Standard Set Forth in the *Spalding* Decision

In *Spalding*, the district court ordered a patentee to produce an internal corporate "invention record" pertaining to the invention of what eventually became the patent-in-suit, concluding that such a communication was not privileged.[9] On appeal, the federal circuit vacated the district court's order to produce the invention record.[10] The appellate court held that the corporation's invention record was protected by the attorney-client privilege.[11]

The federal circuit began its analysis by deciding whether it must apply regional circuit law or its own law to the privilege question. The court concluded that whether an invention record qualifies as a privileged document is a question unique to patent law because the invention record relates to an invention submitted for consideration for possible patent protection; it thus clearly implicates substantive patent law.[12] Thus freed from possibly conflicting decisions by other circuit courts, and applying its own law in this case of first impression, the federal circuit held that "an invention record constitutes a privileged communication, as long as it is provided to an attorney 'for the purpose of securing primarily a legal opinion, or legal services, or assistance in a legal proceeding.'"[13] The court concluded that the invention record at issue was privileged because it "was prepared and submitted primarily for the purpose of obtaining legal advice on patentability and legal services in preparing a patent application."[14]

---

7. 203 F.3d 800 (Fed. Cir. 2000) (en banc).

8. Whether the privilege remains if the communications were shared with a non-attorney patent agent is addressed in Section III.B.

9. An invention record is a standard form "generally used by corporations as a means for inventors to disclose to the corporation's patent attorneys that an invention has been made and to initiate patent action. They are usually short documents containing space for such information as names of inventors, description and scope of invention, closest prior art, first date of conception and disclosure to others, dates of publication, etc." 203 F.3d 800, 808 n.2 (Fed. Cir. 2000) (en banc).

10. *Id.* at 808.

11. *Id.*

12. *Id.* at 804.

13. *Id.* at 805 (citations omitted).

14. 203 F.3d at 806.

The fact that the invention record included technical information, or that the technical information might eventually be made public when a patent is issued, did not change the privileged nature of the document. As the federal circuit explained, "that much of the technical information in one form or another finds its way into the patent application, to be made public when the patent issues, should not preclude the assertion of the privilege over the communication in which that information was disclosed to the attorney."[15]

In dicta, the court addressed the *Jack Winter*[16] line of district court decisions, which held that the transmission of technical information to an attorney and documents relating to patent prosecution were not privileged because the attorney was acting merely as a "conduit" between the client and the U.S. Patent and Trademark Office (USPTO).[17] The federal circuit distinguished *Jack Winter* and its progeny as "not deal[ing] specifically with invention records" and concluded that, in any event, it was not bound by those decisions.[18] The federal circuit concluded that "the better rule [regarding privilege] is the one articulated in [*Spalding*]."[19]

B. District Court Cases Applying *Spalding*

Under *Spalding*, not all invention and patent prosecution-related communications are privileged. Strictly speaking, the federal circuit's holding was limited to invention records submitted to patent counsel for the purpose of obtaining legal advice on patentability. Nevertheless, the court's choice of law analysis, and its criticism of the "conduit" theory, fundamentally changed the privilege landscape. Consequently, armed with the reasoning of *Spalding*, a patent owner is far more likely to prevail in asserting privilege over many different types of documents and communications commonly created in the course of the conception, reduction to practice, and patenting of an invention.

For example, in *Martin Marietta Materials, Inc. v. Bedford Reinforced Plastics, Inc.*,[20] the district court applied *Spalding* and held communications between a client and counsel regarding prior art and the duty to disclose material information to the USPTO were privileged.[21] The privileged communications included "relevant technical information" that was required to "evaluate patentability and/or to prepare a patent application."[22]

---

15. *Id.* (citing Knogo Corp. v. United States, 213 U.S.P.Q. 936, 941 (Ct. Cl. 1980)); *see also* Carl Zeiss Jena GmbH v. Bio-Rad Labs., Inc., 2000 WL 547047, at *1 (S.D.N.Y. May 4, 2000) (finding *Spalding* "squarely on point" and concluding that plaintiff's invention disclosure documents were protected by the attorney-client privilege).

16. Jack Winter, Inc. v. Koratron Co., 50 F.R.D. 225, 228 (N.D. Cal. 1970).

17. *Spalding*, 203 F.3d at 806 n.3 (citing *Jack Winter*, 50 F.R.D. at 228, among other cases).

18. *Id.*

19. *Id.*

20. 227 F.R.D. 382 (W.D. Pa. 2005).

21. *Id.* at 394.

22. *Id.* The district court subsequently determined that the privilege was waived.

Similarly, in *Innogenetics, N.V. v. Abbott Laboratories*,[23] the district court refused to limit its interpretation of *Spalding* to invention disclosures. The district court broadly held, "[I]f it appears that a document was conveyed from [in-house patent department personnel] to one of [plaintiff's] outside patent lawyers for the purpose of obtaining legal advice concerning the preparation of the priority or patent applications at issue, or was prepared by the outside patent lawyers in response to such a request, then I will deem it privileged."[24]

In *Softview Computer Products Corp. v. Haworth, Inc.*,[25] the court observed that "[t]he *Spalding* court relied in part on *Knogo Corp. v. United States*. . . . The line of cases that follow *Knogo* stand for the proposition that the attorney-client privilege *may* attach to communications regarding patent prosecution, so long as those communications meet the other criteria of the privilege."[26] The district court in *Softview* applied the *Spalding* standard for privilege to all of the withheld documents at issue relating to the patentee's U.S. patent application.[27]

In *McCook Metals L.L.C. v. Alcoa Inc.*,[28] the district court applied *Spalding* in concluding that draft patent applications, invention control reports, inventor questionnaires, and a duty of disclosure reminder form were privileged.[29] With regard to draft patent applications in particular, the court in *McCook* acknowledged that other (pre-*Spalding*) courts had refused to extend the privilege to such documents on the ground that much of the information contained in the drafts eventually was placed in the public domain by means of a successful patent prosecution.[30] The court in *McCook* disagreed with the rationale of those contrary cases because they failed to recognize the legal importance that a first-rate patent attorney adds to the legal protection afforded to the client by the proper legal draftsmanship of an airtight patent that is successfully and properly prosecuted.[31]

In *Ergo Licensing, LLC v. Carefusion 303, Inc.*,[32] the defendant sought to compel a patentee's documents that the defendant characterized as "drafts of Patent Office forms." The district court acknowledged that "[c]ase law differs on the question of whether drafts of documents intended to be filed with a government agency, and thus intended to be public, are covered by the attorney-client privilege." The district court followed the reasoning articulated in *In*

23. 2006 WL 6091309 (W.D. Wis. Aug. 14, 2006).

24. *Id.* at *10.

25. 2000 WL 351411 (S.D.N.Y. Mar. 31, 2000).

26. *Id.* at *8–9 (emphasis added) (citations omitted).

27. *Id.* Unfortunately, the district court's opinion fails to describe the precise nature of the prosecution documents it considered.

28. 192 F.R.D. 242 (N.D. Ill. 2000).

29. *Id.* at 252–53.

30. *Id.* at 253 (citing Applied Telematics, Inc. v. Sprint Commc'ns Co., L.P., 1996 WL 539595 (E.D. Pa. Sept. 18, 1996)); *see also* Sneider v. Kimberly-Clark Corp., 91 F.R.D. 1, 5 (N.D. Ill. 1980).

31. 192 F.R.D. at 253.

32. 263 F.R.D. 40, 45 (D. Me. 2009).

re Rivastigmine Patent Litigation,[33] a 2006 district court decision that analyzed post-*Spalding* cases and concluded the "emerging trend" was to apply the attorney-client privilege to drafts of patent applications. The district court in *Ergo Licensing* likewise held the "draft Patent Office forms" that were in issue "are draft documents that are also covered by the attorney-client privilege."[34]

Other cases that have applied *Spalding* in upholding a claim of attorney-client privilege to prevent discovery of documents and communications relating to patent preparation, prosecution, or opinions include:

- *Bergstrom, Inc. v. Glacier Bay, Inc.*[35]—inventors' communications to attorney of prior art either before the patent application was filed or before the patent issued were privileged.
- *Carl Zeiss Vision International GmbH v. Signet Armorlite, Inc.*[36]—clearance opinion provided by counsel to clients was privileged under *Spalding*.
- *Eastman Kodak Co. v. Agfa-Gevaert N.V.*[37]—a document included within invention record will be regarded as part of the whole invention record and privileged unless the party seeking discovery of the individual document demonstrates a reason why the document is a nonprivileged "attachment."
- *Park v. Cas Enterprises, Inc.*[38]—emails regarding patent prosecution as well as drafts of documents that were to be filed in the USPTO were privileged under *Spalding*.
- *Probert v. Clorox Co.*[39]—granting protective order to prevent defendant from deposing plaintiff's patent counsel concerning the invention, prosecution, and interpretation of the patent-in-suit because the subjects of the deposition were likely to involve privileged communications under *Spalding*.
- *Shire Development, Inc. v. Cadila Healthcare Ltd.*[40]—communications reflecting strategies for patent infringement avoidance, although not "as formal as" an invention record, are privileged under *Spalding*.
- *Games2U, Inc. v. Game Truck Licensing, LLC*[41]—prior art documents exchanged between attorney and client and not shared with third parties, as well as draft patent applications, attorney notes, and written

---

33. 237 F.R.D. 69, 85–86 (S.D.N.Y. 2006).
34. 263 F.R.D. at 45.
35. 2010 WL 257253, at *4 (N.D. Ill. Jan. 22, 2010).
36. 2009 WL 4642388, at * 2 (S.D. Cal. Dec. 1, 2009).
37. 2006 WL 1495503, at *4 (W.D.N.Y. Apr. 21, 2006) (hesitating to dissect the invention record without good cause in accordance with *Spalding*).
38. 2009 WL 3565293, at *4 (S.D. Cal. Oct. 27, 2009).
39. 258 F.R.D. 491, 498–99 (D. Utah 2009).
40. 2012 WL 5247315, at *3–5, 7 (D. Del. June 15, 2012).
41. 2013 WL 4046655, at *4, 7–8 (D. Ariz. Aug. 9, 2013).

communications from and to client concerning patentability, are all privileged under *Spalding*.

- *Verinata Health, Inc. v. Ariosa Diagnostics, Inc.*[42]—invention disclosure forms attached to emails were privileged under *Spalding*, although the emails themselves were not.
- *California Institute of Tech. v. Broadcom Ltd.*[43]—invention disclosure sent to an internal intellectual property committee responsible for determining whether to commission preparation and filing of a patent application was a privileged implied request for legal advice as in *Spalding*.

The *Spalding* decision also has been applied in section 337 investigations before the U.S. International Trade Commission. For example, in *In the Matter of Certain Short Wavelength Semiconductor Lasers & Products Containing Same*, the administrative law judge (ALJ), citing *Spalding* with approval, concluded complainant's invention record was privileged.[44]

C. The Limits of the *Spalding* Decision

District courts have applied *Spalding* beyond invention records to a host of other communications and documents that typically are created in the course of patenting an invention, including documents that contain only technical information. Regardless of how the communication is labeled, however, it must still satisfy the other *United Shoe* requirements for the privilege to apply.[45]

1. Forwarding Nonprivileged Records Not Privileged

Even under the *Spalding* standard, the purpose of the communication must be primarily for or in connection with legal advice or legal services.[46] The invention record at issue in *Spalding* was submitted by the inventors to Spalding's corporate legal department for the purpose of making a patentability determination.[47] In contrast to *Spalding*, if an attorney is merely forwarding documents or communications between the client and a governmental agency (such as

42. 2017 U.S. Dist. LEXIS 103630, at *2–3 (N.D. Cal. July 5, 2017).

43. 2018 WL 1468371, at *3 (C.D. Cal. Mar. 19, 2018).

44. 2008 ITC LEXIS 1248, at *5 (ITC June 24, 2008). Unfortunately for the complainant in that particular investigation, the ITC concluded under the circumstances the privilege had been waived. *See id.*

45. McCook Metals L.L.C. v. Alcoa Inc., 192 F.R.D. 242, 255 (N.D. Ill. 2000) (rejecting privilege assertion for technical drawings, sketches, tables, and test results produced from the inventors and sent to in-house patent counsel, on the basis that "[t]he documents themselves contain no request for legal advice, nor is any given, and thus fall outside the ambit of the privilege"). *See also* Prowess, Inc. v. Raysearch Labs. AB, 2013 WL 247531, at *3 (D. Md. Jan. 18, 2013) (internal citations omitted) (holding that draft patent applications and documents created/received by unknown persons and "relating to 'exclusively technical data for inclusion in patent filings are not protected' under the attorney-client privilege.").

46. *In re Spalding Sports Worldwide, Inc.*, 203 F.3d 800, 805 (Fed. Cir. 2000).

47. *Id.*

the USPTO or a foreign patent office), without providing any legal analysis or response to request for legal advice or services, then a court could conclude no privilege attaches to the substance of such communications.[48] In determining whether a particular document constitutes a request for legal advice, courts look to the overall tenor of the document to determine if such a request was either expressed *or* implied.[49]

2. Communications Lacking Confidential Information or Attorney Involvement Not Privileged

In addition, under the *Spalding* test for privilege, the attorney-client communication must still be confidential and involve an attorney providing legal advice to qualify for protection.[50] For example, one district court, applying *Spalding early on*, concluded that a memorandum of a conference with the patent examiner did not reveal any "confidential communications or advice" and status reports regarding a patent application did not reveal any "client confidences or legal analysis."[51] Another district court, applying *Spalding* early on, found that an aerospace industry summary of patent applications, patents, and invention reports stating the summary did not contain legal analysis or legal conclusions was not protected by the attorney-client privilege.[52]

With respect to draft patent applications, in *High 5 Games, LLC v. Marks*, a retired district court judge acting as special master applied *Spalding* in finding that the plaintiff failed to establish that its draft patent applications were communications to or from an attorney.[53] The special master reasoned that a draft patent application is "not an inherently privileged document" and that the draft patent applications lacked attorney involvement.[54] Further highlighting that an attorney's involvement cannot be assumed, in *Endo Pharms. Inc. v. Mylan Pharms. Inc.*, the district court found that an invention record was not protected by the attorney-client privilege given it was not established that the invention record was ever received by GlaxoSmithKline's patent group or any

48. *See, e.g.*, Softview Computer Prods. Corp. v. Haworth, Inc., 2000 WL 351411, at *9 (S.D.N.Y. Mar. 31, 2000) (transmittal letters, cover sheets, and other documents relating to patent prosecution not privileged); *McCook Metals*, 192 F.R.D. at 253–54 (transmittal letters and cover sheets, and communications from third party, are not privileged).

49. *Spalding*, 203 F.3d at 806.

50. *Id.* at 805 (citing Shearing v. Iolab Corp., 975 F.2d 1541, 1546 (Fed. Cir. 1992) ("The privilege protects a client's confidential communications to an attorney necessary to obtain legal counseling.")). *See, e.g.*, MediaTek Inc. v. Freescale Semiconductor, Inc., 2013 WL 5594474, at *4 (N.D. Cal. Oct. 10, 2013) (holding that a consultant's technical report on patents is not privileged under *Spalding* where the privilege log does not identify even one attorney who received the report and the report contained no hints of rendering legal advice).

51. Softview Computer Prods. Corp. v. Haworth, Inc., 2000 WL 351411, at *10 (S.D.N.Y. Mar. 31, 2000).

52. *McCook Metals*, 192 F.R.D. at 253.

53. 2019 WL 2067672, at *4–5 (D.N.J. May 10, 2019).

54. *Id.* at *5.

attorney within the group.[55] The court explained that *Spalding* requires "more than mere speculation or belief that the record will eventually be reviewed by a legal department or attorney in that department."[56]

A privilege log entry suggesting attorney involvement can fall short in establishing the attorney-client privilege if the prosecution-related document itself does not reflect attorney involvement. For example, in *RTC Indus. Inc. v. Fasteners for Retail, Inc.*, the privilege log entries represented that the redacted portions were an "email chain providing information for the purpose of obtaining legal advice and reflecting legal advice" regarding prosecution.[57] Yet, although the redacted portions did "touch on legal issues related to patent prosecution," the court found the email chain lacked attorney authors or recipients and any indication that the discussion was carried out at the behest of attorneys or to obtain information for attorneys.[58]

3. Primarily Business Documents Not Privileged

The privilege also does not apply to documents relating primarily to business matters.[59] Whether a communication or document is "primarily" related to business or is "primarily" related to legal matters may not be easy to decide.[60] In *In re Diagnostics Systems Corp.*, the federal circuit denied a petition for writ of mandamus seeking to overturn a district court's order requiring plaintiff to turn over approximately 550 documents previously withheld on the basis of either privilege or work product.[61] The district court held that the documents were created by certain attorneys who were "functioning primarily in the capacity of corporate executives furthering the business goals" of the company.[62] The federal circuit declined to review the documents de novo absent a showing of "clear error" and held plaintiff had failed to meet its burden to establish a "clear and indisputable error" in the district court's determination.[63]

---

55. 2013 WL 12152480, at *2 (D. Del. May 14, 2013).

56. *Id.*

57. 2019 WL 5003681, at *20 (N.D. Ill. Oct. 8, 2019).

58. *Id.* at *21.

59. *See, e.g.*, Itoba Ltd. v. LEP Group PLC, 930 F. Supp. 36, 43 (D. Conn. 1996); *In re Brand Name Prescription Drugs Antitrust Litig.*, 1995 WL 663684, at *3 (N.D. Ill. Nov. 6, 1995); AMP, Inc. v. Fujitsu Microelectronics, Inc., 853 F. Supp. 808, 830 (M.D. Pa. 1994), *appeal dismissed*, 47 F.3d 1180 (Fed. Cir. 1995); Baxter Travenol Labs., Inc. v. Abbott Labs., 1987 WL 12919, at *6 (N.D. Ill. June 17, 1987); Duplan Corp. v. Deering Milliken, Inc., 397 F. Supp. 1146, 1167 (D.S.C. 1974).

60. United States v. (Under Seal), 748 F.2d 871, 875 (4th Cir. 1984), *vacated on other grounds*, 757 F.2d 600 (4th Cir. 1985) (since patent examiner is a third party to whom the eventual communication will be disclosed, the communication is not intended to be confidential and therefore is not privileged); P.&B. Marina, L.P. v. Logrande, 136 F.R.D. 50, 56 (E.D.N.Y. 1991), *aff'd*, 983 F.2d 1047 (2d Cir. 1992) ("Drafts of letters or documents to third parties lack the requisite confidentiality to be protected under the attorney-client privilege.").

61. 328 F. App'x 621, 622 (Fed. Cir. 2008) (unpublished and nonprecedential).

62. *Id.*

63. *Id.* at 623.

In *In re Google, Inc.*, the federal circuit declined to grant a petition for writ of mandamus regarding an allegedly inadvertently produced email from a Google engineer requesting management feedback on technical alternatives to Java and copying Google in-house counsel.[64] The district court rejected Google's claim that the email was protected by attorney-client privilege or the work-product immunity doctrine. In a nonprecedential decision, the federal circuit found no abuse of discretion in the district court's determination that Google failed to demonstrate the purpose of the email communication was to further in-house counsel's provision of legal advice or investigation of an anticipated infringement suit.[65] Based on the email's own explanation of its purpose, the federal circuit noted that the email was directed to a "negotiation strategy as opposed to a license negotiation as a component or legal strategy."[66]

Even an invention record might be created for a business purpose versus a legal purpose and thus not be protected by the attorney-client privilege. For example, in *Degui Chen v. Jung*, the inventor provided the invention report to a university's intellectual property office that did not have any attorney employees, and that office, one-and-one-half months later, sent the invention record to outside counsel.[67] The court therefore found the invention report was "used first for non-legal business purposes" and the subsequent use by outside counsel did not make the invention report privileged.[68]

Similarly, in *Raytheon Co. v. Cray, Inc.*, an invention record ("invention disclosure") was created for a business purpose.[69] Raytheon's invention disclosure questionnaires went through a technical review by an invention review committee followed by a business review by a patent evaluation committee.[70] If the questionnaire was approved at both levels, then the questionnaire was provided to outside counsel for preparing a patent application.[71] The magistrate judge thus found Raytheon's invention disclosure questionnaires had an "underlying business purpose" and were not created to obtain legal advice.[72]

The distinction between a legal purpose and business purpose has also come into play with respect to patent rankings. For example, in *TCL Commc'ns. Tech Holdings Ltd. v. Telefonattenbologet LM Ericsson*, the district court agreed with the magistrate judge's determination that the record did not show Ericsson's "relevancy rankings" were made for the purpose of obtaining legal advice, and in fact the record suggested the rankings were for a "primarily

64. 462 F. App'x 975 (Fed. Cir. 2012) (unpublished and nonprecedential).
65. *Id.* at 978.
66. *Id.*
67. 2018 WL 7500275, at *1 (C.D. Cal. Dec. 27, 2018).
68. *Id.* at *2.
69. 2017 WL 2426266, at *2 (E.D. Tex. June 5, 2017).
70. *Id.* at *1.
71. *Id.*
72. *Id.* at *5.

business purpose."[73] The court reasoned that Ericsson's assertions on the usefulness of the rankings in the "general process of patent prosecution" did not "properly account for the differences between the *legal* aspects of patent prosecution (e.g., determinations of patentability), and the *business* aspects of patent prosecution (e.g., usefulness to the business of obtaining a patent in a particular field, determinations of willingness to spend a certain amount of resources to obtain a particular anticipated patent, time management of patent prosecutors)."[74] Contrastingly, in *FTC v. Qualcomm Inc.*, a district court found that Qualcomm's internal ratings of its patents and patent applications were privileged legal assessments based on attorney decisions about the scope, validity (or patentability), and enforceability of the patents and patent applications.[75] Citing *Spalding*, the court described the ratings as "quintessential legal determinations about the strength of Qualcomm's patent rights" that are "created for the purpose of informing Qualcomm's litigation and patent prosecution strategy[.]"[76] In response to the FTC's argument that the ratings were also used for commercial decisions, the court explained that "[p]rivilege is not defeated merely because the client may in turn utilize privileged legal advice to make real-world business decisions."[77]

4. Facts about Prior Art Searches May Not Be Privileged

Whether the results of a prior art search are privileged in the aftermath of *Spalding* still is not entirely clear. Before the federal circuit's decision in *Spalding*, a number of district courts had held that prior art searches and prior art studies in general were not privileged because they did not contain or reflect information obtained in confidence from the client.[78] In *Spalding*, the accused infringer similarly argued a portion of Spalding's invention record that included a list of prior art was not privileged because that portion of the record did not request legal advice.[79] The federal circuit rejected this argument, finding it was unnecessary to "dissect" the document to separately evaluate each of its components.[80] According to the court in *Spalding*, it is enough that the overall tenor of the document indicates that it is a request for legal advice or services.[81]

Based upon the broad standard set forth in the *Spalding* decision, a document containing a prior art search would probably be considered privileged because, in most cases, the primary purpose of conducting a prior art search is

---

73. 2016 WL 6921124, at *2–3 (C.D. Cal. May 3, 2016).

74. *Id.* at *2.

75. 2018 WL 2317835, at *3 (N.D. Cal. May 22, 2018).

76. *Id.* at *3–4.

77. *Id.* at *4.

78. *See, e.g.*, Glaxo, Inc. v. Novopharm Ltd., 148 F.R.D. 535, 540 (E.D.N.C. 1993); *Baxter Travenol Labs.*, 1987 WL 12919, at *12.

79. *In re Spalding Sports Worldwide, Inc.*, 203 F.3d 800, 806 (Fed. Cir. 2000).

80. *Id.*

81. *Id.*

either to evaluate patentability or to aid counsel in the preparation of a patent application.[82] For instance, in *Promontory Interfinancial Network, LLC, v. Anova Financial Corp.*, the court refused to compel the patentee to produce a letter containing prior art search results because the letter also contained the patent counsel's analysis of those results.[83]

On the other hand, facts relayed about a prior art search, such as whether or how a prior art search was conducted, may not be privileged.[84] Indeed, in *Lakewood Engineering and Mfg. Co. v. Lasko Products, Inc.*, the court compelled the patentee to provide the accused infringer "with the dates of all prior art searches conducted with respect to the subject matter of the [patents at issue]" because that information was "factual in nature and [did] not seek to probe [the patentee] on advice given by its counsel or the mental impressions, thoughts, or other protected work product of its counsel."[85]

5. *Choice of Law Limitations*

The *Spalding* decision's choice of federal circuit law has no application when the communications in question are not unique to patent law, or are not affected by substantive patent law. Thus, for example, when the communication or document in question relates to patent licenses or similar types of contractual issues, the law of the regional circuit, and not the federal circuit, most likely will be applied in determining whether the communication is privileged.[86]

---

82. *See id.* ("[A]n attorney cannot evaluate patentability or prepare a competent patent application without knowing the prior art and obtaining relevant technical information from the inventors."); *see also* Games2U, Inc. v. Game Truck Licensing, LLC, 2013 WL 4046655, at *4 (D. Ariz. Aug. 9, 2013) ("Prior art and technical documents are privileged if between an attorney and her client in the context of legal counsel."); Martin Marietta Materials, Inc. v. Bedford Reinforced Plastics, Inc., 227 F.R.D. 382, 394 (W.D. Pa. 2005) (prior art search was privileged); Takeda Chemical Industries, Ltd. v. Alphapharm Pty., Ltd., 2005 WL 1678001, at *3 (S.D.N.Y. July 19, 2005) (Generic drug manufacturers "regularly conduct at least initial patent searches, including those that identify the existence of relevant patents and that shed light on the vulnerability of those patents to an attack of invalidity based on prior art, and do analyses of those searches in the ordinary course of their business.").

83. 2014 WL 12544494, *3–*5 (E.D. Va. 2014); *see also* MPT, Inc. v. Marathon Labels, Inc., 2006 WL 314435 (N.D. Ohio 2006) (denying motion to compel patentee to produce redacted portions of a search report generated by a patent agent hired by the prosecuting attorney to perform the search where those redactions contained narratives by the patent agent of how the prior art found in the search compared to the features of the invention since that communication was protected by the attorney-client privilege).

84. *See, e.g.*, Sprint Commc'ns Co., L.P. v. Comcast Cable Commc'ns, 2014 WL 1569963, at *6 (D. Kan. Apr. 18, 2014) (testimony regarding acts performed by counsel in searching for prior art, and information that counsel's review of prior art led it to conclude the company had a patentable invention, held not privileged because it only revealed counsel's "ultimate legal conclusion, not any substantive communication or attorney analysis behind the conclusion"); Clare v. Ford Motor Co., 2004 U.S. Dist. LEXIS 31461, at *2–6 (E.D. Tex. June 10, 2004) (collecting cases holding that party could discover dates of searches, persons requesting search, identity of patents and information referred to in any of the searches, and locations of search, because such information was "factual in nature and not privileged").

85. 2003 WL 1220254, at *5 (N.D. Ill. 2003).

86. *Spalding*, 203 F.3d at 804 (citing *In re Regents of the Univ. of Cal.*, 101 F.3d 1386 (Fed. Cir. 1996)). *See also* McCook Metals L.L.C. v. Alcoa Inc., 192 F.R.D. 242, 251 (N.D. Ill. 2000) (applying Seventh Circuit

D. Patent Prosecution Documents as Work Product

In patent litigation, the owner of the patent-in-suit sometimes asserts that documents prepared in connection with patent prosecution activities are immune from discovery as attorney work product. Some district courts have held that the work-product immunity doctrine does *not* extend to preparation for ex parte proceedings, such as patent prosecution.[87] Those courts that reject an immunity theory for prosecution documents reason that the mere fact that a document is prepared when litigation is foreseeable does not mean that the document was prepared in anticipation of litigation.[88] To qualify as work product, some courts require that the document must be prepared *because of* the prospect of litigation when the preparer faces an actual claim or a potential claim following an actual event or series of events that reasonably could result in litigation.[89] Patent prosecution documents thus ordinarily cannot be protected as work product because they are not typically created in anticipation of litigation.[90] As one district court recently remarked, "[T]here is a general consensus among courts that the work product doctrine does not apply to patent prosecution work because patent prosecution is not an adversarial, litigation-type proceeding, but a wholly ex parte proceeding before the PTO."[91]

The district court in *Bristol-Myers Squibb Co. v. Rhone-Poulenc Rorer, Inc.*[92] rejected the proposition that patent prosecution documents are work product. The court reasoned that documents relating to or in furtherance of the prosecution of a patent application are not work product because the primary motivating purpose behind the performance of the work is to obtain a patent.[93] The court further held that patent prosecution documents are not created "in anticipation of or concerning litigation."[94] A patent prosecution is not adversarial, but rather proceeds ex parte.[95] Since the purpose of the work-product

---

law to whether licensing and contractual documents are privileged); Wi-LAN, Inc. v. LG Elecs., Inc., 684 F.3d 1364, 1368 (Fed. Cir. 2012) (applying Ninth Circuit law to privilege waiver issues not unique to patent law).

87. Bulk Lift Int'l Inc. v. Flexcon & Sys., Inc., 122 F.R.D. 482, 491 (W.D. La. 1988), *aff'd*, 122 F.R.D. 493 (1988) (quoting *Choat v. Rome Indus., Inc.*, 462 F. Supp. 728, 732 (N.D. Ga. 1978)); *but see* Hewlett-Packard Co. v. Bausch & Lomb, Inc., 116 F.R.D. 533 (N.D. Cal. 1987) (finding draft expert declaration prepared for patent reexamination was discoverable, but outside counsel's draft reply prepared for patent reexamination was protected by the work product doctrine).

88. Softview Computer Prods. Corp. v. Haworth, Inc., 2000 WL 351411, at *12 (S.D.N.Y. Mar. 31, 2000); Stryker Corp. v. Intermedics Orthopedics, Inc., 145 F.R.D. 298, 302 (E.D.N.Y. 1992) ("This court rejects the theory that litigation is a 'possibility' in every patent application.").

89. Nat'l Union Fire Ins. Co. v. Murray Sheet Metal Co., 967 F.2d 980, 984 (4th Cir. 1992).

90. Bristol-Myers Squibb Co. v. Rhone-Poulenc Rorer, Inc., 1998 WL 2829, at *4–5 (S.D.N.Y. Jan. 6, 1998) (holding that patent prosecution is not work product); *Stryker Corp.*, 145 F.R.D. at 304 (same).

91. Cave Consulting Group, Inc. v. OptumInsight, Inc., 2016 WL 7475820, at *10 (N.D. Cal. Dec. 29, 2016).

92. *Bristol-Myers*, 1998 WL 2829, at *4–5.

93. *Id.* at *13–14.

94. *Id. See also* Burlington Indus., Inc. v. Rossville Yarn, Inc., 1997 WL 404319, at *2 (N.D. Ga. June 3, 1997); *Stryker Corp.*, 145 F.R.D. at 304.

95. *Bristol-Myers*, 1998 WL 2829, at *4.

privilege is to protect the adversarial process,[96] normally there is no basis for extending this form of privilege to patent prosecutions.

In contrast, certain district courts distinguish between documents created for a patent appeal process versus other prosecution documents. For example, in *McCook Metals*, the district court held that the materials drafted during and for a pending appeal to the Board of Patent Appeals and Interferences were protected by the work-product doctrine.[97] The court reasoned that the patent appeal procedure was an adversarial proceeding like the patent reexamination process with "characteristics of litigation" and therefore constituted "litigation" for purposes of the work-product doctrine.[98]

Some district courts have extended work-product immunity to documents prepared in connection with patent prosecution activities if it is shown that the work also was performed in anticipation of litigation.[99] In *In re Application of Minebea Co., Ltd.*,[100] for example, a patentee sought work-product protection for prosecution-related documents that were created before the patent issued. The district court upheld the immunity claim and explained:

> Generally, work performed by an attorney to prepare and prosecute a patent application does not fall within the parameters of the work-product protection . . . since the prosecution of a patent application is a non-adversarial, ex parte proceeding. . . . This rule does not, however, preclude application of the work product protection to work performed to prosecute a patent application if it was also performed in anticipation of or concerning litigation.[101]

The court in *Minebea* concluded that information pertaining to the patent prosecution was subject to work-product immunity if it was prepared on or after the date that the patentee anticipated litigation, regardless of the fact that the patent did not issue until almost one year later.[102] According to some courts, the crucial date for applying work-product immunity is the date upon which the party asserting the work-product doctrine anticipated litigation regarding the patent, not when the patent was issued.[103]

---

96. Hickman v. Taylor, 329 U.S. 495 (1947).

97. 192 F.R.D. at 262.

98. *Id.*

99. *See, e.g.*, Elkay Mfg. Co. v. Ebco Mfg. Co., 1995 U.S. Dist. LEXIS 473, at *35 (N.D. Ill. Jan 13, 1995) ("[G]iven that there is precedent for extending work-product immunity to *draft* patent applications prepared in anticipation of litigation, it is not unreasonable to extend the benefit of the immunity to the applications themselves.").

100. 143 F.R.D. 494, 500 (S.D.N.Y. 1992).

101. *Id.* at 499.

102. *Id.* at 501.

103. Softview Computer Prods. Corp. v. Haworth, Inc., 2000 WL 351411, at *12 (S.D.N.Y. Mar. 31, 2000) (holding that certain prosecution documents were properly withheld as work product where the patentee alleged that competitors introduced competing model one week after it filed the patent

The attorney-client privilege protecting documents relating to a patent application may extinguish if the inventor in possession of such documents leaves his or her employment or the employer ceases to exist. The district court in *Trading Techs. Int'l, Inc. v. GL Consultants, Inc.*, for example, found that when an inventor left his employment and maintained possession of certain documents relating to prosecution of his patent application, the inventor could not assert privilege over his documents because the privilege remained with his employer and did not travel with the inventor.[104] The court further held that his former employer also could not assert the privilege because it no longer existed and thus lost its "interest in protecting its communications."[105] Finally, the court refused to extend the privilege to the current owner of the patent at issue because that owner never came into possession of the documents at issue.[106] The court thus ordered production of the vast majority of withheld documents.

III. Communications with Patent Agents and Foreign Counsel as Privileged

A. Who Qualifies as an "Attorney"

It is axiomatic that for the privilege to apply there must be a communication between a client and an attorney. What does "attorney" mean, exactly, in this context? Under the often-cited test for privilege formulated in *United Shoe*, an attorney "is a member of the bar of a court" (or his or her subordinate).[107] Although this requirement seems straightforward enough, interesting things can happen if either (1) the "attorney," though licensed to practice law at some point in his or her career, is at the time of the communication on inactive status, or (2) the "attorney" is not really an attorney at all, but the client nevertheless *believes* that the supposed "attorney" is, in fact, a bar member. Both of these scenarios arose in *Gucci America, Inc. v. Guess?, Inc.*[108]

In *Gucci*, a trademark infringement case, plaintiff withheld as privileged various, internal communications with its "in-house legal counsel."[109] Apparently unbeknownst to plaintiff, the in-house counsel had voluntarily taken "inactive" status with the California state bar prior to joining the plaintiff's company, and he remained inactive throughout his tenure with the company.[110]

---

application, and the patentee showed that it believed those models would infringe its patent once issued. The court held that "the challenged documents . . . reflect that counsel's claim drafting and prosecution of the patent application were informed by Haworth's anticipation of litigation against its competitors once the '798 patent issued.").

104. Trading Techs. Int'l, Inc. v. GL Consultants, Inc., 2012 WL 874322, at *3 (D. Ill. Mar. 14, 2012).

105. *Id.* at *4.

106. *Id.* at *2.

107. United States v. United Shoe Mach. Corp., 89 F. Supp. 357, 358–59 (D. Mass. 1950).

108. 2010 WL 2720079 (S.D.N.Y. June 29, 2010), *rev'd*, 2011 WL 9375 (S.D.N.Y. Jan. 3, 2011).

109. *Gucci Am.*, 2011 WL 9375, at *1.

110. *Id.*

Plaintiff first asserted that its in-house counsel was still an "attorney" in that he was a "member" of the California state bar, albeit an inactive one.[111] The magistrate judge rejected this argument, stating the in-house counsel "did not possess the type of bar membership that authorized him to engage in the practice of law" and that California state law "explicitly limits the practice of law to active [bar] members."[112] However, the reviewing court found this analysis incorrect in the determination of a client's right to invoke the attorney-client privilege.[113] A client should not be penalized for an attorney's inactive status because "[t]he purpose of the privilege is to protect the client's communication, and to encourage full and frank disclosure when seeking legal advice, which is why the client holds the privilege and only the client can assert or waive it."[114]

Additionally, the district judge rejected the magistrate's refusal to apply the "mistake" exception. Contrary to the magistrate's finding that "Gucci, as a corporation, must have conducted due diligence, or taken reasonable precautions to determine that its counsel was authorized to practice law," the district judge found that the responsibility to avoid engaging in the unauthorized practice of law falls on the attorney.[115] Gucci was reasonable in its belief that an attorney-client relationship had been established.[116] Accordingly, the district judge set aside the order of the magistrate judge and granted the motion for a protective order.[117]

While *Gucci* provides an exception to the attorney requirement, it appears to be limited to those cases where a non-attorney holds himself out as an attorney and the client reasonably believes the individual is, in fact, an attorney. This principle has been applied in patent cases.[118] Generally speaking, however, courts reject claims based on attorney-client privilege when the putative "attorney" is not licensed.[119]

---

111. *Id.*

112. *Gucci Am.*, 2010 WL 2720079, at *5.

113. *Gucci Am.*, 2011 WL 9375, at *4.

114. *Id.* at *4; *see also In re Grand Jury Subpoena Duces Tecum*, 112 F.3d 910, 923 (8th Cir. 1997) (collecting cases in which a party's reasonable mistake of fact provides exception to general rule that only communications with a licensed attorney representing that party are covered by the attorney-client privilege).

115. *Id.* at *6.

116. *Id.*

117. *Id.*

118. *See, e.g.*, Optimize Tech. Solutions, LLC v. Staples, Inc., 2014 WL 2728596, at *1–2 (E.D. Tex. June 16, 2014) (holding in patent infringement case that privilege applied to communications with unlicensed law school graduate based on putative client's reasonable belief the individual was an attorney).

119. *See, e.g.*, Anwar v. Fairfield Greenwich Ltd., 982 F. Supp. 2d 260, 265 (S.D.N.Y. 2013) ("The general rule under United States law is that only communications between a represented party and that party's licensed attorneys are subject to the attorney-client privilege. . . ."); *see also* Shukh v. Seagate Tech., LLC, 848 F. Supp. 2d 987, 993–94 (D. Minn. 2011) (rejecting argument that privilege did not apply based on a state rule that requires in-house counsel to be licensed in the state where counsel works

B. Communications with U.S. Patent Agents

Registered patent agents are authorized to practice law, albeit limited to practice in patent matters before the USPTO.[120] U.S. registered patent agents thus may prepare and prosecute patent applications; consult with or give advice to clients in contemplation of filing a patent application; draft the specification or claims of a patent application; draft an amendment or reply to an Office Action; or draft a communication for an interference, reexamination, and any other proceeding before the Patent Trial and Appeal Board.[121]

Despite these similarities with attorneys, patent agents obviously are not members of the bar of any "court." The issue sometimes arises in patent litigation of whether communications between a client and a U.S. patent agent are protected by the attorney-client privilege. Until recently, "there [was] no consensus on whether, and to what extent, the attorney-client privilege applies to non-attorney patent agents."[122] Indeed, whether privilege extends to client communications with non-attorney patent agents has been a long-standing question with divided opinions throughout the district courts. But the federal circuit recently provided answers and acknowledged a patent-agent privilege when it granted mandamus in *In re Queen's University at Kingston*.[123]

In a patent infringement suit against Samsung, Queen's University refused to produce communications with its patent agents, asserting that those communications were privileged.[124] After holding a hearing, the district court granted Samsung's motion to compel production, finding that communications between Queen's University and their non-attorney patent agents were not protected by the attorney-client privilege.[125]

Queen's University petitioned for a "writ of mandamus directing the district court to withdraw its order compelling the production of [its] communications with its non-attorney patent agents on grounds that the communications are privileged."[126] The federal circuit granted review on the issue of whether a patent-agent privilege should be acknowledged.[127]

The federal circuit began its analysis by referencing *Sperry,* where the Supreme Court had found that "the preparation and prosecution of patent applications for others constitutes the practice of law."[128] Confirming that

---

and finding communications with in-house attorney were still privileged because the attorney was a member of the bars of other jurisdictions, including the District of Columbia and the USPTO).

120. A "registered patent agent" is an individual who is licensed to practice before the USPTO in patent matters. 37 C.F.R. § 11.6(b).

121. 37 C.F.R. § 11.5(b)(1) (defining scope of authorized practice before the USPTO in patent matters).

122. E.I. du Pont de Nemours & Co. v. Macdermid, Inc., 2009 WL 3048421, at *2 (D.N.J. Sept. 17, 2009) (surveying conflicting cases) (unpublished).

123. *In re* Queen's University at Kingston, 820 F.3d 1287 (Fed. Cir. 2016).

124. *Id.* at 1290.

125. *Id.*

126. *Id.* at 1289.

127. *Id.* at 1294.

128. *Id.* at 1296 (*citing* Sperry v. Florida, 373 U.S. 379, 383 (1963)).

patent agents are engaged in the practice of law itself, the court reasoned that the justification for the traditional attorney-client privilege, based on the need for candor between the client and the legal professional during prosecution of a patent, would seem to apply with equal force to patent agents.[129]

As noted by the federal circuit, the *Sperry* decision had also emphasized that Congress authorized and continues to permit the practice of law by patent agents by allowing such agents to represent applicants before the Patent Office.[130] The court then held that "[t]o the extent Congress has authorized nonattorney patent agents to engage in the practice of law before the Patent Office, reason and experience compel us to recognize a patent-agent privilege that is coextensive with the rights granted to patent agents by Congress. A client has a reasonable expectation that all communications relating to 'obtaining legal advice on patentability and legal services in preparing a patent application' will be kept privileged."[131] Despite a presumption against the recognition of new privileges, the federal circuit turned to "reason and experience" to "recognize a patent-agent privilege that is coextensive with the rights granted to patent agents by Congress."[132]

As to the limits of the patent-agent privilege, the federal circuit explained that the regulations promulgated by the Patent Office help define the scope of communications covered by the patent-agent privilege.[133] Thus, the patent-agent privilege extends only to communications reasonably necessary and incident to the prosecution of a patent before the Patent Office, or other patent-related proceedings authorized by the regulations.[134] When a U.S. patent agent goes beyond that limited role, his or her "status" as a patent agent provides no special protection to assert the patent-agent privilege. As explained by the court in *Queen's University*,

> Communications that are not reasonably necessary and incident to the prosecution of patents before the Patent Office fall outside the scope of the patent-agent privilege. For instance, communications with a patent agent who is offering an opinion on the validity of another party's patent in contemplation of litigation or for the sale or purchase of a patent, or on infringement, are not reasonably necessary and incident to the preparation and prosecution of patent applications or other proceeding before the Office.[135]

129. *Id.* at 1296.
130. *Id.*
131. *Id.* at 1298 (*citing Spalding*, 203 F.3d at 806).
132. *Id.* at 1294, 1298.
133. *In re* Queen's University at Kingston, 820 F.3d at 1301.
134. *Id.*
135. *Id.* at 1301–02 (internal citations omitted).

This limitation is consistent with the general rule that the attorney-client privilege does not apply to communications with an attorney who is acting in a nonlegal capacity.[136] For example, communications between a client and a U.S. patent agent concerning the licensing or enforcement of an *issued* patent ordinarily would not be covered under the patent agent privilege unless the patent agent is acting under the supervision or control of an attorney. This is because the USPTO bar membership does not extend to litigation or licensing.[137]

Accordingly, in patent infringement cases, district courts have applied *Queen's University.*[138] *For example, in Onyx Therapeutics, Inc. v. Cipla Ltd.,*[139] *the district court found the patent-agent privilege did not apply to communications by a scientist seeking advice from a patent agent about the patent landscape as part of planning development of new chemical formulations. Because the advice was not sought to seek* patent *protection on already-developed products, the court found the communications were not "reasonably necessary and incident" to prosecution.*[140] *In Shopify Inc. v. Express Mobile, Inc., we have another instance of a district court applying Queen's University and finding that the patent-agent privilege did not apply to certain patent agent communications.*[141] *The court found two categories of communications—communications relating to patent infringement and communications that failed to mention preparation or prosecution of patent applications—were not reasonably necessary and incident to the preparation and prosecution of patent applications.*[142]

Some courts may not recognize the patent agent-client privilege if it is being asserted in a nonpatent case. For instance, in *In Re Andrew Silver,* a Texas appellate court refused to recognize the privilege, affirming the trial court's decision to do the same.[143] In this breach of contract suit brought by a patentee against a defendant that was marketing the claimed invention, the defendant sought discovery of all communications shared between the plaintiff-applicant and the patent agent who prosecuted the patent at issue.[144] The trial court rejected the plaintiff's assertion of the patent agent-client privilege and compelled production of those documents.[145] The plaintiff sought mandamus review.[146] Ultimately, the plaintiff's request for relief was denied by the Texas appellate

136. *See, e.g., In re Lindsey*, 158 F.3d 1263, 1270 (D.C. Cir. 1998).

137. Patent agents are expressly authorized to practice in post-issuance proceedings before the PTAB. *See* 37 C.F.R. § 11.5(b)(1).

138. *See, e.g.,* TCL Communications Technology Holdings Ltd. v. Telefonaktenbologet LM Ericsson, 2016 WL 6921124, at *3 (C.D. Cal. May 3, 2016) (recognizing the patent agent-client privilege). But see Luv N'Care, Ltd. v. Williams Intellectual Prop., 2019 WL 2471318, at *4 (D. Col. June 12, 2019) ("[T]he Court assumes, without deciding, that the patent-agent privilege applies in the Tenth Circuit.").

139. 2019 WL 668846, at *3 (D. Del. Feb. 15, 2019).

140. *Id.*

141. 2020 WL 4732334, at *3–4 (N.D. Cal. Aug. 14, 2020).

142. *Id.* at *4.

143. *In re* Silver, 500 S.W.3d 644, 646 (Tex. App. 2016).

144. *Id.* at 645–46.

145. *Id.*

146. *Id.* at 646.

court in an opinion declaring that "*Queen's University* is not binding [on Texas courts]," and that "[n]o Texas statute or rule recognizes or adopts a patent-agent privilege."[147] The court reasoned:

> The Federal Circuit applies its own law for substantive and procedural issues if those issues are "intimately involved in the substance of enforcement of the patent right." 820 F.3d at 1290. This includes determination of whether documents are discoverable "in a patent case because they relate to issues of validity and infringement." . . . This case is not a patent infringement case. It is a breach of contract case governed by Texas law. The underlying dispute does not involve a determination of the validity of the patent or whether Tabletop Media, LLC infringed on the patent. The Queen's University court expressly excluded such cases from the scope of the privilege, and neither this Court nor the trial court is required to apply federal patent law to the merits of the case. Where, as here, the substantive claims are governed by state law, the state privilege law also applies. Texas does not recognize a patent-agent privilege, and we decline to create a new common law privilege.[148]

C. Communications with Foreign Patent Agents and Foreign Attorneys

When the communication involves a *foreign* attorney or patent agent and his or her client, the privilege analysis is more complex. In many foreign countries, attorneys at law do not prepare or prosecute patent applications. Often this service is provided by the equivalent (by training and background) of a U.S. patent agent. Nevertheless, it is not unusual for an individual who meets a U.S. practitioner's definition of a "patent agent" (i.e., a non-attorney technical specialist who is not a general attorney at law but who is nonetheless authorized by the law of a foreign country to prepare and prosecute patent applications before the patent office of a foreign country) to be referred to as a "patent attorney."[149] While the nomenclature may be cause for some confusion, courts look beyond the individual's "attorney" title and focus instead on the individual's qualifications in his or her home country.[150]

---

147. *Id.*

148. *Id.*

149. *See, e.g., Willemijn Houdstermaatschaapij BV v. Apollo Computer, Inc.*, 707 F.Supp. 1429, 1444 n. 21 (D.Del. 1989) ("[V]irtually all *patent attorneys* in Europe have *only* a technical or scientific background and, with rare exceptions, have no legal training and are not members of the bar."); Cadence Pharms., Inc. v. Fresenius Kabi USA, LLC, 996 F. Supp. 2d 1015, 1022 (S.D. Cal. Feb. 3, 2014) ("Despite their title, German patent agents perform services similar to patent attorneys in the U.S., receive confidential legal communications from their clients and render legal advice.").

150. *See Cadence Pharms.*, 996 F. Supp. 2d at 1022 ("Because of the attorney-like functions of German patent agents and because of their clients' expectation of confidentiality, U.S. policy interests will not

That does not end the analysis. An issue that is frequently raised in patent litigation is whether communications with such foreign (i.e., non-United States) "patent agents" (or "patent attorneys") are privileged in a U.S. litigation. This issue can arise, for example, when a patent involved in a U.S. litigation has foreign counterparts and the defendant seeks discovery relating to the foreign counterparts.[151]

Determining whether the attorney-client privilege applies to communications involving clients and foreign patent agents or foreign attorneys "has not always been simple or consistent."[152] Neither the federal circuit, nor any other circuit court, has issued to date a published decision that analyzes the scope or applicability of a foreign patent agent or foreign patent attorney privilege in U.S. litigation.[153] It thus remains largely unclear how *Queen's University* will impact this analysis in U.S. courts. As some guidance, in *Knauf Insulation, LLC v. Johns Manville Corp.*, a district court based on *Queen's University* addressed the application of the patent-agent privilege to communications with foreign agents (e.g., a U.K. patent agent called a "patent attorney") and held that the patent-agent privilege applied to the U.K. patent attorney's communications with the patentee that were made within the scope of the attorney's authority as a U.K. patent attorney.[154]

Most courts begin the analysis with Federal Rule of Evidence 501, which provides that federal law determines whether an evidentiary privilege may be invoked.[155] Although there are a few district courts that have refused to recognize an attorney-client privilege for foreign patent agents under *any* circumstances,[156] most federal courts that have published decisions on this issue have utilized a two-step analysis.

First, the court decides which country's law to apply.[157] If the court determines that U.S. law applies, then the court will typically apply the *United Shoe* standard (or some variation of it) and determine, based on that standard,

---

be violated by recognizing privilege protections under German law for German patent agent's communications with foreign clients concerning the prosecution of European patents.").

151. *See, e.g.*, W.L. Gore & Assoc., Inc. v. C.R. Bard, Inc., 2014 WL 3950663, at *12 (D. Del. Aug. 8, 2014) (accused infringer attempts to rely on representations made by applicants during prosecution of related foreign counterpart application as extrinsic evidence to support proposed claim construction).

152. Golden Trade, S.r.L. v. Lee Apparel Co., 143 F.R.D. 514, 518 (S.D.N.Y. 1992).

153. The federal circuit has issued one unpublished, nonprecedential decision that touches on the foreign agent privilege issue but fails to provide any substantive analysis. *See In re* IPCom GmbH & Co., KG, 428 F. App'x 984, 985 (Fed. Cir. 2011) (denying petition for writ of mandamus) (unpublished and nonprecedential).

154. 2019 WL 4832205, at *2–6 (S.D. Ind. Oct. 1, 2019).

155. 143 F.R.D. at 517 (citing United States v. Goldberger & Dubin, P.C., 935 F.2d 501, 505 (2d Cir. 1991)).

156. *See, e.g.*, Duttle v. Bandler & Kass, 127 F.R.D. 46, 52 (S.D.N.Y. 1989); Burlington Indus. v. Exxon Corp., 65 F.R.D. 26, 40 (D. Md. 1974); *accord* Status Time Corp. v. Sharp Elecs. Corp., 95 F.R.D. 27, 32–33 (S.D.N.Y. 1982).

157. The party seeking to use a foreign law must demonstrate that a conflict exists between the foreign law and the U.S. law. *See, e.g.*, *In re IPCom GmbH & Co. KG*, 428 F. App'x at 985–86 (citing Hartford

whether the communication with the foreign agent is privileged by those standards. If the court determines it must apply foreign law, on the other hand, the court must decide whether, as a threshold matter, the particular foreign law in question recognizes an evidentiary privilege for the individual patent professional (agent or attorney). If the foreign law recognizes such a privilege in general, the remaining issue is whether the particular communication in question satisfies the test for privilege under foreign law. If the district court concludes that an attorney-client privilege exists under foreign law, and the communication meets the foreign country's test for privilege, then as a matter of comity the district court should treat the communication as privileged from disclosure in a U.S. legal proceeding.[158]

1. Whose Law to Apply

The "choice of law" rule that district courts have applied in their analysis of the foreign agent or foreign attorney privilege question has been determined to date by regional circuit law only and not by any published, precedential federal circuit decision. The unpublished per curiam decision of the federal circuit in *In re IPCom GmbH & Co., KG*, while hinting at choice of law, fails to provide any meaningful analysis of the issue. At issue in *IPCom* was whether the district court erred in applying U.S. law instead of German law when it required a patentee to produce foreign prosecution documents and the patentee had withheld the documents as privileged under German law.[159]

At the outset the federal circuit stated, "[f]or German law to apply, [the patentee] would first have to establish a conflict exists between German and United States law."[160] In support of this statement, the court cited the U.S. Supreme Court's decision in *Hartford Fire Insurance Co. v. California*.[161] In *Hartford Fire*, the Supreme Court addressed whether the court should refrain from exercising jurisdiction against a foreign entity under the Sherman Act based on principles of "international comity" where the allegedly wrongful conduct at issue was legal in the foreign country.[162] The Supreme Court held "no" and noted, "The fact that conduct is lawful in the state in which it took place will not, of itself, bar application of the United States antitrust laws" even where the foreign state has a strong policy to permit such conduct.[163]

Fire Ins. Co. v. California, 509 U.S. 764, 798 (1993)) (The party seeking to apply German law failed to demonstrate how the application of German law would alter the outcome.).

158. *See, e.g.*, McCook Metals L.L.C. v. Alcoa Inc., 192 F.R.D. 242, 256 (N.D. Ill. 2000).

159. 428 F. App'x 984, 985 (Fed. Cir. 2011).

160. *Id.* (citing Hartford Fire Ins. Co. v. California, 509 U.S. 764, 793 (1993) (limiting the application of international comity doctrine to cases in which "there is in fact a true conflict between domestic and foreign law")).

161. 509 U.S. 764 (1993).

162. *Id.* at 798–99.

163. *Id.* at 799.

Although the Supreme Court in *Hartford Fire* did state that "the only substantial question in this litigation is whether 'there is in fact a true conflict between domestic and foreign law,'" that was not in the context of a choice of law analysis.[164] In any event, the federal circuit in *In re IPCom GmbH & Co., KG* concluded that the patentee failed to meet its burden of showing a conflict between German and U.S. law.[165] The court further rejected the contention that the German law firm, which was the custodian of the documents, was legally obligated under German ethics laws to maintain these communications as confidential and concluded the district court presumably found the law firm was "at least partially at fault."[166] It is unclear what affect, if any, the nonprecedential opinion in *In re IPCom GmbH & Co., KG* will have on the analysis of or the test to apply in the choice of law context regarding attorney-client privilege.

While there is currently no uniform set of choice of law rules that applies to patent cases considering the foreign privilege issue, some district courts follow the "touching-base" rule.[167] The touching-base rule has been described as follows:

> [C]ommunications by a foreign client with foreign patent agents "relating to assistance in prosecuting patent applications in the United States" are governed by American privilege law whereas communications "relating to assistance in prosecuting patent applications in their own foreign country" or "rendering legal advice . . . on the patent law of their own country" are, as a matter of comity, governed by the privilege "law of the foreign country in which the patent application is filed," even if the client is a party to an American lawsuit.[168]

Those courts that apply the touching-base approach look to the foreign law of privilege only where those communications relate solely to activities outside of the United States.[169] Under this general approach, "[i]f a communication with a foreign patent agent involves a foreign patent application, then as a matter of comity, the law of that foreign country is considered regarding whether that law provides a privilege comparable to the attorney-client privilege."[170] Under

164. *See id.* at 798.

165. 428 F. App'x at 985.

166. *Id.* at 986.

167. *See, e.g.*, Philips N. Am. LLC v. Fitbit LLC, 2022 WL 252392, at *5–6 (D. Mass. Jan. 27, 2022) (applying touching-base analysis to privilege claims); Anwar v. Fairfield Greenwich Ltd., 982 F. Supp. 2d 260, 264 (S.D.N.Y. 2013) (same); Odone v. Croda Int'l PLC, 950 F. Supp. 10, 12–13 (D.D.C. 1997) (same); *In re Ampicillin Antitrust Litig.*, 81 F.R.D. 377, 391 (D.D.C. 1978) (same); Duplan Corp. v. Deering Milliken, Inc., 397 F. Supp. 1146, 1169 (D.S.C. 1975) (same).

168. Golden Trade, S.r.L. v. Lee Apparel Co., 143 F.R.D. 514, 520 (quoting *Duplan Corp.*, 397 F. Supp. at 1170). *See also* VLT Corp. v. Unitrode Corp., 194 F.R.D. 8, 15 (D. Mass. 2000).

169. *See Golden Trade*, 143 F.R.D. at 520 (citing cases).

170. *In re Rivastigmine Patent Litig.*, 239 F.R.D. at 356; Softview Computer Prods. Corp. v. Haworth, Inc., 2000 WL 351411, at *11 (S.D.N.Y. Mar. 31, 2000) (quoting Bristol-Myers Squibb Co. v.

a strict interpretation of the touching-base approach, however, even a minimal amount of contact with the United States would preclude the application of foreign law to the question of privilege.[171]

Some courts have criticized the touching-base approach as too rigid. Those courts have observed that under the touching-base standard, a document could touch base with the United States if it merely emanated here or if it simply mentioned a U.S. patent.[172]

Other district courts have applied a balancing test to the choice of law question.[173] Under the balancing test, the district court or other administrative fact-finder attempts to ascertain which country has the dominant interest in the communication, considering such interests as the parties to and substance of the communication, the place where the relationship was centered at the time of the communication, the needs of the international system, and whether the application of foreign privilege law would be clearly inconsistent with important policies embedded in federal law.[174] Some district courts view the traditional approach as being more consistent with the *Restatement (Second) of Conflicts*.[175] The "traditional" approach has been described as looking to the law of the country that has "'the most direct and compelling interest' in whether [the] communications should remain confidential."[176]

Finally, some district courts have endorsed a combination of the touching-base and traditional tests. Under the combination approach, the district court applies a touching-base analysis to those communications that have no connection, or only an incidental connection, to the United States, and it applies the traditional approach to those communications that have more than an incidental connection to the United States.[177]

2. Determining Privilege under Foreign Law

If the court decides the foreign patent agent (or foreign attorney) privilege question should be decided pursuant to foreign law, the court next decides whether the law of the applicable foreign country recognizes an evidentiary

---

Rhone-Poulenc Rorer, Inc., 1998 WL 158958, at *1 (S.D.N.Y. Apr. 2, 1998)); *see also Adver. to Women, Inc. v. Gianni Versace S.p.A.*, 1999 WL 608771, at *2 (N.D. Ill. Aug. 4, 1999).

171. *VLT*, 194 F.R.D. at 15.

172. *Id.*

173. *Id.*; *see also* Smithkline Beecham Corp. v. Apotex Corp., 193 F.R.D. 530, 536 n.6 (N.D. Ill. 2000); *Golden Trade*, 143 F.R.D. at 521.

174. *VLT*, 194 F.R.D. at 15; *see also* Bayer AG v. Barr Labs., Inc., 1994 WL 705331, at *4–5 (S.D.N.Y. Dec. 16, 1994); *Golden Trade*, 143 F.R.D. at 521.

175. *VLT*, 194 F.R.D. at 16 (quoting Restatement (Second) of Conflict of Laws § 139(2) (1988 Rev.) ("[W]hen the sovereign with the most significant relationship with the communication recognizes a privilege not recognized in the forum state, the communication should be disclosed under the policy of the forum state unless the foreign state's interest overrides.")).

176. Astra Aktiebolag v. Andrx Pharms., Inc., 208 F.R.D. 92, 98 (S.D.N.Y. 2002).

177. *VLT*, 194 F.R.D. at 15 (applying a combination approach).

privilege for communications with such foreign patent attorneys or agents.[178] In every case, "[t]he burden is on the party asserting the privilege to provide the court with the applicable foreign law, and [to] demonstrate that the privilege applies to the documents it seeks to exclude from discovery."[179]

Some district courts have gone so far as to hold that the party seeking to establish the privileged nature of foreign patent agent communications involving multiple countries must show the privilege is recognized "for each and every country for which it claims the privilege."[180] Normally, to meet this burden, the party asserting the privilege will need to "provide affidavits from legal experts in the laws of these countries stating the applicable law of the attorney-client privilege, and demonstrating that the law supports the privilege asserted."[181] A number of courts that have addressed this issue have also explained that the privilege for foreign patent agents, like privilege in other contexts, is "strictly construed, and all doubts should be resolved in favor of disclosure."[182]

Even if the party seeking to withhold documents or oral communications shows that patent agent communications are eligible for privilege protection under the law of the applicable nation, it must still show that each communication it has withheld satisfies the requirements of that country's privilege law. Thus, for example, some countries do not provide any protection to documents intended to be filed with the foreign patent office, or information reporting on actions taken by the foreign patent office, since that information would not be considered confidential.[183]

As a practical matter, convincing a judge whether a particular country's law recognizes an evidentiary privilege for foreign patent agent communications

178. *See In re Rivastigmine Patent Litig.*, 237 F.R.D. 69, 75 (S.D.N.Y. 2006) (analyzing privilege claims under the laws of various countries); Saxholm AS v. Dynal, Inc., 164 F.R.D. 331, 337–38 (E.D.N.Y. 1996) ("The plaintiffs here have similarly failed to provide evidence that the attorney-client privilege applies to communications with their foreign patent agents regarding Danish patent applications, and this court accordingly finds that their claims of privilege are not substantiated."); Santrade Ltd. v. Gen. Elec. Co., 150 F.R.D. 539, 546 (E.D.N.C. 1993) ("The burden, therefore, rests upon Sandvik to show, as to each country, that 'the attorney-client privilege extends to patent attorneys and/or patent agents and that the communications were intended to be confidential and not merely passed on to a patent examiner.'") (quoting Burroughs Wellcome Co. v. Barr Labs., Inc., 143 F.R.D. 611, 617 (E.D.N.C. 1992)).

179. *Smithkline Beecham Corp.*, 193 F.R.D. at 535 (citing McCook Metals L.L.C. v. Alcoa Inc., 192 F.R.D. 242, 256 (N.D. Ill. 2000)).

180. *McCook Metals*, 192 F.R.D. at 256.

181. *Id.*; *see also* Burroughs Wellcome Co. v. Barr Labs., Inc., 143 F.R.D. at 617 ("The burden rests upon BW Co. to establish that, as to each country, the attorney-client privilege extends to patent attorneys and/or patent agents *and* that the communications were intended to be confidential and not merely passed on to a patent examiner.").

182. *McCook Metals*, 192 F.R.D. at 256.

183. *Id.* at 257; *see also* Burroughs Wellcome Co. v. Barr Labs., Inc., 143 F.R.D. at 616; Baxter Travenol Labs., Inc. v. Abbott Labs., 1987 WL 12919, at *7–9 (N.D. Ill. June 17, 1987); Foseco Int'l Ltd. v. Fireline, Inc., 546 F. Supp. 22, 25–26 (N.D. Ohio 1982); Mendenhall v. Barber-Greene Co., 531 F. Supp. 951, 954 (N.D. Ill. 1982).

can be a difficult, time-consuming, and expensive task. Furthermore, as some of the following cases illustrate, the outcome of such privilege contests can be unpredictable. Indeed, in some cases, district courts attempting to ascertain the law of the same foreign country have reached different conclusions as to whether that country recognizes an evidentiary privilege for confidential communications with foreign patent agents/attorneys.

a. Japan

A number of district courts have considered whether Japanese law recognizes an evidentiary privilege for communications with Japanese patent agents (*benrishi*) or Japanese attorneys (*bengoshi*) that is similar to the attorney-client privilege in the United States. Prior to 1998, most of the U.S. district courts that considered this issue and had issued published decisions concluded that there was no privilege that covered communications with either a Japanese patent agent or patent attorney.[184]

In 1998, Japan amended its Code of Civil Procedure. The revised law expressly extended an evidentiary privilege both to Japanese *benrishi* and *bengoshi*.[185] The change to the code also retroactively applied to documents that were created before the 1998 amendment, as well as to subsequent documents.[186] District courts that have since interpreted the revised law of Japan (i.e., post-1998) now recognize an evidentiary privilege for confidential communications between a client and a Japanese patent agent or attorney.[187]

For example, in *Eisai Ltd. v. Dr. Reddy's Laboratories, Inc.*,[188] the district court concluded that an attorney-client privilege exists under Japanese law because *benrishi* may refuse to testify about facts they should keep secret and the holder of documents can refuse to produce them.[189] Moreover, those district courts that have considered this issue under Japanese law have concluded that the changes made to the Code of Civil Procedure of Japan do not offend fundamental principles of American justice or public policy, and that they should, therefore, be embraced as a matter of comity in a U.S. patent litigation.[190]

---

184. *Santrade*, 150 F.R.D. at 547 (no privilege for either Japanese patent agent or attorney); *Burroughs Wellcome*, 143 F.R.D. at 623–24 (no privilege for Japanese patent agent); Alpex Computer Corp. v. Nintendo Co., 1992 WL 51534, at *1–3 (S.D.N.Y. Mar. 10, 1992) (same); *Detection Sys.*, 96 F.R.D. at 156 (same).

185. OKI Am., Inc. v. Advanced Micro Devices, Inc., 2006 WL 2547464, at *3 (N.D. Cal. Aug. 31, 2006); Murata Mfg. Co. v. Bel Fuse Inc., 2005 WL 281217, at *2–3 (N.D. Ill. Feb. 3, 2005); Knoll Pharms., Inc. v. Teva Pharms. USA, Inc., 2004 WL 29966964, at *3–4 (N.D. Ill. Nov. 22, 2004).

186. *See* Eisai Ltd. v. Dr. Reddy's Labs., Inc., 406 F. Supp. 2d 341, 345 (S.D.N.Y. 2005).

187. VLT Corp. v. Unitrode Corp., 194 F.R.D. 8, 17 (D. Mass. 2000) ("[T]he court believes that Japanese law would treat the [document in question] as privileged."). *See also* Murata Mfg. Co. v. Bel Fuse, Inc., 2005 WL 281217, at *3 (N.D. Ill. Feb. 3, 2005) (stating that "it seems clear that Japanese law extends the attorney-client privilege to confidential communications involving patent agents or attorneys").

188. 406 F. Supp. 2d 341 (S.D.N.Y. 2005).

189. *Id.* at 343.

190. *Id.*

b. France

Whether France recognizes an attorney-client privilege for communications with French patent agents has been the subject of differing views.[191] In *Bristol-Myers Squibb Co. v. Rhone-Poulenc Rorer, Inc.*,[192] the Southern District of New York, after a thorough analysis of competing expert testimony, concluded French law recognizes no testimonial privilege for patent agents.[193] Other federal district courts, however, have found that French law does recognize an evidentiary privilege for confidential communications between a client and a French patent agent.[194]

For example, in *Duplan Corp. v. Deering Milliken, Inc.*,[195] the district court held that, as a matter of French law, communications to or from French patent agents who are acting as patent counsel in France are protected from discovery in the United States by the attorney-client privilege. The district court concluded the attorney-client privilege protects communications with French patent agents who "are rendering legal advice to foreign corporate control group members, their representatives, or foreign attorneys on the patent law of their own country."[196]

In response to the *Bristol-Myers Squibb Co.* decision, the French Parliament passed Article L. 422-11, which intended to create an attorney-client privilege between "industrial property attorneys" and their clients.[197] Even with this revision, however, the situation in France is complicated in part because different titles are associated with different intellectual property professionals. For example, "industrial property attorneys" may act as patent agents. Thus, it would appear that Article L. 422-11 establishes an attorney-client privilege between all French patent agents and their clients.[198] However, not all French

---

191. McClarin Plastics, Inc. v. LRV Acquisition Corp., 1999 WL 507188, at *4 (Fed. Cir. July 12, 1999) (declining to decide whether communications with French patent agents are or are not privileged).

192. 188 F.R.D. 189, 200 (S.D.N.Y. 1999).

193. *See also In re Rivastigmine Patent Litig.*, 237 F.R.D. 69, 92 (S.D.N.Y. 2006) (no privilege found where plaintiff failed to present evidence of French law).

194. *See* McCook Metals L.L.C. v. Alcoa Inc., 192 F.R.D. 242 (N.D. Ill. 2000) (privilege applies for communications between French patent agents and their clients); Duplan Corp. v. Deering Milliken, Inc., 397 F. Supp. 1146, 1170 (D.S.C. 1974); *see also* Baxter Travenol Labs., Inc. v. Abbott Labs., 1987 WL 12919, at *8 (N.D. Ill. June 17, 1987) (recognizing privilege for confidential communications between French patent agents and client) (dicta).

195. 397 F. Supp. 1146, 1170 (D.S.C. 1974).

196. *Id.* at 1171.

197. *See* Commissariat a L'Energie Atomique v. Samsung Elecs. Co., 245 F.R.D. 177, 182 (D. Del. 2007). Specifically, Article L. 422-11 provides:

> In all matters and for all services referred to in Article L. 422-1, the industrial property attorney shall observe professional secrecy. Such secrecy extends to all consultations addressed to or destined to his client, to professional correspondences exchanged with his client, a colleague or attorney, to discussion notes, and more generally, to all the documents of the file.

198. *Id.*

patent agents are industrial property attorneys.[199] Further complicating the analysis, French patent agents licensed before 1990, when the title of industrial property attorney was created, are now considered to be licensed under a "special list."[200] In *Commissariat a L'Energie Atomique v. Samsung Electronics Co.*, the District of Delaware concluded that the provisions of Article L. 422-11 do not apply to those French patent agents practicing on the "special list."[201]

Therefore, even following the passage of Article L. 422-11, courts are still left with the task of determining whether an evidentiary privilege attaches to communications between a French patent agent who is not an industrial property attorney and his or her clients.

c. Germany

Several district courts have concluded that an evidentiary privilege applies under German law comparable to that accorded to U.S. attorneys. Those district courts have thus found that confidential communications between German patent agents and their clients are privileged.[202] In one decision, a district court, interpreting German law, applied the privilege to encompass both communications with German patent agents as well as to a "non-lawyer patent manager" working for, and at the direction of, the German company's "Patent Department."[203] At least one district court concluded that German law recognizes no patent agent privilege; however, it appears that in that particular case, the patentee failed to present sufficient evidence of German law to sustain its burden of proof.[204]

These different results emphasize the importance of proof in establishing the existence of a foreign privilege. Normally, such proof is provided by legal expert testimony or affidavits on the substance of foreign law and whether that foreign law recognizes an evidentiary privilege for patent agent communications.[205]

---

199. *Id.*

200. *Id.*

201. *Id.* at 190. This case provides an excellent discussion of the evolution of French law insofar as it relates to privilege in the context of intellectual property matters.

202. *See* Astra Aktiebolag v. Andrx Pharms., Inc., 208 F.R.D. 92, 99–100 (S.D.N.Y. 2002) (client communications with German patent agent privileged); McCook Metals L.L.C. v. Alcoa Inc., 192 F.R.D. 242 (N.D. Ill. 2000) (privilege applies for communications between German patent agents and clients); Softview Computer Prods. Corp. v. Haworth, Inc., 2000 WL 351411, at *9 (S.D.N.Y. Mar. 31, 2000) (German law protects communications between a patent agent and his or her clients.); *Santrade Ltd. v. Gen. Elec. Co.*, 150 F.R.D. 539, 548 (E.D.N.C. 1993) (same); Golden Trade, S.r.L. v. Lee Apparel Co., 143 F.R.D. 514, 524 (same).

203. Cadence Pharms., Inc. v. Fresenius Kabi USA, LLC, 996 F. Supp. 2d 1015, 1019–1022 (S.D. Cal. 2014).

204. Baxter Travenol Labs., Inc. v. Abbott Labs., 1987 WL 12919, at *9 (N.D. Ill. June 17, 1987).

205. *See* 2M Asset Mgmt., L.L.C. v. Netmass, Inc., 2007 WL 666987, at *3 (E.D. Tex. Feb. 28, 2007); *Astra Aktiebolag*, 208 F.R.D. at 99–100.

d. United Kingdom

Whether communications between British patent agents and their clients are privileged under the law of the United Kingdom has been the subject of a number of published decisions.[206] To date, those decisions uniformly hold U.K. law recognizes the privilege.

For example, in *In re Rivastigmine Patent Litigation*,[207] the patentee withheld communications between it and its U.K. law firm regarding the prosecution of a foreign counterpart patent. According to the district court, the patentee provided evidence sufficient to demonstrate that U.K. law recognizes a privilege for communications regarding patent matters between a client and a patent agent (also referred to as a patent attorney) registered in the United Kingdom, a patent agent registered with the European Patent Office, or a partnership of patent agents and attorneys.[208] At least one district court has limited such a privilege "only to patent agent communications concerning formal patent proceedings before the appropriate British tribunals."[209]

e. South Korea

At least one district court has concluded that an evidentiary privilege can exist between a South Korean attorney and client notwithstanding the fact that South Korean law itself does not recognize an attorney-client privilege or work-product doctrine.[210] In *Astra Aktiebolag v. Andrx Pharmaceuticals, Inc.*, the court applied U.S. privilege law notwithstanding the fact that the contested communications and work product did not "touch base" with the United States.[211] The court held that the Korean communications were not discoverable because many documents would have been privileged under American law and, thus, would not have been discoverable under Korean law.[212] Because "virtually no disclosure [or discovery] is contemplated" by Korean attorneys in their practice of law, the court reasoned that comity and U.S. public policy outweighed the application of a nonexistent Korean privilege law that would have required disclosure of the communications and documentation.[213]

---

206. *See, e.g.*, Smithkline Beecham Corp. v. Apotex Corp., 193 F.R.D. 530, 535 (N.D. Ill. 2000) ("Communications with patent agents have been deemed to be privileged under British law since 1968. At that time, the Civil Evidence Act extended the privilege to communications with patent agents."); *accord In re Ampicillin Antitrust Litig.*, 81 F.R.D. 377, 391 (D.D.C. 1978); Duplan Corp. v. Deering Milliken, Inc., 397 F. Supp. 1146, 1169–70 (D.S.C. 1974).

207. 237 F.R.D. 69 (S.D.N.Y. 2006).

208. *Id.* at 109.

209. Mead Digital Sys., Inc. v. A.B. Dick Co., 89 F.R.D. 318, 320–21 (S.D. Ohio 1980).

210. *Astra Aktiebolag*, 208 F.R.D. at 101–02 (finding communications between Astra employees, Astra's in-house counsel, and Astra's outside Korean counsel, regarding Korean court procedure, Korean patent office procedure, and various issues of trial strategy, privileged).

211. *Id.* at 102.

212. *Id.*

213. *Id.*

f. People's Republic of China

Until 1997, when the Law of the People's Republic of China on Lawyers (Lawyer's Law) became effective, the People's Republic of China did not protect the confidential information of a client. Article 33 of the Lawyer's Law states that "[a] lawyer should keep state secrets and a litigant's commercial secrets learned through conducting the business activities of a lawyer's practice, and should not disclose the privacy of litigants."[214] While this provision created something akin to an attorney-client privilege, it was without teeth. To be sure, Article 70 of the Law of Civil Procedure of the People's Republic of China (Civil Procedure Law) established an obligation upon attorneys to testify at trial if any facts are known that are relevant to the case.[215] This provision of the Civil Procedure Law, combined with the section of the Lawyer's Law that allows the court to revoke an attorney's license if facts are concealed from the court,[216] effectively prevented meaningful protection of confidential communications between attorney and client.

In 2008, however, China amended the Lawyer's Law to include an affirmative duty to protect clients' confidential information and added a provision to eliminate the obligation placed on attorneys to testify at trial.[217] While client-confidentiality requirements in the People's Republic of China have been strengthened,[218] the current form of the Lawyer's Law has not explicitly established an evidentiary privilege. At least one (nonpatent) case has expressly held, "Chinese law does not recognize the attorney-client privilege or the work-product doctrine."[219]

g. European Patent Attorney

The European patent attorney, while not an attorney at law, provides his or her clients with patentability opinions, prepares and prosecutes patent applications, and provides opinions relating to the validity or infringement of a European patent or application. In the hopes of strengthening European

214. Law of the People's Republic of China on Lawyers, art. 33 (promulgated by the Standing Comm. Nat'l People's Cong., May 15, 1996, eff. Jan. 1, 1997).

215. Law of Civil Procedure of the People's Republic of China (promulgated by the 4th session of the 7th Nat'l People's Cong., Apr. 9, 1991). *See also* Gui Hongxia & Li Xiang, *Attorney-Client Privilege: Extended to Foreign Lawyers in China?*, China L. Insight (Apr. 1, 2009), http://www.chinalawinsight.com/2009/04/articles/corporate/attorneyclient-privilege-extended-to-foreign-lawyers-in-china/.

216. Law of the People's Republic of China on Lawyers, art. 45 § 1 (promulgated by the Standing Comm. Nat'l People's Cong., May 15, 1996, eff. Jan. 1, 1997).

217. *See* Gui Hongxia & Li Xiang, *Attorney-Client Privilege: Extended to Foreign Lawyers in China?*, China L. Insight (Apr. 1, 2009), http://www.chinalawinsight.com/2009/04/articles/corporate/attorney client-privilege-extended-to-foreign-lawyers-in-china/.

218. *See* Wultz v. Bank of China Ltd., 979 F. Supp. 2d 479, 492–93 (S.D.N.Y. 2013) (internal citations omitted) ("While violations of confidentiality may trigger certain sanctions under Chinese law, including suspension of legal license and potential criminal punishment, the duty of confidentiality is an ethical obligation and not an evidentiary protection analogous to the attorney-client privilege or work-product doctrine.").

219. *Id.*

patent attorneys' efforts to resist discovery of confidential client communications, the European Patent Convention was revised in December of 2007 to include an attorney-client privilege.[220] The privilege prevents any communication or document relating to the duties of a European patent attorney from being disclosed in proceedings before the European Patent Office unless the privilege is waived by the client.[221] At least two district courts have recognized the existence of an evidentiary privilege for confidential communications between European patent attorneys and their clients.[222]

IV. Attorney-Client Privilege in Patent-Related Administrative Proceedings

A. Section 337 Investigations before the International Trade Commission

Section 337 of the Tariff Act of 1930 (19 U.S.C. section 1337) prohibits importation of a product into the United States that infringes a valid U.S. intellectual property right.[223] If a violation of section 337 is found, the International Trade Commission (ITC) can issue an exclusion order banning the importation of the infringing product into the United States.[224] Discovery begins shortly after the commencement of an ITC investigation and proceeds in a similar, although expedited, fashion as compared to traditional discovery practice at the district court level. Discovery disputes are governed by the ITC Rules and a set of "ground rules" promulgated by the ALJ presiding over the investigation. Although the ground rules applicable to any investigation are specific to

---

220. *Rule 153, Attorney Client Evidentiary Privilege, Decision of the Administrative Council of 07.12.2006* (CA/D 10/06), 2007 O.J. Spec. Ed. (E.P.O. R. 153) 8.

221. Specifically, Rule 153 of the European Patent Convention provides:

> (1) Where advice is sought from a professional representative in his capacity as such, all communications between the professional representative and his client or any other person, relating to that purpose and falling under Article 2 of the Regulation on discipline for professional representatives, are permanently privileged from disclosure in proceedings before the European Patent Office, unless such privilege is expressly waived by the client.
>
> (2) Such privilege from disclosure shall apply, in particular, to any communication or document relating to:
>
> (a) the assessment of the patentability of an invention;
>
> (b) the preparation or prosecution of a European patent application;
>
> (c) any opinion relating to the validity, scope of protection or infringement of a European patent or a European patent application.

222. *See* Sanofi-Synthelabo v. Apotex Inc., 299 F. Supp. 2d 303, 307–08 (S.D.N.Y. 2004) (finding that communications between Sanofi and its outside European patent attorney were privileged, but ultimately that the privilege had been waived); Solvay, S.A. v. Honeywell Specialty Materials, L.L.C., No. 06-557-SLR (D. Del. Jan. 16, 2008) (order specifically recognizing the existence of a European patent attorney-client privilege) (unpublished).

223. *See* 19 U.S.C. § 1337(a)(1)(B)–(D) (2010).

224. *See id.* § 1337(d).

the presiding ALJ, most ALJs require a "meet and confer" before a discovery-related motion is filed.[225]

The ITC rules provide for discovery of any matter, not privileged, that is relevant to a claim or defense of a party, and thus, they do not track the recent changes to the Federal Rules.[226] The ITC has stated that "the scope of discovery has been held to be broad."[227] Prior to June 30, 2013, traditional privilege rules based upon federal common law and decisions promulgated by the ALJs and commissioners applied during the course of discovery in an ITC investigation.[228] At least one ALJ has recognized an attorney-client privilege for communications relating to the conception and patenting of an invention.[229] With respect to patent agents, an ALJ has found that "confidential communications between a patent agent and his client in connection with a patent prosecution [are privileged;] however, communications between the patent [agent] and client not related to patent prosecutions and in the realm of the general practice of law are not privileged."[230]

ALJs at the ITC also have, in some cases, extended the attorney-client privilege to communications with foreign attorneys and foreign non-attorney patent agents in connection with confidential communications that arise out of patent drafting and prosecution.[231] However, as in district court litigations,

---

225. Some ALJs require a "discovery committee" to be formed and provide that "[n]o motion to compel discovery may be filed unless the subject matter of the motion has first been brought to the Discovery Committee and the Committee has reached an impasse in resolving the matter." *See Certain RF Capable Integrated Circuits & Prods. Containing the Same*, Inv. No. 337-TA-982, Order No. 2 at § 4.1.1 (U.S.I.T.C. Jan. 21, 2016).

226. 19 C.F.R. § 210.27(b).

227. *See, e.g., In re Certain Silicon Microphone Packages & Prods. Containing Same*, Inv. No. 337-TA-888, Order No. 35, at 5 (U.S.I.T.C. Apr. 15, 2014).

228. A Lawyer's Guide to Section 337 Investigations before the U.S. International Trade Commission 117–18 (Tom M. Schaumberg ed., 2010). Schaumberg notes that because extensive pre-filing due diligence is required before submitting a complaint to the ITC, questions may arise as to whether communications and work product conducted pre-complaint will be protected by an evidentiary privilege. In recognizing that an evidentiary privilege normally attaches, Schaumberg makes three general observations: First, tests conducted specifically for the purpose of determining whether to file a lawsuit, at the request of counsel and not performed for other purposes within the regular course of business, are protected as privileged. Second, the identity of entities whose existence as a possible infringer became known solely through the investigatory efforts of counsel or their agents constitutes protected work product. Third, the rationale for not alleging infringement by certain entities is protected by attorney-client privilege (and likely work product as well). *Id.* at 118. Work-product immunity is also extended to tests and data collected for the purpose of determining whether a complaint should be filed. *Id.*

229. *Id.* at 118 (citing *Certain Anisotropically Etched One Megabit & Greater DRAMS, Components Thereof, & Prods. Containing Such DRAMS*, Inv. No. 337-TA-345, Comm'n Op. at 3 (U.S.I.T.C. Sept. 22, 1993)).

230. Donald Knox Duvall et al., Unfair Competition and the ITC: Actions before the International Trade Commission under Section 337 of the Tariff Act of 1930 § 4:41, at 227 (2009 ed.) (citing *Commercial Food Portioners*, Inv. No. 337-TA-339, Order No. 32 (Dec. 9, 1992)).

231. *See* A Lawyer's Guide to Section 337 Investigations before the U.S. International Trade Commission 119–22 (Tom M. Schaumberg ed., 2010). Schaumberg points to multiple Orders

the party asserting the privilege must first establish (1) what country's law applies; (2) whether the law of the foreign country recognizes the right of the foreign attorney, or non-attorney patent agent, to render advice "in confidence in connection with a patent application in that country"; and (3) if a foreign privilege does exist generally, whether its requirements were met in the present case.[232]

Effective June 20, 2013, the ITC amended its Rules of Practice and Procedure codified in Part 210 of Title 19 of the Code of Federal Regulations. In its notice of final rulemaking, the ITC stated it was amending its rules, in part, because of the "litigation costs necessary to protect against waiver of attorney-client privilege or attorney work product."[233] Furthermore, the ITC noted that "no Commission rule requires the production of a privilege log when a person withholds materials from discovery based on an assertion of privilege or work product protection."[234] Consequently, the ITC now has a specific set of uniform procedures relating to claiming attorney-client privilege or work-product protection.[235]

The ITC rules require that within ten days of making a claim that information sought in a discovery request is privileged, the responding party must produce a privilege log separately identifying each withheld communication and providing information necessary for the requester to assess the claim.[236] This logging requirement may be waived by agreement of the parties.[237] The ITC rules further provide a clawback procedure for documents claimed as privileged that were inadvertently produced.[238] The rules also provide a schedule for quickly bringing to the ALJ's attention any disputes over a claim of privilege or work product.[239]

The ITC "clawback" rule does not "supplant any applicable waiver doctrine," and ALJs are expected to "apply federal and common law when determining the consequences of any allegedly inadvertent disclosure."[240] In one post-rule-change investigation, for example, the ALJ concluded under traditional federal common law principles that the privilege had been waived as

---

from various ALJs extending the attorney-client privilege to foreign attorneys or patent agents. *See, e.g., Certain Tape Dispensers*, Inv. No. 337-TA-354, Notice to All Parties, at 1 (July 19, 1993); *Certain Integrated Circuit Telecomm. Chips & Prods. Containing Same, Including Dialing Apparatus*, Inv. No. 337-TA-337, Order No. 109, at 3 (U.S.I.T.C. Nov. 23, 1992).

232. *See* A Lawyer's Guide to Section 337 Investigations before the U.S. International Trade Commission 122 (Tom M. Schaumberg ed., 2010) (quoting *Certain Fluidized Bed Combustion Sys.*, Inv. No. 337-TA-213, Order No. 14, at 1 (U.S.I.T.C. June 21, 1985)).

233. *See* 78 Fed. Reg. 29618, at 29622 (May 21, 2013) (final rule).

234. *Id.*

235. *Id.*; *see* 19 C.F.R. § 210.27(e) (June 30, 2013).

236. 19 C.F.R. § 210.27(e)(1).

237. *Id.* § 210.27(e)(3).

238. *Id.* at § 210.27(e)(2).

239. *Id.*

240. 78 Fed. Reg. 29618, at 29622 (May 21, 2013).

to a particular document because the document was disclosed to third parties to the attorney-client relationship.[241] In a more recent investigation, the ALJ denied respondent's request to compel production of a document that complainant clawed back, after finding the document to be privileged because it was "used or received by an attorney to provide legal advice."[242]

B. Proceedings before the Patent Trial and Appeal Board

Practice before the USPTO has changed significantly as a result of the enactment of the Leahy-Smith America Invents Act (AIA).[243] One of the most significant features of the AIA is the first-to-file provision, which effectively removed the option of an interference for most new patent applications. Nevertheless, patent interferences remain viable for many patent applications containing claims entitled to filing dates prior to March 16, 2013. Since both pre-AIA interferences and post-AIA proceedings involve discovery to some extent, issues of privilege may arise in administrative proceedings before the USPTO.

By way of background, until passage of the AIA, patent interferences were a unique and important feature of the U.S. patent system. Interferences were declared and administered before what was then called the Board of Patent Appeals and Interferences (BPAI) of the USPTO "to determine any question of patentability or priority of invention between two or more parties claiming the same patentable invention."[244] The administrative patent judges (APJs) of the BPAI could enter an order allowing for limited discovery in an interference.[245]

Under the AIA, the BPAI has been replaced by the Patent Trial and Appeal Board (PTAB). There are three main types of PTAB trial proceedings: inter partes review (IPR), post-grant review (PGR), and covered business method review (CBM).[246] One aspect of these patent challenge procedures is the provision of limited discovery regarding the publications and patents raised as grounds to invalidate a patent. Under the AIA, the USPTO director is required to implement regulations "setting forth standards and procedures for discovery of relevant evidence, including that such discovery shall be limited to—(A) the deposition of witnesses submitting affidavits or declarations; and (B) what is necessary in the interest of justice."[247]

241. *In re Certain Silicon Microphone Packages & Prods. Containing Same,* Inv. No. 337-TA-888, Order No. 35, at 5 (U.S.I.T.C. Apr. 15, 2014) (citing FED. R. EVID. 502 and finding privilege waived); *see also In re Certain Sleep-Disordered Breathing Treatment Sys. & Components Thereof,* Inv. No. 337-TA-879, Order No. 18, at 3-4 (U.S.I.T.C. Mar. 6, 2014) (same).

242. *In re Certain Single-Molecule Nucleic Acid Sequencing Systems and Reagents, Consumables, and Software for Use with Same,* Inv. No. 337-TA-1032, Order No. 9, at 1–2 (U.S.I.T.C. May 9, 2017).

243. 125 Stat. 284, Pub. L. No. 112-69, Sept. 16, 2011.

244. 35 U.S.C. § 135(a) (Pre-AIA).

245. 37 C.F.R. § 41.150 (Pre-AIA).

246. The "transitional" CBM program expired on September 16, 2020. 125 Stat. 284, Pub. L. No. 112-69, Sept. 16, 2011, § 18(a)(3)(A).

247. 35 U.S.C. § 316(a)(5).

The PTAB rules governing post-grant procedures are designed to address the abbreviated length of post-grant proceedings and avoid the lengthy amount of time spent on discovery in a federal civil trial. One result of the limited discovery rules before the PTAB is that they appear to minimize the potential for conflicts over claims of attorney-client privilege or work-product immunity.

The first PTAB case to provide guidance on the scope of discovery in an IPR is *Garmin International, Inc. v. Cuozzo Speed Technologies, LLC.*[248] In *Garmin*, the PTAB discussed "routine discovery" and "additional discovery." The PTAB explained that "[u]nder 37 C.F.R. § 41.51(b)(1)(i), '[u]nless previously served or otherwise by agreement of the parties, any exhibit cited in a paper or in testimony must be served with the citing paper or testimony.' Under 37 C.F.R. § 41.51(b)(1)(iii), '[u]nless previously served, a party must serve relevant information that is inconsistent with a position advanced by the party during the proceeding concurrent with the filing of the documents or things that contain the inconsistency' [*privileged information excepted*]."[249]

According to *Garmin*, "additional discovery" will be allowed only for deposing affiants or declarants, and for "what is otherwise necessary in the interest of justice."[250] The PTAB stated the scope of discovery is "significantly different from the scope of discovery generally available under the Federal Rules of Civil Procedure" and "is limited as compared to that available in district court litigation."[251] The PTAB, noting legislative history that indicated the USPTO "will be conservative in its grants of discovery," specified five factors that control whether additional discovery will be granted in the "interest of justice."[252] One such factor, which is frequently the subject of district court disputes over privilege, is a party's litigation position. The PTAB in *Garmin* explained: "Asking for the other party's litigation positions and the underlying basis for those positions is not necessary in the interest of justice. The Board has established rules for the presentation of arguments and evidence. There is a proper time and place for each party to make its presentation. A party may not attempt to alter the Board's trial procedures under the pretext of discovery."[253]

Further demonstrating both the limited scope of discovery, and the PTAB's unwillingness to allow parties before the USPTO to engage in privilege disputes, is the decision in *Arkema France v. Honeywell International Inc.*[254] In *Arkema*, the petitioner requested authorization to file a motion to compel patent owner

248. IPR2012-0001, Paper No. 26 (P.T.A.B. Mar. 5, 2013).

249. *Id.* at 3 (emphasis added).

250. *Id.* at 5 (citing AIA); *see also* 37 C.F.R. § 42.51(b)(2) ("The moving party must show that such additional discovery is in the interests of justice.").

251. *Id.*

252. *Id.* at 5–7 (citations omitted).

253. *Id.* at 6.

254. IPR2015-00915, Paper No. 22, at 4 (P.T.A.B. Feb. 25, 2016).

to produce unredacted copies of two exhibits in order to show the date that certain activities occurred.[255] The patent owner asserted that "the redacted material [was] protected by the attorney client privilege," while the petitioner argued that the privilege had been waived.[256] The PTAB denied the request, concluding that "briefing on a motion to compel [was] not warranted under the circumstances." The PTAB explained that petitioner's request did not persuade the board that patent owner's privilege had been waived, while noting that petitioners did not intend to rely on the substance of the information sought, but rather to show the date that certain activity took place.[257] Accordingly, the PTAB concluded that petitioner failed to demonstrate its request for a privilege log was "necessary in the interest of justice."[258]

Given the limited right to discovery in PTAB proceedings, and in light of cases such as *Arkema,* it appears unlikely that the PTAB will be a breeding ground for disputes over the attorney-client privilege or the work-product doctrine. Although each case is different, as a general matter, there may be few circumstances in which a party in a PTAB proceeding will be able to demonstrate production of privileged or work-product material is "in the interest of justice."

The question of whether patent agent communications are exempt from discovery frequently arises in PTAB proceedings. In 2014, the USPTO launched an outreach initiative to solicit comments and address concerns regarding the treatment of confidential communications between clients and non-attorney patent practitioners.[259] In October 2016, the USPTO published a proposed privilege rule for patent agents in PTAB and other office proceedings, stating that "communication[s] . . . reasonably necessary or incident to the scope of the patent practitioner's authority shall receive the same protections of privilege as if that communication were between a client and an attorney authorized to practice in the United States."[260] In November 2017, the USPTO published the final rule establishing a privilege applicable to patent agents, including foreign patent agents permitted to practice before the USPTO in a limited capacity.[261]

C. PTAB Documents as Work Product

Documents prepared and communications made in connection with proceedings before the Patent Trial and Appeal Board under the America Invents Act

255. *Id.* at 1, 3.

256. *Id.* at 2.

257. *Id.* at 3.

258. *Id.*

259. USPTO, Summary of Roundtable and Written Comments: Domestic and International Issues Related to Privileged Communications Between Patent Practitioners and Their Clients (2015).

260. Rule Recognizing Privileged Communications Between Clients and Patent Practitioners at the Patent Trial and Appeal Board, 81 Fed. Reg. 71653 (Oct. 18, 2016).

261. 37 C.F.R. § 42.57; Rule on Attorney-Client Privilege for Trials Before the Patent Trial and Appeal Board, 82 Fed. Reg. 51570-75 (Nov. 7, 2017).

are more likely to qualify for work-product immunity in co-pending or subsequent federal court proceedings. For example, in *Personal Audio LLC v. Togi Entertainment, Inc.*, a nonparty moved to quash a deposition subpoena served by plaintiff in a patent infringement action pending in the Eastern District of Texas.[262] The third party had filed an inter partes review (IPR) challenging the validity of the patent-in-suit.[263] The subpoena included topics relating to whether the nonparty was "acting under the control, direction, or influence of any of the defendants in the Texas case when it filed the IPR."[264] The third party moved to quash the subpoena on multiple grounds, including attorney-client privilege and work-product immunity.[265] The party seeking the discovery argued it was relevant because if the defendants in the Texas action induced the nonparty to file the IPR petitions, then "defendants will be collaterally estopped from asserting their invalidity defenses in the district court" pursuant to 35 U.S.C. section 315(e)(2).[266] The district court granted the motion to quash because the discovery was speculative, since the USPTO had not yet issued a final decision in the IPR.[267] Other district courts have likewise refused discovery relating to still-pending IPR petitions as premature, hence speculative.[268]

As the popularity of IPR proceedings expands and continues to involve patents in litigation, district courts have increasingly considered the extent to which the work-product immunity and attorney-client privilege doctrines apply to communications and documents from or relating to such USPTO proceedings. Given the adversarial nature of IPR proceedings, it appears more likely that a party involved in such proceedings will have a better chance of protecting documents under the work-product immunity doctrine than they otherwise might have had in a traditional ex parte patent prosecution.

For instance, the court in *Broadband iTV, Inc. v. Hawaiian Telecom* relied on the legislative intent to "convert[] inter partes reexamination from an examinational to an adjudicative proceeding" in holding that IPR-related communications were privileged and confidential. The court went on to explain that "both work product and attorney-client privilege apply to [ ] communications,

---

262. 2014 WL 1318921, at *1 (N.D. Cal. Mar. 31, 2014).

263. *Id.* at *1.

264. *Id.*

265. *Id.* at * 2.

266. *Id.* (quoting section 315(e)(2), which states, "[t]he petitioner in an inter partes review of a claim in a patent . . . that results in a final written decision under section 318(a), or the real party in interest or privy of the petitioner, may not request or maintain a proceeding before the Office with respect to that claim on any ground that the petitioner raised or reasonably could have raised during that inter partes review.").

267. *Id.* at *2–3.

268. *See* VirnetX, Inc. v. Apple, Inc., 2014 WL 6979427, at *2 (N.D. Cal. Mar. 21, 2014) (finding discovery regarding collateral estoppel was premature when PTAB had not issued a final decision in an IPR proceeding).

strategies, and actions [of parties to an] IPR proceeding."[269] Accordingly, the court quashed the plaintiff's subpoena, which requested "[a]ll documents and things that refer to, relate to, or comment upon the Inter Partes Review of the [patent at issue], including the decision to institute th[e] proceeding."[270]

V. Design Around

District courts have generally found that direction of counsel does not make all discovery into designing around patents protected by the attorney-client privilege or work-product doctrine. For example, in *Illumina Inc. v. BGI Genomics Co.*,[271] the magistrate judge held that the defendants' efforts at designing around the patents-in-suit were not protected by the attorney-client privilege or the work-product doctrine. The interrogatories sought details on the changes made or to be made to the accused products by defendants due to defendants' awareness of the patents-in-suit, and the request for production sought documents relating to defendants' efforts to modify the accused products as "influenced" by the patents-in-suit.[272] Disagreeing with the defendants' position that all design around information is privileged, the court, relying on *Upjohn v. Mova Pharm. Corp.*,[273] explained that attorney involvement in the redesign process does not make the process entirely immune from discovery.[274] Because the interrogatories as modified by the court did not ask for information protected by the attorney-client privilege (e.g., "actual attorney-client communications about a design around") or the work-product doctrine (e.g., "attorney-written memo with thoughts and impressions about a design around"), the court ordered the defendants to answer the interrogatories.[275] Similarly, the court ordered the defendants to produce "non-privileged, non-work product documents" in response to the request for production.[276]

In *Visteon Global Techs., Inc. v. Garmin Int'l, Inc.*, a district court, also relying on *Upjohn Co. v. Mora Pharms. Corp.*,[277] held that Garmin in-house counsel's role in the design-around process did not shield him from being deposed about the design-around product.[278] In light of the deposition testimony of Garmin's engineer indicating that the engineer did not review the asserted patent and acted solely at the direction of Garmin in-house counsel, the court

269. 2015 WL 1778432, at *10 (N.D. Cal. Apr. 17, 2015).

270. *Id.*

271. 2020 WL 7047708, at *3 (N.D. Cal. Dec. 1, 2020).

272. *Id.* at *1.

273. 936 F. Supp. 55 (D.P.R. 1996) (finding that documents "concerned primarily with technical or business information" on the "pre-cursor formulations" resulting from the counsel-involved research of the patents-in-suit must be produced).

274. 2020 WL 7047708, at *3.

275. *Id.*

276. *Id.*

277. 936 F. Supp. 55 (D.P.R. 1996).

278. 903 F. Supp. 2d. 521, 530 (E.D. Mich. 2012).

concluded that it was reasonable for the magistrate judge to conclude that Garmin in-house counsel possessed nonprivileged information regarding the design-around product.[279]

When discovery is sought from an expert about a design-around, courts protect against direct or indirect disclosure of attorney mental impressions or theories. For example, in *Sioux Steel Co. v. Prairie Land Millwright Services, Inc.*, the court found that certain deposition questions (e.g., "Were the modifications that you considered to the hinge unit counsel's idea?") asked of a consulting expert were objectionable for seeking opinion work product.[280] The court also emphasized that factual information about the design-around cannot be shielded by having a consulting expert instead of employees make the design modifications.[281]

VI. Waiver of Privilege or Immunity

In patent cases, a voluntary waiver, with respect to a privileged document, reflecting a communication between an attorney and the client in discussing certain subject matter generally waives the privilege as to all contemporaneous communications between that attorney and that client on that subject matter.[282] When a client voluntarily waives the privilege as to some documents that the client considers not damaging and asserts the privilege as to other documents that the client considers damaging, the client may be compelled to produce all documents relating to the matter.[283] The rationale for this rule is that a client cannot be allowed, after disclosing as much as he pleases, to withhold the remainder.[284] The client may elect to withhold or to disclose, but after a certain point any election to withhold becomes final. Likewise, voluntary disclosure of work product to an adversary generally waives the privilege as to other documents on the same subject.[285] Patent cases present numerous issues relating to waiver of privilege and the scope of the waiver.

279. *Id.* at 531.

280. 2021 WL 4967794, at *6–7 (N.D. Ill. May 19, 2021).

281. *Id.* at *7.

282. Duplan Corp. v. Deering Milliken, Inc., 397 F. Supp. 1146, 1169 (D.S.C. 1974).

283. *See In re Seagate Tech., LLC*, 497 F.3d 1360, 1370 (Fed. Cir. 2007) ("[A]sserting the advice of counsel defense waives . . . attorney-client privilege for all communications on the same subject matter, as well as any documents memorializing attorney-client communications."); Fort James Corp. v. Solo Cup Co., 412 F.3d 1340, 1349 (Fed. Cir. 2005) ("The widely applied standard for determining the scope of waiver of attorney-client privilege is that the waiver applies to all other communications relating to the same subject matter.").

284. *See Fort James Corp.*, 412 F.3d at 1349 ("The waiver extends beyond the document initially produced out of concern for fairness, so that a party is prevented from disclosing communications that support its position while simultaneously concealing communications that do not.").

285. *See* United States v. Nobles, 422 U.S. 225, 239 (1975).

A. Inadvertent versus Intentional Waiver

The attorney-client privilege may be lost in a patent case, as in other types of cases, through an inadvertent waiver. These situations typically arise if the party seeking to maintain the privilege (usually but not always a corporate entity) is not careful in maintaining the confidentiality of its privileged documents. In litigation, a party may also waive the privilege inadvertently, such as by error resulting from a careless document production procedure.[286]

According to the advisory committee notes to the 2006 revisions to Federal Rule of Civil Procedure 26(b)(5):

> The Committee has repeatedly been advised that the risk of privilege waiver, and the work necessary to avoid it, add to the costs and delay of discovery. When the review is of electronically stored information, the risk of waiver, and the time and effort required to avoid it, can increase substantially because of the volume of electronically stored information and the difficulty in ensuring that all information to be produced has in fact been reviewed.[287]

The district courts have not uniformly treated the issue of whether an inadvertent production waives the attorney-client privilege. To be sure, some district courts have held that an inadvertent production is never a waiver; some district courts have held that it is always a waiver; and still other district courts have held that it is only a waiver if, in the totality of circumstances, adequate measures were not taken to avoid the disclosure.[288] In fact, some district courts subscribe to all three views.[289]

To alleviate uncertainty and create more uniformity regarding the waiver of privilege (especially when the waiver was inadvertent), legislation was passed in 2008 that created Federal Rule of Evidence 502, Attorney-Client Privilege and Work Product; Limitations on Waiver.[290] FRE 502(a) defines the scope of a waiver of privilege or immunity insofar as it relates to other (undisclosed) communications or information as follows:

> When the disclosure [of a privileged communication or work-product material] is made in a Federal proceeding or to a Federal office or agency and waives the attorney-client privilege or work-product

---

286. *See, e.g.*, *VLT Corp. v. Unitrode Corp.*, 194 F.R.D. 8, 15 (D. Mass. 2000).

287. Fed. R. Civ. P. 26(b)(5), advisory committee's note (2006).

288. *VLT*, 194 F.R.D. at 11.

289. *Id.*

290. S. 2450, 110th Cong. (2008). The act was signed into law on September 19, 2008, and is effective "in all proceedings commenced after September 19, 2008 and, insofar as just and practicable, in all proceedings pending on September 19." Fed. R. Evid. 502.

> protection, the waiver extends to an undisclosed communication or information . . . only if:
>
> 1. the waiver is intentional;
> 2. the disclosed and undisclosed communications or information concern the same subject matter; and
> 3. they ought in fairness to be considered together.[291]
>
> With respect to the issue of inadvertent waivers, FRE 502(b) provides that a disclosure of a privileged communication or work-product material is not a waiver if three conditions are met:
>
> 1. the disclosure is inadvertent;
> 2. the holder of the privilege or protection took reasonable steps to prevent disclosure; and
> 3. the holder promptly took reasonable steps to rectify the error. . . .[292]

FRE 502(b) is intended to avoid protracted battles over waiver in patent cases, which typically involve enormous volumes of documents. As the advisory committee notes to Rule 502 explain, "[t]his concern is especially troubling in cases involving electronic discovery."[293] As one court has noted, electronic discovery may encompass "millions" of documents and to insist upon a "record by record pre-production privilege review, on pain of subject matter waiver, would impose upon parties costs of production that bear no proportionality to what is at stake in the litigation."[294]

For example, in *King Pharmaceuticals, Inc. v. Purdue Pharma L.P.*,[295] a patent infringement case involving the production of millions of documents, the accused infringer asserted that four pages of a document it had produced were privileged and had been inadvertently produced. The disclosure was discovered when plaintiff's counsel used the document during a deposition. The district court agreed that the disclosure of the four pages satisfied FRE 502(b) in that it was very limited in light of the overall production, and that the accused infringer acted promptly under Federal Rule of Civil Procedure 26(b)(5)(B) to notify opposing counsel of the claim and the basis for it. Consequently, the district court ordered patentee's counsel to destroy all copies of the privileged document and not to use or disclose the privileged information.[296] Other courts in patent cases have followed FRE 502(b) in refusing to find a waiver of privilege.[297]

---

291. Fed. R. Evid. 502(a).
292. *Id.* at 502(b).
293. Fed. R. Evid. 502, advisory committee's note (2007).
294. Hopson v. City of Balt., 232 F.R.D. 228, 244 (D. Md. 2005).
295. 2010 WL 2243872 (W.D. Va. June 2, 2010).
296. *Id.* at *1–2.
297. *See, e.g.*, Alcon Mfg. Ltd. v. Apotex Inc., 2008 WL 5070465, at *3–6 (S.D. Ind. Nov. 26, 2008).

Most patent cases involve the entry, prior to discovery, of a protective order to protect confidential information. A patent litigant would be wise to deal with the possibility of an inadvertent production by including an inadvertent disclosure of privileged or work-product materials provision in the protective order. In fact, the protective order solution is specifically addressed in the advisory committee notes to Rule 26(b)(5)(B). Furthermore, FRE 502(d) provides that a court "may order that the privilege or protection is not waived by disclosure connected with the litigation." When parties have stipulated to such a provision, and the district court has entered the parties' agreement as an order of the court, the terms of the protective order control whether an inadvertent production waives privilege.[298]

Whether an inadvertent production results in waiver of the attorney-client privilege can turn on the language of the clawback provision in the protective order and the steps taken to prevent the inadvertent production. For example, in *Shire LLC v. Amneal Pharms.*, the defendants only conducted a remedial investigation after the receiving party, Shire, notified defendants of the inadvertent production.[299] The magistrate judge found that the defendants did not meet their burden under a "literal interpretation" of the clawback provision in the protective order requiring the producing party to discover the inadvertent production.[300] The judge also found that defendants did not meet their burden of showing reasonable steps were undertaken to prevent the inadvertent disclosure, given the document production underwent an "expedited review" that used "analytical software" without any attorney review.[301] The factors considered by the court included the "proportionately small size" of the inadvertent production and the "nearly two months" defendants had to conduct a "thorough document review."[302]

Regardless of whether a protective order controls the issue, the burden rests on the producing party to establish that its disclosure was truly inadvertent.[303] Some district courts have required parties seeking the return of a privileged document allegedly produced inadvertently to act "timely."[304] Moreover, if the producing party is found to have engaged in purposeful or grossly negligent acts in allowing the production of privileged documents, the district

298. *See, e.g., Alcon Mfg.*, 2008 WL 5070465, at *3–6 (finding that inadvertent production did not waive privilege under the terms of the protective order); United States v. Pepper's Steel & Alloys, Inc., 742 F. Supp. 641, 644–45 (S.D. Fla. 1990) (refusing to order production where the protective order provided that there would be no waiver of any privilege); *Eutectic Corp. v. Metco, Inc.*, 61 F.R.D. 35, 52 (E.D.N.Y. 1973) (same).

299. 2014 WL 1509238, at *2 (D.N.J. Jan. 10, 2014).

300. *Id.* at *3.

301. *Id.* at *5.

302. *Id.*

303. *VLT*, 194 F.R.D. at 12 n.2 (quoting Harmony Gold U.S.A., Inc. v. FASA Corp., 169 F.R.D. 113, 116 (N.D. Ill. 1996)).

304. Transonic Sys., Inc. v. Non-Invasive Med. Tech., 192 F.R.D. 710, 715 (D. Utah 2000).

court might very well conclude that their production was not "inadvertent."[305] Indeed, some district courts have also refused to order the return of a privileged document if it was produced because of a mistake of counsel or counsel's exercise of poor judgment, concluding that such conduct was "advertent" and not "inadvertent."[306]

The flip side of the inadvertent waiver is when a patentee or accused infringer knowingly and intentionally discloses privileged or work-product materials to a third party. In such circumstances, and absent an express agreement[307] by the parties in a suit to the contrary, the privileged or work-product status of whatever was disclosed is waived.[308] The issue typically associated with such intentional disclosure is the extent to which the waiver goes beyond the "four corners" of what was disclosed to encompass anything, and everything, relating to the subject matter of what was disclosed.

For example, in *Optimumpath, L.L.C. v. Belkin International, Inc.*,[309] the patentee submitted during prosecution a declaration under 37 C.F.R. § 1.131 to antedate a reference. The declaration itself, and some of its attached documents, reflected privileged communications. The parties disputed the scope of the waiver, with plaintiff seeking a narrow waiver and defendant seeking a broad waiver. The district court concluded that the privilege was waived, and under the facts of that case determined that the subject matter and temporal scope of the waiver would be relatively narrow.[310]

Filing a declaration disclosing a conclusion based on privileged communications can lead to waiver as well. For example, in *Willis Elec. Co. Ltd. v. Polygroup Macao Ltd.*, waiver resulted from an attorney IPR declaration disclosing counsel's conception date conclusion based on privileged communications.[311] The subject matter waiver extended to all communications with counsel relating to the conception date.[312] Similarly, in *Milwaukee Elec. Tool Corp. v. Chervon N. Am., Inc.*,[313] waiver resulted from an attorney IPR declaration disclosing conclusions on conception and diligence, as well as disclosing invention disclosure forms and counsel's communications with inventors about the provisional patent applications. Due to the scope of these disclosures, the subject

305. *See* Amgen, Inc. v. Hoechst Marion Roussel, Inc., 190 F.R.D. 287, 292–93 (D. Mass. 2000) (mistaken production of 200 privileged documents constituting thousands of pages was not inadvertent).

306. *Transonic Sys.*, 192 F.R.D. at 715–16; Vakharia v. Swedish Covenant Hosp., 1993 WL 313523, at *2 (N.D. Ill. Aug. 17, 1993).

307. *See* Fed. R. Evid. 502(e) ("An agreement on the effect of disclosure in a federal proceeding is binding only on the parties to the agreement, unless it is incorporated into a court order.").

308. *See* Fed. R. Evid. 502.

309. 2010 WL 2348665, at *1 (N.D. Cal. June 8, 2010).

310. *Id.* at *3–5.

311. 2020 WL 1934425, at *2–3 (D. Minn. Apr. 22, 2020).

312. *Id.* at *4.

313. 2017 WL 2929522, at *4 (E.D. Wisc. July 10, 2017).

matter waiver extended to all communications with counsel relating to preparation of the patent applications.[314]

Subject matter waiver can also pose a problem when a party selectively produces privileged documents. For example, in *Acantha LLC v. Depuy Orthopaedics Inc.*,[315] Acantha produced privileged communications with its attorneys about a patentability search in an effort to corroborate inventor testimony for predating an alleged prior art reference. Because Acantha took the "affirmative step" of producing the privileged communications describing meetings and documents on conception and diligence, the district court found Acantha could not "selectively hide" behind the attorney-client privilege by withholding other privileged communications on conception and diligence given that "privilege cannot be used as both a sword and a shield."[316] The court though did allow Acantha to redact from the communications any portions unrelated to conception or diligence.[317]

Significantly, Federal Rule of Evidence 502(a) encompasses only intentional waivers of privilege "made in a federal proceeding or to a federal office or agency."[318] What are the consequences when an otherwise privileged communication or attorney work product-protected document is disclosed to a third party *prior to* (not "made in") litigation? This issue was addressed by the federal circuit in *Wi-LAN, Inc. v. LG Electronics, Inc.*[319]

Wi-LAN involved a dispute over whether LG owed royalties to Wi-LAN under a license to Wi-LAN's patents based on LG's use of "V-chip" technology for ratings-based blocking of television programs.[320] LG asserted it owed no royalties under the license because the technology was outside the scope of the licensed patents. Wi-LAN had received a confidential letter from its outside patent counsel that provided a detailed analysis of the Wi-LAN patent rights as applied to the V-chip technology and concluded LG's technology practiced the licensed patents.[321] Evidently hoping the strength of its counsel's opinion would cause LG to change its prior position on royalties, Wi-LAN intentionally forwarded the opinion letter to LG. After LG maintained its position, Wi-LAN filed suit for patent infringement.[322]

LG served a subpoena on Wi-LAN's outside counsel seeking documents and testimony relating to the subject matter of the opinion letter. The law firm moved to quash, arguing in part based on Rule 502(a) that, in fairness, the

314. *Id.*
315. 2017 WL 5186376, at *4–5 (E.D. Wisc. Nov. 8, 2017).
316. *Id.* at *5–6.
317. *Id.* at *6.
318. FED. R. EVID. 502(a).
319. 684 F.3d 1364 (Fed. Cir. 2012).
320. *Id.* at 1366–67.
321. *Id.* at 1367.
322. *Id.*

scope of the waiver should be limited to the opinion letter itself.[323] After the district court rejected the law firm's argument and held it in contempt, the firm appealed the contempt order.[324]

As a threshold matter, the federal circuit determined regional law (here the Ninth Circuit) applied because the issues concerned were not unique to patent law.[325] The question raised on appeal was whether, in determining the scope of the waiver, the Ninth Circuit would apply Rule 502(a)'s fairness balancing test to a prelitigation waiver, or if it would instead conclude the waiver extended to "all communications on the same subject matter."[326] Since the Ninth Circuit had not spoken on this issue, the federal circuit's opinion analyzed what the regional circuit would have done had it been presented with this question.

The federal circuit analyzed both Ninth Circuit and other regional circuit case law. It held the Ninth Circuit would have agreed with "the heavy weight of current authority that comes down on the side of employing fairness considerations to decide the scope of waivers."[327] Finding error in the district court's rejection of considerations of fairness, the federal circuit vacated the contempt order and instructed the district court to consider as part of its waiver analysis "whether LG would be unfairly prejudiced by Wi-LAN's assertion of privilege against discovery into attorney-client communications beyond the four corners" of the opinion letter.[328]

Writing in a separate *dubitante*[329] opinion, Judge Reyna expressed doubt as to whether "a trend in the law" exists such that "there must be a fairness balancing in the context of express extrajudicial waivers."[330] Judge Reyna explained "my instinct tells me the majority could be correct" but "I find that even a route that lies opposite the route charted by the majority is as good a route as any."[331]

B. Advice-of-Counsel Defenses by Accused Infringer

Patent infringement is a strict liability tort, and thus, generally speaking, the accused infringer's mental state is irrelevant.[332] There are two notable exceptions to this general rule.

The first exception relates not to liability itself but to damages; in particular, when a patentee alleges the infringement (whether direct or indirect) was

323. *Id.*

324. *Id.* at 1368; *see also* 28 U.S.C. § 1295(a).

325. *Id.* at 1368.

326. *Id.* at 1369–70.

327. *Id.* at 1373.

328. *Id.*

329. Latin for "doubting," the term is used to signal that the judge questions whether the decision rendered is correct. BLACK'S LAW DICTIONARY 499 (6th ed. 1990).

330. 684 F.3d at 1374 (Reyna, J., *dubitante*).

331. *Id.*

332. Commil USA, LLC v. Cisco Sys., Inc., 135 S. Ct. 1920, 1926 (2015).

willful. Complaints for patent infringement commonly include an allegation of willfulness, along with a plea for enhanced damages and attorneys' fees.[333] As discussed next, where an accused infringer is alleged to have acted willfully, evidence that the accused infringer relied upon competent legal advice could be relevant to whether or not the accused party acted willfully.

The second exception is when the claim is for actively inducing infringement under 35 U.S.C. section 271(b). In 2008, the federal circuit clarified that inducement requires that the alleged infringer knowingly induced the acts of another that directly infringe the patent, and that it did so with a specific intent to cause the other to infringe—that is, the accused infringer "knew or should have known his actions would induce actual infringements."[334] To show the requisite intent, both direct and circumstantial evidence of the accused infringer's state of mind may be used.[335]

In *Global-Tech Appliances, Inc. v. SEB, S.A.*, the Supreme Court overturned the "should have known" part of the inducement standard and clarified that to succeed in proving a claim for induced infringement under 35 U.S.C. section 271(b), a patentee must prove the accused infringer had "knowledge that the accused acts constitute patent infringement."[336] The Court clarified that while "deliberate indifference to a known risk that a patent exists" does not satisfy the knowledge requirement, actual knowledge may be proven under the doctrine of willful blindness.[337] Although *Global-Tech* did not involve any claim of privilege, the Court's holding touched on the possible utility of an exculpatory opinion of counsel as part of a defense to a claim of induced infringement.[338] When an accused infringer elects to rely on an opinion of counsel, it waives the attorney-client privilege to some extent.[339] The issues of the scope of the waiver (both in terms of the subject matter of the waiver and its temporal scope), and whether that waiver extends to attorney work product (including the work product of trial counsel), have been the subject of much litigation. As discussed in the following, the evolution of the law on waiver has arisen mostly in the context of the federal circuit's willfulness jurisprudence,

333. One survey, though dated, put the figure at over 90 percent. *See* Kimberly A. Moore, *Empirical Statistics on Willful Patent Infringement,* 14 Fed. Cir. B.J. 227, 232 (2005). One more recent publication states that findings of willful infringement dropped by about 10 percent in the three years after *In re Seagate* than in the three years before. *See* Christopher B. Seaman, *Willful Patent Infringement and Enhanced Damages after In re Seagate: An Empirical Study,* 97 Iowa L. Rev. 417, 441–42 (2012).

334. DSU Med. Corp. v. JMS Co., 471 F.3d 1293, 1306 (Fed. Cir. 2006) (quoting Manville Sales Corp. v. Paramount Sys., Inc., 917 F.2d 544, 553 (Fed. Cir. 1990)).

335. *Id.*

336. 131 S. Ct. 2060, 2068 (2011).

337. *Id.* at 2068–69.

338. *See, e.g.*, Broadcom Corp. v. Qualcomm Inc., 543 F.3d 683, 699 (Fed. Cir. 2008) (applying "knew or should have known" standard) (quoting *DSU*, 471 F.3d at 1305).

339. F & G Scrolling Mouse, L.L.C. v. IBM Corp., 190 F.R.D. 385, 391 (M.D.N.C. 1999).

although the end result should apply with equal force when the issue is raised in the context of induced infringement.

1. The *EchoStar* Decision

In *In re EchoStar Communications Corp.*,[340] an accused infringer relied on an exculpatory opinion from in-house counsel as a defense to willful infringement.[341] After commencement of the litigation, the accused infringer obtained, but chose not to rely upon, an opinion from outside legal counsel.[342] The district court held that the accused infringer waived the attorney-client privilege and work-product immunity by relying on the advice of its in-house counsel, and that the waiver extended to both in-house and outside opinion counsel.[343] The district court ordered the accused infringer to produce all pre-suit and post-suit communications relating to the opinions it received.[344] In addition, the district court ordered production from the outside opinion counsel of any attorney work product regarding the opinions—even if such work product was not communicated to the accused infringer.[345]

The federal circuit affirmed in part the district court's order. The appeals court held that by relying on advice of its in-house counsel, the accused infringer (EchoStar) waived the attorney-client privilege with respect to any communications involving the same subject as the opinion.[346] The waiver included communications with in-house counsel as well as the outside law firm.[347] However, the federal circuit reversed that part of the district court's decision that had ordered production of attorney work product that was *not* communicated from the outside opinion counsel to its client.[348]

The federal circuit in *EchoStar* identified three categories of work product relevant in addressing the opinion-of-counsel defense:

1. Documents embodying communications between the client and attorney pertaining to the subject matter of the case, such as an opinion letter
2. Documents analyzing issues, but not communicated to the client, reflecting an attorney's mental impression with respect to the subject matter of the case

340. 448 F.3d 1294 (Fed. Cir. 2006).
341. *Id.* at 1297.
342. *Id.*
343. *Id.*
344. *Id.*
345. *Id.*
346. 448 F.3d at 1299.
347. *Id.*
348. *Id.* at 1303–04.

3. Documents not communicated between the client and attorney, but that discuss communications relating to the subject matter between the client and attorney[349]

The court further concluded that the second category, uncommunicated work product, was not subject to the waiver because such uncommunicated work product has little or no bearing on the state of mind of the accused infringer.[350] The court affirmed the district court regarding the scope of the waiver of privilege with respect to the first and third categories of work product.

The *EchoStar* decision did not expressly address whether the waiver extended to work product of trial counsel. Nevertheless, in a footnote, the court stated that the waiver extended to advice and work product communicated after the litigation commenced.[351] This statement by the federal circuit led to much litigation over whether the scope of the waiver should be extended to the accused infringer's trial counsel.

One district court, applying *EchoStar*, concluded that the waiver extends to trial counsel in respect to privileged and work-product documents that contain advice related to the advice given by opinion counsel.[352] Other district courts extended the waiver to trial counsel's communications that question or contradict the opinion provided by the counsel that authored the opinion.[353] Still other district courts construed the waiver even more broadly, holding that any communications with trial counsel concerning the subject matter of infringement should be produced.[354]

2. The *Seagate* Decision

In 2007, the federal circuit rewrote the law of willful infringement in *In re Seagate Technology, L.L.C.*,[355] an en banc decision that reviewed a district court order compelling an accused infringer to produce all communications between it and any counsel, including its trial counsel, on the issues of infringement, invalidity, and enforceability of the patents-in-suit. The court's decision was significant in several respects.

First, the court held that proof of willful infringement requires "at least a showing of objective recklessness," which means "an objectively high likelihood that [the infringer's] actions constituted infringement of a valid patent."[356] The court in *Seagate* thus overruled the "affirmative duty of care" standard of

349. *Id.* at 1302.

350. *Id.* at 1302–04.

351. *Id.* at 1302 n.4.

352. Informatica Corp. v. Bus. Objects Data Integration, Inc., 2006 WL 2329460, at *3 (N.D. Cal. Aug. 9, 2006).

353. Intex Recreation Corp. v. Team Worldwide Corp., 439 F. Supp. 2d 46, 52 (D.D.C. 2006).

354. *See* Convolve, Inc. v. Compaq Computer Corp., 224 F.R.D. 98, 109–110 (S.D.N.Y. 2004), vacated by *In re* Seagate Technology, L.L.C., 497 F.3d 1360 (Fed. Cir. 2007).

355. 497 F.3d 1360 (Fed. Cir. 2007), *abrogated in part by* Halo Elecs., Inc. v. Pulse Elecs., Inc., 136 S. Ct. 1923, 1928 (2016).

356. *Id.* at 1371.

proof for willfulness that had governed patent cases since that standard was first announced, in 1983, in *Underwater Devices, Inc. v. Morrison-Knudsen Co., Inc.*[357] The court in *Seagate* explained that "[b]ecause we abandon the affirmative duty of due care [standard], we also reemphasize that there is no affirmative obligation to obtain [an] opinion of counsel."[358] This component of *Seagate* was later abrogated by the Supreme Court in *Halo*, as discussed further later.[359]

Second, the court held that, as a general rule, where the opinion-authoring attorney and trial attorney are different, the waiver of privilege caused by reliance on an opinion-of-counsel defense to willfulness does *not* constitute a waiver of the attorney-client privilege for the client's communications with its trial counsel.[360] The court explained that this rule was not absolute, and that it was possible for district courts in "unique" circumstances (such as when a party or its counsel engages in what the court referred to as "chicanery") to extend the waiver of attorney-client privilege to its trial counsel.[361]

Third, the court held that, absent exceptional circumstances, the waiver resulting from an accused infringer's reliance on an opinion-of-counsel defense to willfulness does not extend to trial counsel's work product. The court explained that "trial counsel's mental processes . . . enjoy the utmost protection from disclosure."[362] As it did with the issue of privilege, the court in *Seagate* left open the possibility that a situation might arise in which the waiver of work-product immunity could be extended to trial counsel.

Apart from any issue of waiver of work product, the court in *Seagate* reiterated the general standard for discovery of attorney work product. Under this general rule, which is not unique to patent cases, "non-opinion" work product is not discoverable, unless the party seeking the discovery makes a showing of substantial need for the materials and undue hardship without it. Furthermore, "opinion work product" (i.e., the mental impressions, thought processes, analyses, and conclusions of counsel) is generally not discoverable absent "exceptional circumstances."[363] Thus, the general standards for discovery of attorney work product in patent cases were not altered by the *Seagate* decision.

3. Post-*Seagate* Decisions

A number of district courts applied the federal circuit's decisions in *EchoStar* and *Seagate* in defining the scope of the waiver when an accused infringer wishes to rely upon an advice-of-counsel defense. Those courts refused to extend the waiver to trial counsel unless there were "exceptional circumstances."

357. 717 F.2d 1380 (1983).
358. *Seagate*, 497 F.3d at 1371.
359. 136 S. Ct. 1923 (2016).
360. *497 F.3d* at 1373.
361. *Id.* at 1374–75.
362. *Id.* at 1375–76.
363. *Id.* at 1375.

a. Waiver Extended to Trial Counsel

In *Tyco Healthcare Group L.P. v. E-Z-EM, Inc.*,[364] the district court held that when opinion-authoring counsel was an active member of the accused infringer's trial team, "exceptional circumstances" existed that warranted discovery of trial counsel's privileged communications and work product.

In *Tyco*, the patentee filed suit in 2007 alleging willful infringement. The accused infringer, E-Z-EM, received its first notice of infringement when it was served with the complaint. Several weeks after the lawsuit was filed, an attorney (Scott) with the law firm of Alston & Bird provided E-Z-EM with an opinion letter relating to the subjects of claim construction, invalidity, noninfringement, and unenforceability. E-Z-EM retained Alston & Bird as trial counsel, and Scott was a member of its trial team and participated actively in the case.

In March 2010, E-Z-EM produced the opinion letter intending to rely upon it in defense of the willfulness allegation.[365] Plaintiff filed a motion to compel production of every item on defendant's privilege log, as well as other communications that were not identified on the log.[366]

The district court noted that even under the *Seagate* standard, "trial courts remain free to exercise their discretion in unique circumstances to extend waiver to trial counsel."[367] The court held that by having Scott participate on the trial team, the defendant "blurred" the distinction between the distinct functions of trial counsel and opinion counsel.[368] The court further held that, if the opinion was prepared in light of trial strategy, the plaintiff had a right to discovery of such information.[369]

The district court thus concluded that this was a case of "unique circumstances" envisioned by *Seagate*, and the court found a broad waiver.[370] In particular, the court held that E-Z-EM waived the attorney-client privilege for all communications on the subjects included in the opinion letter.[371] The court further found that the waived communications included those between (1) the opinion author and the client, (2) the opinion author and the rest of the trial team, and (3) the trial team and the client.[372] The court also concluded that E-Z-EM waived work-product immunity for all attorney work product on the same subject matter included in the opinion letter to the extent that such work product was communicated to the client.[373]

---

364. 2010 WL 2079920 (E.D. Tex. May 24, 2010).
365. *Id.* at *1.
366. *Id.*
367. *Id.* at *2 (quoting *Seagate*, 497 F.3d at 1374–75).
368. *Id.* at *3.
369. *Id.*
370. *Id.*
371. *Id.*
372. *Id.*
373. *Id.*

In another case where the opinion co-author was a member of the defendant's trial team, the district court subject to certain conditions permitted a deposition of the opinion co-author also acting as trial counsel. For example, the court instructed that trial counsel would not be deposed about trial-related communications or strategies, non-disclosed work product, or counsel's state of mind.[374]

b. Waiver Not Extended to Trial Counsel

In *Duhn Oil Tool Inc. v. Cooper Cameron Corp.*,[375] defendant asserted an opinion-of-counsel defense to plaintiff's charge of willful infringement. The opinion was on the subject of noninfringement. The authors of the opinion were from a different law firm than trial counsel. The opinion-authoring attorneys were deposed and communications between them and the client were produced. Defendant refused to produce any communications with what it characterized as "trial counsel," citing *Seagate*.[376]

Plaintiff thereafter noticed the deposition of defendant's "in-house counsel" (Vyas) and sought his testimony, documents relating to the opinions received from opinion counsel, and additional (allegedly undisclosed) opinions. According to plaintiff, Vyas and defendant's trial counsel were conducting "a separate infringement analysis" (presumably meaning separate from that of opinion counsel), and they were providing advice to the defendant on design-around options.[377] Plaintiff argued that it was entitled "to review 'the full extent of communications and the information Mr. Vyas and [defendant] considered, as well as any other opinions regarding the subject of infringement.'"[378]

Defendant resisted this discovery, asserting that Vyas was actually its "in-house *trial* counsel," and that as such, his communications were privileged and immune from discovery under *Seagate*.[379] Presumably to buttress this assertion, one month *after* plaintiff's motion to compel was filed, Vyas filed an application to appear pro hac vice (which the district court judge signed the next day).[380]

The court granted plaintiff's motion to compel. At the outset, the court remarked that Vyas had never before during the three-year history of the litigation been identified as anything other than "in-house counsel."[381] The court

374. *See, e.g.*, NewRiver, Inc. v. Newkirk Prods., Inc., 2008 WL 5115244, at *3–4 (N.D.N.Y. Dec. 4, 2008) (where co-author of opinion also served as trial counsel, court permitted the deposition of trial counsel but strictly limited the scope of the waiver only to certain prelitigation communications and not to post-litigation communications or work product).

375. 2009 WL 3381052 (E.D. Cal. Oct. 15, 2009).

376. *Id.* at *2.

377. *Id.*

378. *Id.*

379. *Id.* at *15.

380. *Id.*

381. *Id.*

further explained that it "is free to exercise its discretion in 'unique circumstance to extend waiver to trial counsel.'"[382] It concluded that "this case presents unique circumstances justifying its finding."[383] The court ordered Vyas's deposition testimony to cover the period in time prior to the date when he filed his pro hac vice application. For the time period *after* the pro hac vice application was filed, Vyas would be considered "trial counsel" and was not subject to discovery under *Seagate*.

c. Other Waiver Examples Post-Seagate

Where there was no issue over the separate identities of trial counsel and opinion counsel, other cases, decided post-*Seagate*, have limited the scope of the waiver to opinion counsel without implicating trial counsel's privilege or work product. Thus, unless there is something unique or unusual about the circumstances, courts generally will not extend the waiver to post-litigation communications with trial counsel. Furthermore, in circumstances where the opinion was received prior to the initiation of the litigation, courts following *Seagate* have limited the temporal scope of the waiver only to the pre-suit documents and communications on the grounds that any of the post-suit documents or communications were of "marginal value" to the willfulness inquiry.[384]

An additional point to note is that not all allegedly improper disclosures of advice of counsel at trial will warrant reversible error or a new trial. For example, in *ePlus, Inc. v. Lawson Software, Inc.*,[385] defendant's witness testified in response to defense counsel's questioning that it had solicited a "lay opinion" from one of its employees to the effect that after the employee had learned about the lawsuit he read the patents and concluded defendant was not infringing.[386] Plaintiff's counsel, on redirect examination, asked whether defendant had obtained a legal opinion of any kind, to which the defense witness answered affirmatively.[387] When plaintiff's counsel sought to ask whether

---

382. *Id.*

383. *Id.*

384. *See, e.g.*, V. Mane Fils, S.A. v. Int'l Flavors & Fragrances Inc., 2009 WL 1968925, at *5–6 (D.N.J. July 1, 2009) (refusing request to order production of post-suit documents pertaining to willful infringement); Se-Kure Controls, Inc. v. Diam USA, Inc., 2008 WL 169029, at *3 (N.D. Ill. Jan. 17, 2008) (requiring production of communications prior to the filing of the litigation); SPX Corp. v. Bartec USA, L.L.C., 247 F.R.D. 516, 526–27 (E.D. Mich. 2008) (communications with trial counsel that postdate the filing of the litigation "most likely have bearing on the question of willfulness or [defendant's] reliance upon counsel's advice to shape its accused pre-suit conduct"); Convolve, Inc. v. Compaq Computer Corp., 2007 WL 4205868, at *5 (S.D.N.Y. Nov. 26, 2007) (following *Seagate* and holding that "there is no basis here for taking discovery of in-house counsel's communications after the litigation was commenced").

385. 2011 WL 3584313 (E.D. Va. Aug. 12, 2011), *vacated in part on other grounds*, 700 F.3d 509 (Fed. Cir. 2012).

386. 2011 WL 3584313, at *9.

387. *Id.*

defendant had produced the opinion to plaintiff during discovery, defendant objected, and the court shut down the line of questioning.[388] The court later struck the question and gave a limiting instruction to the jury.[389]

Defendant argued posttrial that even though the court sided with defendant, plaintiff "unfairly created an inference in the jury's mind that [defendant] secured an unfavorable legal opinion and behaved improperly by failing to disclose this opinion to [plaintiff]."[390] The court rejected this argument, finding defendant suffered no prejudice and even if there were prejudice it was cured by its instruction to the jury.[391] The district court further held that the Fourth Circuit follows the presumption that the jury obeys the limiting instructions of the district court.[392] The court thus concluded no "miscarriage of justice" occurred warranting a new trial on infringement.[393]

4. The *Halo* Decision

In 2016, the Supreme Court in *Halo Electronics Inc. v. Pulse Electronics*[394] abrogated the *Seagate* willfulness test, holding its objectively reckless standard to be "unduly ridged."[395] Halo involved the appeal of two cases where, in both, the juries found willful infringement or a high probability of willful infringement. However, the federal circuit found no willful infringement in both cases, based on the Seagate test. The Court acknowledged that in many respects, the Seagate test reflected a sound recognition that enhanced damages are appropriate only in egregious cases under section 284, but ultimately found the test to be "unduly rigid, and . . . impermissibly encumbers the statutory grant of discretion to district courts."[396] The Court explained,

> The principal problem with *Seagate's* two-part test is that it requires a finding of objective recklessness in every case before district courts may award enhanced damages. Such a threshold requirement excludes from discretionary punishment many of the most culpable offenders, such as the "wanton and malicious pirate" who intentionally infringes another's patent—with no doubts about its validity or any notion of a defense—for no purpose other than to steal the patentee's business. Under *Seagate,* a district court may not even consider

388. *Id.*
389. *Id.*
390. *Id.*
391. *Id.*
392. *Id.* (citing Hinkle v. City of Clarksburg, W. Va., 81 F.3d 416, 427 (4th Cir. 1996) and United States v. Francisco, 35 F.3d 116, 119 (4th Cir. 1994)).
393. *Id.*
394. 136 S. Ct. 1923 (2016).
395. *Id.* at 1932 (*quoting* Octane Fitness LLC v. ICON Health & Fitness, Inc., 134 S. Ct. 1749, 1755 (2014)).
396. *Id.*

> enhanced damages for such a pirate, unless the court first determines that his infringement was "objectively" reckless. In the context of such deliberate wrongdoing, however, it is not clear why an independent showing of objective recklessness—by clear and convincing evidence, no less—should be a prerequisite to enhanced damages.[397]

The Supreme Court explained that section 284 "imposes no specific evidentiary burden" and allows district courts to punish a variety of culpable behaviors, such that the district should exercise their discretion in a manner free from the inelastic constraints of the *Seagate* test.[398] The Supreme Court's relaxing of the willfulness standard thus has the potential to broaden the scope of waiver concerns.

5. Post-*Halo* Decisions

In *Visteon Global Technologies, Inc. v. Garmin International, Inc.*,[399] an action for patent infringement against Garmin, Visteon alleged that Garmin's infringement was willful.[400] Visteon sought to introduce evidence at trial that Garmin obtained opinions of Garmin's in-house counsel regarding all asserted patents. Garmin elected not to waive attorney-client privilege with respect to those opinions and not to use them at trial.[401] Garmin moved in limine to prevent Visteon's arguments regarding Garmin's opinions of counsel.[402]

The court permitted Visteon to submit evidence of Garmin's failure to provide an opinion of counsel at trial, but the court prohibited Visteon from submitting evidence that Garmin had obtained opinion of counsel but decided to maintain attorney-client privilege and not produce that opinion at trial.[403] The court commented that such a ruling "strikes an appropriate balance between disallowing the prohibited adverse inference to Garmin of an unfavorable opinion of counsel while at the same time preserving Visteon's right to argue to the jury that Garmin's failure to produce such an opinion for trial can be considered as a factor in the jury's determination of willfulness."[404]

In *Krausz Industries Ltd. v. Smith-Blair. Inc.*,[405] the court expanded that scope of waiver when a defendant asserted an opinion of counsel defense against willful infringement claims. At the time that defendant Smith-Blair launched its allegedly infringing product ("Top-Bolt"), it had engaged the services of

---

397. *Id.* (internal citations omitted).
398. *Id.* at 1933–34.
399. 2016 WL 4396085 (E.D. Mich. Aug. 18, 2016).
400. *Id.* at *1.
401. *Id.* at *5.
402. *Id.*
403. *Id.*
404. *Id.*
405. Krausz Industries Ltd. f/k/a Krausz Metal Industries Ltd. v. Smith-Blair Inc. & Sensus USA Inc., 2016 WL 10538004 (E.D.N.C. Dec. 13, 2016).

the Wood Herron law firm to analyze whether the Top-Bolt would infringe Krausz's patent.[406] Wood Herron then issued opinion letters concluding that the product would not infringe.[407]

Krausz initiated a patent infringement lawsuit against Smith-Blair in August 2012, whereby Smith-Blair hired the Smith Anderson law firm as its trial counsel in January 2013.[408] Smith Anderson claimed that it occasionally sought input from Wood Herron, given their familiarity with the '556 patent.[409]

Smith-Blair disclosed its intention to rely on Wood Herron's opinion as part of its defense against claims of willful infringement and subsequently submitted a copy of a Wood Herron opinion letter.[410] However, the parties disagreed over whether the waiver arising from opinion of counsel defenses would extend to communications occurring after litigation began.[411] Krausz argued that the waiver applies to a vast array of topics with no temporal scope, while Smith-Blair maintained that waiver applies only to communications regarding infringement of the '556 patent that occurred prior to litigation commencing.[412]

Krausz noted that the court in *In re EchoStar* extended the waiver beyond the time of filing the lawsuit if the patentee alleged ongoing willful infringement. However, Smith-Blair argued that *Halo* limits *In re EchoStar's* applicability to only prelitigation conduct in assessing whether infringement was willful.[413] The court agreed with Krausz and noted the following:

> Here, Krausz alleges that Smith-Blair is engaged in ongoing willful infringement, and, therefore, Smith-Blair's post-filing conduct will be relevant to the question of whether it has engaged in the kind of egregious behavior that justifies an award of enhanced damages. *See Halo Electronics*, 136 S. Ct. at 1933 (explaining that "Section 284 allows district courts to punish the full range of culpable behavior"). In light of the appropriate scope of the court's inquiry on the question of enhanced damages, there is no reason to restrict the temporal scope of the waiver resulting from the assertion of an advice of counsel defense to pre-litigation communications.[414]

---

406. *Id.* at *2.
407. *Id.*
408. *Id.*
409. *Id.*
410. *Id.* at *2.
411. *Id.*
412. *Id. at *4.*
413. *Id.* at *5 ("[Smith-Blair's] position is based upon the Supreme Court's statement in *Halo Electronics* that 'culpability is generally measured against the knowledge of the actor at the time of the challenged conduct' and the Federal Circuit's comment in *In re Seagate* that 'willfulness ordinarily will depend on an infringer's prelitigation conduct.").
414. *Id.* at *5.

By involving Wood Herron in the substantive defense of litigation, Smith-Blair "engaged in the type of conduct that justifies allowing discovery into any communications either involving or relaying information from opinion counsel to Smith-Blair, its trial counsel, or its in-house counsel."[415] However, the court restricted the scope specifically to communications involving whether Smith-Blair's product infringes the '556 patent.

6. Advice of Counsel after the AIA

Under the America Invents Act, section 298 was added to Title 35 of the U.S. Code. Titled "Advice of Counsel," section 298 states: "The failure of an infringer to obtain the advice of counsel with respect to any allegedly infringed patent, or the failure of the infringer to present such advice to the court or jury, may not be used to prove that the accused infringer willfully infringed the patent or that the infringer intended to induce infringement of the patent."[416] Section 298 applies only to lawsuits commenced on or after January 14, 2013, without regard to the issue date of the patent.[417]

In one post-AIA action, *On Track Innovations Ltd. v. T-Mobile USA, Inc.*, the district court permitted a plaintiff-patentee to amend its complaint after fact discovery closed to add a claim for induced infringement.[418] The accused infringer argued it was prejudiced by the late amendment since, without previous notice of induced infringement claims, it had no reason to seek an opinion of counsel.[419] The defendant further noted that an opinion of counsel could be relevant to the intent element of the new inducement claim.[420] The court rejected defendant's prejudice argument for two reasons. First, the court noted that expert discovery had not closed and "there is no reason this evidence cannot now be obtained."[421] Second, the court relied on section 298 as foreclosing any prejudice based on the absence of an opinion, explaining that "while OTI is free to argue that an opinion of counsel letter obtained after the allegedly infringing acts is immaterial to T-Mobile's intent at the time, it is statutorily barred from arguing that any failure to obtain the advice of counsel with respect to the '043 Patent is probative of T-Mobile's intent to induce infringement."[422]

After *Global-Tech,* it remained unclear whether opinions of counsel advising on issues other than infringement would be relevant in response to a claim

---

415. *Id.* at *1.

416. 35 U.S.C. § 298.

417. *Id.* § 1(n).

418. 2014 WL 406497, at *5 (S.D.N.Y. Feb. 3, 2014).

419. *Id.* at *3.

420. *Id.* (citing *Bettcher Indus., Inc. v. Bunzl USA, Inc.*, 661 F.3d 629, 649 (Fed. Cir. 2011) (opinion of counsel regarding noninfringement "admissible, at least with respect to [defendant's] state of mind and its bearing on indirect infringement").

421. 2014 WL 406497, at *3.

422. *Id.* at *3 (citing 35 U.S.C. § 298).

for induced infringement. In *Global-Tech*, the Supreme Court stated that the mens rea requirement concerns whether the accused infringer had "knowledge that the accused acts constitute patent *infringement*."[423] What remained unclear was whether *Global-Tech* was to be interpreted to preclude reliance on opinions regarding other legal defenses to a claim of infringement, such as invalidity or inequitable conduct. This issue was addressed by the Supreme Court in *Commil USA, L.L.C. v. Cisco Systems, Inc.*[424]

While *Commil* was before the federal circuit, a divided panel held that the district court erred in refusing to allow the accused infringer from presenting evidence at trial of its good-faith belief of invalidity to rebut the allegation of induced infringement.[425] The court stated, "We see no principled distinction between a good-faith belief of invalidity and a good-faith belief of non-infringement for the purpose of whether a defendant possessed the specific intent to induce infringement of a patent" since, as a matter of law, "one cannot infringe an invalid patent."[426] Accordingly, the court held, "a good-faith belief of invalidity is evidence that may negate the specific intent to encourage another's infringement, which is required for induced infringement."[427]

But the Supreme Court disagreed, noting that liability for infringement is separate from issues of invalidity.[428] The Court noted that there are practical reasons not to create a defense of belief of invalidity, since accused inducers have proper ways of obtaining a ruling to that effect, such as seeking an ex parte reexamination.[429] The decision thus narrowed the possible utility of exculpatory opinion of counsel defenses, holding that the good-faith belief of a patent's invalidity is not a defense to induced infringement.[430] Opinion letters addressing patent invalidity are no longer a basis to "negate the scienter

---

423. 131 S. Ct. at 2068 (emphasis added).

424. 135 S. Ct. 1920, 1926 (2015).

425. Commil USA, LLC v. Cisco Systems, Inc., 720 F.3d 1361, 1367 (Fed. Cir. 2013), *reh'g en banc denied*, 737 F.3d 699 (Oct. 25, 2013), *vacated*, 135 S. Ct. 1920 (2015).

426. 720 F.3d at 1368 (citing Prima Tek II, L.L.C. v. Polypap, S.A.R.L., 412 F.3d 1284, 1291 (Fed. Cir. 2005) ("there can be no . . . induced infringement of invalid patent claims"), and *Richdel, Inc. v. Sunspool Corp.*, 714 F.2d 1573, 1580 (Fed. Cir. 1983) ("The claim being invalid there is nothing to be infringed.")).

427. *Id.* at 1368; *see also* VNUS Med. Techs., Inc. v. Diomed Holdings, Inc., 2007 WL 2900532, at *2 (N.D. Cal. Oct. 2, 2007) (denying plaintiff's motion for summary judgment on induced infringement based, in part, on an opinion of counsel that the patents-in-suit were invalid); DataQuill Ltd. v. High Tech Computer Corp., 887 F. Supp. 2d 999, 1014 (S.D. Cal. 2011) (indicating that a belief of invalidity may present a triable issue of fact as to intent to induce infringement); *see also* Lemley, *Inducing Patent Infringement*, 39 U.C. DAVIS L. REV. 225, 243 (2005) ("[I]t is not reasonable to assume that merely because a defendant is aware of the existence of a patent, he intended to infringe it. He may believe the patent invalid. . . .").

428. 135 S. Ct. at 1922 ("Because induced infringement and validity are separate issues and have separate defenses under the Act, belief regarding validity cannot negate § 271(b)'s scienter requirement of "actively induce[d] infringement.").

429. *Id.*

430. 135 S. Ct. at 1928.

required under § 271(b)."[431] Taken together, the Supreme Court's *Global-Tech* and *Commil* decisions "require a showing of the accused infringer's subjective knowledge as to the underlying direct infringement."[432]

C. Waiver Based on Crime-Fraud Exception

Issues of intent in patent cases are not limited to the accused infringer's state of mind. In many patent cases, the accused infringer alleges that the patent-in-suit is unenforceable because the patentee committed inequitable conduct during proceedings before the USPTO. In *Therasense, Inc. v. Becton, Dickinson & Co.*, the federal circuit tightened the standard for proving inequitable conduct.[433] Under *Therasense*, a patent may be unenforceable based on clear and convincing evidence that the patentee/applicant knowingly made a material misrepresentation or knowingly omitted a material fact with specific intent to deceive the USPTO.[434] The test for materiality in most cases is whether the patent would have issued but for the misstatement or omission, also referred to as "but for" materiality.[435] The federal circuit further explained that "but for" materiality was akin to the reliance element of common law fraud.[436]

An assertion of inequitable conduct places into issue the state of mind of the inventor, prosecuting attorney, and/or in-house personnel who were substantially involved in the prosecution of the patent-in-suit. When inequitable conduct is an issue, the alleged infringer may attempt to "pierce" the patentee's attorney-client privilege under what is commonly referred to as the crime-fraud exception. This exception addresses communications made by the client to the attorney in furtherance of an ongoing or future crime or fraud.[437]

As aptly explained by Justice Benjamin Cardozo: "A client who consults an attorney for advice that will serve him in the commission of a fraud will have no help from the law. He must let the truth be told."[438] To pierce the privilege, the movant "must demonstrate that there is a reasonable basis to suspect (1) that the privilege holder was committing or intending to commit a crime or fraud, and (2) that the attorney-client communication or attorney work product was used in furtherance of that alleged crime or fraud."[439]

---

431. *Id.*

432. Unwired Planet, LLC v. Apple Inc., 829 F.3d 1353, 1364 (Fed. Cir. 2016) (finding the district court's reliance on the objective strength of defendant's noninfringement argument erroneous since it precluded a finding of induced (or contributory) infringement).

433. 649 F.3d 1276 (Fed. Cir. 2011) (en banc).

434. *Id.* at 1291.

435. *Id.* at 1292. An exception to requiring evidence of "but for" materiality is when the patentee engages in "affirmative egregious misconduct," such as the filing of an "unmistakably false affidavit." *Id.* at 1292–93.

436. *Id.* at 1295.

437. United States v. Zolin, 491 U.S. 554, 563 (1989); Clark v. United States, 289 U.S. 1, 15 (1933); *In re Antitrust Grand Jury*, 805 F.2d 155, 162 (6th Cir. 1986).

438. *Clark*, 289 U.S. at 15.

439. *In re Grand Jury*, 705 F.3d 133, 155 (3d Cir. 2012).

The precise level of proof required to succeed on a motion to compel based on the crime-fraud exception is subject to some debate. The traditional definition requires the party invoking the exception to provide "prima facie evidence that it has some foundation in fact."[440] But "prima facie" is a slippery standard, and the Supreme Court has since recognized that it has resulted in "some confusion" among the lower courts.[441]

According to the federal circuit, to invoke the crime-fraud exception in a patent case, the party challenging the privilege "must make a *prima facie* showing that the communication was made 'in furtherance of' a crime or [common law] fraud."[442] As one district court explained in denying a motion to pierce a patent holder's privilege, "The fraud element of the crime-fraud exception must be demonstrated by evidence such that 'the proposed factual basis must strike a prudent person as constituting a reasonable basis to suspect the perpetration or attempted perpetration of a . . . fraud, and that the communications were in furtherance thereof.'"[443]

To establish a fraud, the party challenging the privilege must show (1) a misrepresentation of a material fact, (2) with intent to deceive, (3) reliance upon the misrepresentation by the party deceived, and (4) resultant injury.[444] Common law fraud includes both affirmative misrepresentations of a material fact, as well as a failure to disclose a material fact.[445]

In establishing the fraud necessary for an accused infringer to attempt to pierce the patentee's privilege in a patent infringement case, the most difficult areas usually involve making the requisite prima facie showings of deceptive intent and detrimental reliance. Rarely is there a "smoking gun" that unequivocally establishes intent to deceive the USPTO.[446] Thus, proof of deceptive intent must ordinarily be inferred from the facts and circumstances surrounding the applicant's conduct.[447] While there must be a factual basis for a finding of deceptive intent,[448] the withholding of a material prior art reference can, in some cases, warrant the inference of intent to deceive the USPTO.[449] "In a case involving nondisclosure of information, clear and convincing evidence must

---

440. *Clark*, 289 U.S. at 15.

441. *Zolin*, 491 U.S. at 563 n.7.

442. *In re Spalding Sports Worldwide, Inc.*, 203 F.3d 800, 807 (Fed. Cir. 2000).

443. Ergo Licensing, L.L.C. v. Carefusion 303, Inc., 263 F.R.D. 40, 46 (D. Me. 2009) (quoting Fuller v. Interview, Inc., 2009 WL 3241542, at *3 (S.D.N.Y. Sept. 30, 2009)).

444. *Spalding*, 203 F.3d at 807.

445. *See, e.g.*, Restatement (Second) of Torts 551(1).

446. Paragon Podiatry Lab., Inc. v. KLM Labs., Inc., 984 F.2d 1182, 1189–90 (Fed. Cir. 1993); LaBounty Mfg., Inc. v. U.S. Int'l Trade Comm'n, 958 F.2d 1066, 1076 (Fed. Cir. 1992).

447. Molins PLC v. Textron, Inc., 48 F.3d 1172, 1180–81 (Fed. Cir. 1995).

448. Hebert v. Lisle Corp., 99 F.3d 1109, 1116 (Fed. Cir. 1996) (citing Kingsdown Med. Consultants Ltd. v. Hollister, Inc., 863 F.2d 867 (Fed. Cir. 1988)).

449. Baxter Int'l, Inc. v. McGaw, Inc., 149 F.3d 1321, 1330 (Fed. Cir. 1998) (affirming district court's determination that withholding highly material prior art manifested a culpable state of mind sufficient to warrant a finding of an intent to deceive the USPTO).

show that the applicant made a deliberate decision to withhold a known material reference."[450]

Prior to *Therasense*, courts were split on the question of whether, in addition to meeting the common law standard for fraudulent intent, the party seeking to invoke the crime-fraud exception must also establish that the USPTO relied on the misrepresentation. Some district courts held that reliance need not be proven.[451] Other district courts reached the contrary conclusion.[452] In *Nobelpharma AB v. Implant Innovations, Inc.*, for example, the district court held that "[t]he fact misrepresented must be 'the efficient, inducing, and proximate cause, or the determining ground' of the action taken in reliance thereon."[453] Although it is dicta in that case, the federal circuit's decision in *Spalding* also contains language suggesting that proof of reliance is necessary to pierce privilege.[454] Post-*Therasense*, the reliance element of common law fraud has collapsed into the "but for" element of inequitable conduct.[455]

District courts also have grappled with what showing a party must make in order to establish the intent element of fraud. In *Therasense*, the court held that to satisfy the intent prong for inequitable conduct, specific intent to deceive must be the "single most reasonable inference."[456] Notably, *Therasense* did not involve the crime-fraud exception to the attorney-client privilege. In *Unigene Laboratories, Inc. v. Apotex, Inc.*, the federal circuit, in a post-*Therasense* opinion, upheld a district court's denial of an alleged infringer's motion to breach the attorney-client privilege under the crime-fraud exception.[457]

In *Unigene*, the district court declined to find a patent applicant's failure to disclose an allegedly material prior art reference, as well as errors in a table included in the specification, was material and further failed to find sufficient evidence of fraudulent intent.[458] Applying federal circuit law to the crime-fraud issue, the court held that "[a] party must establish *Walker-Process* fraud, also known as common law fraud, to successfully pierce the attorney-client privilege under the crime-fraud exception."[459] With respect to the intent standard, the court in *Unigene* stated, "A finding of common law fraud in the

450. *Molins*, 48 F.3d at 1181.

451. Manville Sales Corp. v. Paramount Sys., Inc., 1987 WL 16888, at *2–5 (E.D. Pa. Sept. 11, 1987); Synair Corp. v. Am. Indus. Tire, Inc., 645 F. Supp. 1080, 1085 (S.D. Tex. 1986).

452. *See, e.g.*, Domestic Sales Corp. v. Intertherm, Inc., 1988 WL 492342, at *12 (N.D. Ind. Mar. 28, 1988); Research Corp. v. Gourmet's Delight Mushroom Co., 560 F. Supp. 811, 820 (E.D. Pa. 1983).

453. 141 F.3d 1059, 1070 (Fed. Cir. 1998) (quoting *Norton v. Curtiss*, 433 F.2d 779, 794 (C.C.P.A. 1970)).

454. *In re Spalding Sports Worldwide, Inc.*, 203 F.3d 800, 806–07 (Fed. Cir. 2000).

455. Therasense, Inc. v. Becton, Dickinson & Co., 649 F.3d 1276, 1295 (Fed. Cir. 2011) (en banc) (holding that "reliance" in the context of common law fraud "is equivalent to the but-for test for materiality set forth in this opinion").

456. *Id.* at 1290.

457. 655 F.3d 1352, 1355 (Fed. Cir. 2011).

458. *Id.* at 1357.

459. *Id.* at 1358 (citing Walker-Process Equip., Inc. v. Food Mach. & Chem. Corp., 382 U.S. 172, 177 (1965)).

patent context 'must be based on independent and clear evidence of deceptive intent.'"[460] The court in *Unigene* did not cite *Therasense* anywhere in its opinion, relying instead upon its much earlier pronunciations (specifically *Spalding* and *Nobelpharma*) of the elements of the crime-fraud exception in patent cases. The federal circuit held the district court did not abuse its discretion in refusing to pierce the privilege "because the record is devoid of sufficient intent evidence."[461]

In *Shelbyzyme, L.L.C. v. Genzyme Corp.*, the district court denied a motion to reconsider its order granting in part a defense motion for production of privileged documents based on the application of the crime-fraud exception.[462] The district court inferred deceptive intent from the contents of an email and rejected plaintiff's assertion that intent to deceive was not the "single most reasonable inference."[463] The district court noted based on *Unigene* that it "is unconvinced that the *Therasense, Inc.* standard has been imported into the crime-fraud context."[464] The court also concluded that, under the circumstances, intent to deceive was in fact the single most reasonable inference.[465] Accordingly, the district court denied the motion for reconsideration.[466]

The patentee thereafter filed a petition for writ of mandamus with the federal circuit.[467] The circuit court denied the petition, holding "the court is not prepared to disturb on the limited record before us" the district court's disclosure order.[468] Finally, the court further stated plaintiff "has alternative avenues to obtain meaningful review of its arguments after trial."[469] As for the "meaningful review" statement, one might question its accuracy since once the privileged documents are produced, they are no longer confidential; plaintiff may not "unring the bell" even if ultimately successful on appeal.[470] In deciding whether the requirements of the crime-fraud exception have been satisfied in a particular case, the district court may review the disputed documents in camera.[471] In fact, some courts hold that in camera review is required

---

460. *Id.* at 1358–59 (quoting *Spalding*, 203 F.3d at 803).

461. *Id.* at 1359.

462. 2013 WL 3229964, at *1, 6 (D. Del. June 25, 2013).

463. *Id.* at *2 n.2.

464. *Id. But see In re Method of Processing Ethanol Byproducts & Related Subsystems ('858) Patent Litig.*, 2014 WL 2938183, at *5 & nn. 6–7 (S.D. Ind. June 30, 2014) (holding that distinction in *Spalding* between common law fraud and inequitable conduct has been "substantially eroded by *Therasense*," and that in the context of the crime-fraud exception, intent to deceive "must be the single most reasonable inference").

465. *Id.*

466. *Id.* at *26.

467. *In re Shelbyzyme L.L.C.*, 547 Fed. Appx. 1001 (Fed. Cir. Dec. 12, 2013) (nonprecedential).

468. *Id.* at 1002.

469. *Id.*

470. *See* United States v. Lowis, 174 F.3d 881, 885 (7th Cir. 1999) (noting "unring the bell is a good analogy and can save a lot of words in making the point" regarding prejudice to a party based on evidentiary ruling).

471. *Zolin*, 491 U.S. at 565–70.

before the court can order the production of documents that would otherwise be privileged.[472] The evidentiary showing that is necessary in order to justify in camera review is less than the showing necessary to actually overcome the privilege.[473] All that is required to justify in camera review is "a factual basis adequate to support a good faith belief by a reasonable person that [the court's] review of the materials may reveal evidence to establish the claim that the crime-fraud exception applies."[474]

For example, in *Global Tubing, LLC v. Tenaris Coiled Tubes, LLC*, the district court conducted an in camera review and granted a motion to compel production of a clawed back draft inventor affidavit.[475] The affidavit included the following statement about the CYMAX brochure: "I am not sure it is a good idea to disclose this document."[476] The motion to compel raised whether withholding portions of the CYMAX brochure from the USPTO amounted to fraud that vitiated the attorney-client privilege under the crime-fraud exception.[477] Based on the internal discussion of the CYMAX brochure, its overlap with the asserted patent, and the decision to "dissect" and withhold certain portions of the brochure, the court found a sufficient showing that a reasonable person would expect the draft affidavit to contain evidence of fraud, thereby justifying in camera review of the "offending paragraph" in the affidavit.[478] Based on its in camera review, the court found that the paragraph included a "rare example of direct evidence of an intent to defraud" and was not a privileged communication because a communication about "future fraudulent conduct" is not protected.[479] Not only did the court find that the accused infringer made a prima facie showing that the CYMAX brochure and its Specifications section were material to the prosecution of the asserted patent, but also the court found that the inventor affidavit filed with the USPTO, due to its false nature, constituted egregious misconduct.[480] Thus, the court concluded that the accused infringer established a prima facie case that the affidavit contained evidence that the "attorney-client relationship was used in furtherance of committing a fraud on the PTO" and required production of the withheld documents relating to the CYMAX brochure.[481]

A patentee that is accused of inequitable conduct may want to rely upon an opinion of the patentee's counsel that the patent owner acted in good faith or did not intend to deceive the USPTO. The federal circuit apparently has not

472. *In re Antitrust Grand Jury*, 805 F.2d 155, 168–69 (6th Cir. 1986).
473. *Zolin*, 491 U.S. at 570–72.
474. *Id.* at 572 (internal quotes and citation omitted).
475. 2021 WL 1169322, at *1, 8, 12 (S.D. Tex. Mar. 26, 2021).
476. *Id.* at *8.
477. *Id.* at *3, 5.
478. *Id.* at *3, 8.
479. *Id.* at *8.
480. *Id.* at *9 & n.9.
481. *Id.* at *10–12.

decided whether such an assertion would result in a waiver of privilege.[482] Applying the reasoning of *Seagate*, at least one district court that has considered this issue concluded that a patentee who relies upon privileged communications to establish a "good faith" defense to inequitable conduct waives the attorney-client privilege as to all other communications relating to the same subject matter.[483] In determining the scope of the waiver, the district court applied the standard set forth by the federal circuit in *Fort James Corp. v. Solo Cup Co.*[484] The district court concluded that "the waiver applies not only to otherwise privileged communications between the attorney and client, but also to any of the attorney's documents which reflect the substance of such advice, even if such documents would otherwise be immune from discovery under the work-product doctrine."[485] The court noted that the scope of the waiver did not extend to work product that was not communicated to the client.[486]

VII. Conclusion

There have been many published decisions on the subject of privilege and immunity in patent cases. Unfortunately, few of those decisions are from the federal circuit, which has exclusive appellate jurisdiction in patent cases. Consequently, it can be difficult in any particular patent case to draw bright-line rules or to know with reasonable certainty how a district court will rule on a particular privilege or work-product issue. Because of this uncertainty, parties who anticipate litigating patent rights would be wise *not* to assume that documents they thought might be privileged will, in fact, be treated that way by the district court judge.

As a general rule, parties should be careful not to make potentially embarrassing written admissions or concessions on critical issues such as patent scope, validity, or infringement, as such admissions may be discoverable. Finally, parties should also be cautious in the way they handle and disseminate legal advice, and they would be wise to institute practices to strictly limit the disclosure of such advice and to take measures that protect the confidentiality of legal advice.

482. *See* Brigham & Women's Hosp., Inc. v. Teva Pharms. USA, Inc., 707 F. Supp. 2d 463, 470 (D. Del. 2010).

483. *Id.* at 471.

484. 412 F.3d 1340, 1349–50 (Fed. Cir. 2005) (finding reversible error in the district court's determination of the scope of waiver stemming from produced opinions on applicability of the on-sale bar).

485. Brigham & Women's Hosp., Inc. v. Teva Pharms. USA, Inc., 707 F. Supp. 2d at 472.

486. *Id.* at 472 n.8.

CHAPTER 11

Litigating Attorney-Client Privileges under the United States Bankruptcy Code and the Federal Rules of Bankruptcy Procedure

TOBY L. GERBER AND JANE A. GERBER

Tips for Asserting Protection in Bankruptcy	**Tips for Opposing Protection in Bankruptcy**
• Identify the party controlling the privilege within the bankruptcy proceeding. • If a party other than the pre-petition holder controls the privilege, or control is in dispute, seek court order authorizing new holder to control the privilege. • Assert protections of common interest doctrine. • Guard against inadvertent sending of privileged information and promptly take steps to correct. • If crime/fraud exception or *Garner* exception is asserted, seek to keep such exceptions from being extended in bankruptcy matters. • Argue damage to debtor by waiver is significant and waiver would not significantly benefit creditors of the estate.	• Assert that a debtor claiming the privilege no longer controls the privilege by virtue of the Bankruptcy Code. • Argue that the party asserting the privilege does not have the requisite qualifications to assert the privilege. • Challenge asserted application of the common interest doctrine. • Seek and assert waiver of the privilege by the debtor-in-possession, bankruptcy trustee, examiner, committee, or other party controlling the privilege. • Argue exceptions to privilege under crime/fraud and *Garner* decision. • Argue maintenance of the privilege for benefit of the debtor is outweighed by Bankruptcy Code goal of maximizing recovery to creditors.

I. Privilege Disputes in Bankruptcy Are Different Than in Other Courts Because the Bankruptcy Code Operates to Transfer Control of the Privilege from a Debtor to Its Bankruptcy Fiduciary

At the heart of any attorney-client or work-product privilege dispute in a proceeding under the United States Bankruptcy Code[1] is the question of "who controls the privilege?" Outside bankruptcy, the question is typically answered through identification of the attorney's client, along with the client's protected rights and powers in respect of the privilege. In bankruptcy however, identification of who originally controlled the privilege is only the beginning of the process.[2]

The Bankruptcy Code operates under the legal fiction that a debtor's property and associated rights and privileges become "property of the bankruptcy estate."[3] In all Chapter 7 and Chapter 11 cases,[4] the bankruptcy estate must be administered by a fiduciary. In Chapter 7, the fiduciary is a Chapter 7 trustee.[5] In Chapter 11, the debtor serves as debtor-in-possession unless a Chapter 11 trustee is appointed.[6]

The bankruptcy fiduciary is responsible for investigating the debtor's financial affairs; for marshalling, protecting, and reorganizing or liquidating

1. 11 U.S.C. §§ 101 *et seq.* (the Bankruptcy Code).

2. "[F]ederal common law governs control of a debtor's privilege. The question of privilege asserted in bankruptcy court is a procedural question and existing federal law is to be used." Gottlieb v. Fayerman (*In re* Ginzburg), 517 B.R. 175, 182 (Bankr. C.D. Cal. 2014) (citations omitted). The Bankruptcy Code creates "a two-part scheme for turnover of property of the estate or other information related to the debtor's property or financial affairs." Keller v. Blinder (*In re* Blinder, Robinson & Co., Inc.), 140 B.R. 790, 792 (D. Colo. 1992). Section 542(a) requires anyone holding property of the estate to deliver it to the trustee. Section 542(e) authorizes a court, "[s]ubject to any applicable privilege, . . . [to] order an attorney, accountant, or other person that holds recorded information . . . relating to the debtor's property or financial affairs, to turn over or disclose such recorded information to the trustee." Bankruptcy Code § 542(e). "Congress's purpose in adding § 542(e) to the Code was 'to restrict . . . the ability of accountants and attorneys to withhold information from the trustee,' and thus to eliminate their leverage, under State-law lien provisions, to command payment before other creditors by withholding information needed to administer the estate." Foster v. Hill (*In re* Foster), 188 F.3d 1259, 1265 (10th Cir. 1999) (citations omitted).

3. The commencement of a bankruptcy case creates an estate comprised of (with some exceptions) "all legal or equitable interests of the debtor in property as of the commencement of the case." Bankruptcy Code § 541(a)(1).

4. The discussion in this chapter is limited to typical proceedings under Bankruptcy Code chapters 7 (liquidation) and 11 (reorganization), however nearly identical concepts of "property of the estate" and the role of a trustee fiduciary exist under certain specialized subchapters of Chapter 11 and under other chapters of the Bankruptcy Code. *See* Bankruptcy Code §§ 1161–1174 (railroad reorganizations), §§ 1181–1195 (small business reorganizations), §§ 1201–1232 (relating to family farmers or fishermen with regular annual income), and §§ 1301–1330 (relating to individuals with regular income). In contrast, such concepts do not exist under Bankruptcy Code Chapter 9, governing the adjustment of debt of municipalities.

5. Bankruptcy Code §§ 701–702.

6. Bankruptcy Code §§ 1101(a), 1104.

the debtor's assets; and for maximizing the value distributed to creditors in accordance with the priorities of applicable law. Bankruptcy courts typically cite the fiduciary's duty to maximize distributions to creditors as the primary justification for placing control of the debtor's privileges in the fiduciary's hands.[7]

Exercise of fiduciary duties involves gathering and using information from the debtor, including confidential material that may be subject to the attorney-client privilege or work-product doctrine. With control of the privilege, the fiduciary may assert or waive the privilege in furtherance of her duties.

II. The Attorney-Client Privilege of a Company in Bankruptcy Is Controlled by Whoever Manages the Company in Bankruptcy

Outside bankruptcy, management is empowered to assert or waive a corporation's attorney-client privilege.[8] Commencement of a corporate bankruptcy case shifts that control to the bankruptcy fiduciary in both Chapter 7 and Chapter 11.

In 1985, the United States Supreme Court confirmed in *Commodity Futures Trading Commission v. Weintraub*[9] that upon the trustee's waiver of the corporate debtor's privilege, the Bankruptcy Code required a corporate debtor's attorney to disclose all information relating to the debtor's property and financial affairs to the bankruptcy trustee, and held that the estate fiduciary held control of the attorney-client privilege applicable to such information. The *Weintraub* Court explained that the transfer of control of the corporate privilege to the trustee was based on the Bankruptcy Code's goal of maximizing the value of the estate to creditors.[10] Pursuant to section 542(e):

> Subject to any applicable privilege, after notice and a hearing, the court may order an attorney . . . that holds recorded information . . . relating to the debtor's property or financial affairs, to disclose such recorded information to the trustee. . . . [t]he legislative history also makes clear

---

7. Whether this justification withstands scrutiny may be subject to debate and is outside the scope of this discussion; however, as noted *infra*, bankruptcy courts are frequently called upon to balance the goal of maximizing returns to creditors against the harm caused to an individual debtor by disclosure of otherwise privileged information.

8. Whether a corporation can assert the attorney-client privilege depends on "whether the corporation is 'dead' as opposed to being in some other state, such as a windup phase, bankruptcy or liquidation, or having merged into or been acquired by a successor." Red Vision Sys., Inc. v. Nat'l Real Estate Information Servs., L.P., 2015 Pa. Super. 5, 108 A.3d 54, 65 (Pa. Super. 2015); *see also* Trading Techs. Int'l, Inc. v. GL Consultants, Inc., 2012 WL 874322, at *4 (N.D. Ill. Mar. 14, 2012) (citation omitted).

9. 471 U.S. 343 (1985).

10. *Id.* at 353.

> that Congress did not intend to give the [corporate] debtor's directors the right to assert the corporation's attorney-client privilege against the [bankruptcy] trustee. Indeed, statements made by Members of Congress regarding the effect of [said provision] "specifically deny any attempt to create an attorney-client privilege assertable on behalf of the debtor against the trustee."[11]

Importantly, *Weintraub* does not apply to an individual's bankruptcy proceeding.[12]

In most corporate Chapter 11 cases, the corporation becomes the debtor-in-possession, with management transformed into a fiduciary to creditors, and remaining in control of the privileges. The bankruptcy court, for cause, may order replacement of management and the debtor-in-possession with a Chapter 11 trustee.[13] Thus, in a common corporate bankruptcy proceeding, a fiduciary holds control of the privilege, with the power to assert or waive it in accordance with the best interests of the estate.

The principal duties of a fiduciary in a corporate Chapter 11 are to "investigate the acts, conduct, assets, liabilities and financial condition of the debtor, the operation of the debtor's business and the desirability of the continuance of such business and any other matter relevant to the case or to the formulation of a plan."[14]

The Bankruptcy Code also grants an estate fiduciary powerful legal tools, including authority and standing to bring actions on behalf of the estate for turnover of property from third persons, to object to and subordinate claims and interests, to avoid and recover fraudulent and preferential transfers, and to pursue a debtor's claims against third parties, including insiders of the debtor.[15] These activities frequently result in litigation and involve disputes over assertion and waiver of the attorney-client privilege and the work-product doctrine.

---

11. *Id.* at 350–51 (citations omitted).

12. *Weintraub* held that management continued its control of the corporate privilege in bankruptcy as part of its fiduciary responsibilities as debtor-in-possession, in comparison to the rights of an individual debtor. "[A] corporation, as an inanimate entity, must act through agents. . . . An individual, in contrast, can act for himself; . . . no 'management' . . . controls a solvent individual's attorney-client privilege. If control over that privilege passes to a trustee [of an individual debtor], it must be under some theory different from the one that we embrace in this case." *Id.* at 356–57 (citation omitted). *See In re Foster*, 188 F.3d 1259, 1265–66 (10th Cir. 1999).

13. Chapter 11 trustees shall be appointed "for cause, including [the debtor's] fraud, dishonesty, incompetence, or gross mismanagement of the affairs of the debtor by current management, either before or after commencement of the case . . . or if such appointment is in the interests of creditors. . . ." Bankruptcy Code § 1104(a)(1)–(2).

14. Bankruptcy Code § 1106(a)(3). Similar duties exist for a corporate Chapter 7 trustee. *See* Bankruptcy Code § 704.

15. *See, e.g.*, Bankruptcy Code §§ 502, 510, 523, 542, 543, 547, 548, 549, and 550.

In the course of most Chapter 11 proceedings, the debtor-in-possession, acting through management, may be conflicted in performing certain of its duties, including administering the estate, pursuing third-party claims pre-confirmation, administering a plan, litigating third-party claims post-confirmation, and liquidating assets because the interests of the estate may be adverse to the corporation's insiders. Where such a conflict hampers the debtor-in-possession's performance of its duties (and appointment of a Chapter 11 trustee is not appropriate), the bankruptcy court may be asked to appoint an unconflicted party[16] to act on behalf of the estate. Typically, the scope of the appointment is limited to specific matters such as actions to avoid a transfer or recover property of the estate. In such situations, however, bankruptcy courts and district courts sitting in bankruptcy do not necessarily view such appointees as fiduciaries qualified to exercise control of the corporation's privilege.[17]

III. The Attorney-Client Privilege of an Individual in Bankruptcy Generally Remains with the Individual unless the Bankruptcy Trustee Can Establish an Exception to the Privilege

In Chapter 7, a trustee is appointed to marshal, administer, and liquidate the property of the estate, including intangible assets such as claims against third parties. In the rare individual Chapter 11, the debtor herself may act as a debtor-in-possession with the powers of a bankruptcy trustee. In either case, control of the attorney-client privilege remains with the individual debtor

---

16. Courts have granted standing to official committees, examiners, plan trustees, litigation trustees, and liquidating trustees, among others. *See In re* Boileau, 736 F.2d 503 (9th Cir. 1984) (holding than an examiner appointed with expanded powers by stipulation of the parties held the authority to waive the debtor's attorney-client privilege); Am. Int'l Specialty Lines Ins. Co. v. NWI-I, Inc., 240 F.R.D. 401 (N.D. Ill. 2007) (finding that entities created under a bankruptcy plan that were transferred certain of the debtor's assets but were not in control of the debtor's business did not result in a transfer of the debtor's privilege); Official Comm. of Unsecured Creditors v. Fleet Retail Fin. Group (*In re* Hechinger Inv. Co. of Del., Inc.), 285 B.R. 601 (D. Del. 2002) (finding that the liquidating trust created pursuant to the debtor's confirmed plan controlled the privilege, but also finding that the liquidating trust's efforts to preserve that privilege was inadequate and therefore any privilege was waived).

17. The Bankruptcy Code also authorizes other parties-in-interest to access information regarding the pre-petition debtor and, in some cases, to administer property of the estate including the estate's legal claims against the pre-petition debtor and other third parties. Bankruptcy Code § 1102 authorizes appointment of an official committee to represent the interests of creditors of the estate, and Bankruptcy Code § 1103 authorizes the committee to investigate the acts, conduct, and financial affairs of the debtor. Since a committee does not have management powers akin to the debtor-in-possession or a Chapter 11 trustee, courts have been reluctant to find that committees should be granted control over the attorney-client privilege, even when appointed to pursue claims which the debtor-in-possession cannot or will not investigate or pursue. *In re* Big M, Inc., 2013 WL 1681489 (Bankr. D. N.J. Apr. 17, 2013) (the power to assert or waive attorney-client privilege does not pass to a committee asserting causes action on behalf of the estate because the committee is a fiduciary only to the creditor body, not to the estate itself), *citing G-I Holding, infra.*

and does not pass to a fiduciary, at least until a valid reason is established for another party-in-interest to exercise control or by establishment of an exception to the privilege.

Bankruptcy courts have noted that an individual debtor has limited fiduciary duties to the bankruptcy estate and, unlike a corporate debtor, retains important legal rights separate from her interests in the property that forms the bankruptcy estate. As stated in *In re Mack Industries, Ltd.*,[18] a Chapter 7 debtor has statutory duties[19] to cooperate with the trustee and surrender property and related recorded information, but no fiduciary responsibilities. Some courts believe that the Chapter 7 trustee should have no role in asserting or waiving the attorney-client privilege.[20]

Individual bankruptcy cases also create a difficult issue over control of the attorney-client privilege that arises when a Chapter 7 trustee seeks authority to waive an individual debtor's privilege and disclose otherwise confidential information that would harm the debtor in matters unrelated to the bankruptcy estate. However, most courts hold that an individual Chapter 7 debtor's privileges do not transfer to the trustee.[21] Other courts take a balancing approach that weighs potential harm to the individual Chapter 7 debtor by allowing the trustee to control the debtor's privileges against the trustee's need for privileged information in the administration of the estate.[22]

In *In re Bazemore*,[23] the court compared the importance of the underlying purposes of the attorney-client privilege (promoting full and frank discussions in an attorney-client relationship by sanctifying the confidential nature of the relationship) and the potential harm caused by disclosure of confidential information, on the one hand, with the benefits to estate of enabling the Chapter 7 trustee to access information helpful to maximizing distributions to creditors. The test is fact-sensitive and requires a case-by-case application.[24]

---

18. 606 B.R. 313, 319 (Bankr. N.D. Ill. 2019).

19. Bankruptcy Code § 521(a)(3), (4).

20. *See, e.g., In re* Miller, 247 B.R. 704 (Bankr. N.D. Ohio 2000) (information from debtor's former attorney might be used in criminal prosecution of debtor; denying trustee access did not significantly hamper trustee's ability to represent estate and maximize recovery to creditors).

21. *In re* Smith, 24 B.R. 3, 5 (Bankr. S.D. Fla. 1982); *In re* Ingram, 1999 WL 33486089, *5–6 (Bankr. D.S.C. 1999); *In re* Bounds, 443 B.R. 729, 734–35 (Bankr. W.D. Tex. 2010); *In re Hunt*, 153 B.R. 445, 454 (Bankr. N.D. Tex. 1992).

22. *In re* Bame, 251 B.R. 367, 376 (Bankr. D. Minn. 2000); *In re* Miller, 247 B.R. 704, 709 (Bankr. N.D. Ohio 2000); *In re Rice*, 224 B.R. 464, 469 (Bankr. D. Or. 1998); *In re* Bazemore, 216 B.R. 1020, 1024 (Bankr. S.D. Ga. 1998). *See also* Foster v. Hill (*In re* Foster), 188 F.3d 1259, 1265 (10th Cir. 1999) (remanding the case so that the bankruptcy court could determine whether the documents from pre-petition civil litigation were attorney-client privileged, whether the Fifth Amendment barred pre-petition counsel from producing the documents, and whether the trustee's need for the information outweighed any harm to the debtor).

23. 216 B.R. 1020, 1024 (Bankr. S.D. Ga. 1998).

24. *See* Whyte v. Williams (*In re* Williams), 152 B.R. 123 (Bankr. N.D. Tex. 1992) (liquidating trustee succeeded to the debtor-in-possession as fiduciary to the estate under a confirmed Chapter 11 plan).

In *Gottlieb v. Fayerman (In re Ginzburg)*,[25] however, the bankruptcy court refused to apply the *Bazemore* balancing test, relying on the Supreme Court's decision in *Swidler & Berlin v. United States*.[26] In *Swidler*, the Court refused to recognize any exception to the attorney-client privilege based upon a test that weighs the importance of the information sought against the client's interest in preserving the privilege.[27] "Thus, federal common law simply prohibits the balancing of the trustee's duties and need for the information with debtor's attorney client privilege."[28]

IV. Balancing the Benefits of a Fiduciary's Control over the Attorney-Client Privilege against the Damage to the Corporate Debtor

In contrast, courts generally need not apply a *Bazemore* test to a corporation's attorney-client privilege if the debtor-in-possession or a Chapter 11 trustee controls the privilege. Bankruptcy fiduciaries have no obligation to manage the attorney-client privilege for the benefit or protection of the pre-petition debtor or debtor's insiders.[29]

This is especially evident in matters in which the estate, on the one hand, and the pre-petition debtor's management, shareholders, or principals, on the other, are adverse. As a practical matter, a debtor-in-possession operated by pre-petition management is not likely to pursue claims against corporate insiders or to waive the debtor's attorney-client privilege or work-product

25. 517 B.R. 175 (Bankr. C.D. Cal. 2014).

26. 524 U.S. 399 (1998). *Swidler* addressed a federal grand jury subpoena for notes from an attorney's initial consultation with a client who later died. The Court rejected the argument that the public interest in determining whether a crime had been committed outweighed the importance of confidentiality, even after the client had died. Central to this reasoning was that "the loss of evidence admittedly caused by the privilege is justified in part by the fact that without the privilege, the client may not have made such communications in the first place. This is true of disclosure before and after the client's death." *Id.* at 408 (citation omitted).

27. *Id.* at 409.

28. Gottlieb v. Fayerman (*In re* Ginzburg), 517 B.R. 175, 182 (Bankr. C.D. Cal. 2014).

29. A bankruptcy trustee, entrusted with the vast responsibilities of a corporation, has the power to waive the corporation's attorney-client privilege with respect to prebankruptcy communications. *See* Commodity Futures Trading Comm'n v. Weintraub, 471 U.S. 343, 358 (1985). Courts have also interpreted *Weintraub* to recognize a bankruptcy fiduciary's right to assert or waive the attorney-client privilege of a special committee to the debtor's board of directors. *See In re* Tribune Co. Fraudulent Conveyance Litig., Case No. 11-cv-02296 (RJ) (S.D.N.Y. 2012) (ECF No. 7245) (trustee of litigation trust appointed under Chapter 11 plan succeeded to control of privilege of dissolved special committee to board which had reviewed disputed LBO transaction); *In re* China Med. Techs. Inc., 539 B.R. 643 (S.D.N.Y. 2015) (liquidator in Chapter 15 proceedings succeeded to control of pre-petition audit committee privilege), *but see In re* BCE West LP, 2000 WL 1239117 (S.D.N.Y. 2000) (finding special committee's privilege was legally "distinct" from board's privileges and denying litigation trustee control of the committee's privilege).

privileges with respect to matters involving such a claim.[30] In such cases (and absent appointment of a Chapter 11 trustee), bankruptcy courts have granted standing to other parties-in-interest, usually an official committee of creditors, to pursue the action against insiders.

However, in such situations, most courts have refused to extend *Weintraub*'s holding (corporate privilege is controlled by the party responsible for management of the bankruptcy estate) to a creditors' committee whose fiduciary responsibilities run only to the creditors of the estate, even when successful pursuit of the claim will benefit the entire estate.

In *Official Committee of Asbestos Claimants of G-I Holding, Inc. v. Heyman*,[31] the committee was appointed to prosecute the Chapter 11 estate's fraudulent claims against the debtor and its principal, including challenging a spin-off transaction allegedly structured to separate important corporate assets from asbestos liabilities.[32] The debtor asserted the attorney-client privilege and refused to produce information and communications developed in connection with the transaction. The committee offered three theories why the privilege was not applicable: (1) *Weintraub*'s holding that corporate insiders cannot withhold information from a bankruptcy trustee should apply to a duly-authorized committee; (2) the fiduciary exception of *Garner v. Wolfinbarger*[33] defeated the corporation's assertion of the privilege; and (3) the fraud exception to attorney-client privilege applies to fraudulent transfer claims. The *G-I Holding* court refused to extend *Weintraub*'s holding that control of the privilege was incidental to the managerial powers of a Chapter 11 trustee, finding that the committee's powers were not the same as those of a Chapter 11 trustee. As such, the committee could not exercise the powers of a debtor-in-possession or Chapter 11 trustee and thus did not control the privilege. The court also rejected the committee's invocation of the fraud exception for failure to establish probable cause that a fraudulent transfer took place.[34]

The court instead focused on *Garner*'s "good cause" requirement and applied the fiduciary exception to the privilege, finding that an insolvent debtor

30. If the debtor-in-possession commenced an action against the debtor's principal, it would create a situation in which the principal, as the control person of the debtor-in-possession, would be giving directions to its attorneys as a plaintiff; and the same principal, as a defendant, would be giving directions to her attorneys as defendant. Said one candid debtor's attorney: "I think it's an understatement to say that is not going to happen." Official Comm. of Asbestos Claimants of G-I Holding, Inc. v. Heyman, 342 B.R. 416, 422 (S.D.N.Y. 2006).

31. 342 B.R. 416 (S.D.N.Y. 2006).

32. The use of a spin-off or "divisive merger" to separate mass tort liabilities from a corporation's core assets, often known as the "Texas Two-Step," is a relatively new, controversial bankruptcy strategy. Liabilities are transferred to the newly created entity along with limited assets. The new entity promptly files a voluntary bankruptcy petition and a proposed plan to use only the limited property of the bankruptcy estate to resolve the tort claims.

33. 430 F.2d 1093 (5th Cir. 1970) (if "good cause" exists, a fiduciary cannot assert the privilege to prevent disclosure to its constituency of information bearing on performance of its fiduciary duties).

34. 342 B.R. at 427.

owed a fiduciary duty to its creditors, that the official committee represented the estate's creditors, and thus was a beneficiary of the debtor's fiduciary duties. Moreover, since the committee had standing to pursue an apparently meritorious claim against the debtor, it had a substantial need to discover the information. Thus "good cause" existed to require disclosure of the privileged information under the so-called fiduciary exception to the privilege.[35]

In *In re HH Liquidation, LLC,*[36] a committee was granted standing to pursue fraudulent transfer and breach of fiduciary claims against the debtors and insiders in connection with pre-petition asset transfers, but the stipulation of standing reserved the right of the debtors to assert privilege objections. The court denied the committee access to allegedly privileged information on grounds that (1) *Weintraub* is applicable only to Chapter 7 trustees, and (2) under applicable Third Circuit law, absent a fiduciary responsibility to the entire estate (e.g., management duties), the committee had to establish the debtor had a duty to its creditors at the time the privileged communication took place in order to control the privilege, citing *Teleglobe Communications v. BCE.*[37] The Delaware court held that the committee could not gain control of the privilege unless it proved that the debtor was insolvent at the time the privileged communications occurred, insolvency being the linchpin to shifting the corporation's fiduciary responsibilities to its creditors.

While management may retain control of the attorney-client and work-product privileges, committees in Chapter 11 cases frequently target management, equity, and insiders under Bankruptcy Code section 548, which authorizes recovery of fraudulent transfers, including those made by the debtor with actual fraudulent intent. The statute also provides a defense to a transferee who has taken the transfer in good faith and for value. Bankruptcy courts have held that a transferee availing herself of the "good faith" defense places issues of her knowledge and intent at issue, and thereby waives her attorney-client and work-product privileges as to documents relevant to those issues.[38]

In addition, Bankruptcy Code section 1104(c) authorizes appointment of an examiner to investigate the affairs of the estate.[39] Whether the examiner will gain control of the privilege however appears to be governed by the specific powers granted in the order appointing her, as observed in *In re*

35. *Id.* at 424–25.

36. 571 B.R. 97 (Bankr. D. Del. 2017).

37. Teleglobe Commc'ns v. BCE, Inc. (*In re* Teleglobe Commc'ns Corp.), 493 F.3d 345, 367 (3d Cir. 2007) (unless a corporation is insolvent, it has no fiduciary duties to its creditors).

38. *In re* Mongelluzzi, 568 B.R. 702 (Bankr. M.D. Fla. 2017); *see In re Gibco*, 185 F.R.D. 296 (D. Colo. 1997).

39. *See In re* Residential Capital, LLC, 474 B.R. 112 (Bankr. S.D.N.Y. 2012); Loral Stockholders Protective Commc'n v. Loral Space & Commc'n, Ltd. (*In re* Loral Space & Commc'n, Ltd.), 2004 WL 2979785 (S.D.N.Y. Dec. 23, 2004); *In re* YC Atlanta Hotel, LLC, 630 B.R. 348 (Bankr. N.D. Ga. 2021).

Boileau.[40] However, most examiners are appointed to more limited duties listed in Bankruptcy Code section 1106(a)(4)(A) and ". . . except to the extent that the court orders otherwise, any other duties of the trustee that the court orders the debtor in possession not to perform."[41] Without express court authority to waive the privilege, the examiner is unlikely to exercise control over the privilege.

Finally, upon confirmation and effectiveness of a Chapter 11 plan, a "plan trustee," liquidating trustee, and or litigation trustee may be appointed to administer, market, and liquidate assets of the estate to create funds for distribution to creditors under the plan. Those assets may include property such as claims that implicate exercise of the pre-petition privileges; as such the post-confirmation fiduciary may, but not necessarily, wind up in control of the privilege.[42] Ultimately, it would appear that the best practice to ensure both clarity and a plan trustee's right to control a debtor's privilege is for the plan itself to expressly authorize a transfer of control.

V. Consideration of the Common Interest Doctrine in Bankruptcy

Although the various constituencies within a bankruptcy proceeding are typically adverse to each other, reorganization and restructuring proceedings are almost always based upon compromise and shifting alliances in order to reach an orderly resolution of the debtor's affairs. As the alliances are formed to further common goals and the need for privileged information arises, application of the joint defense/common interest privilege often comes into play.

The common interest doctrine permits parties with common interests to coordinate their legal positions through sharing otherwise privileged communications and information without waiving the privilege. The doctrine is commonly understood to require "(1) the communication was made by separate parties in the course of a matter of common interest; (2) the communication

---

40. 736 F.2d 503 (9th Cir. 1984) (holding that the examiner had authority to waive debtor's attorney-client privilege). The *Boileau* court held that because the examiner had been appointed by stipulation with expanded powers similar to that of a trustee, including to maximize the value of the estate, he could waive the privilege. The court noted: "Our holding is not to be understood as a ruling on the authority of an examiner to waiver the attorney-client privilege. We simply hold that under the particular facts of this case the waiver authority resided in the examiner." *Id.* at 506.

41. *See, e.g., In re* Metro. Mortg. & Secs. Co., No. 04-00757, Order (Apr. 9, 2004) (Bankr. E.D. Wash. Apr. 9, 2004) (ECF No. 535) ("[T]he Examiner shall have the power to waive, on an issue-by-issue basis, the attorney-client privilege of the Debtors' estates with respect to prepetition communications relating to matters investigated by the Examiner.").

42. Whyte v. Williams (*In re* Williams), 152 B.R. 123 (Bankr. N.D. Tex. 1992) (liquidating trustee succeeded to the debtor-in-possession as fiduciary to the estate under a confirmed Chapter 11 plan); *but see* Foster v. Hill (*In re* Foster), 188 F.3d 1259, 1268 (10th Cir. 1999) (apparently limiting *Williams* to matters in which there is no harm to the debtor).

was designed to further that effort; and (3) the privilege has not otherwise been waived."[43]

In bankruptcy, a debtor may need to share privileged information with a committee, with non-debtor affiliates, or other parties for purposes of administration of the estate or confirmation of a plan. The privilege might otherwise be waived but for application of the common interest doctrine; however bankruptcy presents a rather complicating factor in that there are fundamental adverse relationships among the constituencies that are sometimes temporarily set aside to achieve specific goals. Whether such alliances amount to a "common legal interest" requires analysis on a case by case basis.

In *In re Leslie Controls, Inc.*,[44] prior to filing bankruptcy, the debtor shared privileged information with respect to asbestos insurance coverage with an ad hoc committee of asbestos claimants and the future claims representative.[45] After the bankruptcy was filed, the insurers sought the shared information from the debtor in connection with a coverage dispute before the bankruptcy court, asserting that the privilege had been waived. The court held that debtor, the ad hoc committee, and the future claims representative held a common legal interest, particularly preserving and maximizing the insurance available to pay asbestos claims, even though those parties may have been adverse on other questions (e.g., such as liability and amount of a particular creditor or constituency recovery). In fact, the scope of the privilege is limited by the scope of the common legal interest, such that communications relating to matters in which the parties hold adverse interests lose any privilege.[46]

The *Leslie Controls, Inc.* court noted that other courts have held that pre-bankruptcy plan negotiations between a debtor and its creditors might present a somewhat different dynamic and a different result:

> The common interest exception does not protect information exchanged among parties simply because they are negotiating toward what they hope will be an agreement. During negotiations, adverse parties "ha[ve] no common interest, and indeed, their interests [a]re in conflict—each [party] want[s] to get the best deal from the other [ ], and to the extent that one succeed[s] in its goal, the other suffer[s]." As a result, until an agreement is actually reached, it is not "objectively reasonable for [a negotiating party] to believe that" a communication of privileged material to other negotiating parties "was confidential"

43. *In re* Cherokee Simeon Venture I, LLC, 2012 WL 12940975, at *2 (Bankr. D. Del. May 31, 2012).

44. 437 B.R. 493 (Bankr. D. Del. 2010).

45. The common interest doctrine has been upheld for communications among other bankruptcy constituencies. *See, e.g.*, *In re* Tribune Co., 2011 WL 386827 (Bankr. D. Del. Feb. 3, 2011) (communications among unsecured creditors and secured creditors); *In re* Mortgage & Realty Trust, 212 B.R. 649 (Bankr. C.D. Cal. 1997) (communications among debtor's counsel, debtor's responsible officer and creditor committee counsel).

46. 437 B.R. at 500.

> and thus protected by the common interest privilege because, while negotiating parties "may all have hoped for a successful outcome, [ ] each side is representing its or their own interest, and a successful outcome was not assured."[47]

Denial of protection for pre-agreement communications appears to be based upon a belief that a common interest is not formed until an agreement is reached. Once reached, the parties then have a common interest for successful performance of the agreement.[48] But in situations where the parties have both common and adverse interests, the court should examine whether the shared information was disclosed in furtherance of the common legal interest, and, if so, the privilege is preserved.[49]

Bankruptcy cases are further complicated by the typical interconnection (and sometimes blurring) of common legal interests (covered by the privilege) with common financial interests (not covered). In *In re Simplexity, LLC*,[50] after settling with a senior secured creditor accused of wrongful acts against the estate, the Chapter 7 trustee sued the debtor's former management for similar actions, claiming management, not the secured creditors, was responsible for the debtor's misfortune.[51] The Chapter 7 trustee asserted that communications and information shared among the Chapter 7 trustee, his counsel, and the secured creditor was protected by the common interest doctrine because the secured creditor would share in any recovery from management. The court, however, determined that common interest to be financial rather than legal and held the doctrine inapplicable, finding that the secured creditor had no legal exposure to the Chapter 7 trustee or to the management defendants. "Instead, [the secured creditor] sits on the sidelines and hopes that the Trustee, . . . will achieve success, collect on a judgment, and pay [the secured creditor] its share of the proceeds. Surely that is a financial interest, not a legal one."[52]

In addressing the common interest doctrine, whether asserting or opposing its application, it is vital to specifically identify the claimed common legal interest, and, recognizing that many issues may be contained within the alleged privileged communications, identify the particular issues on which the parties' interests may diverge. Additionally, any resolution of negotiations (e.g., a settlement agreement or plan term sheet) should be memorialized such that a common legal interest for success of the agreement will be recognized.

---

47. 437 B.R. at 502 (*citing* Louisiana Mun. Police Employees Retirement Sys. v. Sealed Air Corp., 253 F.R.D. 300, 309 (D.N.J. 2008)). Denial of protection for pre-agreement communications appears to be based upon a belief that a common interest is not formed until an agreement is reached. Once reached, the parties then have a common interest for successful performance of the agreement.

48. *But see In re* Teleglobe Commc'ns Corp. 493 F.3d 345.

49. 437 B.R. at 502–03.

50. 584 B.R. 495 (Bankr. D. Del. 2018).

51. *Id.*

52. *Id.*

CHAPTER 12

Communications with Public Relations Consultants

MARK D. HINDERKS

Tips for Asserting Protection	Tips for Opposing Protection
• Develop and document litigation-focused goals for public relations (PR) consultation (not PR-focused goals relating to client's image or market presence) and only reveal information to PR consultants that is tied to that goal, that is, to enable legal advice. • Alternatively, protection may be available in some circumstances if PR consultant is the "functional equivalent" of a client employee or decision-maker; requires fact-supported integration with client, and expected responsibility for dealing with legal matters. • Avoid blanket inclusion of PR consultants on all legal team communications. • Claim work-product protection in addition to attorney-client privilege; although it may be overcome in some circumstances with a showing of need, the work-product doctrine often applies when attorney-client privilege does not.	• Characterize adversary's sharing of information with PR consultants as for ordinary public relations purposes, not necessary or indispensable to enable legal advice. • Examine involvement of PR professionals to undermine their status as a proxy for the client in the attorney-client relationship, particularly focus on any lack of responsibility for legal matters and absence of decision-making authority for the client. • Look for ways to categorize communications with PR professionals as broad and business related, beyond the narrow pigeonholes of recognized protection.

I. The Nature of the Issue

Many high-profile cases or cases involving high-profile clients involve an intersection of public relations and law. The public perception and news coverage of the matter may influence prosecutorial decisions, and may subtly have an effect on courts and potential members of the jury pool. In addition, for a client whose business is providing products or services to customers, the public relations impact of a threatened or actual case may be as impactful as potential legal consequences. In this context, attorneys must decide whether, to what extent, and how to involve public relations professionals or "crisis management" consultants in communications with the legal team and client representatives in order to obtain the benefit of their specialized knowledge to achieve the client's goals related to the litigation (and beyond).

Attorneys are trained in legal analysis, fact gathering, and advocacy before tribunals, and generally not trained in the effective ways to influence a broader audience that may be relevant to a litigation matter, or the potential effect of other influences in the press or social media on audiences relevant to the litigation. These things may require translation and input by trained professionals in the field. In addition, a client's goals may extend beyond the litigation itself, for example, to preserve or advance its position in the marketplace. Lawyers and clients may believe that the most efficient way to marry these goals around a particular case or matter is to include PR consultants in the stream of communications and meetings between legal team and client representatives, and involve them in the decision-making relating to litigation-specific goals, as well as the client's broader PR concerns arising because of the litigation. This approach may not align with, and may waive protection afforded by, the attorney-client privilege.

What happens to confidential communications that were divulged to the PR firm once discovery takes place and the opposition requests disclosure of all nonprivileged communications? Can the attorney successfully invoke the attorney-client privilege to protect the communications shared with the PR firm? The answer most often depends upon the clarity of purpose in relation to the litigation for which the PR firm has been retained, and the consistency of the communications shared with that defined purpose. Even then, the path to attorney-client privilege protection of communications with public relations consultants is often an uphill climb. In many cases, the work-product doctrine is a more readily available source of protection, albeit limited in scope.

II. The Attorney-Client Privilege and Third-Party Consultants

The attorney-client privilege protects certain communications between lawyers and their clients from being disclosed to an opponent.[1] Usually, sharing confidential attorney-client communications with someone other than the client or lawyer, or having a third party present when the privileged communications are divulged, destroys the confidentiality prerequisite of the attorney-client

1. Fed. R. Evid. 501, 502.

privilege and renders the communications discoverable. Two exceptions to this principle have developed related to outside consultants.

First, the privilege may extend to confidential attorney-client communications disclosed to third parties if, inter alia, the third party's involvement is necessary to facilitate or enable the lawyer to give legal advice.[2] Communications among client, attorney, and the third party remain privileged and confidential if they are made in confidence and for the purpose of obtaining legal advice from the attorney, as distinguished from advice of the third-party professional not related to the attorney's legal advice.[3] Whether the third party was necessary to assist in the rendition of legal services is the important inquiry in determining whether the third party's presence during otherwise privileged communications maintains or destroys the attorney-client privilege.

In the leading case of *United States v. Kovel*, the United States Court of Appeals for the Second Circuit held that the presence of an accountant during communications between the lawyer and client did not cause a waiver of privilege, when the accountant's involvement was necessary to translate or explain accounting information being communicated to the lawyer in order to facilitate legal advice.[4] Building upon the established principle that interpreters and others necessary to literally translate communications between lawyer and client are within the umbrella of privilege,[5] the *Kovel* court extended this by analogy to the professional services of an accountant in that case:

> Accounting concepts are a foreign language to some lawyers in almost all cases and to almost all lawyers in some cases. Hence the presence of an accountant, whether hired by the lawyer or by the client, while the client is relating a complicated tax story to the lawyer, ought not destroy the privilege . . . the presence of the accountant is necessary, or at least highly useful, for the effective consultation between the client and the lawyer which the privilege is designed to permit. . . . What is vital to the privilege is that the communication be made in confidence for the purpose of obtaining legal advice from the lawyer. If what is sought is not legal advice but only accounting service . . . or if the advice sought is the accountant's rather than the lawyer's, no privilege exists.[6]

2. United States v. Kovel, 296 F.2d 918, 922 (2d Cir. 1961); *In re* Grand Jury Subpoenas Dated March 24, 2003, 265 F. Supp. 2d 321, 325 (S.D.N.Y. 2003).

3. United States v. Kovel, 296 F.2d 918, 922 (2d Cir. 1961).

4. *Id.*

5. *Id.* at 921–22. *See, e.g.*, U.S. v. Salamanca, 244 F. Supp. 2d 1023, 1025 (D.S.D. 2003) (translator "literally became the voice through which [the client] and his attorney could speak").

6. *Id.*

The rationale of *Kovel* has been subsequently applied to many types of third-party consultants, including PR professionals.[7] Some courts have applied its reasoning more narrowly, looking for the ability to analogize the third-party consultant's role to that of a translator, while others have approached it more broadly, looking to determine whether the third-party consultant at least facilitated the attorney's ability to provide legal advice.[8]

Second, privilege may also extend to confidential attorney-client communications disclosed to third parties if the consultant, although not employed by the client, is acting in essence as the client in the context of the litigation. In *In re Bieter Co.*, the United States Court of Appeals for the Eighth Circuit held that a real estate professional who served as the client's representative, although working as an independent contractor, was the "functional equivalent" of the client's employee, so that disclosure of privileged information to him did not destroy the privilege.[9] In doing so, the court found "no principled basis to distinguish . . . [the consultant's] role from that of an employee, and his involvement in the subject matter of the litigation makes him precisely the sort of person with whom a lawyer would wish to confer confidentially in order to understand . . . [the client's] reasons or seeking representation."[10] The functional-equivalent-of-the-client rationale of *Bieter* has also been applied in the context of PR professionals, albeit with limited success, to achieve protection.

III. When Does a PR Consultant's Involvement Have a Sufficient Nexus to Legal Advice?

The common thread of cases addressing this question is a tension between characterizing a PR professional's work as related to a focused litigation purpose or as general business-as-usual public relations work to advance the client's image in the marketplace. Many courts apply a very difficult standard, requiring the PR consultant's involvement in communications to be "necessary," "reasonably necessary," or "nearly indispensable" to the attorney's delivery of legal advice or service. Some apply what appears to be a more flexible requirement that the involvement "facilitate" the giving of legal advice.

In re Grand Jury Subpoenas Dated March 24, 2003 is a popular opinion for proponents of applying attorney-client privilege protection to communications among attorneys, clients, and PR firms.[11] In this case, the U.S. government was investigating Company and Target, a high-profile former employee of Company.[12] Target's attorneys hired Firm, a public relations firm, as part

---

7. *E.g.*, *In re* Grand Jury Subpoenas dated March 24, 2003, 265 F. Supp. 2d 321 (S.D.N.Y. 2003).

8. *See* Michele DeStefano Beardslee, *The Corporate Attorney-Client Privilege: Third Rate Doctrine for Third Party Consultants*, 62 SMU L. Rev. 727, 746–47 (2009).

9. 16 F.3d 929, 939–40 (8th Cir. 1994).

10. *Id.* at 938.

11. 265 F. Supp. 2d 321 (S.D.N.Y. 2003).

12. *Id.* at 322. The court intentionally used generic names to identify the parties.

of their defense of Target out of a concern that negative, unbalanced press coverage would create enough public pressure to push federal prosecutors to bring charges against Target.[13] Witness, an employee of Firm, claimed that Firm was hired to pursue favorable media coverage that reached the prosecutors and regulators responsible for making the decisions on bringing charges against Target.[14]

The government subpoenaed Firm and Witness, seeking documents and testimony before a grand jury regarding Firm's and Witness's interactions with Target.[15] Target's attorneys and Firm cited the attorney-client privilege in their attempt to limit the production of documents and testimony from Witness and Firm.[16] Target had communicated by email and through direct conversations with differing combinations of Witness, Firm, and attorneys; Target communicated directly with Witness without attorneys present; and Firm interacted with Target's attorneys without Target present.[17]

The court analyzed the scope of the attorney-client privilege under federal common law because the dispute was entirely federal in nature.[18] The court stated that its analysis would be framed by *Kovel*'s holding that the privilege protects communications that are revealed to, or include, persons assisting the lawyer in the rendition of legal services.[19] Target's lawyers argued that outside help, in the form of Firm, was needed to achieve its goal of creating a balanced media climate for prosecutors to make an unbiased decision on whether to bring charges against Target.[20] The predominant issue before the court was whether this outside help related to the rendition of legal advice.[21]

Before arriving at its ultimate conclusion, the court observed that in some circumstances, the "advocacy of a client's case in the public forum" is important to "the client's ability to achieve a fair and just result in pending or threatened litigation."[22] The court noted that the public relations services provided by Firm to Target and Target's lawyers were "needed" and were "not a matter for amateurs."[23] Questions such as whether the client should address the media, whether to do so directly or through others, whether and to what extent

13. *Id.* at 322–23.

14. *Id.* at 323.

15. *Id.*

16. 265 F. Supp. 2d at 323.

17. *Id.* at 324.

18. *Id.*; *see* FED. R. EVID. 501. At least one court has noted that federal common law privilege doctrine is broader and more protective of privilege than certain state law, specifically California and New York. Behunin v. Superior Court, 9 Cal. App. 5th 833, 851, 215 Cal. Rptr. 3d 475 (2017).

19. 265 F. Supp. 2d at 325–26.

20. *Id.* at 326.

21. *Id.* The court stated that a client's confidential communications to a non-testifying expert retained by the lawyer to assist the lawyer in preparing the client's case are likely privileged. *Id.*

22. 265 F. Supp. 2d at 330.

23. *Id.*

to comment on specific allegations, and "a host of others" should be decided with "careful legal input."[24]

Based on this need for a targeted public relations strategy in order to properly advance Target's legal goals, the court found (1) confidential communications (2) between lawyers and public relations consultants (3) hired by lawyers to assist them in dealing with the media in cases such as this (4) that are made for the purpose of giving or receiving advice (5) directed at handling the client's legal problems are protected by the attorney-client privilege.[25] The court concluded that certain "fundamental" functions of attorneys (advising clients of legal risks of speaking publicly, seeking to avoid or narrow charges brought against the client, seeking acquittal or vindication) would be hampered if attorneys were not allowed to confidentially discuss facts and strategies with public relations consultants.[26]

In contrast, in *Calvin Klein Trademark Trust v. Wachner*, a district court had taken a narrower view, holding that that the attorney-client privilege did not protect from disclosure communications between a PR firm and the attorneys representing Calvin Klein (CK).[27] Before a lawsuit was filed, CK's attorneys hired a PR firm to act as a consultant in connection with their representation of CK.[28] CK's attorneys claimed their communications with the PR firm were protected by attorney-client privilege when disclosure was requested by the opposing party.[29] The court was unconcerned with the parties' explanations for why a PR firm was retained, noting that the communications appeared to be about "how to put the 'spin' most favorable to CK on successive developments in the ongoing litigation."[30]

The court first noted that few of the documents in issue involved confidential communications from the client.[31] The documents were mostly communications between the PR firm and the attorneys, and the court found that even though these communications were important to the ultimate legal advice given to the client, this was not sufficient to trigger protection from disclosure within the attorney-client privilege.[32] "[T]he privilege protects communications between a client and an attorney, not communications that prove important to an attorneys' legal advice to the client."[33] Next, the court found

24. *Id.*

25. *Id.* at 331.

26. *Id.* at 330. An attorney did not need to be present for communications between Target and Firm in order to have the communications remain protected by the attorney-client privilege *as long as* the communications were directed at giving or obtaining legal advice. *Id.*

27. 198 F.R.D. 53 (S.D.N.Y. 2000).

28. *Id.* at 54. It is also worth noting that the same PR firm was already working directly for Calvin Klein before being retained by the attorneys.

29. *Id.*

30. *Id.*

31. *Id.*

32. *Id.*

33. *Id.* (citing United States v. Ackert, 169 F.3d 136, 139 (2d Cir. 1999)).

that the services being performed by the PR firm did not improve or facilitate comprehension of the communications between the attorneys and the client, that is, they did not serve a *Kovel*-like translation function.[34] The court stated that the PR firm's services of "reviewing press coverage, making calls to various media to comment on litigation, or finding friendly reporters," while potentially helpful to forming legal strategy, did not enable counsel to better understand aspects of the client's communications for the rendering of legal advice.[35] Finally, the court found that the services the PR firm was performing were not materially different from those that an ordinary public relations firm would have performed if hired directly by the client, and the court declined to expand the attorney-client privilege to include an attorney sharing confidential client communications with the PR firm.[36]

In distinguishing the rationale of *Calvin Klein* from its own case, the court in *In re Grand Jury Subpoenas* contrasted the "ordinary public relations advice" from the PR firm in *Calvin Klein* with its finding that the PR firm in the case before it advanced the specific legal goal of using the public campaign to help avoid an indictment.[37] Recall that the PR firm in *In re Grand Jury Subpoenas* was hired for the specific purpose of impacting the media message delivered to prosecutors and investigators, not just the public at large (although the court noted that in some cases advocacy in a public forum could be important to obtaining a fair trial), so that the attorneys' goal of avoiding an indictment of their client could be achieved.[38] The PR firm was involved to assist the attorney in relaying to the client the legal advice of how to present the client and a message to the media (when to speak to the media, what to say, etc.) in the hope that the presentation would influence the prosecutors.[39] The specific legal goal of hiring the PR firm to assist the lawyers in avoiding an indictment for the client was persuasive in the court's determination that sharing confidential communications did not waive the attorney-client privilege.

Other courts have also found that the attorney-client privilege is waived if otherwise-privileged client communications are disclosed to PR firms that do no more in the case than perform "normal" PR firm functions. *Haugh v. Schroder Investment Management North America Inc.* concerned whether the attorney-client privilege protected documents that were sent from a plaintiff to the attorney-hired PR firm and to the attorney.[40] The court found that the communications between the plaintiff and the PR firm and between the PR firm and the attorney were not necessary for the attorney to provide legal advice to

34. *Id.* at 54–55.

35. *Id.* Contrast this with the "translation" exception from United States v. Kovel, 296 F.2d 918, 922 (2d Cir. 1961).

36. *Id.* at 55.

37. *In re* Grand Jury Subpoenas, 265 F. Supp. 2d at 329.

38. *Id.* at 323–24.

39. *Id.* at 330.

40. 2003 WL 21998674, at *2 (S.D.N.Y. Aug. 25, 2003).

the client.[41] The documents/communications were "consistent with the design of a public relations campaign" and did not contribute to any legal advice given by the attorney.[42] "Since [plaintiff] has failed to show that the communications were made for the purpose of obtaining legal advice from her attorney as opposed to public relations advice from [the PR firm], the communications are not protected by the attorney-client privilege."[43]

The *Haugh* court distinguished its conclusion with *In re Grand Jury Subpoenas* by noting that the PR firm in that case was hired to assist counsel in creating a media climate in which prosecutors might feel less pressure to indict the client.[44] The plaintiff in *Haugh* did not identify any legal advice that required the assistance of a public relations consultant, nor did it identify a specific nexus between the consultant's work and the attorney's role in preparing plaintiff's complaint or case for the court.[45]

The necessity of a strong and identifiable nexus between the work of the public relations consultant and either specific litigation goals or expertise needed to facilitate communication between lawyer and client has been a requirement in many subsequent cases refusing to include communications with PR consultants under the umbrella of attorney-client privilege. The courts in these cases typically state that in order to be protected, the work of the PR firm would have to be "necessary," "tied to a specific litigation task that the attorneys needed to accomplish," "reasonably necessary," or "nearly indispensable" to the provision of legal services in the matter.[46]

For example, in *Anderson v. SeaWorld Parks and Entertainment, Inc.*,[47] following the premier of the film *Blackfish*, critical of SeaWorld, its counsel retained crisis management public relations firms "'to work with counsel . . . in developing legal strategy including potential litigation,' among other duties."[48] In subsequent litigation, most of the documents reflecting communications with these firms were produced, but some were withheld or redacted under claim

41. *Id.* at *3.

42. *Id.*

43. *Id.* The court found that all of the documents that were not protected by the attorney-client privilege *were* protected by the work-product doctrine because they were prepared in anticipation of litigation and had an impact on litigation strategy. *Id.* at *4.

44. *Id.* at *3.

45. 2003 WL 21998674, at *3.

46. *See, e.g., In re* Signet Jewelers Ltd Sec. Lit., 332 F.R.D. 131, 136 (S.D.N.Y. 2019) (communications with PR firms were not to perform a specific litigation task to advance attorneys' litigation goals, constituted messaging and other public relations activities directed to "burnishing Signet's image"); Bousamra v. Excela Health, 653 Pa. 365, 210 A.3d 967 (2019) (privilege waived by disclosure to PR professional when the third party's presence was neither indispensable to the lawyer giving legal advice or facilitated the lawyer's ability to give legal advice to the client); Breuder v. Board of Trustees, 2021 WL 4125084, at *6–7 (Sept. 9, 2021) (crisis management consultant not "nearly indispensable" based on either provision of expertise to counsel necessary to render legal advice, or necessary to facilitate communications with client).

47. 329 F.R.D. 628 (N.D. Cal. 2019).

48. *Id.* at 632.

of privilege.[49] The court held it is "not enough that the third party weighs in on legal strategy" in order to be "reasonably necessary" for an attorney's purpose; rather "the third party must facilitate communication between the attorney and client.[50] It found that the PR consultants provided advice to predict public reaction to legal activities and how best to present those activities to the public and other entities, insufficient for privilege protection.[51]

A few cases have extended attorney-client privilege protection based on the involvement of PR professionals in advising lawyers about how best to influence the publicity around a case as an element of litigation strategy,[52] or when the PR professionals are communicating to obtain legal advice for the benefit of the client from the client's lawyers about their work for the client.[53]

The clear conclusion from these cases is that protection of communications with independent public relations consultants under the umbrella of attorney-client privilege is limited. It may be efficient to allow a PR firm to review attorney-client communications or participate in meetings with the client in order to better facilitate the purpose of the PR firm's presence on the team, yet the cases reveal the difficult task in convincing a court that the communications should remain protected by the attorney-client privilege. Generally, the PR firm must be hired to accomplish a specific litigation goal and be necessary to that goal, as evidenced in *In re Grand Jury Subpoenas*, for example, using media to influence prosecutors or specific targets rather than the general public.

In theory, one can also establish protection if the consultant was engaged to "translate" confidential communications in some way so that the lawyer may better assist the client, but it has proven difficult to bring a public relations consultant within the same type of necessity as the accounting expert in *Kovel* as an intermediary between client and lawyer. Merely hiring a PR firm for consulting and media strategy or crisis management is not enough to establish a nexus between the giving and receiving of legal advice.

IV. The PR Firm as the "Functional Equivalent" of the Client

A PR firm's presence in communications between lawyer and client may also be protected by the attorney-client privilege if the PR firm was acting on behalf

---

49. *Id.*

50. *Id.*

51. *Id.*

52. *See* Stardock Sys., Inc. v. Reiche, 2018 WL 6259536, at *6 (N.D. Cal. Nov. 30, 2018) (Because PR firm was hired directly by counsel to provide advice on PR as an element of litigation strategy, attorney-client privilege extends to communications between counsel and PR firm pertaining to giving and receiving legal advice about the appropriate response to the lawsuit and making related public statements.).

53. *See* Sandoz Inc. v. Lannett Co, Inc., 2021 WL 5139975, at *4 (E.D. Pa. Nov. 4, 2021) (active involvement of PR consultant in seeking legal advice from client's counsel on draft PR statement makes communication "necessary for legal advice," distinguishing Bousamra v. Excel Health, 653 Pa. 365, 210 A.3d 967 (2019)).

of the client not independently but as the "functional equivalent" of the client, similar to the consultant in *In re Bieter Co.*, discussed earlier in the chapter. In conceptual terms, this argument characterizes the PR firm as a stand-in for or functional part of the actual client on the legal matter at issue, rather than as a stand-alone third party. This removes the need for any third-party waiver analysis relating to the confidentiality element of privilege.

Viacom, Inc. v. Sumitomo Corp. (In re Copper Mkt. Antitrust Litig.) provides a basic illustration of how a PR firm can be viewed by a court as the functional equivalent of the client.[54] A foreign company that was sued in the United States hired an American PR firm because it had no prior experience in dealing with issues related to high-profile U.S. litigation or in dealing with Western media.[55] The PR firm worked out of the company's foreign office with the company's own communications department.[56] The PR firm was the company's spokesperson when dealing with Western media while the company's communications department handled its domestic media.[57] The PR firm also coordinated with the company's U.S. counsel and "prepared many drafts of the documents [press releases], incorporating legal advice from [U.S. counsel] and [the company's] in-house counsel."[58] "[The PR firm] had the authority to make decisions on behalf of [the company] concerning its public relations strategy."[59] The court found:

> [The PR firm] was the functional equivalent of an in-house public relations department with respect to Western media relations, having authority to make decisions and statements on [company's] behalf, and seeking and receiving legal advice from [company's] counsel with respect to the performance of its duties.[60]

In considering whether to apply the attorney-client privilege to agents engaged by but not employed by the company, the court looked to whether the corporation's agents possessed the information needed by the corporation's attorneys in order to render "informed legal advice."[61] The court found that "there is no reason to distinguish between a person on the corporation's payroll and a consultant hired by the corporation if each acts for the corporation and possesses the information needed by attorneys in rendering legal advice."[62] For purposes of the attorney-client privilege, the PR firm could be

54. 200 F.R.D. 213 (S.D.N.Y. 2001).
55. *Id.* at 215.
56. *Id.*
57. *Id.* at 215–16.
58. *Id.* at 216.
59. *Id.*
60. *Id.*
61. *Id.* at 218–19 (citing Upjohn Co. v. United States, 449 U.S. 383, 391 (1981)).
62. *Id.* at 219.

equated with the company because it was incorporated into the company's staff, its communications with company's attorneys were for the purpose of obtaining legal advice, and it possessed authority to make decisions on behalf of the company.[63] Confidential communications between the PR firm and counsel, PR firm and company, and any other combination that were made for the purpose of facilitating the rendition of legal services to the company were protected from disclosure.[64]

In *F.T.C. v. GlaxoSmithKline*, the Court of Appeals for the District of Columbia followed the reasoning in *Viacom* by holding that corporate communications between a corporation, its attorneys, and its PR firm were protected by the attorney-client privilege.[65] In that case, counsel worked with a PR firm in the same manner it did with full-time corporation employees: some PR firm employees worked full time with the corporation's team, and, as a result, the PR group became completely involved with the company's litigation and legal strategies.[66] The communications among counsel, the PR firm, and the corporation were protected under the attorney-client privilege.[67]

In contrast, in *LG Electronics USA, Inc. v. Whirlpool Corp.*, without deciding whether the Seventh Circuit would adopt the "functional equivalent" test (which it also termed a de facto employee doctrine), the court held that it would not have been met in that case.[68] Whirlpool's communications with agencies it hired on a regular basis to perform marketing, PR, and advertising were at issue on a motion to compel documents listed on a privilege log.[69] The court found that the agencies were closely supervised by Whirlpool, and lacked authority to make decisions on behalf of the company:

> Whirlpool's agencies may prepare its marketing materials, but Whirlpool . . . exercises the final say in all of its advertisements, closely

63. *Id.*

64. *Id.*

65. 294 F.3d 141, 148 (D.C. Cir. 2002). Contrast with *In re* Riddell Concussion Reduction Litig., 2016 WL 7108455 (D.N.J. Dec. 5, 2016).

66. *Id.*; *see also* Schaeffer v. Gregory Village Partners, LP, 2015 WL 166860 (N.D. Cal. Jan. 12, 2015) (in a contamination case, the head of a PR firm was considered a functional employee of the client—and her communications with the client and attorneys were considered privileged—when she acted as the public face of the client and spoke/acted on behalf of the client in front of a water quality control board, other city neighbors, and the plaintiffs; her interactions with all parties were coordinated with the defendants' attorneys, and she provided information to the attorneys that was useful and necessary to evaluate legal strategy for the client).

67. F.T.C. v. GlaxoSmithKline, 294 F.3d 141, 148 (D.C. Cir. 2002). *See also In re* Johnson & Johnson Talcum Powder Prods. Marketing, Sales Practices, and Prods. Liab. Litig., 2021 WL 3144945, at *8–9 (D.N.J. July 26, 2021) (confidential communications with outside firms retained to augment corporate communications department in "highly sensitive atmosphere" were necessary to advance and facilitate the representation, and PR firms were within the scope of "broad practical approach" to determining the functional equivalent to employee status).

68. 661 F. Supp. 2d 958, 965 (N.D. Ill. 2009).

69. *Id.* at 959–60.

> monitors all agency work, and retains all rights in the agencies' work product. Whirlpool claims that "[i]t would be effectively impossible for Whirlpool employees to communicate critical information to their agency counterparts, if they could not discuss legal issues or the Law Department's input," . . . but this misconstrues the scope of the attorney-client privilege. To the extent that agencies need to be informed, Whirlpool's non-legal employees may screen counsel's legal advice and communicate Whirlpool's business concerns to the agencies without revealing Whirlpool's confidential communications to its counsel. . . . Whirlpool does not allow its agencies the freedom to design advertisements without Whirlpool's internal marketing approval.[70]

At first glance, there appear to be inconsistencies in the "functional equivalent" cases, some requiring that the outside consultants literally act as the client with decision-making authority to meet the test, while others focus on whether the consultant is filling an employee role that encompasses consultation with legal counsel, whether or not the consultant possesses final authority on a matter (of course, many employees within the privilege umbrella also do not have that authority). But, these are highly fact-intensive cases, leaving room for counsel seeking to rely upon them to develop fact-based arguments about a variety of factors that could be said to make a consultant look more or less like an employee whose communication are subject to attorney-client privilege.

V. Application of the Work-Product Doctrine

Documents provided to a PR firm by counsel, or created by a PR firm may be protected from discovery and remain confidential under the work-product doctrine, without many of the same concerns that affect application of the attorney-client privilege. In general, documents and tangible things prepared by a party or its representative in anticipation of litigation are protected.[71] Unlike the test for invoking attorney-client privilege in this context, the predominant purpose of the work product does not have to be to assist with the litigation, it need only to have been prepared or obtained (including by investigation) because of the prospect of litigation.[72] There are two types of work product: opinion work product reflecting the mental impressions, conclusions, opinions, and legal theories of counsel, with heightened protection; and fact

70. *Id.* at 965 (citations omitted). *See also* Universal Standard Inc. v. Target Corp., 331 F.R.D. 80 (S.D.N.Y. 2019) (PR firm not functional equivalent of employee where it lacked authority to issue press releases, and most importantly, there was no evidence the PR firm sought legal advice from corporate counsel to guide its work).

71. Fed. R. Civ. P. 26(b)(3).

72. United States v. Adlman, 134 F.3d 1194, 1202 (2d Cir. 1998).

work product, which is protected subject to disclosure only upon a showing of substantial need and an inability to obtain the substantial equivalent without undue hardship.[73] Most importantly as concerns protection for documents disclosed to or created by third party public relations consultants, the standard for waiver is much different: protection is not waived by mere disclosure to a third party, it is waived only when the disclosure is to an adverse party or in a manner that increases the opportunity for adversaries to obtain the information.[74]

Accordingly, several cases have afforded work-product protection to documents shared by counsel with PR consultants, when the prepared-in-anticipation-of-litigation prerequisites for that protection have otherwise been met, even in circumstances in which the attorney-client privilege was held not to apply.[75] This is not a way to protect all communications with public relations professionals relating to their public relations advice, but could provide some protection to documents evidencing legal strategy or factual information assembled for the litigation that counsel wishes to share with the professionals to provide a basis for their work or discussion with them.

---

73. *E.g.*, *In re* Signet Jewelers Ltd Sec. Lit., 332 F.R.D. at 138; Pearlstein v. BlackBerry Ltd, 2019 WL 1259382 (Mar. 19, 2019); Bousamra v. Excela Health, 653 Pa. 365, 383–84, 210 A.3d 967, 977–78 (2019).

74. *Id.* at 7.

75. *E.g.*, *In re* Johnson & Johnson Talcum Powder Products, Sales Practices, & Products Liability Litig., 2021 WL 3144945, at *9 (public relations consultants were not adversaries, therefore no waiver of work product by disclosure to them); Anderson v. SeaWorld Parks and Entm't, Inc., 329 F.R.D. 628, 635–38 (N.D. Cal. 2019) (disclosure of otherwise protected documents to PR consultants did not waive work product protection although communications with consultants held not to be within protection of attorney-client privilege); Calvin Klein Trademark Trust v. Wachner, 198 F.R.D. 53, 55–56 (S.D.N.Y. 2000) (attorney work product provided to PR firm did not lose work product protection, although communications with consultant not within attorney-client privilege); Bousamra v. Excela Health, 653 Pa. 365, 384–87, 210 A.3d 967, 977–80 (2019) (work-product protection not waived by disclosure to PR professionals, remanded for factual findings); America's Test Kitchen, Inc. v. Kimball, 35 Mass. L. Rptr. 75, 2018 WL 2049490, at *6–7 (disputed communications with public relations firms hired for crisis management were prepared because of the prospect of litigation and protected by the work-product doctrine).

CHAPTER 13

Insurance Settings

KIRK PASICH

Tips to Protect the Attorney-Client and Work-Product Privileges
1. Ensure the predominant purpose of the communication relates to a defense against the claim. 2. Include appropriate language in any communication, such as "This letter provides information that may assist the counsel retained to defend us against the claim . . . ." 3. Ensure that the communication is made with the expectation of confidentiality. State in communications among insureds and defense counsel that communications are confidential and for the purpose of the defense against a claim. 4. If the insurer wants to interview the insured's employees, determine in advance the purpose of the interviews. If the purpose is with respect to the defense of a claim or suit, confirm that purpose in writing. If the purpose is as part of a coverage investigation, consider possible privilege implications. 5. Keep in mind that if an insured and/or insurer is represented by coverage counsel in its communications and meetings with its insurers, an appearance may be created that the meeting is not pursuant to a common interest (e.g., defense of a suit against the insured), but rather is adversarial (e.g., because there is a coverage dispute). The purpose of the meeting should be clearly stated, with any discussion of coverage issues segregated. 6. Know which jurisdiction's law will apply and what that law is with respect to communications among insureds, insurers, and counsel *before* the communications occur, if possible.

Tips to Challenge the Assertion of the Attorney-Client and Work-Product Privileges
1. If there is a reservation of rights, determine whether the reservation creates a conflict of interest entitling the insured to control its defense and refuse to share privileged information relating to the conflict. 2. Offer to discuss those issues where there is a common interest (such as the insured's potential exposure and settlement opportunities)—and to do so without the presence of either parties' coverage counsel. 3. In California, consider California Civil Code section 2860(d) requirement: "[I]t shall be the duty of [independent] counsel and the insured to disclose to the insurer all information concerning the action except privileged materials relevant to coverage disputes, and timely to inform and consult with the insurer on all matters relating to the action." 4. Know which jurisdiction's law will apply and what that law is with respect to communications among insureds, insurers, and counsel *before* communications occur, if possible.

I. Introduction

When there has been an accident, an occurrence, a claim made, or some other event that may be covered by insurance, an insured typically communicates with its insurer. This initial communication is typically followed by additional communications, by the transmittal of information, and even by the insurer interviewing employees and potential witnesses. There are often at least two purposes behind these communications. First, the insured typically communicates with its insurers so that it may obtain the benefit of the insurance coverage it purchased. This obviously includes a defense against and indemnification for any claims. Second, the insurer may want to investigate the claim and related events to determine whether the claim is covered and whether its obligations are excused because of the insured's conduct or because of an exclusion.

Upon receiving notice of an actual or potential claim, the insurer has a duty to investigate. This duty extends not only to the facts regarding the claim and the insured's potential exposure, but also to the facts that support coverage for the claim. As the California Supreme Court has explained:

> [T]he insurer cannot deny the claim "without fully investigating the grounds for its denial." To protect its insured's contractual interest in security and peace of mind, "it is essential that an insurer fully inquire into possible bases that might support the insured's claim" before denying it. By the same token, denial of a claim on a basis unfounded in the facts known to the insurer, or contradicted by those facts, may be deemed unreasonable. ". . . The insurer may not just focus on those facts which justify denial of the claim."[1]

---

1. Wilson v. 21st Century Ins. Co., 42 Cal. 4th 713, 720–21 (2007) (citations omitted); Egan v. Mut. of Omaha Ins. Co., 24 Cal. 3d 809, 819, 620 P.2d 141, 169 Cal. Rptr. 691 (1979), *cert. denied and appeal dismissed,* 445 U.S. 912 (1980). *See also* Allan D. Windt, Insurance Claims and Disputes § 2.5, at 20–21 (6th ed. 2013) ("The implied covenant of good faith and fair dealing in the policy should necessarily require the insurer to conduct any necessary investigation in a timely fashion and to conduct a reasonable investigation before denying coverage."); Harner v. USAA Gen. Indem. Co., 497 F. Supp. 3d 901, 911 (S.D. Cal. 2020) ("Delayed payments because of '"inadequate or tardy investigations" . . . may also breach the implied covenant.'"); Armas v. USAA Cas. Ins. Co., 2019 WL 3333279, at *6 (N.D. Cal. July 24, 2019) ("The insurer's investigation of an insured's claims must be thorough, including 'diligently search[ing] for evidence which supports its insured's claim.' As part of this investigation, '[a]n insurance company may not ignore evidence which supports coverage. If it does so, it acts unreasonably towards its insured and breaches the covenant of good faith and fair dealing.'" (citations omitted)); Lennar Corp. v. Transamerica Ins. Co., 227 Ariz. 238, 246, 256 P.3d 635, 643 (Ariz. Ct. App. 2011) ("[A]n insured may suffer injury when an insurer sues over the meaning of a disputed policy term and . . . effectively ignores an obligation to reasonably investigate the claim during the ensuing protracted legal proceedings."); Chi. Title Ins. Co. v. AMZ Ins. Servs., Inc., 188 Cal. App. 4th 401, 428, 115 Cal. Rptr. 3d 707, 730 (2010) (a genuine dispute as to the existence and amount of coverage "'does not relieve an insurer from its obligation to thoroughly and fairly investigate, process and evaluate the insured's claim'") (quoting Wilson v. 21st Century Ins. Co., 42 Cal. 4th 713, 723, 171 P.3d 1082 (2007)).

During its investigation, the insurer may create and compile various documents relating to the defense against the claim and to its coverage determination. These documents often include documents relating to the substantive merits of the claim asserted against the insured and to coverage defenses the insurer may wish to assert, such as the defense that the insured expected and intended to inflict the injury claimed by the underlying plaintiff. The investigatory documents may include witness statements, post-accident reports, assessments by claims adjusters, or advice letters from in-house or outside counsel, and communications from attorneys defending the insured against the claim.

When the insured and the insurer are working together to defend a claim, neither will want their communications or the results of the insurer's investigation revealed to the underlying claimant or potential claimants. The attorney work-product doctrine may offer the parties some protection from disclosure.

Likewise, when the insured and an insurer are embroiled in a coverage dispute, neither usually wants third parties to have access to their documents, but both want and claim a right to access the other's documents. For example, the insured often will seek to discover all information the insurer may have in its claims file in order to determine why the insurer denied coverage and if that denial was in bad faith.

In turn, the insurer may want access to documents found in the underlying defense counsel's files and to documents that might show that there is no coverage because the insured intended to inflict injury—the very documents the underlying plaintiff will want to use to establish the insured's liability. In this situation, there is a real tension between the parties' efforts to litigate their coverage dispute and the need to avoid creating the very liability for which the insured is seeking a defense from the insurer. To the extent possible, this issue should be avoided because an insurer should not be able to create the very liability it is supposed to be defending its insured against by attempting to establish that it has no duty to indemnify the insured.[2]

---

2. *See* Tews Funeral Home, Inc. v. Ohio Cas. Ins. Co., 832 F.2d 1037, 1046 (7th Cir. 1987) (a determination of the duty to indemnify "is premature while the underlying action is pending if the indemnity decision would require a court to adjudicate facts in the underlying dispute"); Montrose Chem. Corp. v. Superior Court, 6 Cal. 4th 287, 301, 861 P.2d 1153, 24 Cal. Rptr. 2d 467 (1993) ("To eliminate the risk of inconsistent factual determinations that could prejudice the insured, a stay of the declaratory relief action pending resolution of the third party suit is appropriate when the coverage action turns on facts to be litigated in the underlying action."); Cal-Farm Ins. Co. v. TAC Exterminators, Inc., 172 Cal. App. 3d 564, 572, 218 Cal. Rptr. 407 (1985) (when underlying action has not yet been tried, "the resolution of coverage must be determined by accepting as true all the allegations contained in the complaint in the underlying action"); *see also* Santa's Best Craft, LLC v. St. Paul Fire & Marine Ins. Co., 611 F.3d 339, 350–51 (7th Cir. 2010) ("[A]n insured is not required to apportion its liability for different claims because that would either require the coverage litigation to be a retrial of the merits of the insured's underlying lawsuit and/or would discourage settlement because the insured would essentially have to prove its own liability for the underlying conduct even if it had not made that concession in arriving at a settlement."); Entercom Sacramento, LLC v. Am. Home Assurance Co., 2008 WL 2025015, n.4 (N.D.

However, regardless of how or when a coverage dispute is resolved, there frequently are questions over who has access to what information. Generally speaking, these questions include the following:

- Is information gathered by an insurer in its investigation of a claim protected from discovery by a third-party claimant?
- Is information gathered by an insurer in its investigation of a claim protected from discovery by the insured?
- Are the underlying defense files protected from disclosure to an insurer?
- Are communications between insurers and insureds protected from disclosure to third-party claimants?

There typically is no privilege known as the "insured-insurer" privilege.[3] However, most states recognize that communications between an insured and an insurer are protected by the attorney-client privilege, at least to the extent the communication relates to the defense of the claim. A minority of the states and at least some federal courts have reached a contrary conclusion, holding that such communications are *not* protected by the attorney-client privilege.[4]

II. Application of the Attorney-Client Privilege: The Majority View

As noted earlier, the majority view is that an insured's communications to its insurers regarding a possible claim or other event potentially covered by insurance may be covered by the attorney-client privilege. Courts following the majority view typically hold that an insured's communications to its insurers generally are protected from disclosure by the attorney-client privilege. This

---

Cal. May 8, 2008) ("Stay of a declaratory relief action to determine coverage is often in order when the coverage question turns on facts to be litigated in the underlying third party action '[t]o eliminate the risk of inconsistent factual determinations that could prejudice the insured.'" (citation omitted)).

3. *See* Lectrolarm Custom Sys., Inc. v. Pelco Sales, Inc., 212 F.R.D. 567, 571 (E.D. Cal. 2002) ("Federal courts have never recognized a blanket privilege regarding insured-insurer communications."); Fox Paine & Co. v. Houston Cas. Co., 37 N.Y.S.3d 207, 2016 WL 1602747, at *22 (2016) (citing *Lectrolarm* for proposition that "where an insurer is providing a defense to an insured under a reservation of rights, a common-interest privilege applies only to communications which are part of an ongoing and joint effort to set up a common defense strategy, but rejecting common interest when there was no showing of "shared legal interest"); *cf.* Grewell v. State Farm Mut. Ins. Co., 102 S.W.3d 33, 37 (Mo. (*en banc*) 2003) ("[The] insurance policy required [the insurers] to defend [the insureds] when they became subject to a claim covered by that policy. As such, [the insureds'] communications with [the insurers] are subject to a privilege analogous to that between an attorney and her client.").

4. *Cf.* Cutchin v. State, 143 Md. App. 81, 90–91, 792 A.2d 359 (2002) (acknowledging two views, but noting that the decisions involved "turn on their facts and few, if any, truly stand for the proposition that all insured-liability or indemnity insurer communications are privileged, or the proposition that none are privileged").

means that communications about potentially covered events are protected by the privilege against disclosure to third parties, including potential claimants.[5]

This approach is premised on the theory that communications from an insured to an insurer are primarily made so that the information communicated can be relayed to the attorney retained by the insurer to defend the insured. As the Illinois Supreme Court explained in the leading decision supporting the broad approach:

> [B]y the terms of the common liability insurance contract, the insured effectively delegates to the insurer the selection of an attorney and the conduct of the defense of any civil litigation. The insured is ordinarily not represented by counsel of his own choosing either at the time of making the communication or during the course of litigation. Under such circumstances we believe that the insured may properly assume that the communication is made to the insurer as an agent for the dominant purpose of transmitting it to an attorney for the protection of the interests of the insured.[6]

---

5. *See, e.g.*, Morris v. Daimler Trucks N. Am., LLC, 535 F. Supp. 3d 803, 808 (S.D. Ill. 2021) ("Under Illinois law, a statement given in confidence by an insured to an insurer is privileged where the insurer is under an obligation to defend the insured, even if it never actually retains a lawyer to represent the insured."); Metroflight, Inc. v. Argonaut Ins. Co., 403 F. Supp. 1195, 1197–98 (N.D. Tex. 1975) (there is a privilege for communications from insured to insurer regarding facts of claim when intended to assist counsel in defense); Bellmann v. Dist. Court, 187 Colo. 350, 353, 531 P.2d 632 (1975), *overruled on other grounds*, Kay Labs., Inc. v. Dist. Court, 653 P.2d 721 (Colo. 1982); Grand Union Co. v. Patrick, 247 So. 2d 474, 475 (Fla. Dist. Ct. App. 1971); People v. Ryan, 30 Ill. 2d 456, 460–61, 197 N.E.2d 15 (1964); State *ex rel.* Cain v. Barker, 540 S.W.2d 50 (Mo. 1976); *see also* United States v. Hoeffner, 254 F.R.D. 302, 307 (S.D. Tex. 2008) ("Here, the Court finds the documents requested in the subpoenas seek communications that were prepared to assist with the defense of claims against Liberty Mutual, Travelers, National Casualty, Continental Casualty, and National Union's insureds. Because compliance with the subpoenas would require the disclosure of privileged and protected matter to which no exception to waiver would apply, and any disclosure would necessarily waive these privileges, the Court finds compliance would be unreasonable and oppressive under Rule 17(c)(2)."); Landmark Screens, LLC v. Morgan, Lewis & Bockius LLP, 2010 WL 289858, at *4 (N.D. Cal. Jan. 15, 2010) (recognizing "that communications between an insured to his liability insurance company about a potential claim is treated as a privileged communication").

6. People v. Ryan, 30 Ill. 2d 456, 460–61, 197 N.E.2d 15, 17 (1964). *See also* Scripps Health v. Superior Court, 109 Cal. App. 4th 529, 535, 135 Cal. Rptr. 2d 126 (2003) ("It has long been recognized that communications made by an insured to his 'liability insurance company, concerning an event which may be made the basis of a claim against him covered by the policy, is a privileged communication, as being between attorney and client, if the policy requires the company to defend him through its attorney, and the communication is intended for the information or assistance of the attorney in so defending him.'"); Bellmann v. Dist. Court, 187 Colo. 350, 353, 531 P.2d 632, 634 (1975), *overruled on other grounds*, Kay Labs., Inc. v. Dist. Ct. of Pueblo Cnty., 653 P.2d 721 (Colo. 1982) ("Since control of [the insured's] defense rested entirely with [the insurer] and counsel retained by [it], we hold that the insurance investigator who took the [insured's] statement was, in effect, an agent of the attorneys for the purpose of acquiring and transmitting this information to them."); Grand Union Co. v. Patrick, 247 So. 2d 474, 475 (Fla. Dist. Ct. App. 1971) (communication of accident report to insurer protected by attorney-client privilege because communication was, in essence, a communication between insured and counsel to benefit the defense of the case); Braglia v. Cephus, 146 Ill. App. 3d 241, 249, 496 N.E.2d 1171, 1176 (1986)

Even under the majority view, not necessarily all communications to insurance-related entities are protected. For example, in *Shere v. Marshall Field & Co.*,[7] the insured's safety director prepared a claim report on a form supplied by an independent adjusting service retained by the insured and one of its insurers. When the injured claimant sought to compel production of the report in the lawsuit against the insured, the insured was ordered to produce the report. The insured's attorney was subsequently held in contempt for refusing to produce the report. The Illinois Appellate Court affirmed, stating:

> In the instant case the statement was given by the Director of Safety to Safety and Claims Service. Safety and Claims Service is an independent contractor retained by both defendant and by defendant's

---

(following *Ryan*); Martin v. Clark, 92 Ill. App. 3d 518, 519, 415 N.E.2d 30, 32 (1980) (following *Ryan* and holding that statement given by insured to insurer "was protected by the attorney-client privilege and . . . should not have been subject to discovery"); State *ex rel.* Tillman v. Copeland, 271 S.W.3d 42, 46–47 (Mo. Ct. App. 2008) (statements made by insured to insurer were privileged where the communication was intended to assist the attorney defending the insured); Crowe v. Booker Transp. Servs. Inc., 2013 WL 394184, at *5 (W.D. Mo. Jan. 30, 2013) (following *Tillman*); Wielgus v. Ryobi Techs., Inc., 2010 WL 3075666, at *4 (N.D. Ill. Aug. 4, 2010) ("The Supreme Court of Illinois has also extended the attorney-client privilege to communications between an insured and insurer where the insurer owes an obligation to defend the insured. The rationale for the extension of the privilege is that agents of insurers serve as a communication conduit between an insured and the attorney to be retained by the insurer for the benefit of the insured and his or her defense.") (citations omitted); Holland v. Schwan's Home Serv. Inc., 992 N.E.2d 43, 85 (Ill. App. 2013) ("To extend the attorney-client privilege to an insurer, the party asserting the privilege must prove: (1) the identity of the insured, (2) the identity of the insurance carrier, (3) the duty to defend a lawsuit, and (4) that a communication was made between the insured and an agent of the insurer. . . ."); Vroman v. Wenciker, 2013 WL 623575, at *6 (Ill. App. Feb. 19, 2013) ("The attorney-client privilege extends to communications between an insurer and insured where the insurer has a duty to defend. . . ."); 81 AM. JUR. 2D *Witnesses* § 396 (2010) (under the broad approach, the insurer "is regarded as a mere intermediate agent to transmit the communications to the attorneys of its claims department or to an eventual trial attorney if an action is brought"); John P. Ludington, Annotation, *Insured-Insurer Communications as Privileged*, 55 A.L.R.4th 336, 342 (2008). In fact, the *Restatement of the Law Governing Lawyers* recognizes this broad approach. The *Restatement* provides:

> [C]ommunications between the lawyer and representatives of the insurer concerning such matters as progress reports, case evaluations, and settlement should be regarded as privileged and otherwise immune from discovery by the claimant or another party to the proceeding. Similarly, communications between counsel retained by an insurer to coordinate the efforts of multiple counsel for insureds in multiple suits and such coordinating counsel are subject to privilege.

RESTATEMENT (THIRD) OF THE LAW GOVERNING LAWYERS § 134 cmt. f (2000).

The *Restatement* also provides:

> The privilege applies to communications to and from the client disclosed to persons who hire the lawyer as an incident of the lawyer's engagement. Thus, the privilege covers communications by a client-insured to an insurance-company investigator who is to convey the facts to the client's lawyer designated by the insurer, as well as communications from the lawyer for the insured to the insurer in providing a progress report or discussing litigation strategy or settlement. . . .

Id. § 70 cmt. f, illus. 5.

7. 26 Ill. App. 3d 728, 327 N.E.2d 92 (1974).

> excess-public-liability insurer to investigate and adjust claims. However, it is not an insurer. The attorney-client privilege has never been extended to cover communications to such third parties. There was no contractual obligation on the part of Safety and Claims Service to defend as there was in the *Ryan* case, and there is no reason to assume that it was an agent for the defendant's attorneys. We therefore find no reason to extend the privilege to the instant independent investigating and adjusting service.[8]

Furthermore, even under the majority view, many courts recognize that the attorney-client privilege does not apply just because there is a communication between an insured and an insurer relating to the defense against a possible claim. Many courts hold that the attorney-client privilege protects communications only if (1) the *dominant purpose* of those communications relates to the defense of the insured by counsel retained by the insurer and (2) the insured had a reasonable expectation of confidentiality.[9]

---

8. *Id.* at 731, 327 N.E.2d at 94. *See also* RESTATEMENT (THIRD) OF THE LAW GOVERNING LAWYERS, § 70 cmt. f, illus. 5 (2000) (recognizing that privilege does not apply to "communications by an insured to an insurance investigator who will report to the company"). *But see* D.I. Chadbourne, Inc. v. Superior Court, 60 Cal. 2d 723, 727, 388 P.2d 700, 36 Cal. Rptr. 468 (1964) (question of fact as to whether privilege attaches when communication from insured's employee to independent contractor employed by insurer for subsequent transmittal to insurer and then to counsel selected by insurer); Gene Compton's Corp. v. Superior Court, 205 Cal. App. 2d 365, 366, 23 Cal. Rptr. 250 (1962) (insured's communication to insurance broker for transmission to insurer privileged), disapproved on other grounds, D.I. Chadbourne, Inc. v. Superior Court, 60 Cal. 2d 723, 388 P.2d 700, 36 Cal. Rptr. 468 (1964); *In re* Tetra Techs., Inc., 2010 WL 1335431, at *5 (S.D. Tex. Apr. 5, 2010) ("Thus, to the extent the communications identified by Plaintiffs between the Defendants, the insurance brokers, and the attorneys fall within this test, or were made to facilitate the rendition of legal services and involve an attorney, the Court holds that they fall within attorney-client privilege and are not subject to discovery."); Flex Energy, LLC v. St. Paul Surplus Lines Ins. Co., 2011 WL 2434095, at *7, n.53 (W.D. La. June 13, 2011) (following *Tetra Tech*); Markwest Hydrocarbon, Inc. v. Liberty Mut. Ins. Co., 2007 WL 1106105, at *3 (D. Colo. Apr. 12, 2007) (independent adjuster is an agent of an insurer and communications with the adjuster are protected by the attorney-client privilege where elements of privilege are met).

9. *See, e.g.*, State v. Anderson, 247 Minn. 469, 477–78, 78 N.W.2d 320 (1956) (statements by insured to insurer not privileged because insured did not sustain burden of establishing that statements had been made for exclusive use in insured's defense and made in confidence); Jacobi v. Podevels, 23 Wis. 2d 152, 155–56 127 N.W.2d 73 (Wis. 1964) (statements by insured to insurance adjuster not privileged because no action pending or threatened and no counsel retained for insured); *see also* TIG Ins. Co. v. Firemen's Ins. Co., 718 F. Supp. 2d 90, 97 n.5 (D.D.C. 2010) ("It is worth noting that the court does not recognize an implicit attorney-client privilege in all insured-insurer communications; instead, this privilege arises only when such communication is for the purpose of pursuing legal representation or the procurement of legal advice."); Kingsway Fin. Servs. v. PricewaterhouseCoopers LLP, 2008 WL 4452134, at *8 (S.D.N.Y. Oct. 2, 2008) ("Generally, the determination of whether the attorney-client privilege attaches to an insured-insurer communication turns on the nature and purpose of the communication. 'Certainly, where the insured communicates with the insurer for the express purpose of seeking legal advice with respect to a concrete claim, or for the purpose of aiding an insurer-provided attorney in preparing a specific legal case, the law would exalt form over substance if it were to deny application of the attorney-client privilege.'") (citation omitted). *See also* Los Angeles County Bd. of Supervisors v. Superior Court, 2 Cal. 5th 282, 302, 386 P.3d 773, 212 Cal. Rptr. 3d 107 (2016) ("[T]he

For example, in *Gene Compton's Corp. v. Superior Court*,[10] the California Court of Appeal considered whether the privilege attached to an accident report prepared by one of the insured's employees, which was subsequently given to the insurer and thereafter to an attorney first appointed by the insurer *after* the insured gave the report to the insurer. The court noted that the evidence before it demonstrated that the communication was made for the predominant purpose of transmittal to the attorney selected to defend the insured and that the information was intended to be confidential. Based on these findings, the court held that this constituted a privileged communication, stating:

> [I]n such circumstances as are here involved the transmission of a privileged communication to the attorney through the agency of an insurance carrier does not destroy the privilege.[11]

The California Supreme Court subsequently disapproved the implication in *Gene Compton's* that communications from an insured to an insurer are privileged as a matter of law.[12] However, the court approved of the "dominant purpose" test and "left intact *Gene Compton's*."[13] Hence, California law is clear that communications may be privileged if the trier of fact decides that the primary purpose for the communications was for transmittal to an attorney at some point during the course of professional employment.[14]

A similar approach was taken in *State v. Pavin*.[15] In *Pavin*, the insured was involved in an automobile accident. Ten days after the accident, he was interviewed in the hospital by an insurance adjuster, who prepared a statement. The insured refused to sign the statement, noting that his mother had been advised by an attorney that he should not do so. Subsequently, the insured was convicted of the crime of fourth-degree death by automobile. One of the key items of evidence admitted against him was the unsigned statement prepared by the insurance adjuster. On appeal, the insured argued that the statement was protected by the attorney-client privilege and had been erroneously admitted into evidence.

---

privilege does not apply to every single communication transmitted confidentially between lawyer and client. Rather, the heartland of the privilege protects those communications that bear some relationship to the attorney's provision of legal consultation.").

10. 205 Cal. App. 2d 365, 23 Cal. Rptr. 250 (1962), *disapproved on other grounds*, D.I. Chadbourne, Inc. v. Superior Court, 60 Cal. 2d 723, 388 P.2d 700, 36 Cal. Rptr. 468 (1964).

11. *Id.* at 379.

12. *See* D.I. Chadbourne, Inc. v. Superior Court, 60 Cal. 2d 723, 739 n.6, 388 P.2d 700, 36 Cal. Rptr. 468 (1964).

13. Travelers Ins. Cos. v. Superior Court, 143 Cal. App. 3d 436, 451, 191 Cal. Rptr. 871 (1983).

14. *Id. See also* Heffron v. L.A. Transit Lines, 170 Cal. App. 2d 709, 718, 339 P.2d 567 (1959) (communication privileged "if the policy requires the company to defend [the insured] through its attorney, and the communication is intended for the information or assistance of the attorney in so defending him").

15. 202 N.J. Super. 255, 494 A.2d 834 (1985).

The New Jersey Superior Court, Appellate Division, rejected this argument. In doing so, the court considered the various approaches taken by other courts, citing to decisions in many other states. The court rejected the notion of a per se privilege, instead finding a fact-based inquiry to be the "better view."[16] It summarized the support for that approach as follows:

> Those cases which have concluded that communications between an insured and his adjuster are not *per se* privileged note that an insurance carrier has the right to review and consider an insured's statement for any legitimate purpose connected with the company's business, such as coverage, cooperation, or renewal. The statement is ordinarily used by the insurer to determine whether and on what basis adjustment of the claim could be attempted. Only if adjustment is not effected and a claim is pursued, will the information be turned over to counsel for use in litigation. If the insured gives a false statement, or a statement which supplies facts regarding some other defense against the insurer's liability under the policy, the insurer can make use of those facts to the detriment of the insured. Thus these cases say that the relationship is not automatically comparable at all stages to that of attorney and client, since it is not at all clear that the insured's interests are being protected by the insurance carrier.[17]

With this reasoning in mind, the court considered the facts before it. The court first noted that the adjuster interviewed the insured within a few days after the accident and before any claim was filed. The court then noted that there was no evidence that the adjuster was acting on instructions of any attorney or that an attorney had even been retained by the insurer. Finally, the court noted that the insured's "expectation of privacy was non-existent" because he did not think of the adjuster as his legal advisor, refusing to sign the prepared statement on the advice of his mother's attorney.[18]

Another court employed the same methodology. In *Lectrolarm Custom Systems, Inc. v. Pelco Sales, Inc.*,[19] the court found that even when an insurer has reserved its rights to deny coverage, there is a "common interest" between the insured and the insurer as to the underlying suit and that, therefore, "disclosure of privileged information by [the insured] to [the insurer] does not waive the attorney client privilege or the work product doctrine."[20] The court explained as follows:

---

16. 494 A.2d at 837.
17. *Id.*
18. *Id.* at 838.
19. 212 F.R.D. 567 (E.D. Cal. 2002).
20. *Id.* at 572.

> [T]he attorney-client privilege is not automatically waived if an otherwise privileged document is disclosed to a third party. The most common situation in which disclosure occurs without waiver is where parties have a common interest. The existence of a common defense allows the parties and counsel allied in that defense to disclose privileged information to each other without destroying the privileged nature of those communications. This "common defense doctrine" also referred to as the "joint defense privilege" expands the application of the privileges to circumstances in which parties are represented by separate counsel but engage in a common legal enterprise.[21]

The court also reasoned that "the threat of production" to a claimant of information shared between an insured and its insurer would "create[] a wedge between the insured and their insurance carrier which is not in the best interests of any of the parties in this or any other litigation."[22]

Thus, under the majority view, communications between insureds and their insurers will be protected because the communications are inherently deemed to be privileged or because they were made for the dominant purpose of protecting the insured's rights, with a reasonable expectation of confidentiality, and/or regarding a subject of common interest (that is, the insured's potential exposure). Therefore, the following questions should be answered affirmatively in order for the communications to be protected from disclosure to third parties (such as governmental agencies and private claimants):

- Was the communication made for the dominant purpose of protecting the insured's rights?
- Was the communication made with a reasonable expectation of confidentiality?
- Was there a "common interest" in the matter to which the communication relates?

21. *Id.* (citations omitted); *see also* United Specialty Ins. Co. v. LIC Contracting, Inc., 2022 WL74157, at *3 (E.D.N.Y. Jan. 26, 2022) ("Where a common interest is found between an insurer and an insured, but the insurer ultimately disclaims coverage, courts have applied the common-interest doctrine to protect communications shared prior to the time the insurer denied coverage to the insured. . . . Courts have also found that insurers do not have to produce their communications with the insured's defense counsel and claims-file documents to the underlying plaintiff; this is because the interests of the insured and the underlying plaintiff are adverse to each other in the underlying actions."); Kingsway Fin. Servs. v. PricewaterhouseCoopers LLP, WL 4452134 (S.D.N.Y. Oct. 2, 2008), at *8 ("[The] fact that the parties are currently adverse in a related action does not alter the fact that [insured] and [insurer] shared a common interest at the time the communications were made.").

22. *Id.* at 573.

III. Application of the Attorney-Client Privilege: The Minority View

Some courts have held that communications between insureds and insurers are not protected by the attorney-client privilege.[23] These courts base their decisions on the theory that communications between an insured and an insurer are unlike communications between a client and an attorney because an insurer may use information it obtains from an insured for purposes that are contrary to the insured's interests. As the Wisconsin Supreme Court has explained:

> When the insured makes such a statement he is ordinarily fulfilling a condition of his policy, requiring him to notify the insurer of the occurrence and circumstances of the accident and to co-operate with the insurer. If the statement be false, the insurer may use it against the insured as foundation for a claim of non-co-operation. If the statement discloses facts giving rise to some other defense against the insurer's liability under the policy, the insurer is doubtless free to make use of those facts.[24]

In *Langdon v. Champion*,[25] the Alaska Supreme Court addressed the applicability of the attorney-client privilege to information compiled in an insurer's files. The court first compared the majority and minority views:

> A shrinking majority of states prohibit discovery of statements made by an insured to his insurer. Most of these courts base their decision on provisions in the insurance policy which require the insurer to defend the insured and the insured to cooperate in the investigation.
>
> . . .
>
> A substantial and growing minority of state courts, on the other hand, have concluded that statements made to an insurer by the insured are generally not protected by the attorney-client privilege. . . . The federal rule is likewise . . . .
>
> Courts adopting this view reason that communications between insured and insurer are not in the same class as communications

---

23. *See, e.g.*, Rogers v. Aetna Cas. & Sur. Co., 601 F.2d 840, 845 (5th Cir. 1979); Jackson v. Kroblin Refrigerated Xpress, Inc., 49 F.R.D. 134, 136–37 (N.D. W. Va. 1970); Gottlieb v. Bresler, 24 F.R.D. 371, 372 (D.D.C. 1959) ("[A] communication received by a liability insurance company from one of its insureds concerning a matter covered by the insurance policy is not a privileged communication."); Longs Drug Stores v. Howe, 134 Ariz. 424, 427–28, 657 P.2d 412, 415–16 (1983); Conley v. Graybeal, 315 A.2d 609, 610 (Del. Super. Ct. 1974); DiCenzo v. Izawa, 68 Haw. 528, 537–38, 723 P.2d 171, 176–78 (1986).

24. Jacobi v. Podevels, 23 Wis. 2d 152, 156, 127 N.W.2d 73, 76 (1964).

25. 752 P.2d 999 (Alaska 1988).

between client and attorney, because the insurer may use its information for purposes inimical to the interests of the insured.[26]

The court then concluded as follows:

> We find the growing minority and federal rule most persuasive. In our opinion, the cases according protection to statements between insurers and insureds have extended the attorney-client privilege into areas in which it was never intended to apply. Moreover, the minority rule is more in line with our policy favoring liberal discovery. . . .
>
> We therefore hold that the attorney-client privilege does not extend to statements made by an insured to his insurer, except in those cases where it can be shown that the adjustor received the communication at the express direction of counsel for the insured. Only in the latter instance do we think it can fairly be said that the adjustor is acting as "one employed to assist the lawyer in the rendition of professional legal services," thus making him a "representative of the lawyer" within the meaning of [Alaska] Evidence Rule 503(a)(4).[27]

IV. Witness Interviews by Insurers or Their Counsel

Even if the attorney-client privilege applies to a particular communication, another question commonly encountered is whether the privilege applies to witness interviews conducted by an insurer or its counsel. As a general rule, the privilege protects interviews with only the "corporation" or certain of its employees. Interviews with nonemployee witnesses typically will *not* be protected.[28] Therefore, interviews by insurers of nonemployee witnesses will not be protected by the attorney-client privilege.

However, some courts have recognized that the privilege should apply to interviews of the insured's employees. In *D.I. Chadbourne v. Superior Court*, the California Supreme Court set forth the rules to be applied in California when an employee communicates with the employer's insurer. The applicability of the various rules turned on the status of the employee in the corporation or in the litigation.[29] According to the court, the attorney-client privilege does not apply in the following situations:

---

26. *Id.* at 1002–03 (citations omitted).

27. *Id.* at 1003–04.

28. *See, e.g.*, Van Alen v. Anchorage Ski Club, Inc., 536 P.2d 784, 787 (Alaska 1975) ("eyewitness" statements taken by insurers not protected by work-product doctrine); D.I. Chadbourne, Inc. v. Superior Court, 60 Cal. 2d 723, 734, 388 P.2d 700, 36 Cal. Rptr. 468 (1964) (attorney-client privilege does not attach to statement by a witness who is not an employee of the client corporation). *See also* Trade Ctr. Props., Inc. v. Superior Court, 185 Cal. App. 2d 409, 411, 8 Cal. Rptr. 345 (1960); Equity Residential v. Kendall Risk Mgmt., Inc. 246 F.R.D. 557, 567 (N.D. Ill. 2007).

29. *Chadbourne*, 60 Cal. 2d at 736–38.

- When an employer directs an employee, at the request of its insurer, to make a statement to the insurer to be communicated to the employer's attorney *if* the insurer has not advised the employer that the employee's statement is to be obtained and used in such a manner;[30]
- When an employee of a defendant corporation is not a codefendant or a person who may be charged with liability, except for a situation where the employee is the natural person to be speaking for the corporation;[31]
- When "an employee has been a witness to matters which require communication to the corporate employer's attorney, and the employee has no connection with those matters other than as a witness," even though his employer required him to make the statement;[32] and
- When an employee "has not been expressly directed by his employer to make a statement, [and the employee] does not know that his statement is sought on a confidential basis (or knowing that fact does not intend [the statement] to be confidential)."[33]

However, the *Chadbourne* court held that the privilege does apply in several situations, including:

- When an employee makes a report as part of his or her normal duties or if the employer requests a report to be made and the dominant purpose of the request is confidential transmission of the report to an attorney;[34] and
- When an employee is a defendant in his or her own right or is a person who may be charged with liability.[35]

These guidelines make sense, given that California follows the "dominant purpose" approach to applying the attorney-client privilege to insured-insurer

---

30. *Id.* at 737–38 (employer's intent controls as to whether privilege applies and if insurer has not advised employer that statement will be obtained for attorney, "it cannot be said that the corporation intended the statement to be made as a confidential communication from client to attorney").

31. *Id.* at 736–37.

32. *Id.* at 737. *See also* Alpha Beta Co. v. Superior Court, 157 Cal. App. 3d 818, 827, 203 Cal. Rptr. 752 (1984) (following *Chadbourne* in holding some information obtained from an employee who had no connection with the litigation other than as a witness not privileged); Costco Wholesale Corp. v. Superior Court, 47 Cal. 4th 725, 734, 219 P.3d 736, 101 Cal. Rptr. 3d 758 (2009).

33. *Chadbourne*, 60 Cal. 2d at 737–38. *See also* Zurich Am. Ins. Co. v. Superior Court, 155 Cal. App. 4th 1485, 1497, 66 Cal. Rptr. 3d 833 (2007).

34. *Chadbourne*, 60 Cal. 2d at 737; *see also* AMCO Ins. Co. v. Madera Quality Nut LLC, 2006 WL 931437, at *9 (E.D. Cal. Apr. 11, 2006) (employee statements made as part of company's internal investigation of insurance fraud were privileged where "dominant purpose was to obtain information with the ultimate intent to provide legal advice"); Sierra Vista Hosp. v. Superior Court, 248 Cal. App. 2d 359, 365, 56 Cal. Rptr. 387 (1967) (privilege applies to report made by hospital administrator whose duties were those of a general business manager and included protection of the employer hospital from "legal action or liability").

35. *Id.* at 736.

communications.[36] They also make sense under the broader approach because they do not unnecessarily interfere with the liberal discovery policy utilized in most jurisdictions.

Other courts have reached similar conclusions. For example, in *Schipp v. General Motors Corp.*,[37] the court held that an insured's recorded statement to her insurer was protected by the attorney-client privilege. The court explained:

> It should have been obvious when [the insured] gave her recorded statement that claims would be made against her and that she would call upon her insurer to defend those claims. . . . [The insured] was entitled to expect that her insurance carrier would engage a lawyer to represent her, which means that she was entitled to view her insurer as her representative for purposes of obtaining legal services. [Her] statement to her insurer was a step in the process of obtaining legal representation pursuant to the insurance contract.[38]

Many other states hold the same view.[39]

Of course, in the minority of states that do not protect insured-insurer communications with the attorney-client privilege, the privilege would not apply to witness interviews.[40]

---

36. *See* Scripps Health v. Superior Court, 109 Cal. App. 4th 529, 533–34, 135 Cal. Rptr. 2d 126 (2003) ("When the corporate employer has more than one purpose in requiring the report, the dominant purpose will control"; report held privileged when one purpose was quality assurance/peer review because "dominant purpose" was attorney review in anticipation of possible litigation); Costco Wholesale Corp. v. Superior Court, 47 Cal. 4th 725, 735, 219 P.3d 736, 101 Cal. Rptr. 3d 758 (2009) ("[T]he dominant-purpose test determines whether the relationship between the attorney and the corporate employee is an attorney-client relationship; if the corporation's dominant purpose in requiring the employee to make a statement is the confidential transmittal to the corporation's attorney of information emanating from the corporation, the communication is privileged.").

37. 457 F. Supp. 2d 917 (E.D. Ark. 2006).

38. *Id.* at 922–23.

39. *See id.* at 919 ("Many states—and what appears to be a majority—have held, depending on varying factors, that . . . a communication [between an insurer and its insured] may be protected by the privilege. . . ."); *see also* Richey v. Chappell, 594 N.E.2d 443, 447 (Ind. 1992) ("[W]e hold that where the policy of insurance requires the insurer to defend claims against the insured, statements from the insured to the insurer concerning an occurrence which may be made the basis of a claim by a third party are protected from disclosure.").

40. *See, e.g.*, Calabro v. Stone, 225 F.R.D. 96, 99 (E.D.N.Y. 2004) ("Federal courts in the Second Circuit have not routinely shielded documents such as accident reports from discovery; rather they have required proof that the material 'is prepared exclusively and in specific response to imminent litigation. . . .' The mere contingency that litigation could result is not sufficient to trigger protection under the work product doctrine. . . . This is particularly true in the insurance context because 'the very business of the producing party is to evaluate claims that may ultimately ripen into litigation.'").

V. The Impact of an Insurer's Reservation of Rights or Declination on the Applicability of the Attorney-Client Privilege

The impact of an insurer's reservation of rights or declination on the applicability of the attorney-client privilege to an insured's communications with its insurers must be considered.

In *Dixie Manufacturing Co. v. Ricks*,[41] the insured's president met with counsel employed by its insurer regarding a lawsuit brought against the insured by an employee. At trial, the attorney was permitted to testify over the insured's objection. The Georgia Supreme Court affirmed on appeal. In doing so, the court emphasized that the attorney had, before meeting with the insured, informed the insured that the insurer was not liable under its policy and that the attorney did not, and would not, represent the insured. In light of these facts, the court concluded that it did "not see how the evidence objected to can be regarded as privileged communications between an attorney and his client."[42]

In *State ex rel. L.Y. v. Davis*,[43] the insurer denied coverage for a potential claim against its insured after receiving from its insured information regarding the claim. When the claimant sued, he requested production of this information, arguing that the insurer's denial of coverage meant that there was no insured-insurer relationship with respect to this claim. The court disagreed, stating:

> If communications between insured and insurer are to be privileged only if the insurer ultimately admits coverage, there is no incentive for the insured to make full disclosure to his insurer. In fact, it may be impossible and, at best, difficult for the insurer to determine whether coverage exists without the insured making a full explanation of the circumstance surrounding the claim.[44]

---

41. 153 Ga. 364, 112 S.E. 370 (1922).

42. *Id.* at 370. *See also* Cont'l Cas. Co. v. St. Paul Surplus Lines Ins. Co., 265 F.R.D. 510, 522 (E.D. Cal. 2010) (insured's communications to insurer were not privileged where insurer made clear it would not defend insured); NL Indus. v. Commercial Union Ins. Co., 144 F.R.D. 225, 231 (D.N.J. 1992) ("To permit insurers, however, unrestrained access to attorney-client communications and work product where those insurers refused to take part in litigation despite notice and an opportunity to participate would distort the 'common interest' doctrine.").

43. 723 S.W.2d 74 (Mo. Ct. App. 1986).

44. *Id.* at 75. *See also* Vicor Corp. v. Vigilant Ins Co., 674 F.3d 1 (1st Cir. 2012) ("Massachusetts law, however, considers an attorney retained by an insurer to represent the insured as the attorney for both. Vicor further argues that the fact that the insurers tendered the underlying defense pursuant to a reservation of rights defeats any claim of a common interest. We disagree. It is undisputed that the primary insurers paid defense counsel and partially funded the settlement with Ericsson. That suffices to rebut Vicor's argument. . . .").

Therefore, the court concluded that "claims [need not] actually be covered before any communications between insured and insurer are privileged."[45]

A Massachusetts court took a similar approach. In *RFF Family Partnership, LP v. Burns & Levinson, LLP*,[46] the insured, a law firm, had been sued for malpractice. Its insurer retained defense counsel on the firm's behalf. Nine months later, the insurer reserved its rights, noting that it had been providing a defense and would continue to do so "under a complete reservation" of rights. The court noted a split in authority as to whether communications between an insurer and appointed defense counsel are privileged when the insurer has reserved its rights. It noted generally that when an insurer retains defense counsel for its insured, "[u]nfettered communications with both clients on a subject of the joint representation is therefore a practical necessity."[47] It reasoned as follows:

> Both are directly interested in the case, its progress and any material developments, counsel's litigation and trial strategy, his assessments of the merits and likelihood of success, his views on whether the case ought to be tried or settled, and myriad other issues, many of which require expression of counsel's strategic judgments and mental impressions. In communicating with the insurer on these matters, the attorney is rendering advice and counsel to a client as a necessary aspect of his representation, both of the insurer and of the insured.[48]

The court then turned to the situation before it, where there had been a reservation of rights. It noted the split of authority:

> Some courts have found the issue more complicated (especially, under California law) when there has been a reservation of rights under the policy, and several of these have concluded that in these circumstances, the interests of insurer and insured are sufficiently divergent that the usual assumption—that attorney-client communications are not privileged if sought by either of the two joint clients (insurer and insured), but are privileged as to the outside world—is inapplicable.[49]

It disagreed, stating:

> [E]ven where an insurer has questioned coverage, reserved its rights, but is still providing a defense, communications concerning the

45. *Id.*
46. 32 Mass. L. Rptr. 88 (Mass. Super. Ct. 2013).
47. *Id.* at *3.
48. *Id.* (footnote omitted).
49. *Id.*

> defense between the defense counsel and either the insured or the insurer (or both) are accessible to both, but privileged from outside scrutiny. In such a case there is as yet no binding determination as to coverage. Both the insurer and the insured are potentially at risk on the loss, and each may be expected to take an active interest in the litigation and to require the defense attorney to keep it informed, not only as to matters of public record, but also concerning his mental impressions, strategy and judgment on issues relating to liability, but not coverage. On liability issues, the interests of the two clients are and remain in full accord.[50]

Therefore, the court concluded:

> [E]ven after issuance of a reservation of rights, the insurer and the insured still share a common interest in bringing the case to a successful conclusion. They ought to be permitted also to share information in furtherance of that common goal, without fear of discovery by those whose interests may be inimical to their own.[51]

Thus, it seems that at least until such time as the insurer makes it clear to the insured that it will not provide a defense and will not be retaining counsel for the insured, the attorney-client privilege arguably should apply if the dominant purpose of the communications is for transmittal to an attorney. However, if the insured communicates with the insurer knowing that the insurer will not provide a defense, it seems the communications arguably would not be privileged.

As for the impact of reservations of rights, courts have reached varying conclusions. With a reservation of rights, the insurer typically assumes the defense against the claim. Thus, there is no reason to treat communications from an insured relating to the defense of the claim any differently than they would be treated if the insurer assumed the defense without a reservation of rights. In fact, such a result is consistent with the *Restatement of the Law Governing Lawyers*. As noted earlier, the *Restatement* recognizes that communications between the defense lawyer and the insurer's representatives "should be regarded as privileged and otherwise immune from discovery by the claimant or another party to the proceeding."[52]

---

50. *Id.* at *4.

51. *Id.* at *5.

52. Restatement (Third) of the Law Governing Lawyers § 134 cmt. f (2000). *See* Lectrolarm Custom Sys., Inc. v. Pelco Sales, Inc., 212 F.R.D. 567, 571–73 (E.D. Cal. 2002) (rejecting underlying plaintiff's request for production of documents from insurer even though insurer had reserved rights, noting that "common defense doctrine" preserved attorney-client privilege).

However, not all courts agree. For example, in *Continental Casualty Co. v. St. Paul Surplus Lines Insurance Co.*,[53] an equipment lessee's insurer sued the equipment manufacturer's insurer. Both the lessee and the manufacturer tendered their defense to the lessee's insurer. The lessee's insurer agreed to defend the lessee, but initially refused to defend the manufacturer and, in fact, paid for the lessee's cross-suit against the manufacturer. However, two years later it agreed to defend the manufacturer and paid for independent defense counsel for the manufacturer. The manufacturer's insurer did not defend either party. Its policy was subject to a self-insured retention and gave it the right, but not the duty, to defend the insured. After the lessee's insurer settled the underlying lawsuit, it sought contribution from the manufacturer's insurer. It also sought discovery of communications among the manufacturer, the manufacturer's insurer, and independent defense counsel. The court permitted the discovery. It ruled that "the privileged relationship relates only to communications between [independent defense counsel] and his client, [the manufacturer], and not to [the manufacturer's insurer]."[54] The court explained:

> [W]hile the conflict of interest is explicit between an insured and a defending insurer that reserved its rights, such a conflict is also objectively manifested between an insured and a non-defending insurer that retains its own interests in the outcome of the litigation while sitting on the sidelines.[55]

The manufacturer, its insurer, and defense counsel argued that the privilege should apply to their communications because while the insurance policy did not require that the manufacturer's insurer defend the manufacturer, it did give the insurer "the right to investigate or defend and did require [the manufacturer] to provide information to [the insurer] about the [underlying] action."[56] They also argued that

> a failure to extend the privilege to those communications "would place an insured in a position of having to choose between violating the terms of the insurance contract and opening its confidential communications to the world."[57]

The court disagreed: "In California, evidentiary privileges are statutorily created and must be strictly construed."[58] It noted that California Civil Code

---

53. 265 F.R.D. 510 (E.D. Cal. 2010).
54. *Id.* at 523.
55. *Id.* at 525.
56. *Id.*
57. *Id.* at 521.
58. *Id.* at 518.

section 2860 protects the attorney-client privilege as to communications shared with the insured's insurer when the insurer is defending the insured under a reservation of rights. However, it emphasized that any "disclosure and cooperation requirements do not require the disclosure of privileged material."[59] It then held:

> [T]he attorney-client privilege has never been extended to cover communications among an insured, defense counsel, and an insurer that is not defending its insured without reservation, let alone an insurer that is not defending its insured at all. This court does not find any justification for creating a new privilege to cover those communications.[60]

The court reached a similar conclusion in *Lincoln General Insurance Co. v. Ryan Mercaldo LLP*.[61] There, an insurer had agreed to defend a lawsuit against its insured subject to a reservation of rights. It retained counsel to do so. Thereafter, it retained another firm to provide a coverage opinion. Based on that opinion, the insurer denied coverage in the underlying action against its insured and withdrew its defense. Subsequently, the insurer sued the firm that

59. *Id.* at 520 (citing Cal. Civ. Code § 2860(f); Assurance Co. of Am. v. Haven, 32 Cal. App. 4th 78, 90, 38 Cal. Rptr. 2d 25 (1995) ("[T]he duties specified in Civil Code section 2860 that *Cumis* counsel owes the insurer are limited to the duties to disclose, inform, consult and cooperate regarding *non-privileged* information.")).

60. 265 F.R.D. at 525. *See also* Enns Pontiac, Buick & GMC Inc. v. Flores, 2011 WL 6181924, at *4 (E.D. Cal. Dec. 13, 2011) ("Federal courts have never recognized a blanket privilege regarding insured/insurer communications. . . . When the insurer defends under a reservation of rights, denying the duty to indemnify on some or all claims, the communications between the insured and the carrier are not privileged per se."); Kaufman & Broad Monterey Bay v. Travelers Prop. Cas. Co of Am., 2011 WL 2181692, at *5 n.2 (N.D. Cal. June 2, 2011) (distinguishing *Compton* and stating that when an insurer defends under a reservation of rights, there is a tension between the insurer and insured "because the insurer essentially makes it clear that it has reserved the right to later deny coverage as to both indemnity and defense if facts support it. And, '[t]he presence of that tension is fundamentally inconsistent with a basic requirement of all attorney-client relationships: the requirement that the client have a reasonably based expectation that the communications will not be used against the client.'"); Hansen v. State Farm Mutual Auto. Ins. Co., 2012 WL 6205722, at *10 (D. Nev. Dec. 12, 2012) (whether reservation of rights results in conflict between insurer and insured to be determined on case-by-case basis); Vt. Gas Sys. v. U.S. Fid. & Guar. Co., 151 F.R.D. 268, 277 (D. Vt. 1993) (The common interest doctrine does not apply "where there is an adversarial relationship between the insured and insurer as to whether coverage exists, the parties have never shared the same counsel or litigation strategy and the documents at issue were prepared in an atmosphere of uncertainty as to the scope of any identity of interest shared by the parties."); Heffron v. L.A. Transit Lines, 170 Cal. App. 2d 709, 718, 339 P.2d 567 (1959) (communication privilege "if the policy requires the company to defend [the insured] through its attorney, and the communication is intended for the information or assistance of the attorney in so defending him"); Sawyer v. Sw. Airlines, 2002 WL 31928442, at *3 (D. Kan. Dec. 23, 2002) (underlying plaintiff's motion to compel production of documents exchanged between insured and insurer denied because insured and insurer, who had duty to defend, "have an interest in common . . . that [is] of a legal and not commercial nature").

61. 2015 WL 12672142 (S.D. Cal. July 15, 2015).

provided the coverage opinion, alleging malpractice. In that action, the insurer and the law firm disagreed as to whether communications between the insurer and the defense counsel after the insurer denied coverage were subject to the attorney-client privilege. The court found that the insurer "severed the tripartite relationship" when it disclaimed its duty to defend. It reasoned that at that point, "there was no longer a common interest between the insurer and insured with regard to the [underlying] claim. . . . At that point, any communications between [the insurer] and [defense counsel] were no longer made in the course of an attorney-client relationship and were not privileged."[62] The court also rejected the insurer's argument that because it continued to pay for the defense counsel's services for several months after denying coverage, the communications were still privileged. It noted that "payment alone does not establish an attorney-client relationship."[63]

California had addressed this issue at least in part by statute. California Civil Code section 2860, which governs an insured's right to select counsel when there is a conflict of interest between insured and insurer, requires that the insured disclose to the insurer all information concerning the action except privileged materials relevant to coverage disputes.[64] Section 2860(d) provides that "[a]ny information disclosed [to the insurer] by the insured or by independent counsel is not a waiver of the privilege as to any other party."[65] Thus, in California, an insurer's declination or reservation should not affect the applicability of the attorney-client privilege, at least when section 2860 applies.

In *Bank of America, N.A. v. Superior Court*,[66] a title insurer retained counsel to prosecute a subrogation action on behalf of its insured against a bank. That bank sought discovery of communications between the insured's counsel and the title insurer. The trial court denied the insured's motion to quash and the insured brought a petition for a writ of mandate. The court of appeal found that the title insurer's retention of counsel to represent its insured was "sufficient to establish a tripartite attorney-client relationship" between the insured, counsel, and the insurer.[67] The court noted that the parties had "formed a 'loose partnership, coalition of alliance' that was directed to the 'common goal' of protecting [the insured's] security position, and communications exchanged among them are privileged."[68]

The court next held that the attorney-client relationship existed even though the insurer had reserved its rights. It held, "A reservation of rights in itself does not create a disqualifying conflict requiring the appointment of

62. *Id.* at *2.
63. *Id.*
64. Cal. Civ. Code § 2860.
65. *Id.*
66. 212 Cal. App. 4th 1076 (2013).
67. *Id.* at 1090.
68. *Id.* at 1091 (citation omitted).

Cumis counsel."[69] The court also noted that the insurer "retained [counsel] to represent [the insured], there is no evidence [the insured] independently retained [the counsel], [the insured] made no demand for *Cumis* counsel, and neither [the insurer] nor [the insured] has ever asserted [counsel] has been acting as *Cumis* counsel."[70]

The court then pointed out that even if the insurer's reservation of rights created a disqualifying conflict of interest, its ruling would be the same. It explained that "the right to invoke the conflict would belong solely" to the insured, and that the adversary "cannot assert [the insured's] right to *Cumis* counsel in order to create a waiver of the attorney-client privilege and attorney work product doctrine as to communications between [counsel] and the insurer."[71] It also pointed out that if the counsel were serving as *Cumis* counsel, then it would have a duty under Civil Code section 2860(d) to disclose to the insurer information other than privileged information regarding coverage issues and that the disclosure would not be a waiver of the privilege as to anyone else.[72]

VI. Application of the Work-Product Doctrine

The work-product doctrine may offer some protection to communications between an insured and an insurer and also may prevent discovery by third parties of information contained in the insurer's claims files. The purpose of the doctrine is to assure the lawyer the "opportunity to work 'with a certain degree of privacy, free from unnecessary intrusion by opposing parties and their counsel.'"[73] Under this doctrine, an attorney's mental impressions and work product, at least to the extent generated in anticipation of litigation, will be discoverable only upon a showing of "good cause."[74] "Fact" work product, which includes "non-legal opinions and thoughts about the facts [of the claim]," is discoverable upon the moving party's showing of substantial need and undue hardship. Conversely, "opinion" work product may be more difficult to discover. Opinion work product consists of the attorney's "mental impressions, conclusions, opinions or legal theories."[75] Consequently, the

---

69. *Id.*
70. *Id.* at 1092.
71. *Id.*
72. *Id.* at 1093.
73. Conn. Mut. Life Ins. Co. v. Shields, 16 F.R.D. 5, 8 (S.D.N.Y. 1954); Linde v. Arab Bank, PLC, 608 F. Supp. 2d 351, 357 (S.D.N.Y. 2009).
74. *See* Hickman v. Taylor, 329 U.S. 495, 510 (1947).
75. Fed. R. Civ. P. 26(b)(3). Duplan Corp. v. Moulinage et Retorderie de Chavanoz, 509 F.2d 730, 732 (4th Cir. 1974), *cert. denied*, 420 U.S. 997 (1975). *See also In re* Murphy, 560 F.2d 326, 334 (8th Cir. 1977); United States v. Deloitte LLP, 610 F.3d 129, 135 (D.C. Cir. 2010) (opinion work product is "virtually undiscoverable").

claims adjusters' and counsel's thoughts regarding a claim should be insulated from third-party discovery. Thus, if a claims adjuster has a law degree or if claims assessment is performed by either in-house or outside counsel, the insured and/or its insurers can seek to invoke the doctrine.

The Federal Rules of Civil Procedure state that materials prepared in "anticipation of litigation" are not discoverable unless the moving party has "substantial need of the materials" and is unable "without undue hardship [to] obtain the substantial equivalent [of the materials] by other means."[76] This rule applies to documents prepared by a party's representative, including its insurer.[77] It even can extend to documents prepared by a nonlawyer.[78] Thus, if the material was not prepared in anticipation of litigation, but instead was prepared as part of the ordinary course of business, the work-product doctrine will not protect it from discovery. Whether documents have been prepared in anticipation of litigation or in the ordinary course of business will be determined on a case-by-case basis.[79] Further, many courts have held that the privilege must be asserted on a document-by-document basis, as opposed to asserting the privilege over all the materials at issue.[80]

However, there is no bright-line standard delineating the scope of the work-product doctrine. Jurisdictions following the federal rule have adopted both majority and minority views, while other jurisdictions, including California, have developed their own standards.[81] Consequently, whether the doctrine applies to protect documents from disclosure can be determined only by reference to the applicable standard in the particular jurisdiction.

---

76. Fed. R. Civ. P. 26(b)(3)(A).

77. *Id.*

78. Diversified Indus., Inc. v. Meredith, 572 F.2d 596, 603 (8th Cir. 1977); Sandra T.E. v. S. Berwyn Sch. Dist. 100, 600 F.3d 612, 622 (7th Cir. 2010); United States v. Deloitte LLP, 610 F.3d 129, 139–40 (D.C. Cir. 2010).

79. *See* Pete Rinaldi's Fast Foods, Inc. v. Great Am. Ins. Cos., 123 F.R.D. 198, 202 (M.D.N.C. 1988); Upjohn Co. v. United States, 449 U.S. 383, 396–97 (1981).

80. *See, e.g.*, Auto-Owners Ins. Co. v. Totaltape, Inc., 135 F.R.D. 199, 202 (M.D. Fla. 1990) ("[t]he trend in lower federal courts is to analyze work product claims concerning insurance claims files on a case by case basis"); Burr v. United Farm Bureau Mut. Ins. Co., 560 N.E.2d 1250, 1256 (Ind. Ct. App. 1990) ("the privilege must be asserted on a document by document basis and with the utmost clarity"); AIU Ins. Co. v. TIG Ins. Co., 2008 WL 4067437, at *14 (S.D.N.Y. Aug. 28, 2008) (when determining whether insurance claims files were properly withheld, "rather than determine that the work-product doctrine applies based on a categorical presumption, the better course here is to engage in a fact-specific inquiry to determine whether each document was created in anticipation of litigation"), *order modified on reconsid.*, 2009 WL 1953039 (S.D.N.Y. July 8, 2009).

81. *See* BP Alaska Exploration, Inc. v. Superior Court, 199 Cal. App. 3d 1240, 1250 (1988) ("federal law is not controlling in California").

VII. The Majority View: Information in an Insurer's Claim Files Is Collected in the Ordinary Course of Business

If the documents at issue were not prepared or collected in anticipation of litigation, then the work-product doctrine will not apply and the documents will be discoverable upon a showing of relevance.[82]

Among the states that follow the federal rule, the majority view recognizes that a significant part of an insurer's business is to investigate and assess claims. As the Colorado Supreme Court explained:

> Because a substantial part of an insurance company's business is to investigate claims made by an insured against the company or by some other party against an insured, it must be presumed that such investigations are part of the normal business activity of the company and that reports and witness' statements compiled by or on behalf of the insurer in the course of such investigations are ordinary business records as distinguished from trial preparation materials.[83]

Based on this rationale, these courts hold that unless the insurer's investigation was performed at the request of or under the direction of counsel, all materials resulting from the investigation are "conclusively presumed to have been made in the ordinary course of business and not in anticipation of litigation."[84]

---

82. Thomas Organ Co. v. Jadranska Slobodna Plovidba, 54 F.R.D. 367, 370 (N.D. Ill. 1972).

83. Hawkins v. Dist. Court, 638 P.2d 1372, 1378 (Colo. 1982); Bronsink v. Allied Prop. & Cas. Ins., 2010 WL 786016, at 1576543, at *2 (W.D. Wash. Mar. 4, 2010) ("In the insurance context, materials prepared as part of claims investigation are generally not considered work product due to the industry's need to investigate claims. Such materials are part of the ordinary course of business unless there is a sufficiently concrete connection between the investigation and potential litigation."); Barnard Pipeline, Inc. v. Travelers Prop. Cas. Co. of Am., 2014 WL at *4 (D. Mont. Apr. 17, 2014) ("Often, in insurance bad faith litigation, the work product doctrine does not apply to materials that are generated before the insurer has formally denied the insured's claim because such materials are prepared as part of the ordinary course of business. . . ."); City of Glendale v. Nat'l Union Fire Ins. Co., 2013 WL 1797308, at *12 (D. Ariz. Apr. 29, 2013) (following *Bronsink*); *cf.* Underwriters Ins. Co. v. Atlanta Gas Light Co., 248 F.R.D. 663, 668 (N.D. Ga. 2008) ("As the federal courts have generally recognized: '[W]hen a liability insurer investigates a third party claim, the investigation is made in anticipation of claims, which, if denied, likely will lead to litigation. For this reason it is logical to conclude that, while files generated in relation to first party claims are made in the ordinary course of business and are discoverable, files generated during the investigation of third party claims are made in anticipation of litigation and are not discoverable.'").

84. Henry Enters., Inc. v. Smith, 592 P.2d 915, 920 (Kan. 1979). *Accord* Charter Oak Fire Ins. Co. v. Am. Capital, Ltd., Civil No. DKC 09-100, slip. op. at 2 (D. Md. July 24, 2013, filed Nov. 6, 2013), https://1.next.westlaw.com/Link/Docket/I01ABAE66E40911DDBC7BF97F340AF743/Blob/ecf/MDDCT-DW/godls,09315539638/8-09CV00100_DocketEntry_11-06-2013_255.pdf?courtNorm=MD-DCT&courtnumber=1058&casenumber=8%3a09-CV-00100&originationContext=document&transitionType=DocumentImage&contextData=(sc.Default)&uniqueId=860da90a-d97a-4788-9ba9-88ed78118746&ppcid=d4c85b2231d34b0ea0bbb7617160d01b&attachments=false&localImageGuid=I65a45c8068d

In fact, even if the insurer retains a law firm to perform the claims assessment, this will not necessarily protect the claims file information from discovery.[85]

However, the federal courts following the majority rule offer no clear guidelines regarding the level of certainty needed to transform investigative material from work performed in the ordinary course of business to work performed in anticipation of litigation. Some courts note that the "[m]ere likelihood of litigation in the future is insufficient for invoking the privilege. Rather, the probability of litigation must be substantial and the commencement of litigation imminent."[86] For these courts, "[t]he mere contingency that litigation may result is not determinative. . . . While litigation need not be imminent, the primary motivating purpose behind the creation of a document or investigative report must be to aid in possible future litigation."[87]

511e39132aa78075319d7 ("[I]nvestigative reports prepared prior to a coverage decision are generally prepared in the ordinary course of business. To enjoy work-product protection, the insurer must present 'specific evidentiary proof of objective facts demonstrating a resolve to litigate.'"); Illiana Surgery & Med. Ctr. LLC v. Hartford Fire Ins. Co., 2008 WL 4976211, at *2 (N.D. Ind. Nov. 18, 2008) ("Claim file materials that are part of a factual evaluation or investigation into an insured's claim, if created before a final coverage decision has been made, are presumed to have been prepared in the ordinary and routine course of the insurer's business."); Harper v. Auto-Owners Ins. Co., 138 F.R.D. 655, 663 (S.D. Ind. 1991) ("[A] document or thing produced or used by an insurer to evaluate an insured's claim in order to arrive at a claims decision in the ordinary and regular course of business is not work product. . . ."); W. Nat'l Bank v. Emp'rs Ins., 109 F.R.D. 55, 57 (D. Colo. 1985); APL Corp. v. Aetna Cas. & Sur. Co., 91 F.R.D. 10, 17 (D. Md. 1980) ("[W]hile litigation often results from an insurance company's denial of a claim, it cannot be said that any document prepared by an insurance company after such a claim has arisen is prepared in anticipation of litigation within the meaning of Rule 26(b)(3)."); Benton v. Brookfield Props. Corp., 2003 WL 21746902, at *2 (S.D.N.Y. July 29, 2003) ("An insurance company's decision whether to afford coverage is part of its normal business decision-making and does not constitute work-product even though the insurance company may face the prospect that if coverage is denied, the insured will commence litigation against it."); Langdon v. Champion, 752 P.2d 999, 1007 (Alaska 1988) ("An insurance company routinely investigates possible claims whether or not there is any possibility of litigation, and we do not believe that [the work-product doctrine] was intended to insulate insurers from discovery merely because they regularly deal with potential claims.").

85. *See* Mission Nat'l Ins. Co. v. Lilly, 112 F.R.D. 160, 163 (D. Minn. 1986); Meighan v. Transguard Ins. Co. of Am., 298 F.R.D. 436 (D. Iowa. 2013) (following *Mission*); Tilden-Coil Constructors, Inc. v. Landmark Am. Ins. Co., 2010 WL 3789104, at *2 (W.D. Wash. Sept. 23, 2010) (even though attorney drafted denial letter, letter was part of ordinary course of the insurer's business of claim determination); Am. Home Assurance Co. v. United States, 2009 WL 3245445, at *3 (D.N.J. Oct. 7, 2009) ("simple involvement of counsel in an insurer's claim investigation does not transform the investigation to one undertaken in anticipation of litigation"); Providence Piers, LLC v. SMM New England, Inc., 2014 WL 11532189, at *4 (D.R.I. Mar. 25, 2014) ("It is well settled that evidence that the insurer has involved its counsel in its claim investigation does not transform the investigation to one undertaken in anticipation of litigation.").

86. Stauffer Chem. Co. v. Monsanto Co., 623 F. Supp. 148, 152 (E.D. Mo. 1985).

87. Janicker v. George Wash. Univ., 94 F.R.D. 648, 650 (D.D.C. 1982); Schwarz & Schwarz of Va. L.L.C. v. Certain Underwriters, 2009 WL, 1043929, at *2 (W.D. Va. Apr. 16, 2009) ("Thus, there is no bright-line test for when work product protection applies for insurance companies, and instead courts must undertake a case-by-case analysis. 'This approach realistically recognizes that at some point an insurance company shifts its activity from the ordinary course of business to anticipation of litigation.' The 'pivotal point' is when the probability of litigation becomes 'substantial and imminent,' or stated otherwise, when litigation becomes 'fairly foreseeable.'") (citations omitted).

Other courts have focused not on the pendency of litigation, but rather on the document itself. "[T]he test should be whether, in light of the nature of the document and the factual situation in the particular case, the document can fairly be said to have been prepared or obtained because of the prospect of litigation."[88]

Thus, under the majority federal view, information in an insurer's claim files should not be deemed to be work product unless the insurer proves, on a document-by-document basis, that the information was prepared in anticipation of litigation.

VIII. The Minority View: Information in an Insurer's Claim File Is Collected in Anticipation of Litigation

Under the minority view, courts accept that all insurer investigations generally are undertaken in anticipation of litigation. As the Iowa Supreme Court observed:

> In our litigious society, when an insured reports to his insurer that he has been involved in an incident involving another person, the insurer can reasonably anticipate that some action will be taken by the other party. The seeds of prospective litigation have been sown, and the prudent party, anticipating this fact, will begin to prepare his case. Although a claim may be settled short of the instigation of legal action, there is an ever-present possibility of a claim's ending in litigation. The recognition of this possibility provides, in any given

88. *APL*, 91 F.R.D. at 15 (citation omitted). *See* Cowie v. State Farm Fire & Cas. Co., 2007 WL 2077619, at *2 (E.D. Tenn. July 17, 2007) ("The dispute in this case centers on the meaning of 'in anticipation of litigation.' This phrase, as it applies to insurance companies, presents an especially thorny problem because insurance companies, by the very nature of their business, have a duty to investigate claims. . . . Nevertheless, a number of courts in other jurisdictions have been faced with this particular discovery dilemma . . . and a majority of them have applied a standard based on whether the documents were prepared primarily for the purpose of adjusting the claim or primarily in anticipation of litigation. . . . To answer the question of the primary purpose of a document, the court must engage in a fact intensive analysis on a case-by-case basis."); William A. Gross Constr. Assocs. v. Am. Mfrs. Mut. Ins. Co., 262 F.R.D. 354, 360 (S.D.N.Y. 2009) ("'Where a document was created because of anticipated litigation, and would not have been prepared in substantially similar form but for the prospect of that litigation, it falls within Rule 26(b)(3).' Where the threat of litigation is accompanied by a non-litigation purpose for the generation of the documents at issue, "[w]hether there is work product protection turns on whether the material 'would have been prepared irrespective of the expected litigation . . . .'" (citations omitted)); Gov't Emps. Ins. Co. v. Saco, 2013 WL 5502871, at *2 (E.D.N.Y. Oct. 2, 2013) (following *William A. Gross*); Amica Mut. Ins. Co. v. W.C. Bradley Co., 217 F.R.D. 79, 83 (D. Mass. 2003) ("Coverage investigations by insurance companies are not *per se* conducted in anticipation of litigation, and a determination as to whether documents generated during such investigations were prepared in anticipation of litigation, as opposed to in the ordinary course of business, should be made on a case-by-case basis."); Henderson v. Zurn Indus., Inc., 131 F.R.D. 560, 570–71 (S.D. Ind. 1990) (same).

> case, the impetus for the insurer to garner information regarding the circumstances of a claim.[89]

Based on this rationale, these courts conclude that most information in an insurer's claim files is protected from discovery by the work-product doctrine.[90]

While the minority view may not permit the insured to discover certain claim documents in coverage litigation against an insurer, it does protect the insured and the insurer from being forced to disclose potentially damaging documents to an underlying claimant. Furthermore, the protection afforded under the minority view may vary, depending upon who is seeking access to the material in question. As one court explained:

> When the party seeking the work product does not have a special relationship with the insurer, different considerations may apply. For example, in investigations of an accident, because of potential claims by the third party against the insured, the possibility of litigation might arise at an earlier time. However, when the claim is made by its insured, an insurance company cannot in good faith contend that there is a reasonable possibility of litigation with respect to every claim submitted to it.[91]

89. Ashmead v. Harris, 336 N.W.2d 197, 201 (Iowa 1983) (quoting Fireman's Fund Ins. Co. v. McAlpine, 391 A.2d 84, 89–90 (R.I. 1978)). A South Dakota case, *Taylor v. Pilot Travel Centers*, LLC, 2011 WL 542123, at *4 (S.D. Feb. 8, 2011), states that Ashmead "was expressly overruled by the Iowa Supreme Court in Wells Dairy, Inc. v. American Ind. Refrigeration, Inc., 690 N.W.2d 38, 48 (Iowa 2004)." In fact, *Wells* did not expressly overrule *Ashmead* or discuss the quoted language. *Wells* lays out the rule as follows: "Accordingly, we hold that the overarching inquiry in determining whether a document was prepared in anticipation of litigation is 'whether, in light of the nature of the document and the factual situation in the particular case, the document can fairly be said to have been prepared or obtained because of the prospect of litigation.'" *Wells Dairy*, 690 N.W. 2d at 48 (quoting 8 Wright & Miller § 2024, at 198–99). If documents "would have been created in essentially similar form irrespective of the litigation[,] . . . it [cannot] fairly be said that they were created 'because of' actual or impending litigation." *Id.* at 48. *See Ex parte* Nationwide Mut. Ins. Co., 898 So. 2d 720, 723 (Ala. 2004) (individual injured in automobile accident was undergoing surgery; therefore, insurer "could have reasonably concluded that its insured would be sued"); Liberty Mut. Fire Ins. Co. v. Kaufman, 885 So. 2d 905, 910 (Fla. Ct. App. 2004) ("Generally, an insurer's claims and litigation files constitute work product and are protected from production.").

90. *See* Almaguer v. Chi., R.I. & P.R.R. Co., 55 F.R.D. 147, 148 (D. Neb. 1972).

91. Pete Rinaldi's Fast Foods, Inc. v. Great Am. Ins. Cos., 123 F.R.D. 198, 202 (M.D.N.C. 1988). *See also* Henderson v. Zurn Indus., Inc., 131 F.R.D. 560, 571 n.11 (S.D. Ind. 1990) (court acknowledged a difference between third-party claims against an insurer and direct first-party claims; "one would expect there to be more litigation on third-party claims than on direct first-party contract actions, with a resultant increased anticipation of such litigation in the third-party context"); Underwriters Ins. Co. v. Atlanta Gas Light Co., 248 F.R.D. 663, 668 (N.D. Ga. 2008) ("As the federal courts have generally recognized: '[W]hen a liability insurer investigates a third party claim, the investigation is made in anticipation of claims, which, if denied, likely will lead to litigation. For this reason it is logical to conclude that, while files generated in relation to first party claims are made in the ordinary course of

While courts have split on the discoverability of some or all information in an insurer's claim fails, their analysis appears to depend on the specific facts involved.[92]

IX. The California View

Not all jurisdictions follow the federal statute. California, for example, has a statute protecting work product from disclosure that is broader than the federal rule. In California, work product is not discoverable unless denial "will unfairly prejudice the party seeking discovery,"[93] and in no event may a "writing that reflects an attorney's impressions, conclusions, opinions, or legal research or theories" be discovered.[94] The California rule protects work product in all legal contexts, not just work performed in anticipation of litigation.[95]

Furthermore, the policy behind the privilege in California is essentially the same as the federal policy. The privilege is intended to preserve the rights of attorneys to prepare for trial with a certain amount of privacy and to prevent attorneys from reaping the benefits of their opponents' work.[96]

X. Protection of the Work-Product Doctrine

In many insurance coverage cases, there are questions as to the timing of occurrences and the extent of any damage or injury involved. As a result, insurers often seek to discover reports by outside consultants in connection with any underlying litigation. In jurisdictions following the federal rule, the discoverability of these reports will depend upon which view of "anticipation of litigation" the jurisdiction follows. Even if such reports are "work product" in

---

business and are discoverable, files generated during the investigation of third party claims are made in anticipation of litigation and are not discoverable.'").

92. *See, e.g.*, United Nat'l Ins. Co. v. Gunderson, Inc., 2010 WL 11537511, at *3 (D. Minn. May 20, 2010) ("In the context of insurance-coverage disputes, the line between documents prepared in the ordinary course of business and those prepared in anticipation of litigation 'is not always clear because an insurance company investigates claims in the ordinary course of its business.' Courts generally take a case-by-case approach to resolving such disputes. Where the documents in question reflect only 'pure factual investigation of the claim,' the work-product doctrine will not protect the materials from disclosure. Further, an insurer is not permitted to use an attorney as a claims adjuster to shield purely investigative material from discovery. But, if the documents are genuinely prepared in anticipation of litigation, the doctrine will protect the documents from disclosure unless the other party can show a substantial need." (citations omitted)).

93. Cal. Civ. Proc. Code § 2018.030(b).

94. *Id.* § 2018.030(a).

95. *Id.*; Rumac, Inc. v. Bottomley, 143 Cal. App. 3d 810, 812, 192 Cal. Rptr. 104 (1983); Laguna Beach Cnty. Water Dist. v. Superior Court, 124 Cal. App. 4th 1453, 1461, 22 Cal. Rptr. 3d 387, 393 (2004). However, like the federal rule, opinion work product also enjoys absolute immunity in California. *See* BP Alaska Exploration, Inc. v. Superior Court, 199 Cal. App. 3d 1240, 1250, 245 Cal. Rptr. 682 (1988); Rico v. Mitsubishi Motors Corp., 42 Cal. 4th 807, 814, 171 P.3d 1092, 68 Cal. Rptr. 3d 758 (2007).

96. *See* Cal. Civ. Proc. Code § 2018.020(a)–(b).

the underlying litigation, they may be discoverable in the coverage litigation. Courts differ as to whether the work-product protection lapses once litigation or anticipation of litigation has ended or whether it offers "perpetual protection," thereby preventing discovery of the material in later proceedings.[97]

XI. The Limited Protection View

Some courts hold that the protection extends only to documents prepared in anticipation of the specific litigation before the court. "Thus, documents prepared for one case are freely discoverable in another case."[98] Moreover, one court following the limited protection view has required not only that the documents be prepared in preparation for the specific action before the court but also that the parties be adversaries in order for the privilege to apply.

> Here, the sought-after materials were . . . prepared for the mutual benefit of insureds and insurers against a third-party adversary. Insurers were not the adversary from whom the attorney's trial strategies and opinions required protection. Insurers and insureds have only become adversarial since the termination of the primary litigation. While the work-product materials, had they been requested by the third-party opponent in the underlying lawsuit, would have been entitled to protection, the same protection is not warranted here.[99]

XII. The Broad Protection View

However, both the Fourth and Eighth Circuits have held that work product prepared in previous litigation is not discoverable in the current litigation.[100] In *In re Murphy*, the court held that the work-product doctrine protects documents prepared in anticipation of unrelated, terminated litigation. The court reasoned that this protection was consistent with the purpose of the work-product doctrine as announced by the U.S. Supreme Court in *Hickman v.*

97. *See* Levingston v. Allis-Chalmers Corp., 109 F.R.D. 546 (S.D. Miss. 1985); Fed. Trade Comm'n v. Grolier, Inc., 462 U.S. 19 (1983).

98. *Levingston*, 109 F.R.D. at 552. *See* United States v. Int'l Bus. Machs. Corp., 66 F.R.D. 154, 178 (S.D.N.Y. 1974) (documents must be prepared in anticipation of the litigation in which special immunity accorded to such material is sought); Honeywell, Inc. v. Piper Aircraft Corp., 50 F.R.D. 117, 119 (M.D. Pa. 1970) (same); Hanover Shoe, Inc. v. United Shoe Mach. Corp., 207 F. Supp. 407, 410 (M.D. Pa. 1962) (materials must be prepared for case at bar); Wong v. Thomas, 238 F.R.D. 548, 551 (D.N.J. 2007) (prosecutors cannot assert work-product protection for criminal investigation file in subsequent civil suits).

99. Waste Mgmt., Inc. v. Int'l Surplus Lines Ins. Co., 144 Ill. 2d 178, 198, 579 N.E.2d 322 (1991).

100. *See* Duplan Corp. v. Moulinage et Retorderie de Chavanoz, 509 F.2d 730, 736, (4th Cir. 1974), *cert. denied*, 420 U.S. 997 (1975); *In re* Murphy, 560 F.2d 326, 334 (8th Cir. 1977); Pamida, Inc. v. E.S. Originals, Inc., 281 F.3d 726, 731 (8th Cir. 2002).

Taylor,[101] which recognized the attorney's need for enough privacy to perform his duties responsibly and effectively.[102] According to the *Murphy* court,

> What is needed, if we are to remain faithful to the articulated policies of Hickman, is a perpetual protection for work product, one that extends beyond the termination of the litigation for which the documents were prepared. Any less protection would generate the very evils that the Court in Hickman attempted to avoid.[103]

California also appears to follow the Fourth and Eighth Circuit's view of broad protection.[104]

XIII. The Intermediate View

A third approach was recognized in *Levingston v. Allis-Chalmers Corp.*[105] In *Levingston*, the court held that the work-product doctrine applies only when the two suits are related.[106] Thus, to the extent that the underlying litigation and

---

101. 329 U.S. 495 (1947).

102. *Murphy*, 560 F.2d at 333.

103. *Id.* at 334.

104. *See* Fellows v. Superior Court, 108 Cal. App. 3d 55, 62, 166 Cal. Rptr. 274 (1980), *disapproved on other grounds*, Coito v. Superior Court, 54 Cal. 4th 480 (2012) ("[T]he attorney's work product privilege . . . survives the termination of the litigation or matter in which the work product is prepared and may be claimed in subsequent litigation—whether related or unrelated to the prior matter—to preclude disclosure of the attorney's work product."). *See also* Planalto v. Ohio Cas. Ins. Co., 256 F.R.D. 16, 19 (D. Me. 2009) (stating that "the emerging majority of courts" hold that work product extends into subsequent litigation); Jicarilla Apache Nation v. United States, 88 Fed. Cl. 1, 9 (Fed. Cl. 2009) (following broad protection rule).

105. 109 F.R.D. 546 (S.D. Miss. 1985).

106. *Id.* at 552. *Accord* Hercules, Inc. v. Exxon Corp., 434 F. Supp. 136, 153 (D. Del. 1977) ("[T]his Court accepts the 'sounder view' that the documents prepared for one case have the same protection in a second case where the two cases are closely related in parties or subject matter."); Republic Gear Co. v. Borg-Warner Corp., 381 F.2d 551, 557 (2d Cir. 1967); Midland Inv. Co. v. Van Alstyne, Noel & Co., 59 F.R.D. 134, 138 (S.D.N.Y. 1973); Underwriters Ins. Co. v. Atlanta Gas Light Co., 248 F.R.D. 663, 668 (N.D. Ga. 2008) (insurance claims files prepared in anticipation of underlying claim were protected in bad-faith litigation; "Particularly where cases are closely related, courts have generally found that documents produced in anticipation of litigating one case remain protected in a subsequent cases [sic]if they were created by or for a party to the subsequent litigation."); La. Mun. Police Emps. Ret. Sys. v. Sealed Air Corp., 253 F.R.D. 300, 309 n.3 (D.N.J. 2008) ("work-product protection applies to documents prepared for a different case so long as the two cases are closely related in parties or subject matter"); Cohen v. City of New York, 255 F.R.D. 110, 124 (S.D.N.Y. 2008) ("the weight of authority now clearly favors protecting work product that was generated as part of an earlier litigation at least where, as here, that litigation is related to the current suit"). *See also* Anchondo v. Anderson, Crenshaw & Assocs., L.L.C., 256 F.R.D. 661, 672 (D.N.M. 2009) (work-product protection may extend into subsequent litigation but "[i]t is unclear whether the doctrine applies only to subsequent litigation that is closely related to the earlier litigation") (citing Frontier Ref., Inc. v. Gorman-Rupp Co., 136 F.3d 695, 703 (10th Cir. 1998)); Cosmetic Warriors Ltd. v. Lush Day Spa, 2013 WL 5536048, at *3 (D.N.J. Oct. 4, 2013) (adopting the "closely related" test); Billups v. Penn. State Milton S. Hershey Med. Ctr., 2013 WL 4041161, at *7 (M.D. Pa. Aug. 7, 2013) ("There is no dispute that the instant civil action is related to the prior criminal

coverage litigation are deemed to be closely related—as they should be—the underlying defense files should be treated as work product and should not be discoverable in the coverage litigation.[107]

XIV. Waiver of the Work-Product Doctrine under Federal Law

Even if documents qualify as work product, the protection against discovery may be waived. However, determining when the doctrine has been waived may not be easy.

Federal courts are split on what represents a waiver of the attorney work-product doctrine. The majority of federal courts hold that conduct that might constitute a waiver of the attorney-client privilege will not necessarily result in a waiver of the work-product protection. As one court stated:

> We do not consider the strict standard of waiver in the attorney-client privilege context . . . to be appropriate for work product cases. . . . The purpose of the work product doctrine is to protect information against opposing parties, rather than against all others outside a particular confidential relationship, in order to encourage effective trial-preparation. . . . A disclosure made in the pursuit of such trial preparation, and not inconsistent with maintaining secrecy against opponents, should be allowed without waiver of the privilege.[108]

This led the court to conclude that "while the mere showing of a voluntary disclosure to a third person will generally suffice to show waiver of the

---

proceedings . . . , and as such, the correspondence exchanged between the [district attorney and the defendants] containing the opinions and legal theories of the prosecutor are subject to work product protection in this action.").

107. *See* Special Magistrate's Report and Recommendation No. 2, *In re* Tex. E. Transmission Corp. PCB Contamination Ins. Coverage Litig., MDL Docket No. 764 (E.D. Pa. Apr. 8, 1991), *reprinted in* 5 Mealey's Litig. Reports—Ins., No. 23, § C (Apr. 16, 1991).

108. United States v. Am. Tel. & Tel. Co., 642 F.2d 1285, 1299 (D.C. Cir. 1980) (citation omitted). *See also* United States v. Deloitte LLP, 610 F.3d 129, 139–40 (D.C. Cir. 2010) ("While voluntary disclosure waives the attorney-client privilege, it does not necessarily waive work-product protection. . . . [T]he attorney-client privilege and the work-product doctrine serve different purposes: the former protects the attorney-client relationship by safeguarding confidential communications, whereas the latter promotes the adversary process by insulating an attorney's litigation preparation from discovery. Voluntary disclosure waives the attorney-client privilege because it is inconsistent with the confidential attorney-client relationship. Voluntary disclosure does not necessarily waive work-product protection, however, because it does not necessarily undercut the adversary process. Nevertheless, disclosing work product to a third party can waive protection if such disclosure, under the circumstances, is inconsistent with the maintenance of secrecy from the disclosing party's adversary. Under this standard, the voluntary disclosure of attorney work product to an adversary or a conduit to an adversary waives work-product protection for that material." (citations and quotation marks omitted)).

attorney-client privilege, it should not suffice in itself for waiver of the work product privilege."[109]

In contrast, a minority of courts hold that the standard for waiver of the work-product protection is the same as the standard as waiver of the attorney-client privilege—that is, the disclosure or consent to disclosure of work-product material by the holder of the privilege waives it.[110]

Whichever standard is used to determine waiver, most federal courts agree that disclosure to an allied party will not waive the privilege.[111] As stated in *In re Crazy Eddie Securities Litigation*,[112] "Counsel may therefore share work product, including ideas, opinions, and legal theories, with those having similar interests in fully preparing litigation against a common adversary."

This should mean that when an insurer is defending its insured against a "common adversary," disclosure to the insured of any information in the claims file and disclosure to the insurer of defense files should not waive the work-product protection as to third parties, including the underlying claimants.[113] When the insured and insurer are co-parties, this "allied party" or "common adversary" exception to the waiver doctrine protects the insured from disclosing a claims file or insured-insurer communications to third-party claimants.

---

109. *Am. Tel. & Tel. Co.*, 642 F.2d at 1299 (emphasis omitted).

110. *See* D'Ippolito v. Cities Serv. Co., 39 F.R.D. 610 (S.D.N.Y. 1965).

111. Cont'l Oil Co. v. United States, 330 F.2d 347, 350 (9th Cir. 1964); United States v. Gonzalez, 669 F.3d 974, 978 (9th Cir. 2012). *See also* United States v. Deloitte LLP, 610 F.3d 129, 139–40 (D.C. Cir. 2010) (disclosure of work product to auditor did not waive privilege because auditor was not an adversary or a potential adversary); Schaeffler v. United States, 22 F. Supp. 3d 319, 337 n.28 (S.D.N.Y. May 28, 2014) (following *Deloitte*).

112. 131 F.R.D. 374, 379 (E.D.N.Y. 1990); *see also* Am. Eagle Outfitters, Inc. v. Payless ShoeSource, Inc., 2009 WL 3786210, at *3 (E.D.N.Y. Nov. 12, 2009).

113. *See* Bovis Lend Lease, LMB, Inc. v. Seasons Contracting Corp., 2002 WL 31729693, at *4 (S.D.N.Y. Dec. 5, 2002) ("certainly, documents created after litigation has already commenced, when the claims handlers' work has plainly shifted from investigating the initial claim to assisting in the defense of the pending litigation and evaluating litigation exposure, are likely to be covered by the work product doctrine. . . . Similarly, correspondence between an insured and its liability insurer, written 'as a consequence of pending litigation for the purpose of mounting a defense to the claim' is entitled to work product protection."); Kingsway Fin. Servs., Inc. v. PricewaterhouseCoopers LLP, 2008 WL 4452134, at *10 (S.D.N.Y. Oct. 2, 2008) ("Work-product protection may be waived by voluntary disclosure to a party outside the privileged relationship. Work-product protection, however, is only waived when the disclosure is to an adversary or materially increases the likelihood of disclosure to an adversary. In this case, disclosure of materials to an insurer does not waive the work-product protection because such disclosure does not "materially increase the likelihood of disclosure to an adversary.") (internal citations and quotation marks omitted). *See also* Niagara Mohawk Power Corp. v. Stone & Webster Eng'g Corp., 125 F.R.D. 578, 587 (N.D.N.Y. 1989) ("sharing work product material with a friendly party does not waive the work product protection as it applies to an adverse third party"); Nidec Corp. v. Victor Co. of Japan, 2007 WL 2156256, at *1 (N.D. Cal. July 26, 2007) ("For work product, protection is waived where disclosure of the otherwise privileged documents is made to a third party, and that disclosure enables an adversary to gain access to the information.") (internal quotation marks omitted).

XV. Waiver of the Work Product Doctrine under California Law

There is no waiver provision in California Code of Civil Procedure sections 2018.010 *et seq.*, the California statute stating the work-product doctrine. As a result, California courts have not reached a consensus on what standard is to be used to determine if the protection has been waived.

In *Williamson v. Superior Court,*[114] the California Supreme Court held that the fact that parties may be codefendants does not ensure that they are not adversaries. The court specifically recognized that on the facts before it, the sharing of information among codefendants is not necessarily the sharing of information among allied parties. As the court noted, "Each codefendant seeks to disclaim any responsibility for the alleged injuries, and argues that if there is responsibility for the alleged injuries it is due to the failure of the other. Certainly, there exists that relationship which suggests a conflict of interest."[115]

However, in *Fellows v. Superior Court,*[116] the court seemed to follow the rule followed by a majority of federal courts. In *Fellows*, the claimants had brought a bad-faith action against an insurer for failure to settle their uninsured motorist claims after the issue of coverage had been resolved by an arbitrator. The insurer sought production of the files of the claimants' former attorney. The court held that although the attorney had turned the file over to the claimants, this did not constitute waiver of the work-product doctrine.[117] The court also

---

114. 21 Cal. 3d 829, 582 P.2d 126, 148 Cal. Rptr. 39 (1978).

115. *Id.* at 836 (quoting Gorman Rupp Indus., Inc. v. Superior Court, 20 Cal. App. 3d 28, 31, 97 Cal. Rptr. 377 (1971)). *See also* Rockwell Int'l Corp. v. Superior Court, 26 Cal. App. 4th 1255, 1263–64, 32 Cal. Rptr. 2d 153 (1994) ("[W]here the carrier questions the availability of coverage and provides a defense in the third party action subject to a reservation of rights, a conflict exists—because the insured's goal is coverage, which flies in the face of the insurer's desire to avoid its duty to indemnify.").

116. 108 Cal. App. 3d 55, 166 Cal. Rptr. 274 (1980), *disapproved on other grounds*, Coito v. Superior Court, 54 Cal. 4th 480 (2012).

117. *Id.* at 65–66; *see also, e.g.*, Laguna Beach Cnty. Water Dist. v. Superior Court, 124 Cal. App. 4th 1453, 1461, 22 Cal. Rptr. 3d 387, 393 (2004) (holding that attorney did not waive work-product protection by disclosing audit response letters containing work product to his client's auditor: "[B]ased on the contents of the letters, which contain the attorney's thoughts, impressions, and opinions, plus the purpose of the work product doctrine, and the rule that waiver occurs only when work product is disclosed to a third party who has no interest in maintaining the confidentiality . . . of a significant part of the work product, we conclude [the attorney's] audit response letters to [the auditor] remained protected work product.") (internal citations and quotation marks omitted); Meza v. H. Muehlstein & Co., 176 Cal. App. 4th 969, 981–83, 98 Cal. Rptr. 3d 422, 431–33 (2009) (sharing of work product among defense counsel with a common interest did not waive work-product protections: "Under the common interest doctrine, an attorney can disclose work product to an attorney representing a separate client without waiving the attorney work-product privilege if (1) the disclosure relates to a common interest of the attorneys' respective clients; (2) the disclosing attorney has a reasonable expectation that the other attorney will preserve confidentiality; and (3) the disclosure is reasonably necessary for the accomplishment of the purpose for which the -disclosing attorney was consulted. . . . California recognizes the common interest doctrine." (footnotes, citations, and quotation marks omitted)).

held that initiation of a civil action by the claimants against the insurer did not waive the protection:

> [A]uthorization by the attorney to his client to waive the privilege cannot be construed as a waiver in and of itself. Nor can the action of an attorney in disclosing the contents of his file to his client be construed as a waiver by disclosure of the privileged material *since the disclosure* is not to a *disinterested person* . . . but to the client whose interest in nondisclosure is supported by the policy reasons which underlie the creation of the privilege.[118]

Thus, *Fellows* indicates that, like the majority of federal courts, California recognizes that disclosure of work product to persons with a common interest or a common adversary should not waive the work-product privilege.

However, a different conclusion was reached in *Durkin v. Shields (In re Imperial Corp. of America)*.[119] There, the insured's defense counsel provided the directors and officers (D&O) liability insurer with letters assessing the insureds' risk in the underlying litigation and settlement demands. The underlying plaintiffs contended that these letters were not privileged or subject to work-product protection. The insureds argued that even though the D&O insurer did not have a duty to defend (it had a duty to indemnify for defense costs), it shared a "common interest" in the ultimate outcome of the lawsuit so that the privilege should attach to their communications. The court rejected this argument, even though the insurers had signed joint-defense agreements with the insureds and their codefendants. The court held as follows regarding the attorney-client privilege:

> [The insureds' defense counsel] did not have an attorney-client relationship with [the insurer]. [Defense counsel's] letters were not written by or to clients of [defense counsel] and do not reveal any directors' or officers' communications to [defense counsel]. The letters were written for the purpose of apprising [the insurer] of the status of the case, not for seeking or imparting legal advice. [The insurer] did not have a duty to defend the [insureds] and did not defend the [insureds], nor pay their legal expenses. Finally, [the insurer] and [the insureds] did not share common legal representation; rather, [the insurer] had separate representation.[120]

118. 108 Cal. App. 3d at 65–66 (emphasis added).

119. 167 F.R.D. 447 (S.D. Cal. 1995).

120. *Id.* at 452–53. Recent decisions have characterized the holding in *Durkin* as follows: "If a document otherwise protected by work-product immunity is disclosed to others with an actual intention, or reasonable probability, that an opposing party may see the document, the party who made the disclosure cannot subsequently claim work-product immunity." Cal. Sportfishing Prot. Alliance v. Chico

The court then held that any work-product protection had been waived by providing the letters to the insurers:

> At the time [defense counsel] sent the letter to [the claims adjuster], the [insureds] and [the insurer] were not adversaries in litigation. However, there can be no doubt that [defense counsel] was aware that when an insurer has not committed to indemnify its insured after demand has been made to do so, the possibility of a future coverage action pitting the insured against the insurer is a distinct possibility. Therefore, there can be no doubt that [defense counsel] understood that at the time the letter was sent to [the claims adjuster] and copied to [another insurer], . . . litigation between his clients and [the insurers] . . . was a very real possibility. Consequently, [defense counsel's] transmittal of the . . . letter to [the insurers] not only increased the likelihood, but virtually assured, that potential opponents in future litigation would gain access to the disputed documents as well as to [defense counsel's] opinions and thought process regarding his clients' liability.[121]

XVI. Restatement of the Law Liability Insurance

In 2019, the American Law Institute published the long-awaited *Restatement of the Law Liability Insurance.* While this *Restatement* addresses many insurance-related issues, it specifically addresses the confidentiality of communications between insureds and insurers in one section. This section states:

> (1) An insurer or insured does not waive rights of confidentiality with respect to third parties by providing to the insured or the insurer within the context of the investigation and defense of a legal action, information protected by attorney-client privilege, work-product immunity, or other confidentiality protections.
>
> (2) An insurer does not have the right to receive any information of the insured that is protected by attorney-client privilege, work-product immunity, or a defense lawyer's duty of confidentiality under rules of professional conduct, if that information could be used to benefit the insurer at the expense of the insured.[122]

Scrap Metal, Inc., 299 F.R.D. 638, n.6 (E.D. Cal. Feb. 18, 2014); *see also* Skynet Elec. Co. v. Flextronics Int'l Ltd., 2013 WL 6623874, at *4 (N.D. Cal. Dec. 16, 2013).

121. 167 F.R.D. at 454–55.

122. Restatement of the Law Liability Insurance § 11 (2019). See the Comments, Illustrations, and Reporters' Note to this section for a more detailed discussion.

The publication of the *Restatement* may influence the development of the law nationally. As the American Law Institute has stated:

> Restatements are primarily addressed to courts. They aim at clear formulations of common law and its statutory elements or variations and reflect the law as it presently stands or might appropriately be stated by a court.[123]

Indeed, *Restatements* have long been cited and relied upon by courts.

> Restatements are one of the most highly regarded types of secondary authority and have exerted considerable influence on the judicial process. Many courts have adopted Restatement sections verbatim as the law of their jurisdiction. Moreover, many law professors rely on Restatements in their courses as the definitive source of "black letter" law.[124]

Thus, the majority and minority views on the issues addressed here may change, particularly as courts in those jurisdictions that have not issued definitive rulings have the chance to consider the *Restatement*.

XVII. Conclusion

As the preceding demonstrates, all communications between an insured and an insurer should be carefully monitored to ensure, to the extent possible, that the protections afforded by the attorney-client privilege and the work-product doctrine will apply. To the extent there is any doubt, insureds should err on the side of caution insofar as the specifics of what is communicated to insurers (but without violating the duty to cooperate imposed by most insurance policies). Of course, insurers also have reason to tread carefully in this area. After all, if a communication from an insured to an insurer turns out to be the evidence that a claimant uses to establish the insured's liability, it may be the insurer who bears the financial burden, at least to the extent of the aggregate limits of its insurance policy.

---

123. *Id.*, Restatements (Excerpt of the Revised Style Manual approved by the ALI Council in January 2015).

124. Suzanne Ehrenberg & Susan Valentine, *Lecture Notes for Restatements of the Law* (1999), http://www.kentlaw.edu/academics/lrw/tutorials/restate.htm.

CHAPTER 14

Class Actions

ALLAN KANNER AND TIBOR L. NAGY, JR.

I. Introduction

Traditionally, our legal system views disputes as discrete events. A stockbroker defrauded an investor. A phone company breached its contract with a customer. A boss fired a worker. The resulting lawsuit in any of these cases was traditionally a one-on-one fight, or what Professor Chayes has referred to as the "bipolar mode" of litigation.[1]

Today, lawyers might also look for patterns or group wrongs in those same events. For example, in the "boss firing a worker" hypothetical, lawyers may look, in appropriate circumstances, for patterns of discrimination or harassment. Group litigation, and, in particular, the use of class actions, has emerged as a far-reaching alternative to the traditional two-party suit in many areas of the law. This changing conception about the nature and role of litigation in addressing root causes, moreover, has materially altered our view of how an attorney can and should communicate with potential clients. The civil rights and labor movements in particular taught us that it is not only proper, but often desirable, for an informed lawyer to share information with lay people, including potential clients, about their rights. This recognition of the need for the targeted dissemination of information has moved into other substantive areas where systemic wrongs occur, and traditional restraints on lawyer advertising and solicitation have accordingly weakened.

1. Abram Chayes, *The Role of the Judge in Public Law Litigation*, 89 HARV. L. REV. 1281 (1976) (nature of dispute affects procedure); *see also* David Rosenberg, *The Causal Connection in Mass Exposure Cases: A "Public Law" Vision of the Tort System*, 97 HARV. L. REV. 851 (1984) (role of class action).

II. Communications with Nonclients Generally

A. Rules Against Solicitation, Contact with Represented Parties, and Misleading Statements

When dealing with nonclients, lawyers must observe the various rules that govern communications with potential clients and opposing parties. The most important rules with respect to potential clients are states' ethical rules against solicitation. Most states have rules that prohibit in-person and direct telephone solicitation, as well as restrictions on solicitation and advertisements by mail. The goal of such rules is to avoid exploitation of potential clients, especially those in vulnerable situations,[2] and to prevent activities that would undermine the public view of the profession. Model Rule of Professional Conduct 7.3 states the following:

> (a) "Solicitation" or "solicit" denotes a communication initiated by or on behalf of a lawyer or law firm that is directed to a specific person the lawyer knows or reasonably should know needs legal services in a particular matter and that offers to provide, or reasonably can be understood as offering to provide, legal services for that matter.
>
> (b) A lawyer shall not solicit professional employment by live person-to-person contact when a significant motive for the lawyer's doing so is the lawyer's or law firm's pecuniary gain, unless the contact is with a:
>
>> (1) lawyer;
>>
>> (2) person who has a family, close personal, or prior business or professional relationship with the lawyer or law firm; or
>>
>> (3) person who routinely uses for business purposes the type of legal services offered by the lawyer.
>
> (c) A lawyer shall not solicit professional employment even when not otherwise prohibited by paragraph (b), if:
>
>> (1) the target of the solicitation has made known to the lawyer a desire not to be solicited by the lawyer; or
>>
>> (2) the solicitation involves coercion, duress or harassment.

---

2. *E.g.*, Ohralik v. Ohio State Bar Ass'n, 436 U.S. 447 (1978).

> (d) This Rule does not prohibit communications authorized by law or ordered by a court or other tribunal.
>
> (e) Notwithstanding the prohibitions in this Rule, a lawyer may participate with a prepaid or group legal service plan operated by an organization not owned or directed by the lawyer that uses live person-to-person contact to enroll members or sell subscriptions for the plan from persons who are not known to need legal services in a particular matter covered by the plan.

Although there is undoubtedly a right to communicate with nonclients, rules such as these must be strictly followed. That said, abuses likely occur at country clubs and in hospitals every day.

With respect to communications with opposing parties, the most important rules are those barring contacts with parties represented by counsel. Model Rule of Professional Conduct 4.2 explains:

> In representing a client, a lawyer shall not communicate about the subject of the representation with a person the lawyer knows to be represented by another lawyer in the matter, unless the lawyer has the consent of the other lawyer or is authorized to do so by law or a court order.[3]

The rule is meant to prevent undue influence by lawyers on opposing parties.[4] When the opposing party is a corporation, the rule generally applies to management and to any other employees who may have privileged information.[5] In the corporate context, the rule may also apply to former employees.[6]

Both solicitation rules and rules against contact with represented parties of course apply to class actions, as discussed at greater length in the following section. In the class-action context, these rules can be more difficult to interpret and apply, for at least two major reasons. First, many class actions concern matters in the public interest and therefore raise First Amendment issues. Second, courts have been somewhat sloppy in describing the status of putative class actions prior to their actual certification. Thus, in the early stages of a class action, for example, the precise status of putative class members is often unclear. During the precertification and opt-out periods, it can be difficult to

---

3. ABA Model Rules of Prof'l Conduct Rule 4.2 (2013). Even if the represented person initiates the communication, lawyers are prohibited from communicating with the client. *Id.* cmt. 3. The rule does not apply to communications concerning matters "outside the representation." *Id.* cmt. 4. A lawyer has a defense if he does not know the person is represented in the matter discussed. *Id.* cmt. 8.

4. Dubois v. Gradco Sys., Inc., 136 F.R.D. 341, 344 (D. Conn. 1991) (citing G. Hazard & W. Hodes, *The Law of Lawyering: A Handbook on the Model Rules of Professional Conduct* 436 (1988 Supp.)).

5. *E.g.*, Niesig v. Team I, 76 N.Y.2d 363, 558 N.E.2d 1030 (1990).

6. *See* Chapter 8.

determine whether putative class members are actual or potential clients, or whether they are represented parties or nonparties. Plaintiff's counsel, wanting to disseminate information or conduct discovery related to certification, may risk charges of solicitation, especially with respect to class members who have retained other counsel, and defense counsel, wanting to settle claims or investigate the scope of liability, may each risk violating Model Rule 4.2.

Furthermore, because class actions have a public law aspect to them and because the stakes involved are often very high, courts have been particularly sensitive to the potential for misleading and self-serving communications by both plaintiff's and defense counsel. Plaintiff's counsel, for example, might attempt to "drum up" litigation, or convey a misleading sense of urgency about joining a class.[7] Defense counsel, on the other hand, might mislead class members into opting out, or might otherwise misrepresent class members' rights.[8]

B. The Traditional Model: No-Comment Local Rules

To deal with the problem of communications with putative class members, many jurisdictions, following the first edition of the *Manual for Complex Litigation*, initially adopted a prophylactic approach in which the district court adopted a "no comment" local rule or individual judges issued gag orders.[9] Many federal district courts, for example, had local rules that stated something like the following:

> In every case sought to be maintained by any party as a class action, all parties thereto and their counsel are hereby forbidden, directly or indirectly, orally or in writing, to communicate concerning such

---

7. *See, e.g.*, *In re* McKesson HBOC, Inc. Sec. Litig., 126 F. Supp. 2d 1239, 1245 (N.D. Cal. 2000) (counsel's solicitations to potential class members improper because they communicated "a gratuitous air of urgency"); *see also* Katz v. DNC Serv. Corp., 275 F. Supp. 3d 579 (E.D. Pa. 2017) (finding that plaintiff attorneys' website regarding a potential wage-hour claim class action was misleading); O'Connor v. Uber Techs., Inc., 2017 WL 3782101 (N.D. Cal. 2017) (finding that attorneys' e-mail to class members strongly suggested that retention of their firm and no other would preserve their rights).

8. *See, e.g.*, Kleiner v. First Nat'l Bank of Atlanta, 751 F.2d 1193 (5th Cir. 1985) (affirming imposition of substantial sanctions upon defense counsel who had participated in campaign of seeking opt-outs from putative class members); *see also* Smith v. SEECO, Inc., 2017 WL 2221707 (E.D. Ark. 2017) (noting that in negotiating a settlement that encompassed a state and federal class that was preliminarily approved by the state, "defendants maneuvered themselves to do an end-run around the communications barrier in [the federal class action]" that the court "assum[ed] . . . is inappropriate" but, in the name of federalism, denied the federal class action emergency motion for a temporary restraining order, highlighting the murky waters of class communications).

9. Pamela Mathy, *The Validity of Class Action No Comment Rules*, 13 Rutgers L.J. 285, 285 (1982); *see also* Gulf Oil Co. v. Bernard, 619 F.2d 459, 464 n.3 (5th Cir. 1980) (en banc) (noting that both the 1973 and 1977 editions of the *Manual for Complex Litigation* advocated this approach).

> actions with any potential or actual class member, not a formal party to the case, without approval by the Court.[10]

The same result, in jurisdictions that did not have a no-comment local rule, was often achieved by an individual judge's use of blanket protective orders.[11]

No-comment rules have numerous flaws. As an initial matter, they are overly broad prior restraints on speech that almost certainly violate attorneys' First Amendment rights.[12] In addition, the rules often operate to harm the interests of putative class members, preventing them from obtaining much-needed legal advice and hindering the efficient operation of group litigation. In the late 1970s, as class actions became increasingly common, courts began to recognize the problems posed by no-comment rules.[13]

C. *Gulf Oil Co. v. Bernard*: The No-Comment Model Is Cut Back

In 1981, in *Gulf Oil Co. v. Bernard*,[14] the Supreme Court struck down the use of such rules in the federal courts. This case remains instructive. In April 1976, Gulf Oil Company and the Equal Employment Opportunity Commission (EEOC) entered into a conciliation agreement involving alleged discrimination against black and female employees at the company's Port Arthur, Texas refinery. Gulf agreed to cease various allegedly discriminatory practices, to undertake an affirmative-action program covering hiring and promotion, and to offer back pay to alleged victims of discrimination based on a set formula. Gulf began to send notices to the 643 employees eligible for back pay, stating the exact amount available to each person in return for execution within 30 days of a full release of all discrimination claims dating from the relevant time period.

Shortly thereafter, a class action was filed on behalf of all current and former African American employees, alleging racial discrimination in employment and seeking injunctive, declaratory, and monetary relief. Gulf promptly filed a motion for an order limiting communications by parties and their counsel with potential class members. An accompanying brief described the EEOC conciliation agreement, asserting that 452 of the 643 employees entitled to back pay under that agreement had signed releases and been paid by the time the class action was filed. Furthermore, Gulf claimed that one of the attorneys for the class had recently attended a meeting of 75 class members, where he had discussed the case and recommended that the employees not sign the releases sent under the conciliation agreement. The attorney allegedly advised

10. Middle Dist. Fla. Local Rule 4.04(e) (no longer in effect).

11. *See, e.g.*, Gulf Oil Co. v. Bernard, 452 U.S. 89 (1981).

12. Gulf Oil, 619 F.2d at 459.

13. *See, e.g.*, Rodgers v. U.S. Steel Corp., 508 F.2d 152 (3d Cir. 1975); *Gulf Oil*, 619 F.2d at 459.

14. *Gulf Oil*, 452 U.S. at 89.

employees to return checks they already had received, since they could receive at least double the amounts involved through the class action.

The district court, without making any findings of fact, entered a temporary order prohibiting all communications concerning the case from parties or their counsel to potential or actual class members. The court later issued a modified order that imposed a complete ban on all communications concerning the class action between parties or their counsel and any actual or potential class member who was not a formal party, without the court's prior approval. The modified order exempted communications from Gulf describing the EEOC conciliation agreement and making settlement offers to class members. On appeal from a subsequent final order, respondents argued that the limitations on communications imposed by the district court were beyond the power granted to the court in Federal Rule of Civil Procedure 23(d) and were unconstitutional under the First Amendment. A divided panel of the Fifth Circuit affirmed the district court, but on rehearing en banc, that decision was reversed and the district court order was held to be an unconstitutional prior restraint on expression.[15]

The Supreme Court affirmed, though limited its decision to a holding that the district court abused its discretion under Rule 23(d). The Court agreed that "[b]ecause of the potential for abuse, a district court has both the duty and the broad authority to exercise control over a class action and to enter appropriate orders governing the conduct of counsel and parties."[16] Nevertheless, district courts' discretion is "not unlimited." The Court, in a passage that is particularly helpful for determining the scope of district courts' authority to limit communications between class counsel and putative class members, stated the following:

> The order interfered with their efforts to inform potential class members of the existence of this lawsuit, and may have been particularly injurious—not only to respondents but to the class as a whole—because the employees at that time were being pressed to decide whether to accept a backpay offer from Gulf that required them to sign a full release of all liability for discriminatory acts. In addition, the order made it more difficult for respondents, as the class representatives, to obtain information about the merits of the case from the persons they sought to represent.
>
> Because of these potential problems, an order limiting communications between parties and potential class members should be based on a clear record and specific findings that reflect a weighing of the need for a limitation and the potential interference with the rights of the parties. Only such a determination can ensure that the court is

15. *Gulf Oil*, 619 F.2d at 459.
16. *Gulf Oil*, 452 U.S. at 100.

> furthering, rather than hindering, the policies embodied in the Federal Rules of Civil Procedure, especially Rule 23. In addition, such a weighing—identifying the potential abuses being addressed—should result in a carefully drawn order that limits speech as little as possible, consistent with the rights of the parties under the circumstances.[17]

The Court therefore held that blanket prohibitions on communications with potential class members exceeded district courts' authority under Rule 23. No longer could unfounded protective orders, like the one in *Gulf Oil*, and "no comment" local rules, like those found in many districts at the time, be used to manage communications with class members. Notably, the Court also identified particular communications between class counsel and putative class members that *were* appropriate in the precertification setting: informing potential class members of the existence of the lawsuit; advising them to obtain legal advice before signing releases with the defendant; and generally "obtain[ing] information about the merits of the case."[18] The Court thus recognized the fundamental importance of precertification communications with putative class members.

D. The Modern Model: Case Management

Blanket restraints on communications with putative class members are therefore no longer tolerated by most federal courts.[19] In the federal system, *Gulf Oil* makes clear that such restraints violate Rule 23. In state courts, such restraints not only violate public policy and the efficient administration of group litigation, but also are probably unconstitutional.[20]

The void left by the erosion of no-comment rules, however, has not been filled by a new, coherent model of how courts should govern communications with putative class members. Instead, courts and leading authorities continue to disagree about what types of communications are appropriate in different circumstances.[21] In a sense, this, and not some particular set of rules, is what

---

17. *Id.* at 101–02.

18. *Id.* at 101.

19. *See, e.g.*, Gates v. Cook, 234 F.3d 221, 227 (5th Cir. 2000); Wiginton v. Ellis, 2003 WL 22232907, at *3 (N.D. Ill., Sept. 16, 2003); *see also* Slamon v. Carrizo (Marcellus) LLC, 2018 WL 3615989 (M.D. Pa. 2018) (applying *Gulf Oil*); Soto v. O.C. Communications, Inc., 2018 WL 3655414 (N.D. Cal. 2018) ("lawyers are perfectly entitled to reach out to potential collective members—via notice or otherwise—without first seeking court approval") (citing *Gulf Oil*). Some federal district courts, notably the Northern District of Georgia, were slow to eliminate their no-comment local rules. *See infra* discussion of Abdallah v. Coca-Cola Co., 186 F.R.D. 672 (N.D. Ga. 1999); *but see* N.D. Ga. R. 23.1 (2013) (reflecting the change of the district's class-action local rules).

20. *Gulf Oil*, 619 F.2d at 459.

21. *See* Manual for Complex Litigation § 21.12 ("Rule 23(d) authorizes the court to regulate communications with potential class members, even before certification. Such regulations, however, could implicate the First Amendment. . . . Most judges are reluctant to restrict communications between the parties or their counsel and potential class members, except when necessary to prevent serious

the *Gulf Oil* court envisioned: decisions to restrict communications between attorneys and putative class members are supposed to be fact-specific, case-by-case determinations. Although more flexible, this new model is often hard to navigate, and a consideration of what courts typically do in generally applicable situations is therefore useful.

III. Communications with Putative Class Members

The certification process of all class actions has three stages: (1) precertification, (2) the opt-out period (i.e., post-certification but before the end of the opt-out period), and (3) post-certification and post-opt-out period. The stage of the class action determines, in large part, the extent to which a party may communicate directly with potential class members. We consider each stage in turn.

A. Precertification

When an attorney files a complaint on a client's behalf—whether in a traditional or class-action lawsuit—an attorney-client relationship unquestionably exists. There is, however, no such clarity with respect to interactions between class counsel and unnamed class members.[22] The majority view in the federal courts is that an attorney-client relationship does not exist between class counsel and putative class members until the district court certifies the class.[23] In state courts, the predominant view is less clear. One class action treatise

misconduct."). *Compare, e.g.*, THOMAS A. DICKERSON, CLASS ACTIONS: THE LAW OF 50 STATES § 4.06[2], at 4-57 (2001) ("The members of the purported class on whose behalf a class action is instituted are deemed represented by counsel for the class representatives as of the time the complaint is filed with the court."), *with* Atari, Inc. v. Super. Ct., 212 Cal. Rptr. 773, 776 (Ct. App. 1985) ("We cannot accept the suggestion that a potential (but as yet unapproached) class member should be deemed 'a party . . . represented by counsel' even before the class is certified. . . ."). *See also* Craig M. Freeman et al., *Knowledge Is Power: A Practical Proposal to Protect Putative Class Members from Improper Pre-Certification Communication*, 2006 FED. CTS. L. REV. 2 (2006), suggesting the following rule be imposed:

> Before engaging in any communication with a putative class member, the defendant, after informing the putative class member of his identity and the party he represents, must ask a number of simple questions to ensure that the class member is apprized [sic] of her rights that are asserted in the class action and that the class member is not represented by counsel. If the defendant offers to settle the putative class member's claim, there must be a reasonable "cooling off" period to allow the putative class member sufficient time to ponder the offer. The defendant must inform the court and opposing counsel of his communication with the absent class member, as well as its general substance. Such notice allows class counsel to petition the court for a corrective notice if she feels the communication is incorrect or incomplete, or discuss the matter directly with the putative class member. The court, likewise, under its broad powers under Rule 23, can determine on its own if the communication is accurate. If it is not, it can order a corrective notice that disseminates accurate information.

22. *See generally* Debra Lyn Bassett, *Pre-Certification Communication Ethics in Class Actions*, 36 GA. L. REV. 353 (2002).

23. MANUAL FOR COMPLEX LITIGATION § 21.33 (describing how attorney-client relationship is formed after class certification); *see, e.g.*, Reid v. Unilever U.S., Inc., 964 F. Supp. 2d 893, 925 (N.D. Ill.

suggests that an attorney-client relationship is created "as of the time the complaint is filed with the court,"[24] but some states' courts do not take this view.[25]

Whatever court one is in, it is clear that even if no formal attorney-client relationship exists between class counsel and putative class members, unnamed members of the class are *not* mere third parties to the litigation. Instead, they have a unique status in the case that warrants careful treatment by plaintiffs' and defense counsel alike. In this regard, while defendants' attorneys may communicate with potential class members in the "ordinary course of business," they may not give "false, misleading, or intimidating information, conceal material information, or attempt to influence the decision about whether to request exclusion from a (certified) class."[26] Newberg opines that defense counsel can communicate with putative class members "only in the ordinary course of business" and only if "they do not infringe on what some courts have characterized as the *constructive attorney-client relationship* that exists between counsel for class representatives and the members of the class."[27] The key variable is likely to be the nature and purpose of the subject communication.

As a general rule, then, both plaintiffs' and defense counsel are free to communicate with putative class members prior to certification, but these communications are limited. A 2007 American Bar Association formal ethics opinion declares that:

> [b]efore a class action has been certified, counsel for plaintiff and defense have interests in contacting putative members of the class. Model Rules of Professional Conduct 4.2 and 7.3 do not generally prohibit counsel for either plaintiff or defendant from communicating with persons who may in the future become members of the class.[28]

2013) (citing Williams v. Chartwell Fin. Servs., Ltd., 204 F.3d 748, 759 (7th Cir. 2000); *see also* RESTATEMENT (THIRD) OF LAW GOVERNING LAWYERS § 99, cmt. l (2000).

24. THOMAS A. DICKERSON, CLASS ACTIONS: THE LAW OF 50 STATES § 4.06[2], at 4-57 (2001) ("The members of the purported class on whose behalf a class action is instituted are deemed represented by counsel for the class representatives as of the time the complaint is filed with the court.").

25. *Compare, e.g.*, *Atari*, 212 Cal. Rptr. at 776 ("We cannot accept the suggestion that a potential (but as yet unapproached) class member should be deemed 'a party . . . represented by counsel' even before the class is certified. . . ."), *and* Kullar v. Foot Locker Retail, Inc., 191 Cal. App. 4th 1201, 1205, 121 Cal. Rptr. 3d 353, 356 (2011) ("since no class has yet been certified . . . no attorney-client relationship has yet arisen"), *with* Lewis v. Bayer AG, 2002 WL 1472339 (Pa. Com. Pl., June 12, 2002) (holding, without addressing question of whether putative class members were deemed represented by class counsel prior to certification, that defendant was allowed to contact putative class members regarding adverse drug reactions), *and* Kay Co., LLC v. Equitable Prod. Co., 246 F.R.D. 260, 262 (S.D. W. Va. 2007) ("a defendant may discuss settlement offers with putative class members prior to class certification").

26. MANUAL FOR COMPLEX LITIGATION § 21.12.

27. 3 HERBERT NEWBERG & ALBA CONTE, NEWBERG ON CLASS ACTIONS 3d § 15.14, at 15-41 (1992) (emphasis added).

28. ABA Comm. on Ethics & Prof'l Responsibility, Formal Op. 07-445 (2007). The rule further states that "[b]oth plaintiff's and defense counsel must nevertheless comply with Model Rule 4.3." *Id*. This requires the following:

Class counsel are typically free to provide additional information, respond to inquiries, and seek information needed to represent the class.[29] Defense counsel are typically free to make communications in the ordinary course of business and to discuss settlement offers with individual class members, though they must take care not to give false or misleading information or attempt to influence class members in making their decision whether to remain in the class.[30] As the cases discussed next illustrate, however, because of the contentiousness of class-action litigation—as well as the fact that a number of courts still have no-comment local rules—precertification communications with putative class members often end up being governed by a court order.

1. *Jackson v. Motel 6 Multipurpose, Inc.* and *Abdallah v. Coca-Cola Co.* In *Jackson v. Motel 6 Multipurpose, Inc.*, the Eleventh Circuit granted a writ of mandamus vacating a district court's order allowing certain communications between plaintiffs' counsel and putative class members.[31] Two class actions, later consolidated, had been filed against Motel 6, alleging racial discrimination against employees and customers. Because the district court had a no-comment local rule,[32] plaintiffs' counsel moved for an order allowing relief from the rule, and specifically requesting that they be allowed to do the following:

> In dealing on behalf of a client with a person who is not represented by counsel, a lawyer shall not state or imply that the lawyer is disinterested. When the lawyer knows or reasonably should know that the unrepresented person misunderstands the lawyer's role in the matter, the lawyer shall make reasonable efforts to correct the misunderstanding. The lawyer shall not give legal advice to an unrepresented person, other than the advice to secure counsel, if the lawyer knows or reasonably should know that the interests of such a person are or have a reasonable possibility of being in conflict with the interests of the client.

Model Rules of Prof. Conduct 4.3 (2013).

29. Gulf Oil, 452 U.S. 89; Oppenheimer Fund, Inc., v. Sanders, 437 U.S. 340, 354 n.20 (1978); *see also* Manual for Complex Litigation § 21.12.

30. *See, e.g.*, Kleiner, 751 F.2d at 1193; Camp v. Alexander, 300 F.R.D. 617 (N.D. Cal. 2014); Reid v. Unilever U.S., Inc., 964 F. Supp. 2d 893, 926 (N.D. Ill. 2013); Kaszovitz v. Qiao Xing Universal Res., Inc., 2012 WL 3224341, at *3 (S.D.N.Y. Aug. 7, 2012) (citing Christensen v. Kiewit–Murdock Inv. Corp., 815 F.2d 206, 213 (2d Cir. 1987)); Belt v. Emcare Inc., 299 F. Supp. 2d 664 (E.D. Tex. 2003); Turner v. Bernstein, 768 A.2d 24 (Del. Ch. 2000); Smith v. SEECO, Inc., 2017 WL 2221707 (E.D. Ark. 2017) (settlement negotiations in the state case was appropriate); *see also* Manual for Complex Litigation § 21.12; Elizabeth M. Williamson, Comment, *When Talk Isn't Cheap: The Hidden Costs of Communication with Putative Class Members for Class Action Defense Counsel in a Post-Financial Recession World*, 5 Entrepreneurial Bus. L.J. 453, 463 (2010).

31. 130 F.3d 999 (11th Cir. 1997).

32. Middle Dist. Fla. Local Rule 4.04(e) (no longer in effect) ("In every case sought to be maintained by any party as a class action, all parties thereto and their counsel are hereby forbidden, directly or indirectly, orally or in writing, to communicate concerning such actions with any potential or actual class member, not a formal party to the case, without approval by the Court.").

- Establish a toll-free number to which potential class members may call;
- Publish notices of the ongoing litigation in publications nationwide and solicit information about potential class members and their alleged experiences with discrimination at Motel 6 motels;
- Respond to requests for information from those who respond to the advertisements or call the toll-free number;
- Distribute mass mailings to Motel 6 employees soliciting information regarding the plaintiffs' allegations of discrimination at Motel 6 motels; and
- Further communicate ex parte with any "persons who may have knowledge of" the alleged discrimination, except for current Motel 6 management or supervisory employees.[33]

The district court, which had not yet ruled on the motions for class certification, granted the order.

By the time Motel 6's second petition for mandamus was heard, the district court had certified one of the classes, the *Jackson* class, and referred the certification decision of the other class, the *Petaccia* class, to the magistrate. The Eleventh Circuit held that the *Jackson* class was erroneously certified and concluded that "the communications order was an abuse of discretion from the beginning." In a less than convincing opinion, the circuit court focused on the fact that the district court entered the communications order long before it ruled on certification and noted the danger to Motel 6's reputation in concluding that the order was an abuse of discretion:

> The communications order was entered months prior to any decision regarding whether either of the two proposed classes would in fact be certified. While we cannot say that orders authorizing communication with potential class members may never precede class certification, district courts must strive to avoid authorizing injurious class communications that might later prove unnecessary. An order authorizing class communications prior to class certification is likely to be an abuse of discretion when (1) the communication authorized by the order is widespread and clearly injurious and (2) a certification decision is not imminent or it is unlikely that a class will in fact be certified. In such circumstances, the danger of abuse that always attends class communications—the possibility that plaintiffs might use widespread publication of their claims, disguised as class communications, to coerce defendants into settlement—is not outweighed by any need for immediate communications.

33. *Motel 6*, 130 F.3d at 1002.

> The advertisements and mass mailings allowed by the order at issue in the instant petition are nationwide in scope and are surely causing serious and irreparable harm to Motel 6's reputation and to its relationship with its employees. . . . Moreover, the order was entered almost six months prior to the court's decision to certify the *Jackson* class and to refer the *Petaccia* plaintiffs' motion for class certification to a magistrate judge.[34]

The Eleventh Circuit did make an exception for the mass mailings:

> We note, however, that insofar as the district court's February 21 order authorizes the *Petaccia* plaintiffs to conduct mass mailings to Motel 6 employees, it authorizes inquiries and communications that would be allowable as a normal discovery matter, whether the *Petaccia* class is certified or not.[35]

The *Motel 6* decision is wrong for two reasons. First, and most importantly, it adopts precisely the posture toward communications orders that was struck down in *Gulf Oil*: communications between class counsel and putative class members were *presumed* inappropriate unless class counsel could make a showing otherwise. Indeed, the district court's local rule, the lawfulness of which the Eleventh Circuit did not directly address, said exactly that.[36] *Gulf Oil*, however, makes clear that communications between class counsel and putative class members, at least with respect to district courts' authority to interfere with such communications under Rule 23(d), are presumptively valid. District courts should not *authorize* communications prior to certification but rather, based on specific facts in the record, should only *limit* them, and should do that in as narrowly tailored a manner as possible.

Second, it is error to assume, as the Eleventh Circuit did, that an "order authorizing class communications prior to class certification is likely to be an abuse of discretion when . . . a certification decision is not imminent or it is unlikely that a class will in fact be certified."[37] *Gulf Oil* makes clear that the timing or likely outcome of a district court's decision on certification is not nearly as significant as the *Motel 6* court suggests. Not only had the district court in *Gulf Oil not* ruled on certification, but it had also initially dismissed the plaintiffs' complaint as untimely.[38] The Supreme Court, in an opinion that was explicitly meant to "determine the scope of a district court's authority to limit communications from named plaintiffs and their counsel to prospective

34. *Id.* at 1004.
35. *Id.* at 1008 n.19.
36. *See* Middle Dist. Fla. Local Rule 4.04(e) (no longer in effect).
37. *Motel 6,* 130 F.3d at 1004.
38. *Gulf Oil*, 452 U.S. at 97 n.8.

class members,"[39] said *nothing* about the pending decision on certification. Moreover, the Court's conclusion that the no-comment order in the *Gulf Oil* case was improper was specifically based on reasons that make clear that the imminence of a decision on certification is irrelevant:

> The order interfered with their efforts to inform potential class members of the existence of this lawsuit, and may have been particularly injurious—not only to respondents but to the class as a whole—because the employees at that time were being pressed to decide whether to accept a backpay offer from Gulf that required them to sign a full release of all liability for discriminatory acts. In addition, the order made it more difficult for respondents, as the class representatives, to obtain information about the merits of the case from the persons they sought to represent.[40]

Both informing putative class members of the existence of a class action and obtaining information about the merits of the case from them—communications that are indisputably legitimate under *Gulf Oil*—frequently and often necessarily occur long before the district courts' decision on certification.[41]

Despite its flaws, class counsel must be familiar with *Motel 6* to meet defense counsel's likely reliance on it. For example, in *Abdallah v. Coca-Cola Co.*,[42] a widely publicized case filed shortly after *Motel 6*, defendants relied centrally on *Motel 6* in seeking an order to limit class counsel's contact with putative class members. Relying on *Motel 6* and the fact that "the certification decision will not be made at any time in the near future," the district court limited class counsel's ability to communicate with putative class members to responding to unsolicited inquiries. According to the court, "[s]uch communications, when initiated by potential class members and not Plaintiffs' counsel,

39. *Id.* at 91.

40. *Id.* at 101.

41. *See also* Friedman v. Intervet, Inc., 730 F. Supp. 2d 758, 765 (N.D. Ohio 2010). The court in *Friedman* rejected a defendant's argument against an order requiring it to inform any prospective class members that it contacted of the existence of pending litigation. The defendant had invoked *Motel 6*, arguing in part that ultimate class certification was unlikely and therefore limitations on the defendants' communications would be unnecessary. The court, however, ruled that it must balance "concern for unnecessary limitations on defendant's communications against the purposes of Rule 23 and class actions," where unlimited contacts by the defendants could allow them to "reduce their potential liability by encouraging potential class members not to join the litigation." *Id.* (internal citations omitted); *see also Griffin v. Aldi, Inc.*, 2017 WL 1957021 (N.D.N.Y. 2017) (defendant Aldi argued that it was not improper to fail to mention a putative class action in separation agreements with former store managers, to which the court responded "[i]t is far from clear to the Court that it is proper for an employer to seek releases from departing employees without mentioning putative collective or class actions in which they may later be able to participate. Indeed, some district courts have deemed misleading releases that mentioned a pending collective action but failed to provide enough detail about the case." *Id.* at *4–5).

42. 186 F.R.D. 672 (N.D. Ga. 1999).

are neither widespread nor injurious." Because of the *Motel 6* "widespread and injurious" standard, the court ordered plaintiffs' counsel to remove the class-action complaint from a website on which it had been posted subsequent to the filing of the suit.[43]

Notably, the *Abdallah* court also made two rulings that were not based on *Motel 6*. Because of the "inherent danger" that communications by an employer could "deter potential class members from participating in the suit," the court prohibited Coca-Cola "from discussing this lawsuit directly with potential class members, except to the extent it needs to speak with managerial employees to investigate the acts, omissions, and statements they committed that may expose Coca-Cola to liability in this action."[44] Furthermore, the court denied Coca-Cola's request that plaintiffs' counsel be prohibited from contacting employees "deemed to be represented by the Company's counsel," which the company claimed included (1) supervisory and managerial employees, (2) any employees whose acts or admissions could be attributed to Coca-Cola, (3) employees involved in defending the action, and (4) those likely to have privileged information. Though it recognized that the state's ethical rules prohibited ex parte contacts with opposing parties, the court concluded that "upper level employees of Coca-Cola have a right to bring a discrimination claim against their employer. Therefore, to the extent that these employees wish to pursue employment claims against Coca-Cola, they may communicate freely with Plaintiffs and their counsel."[45]

2. *Hammond v. City of Junction City*

Under *Abdallah* and the Model Rules, there is no question that employees have a right to sue their employer, and that in doing so they can retain and communicate with their own counsel. It is worth noting, however, that courts sometimes rely on the principle that no attorney-client relationship exists between class counsel and putative class members until a class is certified to erroneously conclude that class counsel should not be allowed to engage in precertification, ex parte communications with managerial employees who are potential class members, even if the communication relates solely to the development of the class action and does not implicate the corporation's privileged information.

This was precisely the court's ruling in *Hammond v. City of Junction City*,[46] in which the district court held that class counsel's contact with the defendant's

43. *Id.* at 678.

44. *Id.* at 679.

45. *Id.* at 677. *See also* Spratley v. State Farm Mut. Auto. Ins. Co., 78 P.3d 603, 609 (Utah 2003) (holding that attorneys who resigned from State Farm claiming that demands of their jobs would force them to violate attorney ethics rules could, in suit for constructive discharge and retaliation, disclose privileged and confidential information to the extent "reasonably necessary to establish their claim against State Farm"); *see also* A.R. *ex rel.* Root v. Dudek, 2013 WL 5278668, at *11 (S.D. Fla. Sept. 19, 2013).

46. 2002 WL 169370, No. 00-2146 (D. Kan. Jan. 23, 2002).

director of human relations was not only not privileged, since it occurred before certification and therefore before there was an attorney-client relationship, but also violated the ethical prohibition against contacting a party represented by counsel. To avoid such a restraint on precertification communications with putative class members, counsel (1) should emphasize that *Gulf Oil* makes clear that precertification contacts with putative class members are perfectly appropriate and are often essential to the development of a class action,[47] and (2) should directly address any concerns regarding privileged information that corporate employees may have and take specific precautions with respect to such information during any ex parte contacts.[48]

B. The Opt-Out Period

Once a class has been certified, most courts hold that the rules governing communications apply as though each class member is a client of class counsel.[49] Under those rules, in particular Model Rule 4.2, defendants and their counsel ordinarily may communicate with class members or putative class members only through class counsel for plaintiffs.[50] This is so even in opt-out class actions, where many putative class members may elect to opt out before the end of the opt-out period.[51] Thus attorneys other than class counsel, in particular defense counsel and objectors, must take care not to engage in inappropriate communications with the class.[52] Recent court decisions balance the need to monitor the notice process with safeguarding the ability of parties to

47. *See supra* text accompanying note 43–45.

48. *See, e.g.*, Benjamin J. Vernia, *Right of Attorney to Conduct Ex Parte Interviews with Former Corporate Employees*, 57 A.L.R. 5th 633 (1998) (suggesting that attorneys should "establish a script of statements and questions to be followed in all initial contacts with former employees"); *see also* Ellen J. Messing et al., *"Silence Like a Cancer Grows" or "You Talk Too Much?": Ethical and Strategic Issues in Communications by Plaintiff's Counsel with Putative Class Members*, 10 Emp. Rts. & Emp. Pol'y J. 649, 660 (2006).

49. *See* Manual for Complex Litigation § 21.33 ("Once a class has been certified, the rules governing communications apply as though each class member is a client of the class counsel.").

50. *But see* Roberts v. Weim, 130 F.R.D. 416 (N.D. Cal 1988) (denying plaintiff's request for an order requiring prior approval of any communications by defense counsel to putative class members during opt-out period).

51. Newberg suggests the possibility of a less absolute view, premised on the likelihood that at least some putative class members will opt out of the litigation after certification and before the exclusion period expires. *See* 3 Herbert Newberg & Alba Conte, Newberg on Class Actions 3d § 15.15, at 15-43 to 15-44 (1992). Under that view, post-certification communications may still be permissible (albeit potentially hazardous if the court disagrees) on grounds that the putative class member being communicated with retains an independent right to make his or her own decisions until the end of the exclusion period.

52. *See* Clincy v. Galardi S. Enters., Inc., 2010 WL 966639 (N.D. Ga. 2010) (requiring that following conditional class certification, any further written communication by defendant employer to potential opt-in plaintiffs to contain court-prescribed rider acknowledging unlawfulness of attempts by defendant to discourage participation in suit, and further allowing plaintiffs' counsel to contact such potential opt-in class members to discuss action).

communicate.[53] The authority of the court also includes the power to invalidate opt-outs procured through fraud, duress, or other improper conduct.[54]

1. *Kleiner v. First National Bank of Atlanta*

The classic case concerning inappropriate communications by defense counsel at this stage of a class action is *Kleiner v. First National Bank of Atlanta*.[55] *Kleiner* involved what Judge Vance called "a ground-breaking class action against the First National Bank of Atlanta . . . sounding in fraud, RICO and breach of contract."[56] Several weeks after the trial judge certified the class under Rule 23(b)(3), but before the end of the opt-out period, defense counsel sought to obtain discovery from a number of putative class members. Class counsel moved for a protective order, arguing that discovery and unilateral contacts by the bank before the close of the exclusion period would intimidate potential class members and discourage them from participating in the suit. The court granted the order prohibiting the bank's requested discovery, but specifically took the broader question of unsupervised contacts between the bank and class members under advisement pending further briefing.

Several weeks later the bank "seized upon the idea of soliciting class exclusion requests."[57] Defense counsel decided that phone calls would be better than letters and would take advantage of its loan officers' existing relationships. The campaign took place during the judge's two-week vacation and proved very successful: the bank's officers obtained opt-out commitments from 2,800 of the 3,000 putative class members contacted, representing a sum total of $694,997,218 in past or present loans. The district judge was not pleased and held a hearing on the matter, declaring the solicitation scheme unethical

53. *See In re* Cmty. Bank of N. Va. & Guar. Nat'l Bank of Tallahassee Second Mortgage Loan Litig., 418 F.3d 277, 310 (3d Cir. 2005) ("Because the advantage of class action litigation comes at the cost of binding absent class members through the res judicata effect of litigation over which they lack control, the district courts must closely monitor the notice process and take steps to safeguard class members from 'unauthorized [and] misleading communications from the parties or their counsel.'") (quoting Erhardt v. Prudential Grp., Inc., 629 F.2d 843, 846 (2d Cir. 1980)); Hinds Cnty. Miss. v. Wachovia Bank N.A., 790 F. Supp. 2d 125, 134 (S.D.N.Y. 2011) ("The Court's primary purpose in supervising communications is . . . to ensure that potential members receive accurate and impartial information regarding the status, purposes, and effects of the class action."); *see also* Dodona I, LLC v. Goldman, Sachs & Co., 2014 WL 2532478, at *2 (S.D.N.Y. June 2, 2014). *But see* Cox Nuclear Med. v. Gold Cup Coffee Servs., Inc., 214 F.R.D. 696 (S.D. Ala. 2003); McLaughlin v. Liberty Mut. Ins. Co., 224 F.R.D. 295 (D. Mass. 2004) (court improperly restrained communication absent finding of abuse).

54. *See, e.g.*, Wang v. Chinese Daily News, Inc., 623 F.3d 743, 755–56 (9th Cir. 2010) *vacated on other grounds*, 132 S. Ct. 74 (2011); Velazquez v. FPS LP, 2014 WL 1758214, at *3 (S.D. Tex. Apr. 28, 2014); *see also* Guifu Li v. A Perfect Day Franchise, Inc., 270 F.R.D. 509, 518 (N.D. Cal. 2010) ("Defendants have cited no case, and the Court is aware of none, where a defendant employer's ex parte solicitation of opt outs from its workers was upheld as a proper communication, regardless of whether the class was certified or not.").

55. 751 F.2d 1193 (5th Cir. 1985).

56. *Id.* at 1196.

57. *Id.* at 1197.

under Model Rule 4.2 and the district court's local rule banning solicitation of opt-outs. Defense counsel was held to have knowingly participated in the scheme and to have given legal advice in bad faith. He was sanctioned $50,000; was ordered to pay, along with his firm and the bank, all legal fees associated with the hearing and costs for curative notice; and was disqualified from further representation in the case. As a final measure, the district court ruled that the exclusion requests would be voidable following entry of judgment.

The Fifth Circuit affirmed the district court's ruling that the solicitation scheme violated Model Rule 4.2, and further held that the scheme violated the court's protective order.[58] Thus, even though the opt-out period had not ended and many of the bank's customers may very well have elected to opt out, the court of appeals confirmed that class counsel and the putative class members should be treated as though they had an attorney-client relationship. In a cogent discussion of the proper role of trial judges in policing communications with putative class members, Judge Vance went on to discuss the authority of district courts to ban opt-out solicitations under Rule 23. Addressing solicitation requests generally, the court stated:

> When confronted with claims pressed by a plaintiff class, it is obviously in defendants' interest to diminish the size of the class and thus the range of potential liability by soliciting exclusion requests. Such conduct reduces the effectiveness of the 23(b)(3) class action for no reason except to undermine the purposes of the rule. A unilateral communications scheme, moreover, is rife with potential for coercion. If the class and the class opponent are involved in an ongoing business relationship, communications from the class opponent to the class may be coercive. . . . Unsupervised, unilateral communications with the plaintiff class sabotage the goal of informed consent by urging exclusion on the basis of a one-sided presentation of the facts, without opportunity for rebuttal. The damage from misstatements could well be irreparable.[59]

With respect to the specific solicitation scheme in *Kleiner*, the court stated:

> In view of the tension between the preference for class adjudication and the individual autonomy afforded by exclusion, it is critical that the class receive accurate and impartial information regarding the status, purposes and effects of the class action. . . . In this case, the carefully constructed edifice of check and countercheck, notice and reply, was obliterated when the telephones were lifted from their cradles. The Bank's actions obstructed the district court in the discharge of its

58. *Id.* at 1200 n.15.
59. *Id.* at 1202–03.

> duty to "protect both the absent class and the integrity of the judicial process by monitoring the actions before it." The Bank's subterfuge and subversion constituted an intolerable affront to the authority of the district court to police class member contacts. Accordingly, we hold that the trial court had ample discretion under Rules 23(b)(3) and 23(d) to prohibit the Bank's overtures.[60]

The *Kleiner* court went beyond its holding that an attorney-client relationship exists between class counsel and putative class members after certification and emphasized that "it is critical that the class receive accurate and impartial information." Although mindful of *Gulf Oil*, *Kleiner* firmly establishes "the authority of the district court to police class member contacts" when misleading information or other improper influence on putative class members is threatened.

2. *Georgine v. Amchem Products, Inc.*

As *Kleiner* illustrated, class counsel and putative class members are generally held to have an attorney-client relationship during the opt-out period, despite the fact that a number of potential class members may elect to opt out. Typically, then, inappropriate communications with putative class members are not likely to come from class counsel during the opt-out period—though they may, as in *Kleiner*, come from defense counsel. One source of potential communications problems, however, is objectors. After a class has been certified and, as is typically the case, a settlement has been proposed, objecting counsel have a strong incentive to encourage putative class members to opt out. A leading case illustrating this problem is *Georgine v. Amchem Products, Inc.*[61]

In *Georgine*, a massive class of asbestos-exposure victims had been certified by the district court.[62] During the opt-out period, dozens of objectors began a campaign of soliciting opt-outs, primarily through the mass mailing of letters to putative class members. These letters reached over 650,000 potential class members, 236,323 of whom ultimately elected to opt out of the class settlement. Class counsel and the defendants (the "settling parties") in the case filed a joint motion requesting that the court remedy the adverse effects of the opt-out solicitation campaign. In particular, the settling parties sought (1) the negation of all exclusion requests, (2) the creation of a second notice and opt-out period for class members who timely requested exclusion from the class, and (3) the issuance of an injunction requiring that all communications by

60. *Id.* at 1203.

61. 160 F.R.D. 478 (E.D. Pa. 1995). Another potential source of trouble is competing counsel in securities class actions. *See In re* WorldCom, Inc. Sec. Litig., 2003 WL 22701241 (S.D.N.Y. Nov. 17, 2003) (discussing misleading letters sent by securities class action firm to absent class members and ordering curative notice).

62. For an extensive discussion of the history of this litigation, see Georgine v. Amchem Products, Inc., 157 F.R.D. 246, 257–61 (E.D. Pa. 1994).

asbestos plaintiffs' attorneys that concern the class action or settlement bear a "Disclosure Statement."[63]

The court began its analysis by discussing the harm caused by misleading communications to putative class members, and by examining the allegedly misleading communications sent by the objectors:

> Misleading communications to class members concerning litigation pose a serious threat to the fairness of the litigation process, the adequacy of representation and the administration of justice generally. . . . Here, I find that unilateral communications with class members by various attorneys were misleading and made it unlikely that class members, who received these communications or were informed of their contents, made an informed choice to exclude themselves from the class. . . . Many of the letters and advertisements were misleading because they (1) made statements regarding the terms of the settlement that created false impressions about the effect of the settlement on the recipient, e.g., the false statement that opting out is the only way to secure future compensation; asbestos companies can back out of the settlement at any time; and (2) did not reveal the personal interests of the drafters of the letters and advertisements. Moreover, because these communications contained only one-sided attacks on the terms of the settlement without any discussion of the settlement benefits or the existence of the Court-approved notice materials, the effect of the misleading aspects of the communications was compounded.[64]

Georgine illustrates a principled, well-reasoned application of *Gulf Oil.* The court engaged in a thorough review of the record, and decided upon a remedy specifically tailored to remedy the identified harm caused by the misleading communications. Although recognizing the inherent bias on the part of objectors, the court did not attempt to impose any blanket restriction on their communication with putative class members. Indeed, the court seemed legitimately open to the use of forthright communications by objectors: "[T]his Court encourages the free flow of ideas relating to the advantages and disadvantages of the settlement, in order to evaluate the relative merits of conflicting arguments."[65] It is worth noting that of all the misleading characteristics of the contested letters, the one that bothered the court the most was the failure of the objectors to identify their biases: "In the instant case, because none of

63. *Georgine,*160 F.R.D. at 489. Notably, the settling parties elected not to seek an order banning all potentially misleading communications by objectors with putative class members during the second opt-out period. Class counsel specifically informed the court that while they supported the inclusion of a disclosure statement on all future communications, they could not support "any order that would restrain attorney-client communications in any manner." *Id.* at n.11.

64. *Id.* at 490.

65. *Id.* at 495.

the communications at issue revealed to the recipient that the drafter had a financial motive to obtain additional opt-outs, the recipient was not on notice to closely scrutinize the substance of the communications."[66] While objections to proposed settlements are sometimes in the best interests of the class, objectors have no legitimate reason to hide their financial interest in soliciting class members' opt-outs. Courts can and most likely will use their "broad authority to exercise control over a class action" to remedy the effects of any misleading communications.

C. Post-certification, Post-Opt-Out Period

Once a class has been certified and the opt-out period has closed, it is clear that an attorney-client relationship exists between class counsel and all class members who have not opted out.[67] Thus, subject to the requirement of court approval for settlement or dismissal of the suit, class counsel can freely communicate with class members. Moreover, in keeping with the rule against communications with represented parties, defense counsel are barred from communicating with class members, other than through class counsel.[68]

IV. Opt-In Class Actions

Section 216(b) of the Fair Labor Standards Act[69] (FLSA) provides a private right of action for employees to recover unpaid minimum wages and overtime compensation, to redress retaliatory discharges, and to enforce the terms of the Age Discrimination in Employment Act (ADEA). Actions under section

---

66. *Id.* at 496.

67. *See* 3 Newberg & Conte, *supra* note 27, § 15.18, at 15-49.

68. *See also* Williams v. Quinn, 2010 WL 3021576 (N.D. Ill. 2010) (holding that after certification, counsel representing class objectors were barred from initiating contact with additional class members without first seeking permission of the class members' representative counsel); Estakhrian v. Obenstine, 2017 WL 2661616 (C.D. Cal. 2017) ("After a court has certified a class, communications with class members regarding the subject of representation must be through counsel for the class.") (quoting Jacobs v. CSAA Inter-ins., 2009 WL 1201996 (N.D. Cal. 2009)); Speaks v. U.S. Tobacco Cooperative, Inc., 2020 WL 1485965, at *8 (E.D. N.C. 2020) (citing 3 Herbert Newberg & Alba Conte, Newberg on Class Actions § 9.9 (1992) (holding that defense counsel did not violate Model Rule 4.2 because they communicated with the putative class through the plaintiff's counsel)). Even responding to a seemingly innocuous email from a class member post-certification may be prohibited. In Mullen v. GLV, Inc., 334 F.R.D. 656 (N.D. Ill. 2020), the court held that defense counsel violated Model Rule 4.2 simply by sending a short reply email to a class member who asked to be removed from an email list. After class certification, two class members had sent a mass email to other class members, providing details about opting out of the class. *Id.* at 660. When a recipient of this mass email forwarded it to the owner of the defendant company, the owner forwarded it to defense counsel. *Id.* Defense counsel then replied directly to the class member who sent the initial email, requesting the names of other class members who wished to be removed from the email list. *Id.* The court held that this short reply violated Model Rule 4.2, even though counsel did not initiate the contact with the class member, and even though it did not find the communication to be coercive. *Id.* at 664–65.

69. 29 U.S.C. §§ 201 *et seq.*

216(b) can be brought individually or as collective actions. Unlike modern class actions, however, section 216(b) actions operate as "spurious" or "opt in" class actions: "No employee shall be a party plaintiff to any such action unless he gives his consent in writing to become such a party and such consent is filed in the court in which such action is brought."[70] The role of notice in these opt-in actions, therefore, is different and arguably even more important than notice in opt-out actions: without notice of the suit and of one's right to opt in, a potential plaintiff literally *cannot* participate in the litigation.

While individual notice is required in opt-out class actions under Rule 23, the federal courts were long divided on the issue of whether a district court even had the authority to facilitate the joinder of section 216(b) class members by approving the sending of notice in opt-in actions brought under FLSA. Some courts held that notice of a proposed action under section 216(b) was neither required nor authorized, and that a district court lacked authority to direct notice to potential class members.[71] Other courts held that such notice was improper solicitation of litigation.[72] On the other hand, several courts concluded that the right to bring a representative action carried with it the right to notify those persons whom the plaintiff wished to represent, and thus approved notification of potential class members.[73]

The split in the lower courts was resolved by the Supreme Court in *Hoffman La-Roche Inc. v. Sperling*,[74] an action brought under ADEA in which plaintiffs sought court-approved notice under section 216(b). Stressing the "wisdom and necessity" of "judicial intervention in the management of litigation" and noting that the rationale of *Gulf Oil* applied in section 216(b) actions, the Court held that "district courts have *discretion*, in appropriate cases, to implement 29 U.S.C. § 216(b) . . . by facilitating notice to potential plaintiffs."[75] Such court-facilitated notice can, for example, serve "the legitimate goal of avoiding a multiplicity of duplicative suits and setting cutoff dates to expedite disposition of the action."[76]

---

70. *Id.* at 216(b).

71. *See* Baker v. Michie Co., 93 F.R.D. 494 (W.D. Va. 1982); McKenna v. Champion Int'l Corp., 747 F.2d 1211 (8th Cir. 1984), abrogated by Hoffmann-La Roche Inc. v. Sperling, 493 U.S. 165 (1989).

72. *Baker*, 93 F.R.D. at 494; Roshto v. Chrysler Corp., 67 F.R.D. 28 (E.D. La 1975).

73. Braunstein v. E. Photographic Labs., Inc., 600 F.2d 335 (2d Cir. 1978); Woods v. N.Y. Life Ins. Co., 686 F.2d 578 (7th Cir. 1982); Riojas v. Seal Produce, Inc., 82 F.R.D. 613 (S.D. Tex. 1979).

74. Hoffman, 493 U.S. at 165; *see also* Mitchell, et al. v. City of San Diego, 2018 WL 3729289 (S.D. Cal. 2018) ("This Court has the power to facilitate Plaintiffs' efforts to notify individuals that might be interested in joining a collective action," citing Hoffman, "[b]ecause trial court involvement in the notice process is inevitable in cases with numerous plaintiffs where written consent is required by statute, it lies within the discretion of a district court to begin its involvement early, at the point of the initial notice, rather than at some later time.") (internal citations omitted).

75. *Id.* at 169 (emphasis added).

76. *Id.* at 172; *see also* Whalen v. United States, 85 Fed. Cl. 380, 388 (Fed. Cl. 2009) (holding that exercise of court discretion in facilitating notice to avoid multiplicity of duplicative suits and to set cutoff dates was appropriate in collective action such as one under Fair Labor Standards Act).

The Court in *Hoffman*, however, specifically refused to examine the details of the notice at issue in the case, and emphasized that it was "confirm[ing] the existence of the trial court's discretion, not the details of its exercise."[77] Furthermore, the Court stated, "We do not address any conflicts between court-authorized notice and communications with potential plaintiffs by counsel."[78] Thus, the Court specifically left open the possibility that a district court could refuse to approve or otherwise facilitate notice to potential plaintiffs in a section 216(b) action, and that notice would have to be accomplished by "communications with potential plaintiffs by counsel" that did not involve the court.[79]

Several pre-*Hoffman* opinions that refused to issue or allow notice under section 216(b) illustrate how courts conceive of the nature and scope of these direct communications between class counsel and potential plaintiffs. In *Dolan v. Project Construction Corp.*,[80] for example, the Court of Appeals for the Tenth Circuit affirmed an order of the district court refusing to issue court-approved notice under section 216(b) and, further, granting a protective order with respect to discovery plaintiffs had sought in order to learn the names and addresses of potential plaintiffs. Although it concluded that court-approved notice was inappropriate, the *Dolan* court expected that plaintiffs' counsel would seek out and contact potential plaintiffs on their own:

> However, recent United States Supreme Court cases regarding legal communication dictate the allowance of a level of reasonable communication by the plaintiff and counsel with those parties he can discover without judicial assistance. . . . Additionally, "an order limiting communications between parties and potential class members should be based on a clear record and specific findings that reflect a weighing of the need for a limitation and the potential interference with the rights of the parties." Although *Gulf Oil* is a case involving a Rule 23 action, the principle of law is applicable to all representative actions.[81]

Thus, under *Dolan*, even if a district court refuses to facilitate notice under section 216(b), it should not interfere with plaintiffs' attorneys' attempts to inform potential class members of the suit, unless such interference is consistent with *Gulf Oil*.

The Seventh Circuit, in another pre-*Hoffman* case, took a different approach. In *Woods v. New York Life Insurance*,[82] the court held that district courts could review and approve communications between section 216(b) plaintiffs and

77. *Id.* at 171.
78. *Id.* at 171 n.2.
79. *Id.*
80. 725 F.2d 1263 (10th Cir. 1984), abrogated by Hoffmann, 493 U.S. at 165.
81. *Id.* at 1269.
82. 686 F.2d 578 (7th Cir. 1982).

potential class members but could not send out notice that was on judicial letterhead or that was signed by a judicial officer. The court addressed the concern, shared by many plaintiffs' attorneys bringing actions under section 216(b), that the judicial imprimatur on the notice was necessary in order to avoid potential solicitation complaints under state law:

> At oral argument the plaintiffs' counsel stated that he wanted the imprimatur in order to shield himself from a possible complaint under state law that he was trying to stir up litigation; but if the notice is approved by a federal court under the authority that we hold it has by virtue of section 16(b) of the Fair Labor Standards Act, any effort by the state to punish the lawyer who mails the notice would violate the supremacy clause of the United States Constitution. It is the court's order, not its letterhead or its clerk's signature, that provides the lawyer with immunity from a state's efforts to prevent communications authorized by section 16(b). Indeed the order may be unnecessary; section 16(b) of its own force may preempt state laws that operate to prevent the representative plaintiff or his counsel from communicating with other (actual or potential) class members; such laws could even raise First Amendment problems.[83]

Notably, however, the *Woods* court did *not* believe that class counsel could freely contact potential plaintiffs, even if the content of the communications was perfectly appropriate. Instead, the court envisioned the following procedure, at least in section 216(b) actions:

> Before this suit was filed, Woods had sent invitations to other members of the class to join with him, and New York Life does not challenge his right to do this. After suit was filed, however, we do not think it would have been proper for Woods or his counsel to have sent out such invitations without first communicating to the defendant's counsel his intention to do so, so that the defendant's counsel would have an opportunity to verify the accuracy of the notice and, if he wished, to move for an order amending the notice or limiting its distribution in an appropriate manner. We cannot find any express basis in rule or statute for inferring either the duty of the plaintiff's counsel to notify the defendant's counsel in this manner or the power of the district court to regulate the content and distribution of the notice to potential class members; but we think both the duty and the power may fairly be inferred from section 16(b) itself and from Rule 83 of the Federal Rules of Civil Procedure, which provides that "in all cases not

83. *Id.* at 581.

> provided for by rule, the district courts may regulate their practice in any manner not inconsistent with" the Federal Rules. Once a section 16(b) action is commenced, the defendant has a vital interest in, and the court a managerial responsibility regarding, the joinder of additional parties plaintiff, and these concerns support the modest duty and power that we infer.[84]

While the *Woods* court recognized the right of class counsel to communicate with potential class members, as well as the potential "First Amendment problems" with state laws interfering with such communications, the court invented a procedure under section 216(b) that, in effect, requires class counsel to obtain approval by either defense counsel or the court before sending out notice to potential class members. Such a requirement is arguably inconsistent with *Gulf Oil*, which the Supreme Court has explicitly held applies to actions under section 216(b).[85]

Finally, in *Goerke v. Commercial Contractors & Supply Co.*,[86] the district court for the Northern District of Georgia adopted the reasoning of the Tenth Circuit in *Dolan* in holding that it had no power under FLSA to authorize notice to potential class members. Because plaintiffs' counsel, like the plaintiffs' attorneys in *Wood*, expressed concern about violating the rules of the State Bar of Georgia, the court specifically addressed the alternative to court-approved notice under section 216(b):

> The denial of this motion, however, does not preclude the plaintiff engaging in protected communication with other potential plaintiffs who can be discovered without intervention by the court. . . . As the Supreme Court has held in *Gulf Oil Company vs. Bernard*, an order limiting communications between parties and potential class members "should be based on a clear record and specific findings that reflect a weighing of the need for limitation and the potential interference with the rights of the parties." There is no question that *Bernard* dealt with a Rule 23 class action, and was based upon the standards of the *Federal Rules of Civil Procedure*. However . . . the rationale behind *Bernard* was equally applicable to a representative action under 216(b). Thus, although this court has found that it has no power to approve and authorize the dissemination of a notice to potential class members, there are forms of protected communication in which plaintiff's counsel can engage with potential class members. As regards plaintiff's fears, expressed in the brief in support of this motion, plaintiff need only make certain that any communications in which he engages

84. *Id.* at 580.
85. *Hoffman*, 493 U.S. at 171.
86. 600 F. Supp. 1155 (N.D. Ga. 1984).

> are directed toward the provision of *notice*, rather than toward active solicitation of individuals to join in the present litigation.[87]

Thus, the *Goerke* court specifically held that in the absence of court-approved notice, class counsel in a section 216(b) action could communicate with potential class members, and such communications would be governed by the principles set forth in *Gulf Oil*. Numerous courts have since reached the same conclusion, holding that the standard set forth in *Gulf Oil* applies to collective actions under section 216(b).[88]

V. Conclusion

As the Supreme Court made clear in *Gulf Oil*, communications between class counsel and putative class members are critical to the prosecution of class actions. Thus, while district courts have broad authority to police these communications, their decision to do so must be based on a clear record and specific findings that reflect a weighing of the need for the limitation and the potential for interference with the rights of the parties. Only such a determination, as the Court itself has stated, "can ensure that the [district] court is furthering, rather than hindering, the policies embodied in the Federal Rules of Civil Procedure, especially Rule 23."[89] Furthermore, the analysis in *Gulf Oil* applies with, if anything, even more force in other class-action contexts. In opt-in class actions under FLSA, furthermore, it is now clear that district courts have the authority to issue notice to putative class members. The fact that class members will not be able to participate in the suit unless they affirmatively opt in strongly suggests that courts should approve and issue notice. At the very least, they should not hinder class counsel from communicating with putative class members.

---

87. *Id.* at 1161 (citations omitted).

88. *See, e.g.*, Forauer v. Vt. Country Store, Inc., 2013 WL 6086202 (D. Vt. Nov. 19, 2013); Howard v. Securitas Sec. Servs., USA Inc., 630 F. Supp. 2d 905, 909 (N.D. Ill. 2009); Maddox v. Knowledge Learning Corp., 499 F. Supp. 2d 1338, 1343 (N.D. Ga. 2007); Parks v. Eastwood Ins. Servs., Inc., 235 F. Supp. 2d 1082, 1085 (C.D. Cal. 2002); Belt v. Emcare, Inc., 299 F. Supp. 2d 664, 667–68 (E.D. Tex. 2003); Jones v. Casey's Gen. Stores, 517 F. Supp. 2d 1080, 1086 (S.D. Iowa 2007); Soto v. O.C. Commc'ns, Inc., 2018 WL 3655414, at *1 (N.D. Cal. 2018); Jones v. Synergies3 Tec Servs., LLC, 2018 WL 3458636, at *3 (E.D. Mo. 2018).

89. Gulf Oil, 452 U.S. at 101–02.

CHAPTER 15

Choice of Law Issues

MARCY HOGAN GREER

Tips for Applying Choice of Law
• Analyze choice-of-law issues before providing a privilege log.
• Do not assume that any choice-of-law determinations as to the substantive claims also govern privilege issues.
• Obtain foreign-law materials to substantiate the privilege in advance of a challenge.
• Consider whether choice-of-law requires time-consuming translation of foreign authorities and expert testimony.

I. Initial Questions Involving Choice of Law

Determining what law governs the application of attorney-client privilege can involve a complicated and nuanced analysis:

- Federal courts entertaining federal questions apply federal common-law governing attorney-client privilege
- Federal courts sitting in diversity apply state law using conflicts of laws principles, using essentially three approaches:
  - Assume that the state that provides the "rule of decision" also provides the privilege law
  - Apply the privilege rules of the forum state
  - Employ the conflicts of law principles of the forum state
- State courts apply state law using the forum's conflicts of laws principles
- If multiple jurisdictions' laws are implicated:
  - Identify all potential jurisdictions whose laws could apply
  - Determine whether there is an actual conflict between the laws (i.e., the result is different depending on which law applies)
  - If no conflict, forum law applies
  - If conflict, engage in choice-of-law analysis

- Determination of law governing a claim or remedy will not necessarily determine the choice of law for a privilege issue.

II. State Courts

Although myriad variations exist beyond the scope of this chapter, state courts typically use two basic choice-of-law approaches: "[t]he older, minority approach, is set forth by the First Restatement of Conflict of Laws and focuses on the location of a particular event. The more modern approach follows the Second Restatement of Conflict of Laws, which directs courts to identify and apply the law of the most interested state."[1] However, unless there is an actual, material conflict between the potentially governing bodies of law, courts will apply the law of the forum.[2] The same result obtains if the party claiming another law applies fails to carry its burden of substantiating the foreign law or the record is unclear.[3] And where there is only a "false conflict"—where there is in actuality only one "jurisdiction with an actual interest in the outcome of the dispute"—the courts are directed to apply the law of the only interested jurisdiction.[4]

The Restatement's position on conflicts of law has been evolving, and, as many states have adopted a version of the Restatement approach, it is important to understand that evolution.

A. First Restatement

Section 597 of the First Restatement requires that "[t]he law of the forum determines the admissibility of a particular piece of evidence."[5]

Courts using the First Restatement approach are divided on whether "privilege law is an evidentiary matter and is therefore categorized as 'procedural' and subject to the law of the forum" or "rules affect[ing] people's

1. Skepnek v. Roper & Twardowsky, LLC, 2014 WL 4377706, at *4 (D. Kan. Sept. 4, 2014) (citing Aselco, Inc. v. Hartford Ins. Grp., 21 P.3d 1011, 1020 (Kan. Ct. App. 2001), and Tartaglia v. Paul Revere Life Ins. Co., 948 F. Supp. 325, 326 (S.D.N.Y. 1996)).

2. Wellin v. Wellin, 211 F. Supp. 3d. 793, 806–07 (D.S.C. 2016).

3. Diamond Offshore Drilling, Inc. v. Black, — S.W.3d —, 2022 WL 2128337, at *6 (Tex. App. June 14, 2022) ("'If the party seeking the application of foreign law fails to provide the necessary information to the trial court, there is a presumption that the law of the foreign jurisdiction is identical to that of Texas.'" (quoting Cal Dive Offshore Contractors Inc. v. Bryant, 478 S.W.3d 914, 921 (Tex. App. 2015)); Laxalt v. McClatchy, 116 F.R.D. 438, 446 (D. Nev. 1987) ("Because the record in this case is insufficient to judge which state has the most significant relationship with these communications, the parties have failed in their burden of proof, and the Court will fall back onto the law of the forum." (citing Cambridge Filter Co. v. Int'l Filter Co., Inc., 548 F. Supp. 1301, 1305 (D. Nev. 1982)).

4. Harrisburg Auth. v. CIT Capital USA, Inc., 716 F. Supp. 2d 380, 391 (M.D. Pa. 2010).

5. Restatement (First) of Conflict of Laws § 597 (1934).

conduct at the stage of primary private activity and should therefore be classified as 'substantive or quasi-substantive.'"[6]

B. Second Restatement

Section 139 of the Second Restatement instead focuses on the state with the "most significant relationship" with the communication, providing that:

> (1) Evidence that is not privileged under the local law of the state which has the most significant relationship with the communication will be admitted, even though it would be privileged under the local law of the forum, unless the admission of such evidence would be contrary to the strong public policy of the forum.
>
> (2) Evidence that is privileged under the local law of the state which has the most significant relationship with the communication but which is not privileged under the local law of the forum will be admitted unless there is some special reason why the forum policy favoring admission should not be given effect.[7]

To apply Section 139, the court must first determine the state having "the most significant relationship with the communication." Comment e of the Restatement explains that:

> [t]he state which has the most significant relationship with a communication will usually be the state where the communication took place, which, as used in the rule of this Section, is the state where an oral interchange between persons occurred, where a written statement was received or where an inspection was made of a person or thing.[8]

After that determination is made, the court must then determine whether the communication is privileged under the state having the most significant relationship and whether it is also privileged under the law of the forum. If both laws consistently treat the communication as privileged (or not privileged), then there is no conflict of law and, concomitantly, no need to engage in conflicts analysis, and the forum state's privilege law will govern.[9] If

6. Wellin v. Wellin, 211 F. Supp. 3d. 793, 801 (D.S.C. 2016) (citing Winthrop Res. Corp. v. Commscope, Inc. of N.C., Civ. A. 2014 WL 5810457, at *1 n.2 (W.D.N.C. Nov. 7, 2014), and quoting *In re* Yasmin & Yaz (Drospirenone) Mktg., Sales Practices & Prod. Liab. Litig., MDL No. 2100, 2011 WL 1375011, at *8 (S.D. Ill. Apr. 12, 2011)).

7. Restatement (Second) of Conflict of Laws § 139 (1971).

8. *Id.* § 139 cmt. e.

9. *See, e.g.*, Baker v. Gen. Motors Corp., 209 F.3d 1051, 1054 (8th Cir. 2000).

the difference between the two states' laws is "outcome determinative," then there is a conflict that requires the next-steps analysis.[10]

C. Most Significant Relationship (MSR)

As noted, when there is an actual conflict in the laws of two or more states as to attorney-client privilege issues, the Second Restatement asks which state has the "most significant relationship with the communication."[11]

Under the Second Restatement approach, the location of the communication and "the state where the relationship between the parties was centered" are usually given particular weight.[12] The state where the communication took place "is the state where an oral interchange between persons occurred, where a written statement was received, or where an inspection was made of a person or thing."[13]

For example, where the principal representative for an insurance company testified that while he was in New York, he contacted outside coverage counsel, retained him by email to provide a formal legal opinion, received that legal opinion, and arranged for telephonic meetings with the counsel and other company employees to meet with the counsel by phone, New York had the most significant relationship to the communications claimed as privileged.[14]

1. Section 139(1): Not Privileged in MSR State; Privileged in Forum

If a conflict exists between the two states, and the MSR state would require disclosure of the communication, then Restatement section 139(1) governs, and the court must consider whether admitting the communication "would be contrary to the strong public policy of the forum."[15]

The reason for this treatment is practical. With respect to the "easier conflict" described in section 139(1)—where laws of the "communication state" require disclosure while the forum would not—the forum's interest in ascertaining the facts is not served by applying its privilege law to prevent disclosure.[16] And the forum's interests in regulating and protecting the relationships

---

10. Gibson v. Chubb Nat'l Ins. Co., 2021 WL 4401434, at *2 (N.D. Ill. Sept. 27, 2021). Another court described a "'true conflict'" as one that "exists 'when the governmental interests of both jurisdictions would be impaired if their laws were not applied.'" Harrisburg Auth. v. CIT Capital USA, Inc., 716 F. Supp. 2d 380, 390 n.17 (M.D. Pa. 2010) (quoting Lacey v. Cessna Aircraft Co., 932 F.2d 170, 187 (3d Cir. 1991)).

11. Restatement (Second) of Conflicts of Law § 139.

12. Gibson v. Chubb Nat'l Ins. Co., 2021 WL 4401434, at *2 (N.D. Ill. Sept. 27, 2021); *see also* McDevitt v. Wellin, 2019 WL 4622088, at *4 (D.S.C. Sept. 24, 2019) (applying South Carolina law to attorney-client privilege issues because parties' relationship was centered in South Carolina where their attorneys and litigation were located); *accord* Wellin v. Wellin, 211 F. Supp. 3d 793, 805–06 (D.S.C. 2016).

13. Rawat v. Navistar Int'l Corp., 2010 WL 1417840, at *3 (N.D. Ill. Apr. 7, 2010) (quoting Restatement (Second) of Conflict of Laws § 139(2) cmt. e).

14. Gibson v. Chubb Nat'l Ins. Co., 2021 WL 4401434, at *2 (N.D. Ill. Sept. 27, 2021).

15. Restatement (Second) of Conflict of Laws § 139(1).

16. 2 Christopher B. Meuller and Laird C. Kilpatrick, Fed. Evid. § 5:8 (4th ed. 2009).

of its citizens are not implicated when the communication or relationship is centered elsewhere.[17] The presumptive decision is disclosure.

2. Section 139(2): Privileged in MSR State; Not Privileged in Forum

Conversely, if the MSR state treats the communication as privileged and the forum does not—the scenario addressed by section 139(2)—then the forum court must admit evidence about the communication "unless there is some special reason why the forum policy favoring admission should not be given effect."[18] This "harder conflict"

> arises when the law of the communication state would hold a matter privileged but the law of the forum state would require disclosure (by not recognizing a privilege or by holding it waived or otherwise inapplicable). Denying the privilege would frustrate the policies and interests of the communication state, but upholding the privilege would frustrate the interest of the forum state in ascertaining facts. This point may appear all the more poignant if the privilege is asserted by an out-of-state litigant against a local party seeking evidence in the forum state during discovery or trial. In this circumstance, however, the privilege claim should usually be honored, for the interests of the communication state are likely to be of overriding significance. Viewed from a utilitarian perspective, the privilege serves the purpose of encouraging and protecting an underlying relationship valuable to society, and the communication state has a legitimate interest in achieving this aim, which will be frustrated if the privilege claim is overruled. Viewed as protective of a right of privacy and of certain ethical or moral considerations underlying confidential relationships, the privilege will again serve its purpose if the claim is upheld, and again the communication state has a legitimate interest in achieving these aims which will be frustrated by overruling the privilege claim, and underscoring the importance of upholding the privilege will often be the fact of reasonable reliance.
>
> In this circumstance, the Second Restatement points toward applying forum law "unless there is some special reason why the forum policy favoring admission should not be given effect."[19]

In determining whether a "special reason" exists to exclude evidence, the forum court should consider:

---

17. *Id.*
18. Restatement (Second) of Conflicts of Laws § 139(2).
19. *Id.*

- The number and nature of the contacts that the state of the forum has with the parties and with the transaction involved;
- The relative materiality of the evidence that is sought to be excluded;
- The kind of privilege involved; and
- Fairness to the parties.[20]

For example, in a contest between New York, as the MSR state, and Illinois forum law, an Illinois court found there were not "special reasons" to deny the effect of Illinois' privilege law—even though some of the "special reason" factors favored New York.[21] The court noted that Illinois was (1) the location of a destroyed house; (2) where the insurance company provided coverage; and (3) the insurance company was accused of violating local law and (4) the coverage analysis sought was highly material to the insured's claim, so the first two comment d factors favored Illinois.[22] It also considered that New York had well-established attorney-client privilege law, while Illinois' "control-group" test is not widely accepted, and the New York representative believed the communications with his counsel were privileged.[23] Because some of the factors favored New York, while others favored Illinois, the court held that Illinois' policy favoring disclosure prevailed.[24] A seminal Illinois case has indicated:

> In view of the fact that Illinois does recognize the privilege, in the first instance, but construes it strictly in the corporate context, **we cannot foresee any situation where a special reason would exist** not to give effect to this clear, strongly articulated policy in favor of another state's broader corporate attorney-client privilege.[25]

Some courts place particular importance on the "recognized" and reliance circumstances: the "forum will be more inclined to give effect to a foreign privilege that is well established and recognized in many states" and "was probably relied upon by the parties.[26] For example, when a communication was made solely in Michigan, which at the time had broader privilege protection than Texas, the Supreme Court of Texas held Michigan's law of privilege to govern.[27] As another example, Delaware's courts have placed a premium on

20. *Id.* § 139 cmt. d; *see also* Ford Motor Co. v. Leggat, 904 S.W.2d 643, 647 (Tex. 1995).
21. Gibson v. Chubb Nat'l Ins. Co., 2021 WL 4401434, at *3 (N.D. Ill. Sept. 27, 2021).
22. *Id.*
23. *Id.*
24. *Id.* at 4 ("Such a holding 'promotes Illinois' discovery-oriented view of the attorney-client privilege. . . .").
25. Sterling Fin. Mgmt. L.P. v. UBS PaineWebber, Inc., 782 N.E.2d 895, 905 (Ill. App. Ct. 2002), *overruled in part on other grounds*, Bridgeview Health Care Center, Ltd. v. State Farm & Cas. Co., 10 N.E.3d 902 (Ill. 2014) (emphasis added).
26. Restatement (Second) of Conflicts of Law § 139.
27. Ford Motor Co. v. Leggat, 904 S.W.2d 643, 648 (Tex. 1995).

its "considerable interest in vindicating the reasonable expectations of those parties that engage in a merger under Delaware law; it further has an interests in defining the scope of all of those reasonable expectations."[28]

The burden of demonstrating both a conflict between the two jurisdictions and "some special reason" for protecting the communication that overcomes the forum's preference for disclosure is on the party claiming the privilege.[29]

D. Third Restatement

As of the date of publication, the Third Restatement is still in draft form, and the American Law Institute is evaluating choice-of-law issues in the specific context of attorney-client privileges. Tentative Draft No. 3, approved by ALI's membership in March 2022, does not address which law governs attorney-client privileges.

E. Greater Interest/Government Interest Tests

Similar to the Second Restatement approach, Pennsylvania courts "weigh the contacts on a qualitative scale according to their relation to the policies and interests underlying the [particular] issue."[30] They are then to apply "the law of the state having the most significant contacts or relationships with the particular issue."[31]

California employs a "government interest analysis" in choice-of-law issues as to privileges that "examine[s] the underlying policies of the state laws involved to determine the respective government interests at stake."[32] Generally speaking[,] the forum will apply its own rule of decision "'unless a party litigant timely invokes the law of a foreign state [and] demonstrate[s] that the latter rule of decision will further the interest of the foreign state and therefore that it is an appropriate one for the forum to apply to the case before it.'"[33]

The District of Columbia uses an "'interest analysis' in which it determines which jurisdiction's underlying policy would be most advanced by having its law applied to the matter."[34]

---

28. 3COM Corp. v. Diamond II Holdings, Inc., 2010 WL 2280734, at *6 (Del. Ch. May 31, 2010).

29. *In re* Teleglobe Commc'ns Corp., 493 F.3d 345, 358–59 (3d Cir. 2007) (failure of party seeking protection to articulate a conflict between Canadian and Delaware law "undercuts BCE's argument particularly given that the Restatement favors the admission of evidence when the law of the forum so requires; thus if applying Canadian law will safeguard the privilege, it is BCE's responsibility not only to highlight the legal conflict, but also to point to 'some special reason' favoring protection." (quoting Restatement (Second) of Conflicts of Law § 139 cmts. c & d.)).

30. Hammersmith v. TIG Ins. Co., 480 F.3d 220, 231 (3d Cir. 2007).

31. *In re* Estate of Agostini, 457 A.2d 861, 871 (Pa. Super. Ct. 1983).

32. Wolpin v. Philip Morris, Inc., 189 F.R.D. 418, 423 (C.D. Cal. 1999) (citing Hurtado v. Sup. Ct., 522 P.2d 666 (Cal. 1974)).

33. *Id.* (quoting Hurtado, 522 P.2d 666).

34. Kuhn & Kogan, CHTD v. Jeffrey C. Mensh & Assocs., Inc., 77 F. Supp. 2d 52, 55 (D.D.C. 1999) (quoting Gatewood v. United States Cellular Corp., 124 F.R.D.504, 506 (D.D.C. 1989)).

When it comes to the attorney-client privilege in particular, a key consideration is a "connection between the communication which the plaintiff sought and the Commonwealth of Pennsylvania."[35] Applying these principles, Judge Scheindlin found New York to have the greater interest in communications between a company's general counsel and executives because all of these individuals were located in New York and "the legal work they discussed occurred in New York," so the communication "lack[ed] a 'direct and explicit connection' to Pennsylvania."[36] Pennsylvania had only a "post hoc connection" because the litigation pending there was "unrelated to the substance of the communication."[37]

Another court in Pennsylvania concluded that New York had a greater interest in protecting communications between its citizen corporation and attorneys "located primarily in New York," where "almost all of the [] employees receiving legal advice were [also] located."[38] By contrast, the forum state had no interest in the privilege issues because there were "no Pennsylvania litigants seeking protection of the attorney-client privilege, meaning that application of New York's law would not impair Pennsylvania's interest in protecting its litigants."[39] That court concluded:

> In light of New York's superior contacts, we believe that CIT probably would have consulted New York law to resolve any attorney-client disputes related to the communications at issue. We believe that these determinations are extraordinary enough to forego the application of Pennsylvania law in favor of New York law. The fact that the New York's attorney-client privilege law is well-established only buttresses this determination.[40]

III. Federal Courts

Rule 501 of the Federal Rules of Evidence provides:

> The common law—as interpreted by United States courts in the light of reason and experience—governs a claim of privilege unless any of the following provides otherwise:

35. Carbis Walker, LLP v. Hill, Barth & King, LLC, 930 A.2d 573, 581 (Pa. Super. Ct. 2007).

36. *In re* MTBE Prods. Liab. Litig., 180 F. Supp. 3d 273, 281 & n.53 (S.D.N.Y. 2016) (quoting Carbis Walker, LLP v. Hill, Barth & King, LLC, 930 A.2d 573, 581 (Pa. Super. Ct. 2007)). Although the *MTBE* case was pending in the Southern District of New York, the parties agreed that Pennsylvania choice-of-law rules applied. *Id.* at 280 & n.44.

37. *Id.* at 281.

38. Harrisburg Auth. v. CIT Capital USA, Inc., 716 F. Supp. 2d 380, 390 (M.D. Pa. 2010).

39. *Id.* at 391.

40. *Id.* at 393.

- the United States Constitution;
- a federal statute; or
- rules prescribed by the Supreme Court.

But in a civil case, state law governs privilege regarding a claim or defense for which state law supplies the rule of decision.[41]

The emphasized sentence clarifies that state law determines the application and extent of privileges but is silent on how to conduct a "horizontal" choice-of-law determination where two or more states have an interest in the communication claimed as privileged. "Federal courts have interpreted this language to require the court to determine the 'availability of an evidentiary privilege' based on the choice of law rules of the forum state."[42]

A. Federal Questions

The federal courts have developed a body of common law that governs the attorney-client privilege in cases involving federal questions.[43] Chapter 1, on Attorney-Client Privilege, discusses the federal common law of privilege.

In patent cases, there is another layer of conflicts analysis—whether the issue is procedural or substantive patent law, as that distinction determines whether the Federal Circuit applies the law of the regional circuit court of appeals or its own precedent.[44] For example, the decision as to whether an "invention record prepared and submitted to house counsel relating to a litigated patent" is protected under the attorney-client privilege is a substantive issue of patent law, and the Federal Circuit applied its own precedent.[45]

In addition, "'a procedural issue that is not itself a substantive patent law issue is nonetheless governed by Federal Circuit law if the issue pertains to patent law, if it bears an essential relationship to matters committed to our exclusive [jurisdiction] by statute, or if it clearly implicates the jurisprudential responsibilities of this court in a field within its exclusive jurisdiction.'"[46]

---

41. Fed. R. Evid. 501 (emphasis added).

42. Wellin v. Wellin, 211 F. Supp. 3d 793, 799 (D.S.C. 2016) (collecting cases).

43. Babych v. Psychiatric Solutions, Inc., 271 F.R.D. 603, 608 (N.D. Ill. 2010) ("In federal court, privileges, including [the] attorney-client privilege, are governed by federal common law, except that privileges are determined by state law for an element of a claim or defense as to which state law provides the rule of decision.").

44. *In re* Spalding Sports Worldwide, Inc., 203 F.3d 800, 803 (Fed. Cir. 2000).

45. *Id.* (citing Institut Pasteur v. Cambridge Biotech Corp. (*In re* Cambridge Biotech Corp.), 186 F.3d 1356, 1358 (Fed. Cir. 1999)).

46. *Id.* (quoting Midwest Indus., Inc. v. Karavan, 175 F.3d 1356, 1359 (Fed. Cir. 1999) (en banc in relevant part), *abrogated on other grounds by* TrafFix Devices, Inc. v. Mktg. Displays, Inc., 532 U.S. 23, 28 (2001)).

The dividing line is where the issue is "unique to patent law."[47] Chapter 10 addresses the attorney-client privilege in patent litigation.

B. Diversity

In diversity cases, Rule 501 directs that "state law governs privilege regarding a claim or defense for which state law supplies the rule of decision."[48] The rule does not further elaborate as to how to make the determination of which "state law" applies when more than one state has an interest in the dispute. Courts and commentators have suggested three different approaches:

- Assume that the state "'which supplies the rule of decision' is the state which also supplies the privilege law;"[49]
- [A]pply the privilege rules of the state in which the federal court sits;[50] or
- [A]pply the conflict of law doctrine of the state in which the federal court sits.[51]

This approach has been characterized and justified as being consistent with the Erie doctrine, "requir[ing] federal courts sitting in diversity to apply the forum state's substantive law, including its choice of law rules."[52] To do so, the court must first identify the states that have a potential interest in the pending case. But before engaging in a choice-of-law analysis, the court must first determine whether there is an actual conflict. A conflict is "actual" when the result is different if one state's laws apply over another's. If there is no conflict—meaning that the court would find implied waiver of the privilege, for example, under any of the potentially applicable state's laws—the courts either pretermit the issue[53] or apply the privilege law of the forum state.[54]

---

47. *Id.*

48. Fed. R. Evid. 501.

49. KL Grp. v. Case, Kay & Lynch, 829 F.2d 909, 918 (9th Cir. 1987) (quoting Charles A.Wright & Kenneth W. Graham, Jr., Federal Practice and Procedure § 5435, 865–69 (1980)); *accord* The Shaw Grp., Inc. v. Zurich Am. Ins. Co., 2014 WL 1784046, at *7 (M.D. La. May 5, 2014).

50. *Id.*

51. *Id.*

52. Shaw Grp., Inc. v. Zurich Am. Ins. Co., 2014 WL 1784046, at *7 (M.D. La. May 5, 2014) (citing Klaxon v. Stentor Elec. Mfg. Co., 313 U.S. 487, 495–96 (1941)); *see also* Miller v. Trans, Press, Inc., 621 F.2d 721, 724, *op. supplemented on denial of reh'g*, 628 F.2d 932 (5th Cir. 1980).

53. KL Grp. v. Case, Kay & Lynch, 829 F.2d 909, 918 (9th Cir. 1987) ("We need not decide the question whether Hawaii or California law applies to the privilege issue in this case because the result is the same under the law of both states.").

54. Shaw Grp., Inc. v. Zurich Am. Ins. Co., 2014 WL 1784046, at *8 (M.D. La. May 5, 2014); *see cf.*, Skepnek v. Roper & Twardowsky, LLC, 2014 WL 4377706, at *5 (D. Kan. Sept. 4, 2014) (finding any error in magistrate judge's choice-of-law analysis to be "harmless" because privilege laws of Kansas and New Jersey "do not appear to differ in any material respect").

C. Communications Affecting Both Federal and State Claims

As Rule 501's Advisory Committee Notes explain, "in diversity cases where the litigation in question turns on a substantive question of State law, and is brought in the Federal courts because the parties reside in different States, the committee believes it is clear that State rules of privilege should apply unless the proof is directed at a claim or defense for which Federal law supplies the rule of decision."[55] The note also indicates that the circumstances where federal law would supply the rule of decision would be rare, "a situation which would not commonly arise."[56]

However, courts have treated pendent, state-law claims within their supplemental jurisdiction as largely irrelevant when they parallel federal claims. For example, an Illinois district court ruled in a suit brought under the Americans with Disabilities Act that the analogous state-law claims were largely irrelevant to the choice-of-law analysis: "The fact that the materials sought may also relate to [the plaintiff's] state law claims does not make state privilege law applicable."[57] In its view, "[a]ll that is required is that the material concern federal claims for federal privilege law to apply—it need not do so exclusively."[58] This view is supported by the Senate Report on Rule 501: "It is also intended that the Federal law of privileges should be applied with respect to pend[e]nt State law claims when they arise in a Federal question case."[59]

D. Transferred Cases

When a case is transferred for convenience purposes under 28 U.S.C. § 1404(a), the transferee court must apply the law of the transferring court.[60]

IV. Special Issues

A. Substantive Law versus Privilege Law

Some jurisdictions hold that a prior determination of the choice of law governing the dispute dictates the governing law for privilege issues as well,

55. Fed. R. Evid. 501 advisory committee's notes (1974).

56. *Id.*; *see also In re* MTBE Prods. Liab. Litig., 2015 WL 1500181, at *3 (S.D.N.Y. Mar. 30, 2015) (applying Pennsylvania, rather than Third Circuit, choice-of-law principles to veil-piercing issue because the suit maintained "its state-law identity" even though the case was removed to federal court based on a federal defense).

57. Wier v. United Airlines, Inc., 2021 WL 1517975, at *4 (N.D. Ill. Apr. 16, 2021) (citing Babych v. Psychiatric Sols., Inc., 271 F.R.D. 603, 609 (N.D. Ill. 2010)).

58. *Id.* at *5.

59. Babych v. Psychiatric Sols., Inc., 271 F.R.D. 603, 609 (N.D. Ill. 2010) (quoting S. Rep. No. 93–1277, at *7059 n.16 (Oct. 18, 1974)).

60. KL Grp. v. Case, Kay & Lynch, 829 F.2d 909, 915 (9th Cir. 1987) ("Change of venue [under § 1404(a)] is not accompanied by a change in the applicable state law."); *see also* Shaw Grp., Inc. v. Zurich Am. Ins. Co., 2014 WL 1784046, at *8 (M.D. La. May 5, 2014) (citing Ferens v. John Deere Co., 494 U.S. 516, 528 (1990)).

reasoning that privilege is a substantive issue.[61] Other jurisdictions employ a rule of "depecage," meaning that they may apply the law of one state to a particular issue and another to a different issue in the same case.[62] In those jurisdictions, a prior determination of the law governing a cause of action or remedy does not necessarily determine which law governs a communication claimed to be privileged.[63]

For similar reasons, those jurisdictions do not consider a choice-of-law provision in an agreement to dictate the applicable law for communications claimed to be privileged.[64]

B. Other Countries' Laws

United States law typically governs communications concerning legal proceedings in the United States or advice regarding American law.[65] However, courts in the United States will typically defer to other countries' privilege laws as to purely overseas communications unless they directly involve the United States. The fundamental inquiry is whether the privileged matter "touch[es] base" with American law, in which case the United States courts are much more likely to find that a United States jurisdiction's laws determine the privilege issue.

"Courts engaging in the 'touch base' analysis defer to the laws of the country that has the 'predominant' or 'the most direct and compelling interest' in whether the challenged communications should remain confidential unless that foreign law is contrary to the public policy of the forum."[66] The jurisdiction having the "predominant interest" is either "the place where the allegedly

---

61. United States Sur. Co. v. Stevens Family Ltd. P'ship, 2014 WL 902893, at *1–2 (N.D. Ill. Mar. 7, 2014) ("Once the court has, by applying appropriate choice of law principles, determined the substantive law applicable to a claim based on state law, the privilege issues are determined by that same state's law.").

62. Shaw Grp., Inc. v. Zurich Am. Ins. Co., 2014 WL 1784046, at *8 (M.D. La. May 5, 2014) (observing that Washington applies a rule of "decepage").

63. *E.g.*, McDevitt v. Wellin, 2019 WL 4622088, at *3–4 (D.S.C. Sept. 24, 2019) ("While South Dakota law governs the substantive legal issues related to the Wellin Family 2009 Irrevocable Trust, the attorney-client privilege issue currently before the court is a discovery issue that is only collateral to the trust" and so, "the court must conduct a traditional choice-of-law analysis under [the forum state's] law." (citing Klaxon Co. v. Stentor Elec. Mfg. Co., 313 U.S. 487, 496 (1941)).

64. *Id.*; *see also* Harrisburg Auth. v. CIT Capital USA, Inc., 716 F. Supp. 2d 380, 391–92 (M.D. Pa. 2010) ("The issue presently before us does not involve any dispute involving the benefits received from, or the obligations imposed by, the provisions of the Sublicensing Agreement; rather, the dispute sub judice relates to issues of discovery and privilege. Consequently, we believe that the issue at bar is collateral to the contract and the choice-of-law provision contained therein.").

65. Veleron Holding, B.V. v. BNP Paribas SA, 2014 WL 4184806, at *4 (S.D.N.Y. Aug. 22, 2014).

66. Cadence Pharms., Inc. v. Fresenius Kabi USA, LLC, 996 F. Supp. 2d 1015, 1019 (S.D. Cal. 2014); *see also* Veleron Holding, B.V. v. BNP Paribas SA, 2014 WL 4184806, at *4 (S.D.N.Y. Aug. 22, 2014).

privileged relationship was entered into or the place in which that relationship was centered at the time the communication was sent."[67]

For example, in *Veleron*, defendant Morgan Stanley argued that either Russia or the Netherlands was the jurisdiction with the "predominant interest" as to documents Veleron had withheld as privileged because the communications occurred in Russia or the Netherlands between Veleron's Russian and Dutch executives with its Russian and Dutch counsel.[68] Veleron countered that the "substance" of the communications were a guaranty agreement governed by British law and investment documents governed by Canadian law.[69] The court rejected Veleron's argument because "the only connection the United Kingdom and Canada have to the communications at issue is through the choice of law clauses in the relevant contracts. . . . Comparatively, Russia and the Netherlands have a strong interest in the uniform application of attorney client privilege law for Russian and Dutch attorneys and for communications that occur in their respective countries."[70] It concluded that "the touch base analysis favors the application of Russian and Dutch attorney-client privilege law to the communications at issue."[71]

In *Cadence Pharmaceuticals, Inc. v. Fresenius Kabi USA, LLC*,[72] the district court was confronted with whether communications in Germany with a patent agent were privileged. The court determined that the communications did not "touch base" with the United States because "[t]he factual record supports the view that the alleged privileged relationship . . . case was centered in Germany at the time of the communications."[73] Consequently, it concluded that "German has 'predominant' or 'the most direct and compelling interest' in whether the Bichlmaier Documents should be treated as confidential."[74] And it applied German privilege law, which recognized a privilege in that context even though the United States would not have.[75]

In patent cases, U.S. courts often look to the law of the country where the advice was given or where the patent application is pending.[76]

---

67. Veleron Holding, B.V. v. BNP Paribas SA, 2014 WL 4184806, at *4 (S.D.N.Y. Aug. 22, 2014) (internal quotations and citations omitted)).

68. *Id.*

69. *Id.* at *5.

70. *Id.*

71. *Id.*

72. Cadence Pharms., Inc. v. Fresenius Kabi USA, LLC, 996 F. Supp. 2d 1015, 1017–18 (S.D. Cal. 2014).

73. *Id.* at 1021.

74. *Id.* (quoting Astra Aktiebolag v. Andrx Pharms., Inc., 208 F.R.D. 92, 98 (S.D.N.Y. 2002)).

75. *Id.* ("Because the legal advice in this case was rendered in Germany and related to the prosecution of European patent applications, as well as the application of a German statute, the connection to the U.S. is incidental" and "[t]he communications at issue thus do not 'touch base' with the U.S.").

76. Golden Trade, S.r.L. v. Lee Apparel Co., 143 F.R.D. 514, 522 (S.D.N.Y. 1992) (Courts of Norway, German, and Israel, where patent applications were pending had "predominant interest" in whether contested communications between Italian corporation and its patent agents located in those

> [A]lthough most American courts have noted that United States patent agents are not attorneys and hence have held them not to come directly within the scope of the attorney-client privilege, the invocation of a comparable privilege for patent agents—whether domestic or foreign—would not be dramatically inconsistent with the rationale underlying the attorney-client privilege, and indeed I note that a number of United States courts have in fact offered such a protection not only for foreign patent agents but for domestic agents as well.[77]

C. Discovery from Nonparties

Third-party discovery disputes present additional layers of complexity in ascertaining privileges when the discovery dispute takes place in a different state from the forum for the underlying lawsuit. Many district courts have taken a pragmatic approach, applying the choice of law principles of the forum state for the discovery dispute.[78] The Reporter's Note to section 139 of the Second Restatement indicates that:

> To date, the courts of the deposition state have refused to admit evidence of a communication privileged under their local law, but it would appear that in all of these cases the deposition state was also the state of most significant relationship with the communication.[79]

The Third Restatement on Conflicts of Law is considering adding language directed to this particular issue, but the draft is not yet publicly available.

V. Engaging the Choice of Law Analysis

When a party fails both to raise and substantiate a source of law other than the forum, courts will apply the forum's law. The reasoning for doing so has been characterized as waiver, default, and a failure to overcome the presumption that the forum's law governs. However, the issue can of such importance that even a belated attempt to raise another jurisdiction's laws might

jurisdictions were privileged; "enforcement of their laws" in the American patent-infringement suit "would not seriously impinge on any significant policy of this forum.").

77. *Id.* at 522–23 (citing Venitron Medical Prods., Inc. v. Baxter Lab., Inc., 186 U.S.P.Q. 324, 325–26 (D.N.J. 1975); *In re* Ampicillin Antitrust Litig., 81 F.R.D. 377, 393 (D.D.C. 1978)).

78. Wolpin v. Philip Morris, Inc., 189 F.R.D. 418, 423 (C.D. Cal. 1999) (collecting cases); Kuhn and Kogan, CHTD v. Jeffrey C. Mensh & Assocs., Inc., 77 F. Supp. 2d 52, 55 (D.D.C. 1999).

79. Restatement (Second) of Conflicts of Laws § 139 Reporter's Note (1971) (citing Palmer v. Fisher, 228 F.2d 603 (7th Cir. 1955), *Ex parte* Sparrow, 14 F.R.D. 351 (N.D. Ala. 1953); Matter of Walsh, 40 Misc.2d 413, 243 N.Y.S.2d 325 (Sup. Ct. 1963); Application of Queen, 233 N.Y.S.2d 798 (Sup. Ct. 1962); Matter of Franklin Washington Trust Co., 148 N.Y.S.2d 731 (Sup. Ct. 1956)).

be considered.[80] Federal Rule of Civil Procedure 44.1 prescribes a process for invoking foreign law:

> A party who intends to raise an issue about a foreign country's law must give notice by a pleading or other writing. In determining foreign law, the court may consider any relevant material or source, including testimony, whether or not submitted by a party or admissible under the Federal Rules of Evidence. The court's determination must be treated as a ruling on a question of law.[81]

The party that invokes a foreign privilege to protect information and documents against discovery bears the burden of proving both (1) the foreign law applies to the privilege issue and (2) the foreign law protects the communication from discovery. If successful, the burden shifts to the opposing party to offer proof to counter the privilege. If a litigant fails to timely invoke foreign law, the default presumption is that the law of the forum state governs.

Many states use a similar approach. For example, Texas requires that proof of the sources and applicability of foreign law to be submitted 30 days before trial.[82]

Once established, the attorney-client privilege does not apply wholesale to a collection of documents; instead the privilege must be determined on a document-by-document basis.[83] Where courts are unable to determine the application of foreign privilege law from a privilege log, they must conduct an in camera review,[84] which can be complicated by the inclusion of documents that must first be translated into English. It is also a good idea to produce the in camera documents with unique Bates numbers or similarly identifying information that is correlated to the items in the privilege log.[85]

---

80. McDevitt v. Wellin, 2019 WL 4622088, at *3 (D.S.C. Sept. 24, 2019) ("While the court certainly does not condone the procedural manner in which the Wellin Children raised this argument, the court deems it appropriate to address for several reasons," including the need to determine "the correct law [as] to this issue [to] ensure a legally sound decision" and the fact that a prior magistrate judge's report and recommendation made a different choice-of-law decision as to similar attorney-client privileged communications.).

81. Fed. R. Civ. P. 44.1.

82. Diamond Offshore Drilling, Inc. v. Black, --- S.W.3d ---, 2022 WL 2128337, at *6 (Tex. App. June 14, 2022) (failure to timely submit source materials to establish the substance of English law resulted in default to Texas law, despite pleading English law claims (citing Tex. R. Evid. 203, Cal. Dive Offshore Contractors Inc. v. Bryant, 478 S.W.3d 914, 921 (Tex. App. 2015), and PennWell Corp. v. Ken Assocs., Inc., 123 S.W.3d 756, 764 (Tex. App. 2003)).

83. Cadence Pharms., Inc. v. Fresenius Kabi USA, LLC, 996 F. Supp. 2d 1015, 1025 (S.D. Cal. 2014) (conducting in camera review of the challenged documents "to determine whether privilege has been properly asserted as to each document").

84. Gucci Am., Inc. v. Guess?, Inc., 2010 WL 3034244, at *2 (S.D.N.Y. July 28, 2010) (collecting cases).

85. *E.g.*, *id.* (ordering that the unredacted, privileged documents "bear legends or Bates-numbers corresponding to the document numbers in the" privilege log).